THE HISTORY OF PSYCHIATRY

BOOKS BY FRANZ ALEXANDER, M.D.

The History of Psychiatry: An Evaluation of Psychiatric Thought and Practice from Prehistoric Times to the Present (with Sheldon T. Selesnick)

Psychoanalytic Pioneers (Franz Alexander, Martin Grotjahn, and Samuel Eisenstein, editors)

The Scope of Psychoanalysis—Selected Papers of Franz Alexander, 1921–1961

The Impact of Freudian Psychiatry (Franz Alexander and Helen Ross, editors)

The Western Mind in Transition

The Criminal, the Judge and the Public: A Psychological Analysis (with Hugo Staub)

Psychoanalysis and Psychotherapy: Developments, Theory, Technique and Training

Twenty Years of Psychoanalysis: A Symposium in Celebration of the Twentieth Anniversary of the Chicago Institute for Psychoanalysis (with Helen Ross)

Dynamic Psychiatry (Franz Alexander and Helen Ross, editors)

Psychosomatic Medicine: Its Principles and Applications

Studies in Psychosomatic Medicine: An Approach to the Cause and Treatment of Vegetative Disturbances (with Thomas M. French)

Fundamentals of Psychoanalysis

Psychoanalytic Therapy: Principles and Applications (with Thomas M. French)

Our Age of Unreason: A Study of the Irrational Forces in Social Life

Roots of Crime: Psychoanalytic Studies (with William Healy)

The Medical Value of Psychoanalysis

The History of Psychiatry: AN EVALUATION OF PSYCHIATRIC THOUGHT AND PRACTICE FROM PREHISTORIC TIMES TO THE PRESENT

BY Franz G. Alexander, M.D.

AND Sheldon T. Selesnick, M.D.

 HARPER & ROW, PUBLISHERS

NEW YORK

Contents

Illustrations follow pages 144 and 272.

Acknowledgments

We would like to express our deep appreciation to those people who, through suggestions, criticisms, and encouragement, helped to bring this book to completion: Dr. Hedda Bolgar, Dr. Sidney Cohen, Dr. Richard Edelman, Dr. Joshua A. Hoffs, Dr. and Mrs. Fred Engreen, Dr. Alan Glasser, Mrs. Fran Goodman, Mrs. Helen Berk, Dr. Eric Marcus, Dr. Rocco Motto, Mrs. Miriam Silinsky, Dr. Zanwil Sperber, Mr. Lawrence Weinberg, Mrs. Rose Berk, and especially to my wife, Rose.

Mr. Don Reed of the University of California at Los Angeles library staff, Miss Kathryn E. Laing and Mr. Richard J. Bammann of the Veterans' Administration, Brentwood, California, library staff were most helpful in research.

We would also like to thank the editorial staff of Harper & Row, especially Mr. Marion S. Wyeth, Jr., Mr. Norbert Slepyan, and Miss Katherine Johnson, for their invaluable advice and assistance.

A very special debt of gratitude is owed to Mrs. Maisie Matula for six years of dedicated devotion to our common task. With her efficient secretarial and editing assistance, along with library work, many apparently insurmountable problems were resolved.

S. T. S.

JULES MASSERMAN

Introduction

No perceptive reader can delve into this book without realizing that its title does it insufficient justice, in the sense of the memorable quatrain of Alexander Pope:

> Let us, since life can little more supply
> Than just to look about us, and to die,
> Expatiate free o'er all this scene of man;
> A mighty maze! but not without a plan.

For this is not merely a history of psychiatry—it is a history of man's eternal fears, his perennial hopes, and the physical, social, and philosophic devices that in various guises evolved into "modern" psychiatry. Goethe properly pointed out that "The history of Science is science itself, the history of the individual the individual," and Halphen added: "History does not turn people into skeptics, but provides a wonderful schooling in prudence."

American psychiatry is especially in need of the broad perspectives that Drs. Franz G. Alexander and Sheldon T. Selesnick have invited us to survey in this book. It beckons toward horizons of place and time even before those of its initial chapters. When, indeed, did man's "history" begin? Should man's history be dated from the two-million-year-old crude artifacts discovered by J. B. Leakey in the Olduvai Gorge or from man's primeval but already artistic imagery as recorded a mere fifteen thousand years ago in the cave paintings at Lascaux and Altamira? With even more direct reference to our special psychiatric interests, do not these paintings and their neighboring sarcophagi show that even Paleolithic man had long since experienced to the highest degree what is often thought of as man's three principal sources of anxiety: his physical well-being, his social securities, and far from least, his immortal place in the universe?

Drs. Alexander and Selesnick begin their history of psychiatry with man's written records of four or five thousand years ago, by which time, as they point out, the Akkadians and Egyptians had already developed quite "modern" answers to man's ultimate anxieties—elaborate technologies, well-organized social systems, and multisymbolic religions. The authors then trace man's physical, transactional, and psychologic development through "Ancient," Classical, Medieval, Renaissance and Romantic times to the medical, sociological and metapsychological aspects of modern psychology. That Alexander and Selesnick do this with scholarly scope and literary charm every reader will soon discover for himself; that they also leave room for additions to or qualifications of their vistas of history is another creditable feature of the book. As examples:

Some readers may not be quite as certain as some psychiatric historians seem to be that man's understanding of himself has necessarily reached its peak in our post-Freudian era. The Minoan culture was in its time zestful, sophisticated, exploratory, creative, and serene for many a century. Those who forever mourn the Golden Age of Greece can point out that Anaximander traced the evolution of inorganic matter to animals and men and that Pythagoras called the brain the organ of the mind, approximated the functions of the nerves, distinguished rational (cerebral) behavior from the instinctive, or emotional, conceived of personal ego and will, and erected a mathematical cosmology, Heraclitus in his book *On Nature,* written nearly two and one half millennia before Hegel or Freud, perceived the eternal struggles and dialectic syntheses between opposites in man's behavior—good and bad, love and hate, and life and death. Plato recognized the origins of dreams, Thucydides analyzed the motives of historic figures, Xenophanes knew well man's need to believe in anthropomorphic myths, and Theophrastus, Aristotle's successor at the Academy of Athens, wrote a highly perceptive anthology of character descriptions easily recognizable in our friends and acquaintances today.

The Greek dramatists transcended all of these in their insights into the complexities of human motivations and tribulations. Consider how Sophocles enriched the legend of Oedipus with a broad spectrum of human relationships: the hidden fears Laius and Jocasta had—and indeed all parents have—of their child's potential ascendancy over them; the restless seekings of Prince Oedipus for his "identity"; the destructive rage of the youth when his presumption of dominance is challenged at the symbolic crossroads leading to Thebes; the unconscious fantasy every man cherishes of recapturing an all-provident mother—and every woman of acquiring an obedient son in marriage. Indeed, considering this kaleidoscope of subtly shaded human transactions, Sophocles himself would have been puzzled had he been told that eventually the term "Oedipus complex" would come to mean only a little boy's deliberate desire to kill his father and copulate with his mother.

Other classicists might contend that not the tragedians of Greece, but its writers of comedy, not only better understood the foibles and follies of mankind but also knew best how to use that most uniquely human asset—a sense of the preposterous that explodes pomposity and pretense. Witness Aristophanes, who in "The Clouds" pictures Socrates, up in the air in a basket, eliciting, with startling Freudian techniques, the free-associative fantasies of Strepsiades, who has come for philosophic counsel about his debts:

soc: Come, lie down here.
STREP: What for?
soc: Ponder awhile over matters that interest you.
STREP: Oh, I pray not there.
soc: Come, on the couch!
STREP: What a cruel fate.
soc: Ponder and examine closely, gather your thoughts together, let your mind turn to every side of things. If you meet with difficulty, spring quickly to some other idea; keep away from sleep.

The "analysis" goes on until Strepsiades, under Socrates' urgings and interpretations, eventually thinks of controlling the waxing and waning of the moon so that the months will cease and his monthly bills never come due. Aristophanes served a lighthearted tradition that has been honored through the ages by masters of merriment (such as Boccaccio, Rabelais, Voltaire, Gilbert, Twain, and Thurber, among others), who have lightened man's burdens through humor—a device, incidentally, often used by Franz Alexander as an effective psychotherapeutic technique.

Glorifiers of the late Middle Ages may feel that the authors of this volume have paid insufficient tribute to the experimental and mathematical genius of Roger Bacon, *doctor mirabiles,* or that no one better anticipated the modern principle of parsimony in philosophic postulates than William of Ockham in his dictum *Essentia non sunt multiplicanda praeter necessitatem.* Desiderius Erasmus and Luis Juan Vives are mentioned in the text, but their admirers may point out that both giants of the fifteenth century, in their personal lives as well as their writings, were courageous humanists in times of widespread disillusionment, arrogance, and opportunistic brutality and that Vives, in particular in his *Commentaries* on Aristotle's *De Anima,* advocated the inductive method as a corrective to what Francis Bacon later called the "worship of the idols of the cave, the tribe and the marketplace"; even more brilliantly, Vives also anticipated Thomas Hobbes's motivational and associationist psychology, without the latter's cynicism and sycophancy. In like manner, Johannes Weyer, John Scotus, and other luminaries down to recent times may be thought by one or another reader to have been similarly neglected or slighted.

Quite the opposite attitude could be taken with regard to the authors' discussion of Sigmund Freud and his works. On the one hand, Alexander and Selesnick do not hesitate to point out Freud's largely unacknowledged indebtedness to Herbart, James, Carus, Von Hartmann, Driesch, Charcot, Bernheim, Forel, Dejerine, and others who preceded him; some of his inconsistencies; and his tolerance of a disciple's policy (cf. the Bleuler correspondence) of excluding from the private preserve of psychoanalysis all who seriously questioned any current dogma. Yet on the other hand, the authors variously characterize Freud as at once an objective observer and an intuitive *menschenkenner;* a strict logician, yet one given to tenuous and unprovable metapsychologic speculations; the first harbinger of scientific psychotherapy, but a pessimist as to its general applicability and clinical results; and withal "one of the most important and influential figures . . . in Western civilization." Future generations may instead regard Freud as a troubled, restless, solitary investigator, a monothetic innovator and an imaginative systematizer and colorful writer, who, though he sometimes represented principles, forces, and their interactions as animated entities somewhat in the manner of Aesop, nevertheless provoked and evoked useful thought about man's behavior, its evolution, and its control. Alternatively, behavioral scientists of the twenty-fifth century may credit Alexander and Selesnick as contemporary prophets and echo their paeans of praise of Freud's greatness. We can speculate that consensual judgment will long since have stopped somewhere between abjuration and adulation, but it is not for the twentieth-century historians to claim such prescience.

Yet, having written this, I shall nevertheless essay an inconsistency by hazarding two other predictions. The first is that our own and future generations will find the considerable space in this book devoted to Franz Alexander's dynamic thinking, psychophysiologic research, and pragmatic modifications of analytic therapy entirely justified by their lasting significance; and the second forecast is that the book itself, because of its high scholarship, predominantly commendable evaluations and judgments, and lucid, vibrant style will remain a landmark in the literature of the history of man. Or better, it will serve as a revolving beacon serves a ship in poorly charted waters: its sweep dispels the shadows of regions already sailed, fixes its own point of reference, and then turns to illuminate the future.

Preface

Dr. Franz Alexander died at the age of 73 in March, 1964, deeply mourned by the psychiatric community and by the entire scientific world. Unfortunately, he did not live to see the publication of this book. His death occurred after we had sent our original manuscript (which we had started together in 1959) to the publisher and shortly after we had begun the extensive revisions that are always necessary in the preparation of a book of this scope. As it was necessary for me to complete the work alone, I must take responsibility for whatever faults may be found therein. Whatever benefits I may have brought to the work were made possible by the presence and then by the continuing influence of Dr. Alexander, who was my teacher, my colleague and my friend.

While Dr. Alexander was a student at the Berlin Psychoanalytic Institute (in 1919 he had become the first student at the fountainhead of talent for the psychoanalytic movement) it was predicted by Freud himself that he would prove to be one of the great contributors to psychiatry. His career more than justified that prediction. From his earliest work to the end of his career, when he was conducting important studies in psychosomatic medicine, his name was identified with creativity in research, writing, and teaching. In addition to many articles and books in the field of psychiatry, he wrote on political theory, literature, ethics, aesthetics, criminology, cultural history, sociology, and other subjects. His was a broad vision of the integral place of psychiatry in the dynamics of Western civilization. For example, in his book *The Western Mind in Transition,* he pointed out the necessity of uniting sociology and psychology into an integrated behavioral science. He brought to his work youthful zeal, an open mind and an ability to build new concepts upon valid tradition. He not only wrote psychiatric history, he made it.

It was my pleasure to meet Dr. Alexander in 1950 and to know the inspiration and understanding he brought to his students. As his colleague I experienced the wit and gracious charm that endeared him to all his co-workers. What Freud said of Sandor Ferenczi, who strongly influenced Dr. Alexander, can be said of Dr. Alexander as well: "He made students of us all."

To the memory of Franz Alexander this book is dedicated.

SHELDON T. SELESNICK

Los Angeles, California
November, 1965

PART **I**

THE AGE
OF PSYCHIATRY

CHAPTER 1

Psychiatry Comes of Age

The mentally ill have always been with us—to be feared, marveled at, laughed at, pitied, or tortured, but all too seldom cured. Their existence shakes us to the core of our being, for they make us painfully aware that sanity is a fragile thing. To cope with their ills man has always needed a science that could penetrate to where the natural sciences cannot probe—into the universe of man's mind.

This need has been answered in many ways. The effort began with witch doctors in the prehistoric past and has, since those primeval times, been embraced by philosophers, physicians, artists, clergymen, scientists, and at last, medical men specially prepared and dedicated to the effort—the psychiatrists. Because mental illness strikes at the very essence of man's nature, because we are all intimately involved in the problem of mental health and have been so from time immemorial, the struggle to understand and to deal with mental illness has encompassed broad areas of our civilization. The evolution of psychiatry has been a central part of the evolution of civilization itself.

Yet for the last three hundred years most of the best scientific minds have dedicated their efforts to the exploration of the physical universe. In this period man has brought about revolutionary changes in his physical, cultural, and social environment. This emphasis on the physical sciences strongly affected medicine, so that medical science became essentially an applied natural science. Medicine too has radically improved the nature of man's existence. Life expectancy has increased, as has the survival rate of newborn infants. The horrors of diseases—from chronic ailments to epidemic outbreaks—have been considerably lessened.

Considering this, it is not surprising that the predominant view of the nature of man was long governed by the concepts of the natural sciences. The outlook of the nineteenth century was that man is an extroverted,

[3

rational being influenced by natural laws. Man's physical being, based as it is upon cellular structures, was viewed as part of a larger universe based on atomic and molecular structures. Such a viewpoint made of man a rational mechanism, a combination of intellectual and moral free will, operating in a context of biological determinants. Given this viewpoint, it was to be expected that medicine would come under the sway of the natural sciences.

However, one branch of medicine dealt with phenomena that defied description in terms of physics and chemistry, physiology and anatomy. Not all men are rational. Not all men possess intellectual and moral freedom. Rather, some men behave strangely, as if under weird compulsions. They may speak incoherently or may be frightened for no apparent reason. They may alternate violently and unaccountably between elation and depression. They may suffer from excessive despair or be unable to use their judgment or be beset by hallucinations and delusions. Such men may even be homicidal or suicidal. Certainly they seem alien to the dominant image of man that natural science created. And even more frustrating to science, the causes of their behavior could not be determined by laboratory methods or even be localized in any one part of the body.

Nonetheless, psychiatry has been long in coming into its own as a major part of medical science, for it did not fit into the dominant rational, materialistic-mechanistic orientation. Instead, it seemed to be a possible means of infiltration into medicine of old demonological concepts, boding a relapse to an age when diseases were thought to be caused by evil spirits. This fear was strengthened by the recognition that psychiatry dealt with psychological concepts much as did the demonology of the primitive ages. Still, the mentally ill required help—or at least watching—and were beyond the physical methods of medicine. Thus, at the same time that psychiatry was suspected, it was also needed, and so was restricted mainly to the custodial care of advanced cases, most of whom were helpless or dangerous to themselves or to others.

While psychiatry was considered a part of medicine, it was kept in a marginal position. The psychiatrist was primarily a custodian and not a healer, and were it not for mental disturbances that apparently were due to physical causes, the psychiatrist would have had no contact with his fellow physicians or even a common language with them. Yet the great majority of mental disturbances, the psychoneuroses and the so-called functional psychoses, the schizophrenias and the manic-depressive conditions, stubbornly refused to be described, understood, or treated by the usual medical approaches. Their symptoms could be observed only as psychological phenomena and their causes were obscure. The psychiatrist therefore remained apart from his fellow doctors.

In our century a scientific revolution has taken place: psychiatry has come of age. On the strength of substantial achievements, it has ceased being medicine's neglected stepchild and has become one of the most prominent fields in medicine.

This advancement was in large part the fruition of thousands of years of study of the human psyche, but it became possible only after Freudian discoveries transformed psychiatry and penetrated general medical thought. Many who started their psychiatric careers in what was still essentially the pre-Freudian era witnessed the changes that made psychiatry a vital field of medicine. They witnessed the necessary introduction of a sound and scientific kind of psychological reasoning that did not appear to threaten medicine with relapse into its magical and animistic origins. Freud's method made it possible to bring the first comprehensive theory of personality based on an effective method of scrupulous, systematic observation and interpretation to the study of the human mind. Equally important was the Freudian development of the new concepts of repression and psychological defenses as well as of a dynamic personality theory. In turn, this method and its resultant discoveries introduced a rational method of treatment for psychoneurotics based on the understanding of the nature and causes of their disease. In spite of the sharp differences between psychoanalysis and other forms of medicine, these accomplishments inexorably brought psychiatry closer to the rest of medicine.

The psychoanalytic movement was neither an accident nor the achievement of a single genius. The advent of psychoanalysis was only one of the manifestations of an ideological revolution in Western civilization, when man's curiosity about his external world began to give place to a new kind of interest. First in philosophy and literature, then in the emergence of the social sciences, and finally in the advent of a new kind of psychology, Western man addressed himself to the challenge of understanding his own personality, to the questions of his destination and the meaning of his life. The psychoanalytic approach of Freud soon became the most effective and comprehensive expression of this search.

If ours has been the age in which psychiatry has developed the means of confronting mental disease with greater assurance of success, it has also been an age in which the dangers that mental illness poses for national health have been realistically recognized. In the last twenty-five years awareness of new means of dealing with mental illness has led the public, the government, and medical men to appreciate that mental illness presents as great a threat to the national well-being as any of the most dreaded physical diseases. It has been estimated that one out of every ten persons in the United States now has some form of mental illness. Thirteen percent of the young men examined by the armed forces are found inadequate for military service because of psychiatric difficulties. One out of every two hospital beds is occupied by a mentally disturbed patient. One and one half billion dollars are lost each year by people who are absent from their jobs because of emotional disorders. We have at last begun to realize the terrific toll that mental illness takes of human potential and production.

To meet this growing challenge, psychiatric education has expanded. In the early 1930's there were fewer than five hundred practicing psychiatrists in the United States. Today there are nearly sixteen thousand. Psychiatry is a pioneering field, which, because of its very nature, must include the study of the total personality. It therefore touches all medical specialties and also the social sciences. Understandably, medical students have become increasingly interested in mental disease and in psychiatry as a specialty to pursue. In fact, psychiatry now ranks third—behind only surgery and internal medicine—as a specialty chosen by physicians. Yet the preparation for practice in this field is perhaps the most arduous in all medicine. The psychiatrist-physician must undergo training comparable to that of his confreres in other medical fields. He must hold a medical diploma and complete an internship and then must serve a three-year training period (residency) under the supervision of trained psychiatrists. He must then spend two years in practice before he is considered qualified to take the board examinations that certify him a psychiatrist. To become a psychoanalyst he must attend a psychoanalytic institute for six hours a week for a four-year period and must at the same time undergo his own personal psychoanalysis. This training is time-consuming and expensive, a contributing factor to the fact that there are only eleven hundred certified psychoanalysts in the United States today.

Contrary to widespread opinion, psychiatry is not as remunerative as are many other medical specialties. Yet the psychiatrist does find great personal gratification in his work, for his is the reward of knowing that he may aid an individual in finding a satisfying way of life when that person, tortured by fear or despair or confusion, cannot find that way on his own.

Furthermore, the close relationship between emotional problems and physical illness has been dramatically illuminated, with the result that hundreds of specialists from other fields of medicine, grateful for the availability of psychiatric training, have entered psychiatric residency programs. In this tendency, and in the development of psychiatric teams in universities and general hospitals, we are perhaps witnessing the alliance between psychiatry and other medical fields that psychiatrists have long known to be vital to the improvement of medical practice.

As the momentum of awareness and involvement gathers, it becomes increasingly evident not only that psychiatry has come of age but also that our civilization may have entered an age of psychiatry. This evolution has meant more than the betterment of psychiatry; it has meant the advancement of all medicine. Man, the benefactor, has come a long way from the first crude probings of the prehistoric witch doctors and ancient physician-priests. The saga of that coming is the subject of this book.

CHAPTER **2**

The Three Basic Trends in Psychiatry

Three basic trends in psychiatric thought can be traced back to earliest times: (1) the attempt to explain diseases of the mind in physical terms, that is, the organic approach; (2) the attempt to find a psychological explanation for mental disturbances; and (3) the attempt to deal with inexplicable events through magic.

We shall try in the following chapters to trace these three ever-present components of psychiatric thought from their beginnings to their present state. The progress of medicine consists in applying psychological and organic theories and methods of treatment to cases where they properly can be applied, and at the same time in gradually removing the magical components from both the psychological and the somatic approaches. Eventually the mutual relationship of the two basic approaches, the psychological and the organic, will have to be clarified. As we shall see, this will lead to a kind of theory of complementarity—a solution which is similar to one that has been proposed by atomic physicists.

The Magical Approach

Primitive man cured his minor troubles through various intuitive, crude, empirical techniques: he cooled his injuries with saliva, alleviated fevers by lying in cold water, extricated foreign matter from his skin as best he could with his fingers, rubbed his wounds with mud, sucked snake bites to rid himself of venom.

The first attempts to explain illness were equally intuitive. The simplest explanation was that diseases "come of themselves," although there was some recognition of cause and effect; for instance, the Bantu know and understand that food goes through the body, that overeating and drinking may cause discomfort, and that purgatives will help to cure it.

But when the causes of an ailment were not obvious, primitive man ascribed them to the malignant influences of either other humans or superhuman beings and dealt with the former by magic or sorcery and the latter through magico-religious practices. In the sense that these methods of care were attempts to change the malevolent consequences psychologically, psychiatry is historically the oldest of the medical specialties.

Primitive medicine may be considered mainly primitive psychiatry. Mental and physical suffering were not separated, and neither were medicine, magic, and religion. Magic was always directed against some mortal or superhuman being who had malevolently inflicted a disease on another. The primitive medicine man quite logically dealt with these beings and with the evil spirits torturing his patient by such human devices as appeal, reverence, supplication, bribery, intimidation, appeasement, confession, and punishment as expressed through exorcism, magical rituals, and incantations. It was felt that disease was caused by something superfluous being added, usually by being "shot" into the body by a sorcerer or god, using blow tubes and darts. The concept of removal from the body involved the primitive's idea of the soul as manifested in dreams, shadows, hallucinations, etc. As long as the body and soul were together, the man would be in good health, but if the soul or part of it left him or were abducted, the man would become ill. According to the belief of each individual tribe, the soul was located in various parts of the body, such as the heart or the kidney. The malicious sorcerer would ensnare the soul of his victim, drawing it from him and thereby creating disease within him.

Another important principle in magic is the idea that two things at a distance from one another can produce an effect upon each other through a secret relationship. Sir James Frazer (1854–1941) called it "sympathetic magic." Two things that look alike affect each other through their *similarity* because they are in sympathy with one another. From this reasoning are derived so-called homeopathic, imitative, and mimetic magic. A medicine man may himself enact his patient's illness and recovery, pretending to be near death, writhing in agony, and then slowly recovering, prompting by mimetic magic the recovery of the dying man. A form of sympathetic magic works through the law of *contiguity,* whereby there is continued action upon each other of things once close but now separated. Thus nail parings and afterbirth were seen as devices for influencing those of whom these things once had been a part. Sympathetic magic lies behind the use of effigies to influence others. An effigy of an intended victim might be formed out of beeswax, as on the Malay Peninsula, and the eye of a figure might be pierced with the intention of causing blindness in the living victim. If death is desired, the effigy is treated as though it had died. The Malays try to create marital trouble by tying the figure of a man and his wife back to back so that they will "look away from each other."

Although on the surface, sympathy between two objects, whether animate or inanimate, appears to be a mechanistic explanation, the important
underlying idea is that these mechanisms—similarity and contiguity—are
used by some evil being for doing harm. The evil intention is, therefore, the
ultimate cause of illness in all these theories. The effect is achieved by the
sorcerer's ability to influence his suggestible victim psychologically. It is no
wonder that in primitive societies the most forceful, enterprising, and often
the most gifted individuals are witch doctors. To sum up, the effect of
magic depends upon the suggestibility of the person on whom the magic is
worked, upon the suggestive power of the influencing magician, and finally
upon a sympathetic connection between objects.

Primitive medicine consisted of psychological procedures aimed at influencing all natural events, including the diseases of body and mind. This
animistic-magical medicine reflects primitive man's view of the universe,
based on his discovery of the psychological laws governing his own
behavior. Earliest man subjectively experienced certain sequences of events
in his own behavior, sequences which appeared to him as natural, self-
evident, axiomatic. It seemed natural to him that he felt angry when
assaulted or afraid when he had the impulse to attack someone who had
previously defeated him. These sequences of events may be called "emotional syllogisms," which do not require explanation or proof. They are felt
as natural and inevitable sequences; they follow the "logic of emotions."
Primitive man possessed this type of knowledge long before he understood
the order of things in the world around him. He could not know that
bacteria caused wounds to become infected, but he did understand how to
use his own body, and he applied this internal and subjective knowledge to
external events. Wind was destructive; hence he assumed an angry being
who blew it to attack him. Rain was sent by spirits to reward or punish him.
Disease was an affliction sent by invisible superhuman beings or was the
result of magic manipulations by his enemies. He animated the world around
him by attributing to natural events the human motivations that he knew so
well from his own subjective experiences. Thus it was logical to him to try to
influence natural events by the same methods he used to influence human
beings: incantation, prayer, threats, submission, bribery, punishment, and
atonement.

Like most theories, demonology contains a nucleus of truth. The fact
that human behavior *can* be explained psychologically is recognizable by
anyone who has analyzed his own actions. The obvious flaw in the thinking
of primitive man was in ascribing to inanimate nature human motivations.

The Organic Approach

In observing events in nature, man began to recognize certain regularities
of temporal sequences. The occurrence of daylight with the rising of the
sun led to the assumption that the sun was the cause of daylight. Yet this

type of causality was different from that derived through internal experiences. Man could also dispel darkness by making fire. This event, however, was different from the phenomenon of sunrise. Man *intended* to make light by fire; he could not observe any such purpose in the sun. Extrapolating his own experiences to explain natural phenomena, he assumed that the sun—or more precisely, a sun god—had its own good reasons for creating light. In other words, primitive man extended the motivational causality of his own actions to all nature.

The problem of the existence or nonexistence of purpose in nature has had a profound effect on the development of science. Medicine progressed as it gradually freed itself from these animistic theories and replaced them with another type of causality—one that was nonpsychological and also applicable to inanimate nature. The natural sciences could develop only after man had replaced his primitive ideas of motivational causality in nature with the recognition of certain regularities in the natural world. Such a recognition was hard in coming and not easy to maintain. The Greek rationalistic philosophers of the seventh and sixth centuries B.C. introduced the foundations of scientific thought, but by the Middle Ages their revolutionary discoveries had been replaced by a resurgence of demonological and religio-magical bias. Only in the last three hundred years, since the Renaissance, has scientific thought achieved true dominance.

Vital to the advancement of science was the growing conviction that eventually all phenomena of life can be described and understood in terms of physics and chemistry, and this conviction soon came to dominate medicine. As a result investigation into the actual makeup of the human body, from the single cell outward, became intense. The human body gradually revealed itself as an extremely complicated physico-chemical apparatus which functioned by converting chemical into mechanical energy. However, even as these discoveries mounted, the problem of purpose reasserted itself. Natural science saw all occurrences in nature as having a cause but not a purpose. Still, in spite of the wealth of evidence which supported a mechanistic approach to understanding the body, the irrefutable fact was that the parts and functions of the body interact in a sensible manner as if animated by a supreme goal—survival. The mechanistic view had led to the teleological conclusion that since man-made machines are always constructed with a use or purpose in view, so also must that most complex of machines, man himself. This led to disturbing questions. Who or what was responsible for the sensible construction of animal organisms, including man, or are such organisms an exception? Must their function and development be explained in terms of purposes instead of causes? And if there is a purpose behind the construction of the living organism, whose purpose is it?

Thus in the early nineteenth century an age-old problem was revived as the biological and medical sciences were threatened by the foreign principle of purpose, as they had been by animism in the prescientific eras. They were saved from this dilemma by the contribution of Darwin and by the concept of stability.

The principal attempt to reintroduce animistic concepts into biology was a theory called "vitalism." Its most outstanding advocate was Hans Driesch (1867–1941), the German zoologist and philosopher, who attributed a directive force, a "vital energy," to all living organisms. He maintained that the living organism cannot be fully understood in mechanical terms and assumed the existence of a form- and direction-giving force as an elementary and independent principle of nature. This vital force was psychological or spiritual. It was purposeful, its purpose being life. It was considered basic and irreducible and could not be traced back to the laws of physics and chemistry. Vitalism did not find many followers, and it has been rejected by almost all biologists and most representative philosophers as a theory that cannot be validated, and above all, as unnecessary, since theoretically all phenomena of life can be explained from the same principles that rule the inanimate world.

The great contribution of Darwin, which helped to save the biological sciences from this relapse into animism, was his concept of natural selection by the survival of the fittest, a concept which explained the purposefulness of living organisms. In Darwin's theory those species and those differences in characteristics within a species which accidentally have the greatest survival value are perpetuated by heredity. Darwinian theory assumed the existence of the instinct of self-preservation, without which the struggle for existence would remain unintelligible. Through the concept of the struggle for survival, *purpose* again was brought into biological theory.

The development of the concept of stability (homeostasis) by Theodor Fechner (1801–1887), Claude Bernard (1813–1878), and an American physiologist, W. Cannon (1871–1945) resolved the dilemma. This principle attributes to the organism a tendency to maintain within itself certain constant conditions necessary to perpetuate its life. Although this actually is a more precise definition of the instinct of self-preservation, its formulation in terms of stability separates it from teleological significance. Essentially, it is like Newton's first law of motion, of bodies tending to *remain* in motion or stationary through inertia. Just as inertia is clearly not purpose, so would homeostasis not be a manifestation of purpose.

On the basis of these developments, the end of the nineteenth century seemed to see the resolution of this age-old problem in the emancipation of all natural processes from psychological forces. The mechanistic concept of the universe appeared to be finally established.

The Psychological Approach

Primitive man did not need a supernatural explanation for a wound inflicted by a sharp weapon. Hence, and in this sense, surgery was the first nonmagical aspect of medicine. But internal diseases, where neither the locus of the trouble nor its causes could be directly observed, required demoniacal explanations. To these nonvisible phenomena man applied the only solid knowledge he possessed, that is, the knowledge of his own motivations, which he acquired from his own direct subjective experience. Since he could successfully explain his normal behavior in psychological terms, why did it take him such a long time to use the same solid knowledge of psychological causality to explain abnormal behavior?

One of the reasons for the delay in the development of a rational psychiatry is that normal behavior does not awaken the need for scientific explanation. We know our strivings, our hopes. We know what hurts our feelings, what pleases us, and how our aims and feelings determine our behavior. At least we think we know. Only when human behavior and feelings become abnormal—for instance, when a person becomes depressed or elated without any obvious reason, when he sees and hears things that do not exist, when he is afraid without being threatened—do we need some special explanation.

Primitive man's explanation of abnormal behavior was that some outside power, an evil spirit, must have taken possession of the sufferer. In short, mental disease, like most physical illness, was to him obviously caused by evil spiritual forces. In principle, man was right when he associated mental disease with psychological forces; what he did not recognize until recently was that these forces were not outside of him, were not caused by magic, but were his own unacceptable desires, fears, and impulses. The essence of mental disturbance is precisely man's inability to face himself, to recognize the feelings and motivations that his conscious self repudiates. In this central phenomenon, which Freud called "repression," lies the reason for the time lag between the development of psychiatry and the rest of medicine. The unacceptable emotions and impulses that man excludes from his consciousness do not cease to exist, and do influence behavior. In the mentally sick they cause irrational neurotic and psychotic symptoms and in normal persons form the imagery of dreams. For modern man to admit that under his civilized surface, and for all his moral and religious beliefs, he still harbors the same untamed and undomesticated sexual and hostile impulses that his savage ancestors had, required a great deal of sincerity and moral courage. Since understanding and treatment of most of the mental disturbances demand precisely the recognition of this fact—that the overwhelming majority of neuroses and psychoses are the manifestations of repressed, unconscious motivations—it is not surprising that the psychological approach in psychiatry, the discovery of the self as something that required special techniques of self-observation and verbal communication, has been the latest chapter in medical thought. Science first described what is farthest from man—the stars—and then described his body, and last of all what is nearest to man, his own personality.

Whenever scientists, philosophers, and psychiatrists came near to a rational evaluation of human nature, humanity shrank back and resorted again and again to magical explanations or deluded itself with pseudo-scientific speculations.

When Aristotle, further developing the views of Socrates and Plato, who believed that the good life could be obtained through self-knowledge and rational thought, succeeded in designing the first rational psychology, he still believed with Plato that the intellect (*nous*) had a superhuman, divine origin. When Hippocrates, the great empirical observer, declared that the sacred disease—epilepsy—was no more sacred than any other affliction and was not the result of the machinations of supernatural spirits, he still believed that melancholia was caused by black bile and could be cured with purgatives. Cicero, several centuries later, objected to the black-bile hypothesis and maintained that melancholia was the result of psychological difficulties. He proclaimed that people were responsible for their emotional difficulties in a psychological sense, that they brought their ills upon themselves and could do something about them. Thus, he laid down the foundations of psychotherapy (for him "philosophy"), but his ideas did not come into their own until the modern era.

St. Augustine, who was the greatest introspective psychologist before Freud and who mercilessly exposed all that he felt as evil in himself, still doubted that man alone, by self-scrutiny, could gain mastery over his carnal passions without seeking the superhuman aid of Divine Grace. Mesmer, as late as the nineteenth century, came near to recognizing the curative power of a psychological phenomenon, hypnotic suggestion, but he attributed it to the effect of "animal magnetism," which he believed flowed through his magical touch from the hypnotist's body into the patient.

It appears, indeed, that man has a deep disinclination to understand the disturbances of his behavior in terms of psychology. He undoubtedly shuns the responsibility which results from such understanding and is ready to blame the spirits, the devil, or even mystical fluids in his body for his abnormal behavior instead of recognizing that it is the result of his own feelings, strivings, and inner conflicts.

The most dramatic example of the threat man felt from a rational approach to human psychology was his return to the most primitive form of demonology during the Renaissance, when in all other fields the rational approach asserted itself vigorously. Studies in anatomy and physiology increased. Art and literature portrayed man realistically, as an individual. Montaigne and Machiavelli dealt with the problems of psychology concretely rather than in terms of Aristotelian abstractions and made strides toward discovering man as a person with all his social and personal problems. Boccaccio and Rabelais were anything but squeamish in depicting the earthy impulses of man, not only with unprecedented realism but with real gusto. Man, during the sixteenth and seventeenth centuries, began to take cognizance of his instinctual vital forces. And during the same period, in a violent reaction against this rapidly advancing psychological enlightenment, demonology reached a new height. Man could not accept responsibility for his impulses, particularly for his sexual drive, which the Renaissance writers and artists exposed so effectively, and had to attribute them to the influence of a foreign agent, to the devil and to the sorcerers and witches who were believed to be his instruments. An unprecedented recrudescence of witch hunting was the response to the progressing trend toward recognizing the instinctual forces of man as a vital part of his own personality.

And the struggle still goes on in our present day. The role of the devil now has been taken over by brain chemistry. No longer a devil but a *deus ex machina,* a disturbed brain chemistry rather than the person's own life experiences, is responsible for mental illness. Whatever the cause of faulty brain chemistry may be, the new conviction is that the disturbed mind can now be cured by drugs and that the patient himself as a person no longer needs to try to understand the source of his troubles and master them by improved self-knowledge. Brain chemistry undoubtedly has a part in all mental processes, in all our strivings, learning, and ambitions, and also in our mental ailments. But brain chemistry cannot be isolated from man, from what is the core of his existence, his personality. Brain chemistry, indeed, can be altered by emotional stress, by anxiety, rage, fear, and hopelessness.

The integration of brain chemistry with psychology is the principal task which psychiatry is facing in our present era.

PART II

FROM THE ANCIENTS THROUGH THE MODERN ERA

CHAPTER **3**

Contributions of the Ancients

The story of psychiatry began when one man attempted to relieve another man's suffering by influencing him. When psychic and physical suffering were not distinguished one from the other, the precursor of the psychiatrist was any man who tended another in pain. The story of psychiatry thus begins with the story of the first professional healer, the medicine man.

In the most primitive society the man who was believed to have mysterious powers, including the ability to cause rain or sunshine, to predict success in war, or to make the crops grow, also had the task of curing the ill. Most often the medicine man was the head priest—not only the chief of the tribe, but also the sorcerer of the clan. Among more advanced races the medicine men formed an elite class, and in general, the higher the culture, the more select was this caste. In some cultures the witch doctor inherited his profession or was appointed to this position because some unusual incident had indicated that he was a special favorite of the gods: for instance, if he had avoided injury in a situation in which another man might have died or been maimed. Frequently a man became a witch doctor after he had had a convulsion or went into a trance and had a hallucination which revealed to him that that was what he should be. This method of selection is especially common among the Osa-Kaffirs of South Africa, some Siberian tribes, and the North American Indians.[1]* A prospective witch doctor must usually undergo rigorous training, including falling sick himself, and an elaborate initiation ceremony. For example, an islander who lives in Indonesia on the island of Nias may be selected because his father was the chief witch doctor and had taught him the magic formulas and the use of the drum, but this alone does not entitle him to inherit this father's position: he also must become ill. Often this illness is a

* Superior numbers refer to Notes, p. 415.

psychosis. During his sickness he is treated by another medicine man, and while he is ill he is instructed in various ritualistic maneuvers. After he is cured, he assists his teacher and pays for the instruction he receives. No professional courtesy is granted to the candidate. The teacher decides when the student is ready to begin his own practice—just as applies to a present-day candidate of a psychoanalytic institute—and a huge banquet celebration marks the granting of his license.

Since dreams and hallucinations are part of selecting a candidate, medicine men pay a great deal of attention to these phenomena. Among the Bantu in Africa, after the candidate has had his revealing dream a medicine man is called to train him. During the period of initiation and training the candidate has to observe taboos, he must make sacrifices, and he *"must confess what he sees in his dreams."*[2] This training procedure is not much less rigorous than that of a candidate of a psychoanalytic institute, who, as a preparatory step, must be freed from his neurotic blind spots by psychoanalysis. And, as in primitive societies, institutes prefer mildly neurotic but curable candidates because of their firsthand acquaintance with neurotic suffering.

However learned and able the medicine man is, he tends to take credit for spontaneous natural cures and also sometimes exploits his fellow men in order to gain more wealth or prestige; these circumstances are not without civilized parallels. Physicians throughout history have used various devices to impress their patients, from smearing their bodies with red paint to wearing a red cloak or using a gold-headed cane. Perhaps modern physicians do not utter incantations, but they may wear caduceus cuff links and prescribe in an esoteric fashion with Latin phrases; as a medical historian rightly asserts, all the hocus-pocus has not gone out of medicine.[3]

Mesopotamia

Since the origins of psychiatry are rooted in the primitive medicine of ancient cultures, we turn our attention to the organized civilizations of ancient times in which medicine was already beginning to find its systematized concepts. One of the earliest of civilizations, the Babylonian, was contemporaneous with predynastic Egypt of about the fourth millennium, before the great pyramids were built and before religion, science, and art were organized. This was at least three thousand years before the flowering of Hebraic culture.

The earliest Babylonians probably emigrated from the mountains of Persia. They were finally conquered, as were their neighbors, by the Semitic chieftain named Sargon (about 2750 B.C.), whose nation was conquered in turn by Hammurabi about 2100 B.C. The Code of the great Hammurabi, who created a centralized government, was written into law and is preserved in cuneiform clay tablets. These are the earliest laws to come down to us in systematized form.

The first Babylonian physicians were priests who taught at the cities of Babylon and Nineveh and were called the Assipu priests. Later there were lay physicians, who were called Asu (A-zu). The priest-doctors dealt with internal illnesses and especially with mental afflictions, which were attributed to demonic possession and cured by magico-religious methods; the lay physicians dealt with external pathological abnormalities usually caused by injury and used more natural means of treatment. The Code of Hammurabi, being a practical code, dealt with law and order; in the main it ignored the priests and dealt primarily with the work of the lay physicians. Since the Babylonians believed in animistic conceptions, the Asu frequently had to supplement his natural methods of treatment with the "sugar coated pills of magic and divination."[4] Indeed, the Asu was the man "who knows the waters," and water played an important role in incantations.

Magical procedures were aided by astrologic and oracular practices. The Babylonians believed that the stars were divine and possessed superior intelligence and that everything in nature had a plan and an intelligence. The menstrual cycle and the exacerbation and remission of certain diseases were held to be closely related to the cyclic activity of celestial bodies. The organs of sacrificed animals were used as auguries. The liver was especially suited for prophecy. Its size, shape, form, and color had prognostic value for the diseased patient in whose behalf the animal was sacrificed. The priestly physicians, who jealously guarded the secret knowledge of this method of divination, were called Hepatoscopists.

Drugs were used, but the most effective treatment was believed to be incantation. The large Babylonian pharmacopoeia has been preserved in the cuneiform tablets; the incantations were not codified, much as a patient's silent prayers are not part of the modern medical textbooks, although the patient may feel that they are as important as his medicine. In fact, the incantation was a powerful psychological tool; as the eminent medical historian Sigerist states: "A system of medicine that was dominated by magic and religion and the purpose of which was to rehabilitate an individual and to reconcile him with the transcendental world obviously included psychotherapy. The soul-searching of the patient who was convinced that he had suffered because he had sinned had a liberating effect; and the rites performed and the words spoken by the incantation priest had a profound suggestive power." From this point of view, Sigerist concludes that "Mesopotamian medicine was psychosomatic in all its aspects."[5]

The spiritual world of the Babylonians was populated by many demons who battled an even greater number of benign spirits or gods. The goddess Ninkharsag, with the aid of eight other goddesses and gods, specialized in different disease syndromes. All physicians had their own personal gods;

the chief deity of the physicians was the healing god, Ninurta, who, with his wife, Gula, was the patron of the healing art. Their symbol was the serpent. The priest first diagnosed the illness, and then he appealed to the particular god who specialized in that disease, and at the same time invoked the deity in charge of the city in which the patient dwelled.

The gods had seven enemies, the evil demons, who headed an army of lesser demons devoted to Ishtar, the goddess of witchcraft and darkness. Each disease had its specific demon. Insanity was caused by the demon Idta. The demons were served by sorcerers, who used the evil eye, special concoctions, and certain ceremonies.

Although the people of Mesopotamia primarily practiced magic and religious medicine, medicine nevertheless owes them a considerable debt because they described many diseases correctly and in detail on their cuneiform tablets. Not only did they discover many medical principles, but they were the first to study the patient's life history. Moreover, under the Babylonians hygiene and social medicine, and above all medical ethics, reached great heights.

In psychiatry, as in all fields of medicine, the codification of the responsibilities of the physician to his patients is indispensable. If Babylonian medicine provided us with nothing more, this was a significant advancement. Babylonian physicians were so renowned that they were frequently called to Egypt on consultations.

Egypt

Although both Babylonians and Egyptians emphasized religion and magic in their medical practices, they differed in some respects. The Babylonians developed a profound mathematical discipline; the Egyptians collected a great many details but often failed to discriminate between fact and imagination. The cuneiform clay tablets of the Babylonians were briefer, more concise than the Egyptian papyrus scrolls, which were lengthy, vague, and at times incomprehensible. It has been said that if the Egyptians had used a "waste papyrus basket" more often, their valuable medical contributions would not have been so buried in the mass of other, useless detail.[6]

Of the two main influences on the people of the Nile, one came from the Orient and the other from Africa. Where Oriental influence held sway, mysticism and priestly medicine were predominant; where contact with nature prevailed, as in African civilization, empiricism was dominant.[7]

Imhotep, the first Egyptian healer of whom we have actual knowledge, lived about 2850 B.C., at the time of the third dynasty. He was the physician to King Djoserin and renowned as a great architect, sage, astronomer, and priest. Eventually, in 525 B.C., when Egypt had become a Persian province, Imhotep was deified as the special god of medicine, replacing in importance the other healing gods in the Egyptian hierarchy.

His temple at Memphis became a medical school and hospital where incubation sleep—a form of psychotherapy that was developed further by Aesculapian priests (see p. 27)—was practiced. Long before the Greeks, the Egyptians in their temples established the type of milieu which in certain aspects was most modern. For example, patients were encouraged to occupy themselves with recreational activities such as excursions on the Nile, concerts, dances, painting and drawing, and other constructive uses of their spare time. These activities must have had therapeutic results, just as they do in our modern hospital settings, where occupational therapy is prescribed. However, the need for supernatural explanations was so great that when cures were achieved they were attributed to the patron saint of the particular temple where the patient resided.

The two most important Egyptian medical papyri now in existence are called the Ebers papyrus and the Edward Smith papyrus, both of which were set down at approximately the same time, about 1550 B.C. The Ebers papyrus deals exclusively with internal medicine and pharmacology, whereas the Smith papyrus describes wounds and surgical management. Successful surgery is a matter of rational procedure, so it is not surprising that the Smith papyrus contains little in the way of religious incantation or magical ritual. The Ebers papyrus, on the other hand, abounds in incantations and occult explanations for diseases whose real etiology was unknown. The Smith papyrus is also important because in it the brain is described for the first time in history, and it shows "clearly that it was recognized as the site of mental functions."[8]

Egyptian physicians knew little about nerves, muscles, or blood vessels. They believed that anatomical parts were governed by specific spirits and that the body was a microcosm that, like the outside world, was composed of four elements. The bones and flesh of the body corresponded to earth. The fluid of the body corresponded to water, and just as the Nile alternately flooded and receded, the body's fluid rose and fell in its pulsating vessels. The heart that warmed the body was the equivalent of sun and fire, and the breath was the equivalent of the wind.

The Egyptians had recognized the emotional disorder that the Greeks later called "hysteria" (hysteron = uterus). They believed that the symptoms were caused by the malposition of the uterus and therefore fumigated the vagina, hoping to lure the vagrant uterus back to its natural position. Fumigation was also a well-known treatment in Greece, where Hippocrates and Plato recommended it without reservation. Even Galen, who opposed many Egyptian ideas, followed uterine-fumigation therapy.

Egyptian physicians were bound to malpractice laws similar to those in the modern world. Traditional practices were recognized, and if the patient died when treated unconventionally, the physician was considered guilty and liable.

Whether the physicians were priests, laymen, magicians, or combinations thereof, by and large Egyptian medicine was predominantly magical and religious. Nevertheless, the papyri reveal excellent observations and detailed descriptions of diseases. Their hygienic prophylactic measures were elaborated by the Hebrews. Unquestionably Egyptian medicine influenced Moses as well as Hippocrates. The Egyptian physicians were as astute in their observations as they were magical in their explanations and esoteric in their teachings.

The Hebrews

The medicine of the people of Israel was greatly influenced by that of their neighbors the Babylonians and the Egyptians. Unlike them, the Hebrews did not have systematic medical texts or inscriptions, but the Talmud—the codification of what originally were oral laws—is full of stories that evidence psychological wisdom. The psychological mechanism of blaming others for one's own sins or sinful ideas, which we call "projection" or "scapegoating," is described anecdotally in Megillah 25, which tells the story of an anti-vice crusader who accused the people of Jerusalem of committing precisely those crimes of which in fact he himself was guilty.[9] Another psychological insight is the one attributed to Rabbi Hunah, who said that good men have wicked dreams, which means, in effect, that he recognized that dreams serve to express wishes that our conscious moral principles forbid. As for psychotherapy, Rabbi Ami recommended diversion as a treatment for mental disorder, and Rabbi Asi advocated that the troubled patient should talk freely about his worries.[10]

The fundamental point of view that characterized early Hebraic medicine and distinguished it from the ancient medicine of Babylon and Egypt was the belief that one God was the source of health and disease. "For I am the Lord that healeth thee" (Exodus xv: 26); "I kill and I make alive; I wound and I heal" (Deuteronomy xxxii:39). Cure of disease therefore was an attribute of the Divine, and the purpose of disease, including madness, was to punish man for his sins.

The most important Hebrew physicians were priests who had special ways of appealing to the Great Healer. Probably the first Hebrew patient on record who tried to separate the roles of priest and physician was King Asa (950–875 B.C.), who, as is reported in II Chronicles xvi:12, "in his disease sought not to the Lord but to the physicians." Eventually, when lay physicians did become established, their practice was restricted, as was the practice of Egyptian and Babylonian lay physicians, so that they had no jurisdiction over the hidden diseases—internal diseases, epilepsy, and mental illnesses. The duties of the doctor-priests were also well defined: they supervised dietary laws and enforced the rules of social hygiene.

Anatomical knowledge was more advanced among the Hebrews than among the Egyptians and Babylonians, for the Bible sanctioned dissection of the sacrificed animals. Almost all organs and structures are mentioned in the Bible—one that never occurs is the human brain—but the most important organ, since it was considered the seat of emotion and intellect, was the heart. Malignant demons were considered the cause of insanity, asthma, and other obscure conditions in biblical accounts; in the Talmud, however, supernatural powers are of less account, and the influence of the Talmud made Hebraic medicine less magical than was the medicine of ancient Babylon and Egypt.

In Deuteronomy (vi:5) it is written, "The Lord will smite thee with madness," which indicates that although demons were considered the precipitating agents of insanity, the supreme controlling force was considered to be Divine. Saul's mental illness, which is carefully described in the first book of Samuel, was thought to have been caused by an evil spirit sent from the Lord. Overcome with depression, Saul tried to persuade his servant to kill him; when the man refused, Saul committed suicide (I Samuel xxxi:4). There are also several biblical descriptions of catatonic excitement and epileptic fits.[11] There is even a description in the Bible of the strange psychosis of lycanthropy (the delusion that one is a wolf) that befell one of the most famous men of ancient times, Nebuchadnezzar (605–562 B.C.), the king who rebuilt Babylon. The Hebraic concern for the sick has always been an important influence on the humanitarian aspects of medicine and psychiatry, and as early as A.D. 490 there was a hospital in Jerusalem solely for the mentally ill.[12]

The Persians

The first great period of Persian medicine began about the middle of the first millennium B.C. and flourished under the rule of Darius the Great, when Persian influence was widespread over the whole Middle East. The primary source of our information about ancient Persian philosophy is the Zendavesta, a volume of which, the Venidad, has several chapters devoted to medicine. The Venidad says there are 99,999 diseases that afflict mankind, all of which are caused by demons. In fact, "Venidad" literally means "the law against demons."

The Persians of the middle of the second millennium embraced a dualistic religion. Ahura Mazda (Ormuzd), who created the world, was the god of goodness and light; he was surrounded by his six angels representing everything that is bountiful. In direct opposition to Ormuzd was Angra Mayniu (Ahriman), who was the spirit of evil and darkness. Because Ormuzd did not have infinite power, he was constantly struggling against Ahriman and the evil genii who were his helpers. Ormuzd delegated the realm of medicine to a powerful angel named Thrita, who became the Persian mythological physician-in-chief, much as Imhotep was the Egyptian and Aesculapius the Greek patron saint of medicine.

Perpetual exorcism was the road toward the good life and the way to defeat the evil influence of Ahriman. Consequently tremendous demands were made upon the ancient Persians to be virtuous, courageous, humble, and charitable.

Fortunately, to help man in his struggle against evil, there arose the prophet Zoroaster (Zarathustra) (c. sixth century B.C.). Zoroaster contributed to the Zendavesta ways in which man could decide on which side of the fence he stood. He must align himself either with the Satan, Ahriman, or with the good, Ormuzd. Aiding Zoroaster in his proselytization of the right road were the priests known as Mah (pronounced Mag), which meant "the greatest ones." It will be recalled that the New Testament tells of the three wise Magi who came from the east to worship the infant Christ. In subsequent years, however, the great Magi lost the high esteem in which they were held and became known as charlatans and tricksters; hence, the connotation to the word "magic."

Like Yang and Yin of the ancient Chinese, in the dualistic concept of the Persians good and evil were constantly at odds; even within the body the battle raged. The forces of the body seek pleasure and therefore evil, and are opposed by the soul, which leans toward goodness and purity.

Although the Venidad mentions three types of physicians—surgeons, herb doctors, and magicians—the emphasis was on magical and religious procedures, and most confidence was placed in spiritual healers. "When physicians compete," said Ormuzd, "knife doctor, herb doctor and word doctor [perhaps the equivalents of our modern surgeon, internist, and psychiatrist], then shall the believer go to him who heals by the holy word for he is a healer of healers and benefits the soul also."[13]

Prophylaxis, hygiene, purity of mind and body, good deeds, and good thoughts were considered the ways to achieve and maintain health. Ethical concepts cannot, however, curb epidemics, and in this sense Persian medicine was not very advanced. It emphasized demonistic theories, as did Babylonian medicine; it also included the kind of religious bias that was present in Egyptian medicine but lacked the more rational and empirical approach to medical practice present in these other two cultures. Furthermore, Persian hegemony in the Middle East ensured that these anthropomorphic, animistic, microcosmic, and spiritualistic theories could survive and be found as remnants in Greek medicine.

The Far East

Ancient Hindu medicine as described in the holy books of the Vedas, a collection of hymns and prayers, comprises the Vedic medical period (to 800 B.C.). Living in the valleys of the Ganges River, where the Aryan tribes settled, was indeed arduous. Petty satraps ruled over small divided principalities. The poverty-stricken populace found comfort in mystical beliefs, especially in the transmigration of the soul, which promised a better lot in the next life. The possibility of redemption through renunciation of worldly pleasures was more highly developed in ancient India than in other ancient lands. Witchcraft and demonology flourished and ascetic hermits and reformers traveled the countryside offering salvation. Ancient Hindu medicine was similar to that of the Persian and Chinese in that its basis is a struggle of the forces of evil (Siva) with the forces of restoration (Vishnu). Since angry demons were purported to inhabit the body, animistic and exorcistic practices and prayers were offered to the gods, especially the great one, Brahma, by the Vedic priests.

The Brahmans, successors to the Vedic priests, possessed "Brahma," or power over the spiritual world, and medical practices were their exclusive domain. In the Brahmanical period (800 B.C.–A.D. 1000) medical texts were written without regard for separating medical practices from incantation rites. Yet the works of Charaka (second century A.D.) and Susruta (fifth century A.D.) suggested that powerful emotions may be related to peculiar behavior.[14] Mystical theories about demoniacal possession described the locations of the offending evil agents. Also located within the body were certain personality characteristics; for example, ignorance was located in the abdomen, passion in the chest, and goodness in the brain. Brahmanical physiology considered that air, bile, and phlegm are vital to all processes of life and that these substances were required in proper proportions to ensure health. This harmonious balance of substances is akin to the humoral theory of the Greek Hippocratics.* Yet it is not known how much communication there was between the precursors to the Hippocratics and the Hindu medical practices. It was not Hindu medicine, however, but Buddhist that has most interested the Western world.

The central factor in the Indian influence on psychiatry is the Buddhist emphasis on the withdrawal of interest from the external world to the inner self. Buddhistic meditation has a definite psychotherapeutic flavor; in fact, it has been advocated not only as a form of psychotherapy for the mentally sick but also as an aid in managing the difficulties of everyday life.

The philosophy of Gautama Buddha (568–488 B.C.), a Hindu prince, stemmed from his shock of discovery of the effects of age, sickness, and death. His inordinate empathy for all things living earned him the name Buddha, signifying the Enlightened One. He developed a psychological technique of meditation for the purpose of arriving eventually at the ultimate stage of nirvana—a tranquil state devoid of all striving and passion. This was to be achieved through a succession of four stages of meditation (jhana), leading back to a nullification of birth, which is the beginning and cause of man's troubles. The goal, therefore, is a psychological and physiological regression to the prenatal state of oblivion, of pure being, in which the difference between subject and object vanishes. In the first stage of jhana the world is renounced as a symbol of evil; contempt for the world results in renunciation of all worldly desires, and the

---

* An extraordinary fact is that the Brahmans also set down detailed accounts of complex surgical procedures, such as rhinoplasty.

meditating monk is beset with sorrow. This is analogous to a state of experimentally induced melancholia. These feelings of sorrow are replaced in the second stage by self-love, a drawing upon the self for all spiritual sustenance. This condition represents a still further regression and re-sembles psychotic states in which interest is completely centered upon the self. In the third stage the feeling of pleasure induced by self-love dimin-ishes into apathy, which is in turn transformed—in the fourth stage—into complete mental emptiness and uniformity. Here the ascetic meditator is exalted above pleasure and pain, is free from love and hate, is indifferent to joy and sorrow, is indifferent indeed toward the whole world, toward gods and men, even toward himself. He emerges free of all emotion. At this point he can remember with ever-increasing clarity all the circumstances of his life down to the least detail. Significantly, recollection of one's whole development has been described by Freud as the aim of psychoanalytic treatment for mental disturbances. However, in Buddhistic training the unwinding of the film of life in a reverse direction goes even further, beyond birth, back through all the previous reincarnations to the very beginning of life, reversing the developments through all previous exis-tences. This is nirvana, the end of the regressive journey through the four stages of jhana, during which all forms of one's previous lives are reexperi-enced in a clairvoyant fashion. That these memories are in fact true may be open to doubt, for it is understandable that a person intent upon flight from the world and the self may, in his spiritual fervor, accept his visions as memories of previous incarnations.

It is difficult to reconcile the goal of absorption, nirvana, which is a completely asocial condition, with Buddhist ethical precepts, healing and devotion to the "welfare and succor of gods and men." Absorption with oneself—withdrawal from the world and society—is an unbridgeable gap between Buddhism and Western psychiatric thought. Psychoanalysis, for example, strives to conquer the self without losing the outside world. A complete withdrawal is a goal alien to the Western cultural tradition, in which man is imbued with a drive toward achievement. This fundamental opposition of ideals explains why the influence of Eastern thought upon the development of psychiatry has been only sporadic. As the extroverted interest of European culture reached its peak in the modern era of science, eventually even psychology assumed the goals and principles of empiricism and experimentation.

Introspection is, however, a basic attribute of man. Through introspec-tion man has an avenue to the universe of which he is a part. This avenue is not contradictory but complementary to the exploration of the physical world. It is not amazing, then, that in the course of history, whenever the problems of social existence impinged forcibly upon him, Western man's concern with himself was aroused and he became more receptive to Oriental philosophy.

CHAPTER 4

The Classical Era

From the Magical Cult of Aesculapius to the
Materialistic World of the Greeks

In Homer's hexametric poems, written about 1000 B.C., people suffering from insanity were thought to have offended the gods, who punished them by causing them to behave strangely. Thus, when deranged, Ulysses plowed sand instead of fields and Ajax killed sheep instead of his enemies. Divinities are mentioned by the score in the Homeric poems, but Aesculapius, who later became the god of medicine, is referred to as a mortal. Homer knew his two sons, Machaeon and Podalirius, as surgeons. It is probable, therefore, that Aesculapius, like the Egyptian Imhotep, was a human being who was deified after his death.

The cult of Aesculapius was influential in Greek medicine for centuries; indeed, it is only in the era of Greek enlightenment in the seventh and sixth centuries B.C. that its predominance began to decline.

Hundreds of Aesculapian temples were built in different parts of the ancient world, most of them in Greece; the foremost of these temples was in Epidaurus. The temples were situated in places of beauty, with adjacent baths, gardens, and hillsides. Possibly the diseased patient gained inspiration and hope from the splendor and magnificence of the Aesculapian temples. Not all who wished treatment were admitted to the temples; if a supplicant's disease was too severe, he was turned away, for the Aesculapian cult depended on its reputation. Once he had been screened and admitted, the patient received instruction in personal cleanliness and dietetics. The most important treatment was temple, or "incubation," sleep. Accounts of what transpired just prior to and during the patient's sleep are not fully in accord. Apparently, while sleeping in the temple the patient would receive dream inspirations or instructions from the Aesculapian priests; the dream was supposed to reveal to the patient what he needed to do to get better. Ludwig Edelstein, an expert on the Aesculapian cult, believes that the patients dreamed of Aesculapius, because they were profoundly influenced by the Aesculapian priests who had told them that they would have such dreams. Edelstein also maintains that the average Greek knew a lot about practical therapeutics, and therefore might easily have had a vision involving an appropriate cure.[1] Other historians hold that the Aesculapian priests were charlatans, who drugged the patients with opium derivatives and then impersonated Aesculapius, tricking the patients into following their advice. All individuals are most suggestible in the period between sleep and waking (hypnagogic state), and this may account for the results of the Aesculapian priests.

Snakes played important roles in the cult of Aesculapius; even his name may be derived from the Greek word for snake (askalabos). The Greeks worshiped the earth and believed that the serpent was the symbol of the power of the underworld and were in great awe when a snake was produced by the Aesculapian priest to lick their wounds. The staff of Aesculapius—a rod with a snake entwined around it—has come to be the emblem of medicine.

Although the magical cult of Aesculapius had extensive influence, there was a lack of cohesiveness and dogmatism among the cultists. The division of Greece into city-states was responsible for a lack of central authority in all fields of life. The priests were not so powerful and organized as they were in other ancient civilizations, nor did religion dominate the daily life of the average Greek as it did the life of the Babylonian or Egyptian. There was generally an absence of religious persecution. Thus in Greece it did not take as long to abandon dogmatism and magical cults as in the other ancient cultures. The Greeks were seafaring men and their contact with neighboring nations was a great stimulation to the earliest philosophical speculators. In the medical schools of Cos, Rhodes, Cnidus, and Cyrene, Eastern influence was great. These schools, along with the Sicilian, attempted to find rational and materialistic explanations for everything. Ultimately, all of Western science, including medicine, began with the rationalistic speculations of a series of unusually gifted Greek philosophers.

The chronological order of the development of scientific thought from cosmological speculations to the study of man and society is not accidental. Man first discovers the stars, then his immediate physical environment, then his body, and only last his personality and the society in which he lives. Nietzsche's thesis that man is farthest removed from what is nearest to him—his own self—has been borne out by historical evidence, ancient and modern. The history of Greek thought offers the neatest demonstration of this universal principle, the explanation of which we are only now beginning to grasp.

For almost two centuries—roughly from 600 to 450 B.C.—the interest of

Greek philosophers was almost exclusively cosmological. This period was followed by the anthropological era (450–400 B.C.), when man himself became the focus of inquiry, gradually continuing into the ethico-socio-logical age of Plato and Aristotle and culminating in the Stoic and Epicurean systems of the Hellenistic period and of Rome.

Matter, force, and motion occupied the interest of the Ionian philosophers. Thales of Miletus (650–580 B.C.) is considered to be the founder of the Ionian school, which dealt with mechanical and materialistic principles. He taught that all matter was created from water. The idea was not at all revolutionary; it had come directly from Egypt, where it was well known that water was necessary for life and probably basic to it. It was new, however, to advance a comprehensive cosmological theory based on a materialistic principle. Thales is considered the father of science, the first philosopher. Aristotle called him the man who made the first attempt to establish "a physical beginning" without mythical presuppositions.[2]

In the Milesian tradition, Anaximenes (570–500 B.C.) sought the primary element fundamental to human life and found it not in water but in air. He claimed that since clouds were formed from the air and since life itself depended upon the inspiration of atmospheric air, it would follow that air was the basic substance of the universe. Heraclitus of Ephesos (536–470 B.C.), also searching for a material source, created a fundamental concept related to rhythmicity. Life and death, health and disease, sleeping and waking, were rhythms that were characteristic of living organisms. The motions of fire, moving upward and downward, symbolically represent this type of dynamic movement, and thus Heraclitus considered fire to be the fundamental element.

Like many Greeks of this period, the Eleatic school, founded by Xenophanes (c. 530 B.C.), considered the earth to be fundamental material. They did not believe that earth, air, water, or fire was each in itself a basic substance, but considered their combination to be fundamental. Pythagoras (580–500 B.C.), whose ideas will be discussed in a later section, believed, like the Eleatic school of Greek philosophers, in the four basic elements. It is said that Pythagoras was impressed by the fact that the burning of fresh wood demonstrated the four basic elements—fire, smoke (air), water, ashes (earth). Pythagoras' influence on the growing materialistic concepts in medicine came by way of his pupils Alcmaeon and Empedocles.

Alcmaeon of Crotona (c. 500 B.C.), unlike his philosopher-teacher, Pythagoras, devoted himself exclusively to medicine and founded the Sicilian school. He may have been the first Greek to experiment with the brains of animals.* He believed that the brain was like a gland that

* Some authorities regard an Eleatic philosopher, Anaxagoras (500–400 B.C.), as the first individual to dissect animals systematically. Although Alcmaeon and Anaxagoras were contemporaries, it is not known whether they had been in communication in regard to their anatomic findings.

secreted thought, much as the lachrymal gland secreted tears, and he tried to trace auditory and visual "channels" to the brain.[3] He thought that inadequate perception was due to a clogging of the channels from the ear and eye to the brain. This interest in body secretions led him to suggest that there were humoral relationships (the interaction of body fluids) that could be the cause of disease. This humoral theory is a source of the physiological doctrines of the Hippocratics. Indeed, Alcmaeon's work *On Nature* was probably the most fundamental text used by pre-Hippocratic writers.

Empedocles (*c*. 490–430 B.C.) was a physician who spent a great deal of his lifetime in Agrigentum, in Sicily. He is considered by some to be the true founder of Italian medicine. He was the first to explain—nineteen hundred years before Darwin—evolution through the survival of the fittest. Empedocles believed that elements were attracted and separated by forces of love and hate, and thus anticipated Freud's concepts of life and death instincts. The historical influence of Empedocles was his elaboration of the four-element theory, which became the basis for the physiological doctrines of the Hippocratics. This theory stated that the four basic elements (fire, earth, water, and air) represented four basic qualities (heat, dryness, moisture, and cold). The four humors of the body were blood, phlegm, yellow bile, and black bile. They were found in the heart, brain, liver, and spleen. An imbalance of these humors was considered to be the basic cause of disease, and one could cure the disease by using drugs that had qualities opposite to the four fundamental qualities—heat, dryness, moisture, and cold.

Hippocrates (460–377 B.C.) applied the speculations of the philosophers of medicine and combined them with bedside observations. Hence he is called the Father of Medicine and was the first to attempt to explain consistently all diseases on the basis of natural causes. For example, Hippocrates wrote that in his opinion those who first considered epilepsy "divine" called it a "sacred malady" to conceal their ignorance of its nature; this skeptical insistence on rational knowledge is the hallmark of the Hippocratic tradition in medicine and swept away the mysticism of the Aesculapians; science could now become an integral part of medicine and psychiatry.

Hippocrates was said to have been born on the island of Cos and to have received his medical education from his father, Heracleides, who was probably a member of the Aesculapiadae. He studied under the Sophists in Athens and made many journeys to Asia Minor but eventually settled in Thessaly, where he spent most of his life. The Hippocratic writings—the *Corpus Hippocraticum*—consists of more than seventy-six treatises on more than fifty subjects; they show such extreme variations in style and content that they are generally taken to be the work of the entire school of medicine at Cos. Cos placed emphasis on treatment and prognosis, as opposed to a rival medical school at Cnidos, which stressed diagnosis. The Hippocratic physicians emphasized observations made on patients as a guide to symptoms. Of the *Corpus Hippocraticum* the treatise on epilepsy stresses that in this illness the brain is diseased; the portion on diet states that most diseases can be prevented by reasonable eating habits. The Hippocratic Oath and the books *On the Law* and *On the Physicians* contain important clinical hints.

The modern medical student learns, on his first day in medical school, the Hippocratic tenet that *vis medicatrix naturae* (it is nature that heals the patient) and that the doctor is merely nature's assistant. Physicians of today learn of the basic principle of harmony—"homeostasis." Hippocratic pathology was founded on the concept of harmony between humors. Medical students learn to think in terms of syndromes—a coherent interconnected group of symptoms—and not in multiple diagnoses based on isolated symptoms. Hippocrates, unlike the Aesculapian priests, did not hesitate to report unsuccessful cases. Physicians today are encouraged to report unsuccessful treatment so that more can be learned about the most difficult diseases. Hippocrates himself claimed that perhaps sixty percent of his difficult cases ended fatally. The modern physician is constantly aware of prognosis, which was stressed first by Hippocrates. Medical therapy of today still utilizes supportive measures introduced by Hippocratic physicians—for example exercise for those suffering from chronic conditions—but that must be used sparingly with acutely ill patients. He considered bathing, dieting, and proper hygiene essential to maintain good health. As far as treatment was concerned, he used bloodletting and purgatives, but only after other measures had been unsuccessful; he prescribed medicinals —for instance, hellebore, an emetic and purgative—especially for patients suffering from insanity but warned about the importance of correct dosage and careful observation of the patient's reactions. Young medical students are warned today with the Hippocratic motto: "If you can do no good, at least do no harm," and heroics on the part of the physician to use drastic medications are frowned upon in good medical centers as they were by the Sage of Cos. Through practical experience, physicians have learned that not only the forces of nature but also the patient's environment must be enlisted to aid the sick person: "Life is short, science is long, opportunity is elusive, experiment is dangerous, judgment is difficult. It is not enough for the physician to do what is necessary, but the patient and the attendants must do their part as well and circumstances must be favorable."[4]

Psychiatry owes a great deal to the Hippocratic emphasis on clinical medicine; it also owes to him the first recognition that the brain is man's most important organ. "Men ought to know that from the brain and from the brain only arrives our pleasures, joys, laughter and jests, as well as our sorrows, pains, griefs and tears . . . wherefore, I assert that the brain is the interpreter of consciousness."[5] Still, he believed that if the brain were plagued by excess moisture, heat, or cold, madness could ensue, and that if the humors were balanced correctly wholesome thoughts would be forth-coming. Intelligence was thought to be due to the inspiration of pneuma (air), which circulates and enters the brain.

The Hippocratic physicians described for the first time organic toxic deliria, as well as the symptom of depression we call melancholia, which they thought was caused by an accumulation of black bile. They also noted the characteristics of puerperal insanity—in modern terms, "postpartum psychosis"—described phobias, and coined the word "hysteria" for a condition, still prevalent, that they thought was specific for women. They thought hysteria was caused by a wandering uterus that had been loosened from its moorings in the pelvic cavity. Perhaps they suspected a sexual origin for hysterical symptoms, inasmuch as they recommended marriage and intercourse as cures for the condition.

The Hippocratics also inaugurated the first classification of mental illness, and one that was extremely rational. They included in this schema epilepsy, mania (excitement), melancholia, and paranoia.* They made the first attempts to describe personality in terms of their humoral theories, and even today we speak of choleric, phlegmatic, sanguine, or melancholy people. Even in our times there have been many attempts at establishing personality profiles on the basis of physiological theories. The Hippocratics had great reputation for their ability to recognize and treat mental illness, and Hippocrates himself appeared as an expert witness at the trial of an insane person. Most significant was that the Hippocratics not only elicited a complete life history of their patients but also recognized the importance of the intimate relationship between doctor and patient.

Psychology Without Demons

The unique contribution of Greek culture to the development of our civilization was its *rational*—although quite primitive—approach to the understanding of nature, man, and society. No other historical event—wars or political upheavals—can be compared in its effect on Western culture to this change in point of view toward the world. It replaced supernatural traditions with a secular belief that natural phenomena have natural explanations. Man's mastery over nature began with this change.†

* The latter term referred to conditions that today would be considered as mental deterioration. Paranoia today designates a type of delusional state of extreme sus-piciousness.

† The change did not come to fruition until some twenty-five hundred years later. Historical materialists—such as the followers of Karl Marx—are inclined to consider changes in the economic structure, in the means of production, as the "basic cause" for ideological changes. Idealists consider the internal logic of thought development as primary; history is the "self-realization" of the human spirit (Hegel). Others believe that the creative genius of exceptional individuals is the *spiritus rector* (guid-ing spirit) of history (Carlyle). According to the principle of multicausality, which

Rationalism as a consistent trend began with the Greek philosophers of the seventh and sixth centuries B.C. It was applied to medicine—even to the study of mental diseases—by Hippocrates in the fourth century. This trend gradually declined after Greek culture reached its peak in Athens, and for all practical purposes disappeared during the long hibernation of human thought—the Dark Ages—to be revived again in the Renaissance, which introduced our present "scientific era."

The first psychological concepts of the philosophers discussed in the previous section were mainly materialistic. Their primary interest was in the physical universe. Psychological forces, however, were recognized as active in the universe. They were conceived as impersonal forces not belonging to individual persons but pervading the whole physical world.

Empedocles of Agrigentum—to whom reference was made previously—was a statesman and physician who derived his fame from elaboration of the concept of the basic elements. While Anaxagoras explained the motion of the basic elements from reason (*nous*), which he conceived as a fine "thought substance," Empedocles saw in love and hate the dynamic agents of the world. Since *nous* represents order and harmony, the universe of Anaxagoras is orderly, goal-directed (teleological), and harmonious. Empedocles saw emotions as the moving forces, and therefore he can be considered the first voluntarist philosopher. There was, however, no differentiation as yet between physical and psychological phenomena; psychic forces were considered as representing a *fine material,* and the materialistic trend remained unchallenged. Pythagoras speculated that since there were four elements, there must be pairs of opposites and that numbers themselves had a basis in reality. This idea was to be prevalent throughout many Greek philosophical writings, as well as in future psychological theories. Pythagoras was the first to stress that the brain is the true organ of man's intellect and the site of mental disease, although it remained for his pupils actually to dissect animal brains. The Pythagoreans experimented in many fields. For example, they were the first to employ music therapy with emotionally ill patients.[6] Diogenes of Appolonia (*c.* 460 B.C.), like Anaxagoras, supported the teleological principle; he attributed to air (pneuma) the quality of rationality, which to him explained the utilitarian construction of the living organism.

The Greek thinkers faced the same dilemma as biologists of modern times do when they try to apply to the living organism mechanistic explanations that worked well for the explanation of physical phenomena.

<hr />

became dominant in modern science, the truth probably consists in an intricate interplay of all these factors: political and economic conditions, the internal logic of thought development, and the emergence of extraordinary men of genius. The ultrascientific mind, which has thoroughly absorbed the teachings of modern theoretical physics, will be inclined to consider chance, the fortuitous but unpredictable and possibly undetermined specific coincidences of these three factors (independent variables), as responsible for shaping man's destiny.

They did not include man—the observer—in their formulations. These early philosophers did not pay attention to psychological and logical problems as such. They were "naïve realists" who accepted the world of the senses as the absolute reality. They did not raise the crucial questions: What is knowledge? What is the nature of observation and reasoning? Neither were they interested in social and ethical problems. The physical universe, and not man, was their primary concern. Their approach to the understanding of the world was still naïve insofar as they were preoccupied only with the nature of things, but not with the nature of man, who observes the world and thinks about it. Reality was still not separated from the *psychological acts of observation and thinking*. To make this step was the accomplishment of the Sophists. Their spiritual origin, however, goes back to Pythagoras.

The Pythagorean school differentiated observation from reasoning, and their emphasis was on the latter, particular on mathematical reasoning. The essence of the world now became the number—mathematics, with its own internal laws and regularities. It became evident that the laws of reasoning were superior, more perfect than those of the world we actually perceive through our senses. The laws of geometry are absolute, having only psychological unity; those of the world of observed facts are only approximations. Only the ideally conceived geometrical figure, which is the creation of the intellect, is perfection. With this emphasis on reason, the foundations for Plato's idealistic philosophy were laid down. The teachings of the Sophists were the connecting link between Pythagoras and Plato. The psychological point of view became explicit when the Sophists—particularly their ablest representative, Protagoras of Thrace (480–410 B.C.)—applied it to observation. Protagoras founded "epistemology," the study of the nature and sources of "knowledge" itself. When the focus of interest shifted from the external world of objects to that of the man who observes them, who sees and hears the objects and reflects about them, the psychological point of view entered Western thought.

We do not perceive objects in the world as they really are. Observation is an interaction (for Protagoras, "motion") between the object and the observer; hence the result of this interaction, which constitutes the content of our perceptions, depends not only upon the nature of the observed object but equally upon the nature of the observer. It is determined by both, but it is different from both. With this the basic tenet of psychophysiology is formulated. Differentiation between objects and the act of perceiving them is clearly established. Since the act of perception is both a physiological and psychological phenomenon, psychology as a special branch of science is recognized. Epistemology, the study of the process of "knowing," is essentially both a psychological and physiological discipline.

Sophists questioned the objective reality of observation and also that of ethical and aesthetic judgment. With Protagoras, the world of absolutes yielded to a world of comparatives in which man became "the measure of all things." The extension of this relativistic concept to ethical-value judgments is responsible for the reputation of the Sophists, who doubted the validity of everything that to common sense appears self-evident. Now moral conduct became for the first time the object of philosophical thought. Without recognizing the influence of the Sophists, this new trend—the turning away of interest from the cosmos toward man, culminating in the teachings of Socrates, Plato, and Aristotle—cannot be understood.

The Sophists' historical significance consisted in shifting the focus of interest from the material outside world to man himself, particularly to his reasoning faculties, something which was initiated by the Pythagoreans. This new direction of thought found in Socrates (470–399 B.C.) a most influential promoter. He shared the basic conviction of Protagoras that man's ability to know the world is limited and that cosmology and metaphysics cannot give certain answers about the nature of the world. But he did believe in knowledge of man's own behavior, holding that by using his reasoning faculties correctly man can arrive at the foundations of a good life—of happiness.

It would be futile to attempt to decide whether or not the course of Greek philosophy, the shift of interest from cosmological speculation to man and his ethical social problems, was the unavoidable result of the internal logic of thought development. Social events—the progressive decline of tradition, the internal political crisis in Athens—undoubtedly had their share in fostering the preoccupation with psychological, ethical, and sociological issues. When the traditional patterns of social life begin to crumble, a man no longer has the necessary detachment to speculate about the world; his interest becomes forcefully drawn back to his own self and to the practical issues that concern him in striving for his own happiness in his daily life. The intellectual climate of Athens in the middle of the fifth century B.C. was ideally suited to further interest in man and his ethical problems, which the Sophists initiated. A leader in this development, Socrates believed that knowledge resides in man and can be elicited through inquiry. From him to Plato (427–347 B.C.) passed the stream of development of rational exploration of man and his world.

Much of Plato's philosophy stemmed from Pythagoras. Pythogoras had absorbed much of the introspective Oriental mentality. For him the psyche had real existence. He believed in the soul.* And even Plato could not entirely divest the soul from the penumbra of Oriental mysticism. Yet he was still more a pagan Greek than an Oriental mystic, and rationalism

---

* Pythagoras had spent a good deal of time in Egypt and was imbued with the doctrine of metempsychosis (transmigration of the soul), along with the theory of immortality. He journeyed to India and from there brought back Oriental theories to Crotona, a Greek colonial city in Italy, where he established his school.

predominates in his writings. The world of Plato is built of psychological entities—ideas—but his psychology is almost entirely speculative. His "ideas" were abstractions.

As we have seen, the Sophists were primarily interested in epistemological questions about the nature of knowledge, of perceptions and primarily of the process of logical reasoning. Plato, in true Pythagorean tradition, considered mathematics the key to the formal properties of the world that are hidden behind a world of appearances. Ideas are absolute, unchangeable, and perfect. The world as we perceive it is changeable and imperfect and represents only an approximation of the only reality, that which consists in the world of ideas. With this thesis Plato introduced into human thought development a new kind of reality: *psychological reality*. The reality of ideas was more reliable to him, more essential than that of the objects conveyed to us by our senses.

If one would remove from Plato's psychology the theoretical superstructure, the little that would remain would be seen to be based on introspective observations and as less antiquated from the vantage point of modern psychology than are the Hippocratic organic explanations of body processes. No philosopher who speculates about the human soul can escape dealing with the eternal mind-body problem. The body can be minimized in importance, but it cannot be talked out of existence.

Plato's speculations about the body and its relation to the world of reasoning, desiring, and feeling contain an astonishing intuitive anticipation of later scientific insight. He recognized that life is a dynamic equilibrium. The body continually builds up matter and gives out waste; life is a perpetual rhythm of depletion and regeneration, as in respiration. For Plato, bodily states are reflections of psychological states. The vital principle of the body is the soul. The seat of reason—the rational soul—is eternal and is placed by God in the head, nearest to heaven. The irrational soul resides in the body. Its superior parts—courage, ambition, and energy—are placed in the heart; its inferior parts—desire, appetites (drives) and nutrition (hunger)—reside below the diaphragm. The whole body is ruled by the rational soul. The souls freely communicate by means of the bodily organs. The basic idea is that in the lower parts the psychological and physiological processes are chaotic and undirected, and they receive their organization and direction from the highest functions of reason. One cannot but be reminded of Freud's concept of the chaotic "id" that gradually comes more and more under the organizing power of the "ego."

In his *Republic* Plato anticipated Freud's dream theory. In sleep the soul attempts to withdraw from external and internal influences, but desires which are commonly unexpressed in the waking state are expressed in dreams. The great difference between Freud's and Plato's dream theories consists in the fact that Plato's was an ingenious intuitive postulation, whereas Freud devised an operational method by which the repressed unconscious content of a dream can be reconstructed and brought into consciousness.

Plato's most significant contribution is that he considered psychological phenomena as total responses of the whole organism that reflect its internal state. The conflict between the disorganized lower appetites and the higher organizing functions of reason is the basis of Platonic psychology.*

Platonic rationalism represented a reorientation toward psychological, ethical, and social phenomena equally as revolutionary as was the Milesian and Eleatic philosophers' rational approach to the surrounding universe. Both schools supplanted the mystical demonological explanations of phenomena: the old cosmologists accomplished this for nature, Plato for psychology. Although these explanations did not contribute substantially to our concrete knowledge of the world and ourselves, they did prepare the intellectual soil for methodical explorations that came about two thousand years later.

The brilliant and almost exclusive methods of Aristotle (384–322 B.C.) of Stagira, a city in Thrace, led to major advances in knowledge and philosophy. His often astonishingly valid observations and the precision with which he classified them influenced many subjects, scientific and nonscientific, including human psychology. He lucidly described the five senses. Touch, he said, is the most important and basic sense; taste is similar, but restricted to touch with the tongue. Both of these senses are in the service of nutrition. Smell, sight, and hearing function through distance. Aristotle recognized that sound is conducted by air, but his explanation of seeing is confused. According to him, all perceptions are conducted to the heart, which is the central organ of the senses. Most of the psychophysiological speculations of Aristotle are of a similar order.

Aristotle's most lasting contributions to psychology are his descriptions of the content of consciousness. He distinguished, obviously on the basis of introspective observation, between sensation, conation (striving), and affection. The affections are desire, anger, fear, courage, envy, joy, hatred, and pity, a list which hardly needs additions. The descriptions of these different affective states are as good as the modern ones, with the possible exception of Spinoza's descriptions, and in some respects more complete than those of modern psychologists. Anger, being derived from subjection to wrongdoing, seeks revenge.† Fear is derived from awareness of danger with the expectation of defeat, while courage is the same but with the

---

* Freud himself may have been little influenced by Plato's writings, yet his basic orientation that emotions, drives, ideas, and memories constitute a kind of reality and are worthy of systematic study because they have consequences upon our behavior and bodily processes had been prepared by Platonic views. The recognition that psychological phenomena have profound reality that cannot be disregarded was never fully eradicated from Western thought.

† This is a more concrete and meaningful statement for the understanding of an angry person's behavior than Freud's concept of an internalized death instinct.

anticipation of success. Imagination is described as the faculty of re-awakening a mental image in the absence of the original object. It depends upon the faculty of the memory. Memory is for Aristotle not merely a passive phenomenon, but an activity. Striving requires imagination, which implies the modern concept that the memory of past successes determines the direction of actions. He considered all sensations as being either pleasurable or painful and regarded thinking as directing striving toward elimination of pain and attainment of pleasure, a concept which anticipates Freud's pleasure-pain principle.

Reason, for Aristotle, is active intellect that itself cannot be explained; it is absolute. It does not depend on experience; it has, as Plato assumed, a Divine origin. This position is not much different from that of most of the later philosophers, including Kant, whose categories of pure reason (*Reine Vernunft*) were absolute and irreducible. It was first challenged in our times by the Pragmatists, who considered reason an organic function in the service of survival, and then more explicitly by Freud, who considered the ego and its reasoning faculties as the imprint of external reality upon the organism which allows the organism to gratify its needs. Accordingly, logical reasoning is seen as ultimately an adaptive function, and logical laws as adaptations of the organism to the laws of nature. Because Aristotle considered reasoning to be Divine and therefore sacrosanct, it was impossible for him to conceive of reasoning as possessing an adaptive function.

Italian Medical Mythology

Medicine in ancient Italy, as medicine in all ancient civilizations, was shrouded in magic and remained in this state until late in the second century, B.C., when rational Grecian medical thought first began to influence Italian physicians.

The earliest conquerors of the Italian peninsula of whom we have any knowledge were the Etruscans, who had probably emigrated into Tuscany from Asia Minor (*c.* 1000 B.C.).

The Etruscans shared the mythologies not only of their immediate neighbors but also of Greece and Egypt. They had deities for every purpose. Apollo and Mars were the main protectors of health; the goddesses Febris and Methitis protected against fevers, Scabies against the itch, and Angina against pain. From the moment a woman met a man to the time that she gave birth, she was protected by the deities. Juga hovered over a woman during her courtship. Cinixia helped loosen her undergarments, Virginensis observed while she was being deflowered, and Pertunda oversaw the insertion. Other goddesses were responsible for the feeding of the prenatal infant, and at the time of delivery ensured the proper head presentation.[7]

About 300 B.C. Rome was the center of a major epidemic, and Roman ambassadors went to seek the advice of the Aesculapian priests at Epidaurus. During the conference between the Roman delegation and the priests, a snake entered the Roman ship anchored in the harbor. When the vessel reached an Italian port the snake swam to shore. When, soon after, the epidemic ceased, Aesculapius and his priest-doctors were credited with its abatement, and the Aesculapian cult flourished for a while in Rome.

The Hellenistic Organic Approach

While Rome was conquering neighboring cities, and while the Aesculapian priests were dominating Roman medicine, more rational medicine was in evidence across the Mediterranean in Alexandria. This city, from its founding in 332 B.C. until Rome politically united the Mediterranean world in the first century B.C., linked Athenian culture to Rome. Euclid, Archimedes, and Eratosthenes were contributing scientific data in geometry, astronomy, physics, and mathematical geography, Herophilus (c. 335–280 B.C.), Aristotle's grandson, and Erasistratus (c. 310–250 B.C.) discovered through actual human dissections important anatomical and physiological facts and have been honored by the titles Father of Anatomy and Father of Physiology respectively. Important to later developments in brain research was that Herophilus described the venous drainage and the coverings of the brain, and Erasistratus explored its cavities.

However, advances in Alexandrian science gradually diminished because of cultist hairsplitting. Sectarian deviationism caught hold not only in economics, politics, and philosophy, but in medicine as well. Herophilists and Erasistratists founded schools dedicated to their masters and quibbled with one another as well as with the Skeptics, Stoics, Epicureans, and Dogmatists.* As often happens when disciples battle one another, reformers came upon the scene to attempt a corrective position; Empiricists held that revered works were not always sources of knowledge and that true scientists relied on experience and observation. Soon the Empiricists not only disregarded the works of Herophilus and Erasistratus but also ignored all anatomical findings.†

During the period of Roman ascendancy in the Mediterranean, the campaigns of the Punic Wars (intermittently from 264 B.C. to 146 B.C.)

---

* Thessalus and Draco of Cos, the sons of Hippocrates, founded the Dogmatist sect, which later thrived in Alexandria and was dedicated to the concept that further medical investigation should cease because Hippocrates had already recorded the essentials. (Over two thousand years later Freud's doctrines had the same fate in the hands of some of his followers.)

† This pattern of sect reverence recurred five hundred years later in Byzantium and contributed to the collapse of Hellenism (see pages 50–52), and again in the late Middle Ages when Aristotle's views became dogmatized by the scholastics (see pages 59–60).

created a need for efficient treatment of wounded soldiers. Much more practical than sending these soldiers home was the establishment of a network of hospitals along the roads leading to Rome. Gradually the Roman hospital system—the first of its kind—became not only efficient but advanced. The wounded were treated by physician-hostages, many of them Greeks, since there were no trained professional physicians in Rome.

By copying and synthesizing, Rome transmitted Greek culture to future civilization. Eventually Rome synthesized and unified Greek medical writings, but before this could take place the Romans had to become more familiar with Greek medical practices. However, supervising magistrates had an economic investment in preventing the rise of a physician class. Slaves or barbers, who practiced a form of unskilled medicine in Rome, paid them or their masters the fees they collected. Furthermore, because Greeks were despised, it took an intrepid soul to journey from Greece to Rome in the hope of finding employment as a physician.

One of the first Greek doctors who came to Rome deliberately to practice medicine was Archagathus (c. 219 B.C.). A well-trained physician, Archagathus was a much better doctor than his competitors and therefore had almost immediate success. Unfortunately he made the mistake of attempting surgery beyond his capabilities and came to be known as "carnifex" ("the butcher"). As a result of his failures, all foreign physicians were expelled from Rome.

Cato (234–149 B.C.), a powerful magistrate, particularly opposed Greek doctors as being dangerous and untrustworthy. This corrupt official wrote books dealing with subjects ranging from agriculture to the treatment of dislocations; one of them, a medical textbook, reads like a sorcerer's handbook and indicates why he was so intent on keeping better-trained doctors out of Rome.

Fortunately for the cause of the transmission of Greek medicine to Rome, another Greek adventurer, Asclepiades, born in Bithynia, 124 B.C., was teaching rhetoric in Rome. Asclepiades had been trained in medicine, philosophy, and oratory in Alexandria and Athens but was not able to practice as a physician in Rome because of the prejudice against Greek doctors. One day, however, a funeral procession passed him, and he could tell from the position of the corpse that it might still be alive. He stopped the funeral procession and began to manipulate the body. When the supposed corpse revived, Asclepiades was hailed as a miraculous physician and was allowed to practice. He promised, *"Curare tuto, celeriter, et jucunde"*—the cure will be safe, quick, and pleasant—and indeed he kept his promise. He prescribed bathing, exercise, massages, and wine—a regimen that pleased his patients and also was noteworthy because it emphasized humane and dignified treatment. Light and airy rooms, music, baths, and massage were supplied not only to physically diseased patients but also to the mentally ill. Asclepiades also emphasized the importance of differentiating between acute and chronic diseases and distinguished hallucinations from delusions. He sympathized with the mentally ill and regarded mental illness as a result of emotional disturbance.

Asclepiades was too good a philosopher to remain aloof from medical theory. His ideas were influenced by the tendency then prevalent in Rome to oppose Greek and especially Hippocratic reasoning. In opposition to Hippocrates' humoral theory, Asclepiades advanced a theory based on solidity. The basis for the solidistic structure could easily become the atom.* Asclepiades' materialistic concept was that man is composed of atoms that attract and repel each other. Between the atoms there are pores, and when atoms did not move in the proper manner, the reason offered was that the pores were blocked. Accordingly, to cure illness, the atoms had to be brought back to their proper motility through mechanical means. This simple doctrine allowed for pleasurable physical therapy and elevated the morale of the patient; it also appealed to the utilitarian and pleasure-seeking Roman mind. What could be a more pleasant way to treat an illness than by the principle of "contraris contrarius"—when "the contrary" meant immersing oneself in a warm tub while drinking chilled vintage wine?

After the fashionable success of Asclepiades, Greek physicians were acceptable in Rome, and by 46 B.C. Julius Caesar had granted them full citizenship.† The theories of Asclepiades had had other consequences as well. Themison (123–43 B.C.), a student of Asclepiades, embellished his teacher's ideas and founded a new school of medical thought, Methodism. Themison's notion was that if tissues were composed of solid atoms between which there were pores, in practice one need only consider the condition of these pores. If the pores were clogged and constricted, it was because of coldness; therefore, the treatment should be to apply heat. If the pores were too lax, the method of treatment should be to apply cold. The simplicity of these systems implied simple therapeutic regimens, and therefore only astringents and laxatives were used. Furthermore, all ailments could be considered as generalized problems, since constriction and relaxation were larger concepts than any local disturbance of the pores.

Simplicity appeals to untrained individuals, and Thessalus of Trales

---

* The Greek atomistic school founded by Leucippus (fifth century B.C.) conceived a mechanistic-materialistic cosmology in which moving atoms destroyed each other or coalesced. The movements of atoms occurred not because of motivations like love or hate, but because of mechanical laws, i.e., as heavier atoms gathered in the center, lighter atoms were forced to the periphery. Democritus (460–360 B.C.) popularized the atom theory, and then Lucretius (95–55 B.C.) elaborated this concept.

† Relieved of the necessity to gain approval, Greek doctors could turn their attention to more scientific pursuits, so that in the next century Largus (c. A.D. 47) experimented with electric physiotherapy in treating the emperor's headaches with electric eels (the first time electriciy was used in medicine), and Dioscorides (c. A.D. 76) devoted his life to describing plants and compiling an exhaustive material medica which remained for one thousand years the basis for medicinal therapy.

(A.D., 10–70), a weaver by trade, memorized these Methodic principles. He became a medical teacher and private physician to Nero. He promised a doctor's degree within a few months to anyone who came to him and paid the fee. The name "Thessalus" has come to stand for a medical charlatan; nonetheless, this quack introduced a practice which today is still important in teaching medical students. Probably because he wished to impress both his patients and his students, Thessalus "taught" Methodism at the bedside of the patient. Another Methodic physician, Soranus (A.D. 93–138), had studied in Alexandria before he came to Rome; he wrote an authoritative biography of Hippocrates and was a specialist in gynecological and pediatric problems. Soranus opposed demonology; he also opposed many of the simple therapies of the Methodist school and in his practice used whatever treatment from whatever school he found to be pragmatically sound. We shall discuss in the next section his crucial observations on diseases of the mind.

Aurelius Cornelius Celsus (25 B.C.–A.D. 50) was a writer on medical subjects and described all phases of human life and experience. During the rule of Tiberius, Celsus made a collection of many of the great medical writings of Greek antiquity, which he translated into Latin. He was probably not a practicing physician; as he was a member of the patrician class, the practice of medicine would have been beneath his dignity. It is curious how the pendulum had swung by this time. Now not only were the Greek writers accepted, but anything which did not contain remnants of Greek thought was disdained. Because Celsus wrote in clear, concise, and picturesque Latin prose, he was considered by some to be the Latin Hippocrates or the Cicero of medicine. He was not bound by any one particular school of thought, although he had the highest respect for the followers of Hippocrates. But unlike the great Greek physician, Celsus did not have pupils and was little appreciated during his lifetime. Celsus stressed the importance of dissection and probably attended autopsies. The Romans were delighted to watch gladiators smash each other's bones but were reluctant to examine the bones after they had been broken; and if it had not been for the emphasis that men like Celsus placed on the importance of dissection, anatomical studies might have died out completely during these years. Celsus believed in demonology to the degree that he considered that some illnesses were due to the anger of the gods; however, by and large he advocated a rational approach to medicine and made accurate observations. One of his concepts—that frightening a patient might cure him by scaring away spirits that possessed him—was still used in the Middle Ages.

In the last century before Christ many physicians became unhappy with the rigidity of the anti-Hippocratic, Methodist theories and searched for a vital principle that would explain health and disease more satisfactorily. They found this principle in *pneuma,* the air, and hence were called Pneumatics. As clinicians, these men were practical and interested in a wide range of treatments; consequently they were also later called Eclectics, because they were not bound by any system of therapy, even though they preferred the humoral theory. Eclecticism in medical philosophy has come to mean choosing from many sources what is thought to be best. Like the Hippocratics, the Eclectics were extremely careful in their descriptions of diseases, and especially in their observations of detail; they subsequently revitalized the original Hippocratic clinical methods. In the early part of the first century A.D. the Eclectics reached their greatest influence with the work of their chief proponent, Aretaeus (A.D. 50–130).

Little is known about Aretaeus, who rarely mentions himself in *De Causis et Signis Morborum,* the only one of his treatises that survives. He was a native of Cappadocia in eastern Asia Minor and probably studied in Alexandria and Egypt. His ideal was Hippocrates; like him he was free of dogma and superstition, offered vivid clinical descriptions of many important diseases, and was deeply concerned with the welfare of his patients. For example, Aretaeus tells us that ointments that would stain bedclothes and are disagreeable to the patient are undesirable.[8]

Aretaeus observed mentally ill patients and did careful follow-up studies on them. As a result he established the fact that manic and depressive states occur in the same individual and that lucid intervals exist between manic and depressive periods. He considered mental illness in terms of its outcome, emphasizing the course of the disease and its prognosis. Aretaeus was the first to describe in detail the personalities of people prior to a mental breakdown (the prepsychotic personality). He also understood that not all persons with mental illness are destined to suffer intellectual deterioration, a fact not adequately emphasized until the twentieth century.

The followers of Asclepiades established Greek doctors in Rome; Celsus compiled Greek medical thought; Aretaeus revitalized Hippocratic observational medicine. The next development in Roman medicine was the appearance of the greatest of the medical writers, Claudius Galenus of Pergamum (A.D. 131–200), whose authority was practically undisputed for the following fifteen hundred years.

Galen began his career as surgeon to the gladiators in Pergamum and as part of his duties prescribed dietary regimens for these athletes. In A.D. 161 his appointment terminated, and the next year he went to Rome, where he contacted fellow Pergamenians who might be in a position to help him. Galen's rise to fame began with his curing of Eudemus, a philosopher, of quartan fever. Over the next four years his illustrious patients included the uncle of the Emperor Ovarus and the son-in-law of Marcus Aurelius. Galen left Rome at the time that an epidemic was reported approaching the Italian coast. Some reports say that he fled because he was afraid he would die in the epidemic; other accounts mention the fact that he went to his home in Pergamum, which was also in the path of the epidemic, and explain that he had simply made enemies in Rome whom he feared.

Galen is said to have written at least four hundred works, of which eighty-three books and at least fifteen commentaries on the Hippocratic writings are still extant. He was a great borrower: he plagiarized, synthesized, embellished, and copied. He utilized the mysticism of Plato, the Stoicism of Zeno, and the anatomical works of Herophilus and Erasistratus, and he had Epicurean tastes. The perpetuation of his influence was due to his staunch advocacy of Hippocrates and his acceptance of a Creator to whom he frequently dedicated his works. Christianity in the Dark Ages could find no exception to Galenic monotheism.

Galen maintained that human anatomy was identical with animal anatomy, a theory that was held until the sixteenth century, when Vesalius proved otherwise. Galen probably observed dissections of human bodies only twice in his life, but his descriptions of bones and muscles are excellent. He observed that brain lesions in animals produce disturbances on the opposite side of the body. He traced seven of the cranial nerves, distinguished between the sensory and motor nerves, and showed that the arteries contained blood. Although he knew that blood was mobile, he never formulated a theory of why or how it circulated. He noted that total severance of the spinal cord in animals resulted in a loss of movement and sensation below the lesion, and he offered the theory that nerves relayed impulses from the brain and the spinal cord.[9]

The weakness of Galenic anatomy lies not only in its reliance upon animal dissection but also in the fact that Galen substantiated his anatomical findings by an appeal to religious philosophy. Galen depended heavily upon the Hippocratics; he believed in the doctrine of the four humors; and he philosophized in the manner of Aristotle and Plato about the teleological principle in physiology. Although he spoke of the brain as the site of the rational soul, he went so far as to maintain that severe emotional disturbance might indicate a lesion in the brain. He did, however, seek an integrating force to link mind and body. As a result he recognized an active organizing principle derived from a spiritual source.

Galen transmitted to the medieval world some rays of Hellenistic culture. Nevertheless, because he codified the primitive notions of his era, he also helped to retard the development of medicine for centuries.

The Psychological Contributions of the Romans

Of the Greek philosophies that influenced Roman thought, two, Epicureanism and Stoicism, were extremely realistic in their approach to the problems of daily life. Neither was a theoretical system comparable to the ideas of the pre-Socratic cosmologists; instead, each offered a set of ethical principles governing human conduct. The ultimate aim of both philosophies was the attainment of happiness, which was to be found in peace of mind and lack of tension—for the Stoics in indifference or apathy, for the Epicureans in inner security. So far as the Stoics and Epicureans were interested in metaphysics, theirs was a thoroughly materialistic philosophy, the atomic theory of Democritus. The world consists of atoms, they believed, and their movements follow their own laws; man's only sensible position is either to conform with these laws and accept the inevitable course of materially predestined events (Stoicism) or to try to extract from them as much pleasure as possible (Epicureanism). The central ethical principle for both Stoic and Epicurean philosophies is "ataraxia," or lack of perturbation. The wise person recognizes that he can achieve happiness only by making himself independent from, or at least unperturbed by, the inexorable, unchangeable course of world events. "Perturbation" thus meant mental distress, a phrase which for centuries—in fact, until just recently—was synonymous with mental disease. Modern psychotropic drugs—tranquilizers—which are used hopefully to free man from his emotional stress, are called "ataractics." It is characteristic of our scientific era that we try to achieve with chemicals the same goal which the ancients tried to reach through philosophy.

The Epicurean mode of reaching a state of happiness was different from that of the Stoic. Epicurus modified Democritus' materialistic, deterministic system to suit his philosophy. He made it not less materialistic but less deterministic. The old atomic doctrine gave to accidental atomic events (chance) an important role in the evolution of the world but taught that in their movement the atoms themselves follow universal laws. In contrast, Epicurus maintained that the atoms have some degree of self-determination. This permitted Epicurus to negate absolute predetermination and lawfulness in nature and vindicate freedom of will. Man can therefore become to some degree independent of the universal unchangeable course of world events and can achieve the ultimate goal—his own happiness. This consists ultimately in seeking pleasure. Epicurus preferred, however, the attenuated higher forms of pleasure to the momentary gratification of the pleasures of the flesh. Full happiness consists in the serene, not tempestuous, enjoyment of these attenuated pleasures.

The ethical goal of the Stoics was like that of the Epicureans—to obtain freedom from emotional stress, which they equated with happiness. The Stoics, however, followed more closely than the Epicureans the original determinism of Democritus. For the Stoics society was an integral part of an internally consistent universe guided by universal unchangeable laws. For them the whole world, including society, is ruled by an intrinsic "world intelligence." The social order—"politicon systema"—is a part of an all-encompassing world order. To promote this rational world (and social order) is the duty of man. He must accept peacefully the universal unchangeable laws of the world and do everything to further them. Lack of perturbance—the lack of emotional stress—consists in submitting to the laws of the universe without rebelling against them. This world intelligence is represented by God. The Stoics' philosophy is pantheistic and prepares the way to Christian monotheism. In itself, however, the contributions of Stoic philosophy without the powerful influence of Jewish monotheism never would have sufficed to introduce the Christian era.

Stoicism and Epicureanism, as practical rather than theoretical philosophies, contributed little to psychology as a basic science. In fact, any predominantly ethical orientation is not conducive to development of psychology as a science. Psychology deals with mental processes as natural phenomena and does not evaluate them from the point of view of good or bad. It is difficult for man to look upon his own nature objectively; he is apt to see in himself only what he wants to see and ignore and repress what he considers as bad and unacceptable. In the ancient world, as in later times, the tendency to evaluate and moralize instead of trying to understand human nature was the greatest obstacle to the development of psychology as a science. Furthermore, the Hellenistic practical and ethical orientation was reinforced, as far as psychology was concerned, in the Roman Empire by the withering away of scientific interest in nature, the human body, and the mind. The psychological thoughts of Plato and Aristotle were too abstract to be applied to the behavior of individual persons. They were actually generalities about human strivings, memory, fantasy, emotions, and drives, and these lofty abstractions were not a suitable basis for explaining individual personalities, let alone the behavior of mentally disturbed patients. On the other hand, although Hellenistic preoccupation with the desirable way of life contributed little toward a scientific psychology, it did prepare the way for the empirical psychotherapy that was a redeeming feature of the otherwise sterile and stagnant medicine of Rome.

It is not surprising, of course, that Roman medicine reflected the characteristic pragmatism of the Roman people. There was little theoretical interest in anatomy and physiology, and the orientation of Roman physicians was strictly empirical: they wanted to make their patients comfortable by pleasant physical therapies. Any procedure—warm baths, massage, music, shocks by electric eels, diet, or well-lighted and pleasant rooms— that produced immediate results and improved the patient's subjective state of mind also increased the physician's reputation, which was all that mattered.

The two most significant Roman contributions to the development of psychiatry were made by a philosopher, Cicero, and a Methodist physician, Soranus. Cicero (106–43 B.C.), who combined the Roman virtue of pragmatism with an exceptional clarity of thought and an unsurpassed ability to penetrate to the heart of a problem, commented on medical matters in his usual pointed way. Although he was not—or perhaps *because* he was not—a physician, he recognized the central significance of mental illnesses and asked "Why for the care and maintenance of the body, there has been devised an art . . . whilst on the other hand the need of an art of healing for the soul has not been felt so deeply . . . nor has it been studied so closely."[10] Cicero stated boldly that bodily ailments could be a result of emotional factors. Hence he might be called the first psychosomaticist. He objected to the black-bile concept of Hippocrates and believed in the psychological causation of melancholia. "What we call furor they call melancholia, as if the reason were affected only by a black bile, and not disturbed as often by a violent rage, or fear, or grief."[11]

In discussing similarities and differences between bodily and mental illnesses, he recognized the fundamental differences between the two. "Herein indeed the mind and the body are unlike; that though the mind when in perfect health may be visited by sickness, as the body may, yet the body may be disordered without our fault, the mind cannot. For all the disorders and perturbations of the mind proceed from a neglect of reason; these disorders, therefore, are confined to men; the beasts are not subject to such perturbations, though they act sometimes as if they had a reason."[12]

This thought is fundamental to modern psychotherapy, for when a person accepts and understands the psychological sources of his mental disturbance, he becomes capable of changing the circumstances that led to his problem. This is also perhaps the clearest statement made by an ancient writer of man's responsibility for his own behavior, normal or morbid. In the same *Tusculan Disputations* Cicero also says: "The cure of grief, and of other disorders, is one and the same, in that they are all voluntary, and founded on opinion; we take them on ourselves because it seems right so to do. Philosophy undertakes to eradicate this error as the root of all our evils: let us therefore surrender ourselves to be instructed by it, and suffer ourselves to be cured; for whilst these evils have possession of us, we not only cannot be happy, but cannot be right in our minds."[13] Today we do not call the cure philosophy, but psychotherapy.

The Methodist physician, Soranus, who has been mentioned above, had a student, Caelius Aurelianus, who put down some of his master's ideas in a volume called *On Acute Disease and On Chronic Disease*. Seventeen chapters in this book are devoted to "phrenitis," diseases of the mind. They were called "phrenitis" because the seat of the mind was considered to be located in the diaphragm, *(phren)*.

Soranus was a most enlightened physician in his attitude toward the mentally ill and refused to treat them harshly. "The place [in which patients with phrenitis should be lodged] should be lighted," he says, "through high windows, for it often happens in this disease that unguarded patients, in their madness, jump out of windows."[14] Whether a patient is placed in a warm room or a cold room should depend upon what the patient feels is most comfortable, and the only time Soranus considered restraint advisable for the excitable patient was when there was a danger that he would injure himself. Whatever restraints were used were to be humanely applied: "Use wool or clothing to protect the places where the ropes are tied, lest the harm done the patients be greater than the advantage gained in keeping them quiet."[15] He was as outspoken in his refusal to treat mental patients harshly as were the great reformists in the latter part of the eighteenth century, who finally released the patients from their chains.

Soranus' management of the mentally ill was directly opposed to methods advocated by Celsus, who believed that rough treatment would frighten a patient out of mental illness. Celsus chained patients, starved them, isolated them in total darkness, and administered cathartics in his efforts to frighten them into health. In contrast, Soranus believed he could reduce the discomfort of the mentally ill by talking to them, and he recommended discussing with the patient his occupation or other subjects that might interest him.

Soranus did not doubt that mental illness was caused by a material disturbance in the organism but tempered this organic point of view by undogmatic and practical measures, the purpose of which was to relieve the mental anguish of the mentally ill. Unlike other Methodists, he was not satisfied to treat excessive tension with relaxing measures and to treat excessive looseness with astringent measures; instead, he believed that theory was secondary to practical consideration of the individual patient. One of the astonishing lessons that Soranus left for psychiatric posterity, and which was often repeated in the history of psychiatry, consists in the fact that even though he described mental illness in terms of an organic mechanical disturbance, he treated the mentally ill by psychological measures. Soranus minimized the utilization of drugs and other physical methods, stressing the importance of the relationship between the physician and the patient.

In Retrospect

The basic orientation of the Greeks, revived during the Renaissance, made possible the further development of all natural sciences, including medicine. We may disregard most ancient theories and observations, but we cannot emphasize too strongly the historical importance of the rationalistic approach, the mentality of ancient Greece, which was inaugurated and established as a tradition during this unique phase of human history—the Classical era.

The early Greek philosophers, those whose naturalistic attitude was revived during the Renaissance, paved the way for Hippocrates and his school by replacing magic-mystical-religious explanations with a rational orientation toward the world and were therefore the true originators of our present era.

Of similar nature was the contribution of the Greeks to the psychological approach. In ancient thought the turning point from cosmological speculations to the study of man can be traced to the appearance of the Pythagorean school. Not only Plato's rationalistic idealism but also Hippocratic medicine can be followed back to Pythagoras. It is understandable that the intellectual turning from the external world to man should have stimulated curiosity about human personality and the human body. In this respect the body has an intermediary position between the external physical world and the inner self. It can be studied as both an external object and as part of self-awareness. It is part of external reality and psychological reality. This recognition was invaluable in man's dawning sense of obligation to know himself.

The view that the essence of nature consists in quantitative relationships between events that can be mathematically formulated was the most powerful blow to the naïve realism of the early philosophers, for whom the world consisted in tangible and visible objects as the ultimate realities. Mathematical reasoning as a psychological function is clearly different from the mere observation of external objects. With the Pythagorean emphasis on mathematical reasoning and on reasoning in general, the focus of interest turned for the first time from external objects to the mind, which reflects about the nature of things.

The two influences emanating from Pythagoras—the one upon Plato, the other upon Hippocrates—are the sources of the separation of psychology from medicine that has persisted until our present era. The unification of these two trends has only begun in the present day.

Although the philosophers and physicians of the Hellenistic and Roman periods were far less revolutionary in their theoretical contributions than were the great early Greek thinkers, their work did add to the mainstream of psychiatric evolution. The spreading of Greek medicine by Asclepiades, the Hippocratic revitalization stimulated by Aretaeus, some of the anatomical compilations of Galen, and the humanization of treatment of the mentally ill by men such as Soranus and Cicero—all these contributions served the development of psychiatry well. In fact, Roman preoccupation with ethical concepts prepared the way for future developments in psychotherapy.

And even though in physiology Galen actually proved to be a retrogressive force for centuries, in the sense that he maintained the Hippocratic position of organismic unity, this greatest of the Hellenistic physicians perpetuated a holistic concept of the organism that is the essence of modern psychiatry and the psychosomatic approach in medicine.

CHAPTER 5

The Medieval Period

Medieval Psychology

The citizens of ancient Greece at the height of their civilization found their inner security in knowledge and reason. The Romans adopted the intellectual heritage of Greece but relied more for their peace of mind on social institutions and on a rational organization of a society supported by equalitarian law, technological achievements, and military might. When these institutions disintegrated and the empire declined, fear, unadulterated and naked, felt by rich and poor alike, became the central dynamic social issue. The collapse of the Roman security system produced a general regression to belief in the magic, mysticism, and demonology from which, seven centuries before, man had been liberated through Greek genius.

The causes underlying the fall of the empire were complex. Among the most important were the pressures from barbaric tribes and the plague. Between the first and fourth centuries A.D. six epidemics killed hundreds of thousands of people and desolated the land. In these times of catastrophe people turned for comfort to supernatural explanations, and Christianity exquisitely satisfied many of the emotional needs of the demoralized masses. Christ was worshiped as the tender of souls and also as healer of the body. Images of Aesculapius from pagan shrines were venerated as images of Jesus the healer. Christian dogma in medicine was all-prevailing. Saints were revered and, as in the pagan past, were invoked to prevent disease. St. Sebastian protected against plagues and St. Job against leprosy; St. Anthony prevented all kinds of diseases, from intestinal upsets to fractures. Christian priests gave advice on healing bodies as well as souls, and priestly scholars recorded for posterity descriptions of miraculous healings. The churches became sanctuaries for sufferers, and as the number of patients coming to the monasteries grew, the churches built hospitals nearby. At Montecassino, St. Benedict of Nursia (A.D. 480–543) laid the foundations for monastic medicine. "The care of the sick is to be placed above and before every other duty . . . the infirmarian must be thoroughly reliable, known for his piety and diligence, solicitous for his charges."[1] Cassiodorus (A.D. 490–585), a philosopher and physician who later became a Benedictine monk, stressed not only the care of the diseased but also the enlightenment of the priestly physician and emphasized the necessity for studying Hippocrates and Galen.

In the fourth century Constantine, seeking the aid of the Christians against his enemies, made Christianity the official religion. The allegiance between the state and church was established. Pope Leo III was supported by Charlemagne, who in turn was christened emperor of the Holy Roman Empire. In the twelfth and thirteenth centuries the crusaders were marching to the Holy Land against the Moslems and were bringing back new thoughts and products from the East. It was during this time that townships prospered, commerce was on the upswing, and the power of feudal lords was beginning to decline, while monarchs achieved supremacy. New nations were carved out of defeated lands. It is no wonder, then, that the Middle Ages has been characterized as an era of amazing contrasts. On the one hand there were examples of tyranny, of destructive plagues, of famine that wiped out hundreds of thousands of people; and on the other hand, stupendous churches were built and principles of chivalry and gallantry and self-sacrifice evolved.

Throughout these hectic periods the unifying influence on all peoples was the Christian faith, along with its counterpart, the Latin language. People were more prepared to face the hardships and discomforts in this world because of the promise of better things in the hereafter.

The constructive influence of religious faith and Christian ethics during these troubled centuries cannot be overrated. This ideological force consoled and strengthened the demoralized and impoverished masses and ensured the continuity of civilization; nonetheless, faith was a jealous mistress. It did not tolerate competition, particularly from science. The medieval motto *credo quia absurdum est* (I believe it because it is absurd) is in opposition to the scientific position, which relies on observation and reason. Rationalism as a social force disappeared, or to be more precise, had to go underground for centuries. The tradition of Greek skeptical empiricism, Alexandrian scholarship, and the practical adaptations of the Greek heritage by the Romans were preserved in monastic libraries and by the Arabs, but these traditions were merely preserved, not developed further. The organizational technique of the Roman Empire was the only dynamic force that survived, as religion was institutionalized on a scale hitherto unknown in human history. The Catholic hierarchy was a clerical replica of the political hierarchy of Rome, Roman laws were the models for canonic laws, and the bishop of Rome was the counterpart of the emperor. This rigidity of organization helped preserve Western culture, but as far as the history of medical ideas is concerned—particularly the ideas that led to modern psychiatry—during the centuries between the decline of Rome and the Renaissance there was not only amost complete stagnation but also a regression to the kind of nonrational thought that had existed before the sixth century B.C.

It is not surprising that in the early part of the Christian era, when organic medicine was at such a complete standstill, the psychological approach to illness retained some vitality. Faith and ethics are related to psychology: saving souls is closely related to curing troubled minds, even though the methods employed are different. The psychiatry of the Middle Ages can be scarcely distinguished from prescientific demonology, and mental treatment was synonymous with exorcism. This is particularly the case in that early heretical doctrine called Manichaeanism, which though Persian and not Christian in its origin had a great appeal in the first Christian centuries. It existed side by side with the orthodox religion, even though it was denounced by men of St. Augustine's authority. This is the dualistic mythology of the never-ending battle of Ormuzd, the good spirit, against Ahriman, the devil that possesses the mentally diseased person's body and mind. In medieval exorcism Christian mythology and prehistoric demonology found a quaint union.

Christian scholastics and Arabian physicians made considerable contributions to humanitarian psychiatric care, particularly during the early Middle Ages, when the Christian spirit of charity was responsible for offering comfort and support to the mentally ill. In the later medieval period, when these early Christian ideals had become debased and reliance upon authority and supernatural explanation for diseases characterized monastic medicine, psychiatric care did deteriorate to the point where it became indistinguishable from demonological exorcism. Originally exorcism was not punishment. The exorcistic rites were directed against the devil who had taken possession of a man's body and soul, not against the man himself.

Edith Wright maintains that medieval laymen had more enlightened attitudes toward mental health than did the professionals, for poetry and other literature present very realistic views of these matters. Wright quotes the story of Yvain, the hero of a French romance who becomes psychotic when he is rejected by his beloved; the cure suggested for the psychosis is to find another love for him. The poem *Amadas* (of the late twelfth century) and later the poem about *Tristan* also indicate an understanding of the idea that emotional crises may result in severe emotional disorders and that they may be corrected by a realistic psychological approach. Wright therefore says, "There existed in France in the 12th, 13th and 14th centuries, a conception of psychosis as a curable illness, caused primarily by an emotional upset. . . ."[2]

Whether insanity was considered the result of emotional upset or diabolic possession during the early medieval period, proper care for the ill individual was a matter of community responsibility. It was not until the fourteenth century that the mentally ill were considered witches and became the victims of persecution. Furthermore, the physical care of the insane was better in the early Middle Ages than it was during the seventeenth and eighteenth centuries. One of the earliest asylums for the mentally ill, the Bethlehem Hospital in London, was originally far different from the snake pit that later became known as Bedlam. In those early days patients were treated with much concern. When they were able to leave the hospital in the care of their relatives, they were given arm badges to wear so that they could be returned to the hospital if their symptoms should recur. These patients received so much attention and sympathy from the community that vagrants often counterfeited badges so they would be taken for former patients of Bethlehem.[3] In the thirteenth century, in Gheel, Belgium, an institution was established to take care of retarded and psychotic children, who were often boarded out to and adopted by sympathetic families in the neighborhood. And a Franciscan monk, Bartholomaeus Anglicus (c. 1480), who wrote about mental illnesses in the prevailing demonological terms of angels and devils, nonetheless recommended rational methods of treatment, baths, ointments, and diets.

All these more or less isolated examples of enlightened rational approaches were but carryovers from the past and not original contributions. They came from Greek tradition. This is why the Byzantine Empire, which preserved Greek culture, became so important for later centuries. The humanitarian aspect of medieval medicine was, however, the contribution of the Judeo-Christian spirit.

Of all medieval authors, the great Church Father, St. Augustine, made the most significant contribution to psychology when he demonstrated that introspection is an important source of genuine psychological knowledge. St. Augustine, as a devout member of the Church, accepted most of its dogmas and superstitions, and believed in Divine revelation as a source of psychological knowledge. However, his addition of introspection as an important tool to the understanding of human psychology was an essential contribution to dynamic psychology. He was the first to describe vividly and in detail subjective emotional experiences, and in doing so he used a methodological principle which is still basic to present-day psychology. Without self-awareness psychology could not exist. Emotions—anger, hope, joy, fear—can be experienced only subjectively; if a person has never experienced anger, there is no way to explain to him what anger is, no matter how precise his information may be regarding physiological changes that accompany anger. St. Augustine's *Confessions* are a profoundly incisive work of self-analysis; as Brett said in his *History of Psychology,* "He stands with the greatest, with Plato and Aristotle, and in one respect superior to them. Psychology reaches a second great climax when its expositor can say that the foundation of the soul is continuous self-consciousness, and thought is simply life reflected into itself."⁴ To paraphrase this sentence: Thought is simply life reflected and perceived by the living organism. St. Augustine was not only the first forerunner of Husserl's phenomenology and of existentialism but also a forerunner of psychoanalysis. Like Kierkegaard centuries later, he used autobiographical confession as the source of psychological knowledge. It was psychoanalysis without a psychoanalyst listening and interpreting the confessions.

Aurelius Augustinus, known as St. Augustine, was born in Tagaste (Numidia, North Africa) in A.D. 354. His father, Patricius, was a pagan, a man of great passions, who lived a loose life and encouraged his son's worldly ambition to pursue a lucrative career as a rhetorician. His mother, Monica, was a pious Christian, and her influence upon her son proved to be stronger than that of his sensuous father. As a young man Augustine had an illicit affair with a woman who bore him a son, and until his baptism in his thirty-third year, his life consisted of a constant internal struggle between his love of God and his desire to express his carnal passions.

He studied rhetoric at Carthage, where he was most influenced by Cicero's writings. In an effort to resolve his inner conflict about good and evil, he became an ardent proponent of the Persian ascetic doctrine of Manichaeanism, but grew disenchanted with this creed after a dispute with an outstanding Manichaean bishop. He spent a year at home with his mother and then returned to Carthage to continue his studies. Monica was tormented by her son's lack of faith, and he reports a dream of hers in which she saw herself and her son standing on the same wooden rule. The rule may be taken as a symbol for the rules of Catholicism, since Augustine considers the dream an expression of her wish to share her way of life with her son and thereby bring him to grace.

St. Augustine's inner conflicts increased as he witnessed and participated in the licentious student life at Carthage. He went to Rome for a short period but no longer felt easy with his Manichaean friends and therefore accepted a position in Milan as a teacher of rhetoric. When he abandoned Manichaeanism he continued the search for a solution to his inner conflicts, at first in Skeptic philosophy, and later in the neo-Platonic school, whose monistic teachings appealed to him. His final determination to abandon carnality came when he fell under the direct influence of Alypius, a friend and pupil of the great churchman Ambrose, and after he had read the epistles of St. Paul.

His concubine had followed him to Milan, and they had become betrothed, but in his fight against sensuality Augustine left her. Total acceptance of Catholicism did not come easily, however, and he did have another affair. The conflict of the flesh opposing the spirit and the spirit opposing the flesh reached a dramatic peak in his thirty-second year and is vividly described in his *Confessions*. He burst into violent sobbing as he prayed to God. "I cast myself down I know not how, under a certain fig-tree, giving full vent to my tears; and the floods of mine eyes gushed out an acceptable sacrifice to Thee. . . . Eagerly then I returned to the place where Alypius was sitting; for there had I laid the volume of the Apostle when I arose thence. I seized, opened, and in silence read that section on which my eyes first fell: Not in rioting and drunkenness, not in chambering and wantonness, not in strife and envying; but put ye on the Lord Jesus Christ, and make not provision for the flesh, in concupiscence. No further would I read; nor needed I: for instantly at the end of this sentence, by a light as it were of serenity infused into my heart, all the darkness of doubt vanished away."[5]

A year later his friend Alypius, Augustine himself, and Augustine's son joined the Church, thus fulfilling Monica's dream. The next year she died content. The description of her death in the *Confessions* is one of the many passages in which St. Augustine, with unsurpassed realism, expressed his never-ending struggle to reconcile earthly emotions with religious ecstasy. "I closed her eyes; and there flowed withal a mighty sorrow into my heart, which was overflowing into tears; mine eyes at the same time, by the violent command of my mind, drank up their fountain wholly dry; and woe was me in such a strife! . . . And being very much displeased that these human things had such power over me . . . with a new grief I grieved for my grief, and was thus worn by a double sorrow."[6] Only after he succeeded in unifying his love for his mother with that felt toward God could he give free flow to his tears. Before God he felt no shame for the weeping that some mortals would have considered weakness.

His son died soon afterward, and from then on Augustine devoted his life to the Church. He founded a monastic religious community in his home town, and two and a half years later he accepted an invitation to serve as a priest at Hyppo, eventually becoming its bishop. He died there in 430 during a siege laid by the Vandals.

As a churchman Augustine took a conservative position against heretics, against the radical policies of the Donatists, who believed in rebaptism and other innovations, and against those who spoke of the basic goodness of human nature. Augustine believed that man is so weak and corruptible that redemption is possible only through Divine Grace, and he maintained this view with uncompromising severity. This attitude was obviously deeply influenced by Augustine's own lifelong internal struggle against his worldly passions, which he was able to conquer only by renouncing them completely and devoting himself wholly to divinity. The controversies in which he became involved allowed Augustine finally to succeed in externalizing his conflicts by fighting his own sinfulness in others; and by attacking his opponents, he attacked all that once was part of his own self.

Sigmund Freud offered as the fulcrum of the psychoanalytic doctrine the point that one cannot combat an invisible enemy, that neurotic disturbances can be conquered only by recognizing through self-revelation their unconscious origin. This principle of uncompromising truthfulness with oneself was also Augustine's guiding impulse. As would Freud centuries later, Augustine unwaveringly assailed the hypocrisy of those who tried to slur over the deep unrevealed motivations that are unacceptable to the conscious personality. Fully aware of the asocial forces of mind, Augustine was pessimistic about human nature, but he saw a way toward mastery of inherent evilness through complete devotion to and dependence upon God as the only source of healing grace.

What makes Augustine so important for the history of psychoanalysis is the psychological methods he used to reach the conclusions on which his religious theories were based. His *Confessions* are an unprecedented example of self-analysis; in this work he methodically presents his earliest memories and bares his soul without reservation. He even tries to reconstruct those early years lost in infantile amnesia on the basis of observations of infants and from whatever memories of his own early childhood he preserved: "And when I was not presently obeyed (my wishes being hurtful or unintelligible), then I was indignant with my elders for not submitting to me, with those owing me no service, for not serving me; and avenged myself on them by tears. Such have I learnt infants to be from observing them; and that I was myself such, they, all unconscious, have shown me better than my nurses who knew it."[7]

Augustine did not believe in the angelic innocence of infants: "The weakness, then, of infant limbs, not its will, is its innocence. Myself have seen and known even a baby envious; it could not speak, yet it turned pale and looked bitterly on its foster-brother. Who knows not this? Mothers and nurses tell you that they allay these things by I know not what remedies. Is that too innocence, when the fountain of milk is flowing in rich abundance, not to endure one to share it? . . . We bear gently with all this, not as being no or slight evils, but because they will disappear as years increase; for, though tolerated now, the very same tempers are utterly intolerable when found in riper years."[8]

Augustine goes on to discuss how children acquire speech, showing that subjective needs are the dynamic power behind this learning process: "Passing hence from infancy, I came to boyhood, or rather it came to me, displacing infancy. Now, did that depart,—(for whither went it?)—and yet it was no more. For I was no longer a speechless infant, but a speaking boy. This I remember; and have since observed how I learned to speak. It was not that my elders taught me words (as, soon after, other learning) in any set method; but I, longing by cries and broken accents and various motions of my limbs to express my thoughts, that so I might have my will, and yet unable to express all I willed, or to whom I willed, did myself, by the understanding which Thou, my God, gavest me, practice the sounds in my memory. When they named any thing, and as they spoke turned towards it, I saw and remembered that they called what they would point out by the name they uttered. And that they meant this thing and no other was plain from the motion of their body, the natural language, as it were, of all nations, expressed by the countenance, glances of the eye, gestures of the limbs, and tones of the voice, indicating the affections of the mind, as it pursues, possesses, rejects, or shuns. And thus by constantly hearing words, as they occurred in various sentences, I collected gradually for what they stood; and having broken in my mouth to these signs, I thereby gave utterance to my will. Thus I exchanged with those about me these current signs of our wills, and so launched deeper into the stormy intercourse of human life, yet depending on parental authority and the beck of elders."[9]

The problems of his later years are presented with the same perspicacity: "In boyhood itself, however (so much less dreaded for me than youth), I loved not study, and hated to be forced to it. Yet I was forced; and this was well done towards me, but I did not well; for, unless forced, I had not learnt. But *no one doth well against his will. . . .*"[10]

He readily admits he disliked basic subjects, but liked to read Vergil's heroic poems. " 'One and one, two;' 'two and two, four;' this was to me a hateful singsong: 'the wooden horse lined with armed men,' and 'the burning of Troy,' and 'Creusa's shame and sad similitude,' were the choice spectacle of my vanity."[11] The philosophy professor of today might be more reticent to admit that cowboy stories excited his youthful mind to a greater extent than basic algebra.

These admissions are the first signs of Augustine's conflict between pleasure and discipline. With advancing years his sense of his own sinfulness grows. Classical literature becomes a source of sexual temptation. From Greek and Latin authors he learns "many a useful word." He quotes Terence as an example of how lust may be excited by "pornographic" verse:

> Viewing a picture, where the tale was drawn,
> Of Jove's descending in a golden shower
> To Danae's lap, a woman to beguile.
> And what God? Great Jove,
> Who shakes heaven's highest temples with his thunder,
> And I, poor mortal man, not do the same!
> I did it, and with all my heart I did it.[12]

St. Augustine confesses how susceptible he was to the "vanities" of the world and how he deceived his parents and teachers, hiding from them his eagerness to see cheap shows and reenact them. He also confesses that he stole when he was sixteen years old, displaying remarkable insight into the motivations for stealing and even for the psychology of kleptomania. "Yet

I lusted to thieve, and did it, compelled by no hunger, nor poverty . . . For I stole *that, of which I had enough,* [italics authors'] and much better. Nor cared I to enjoy what I stole, but joyed in the theft and sin itself. A pear tree there was near our vineyard, laden with fruit, tempting neither for colour nor taste. To shake and rob this, some lewd young fellows of us went . . . and took huge loads, not for our eating, but to fling to the very hogs, having only tasted them. And this, but to do what we liked only, because it was misliked. . . . For if aught of those pears came within my mouth, what sweetened it was the sin."[13]

Augustine does not stop at recognizing the lure of the forbidden fruit; he goes further in his search for secret motivations, demonstrating an understanding of the psychology of adolescent gangs with his discovery that committing a crime in company of others further enhances the gratification derived from it; that is, to use the vocabulary of modern dynamic psychology, he discovers that actions are determined not by a single motive, but by many: "I loved then in it also the company of the accomplices, with whom I did it. . . . For had I then loved the pears I stole, and wished to enjoy them, I might have done it alone, had the bare commission of the theft sufficed to attain my pleasure; nor needed I have inflamed the itching of my desires by the excitement of accomplices. But since my pleasure was not in those pears, it was in the offence itself, which the company of fellow-sinners occasioned."[14]

Augustine's psychological genius is seen in his search to understand the mourning he felt when a dear friend died. He vividly portrays the mourner wallowing in misery and comes close to recognizing that the function of hate in mourning is to help detach oneself from the beloved and lost person. Equally penetrating is his analysis of the love of fame. He recognizes that the admirer of a great man does not admire him for what he says and accomplishes, but wants to be in his place and have for himself the love and admiration of the people. Yet, he asks, why does he not admire persons for their qualities? "Do I love in another what, if I did not hate, I should not spurn and cast from myself?" He resignedly adds: "Man himself is a great deep, whose very hairs Thou numberest, O Lord, and they fall not to the ground without thee. And yet are the hairs of his head easier to be numbered than his feelings and the beatings of his heart."[15]

Augustine refers more than once to those who try to explain man's conduct in physical terms only, thus circumventing individual responsibility and ignoring man's ability to account for his behavior in psychological terms: "Those impostors then whom they style Mathematicians, I consulted without scruple; because they seemed to use no sacrifice, nor to pray to any spirit for their divinations. . . . [They say] 'The cause of thy sin is inevitably determined in heaven'; and 'This did Venus, or Saturn, or Mars': that man forsooth, flesh and blood and proud corruption might be blameless; while the Creator and Ordainer of heaven and the stars is to bear the blame."[16]

Fifteen hundred years ago Augustine believed that a sufferer should understand himself psychologically and correct his behavior. In his great work *De Civitate Dei,* the metaphor he uses to express what life would be like without inner turmoil is that of a city of God ruled by truly religious men whose souls are free of all destructive impulses. The City of God, Augustine says, can not be built by technological or political means. Its appearance requires a change in *inner* values; and it is this sincere concern for psychological matters that makes Augustine's writings so pertinent for twentieth-century psychiatry.

In his *Confessions,* psychology becomes real and concrete; in contrast to the abstract descriptions of Plato and Aristotle, it assumes flesh and blood. St. Augustine's psychology tells about the feelings, conflicts, and anguish of an individual of greatest sincerity and introspective power, and can be justly considered as the earliest forerunner of psychoanalysis.

During the first five centuries after the fall of Rome, monks functioned both as theologians and medical men. The University of Salerno, which came to prominence during the eleventh and twelfth centuries, was instrumental in severing medicine from theology and putting physical healing back into the hands of nonclerical physicians. Psychology, however, was not so fortunate; its connection with magic was not broken, and its ideas remained the property of philosophic theology and medieval scholasticism until well into the fourteenth century. The result was a stagnation of thought about psychological matters, for which St. Thomas Aquinas (1225–1274), a pupil of the great schoolman Albertus Magnus, was to a great degree responsible.

In the thirteenth century Aristotle's natural philosophy had been revived in the West, transmitted from the Greek manuscripts preserved by the Arabs. St. Thomas came to terms with this vital intellectual force by reconciling Aristotle's teachings with Christian dogma through their subordination to religious revelation. Thus the works of the great Greek observer and rationalist were placed in the paradoxical position of being dogmatic impediments to the development of science and free inquiry. Of great importance was Aquinas' description of the separation between the body and the soul. He believed that the body is ruled by the soul but that the soul can exist independent of the body. He held the vegetative functions to be dependent on the alimentary tract and some other organs, and the sensitive faculty as operative through the sensory organs; but he did not see the rational powers as functions of any bodily organ or as dependent on the brain. What St. Thomas did to Aristotle's teachings is a classical example of the common historical pattern that an originally pioneering accomplishment, after becoming institutionalized, can become rigid dogma and the greatest impediment for future development. These and other principles become so institutionalized that even into the eighteenth century Aristotle remained the unyielding fortress of reactionary and oppressive thought.

The influence of St. Thomas in the history of psychiatry thus must be seen as retrogressive.*

The Medieval Organic Approach

During the early years of the Christian era, when the Western world was struggling against the barbarian hordes, the Byzantine Empire was the repository of the Greco-Roman heritage in medicine as in other cultural fields. The earliest Byzantine physician of note was Oribasius (A.D. 325–403), who compiled Greco-Roman medical writings. Oribasius was born in Asia Minor in Pergamum, Galen's birthplace. Oribasius copied Galen's ideas; he also compiled works by Aristotle, Asclepiades, and Soranus. A later compiler, Aetius of Amida (A.D. 527–565), transcribed sixteen books of selections from previous writers. He described three types of "phrenitis" —that is, mental disease—in the anterior, middle, and posterior parts of the brain, affecting memory, reason, and imagination. Alexander of Tralles (A.D. 525–605) and Paul of Aegina (A.D. 625–690) followed Aetius in localizing emotional disturbances in the brain.

Alexander of Tralles achieved worldwide fame—his writings were transcribed into Hebrew, Latin, and Arabic—as did his brother, who was the architect of Santa Sophia in Constantinople. His major work dealt with pathology and therapeutics of internal diseases and took up twelve volumes. He was an excellent observer in the finest Greek tradition; a good example of his attention to detail is his differentiation between various parasites found in the intestine. He described mania and melancholia and recognized that they may occur in the same individual—a rediscovery of the observations of Aretaeus. Like Paul of Aegina, he recommended baths, wines, diets, and sedatives for the mentally deranged, a therapy similar to that used by the Roman Methodists. Paul of Aegina wrote seven volumes entitled *On Medicine*. Most of his writings concerned obstetrics and surgery, the latter subject excellently covered in precise detail. (As we noted above, surgery has always been less hampered by magic and dogma than the other medical fields.) By his own admission, Paul never published anything original and depended completely on the past for his information; in this he was typical of other medieval medical writers who considered that their function was to preserve knowledge without contributing anything new to it.

Byzantine science and medicine, just as did the Byzantine Empire, fought a losing battle against the growing and inevitable fate of Hellenistic

* On the other hand, another scholastic and pupil of Albertus Magnus, Roger Bacon (1214–1292), helped keep alive the empirical-rational tradition. Opposing St. Thomas, Bacon maintained that observation and not deduction can lead to ultimate truth. His contribution to psychiatry was his consideration that mental diseases come from natural causes. This and other ideas caused him to be censored by the Church, which he served as a Franciscan friar, and condemned by Oxford University, where he taught.

decline. Christian dogma, which venerated the authority of Aristotle and Galen, retained for a time its preservative function. This form of preservative function, however, could not forever prohibit the decay of its treasured object, which was rational Grecian science. Hippocratic Dogmatists attempted a similar form of preservation but fortunately they could not stem the tide of scientific experimentation and exploration. A millennium had passed since the Dogmatists, but authority rule remained unquestioned. The scholastics and the monks were to have their millennium, interrupted only briefly by the attempt of Arab scholars to add their preservative to the already overprotected ancient authority.

A fascinating chapter in the history of medical thought begins in the sixth century with the rise of the Arabian Empire, twelve hundred years after the Persian Empire had contributed to the birth of medicine. A prophet, Mohammed, had arisen to unite the Arabic people into a new and flourishing culture, which was spread, as the Arabian conquests expanded their influence, throughout the Western world.

Mohammed was born in 570 in Mecca, and by the time he died, in 632, in Medina, the Arab world was already embracing Islam, the religion of which he was the self-proclaimed prophet. A century later his successors had conquered Syria, Persia, Mesopotamia, Africa, Egypt, Arabia, and Spain, and the Arabian Empire was so gigantic that it had to be split in half for the sake of efficient administration. Baghdad became the Eastern caliphate and Córdoba became the Western. The march of these people, who professed monotheism and one prophet, halted only in 717 at the gates of Constantinople. The grandfather of Charlemagne, Charles Martel, stemmed the Islamic invasion of France at Tours in A.D. 732. It was not until the eleventh century, with the growing power of the Turks, that Arabian military power began to wane. Finally, in the thirteenth century, when the Tartars ravaged Baghdad, the tide of the militant Moslems was destroyed for all time. The Arabs devoured knowledge with almost the same rapidity that they consumed empires. In a sense Mohammed died illiterate; all through his life, however, he admired knowledge, for it was said that "Allah taught man to move the pen." As the Arabs conquered countries, they took manuscripts as part of their loot and thus became the main custodians of ancient knowledge. They also made two contributions that became indispensable tools for the natural sciences—algebra and the concept of zero.

The most important impetus to Arabian medicine was the work of the Nestorians, a religious sect in the lands of Mesopotamia, Syria, and Persia that were conquered by Islamic tribesmen. The Nestorians were followers of Nestorius, who was born in Syria. The date of his birth is uncertain; it is known, however, that he died in exile in A.D. 451 in the Libyan desert. He, like Mohammed, became the leader of a religious sect. He received a

Christian education in Syria, and because of his great reputation as an eloquent monk he was called to Constantinople and served as patriarch of that city from 428 to 431. Nestorius took issue with some Catholic doctrines and was deposed and banished to Arabia. His followers preached in Asia, Syria, Armenia, and even in the distant lands of India and China; but many of the sect, because of persecution, gave up their theological studies and began to work instead at curing sick bodies. They founded medical schools at Edessa in Mesopotamia and Gondischapur in Persia, and their medical missionaries traveled to Salerno and thus established contact with the first and most important medical school in Europe. These "Christians of the Orient," thoroughly grounded in Greek, the language of the city of Constantinople at the time of Nestorius, translated Greek works into Syrian, and then, as Nestorian physicians started to attend important Arabian caliphs, their Syrian works were translated into Arabic. In this way the Nestorians, Syrians by birth and Greeks by education, transmitted Hellenism to Persia and Arabia and put Hippocrates, Aristotle, and Galen in the hands of the Arabs.

The most illustrious among the Arab physicians was Rhazes (A.D. 865–925), the "Persian Galen." Because of his brilliance as a scholar and clinician, he was appointed physician-in-chief to the Baghdad Hospital, one of the first of the ancient hospitals to have a ward devoted to the mentally ill. Rhazes wrote more than two hundred volumes on subjects ranging from medicine and religion to philosophy and astronomy, and his *Liber Continens* was a compilation of all Arabian medical knowledge up to that time.

In the field of psychiatry Rhazes was as good as the finest of the Hippocratic physicians. He was a careful describer of all illnesses, including mental ones. He combined psychological methods and physiological explanations in a way reminiscent of the Hippocratics, and he used psychotherapy in a primitive but dynamic fashion. Rhazes was once called in to treat a famous caliph who had severe arthritis. He advised a hot bath, and while the caliph was bathing, Rhazes threatened him with a knife, proclaiming he was going to kill him. The caliph got up from his knees in the bath and ran; Rhazes left the palace and wrote later to explain the reason for his behavior. "There was . . . a deficiency in the natural caloric and this treatment would have been unduly protracted, so I abandoned it in favor of *psychotherapeusis* and when the peccant humours had undergone sufficient coction in the bath, I deliberately provoked you in order to increase the natural caloric which thus gained sufficient strength to dissolve the already softened humours"[17] (authors' italics).

While some other prominent Arabian physicians used demonological explanations for diseases, Rhazes always fought charlatanism and stood by his principles as a physician and as a man. When the patriarch of Bokhara argued with Rhazes and could not budge the great teacher from his point, he sentenced him to be hit over the head with his own book until the book or the head broke.[18] Rhazes was blinded by this punishment and remained sightless because he would not undergo an operation by a surgeon who was unfamiliar with the anatomy of the eyeball.

Rhazes, like other Arab doctors, was hindered by the fact that the Koran did not permit anatomical dissection. Arabs were not permitted to look on the unclothed body of a woman, and like the Christian Bible, the Koran insisted upon acceptance of authority. Thus Arabian medicine was stymied by lack of intellectual freedom. As Rhazes himself said, "If Galen and Aristotle are of one mind on a subject, then of course their opinion is the right one. When they differ, however, it is extremely difficult to know the truth."[19]

Arabian physicians were not able to make any real contribution to psychiatric theory because they depended entirely on the organic speculations of Hippocrates. But some Arabian physicians were aware that a relationship did exist between physical afflictions and emotions. One woman who suffered from such severe cramps in her joints that she was unable to rise was cured by a physician who lifted her skirt, thus putting her to shame. "A flush of heat was produced within her which dissolved the rheumatic humour."[20]

Avicenna (A.D. 980–1037) was recognized as a child prodigy at the age of ten, when he had memorized the Koran. Before he was twenty he was physician to the royal court, and by the time he was an adult he was considered the most brilliant of all Arabian physicians. His book *The Canon* was a systematic attempt to correlate Aristotelian philosophy, Hippocratic observation, and Galenic speculation. The book became the medical bible in Asia and later in Europe and was used until the dawn of anatomical experimentation in the sixteenth century. Robinson, the medical historian, considered *The Canon* "the most influential textbook ever written."[21] As in Galen's writings, pages of excellent medical exposition are side by side with pages filled with medical trash. Avicenna was the first to use a catheter in patients who had urethral constriction caused by gonorrhea; yet he also advised placing a louse in the meatus of the urethra for patients suffering from urinary retention.[22] That his ideas could be influential for such a long period is an outstanding example of how medical authoritarianism, lacking in creativity, can stand for centuries without a critical word being raised against it.

Avicenna, like Rhazes, attempted to correlate physiological reactions and emotional states. He is said to have treated a terribly ill patient by putting his finger on the patient's pulse and reciting aloud to him the names of provinces, districts, towns, streets, and people. By noticing how the patient's pulse quickened when names were mentioned Avicenna deduced that the patient was in love with a girl whose home Avicenna was able to locate by this digital examination. The man took Avicenna's advice, married the girl, and recovered from his illness.[23]

Avicenna also was concerned with psychotic delusions and their treatment. When one of his patients claimed he was a cow and bellowed like one, Avicenna told the patient that a butcher was coming to slaughter him. The patient was bound hand and foot; then Avicenna proclaimed that he was too lean and had to be fattened, and untied him. The patient began to eat enthusiastically, "gained strength, got rid of his delusion and was completely cured."[24]

During the twelfth century, Avenzoar (1113–1162) and his pupils Averroës (1126–1198) and Maimonides (1135–1204) influenced Arabian medicine by their philosophical speculations. Avenzoar was a Spanish Moslem and one of the few Arabs to raise his voice against Galen. The Arabs, who were opposed to shedding blood and who therefore refused to use the scalpel, used the cautery (a device to kill tissue through the application of hot substances) as their main surgical instrument. It was also used on patients suffering from mental illness, a practice Avenzoar condemned.

Averroës was a confirmed Aristotelian but compromised with religion by maintaining that "there is a double truth," one begotten by faith and the other from "rational philosophy."[25] This compromise was important for medical psychology; it established the tradition of a medical man keeping his religious convictions and still believing in scientific discoveries.

Maimonides, who is better known for his biblical commentaries and his philosophical writings than for his medical treatises, emphasized the mentally hygienic aspects of an ethical life, in the tradition of the Hebraic scholars. He regarded medicine as an art rather than a science, and as an intuitive physician he was far more concerned with the patient as a totality than with his illness. Like Averroës, he considered religious faith and scientific explorations not incompatible and was one of the few voices raised during the Middle Ages against authoritarianism.

Maimonides, Avenzoar, and Averroës represented a humanistic and philosophical force which emanated from the Western caliphate at Córdoba and which was unquestionably influential in the movement to found hospitals in the Moslem Empire. Probably the earliest hospital in Baghdad was erected in the ninth century; by 1160 there were more than sixty hospitals in that city, and Damascus too had an important hospital that cared for the ill without charging them. Another excellent hospital was founded in Cairo in 1283. At Fez, Morocco, an asylum for the mentally ill had been built early in the eighth century, and insane asylums were built by the Arabs also in Baghdad in 705, in Cairo in 800, and in Damascus and Aleppo in 1270.[26] Because the Arabs believed that the insane were somehow divinely inspired and not victims of demons, the hospital care given them was usually benevolent and kindly.

European hospitals, as well as Arabian ones, founded in the early centuries of the Christian era were pervaded by a humane orientation. In

Europe the first one built was probably the hospital in Lyons, founded in A.D. 542. The Hôtel-Dieu was erected in Paris in A.D. 652; probably the first Italian hospital was Santa Maria della Scala, in Siena, built in A.D. 898. In the twelfth century more hospitals were established to take care of crusaders who fell ill or were wounded. The first European hospital devoted entirely to mental patients was built in 1409 in Valencia, Spain.

Cassiodorus and St. Benedict laid the foundations for monastic medicine. The cure of wounds and broken bones required more than faith, however, and the development of an empirical and practical lay medicine was inevitable. For one thing, the monks' medical work was restricted by many ecclesiastical doctrines: performing clerical duties outside of the monastery, collecting fees, and touching flesh were unacceptable practices. When the twelfth-century Clermont and Lateran councils therefore forbade monks to leave monasteries to take care of patients, lay medicine began to evolve at the University of Salerno.

Salerno had always been a cosmopolitan city, and according to legend the school there was founded sometime in the ninth century by a Jew, an Arab, a Greek, and an Italian. The school was nonsectarian and free from provincial bias, and since the port of Salerno itself had always remained open to Arabian influence as well as European, this guaranteed a tradition of Hippocratic observational medicine. At Salerno mystics and priestly therapeutics were conspicuously absent.

Constantinus Africanus (1020–1087), a Jew who became a Christian convert and a Benedictine monk, was responsible for translating the Arabic versions of Hippocrates' teachings into Latin and bringing them to Salerno. The Hippocratic tradition of organic medicine guaranteed once again an emphasis upon pathology of the nervous system, and in particular the brain, in the explanation of mental illness; for example, abscesses of the cerebral ventricles were considered to be the exciting agents of the psychoses and were treated by diet, bloodletting, and drugs. The comforting ministrations (such as hydrotherapy) of the Roman Methodists were also employed, and animals were dissected and the findings recorded. The reputation of the school of Salerno reached its height when, in 1240, Frederick II decreed that it had the sole right, in the bounds of the Holy Roman Empire, to grant an official medical diploma to physicians.

During the thirteenth century lay physicians who maintained the Hippocratic tradition opposed the scholastics, who condemned clinical experimentation. This generalized social conflict also existed on a personal level within the minds of the physicians themselves. For example, Pietro Albano (1250–1316), of the school of Padua, attempted to reunite Aristotelian deductive reasoning with the known facts of medicine and was condemned to death by the Inquisition because he minimized spiritual principles. Arnold of Villanova (1240–1313), of the French school of Montpellier— the counterpart of the Italian Salerno—met a similar fate. Villanova was

tried for heresy because he attempted to amalgamate Hippocratic principles with demon worship. His recommendation for the treatment of
mania is characteristic: "The skin is incised in the fashion of a cross and
the cranium perforated so that the morbific material will pass to the
exterior."[27] Obviously Villanova wanted to give an opportunity for both
demons and morbid vapors to leave the body.

The uncertainty of the age produced much insecurity, and stirred up the
irrational forces always present in men's minds. Magic has always been one
way to deal with the unknown—as witness the medieval explanation of
mental disorder. The theologians believed that man was the center of the
universe; if a person was sane it was because heaven had ordained it, and if
he was mad it was because some external force, some heavenly body, must
have affected him. It was known that the emotionally distressed are most
troubled when they are alone with their thoughts, and the natural conclusion, to the medieval mind, was that troubled minds were being influenced
by the night's most prominent heavenly phenomenon, the moon. Lunacy
literally means a disorder caused by the lunar body; the institutions that
cared for these troubled people were for centuries afterward called "lunatic
asylums."

By and large, throughout the thirteenth and fourteenth centuries, then,
the human body and its organic afflictions were dealt with by lay physicians, but the problems of the mind remained the domain of the clerical
scholars. What did these Church scholars claim caused conflagrations,
epidemics, and the diseases of the soul? Two Dominican monks, Johann
Sprenger and Heinrich Kraemer, advised the faithful that witches were the
culprits. The reasons why their ideas were so wholeheartedly accepted are
complex and again illustrate mankind's eternal search for security regardless of the means.

The Witch Hunt, the Hunters, and Their
Textbook at the Dawn of the Renaissance

Witch hunts arose in Europe just as the spirit of the Renaissance was
beginning to provoke uneasy reactions among the keepers of the status
quo. Feudalism was threatened by the discovery of gunpowder; the invention of the printing press permitted self-education; abuses of the Church
were being attacked by precursors of the Reformation. In addition, severe
plagues occurred that killed fifty percent of the population of Europe.
Social institutions that are beginning to crumble cannot afford political or
religious disaffection, and the Church, the monarchs, and the feudal lords
grouped their forces for defense. This age had to find its scapegoat, and
severe persecution of the Jews did not seem to be enough to stem the
tide.

One of the most important threats arose in the ranks of the Church
itself. Centuries of imposed celibacy had not inhibited the erotic drives of

monks or nuns, and underground passageways were known to connect some monasteries and nunneries. Townspeople often had to send prostitutes to the monasteries in order to protect the maidens of the village. It became increasingly imperative to the Church to start an antierotic movement, which meant that women, the stimulants of men's licentiousness, were made suspect. Men's unsavory impulses could no longer be tolerated, so they were projected upon women under a misogynic banner whose motto was: "Woman is a temple built over a sewer."[28] Women stirred man's passions, therefore they must be the carriers of the devil. Psychotic women with little control over voicing their sexual fantasies and sacrilegious feelings were the clearest examples of demoniacal possession; and in turning against them the Church increased an already mounting fear of the mentally deranged. The thirteenth and fourteenth centuries were marked by mass psychotic movements that terrified the Church because they could not be controlled. In Hungary, for example, in 1231 a group of people appeared whose conviction it was that plagues were caused by individual sins. They marched throughout much of Europe singing hymns, bearing red crosses on their breasts, and carrying whips with knots from which hung iron tongs. As they passed through villages they would display their penitence publicly by whipping themselves and any self-confessed converts they might attract. This brotherhood of flagellants or crossbearers became excessively powerful, so much so that they threatened to usurp the Church's hitherto exclusive prerogative to forgive sinners, and Emperor Charles IV and Pope Clement finally prohibited their organization. However, other groups of malcontents and psychotics continued to emerge; for example, in 1418 thousands of maniacs danced in the streets at Strasbourg in front of spectators who identified themselves with these self-humiliating orgies and thus vicariously relieved their guilt feelings about their own bodily desires.

As soon as the misogynic banner was fully unfurled, the ideology of the mass movement of witch hunting was codified by Johann Sprenger and Heinrich Kraemer, with typical Germanic thoroughness, in their book *Malleus Maleficarum* (*The Witches' Hammer*) (1487), which is both a textbook of pornography and a textbook of psychopathology. *Malleus* was translated into English in 1928 by the Reverend Montague Summers. In 1484 from Pope Innocent VIII they obtained papal approval to publish their "textbook of the Inquisition"; next Maximilian I, the king of Rome, approved their document in 1486; and finally, a year later, the faculty of theology at the University of Cologne approved the *Malleus*. Kraemer and Sprenger thus possessed the backing of the Church, an important university, and the monarch.[29]

The *Malleus* details the destruction of dissenters, schismatics, and the mentally ill, all of whom came under the term "witch." The book is divided into three parts. The first section attempts to prove the existence of devils and witches; if the reader is not convinced by the authors' arguments, it is only because he himself is a victim of witchcraft or heresy. The second part tells how to identify witchcraft; the third part describes how witches are to be tried in civil courts and punished. The favorite way to destroy the devil was to burn his host, the witch. The *Malleus* recommends that if a doctor cannot find a reason for the cause of disease, or "if the patient can be relieved by no drugs, but rather, seems to be aggravated by them, then the disease is caused by the devil."[30] Thus, any unknown disease was thought to be caused by witchcraft; today if no organic reason can be found for a disease it is thought to be psychologically induced. The *Malleus* points out that "All witchcraft comes from carnal lust which is in women insatiable" and that furthermore, "three general vices appear to have special dominion over wicked women, namely, infidelity, ambition and lust. Therefore, they are more than others inclined towards witchcraft who more than others are given to these vices. . . . Women being insatiable it follows that those among ambitious women are more deeply infected who are more hot to satisfy their filthy lusts."[31] The authors of the *Malleus* justified their attack upon women by stating that they came from the inferior rib of Adam and were thus imperfect in their physical structure and soul.

It must also be said that accused witches oftentimes played into the hands of the persecutors. A witch relieved her guilt by confessing her sexual fantasies in open court; at the same time, she achieved some erotic gratification by dwelling on all the details before her male accusers. These severely emotionally disturbed women were particularly susceptible to the suggestion that they harbored demons and devils and would confess to cohabiting with the evil spirit, much as disturbed individuals today, influenced by newspaper headlines, fantasy themselves as sought-after murderers.

The *Malleus* includes many descriptions of the incubi, the male demons who seduce women, and of the succubi, the female demons who sexually violate their male captives. In fact, throughout, the book is replete with pornographic sexual orgies occurring between these demons and their human hosts. Not content with these vivid passages, Kraemer and Sprenger go on to satisfy the voyeuristic impulses of the judging inquisitors by recommending that the witch be stripped and her pubic hair shaved before she was presented to the judges. The rationale for shaving the genitals was that the devil would not be able to hide in the pubic hairs.[32] This huntsman's bible directed against heretics, the mentally ill and women of all stations of life, was responsible for hundreds of thousands of women and children being burned at the stake.

From Charity to Bloodshed—
An Overview of Medieval Contributions

In seeking to evaluate the cultural developments of the Middle Ages, the historian faces the difficult task of appraising complex and heterogeneous trends. Contradictory movements such as the underground trickle of Greco-

Roman tradition, the original pure Christian spirit, regression toward supernatural demonology, and growing Oriental influences were all involved. One's evaluation may well come to depend upon one's selection of the trend he prefers. One can readily admire the charitable accomplishments of the monasteries, the erection of the first hospitals in Europe, the foundation of the first universities, the psychological genius of St. Augustine, the encyclopedic scholarship and deductive finesse of St. Thomas Aquinas, and the enlightened outlook of Avicenna and Maimonides, which stands out sharply against a background of prevailing obscurantism. But one can also deplore the intellectual sterility of the scholastics, the return to prehistoric demonology, and the institutionalization of the vital principles of Christian ethics that led in time to unparalleled excesses of intolerance and injury committed in the name of those principles.

Some clarity can be discovered if one recognizes behind these contradictions the eternal conflict between man's two fundamental psychological principles of attempting to master his insecurity—knowledge and faith. With the failure of the rationalist Greco-Roman experiment, man returned to the security of faith in the supernatural, to an infantile state of helplessness and dependence on something stronger than himself to lead him from panic and confusion. The first five hundred years of the Middle Ages were chaotic, confused, and fearful, made so by wars, famines, and plagues. The Church, with its promise that "the disinherited will inherit the world," offered security to the soul as the Roman law had offered security to the civil body. Entrusted with all of man's ills, monks treated both the soul and the body, and out of this trust came a humane hospital system. Still, while some forms of human suffering might respond to faith, organic calamities might not. Monastic medicine could not stem the tide of empirical knowledge in Western Europe any more than the medicine man could have in antiquity.

The Romans had preserved Greek thought in Constantinople. The Nestorian physicians brought the Grecian manuscripts to Syria and Persia, where the Arabians discovered them. In the twelfth and thirteenth centuries the crusaders brought Arabic contributions back to Western Europe; Constantinus Africanus translated the Arabic works into Latin, and the lay school at Salerno began to flourish. Having come to devote themselves exclusively to philosophical speculations, the monks retained their involvement with the problems of the mind but defaulted medicine to lay physicians, with whom they now vied. The devil was exorcised to cure the mind, and empirical methods began to alleviate organic suffering. The practical psychotherapeutic measures of Avicenna and Rhazes were lost as the scholastics speculated. The great universities in the middle centuries of the Middle Ages contributed information but not ingenuity. The scholastics venerated Aristotelian logic, and the lay physicians revered Hippocrates and Galen. And man's outlook had not moved forward.

By the thirteenth century the trickle of Greek manuscripts became a powerful stream. The influence of Aristotle began to challenge the Christian influence, and the old struggle between faith and reason began to recrudesce. Dogma went into defensive action on the theoretical level. Aristotle was adapted to Christianity through the exclusion of the realistic spirit of his views and the retention of only his deanimated words. Under the attentions of the scholastics, Aristotle's views were deduced from Christian dogma. In the light of such revealed truth, further *exploration*—the inductive approach to knowledge—appeared superfluous. However, this theoretical defensive against free inquiry was insufficient.

Another counterforce to Renaissance enlightenment was the recrudescence of exorcist practices over the next three hundred years. Paradoxically, that period of renewed enlightenment was marked in part by a violent regression toward supernaturalism, which, in the face of the strengthening rebirth of knowledge and exploration, turned to repression of heresies by the sword. The mentally ill were caught up in the witch hunt. Theological rationalizations and magical explanations served as foundations for burning at the stake thousands of the mentally ill as well as many other unfortunates. Those who had written about the mind now wrote death warrants as the tradition of scholastic reasoning in defense of dogma gave way to bloody persecution.

CHAPTER **6**

The Renaissance

Trading among the countries of the Mediterranean was a powerful impetus to the development of sea townships and for the rise of the cosmopolitan merchant and middle classes. Another cultural influence came with the arrival of classical Greek writings preserved by the Arabs, who reintroduced them to the Western world. These were cultural sparks that ignited the short-lived enlightenment of the thirteenth century.

In the fourteenth century and early decades of the fifteenth, an era of plagues, civil strife, wars, corrupt clergical practices, disunity between popes and emperors, and reverence of authority, the slow flame of enlightenment might have been extinguished had it not been for men like Dante, Boccaccio, and Petrarch. These men, the first humanists, led a movement away from the rigid doctrines of the scholastics toward a reawakening of respect for the writings of the Romans and the Greeks. Study of the classics of antiquity in the original, rather than dogmatic commentaries on them, became the ideal of the humanists.

The humanistic movement emphasized a respect for the writings of antiquity, and the consequent revival of Greek learning went hand in hand with a growing contempt for medieval scholasticism, which emphasized the other world of the supernatural. However, humanism was not in itself the essence of the Renaissance, and the humanistic spirit did not free men from the yoke of the authority of antiquity. As Bertrand Russell observed, "Many of them [humanists] had still the reverence for authority that medieval philosophers had had, but they substituted the authority of the ancients for that of the Church. This was, of course, a step towards emancipation, since the ancients disagreed with each other and individual judgment was required to decide which of them to follow."[1] Science, however, cannot substitute one authority for another, since it cannot depend on authority as a source of knowledge. The scientific Renaissance could not begin until man once again began to trust his own experiences more than what he had read in ancient texts.

In the fifteenth century historical circumstances created new sparks of enlightenment, so that by the sixteenth and seventeenth centuries the Renaissance blaze was forever unextinguishable. When the Turks took Constantinople in 1453, a Greek colony of scholars fled to the Western countries, where they translated the original writings of the great ancient scholars. The printing press came into use in the middle of the fifteenth century and provided the means to bring these writings to a growing number of readers. Antiquity now not only could be studied by the most learned of the humanists, but could also be read by greater portions of the public. And yet, the world of the ancients was soon to lose its grip on the minds of men. The real world of today was coming into sharper focus.

The utilization of gunpowder and the discovery of new continents and trade routes contributed to the emphasis on the here and now. Feudal knights and robber barons could no longer protect themselves behind their shields or in their fortresses. A newly prosperous middle class was rising and the old feudal world was collapsing. The supernatural world of the Church and the feudal order were being replaced by the real world of the present. By the sixteenth century Machiavelli was describing the world of political reality, just as Copernicus was describing geophysical reality, and replacing geocentric illusion with heliocentric perspective. The Renaissance painters and anatomists discovered the human body in its full concreteness. Authority and tradition had yielded so completely to the inquiring mind that even the most sacred medieval institutions and concepts were being questioned. Reformers like Calvin, Knox, Wycliffe, Zwingli, and Luther challenged the authority of the Catholic Church, astronomers attacked the celestial concepts of the ancients, and the anatomists attacked the anatomy of Galen. Rabelais and Montaigne, in the sixteenth century, challenged the decadent practices of clergymen and city officials.

Man, as a concrete individual, had been discovered and became the object of the artist and the anatomist. The day had arrived when the artist was to try his hand, and the anatomist his scalpel, toward understanding man in the context of his present. The artists showed how man looked from the outside, the anatomists detailed his inner structure, and finally, the psychologists and the philosophers of the Renaissance described his sensations and feelings. As man began to trust his own senses and his own experiences without relying on the written word of authority, science could enter the Renaissance.

From the perspective of this overall view of the large historical trends, we shall now follow thought development from the fifteenth to the seventeenth century by focusing on the three mainstreams of approach—the organic, the psychological, and the magical.

Developments in Medicine

The medieval view that the naked body is sinful and must be covered was being supplanted by the Renaissance artist's bold representation of the naked human form in its full nude and voluptuous reality. Dynamic representations of the human body in the important works of late-fifteenth- and early-sixteenth-century Italian artists like Leonardo da Vinci, Botticelli, Raphael, Michelangelo, Titian, Tintoretto, and Signorelli contrast markedly with the rigid, unreal, stilted, and unmoving bodies painted during the Middle Ages. Indeed, the human body was as informative to the painters of the Renaissance as it was to the physicians, and it is entirely understandable that sixteenth-century doctors and artists belonged to the same guilds.

The greatest representative of the Renaissance combination of artistic and scientific talent was Leonardo da Vinci (1452–1519), painter, biologist, sculptor, architect, engineer, poet, musician, philosopher, chemist, botanist, geologist, and mechanician. Leonardo understood that the artist needed knowledge of anatomical structure. He studied live and dead bodies and drew what he saw so accurately that his anatomical sketches were used by physicians for many centuries after him. He even sectioned the brain and drew accurately cavities in that organ by his new technique of injecting them with wax. Leonardo went a step further than the humanists, for he made a complete break with authority, including the antique sources to whom the humanists paid homage. "Those who study old authors," said Leonardo, "and not the works of nature are stepsons, not sons of Nature, who is mother of all good authors."[2]

Leonardo's anatomical sketches were relatively unknown to his contemporaries; consequently the idea of sketching the dissected corpse has been attributed not to Leonardo but to the physician Berengarius of Capri (1470–1530). Berengarius believed in making firsthand observations, but he was not completely free of the humanist point of view that the essential discoveries had been made by the scholars of antiquity. Consequently he could not make up his mind whether to follow Galen's word or abide by his own observations. Of great importance is the fact that in 1521 he published some of his work and that his contemporaries were thus able to study his almost accurate sketches of cross sections of the brain. He was, of course, accused of vivisection, just as Herophilus and Erasistratus, the Alexandrian anatomists, had been accused by their contemporaries.

The loudest cry from those who upheld the authority of the ancients was raised against the foremost of all anatomists and the man to whom modern medicine owes its foundations—Andreas Vesalius (1514–1564). Andreas' father, a Belgian from Wessale, was a renowned pharmacist in the Spanish court of Charles V. As a child Vesalius had read ancient anatomical writings and dissected dead animals. The study of anatomy remained his passion, so much so that later, as a student in Paris, where dissection was not permitted, he robbed graves for specimens so that he could continue to study anatomical structure.

Vesalius began his medical education at the University of Paris in 1533 under the guidance of the illustrious anatomists Vidus and Sylvius. Both these men followed Galen, even when what he said contradicted what they saw with their own eyes. Sylvius would state, for example, that since Galen had claimed the thigh bone was curved, if it appeared straight it was because over the years men had worn tight pants and thereby had changed the curvature of the bone. By 1535 Vesalius could no longer abide being taught Galenic anatomy and decided to transfer to the University of Padua, which had a reputation for intellectual freedom. Padua granted him a Doctor of Medicine degree in the last months of 1537 and regarded him so highly that the day after his graduation he was appointed professor of anatomy. In the next six years he wrote *De Humani Corporis Fabrica,* one of the great contributions to Western science.

De Fabrica, published in 1543, the same year that Copernicus issued his treatise revolutionizing the prevailing concepts of the solar system, is an enormous work that includes all aspects of human anatomy, with more than three hundred illustrations by Vesalius' friend Calcar, a student of Titian. The book revolutionized the study of anatomy and once and for all liquidated the writings of Galen, who, as Vesalius was able to prove, had based his descriptions on animal dissections, not on human corpses. *De Fabrica* and Copernicus' treatise represent the beginning of modern science.

Vesalius also established a new method of teaching anatomy at Padua. Instead of sitting in a chair holding a book of Galen's writings and lecturing while a barber dissected the corpse in front of the students, Vesalius stood with his students around the corpse, which he himself dissected, demonstrating his lecture as he went along. Once Vesalius had freed anatomy from theoretical speculation and animal dissection, an accurate study of the human brain was feasible. Vesalius compared the brains of animals and man and showed that they were similar in structure but that the brain of man was larger in comparison to his body weight. In addition, he differentiated between the gray and the white matter of the brain and preserved cross sections of the brain for Calcar to sketch.

Soon after the publication of *De Fabrica* Vesalius was strongly attacked for daring to dispute Galen. Discouraged, and possibly fearing for his life, Vesalius left Padua to join the court of Charles V of Spain, where his father had served, and for the next twenty years lived the life of a court physician. Dissections were few and far between in Spain, and whatever further contributions Vesalius might have made to anatomical research were lost. He died in 1564 in a shipwreck off the Isle of Zante after returning from a pilgrimage to the Holy Land—a pilgrimage that may have been made as penance for his sacrilegious anatomical pursuits.

Reliance on observation rather than on theory was reflected also in the fact that in the sixteenth century physicians began to look at their patients closely and record what they saw. In Italy Giovanni Montanus (1498–1552), in Germany Johann Lange (1485–1565), and in France Jean Fernel (1497–1558) were the prominent clinicians. Realistic observations similar to theirs made their first appearance in the field of mental illness. Johann Weyer (1555–1588) recorded in accurate detail the verbalizations and behavior of the emotionally distressed, and Girolamo Cardano (1501–1576) gave, in his autobiography, a vivid portrait of the psychopathic (antisocial) personality. Gerolamo Mercuriale (1530–1606) wrote essays on melancholia and distinguished various kinds of mania, but it remained for Felix Plater (1536–1614), a professor of anatomy and medicine at Basel, to apply precise observational measures to the mentally ill. Plater tried to classify all diseases, including mental ones, and spent time in Swiss dungeons studying psychologically ill prisoners. Plater considered that most mental diseases were due to some sort of brain damage; he explained sexual fantasies, nonetheless, as the result of possession by the devil or punishment by God. His *Praxis Medica* abounds in rich clinical descriptions reminiscent of Hippocratic writings. Felix Plater, indeed, can be considered a worthy precursor to the nineteenth-century German classifiers of mental disease.

The first advocate of the experimental approach to medicine was Ambroise Paré (1510–1590), who began as a mere barber-surgeon in the army of Francis I. His education was meager and he knew neither Greek nor Latin. French soldiers who had suffered gunpowder wounds were treated, according to ancient custom, with boiling oil. Paré observed that these wounds usually developed severe infections, but when, because of a lack of oil, only bandages were applied to some soldiers' wounds, these healed well without infection. For the rest of his life Paré advocated that wounds be treated simply so that the natural healing processes could occur without interference. Hippocrates had taught this doctrine but had been ignored by centuries of ambitious physicians. Another example of Paré's concern for objective experimentation is the study he made of a certain onion concoction which he had been told was effective in healing wounds. Paré tested this concoction by treating half a burned area with it and leaving the other half untreated, so that he could compare the two results. He used this same concoction on some wounded patients and withheld it from others who had suffered similar wounds. This humble barber, who said, "I dressed him and God healed him," thus introduced the principle of controlled experiments into medical science.

Thirst for more information and knowledge coupled with intellectual freedom kept the experimental method alive in Italian universities, expecially in those of Padua and Venice. Except for the heavy influence of the *Malleus Maleficarum* and the witch hunters, the sixteenth century allowed bright expectations for further progress, since instrumentation and mechanization facilitated in the biological sciences the broadening of the experimental approach.

Developments in Psychology

The glory of the Renaissance began when the word of the classics ceased to be venerated and the spirit of Hellenic intellectual inquisitiveness came to new life and was intensified. It is not our task here to present a detailed appreciation of the many men of letters who first challenged the authoritarian dogma of a Christianized Aristotle. Our interest is rather in whatever contributions toward the development of psychology—in particular the psychological point of view in psychiatry—were made during these centuries. The first indispensable steps toward a more realistic approach to man as a person were taken by the Renaissance humanists, who opposed the scholastics and introduced a fresh point of view about nature and man.

During the thirteenth century a group arose who may be considered the forerunners of the Renaissance humanists: Giovanni Bonaventura (1221–1274) in France, Johannes Eckhart (1260–1328) in Germany, John Duns Scotus (1265–1308), and William of Ockham (1280–1349) and Roger Bacon (1214–1294) in England. Their professions were different: Bonaventura was a religious philosopher, Eckhart a mystic, Bacon a philosopher of science who turned toward psychology. All had one thing in common, however, a realistic and concrete view of *this* world and of nature, including *human* nature. They were voluntarists, which is to say that they considered the intellect merely an instrument that served the basic strivings of man, and their psychology is unmistakably Augustinian in being founded on internal subjective experience. These thirteenth- and fourteenth-century men ventured into a new territory—the world of feelings, strivings, and doubts—and in so doing they rediscovered the individuality of man.

At the time that this move toward psychological realism was accomplished, Giotto, the father of modern painting, was breaking through the depersonalized rigidity of Byzantine formalism and daring to paint Christ as a man among others. In Giotto's work, writes André Malraux, "Psychology was replacing the symbol, and painting in its turn discovered that one of the most effective methods of suggesting an emotion is to picture its expression. . . . To restore to life the slumbering populace of ancient statues, all that was required was the dawn of the first smile upon the first medieval figure. . . . Into Mary's face [Giotto] instills something of that supreme pathos which we find in the suffering of little children. . . ."[3] Scotus, Ockham, and Eckhart, Giotto's philosophical contemporaries, were also reviving, after six hundred years, St. Augustine's concept of the reality of man's inner experiences.

The idea that man's strivings and feelings are dominant and that the intellect is their servant was a complete reversal of the early medieval scholastic position that deductive reasoning is an instrument of revealed truth, which in itself is beyond man's competence. With this reversal psychology became humanized, and the door was opened to the study of man as a biological organism whose psychological faculties serve his will to live. The contributions that these first voluntarists made to the foundations of psychology as a natural science cannot be overrated; it must be noted, however, that the spiritual origin of their thought goes back to St. Augustine's all-important emphasis on self-awareness.

Literature as well as art became more realistic. The literary talents of Rabelais and Boccaccio expressed in a new way the basic, naturally earthy impulses of man, which had been ignored for centuries. Their work indicates that after long years of abstract contemplation and instinctual repression men were becoming realistic about themselves and the world. The senses—both those that convey internal impulses and those that convey perceptions of the external world—were no longer denied, and the negation of the forces of life gave way to acceptance of them. This psychological realism, of course, was only another manifestation that the European mind was being liberated from medieval dogma and once again, for the first time since the Greeks, was finding the natural world of vital concern, the essence of reality.

The fifteenth century is the era of transition between the medieval and the modern worlds. The medieval world had become formalized, Christianity had so lost its spirit that ritual had superseded faith, and the secular world was ruled by a complicated and static system of traditional stereotypes whose complex rigidity is well symbolized in late Gothic architecture. The supernatural world still existed in man's mind but had lost its vitality. Ortega y Gasset speaks of the man of the fifteenth century as living in two worlds, as being "torn away from one system of convictions and not yet installed in another. . . . He still believes in the medieval world, that is to say, in the supernatural other world of God, but he believes it without a living faith. His faith has already become a matter of habit . . . although this does not mean that it is insincere."[4]

The one common denominator among the great intellectual movements of this century, which in many respects appear to contradict each other, is a new confidence in the capacity of man to learn about nature through the use of his own observational and reasoning faculties—to discover truth, in contrast to receiving it through Divine revelation or proving it by syllogistic reasoning. The use of reason and observation to discover truth was a complete departure from the medieval practice of the schoolmen who used deductive reasoning in order to prove revealed truth. This intellectual revolution had begun in the thirteenth century with the rediscovery of Aristotle's philosophy. Aristotle's ideas were used by Albertus Magnus and St. Thomas to support revealed dogma; but then, in the fifteenth century, the humanists de-Christianized Aristotle in spite of their avowed intention of reconciling him with Christianity, and by so doing paved the way for the true Renaissance.

The contribution of the humanists was principally to literature, the arts, and ethical philosophy, and only tangentially to medicine and psychiatry. Psychology had always been more deeply tied to religious tradition than the natural sciences, man's soul being the main object of both, and therefore psychology had to wait the longest to benefit from this spiritual reorientation. As it always had, man's need to find the way to live an ethical life interfered with the development of *psychology as a science*.

The earliest humanists, such as Petrarch (1304–1374), were primarily moralists strongly influenced by Cicero and were bent on reconciling the spirit of the Church with the pagan culture of the classics. Petrarch opposed the Averroëist variety of Aristotelianism; he detested medieval deductive reasoning. He returned to the prescholastic Christian religion, to the religion of St. Augustine, which was based on sincere subjective experience as contrasted with the synthetic rationalistic religion of the schoolmen.

The main significance of humanism is not in the content of its ideas but in its spirit, the discovery of the full concrete complexity of human existence, and above all, a new reliance of man on his own convictions and feelings. Soon, within a century, this self-reliance reached a peak in the "universal man" of the Renaissance. It was reflected by the lives of such picturesque, exuberant personalities as Benvenuto Cellini and Cesare Borgia, in the gigantic musclebound statues of Michelangelo, in the life-exuding paintings of Raphael, Titian, and Veronese. In this emphasis on man's actual feelings and strivings lies the historical significance of humanism, and it is this rediscovery of man in his earthbound existence that gives the expression "humanism" its real justification.

The discovery of man's concrete existence at first took place in the realm of religion, which was the main cultural arena of the age. Desiderius Erasmus (1465–1536), in whom humanism came to its full fruition, was a churchman who, like Petrarch, attacked the formalism and corruption of the Church, the sterile ritual divested of spirit. His *Praise of Folly,* which he wrote while visiting his English friend Sir Thomas More, another great humanist, became one of the most widely read books in Europe.

The humanists' theoretical psychology was either Aristotelian or Platonic and contained little that was original. Pomponazzi (1462–1525), a famous teacher at the University of Padua, was trained both as a philosopher and as a physician; his main contributions dealt with the relation of mind and body and the immortality of the soul. His writings show most impressively the dilemma in which serious thinkers of the era found themselves, squeezed, as they were, between the prevailing traditions of scholastic philosophy and Averroëist Aristotelianism. Pompanazzi tried to compromise. He supported both theses, that the soul is mortal and immortal, that the mind needs the physical equipment of the body to express itself, and also that reason, as Thomas Aquinas preached, has an independent existence. There was little actual observation in his work; he was mainly an interpreter of Aristotle, and the new spirit of the times manifested itself in his writings only in that his restatements were clearer and simpler than those of previous commentators.

More originality was shown by Julius Caesar Scaliger (1484–1558). He discovered the kinesthetic sense, the muscular sense that registers the position of the different parts of the body. He also postulated an idea basic to physiology: that the movements of the body come about by central nerve impulses, or "innervations." He considered instincts to be inherited adaptive habits of behavior, which is how they are viewed today.

Still more modern in his outlook was the Spaniard Juan Luis Vives (1492–1540). He had an active, searching mind and came to psychology through his interest in education. In order to appreciate his significance, we shall have to review his immediate predecessors and contemporaries.

Before Vives, humanists were not primarily interested in science, and particularly not in scientific theory. Their thinking was pragmatic and they considered that their historical function was to help man to find a new way of life. Their ethical orientation came to its fullest expression in the neo-Platonic Academy of Florence, founded by Cosimo de' Medici, where Marsilio Ficino (1433–1499) promulgated his ideas about each man's ability fo find his way to eternal truth and the highest good. Giovanni Pico della Mirandola (1463–1494) went further and espoused the principle that each man is free to determine his own fate, a concept that perhaps more than any other has influenced the developments of the last three centuries. Pico's idea was that only man, in contrast to all other beings, has no fixed state, but is capable, because he is free, of realizing his ideal. This ideal condition can, however, be achieved only through education. Education, which is applied psychology, is the means by which man learns how to make constructive use of his faculty of free choice. Pico's thesis was implemented by Vives, the educator.

Vives was primarily animated by a vital interest in education. His pragmatic orientation produced occasional flashes of insight; for instance, he thought that emotional experience rather than abstract reason plays the primary role in man's mental processes. In order to educate a person and to change his character, it is necessary to understand the complex workings of his mind. Generalizations and abstractions may suffice for writing treatises about human nature, but they have no practical value. Educational psychology must work, said Vives, or it is good for nothing. Vives achieved a concrete psychological orientation in which the abstract knowledge of man was replaced by an appreciation of each man as an individual, different from others.

Building up character through education requires a knowledge of the emotions, or, as Vives called them, the passions. Vives offers a highly realistic description of human passions—love, hate, resentment, envy, jealousy, hope—that is presented according to general principles similar to those of physics. These principles might be called the "logic of emotions." In this sense Vives belongs to those few early psychologists who paved the way toward the science of psychodynamics, but he shared the fate of all the humanists: to be able to make only a scattered beginning, to introduce or emphasize general attitudes rather than to achieve solid knowledge based on systematic observation.

If our yardstick of evaluating past contributions is their modernity, two Renaissance authors deserve highest recognition—Montaigne and Machiavelli. This yardstick of modernity is justified in science, for science is a continuously growing body of knowledge, a truly accumulative type of cultural activity. Michel Eyquem de Montaigne (1533–1592) was anything but a systematic thinker or theoretician. He was a psychological realist, concerned only with the great richness of human feelings, character, and behavior, and not at all with general abstract principles. He was satisfied to understand human actions in psychological and—we may use the term justifiably—"psychodynamic" terms. Niccolò Machiavelli (1469–1527) shared Montaigne's distaste for abstraction. It has become customary to call Machiavelli the first social psychologist, but it would be better to call him the first student of interpersonal relations. His advice to the prince is not primarily based on a knowledge of social dynamics, but on an astute, intuitive knowledge of human interactions, and particularly of the psychology of leadership. What is most characteristic of both Montaigne and Machiavelli is that, unlike the humanists, they distinguished between the psychology of human behavior and morals. They tried to describe how human beings actually behave, without making any moral judgment about their behavior, and for this reason, although neither contributed directly to the development of abnormal psychology or psychiatry, they deserve a place in the history of psychiatry. To view natural phenomena dispassionately, without wishful distortions, is difficult enough; to study human behavior in the same objective manner is perhaps the most difficult of all scientific tasks.

Magic and the Anti-Witch-Hunt Crusade

Despite the advances in technology and science made during the Renaissance, magic continued to be as strong an influence as it had ever been. Even though the fable that the earth is the center of the universe had been destroyed, other myths involving celestial bodies, as found in astrology, survived. In fact, astrological divination was even more popular during the Renaissance than it had been previously. The reason for this seeming paradox is that rational, scientific discoveries very often provoke counterforces of irrationality; although science answers some questions, in so doing it raises others. These unknowns evoke fear and anxiety, which pseudoscientific fantasies attempt to relieve. Thus the science of astronomy, progressing toward the deanimation of nature, was countered by astrology, the aim of which is to reanimate nature. The age that invented the microscope and telescope was for this reason strongly influenced by the horoscope. It is not, however, as though there are two camps—one scientific and the other antiscientific. The fear of deanimation, with the constant need to reanimate, can occur within the same individuals. Some of the greatest scientists of every age have embraced mysticism and practiced magic. The late Middle Ages and early Renaissance were no exceptions. Johannes Kepler (1571–1630), who discovered three of the laws governing planetary motion, on occasion resorted to drawing horoscopes; Rabelais, a bitter foe of charlatanism, also drew horoscopes and called himself "Doctor of Medicine and Professor of Astrology."⁵ Officially, astrology was condemned by the Church, yet it was known that the popes often consulted astrological diviners. Professors of astrology were in high repute in many universities in the Middle Ages and the Renaissance, as were professors of mathematics. Like all wizards, the astrologists remained secure as long as they could boast occasional success in prediction. It could even be claimed that the astrological wizard was the one who caused the desired event. The argument *post hoc ergo propter hoc* (the concept that one event that follows another is caused by the former) influences individuals inclined toward magic, be they the primitive savage, the Renaissance man, or the twentiety-century sophisticate. Reports concerning a favorable prediction by an astrologer would outweigh thousands of false forecasts. Furthermore, magical practice is impressive because it follows a consistent order and becomes ritualized. In this sense men who admired the scientific method of systematic procedure could admire the astrologist's procedures. Thus other magic rituals were impressive to the men of the Renaissance. Sand gazers (geomancers), flour gazers (aleuromancers), and readers of tea leaves rivaled the star gazers in popularity. Men were curious about what the future held and also wanted to understand what their personalities and characters were like and would be like. Astrology emphasized prediction, but some of the other mantic arts combined prospicience with foretelling personality configuration. Outstanding among the readers into individual psyches were the palmists and the physiognomists.

Chiromancy, or palmistry, probably arose in China about 3000 B.C., and from there it spread to all parts of Asia, Greece, and Italy. It was especially popular during the Renaissance, when anatomists discovered that the creases in the human hand serve a definite prehensile function and when painters emphasized the human hand in order to capture the full quality of human expression. The palmists maintained that the shape and size of a person's hand and its various sulci also revealed whether he was charitable, intelligent, pious, brazen, hot-tempered, or impudent. (Should the palmist find that the emperor whose hand he was examining was gifted with favorable personality features, the magician would never have to worry about royal employment.) The first book on palmistry was probably written by a German doctor, Johannes Hartleib, in the early sixteenth century.*

The hand is merely one of the parts of the human body that has been studied in attempts to read human character. Hippocrates believed that the shape of the human body revealed personality features. Aristotle studied the hair, the limbs, and all other portions of the human body to arrive at characterological impressions. He felt that the nose was particularly reveal-ing. A pointed nose like a dog's meant irritability; an aquiline nose indi-cated an eaglelike character. Physiognomy continued to be one of the important tools for diagnosing psychological characteristics throughout the Middle Ages and Renaissance. There were probably more essays and books written on this topic during the sixteenth century than in all of the previous centuries combined.

Furthermore, interest in finding a simple correlation between physical makeup and psychological features remained high long after the Renais-sance. Gall, a brilliant eighteenth-century neuroanatomist, as we will see, concluded that the shape and size of the skull and its superficial protuber-ances revealed important facts regarding the individual's temperament; and Cesare Lombroso, a nineteenth-century Italian anthropologist, maintained that there was a correlation between criminality and facial configuration.

Perhaps the most influential and outstanding Renaissance metoposcopist was Girolamo Cardano, whom many consider to be the systematizer of the correlation of facial lines and expression with character. He was one of the most brilliant physicians of his time, probably as influential as Vesalius, and yet he was a medical charlatan. He was an astute anatomist and a confirmed palmist, and his research in astronomy was paralleled by his horoscopic speculations. Cardano was a highly touted mathematician and lecturer and yet was a firm believer in numerology. He was a confirmed demonologist and a bitter opponent of the witch hunt. Cardano's works are as irreconcilable with one another as were his personality traits. In his time he was deified and vilified, praised and blasphemed. Burckhardt, the greatest authority on the Renaissance, considered Cardano's autobiog-raphy, De Propria Vita (1575), a highly significant biographical study ranking with Benvenuto Cellini's as most revealing of the Renaissance spirit. Yet it was neither astute in introspection nor accurate in detail.

* As recently as the late nineteenth century a French author, Casimir d'Arpentiginy, was trying to correlate the shape of the hand with psychic disposition.[6]

Cardano's autobiography frankly reveals the inconsistencies of his character: "Nature has made me capable in all manual work. It has given me the spirit of a philosopher and ability in the sciences, taste and good manners, voluptuousness, gaiety, it has made me pious, faithful, fond of wisdom, meditative, inventive, courageous, fond of learning and teaching, eager to equal the best, to discover new things and make independent progress of modest character, a student of medicine, interested in curiosities and discoveries, cunning, crafty, sarcastic, an initiate in the mysterious lore, industrious, diligent, ingenious, living only from day to day, impertinent, contemptuous of religion, grudging, envious, sad, treacherous, magician and sorcerer, miserable, hateful, lascivious, solitary, disagreeable, rude, divinator, envious, obscene, lying, obsequious, fond of the prattle of old men, changeable, irresolute, indecent, fond of women, quarrelsome, and because of the conflicts between my nature and soul, I am not understood even by those with whom I associate most frequently."[7]

Cardano's life was a parade of successes and dismal failures, momentary happiness and absolute despondency. His father was a highly respected Milanese lawyer and mathematician who believed in occult practices and who was unable to marry Cardano's mother because she was beneath him socially. After Cardano had received his medical diploma he was denied membership in the society of doctors of Milan because he was illegitimate and therefore was unable to practice there. He was a general practitioner in the small village of Sacco between 1526 and 1532, where he was respected by the community. By this time, however, he had become an inveterate gambler and lost most of whatever money he earned, so that he and his family were forced to live in the poorhouse. It was during this period that he became interested in the scientific exploration of games of chance, and later in his life wrote popular books on the subject. It is said that Cardano discovered the principle of probability before Pascal.

By the 1540's Cardano was lecturing and writing many popular books, one of which—*On the Bad Practices of Medicine in Common Use*—incensed the Milanese medical society. He gained a reputation as a doctor although he was not recognized by the medical authorities, and he may well have been the most widely read medical writer of his time. His subjects ranged from physics, astronomy, mathematics, morality, and immortality to treatises on how to bring up children—although his two sons turned out to be criminals, gamblers, and drunkards. Cardano himself was arrested for heresy in 1570 on the grounds that he had praised Nero for murdering Christian martyrs and had had the audacity to cast the horoscope of Jesus Christ.

Despite Cardano's belief in premonitions, visions, and demons, he at times displayed genuine scientific reasoning. He never brought to fruition many of his brilliant theories; for example, he had devised ways to teach the deaf to learn and even devised means of teaching the blind to read.

Cardano was a great believer in maintaining morale and taught that anyone who believed in himself could overcome the vicissitudes of life—a thesis probably derived from weathering his own misfortunes. Cardano stated his philosophy succinctly: "A man is nothing but his mind. If that be out of order, all's amiss. And if that be well, all the rest is at ease. . . . It was my design by my own example to teach these two things: first, it is nothing but a guilty conscience that can make a man miserable; secondly, constancy of mind helps greatly not only to bear evils but to produce a change of fortune. It is necessary to keep thee from being miserable, to believe *that thou art not so* [italics authors']. Which rule, in one word, may be learned and taught by every man."*[8] Cardano recognized that in order for him to be a successful doctor his patients had to believe in him: "He cures most in whom most believe."[9] The persuasive nature of his manner of presentation allied itself with the patient's wish to be cured, so that in a sense Cardano made the power of suggestion part of his therapeutic efforts. The next two centuries were to further advance the profound influence of suggestion through the ritual of animal magnetism (mesmerism), culminating in nineteenth-century hypnotism.

The greatest suggestionist of the Renaissance was not a physician but a man who had served as a lieutenant in the ranks of Cromwell's army, Valentine Greatrakes (1628–1666), who utilized the popular belief in the efficacy of "the king's touch"—the belief that illness could be cured by the touch of a divinely inspired leader. In Western Europe the first ruler who touched to cure had been Edward the Confessor, in the eleventh century. After him, both in France and England, kings were thought to be able to cure diseases by means of this procedure, and tuberculosis of the neck—the "king's evil"—was popularly supposed to be especially amenable to the hand of the king. Cromwell would not practice the touch ritual, and after Charles I was beheaded in 1649, the king's touch was considered to have been granted to "the divinely inspired" Irish stroker Valentine Greatrakes. At first Greatrakes had few clients, but gradually his practice built up until eventually thousands of patients came to be cured by the impressive Irishman, and "his barns and outhouses were crammed with innumerable specimens of suffering humanity."[10] Walter Bromberg, a psychiatric historian, considers Greatrakes significant because he practiced as a layman a form of psychotherapy that had previously belonged to members of the ruling class.

Astrology, palmistry, the magical touch, suggestion, and other magic practiced during the Renaissance were employed to relieve anxiety and fear. More drastic measures of alleviating anxiety arising from unacceptable impulses were to impute them to certain women and then to persecute and execute the women as witches.

The hangman's noose and the executioner's torch were always in readi-

* In this sense Cardano can be considered one of the forerunners of the French hypnotist, psychotherapist, and autosuggestionist Émile Coué (1857–1926), who will be remembered for his saying "Every day and in every way I am becoming better and better."

ness during those days. It is astonishing that any protests, however feeble, were raised against the witch phobia, yet there were some courageous men who could not sanction manslaughter, even though they believed in the devil. Two of the loudest protesters against the witch hunters are important figures in the history of psychiatry. One, Paracelsus (1493–1541), was an eccentric mystic; the other, Johann Weyer (1515–1588), was a stable observer. Both men were physicians and wielded considerable influence in their world.

Philippus Aureolus Paracelsus was born Theophrastus Bombastus von Hohenheim in Maria-Einsiedeln, Switzerland. As a youngster he preferred to be called Theophrastus after the distinguished scholar who succeeded Aristotle,* but later he Latinized his name, with a characteristic lack of humility, to Paracelsus—"greater than Celsus." (He was so forceful and turbulent that the name Bombastus was appropriated into the language to describe men like him.) His father, Wilhelm von Hohenheim, was a physician who came from a noble family; after his wife had committed suicide, he took his rachitic child to a mining town, where Paracelsus grew up and began his studies of alchemy. In his early teens Paracelsus became a vagabond. He was educated in six cities in three countries; his success as a doctor started in Basel in 1526, when he cured an influential citizen who was sick with a gangrenous leg. He went on to cure the famous theologian Erasmus and was as a result appointed a professor of medicine at Basel University. He immediately embarked on a program of undermining the authority of the ancients. He appealed to the students to trust in him and his experiences instead, and when the students and the faculty demanded his resignation, the stormy iconoclast burned books of Avicenna and Galen and proclaimed "For I tell you boldly that the hair from the back of my head knows more than all your writers put together; my shoe buckles have more wisdom in them than even Galen or Avicenna, and my beard more experience than your whole academy."[11] His outcries against the authorities, ancient and modern, were equaled only by his admonitions for physicians "to follow only in the footsteps of Paracelsus."[12] He lasted at the university less than a year and spent his remaining years wandering again, finally returning to die in Salzburg. His contemporaries said that he died of fatigue brought on by his peregrinations and complicated by an intense thirst for alcohol.

Although Paracelsus was an astrologist, he did not think disease was caused by either the stars or demons. Instead, he believed in a "natural spirit" that utilized the basic alchemical substances—salts, sulfur, and mercury—to form the complex human body. He envisioned the human personality as a whole, as made up of spiritual and corporeal parts inti-

---

* While walking with his students in the botanical gardens (the Lyceum) of Athens, Aristotle was asked by his students to choose a successor. Aristotle asked to be served wines from different area and noted that the blends served by Theophrastus of Lesbos were the sweetest. Aristotle thus chose not his favorite wine but his heir, who went on to become the "Father of Botany."

mately connected with the soul. Mental disease was a disturbance within the internal substance of the body and could not be considered a result of external effects. He believed that all illness, mental or physical, could be cured by the proper medicine, yet he objected to the polypharmacy of the day and prescribed simple drugs in exact dosages. His bitterness and contempt were apparently reserved for authority and never directed at his patients, toward whom he showed only sympathy. He was able to brag that in spite of the fact that he had been driven out of many countries, his patients everywhere loved him.

Paracelsus' obscurantism and proclivity to mysticism rendered his philosophical and psychiatric contributions ambiguous. It has become almost customary in some quarters to claim that a writer who has the germ of an original idea but whose thoughts are ill-defined and confused is not understood because he is beyond the scope of his contemporaries and successors. Had Paracelsus rebelled against the scepter of Galen without insinuating his own dogmatism, he might have rightfully been designated a great medical reformer. On the subject of witch hunting he was unambiguously loud and clear. One of the most tragic iconoclasts in the history of medicine, he was the second physician to speak out lucidly against the code of the witch burners; the first was Agrippa, whose greatest claim to medical fame comes by virtue of the fact that he was the teacher of Johann Weyer.

Johann Weyer, unlike Paracelsus, did not attack authority for the sake of self-advertisement. Weyer was a calm, methodical, and conscientious individual; his goal was to prove that witches were mentally ill and should be treated by physicians rather than be interrogated by ecclesiastics. Weyer was born in 1515 in Grave, in what is now Holland. Little is known about his life; he apparently displayed an immense curiosity, and his father, a commoner, sent him to study under Cornelius Agrippa von Nettesheim (1486–1535), a German physician and philosopher. Agrippa's stirring tract *On the Nobility and Pre-eminence of the Feminine Sex* taught Weyer to empathize with the plight of persecuted women. After three years with Agrippa, Weyer, at nineteen, journeyed to France to study medicine at Paris and Orléans. A brilliant scholar, he was invited by the officials at Arnheim to become their medical officer in 1545, which post he held until 1550, when he became the private physician to Duke William of Cleves. The duke was a chronic depressive, with many relatives who had become insane; he had observed that witches manifested many of the same symptoms as his relatives and sympathized with Weyer's idea that these women were really suffering from mental illness. When, in 1578, the duke suffered transient psychotic episodes as a result of a stroke, he was no longer able to keep the witch hunters under control in his duchies; consequently Weyer had to leave the duke's service, and for the rest of his life he held a post under the protection of Countess Anna of Techlenburg. It is altogether fitting that this man who defended women against the murderous hordes of witch hunters should himself have been protected by a woman.

While he was with Duke William, Weyer journeyed to Julich and Berg to investigate all reported cases of witchcraft. He accumulated data, interviewed both accusers and accused, and then carefully and systematically exploded the accusations with naturalistic explanations. One of the best examples of his method of investigation is the case of a sixteen-year-old girl who believed that the devil put cloth, nails, and needles in her stomach. Weyer carefully examined a piece of cloth that had supposedly come out of her stomach and found that it was damp from saliva only, not from gastric juices, convincing proof that the girl was lying.[13] In one of his pamphlets, *De Commentitiis Jejuniis* (*On Alleged Fasting*), he describes how he discovered the malingering of a ten-year-old girl, who, according to her parents, had neither eaten nor drunk for six months. Weyer took the girl home with him and induced her to confess that her twelve-year-old sister had been secretly feeding her all during this time.

Weyer's careful case studies contain excellent psychiatric descriptions of different mental disturbances. He continued his investigations of the absurdities involved in identifying witchcraft for twelve years, and finally, in 1563, he published *De Praestigiis Daemonum* (*The Deception of Demons*), which four years later he translated into German. *De Praestigiis* is a step-by-step rebuttal of the *Malleus Maleficarum* and reveals that Weyer was neither an embittered, rebellious renegade nor an impious reprobate; he was a reverent, respectful, and religious man whose only contempt was for the hangman. In his introduction Weyer says, "Almost all of the theologians are silent regarding this godlessness [witch burning]. Doctors tolerate it, jurists treat it while still under the influence of old prejudices. . . ." He firmly believed that "those illnesses whose origins are attributed to witches come from natural causes."[14] Weyer was only too aware that all mental illness could not as yet be explained, but he knew "that witches can harm no one through the most malicious will or the ugliest exorcism, that rather their imagination inflamed by the demons in a way not understandable to us—and the torture of melancholy—makes them only fancy that they have caused all sorts of evil. For when the entire manner of action is laid on the scales and the implements therefore examined with careful scrutiny, then soon there is shown clearly before all eyes and more lucid than the day the nonsense and the falsity of the matter."[15] He refers throughout the book to "the perplexed poor old women" who have been accused of witchcraft, and it matters little that Weyer himself believed in the devil and demons, for he was not a devil's advocate. Weyer understood, as did his worthy predecessor Hippocrates, that physicians in their frustration, unable to cure certain maladies, will espouse that the devil has taken his patient. Four hundred years after Weyer, physicians will still maintain that if they cannot cure an illness the patient is "nervous" or "psycho." As had Hippocrates, Weyer fought to prove that mental diseases are neither supernatural nor sacred and that it was his right as a physician to treat people so afflicted. But he could not escape the scorn of people of his age. He was called "Weirus Heriticus" or "Weirus Insanus."[16] It was whispered that he himself was a wizard, otherwise he would not defend them. In our century those who label the psychiatric physician variously "crazy doctor," "headshrinker," or "nut opener" are no wiser than the Renaissance assailants of Johann Weyer.

Zilboorg considered the significance of Weyer to be that he was the "first physician whose major interest turned toward mental diseases,"[17] which he approached by careful observation of individual cases. On the other hand, Weyer did not propound a comprehensive theory of mental diseases; he remained unknown to his contemporaries except as an anti-witch-hunt crusader,* and his psychiatric writings remained largely unnoticed by medical men until he was recently discovered as an early psychiatrist.

*   *   *

The Renaissance marked Western man's reorientation toward reality. Although the battle against superstition was not won during this period, the turning point was reached: Western man was committed to seeking the truth about himself. As we have seen, this commitment was made on many fronts—scientific, philosophical, political, and artistic—and stimulated a broad, composite study of man which would provide a solid foundation for future discoveries. Man's body in all its magnificent complexity was rediscovered. Man's mind and spirit were reilluminated—as they really are. In the work of Vesalius, Paré, Plater, Cardano, Vives, Paracelsus, Weyer, Montaigne, Giotto, Machiavelli, and many other men of genius and courage, a more honestly constructed image of man as a whole began to emerge. Most important, the vital principle of objective observation was reestablished and has proved to be the most valuable and enduring part of the legacy of the Renaissance.

---

* Reginald Scott (in *The Discovery of Witchcraft*, 1584) presented a devastating critique of witch hunting and popularized Weyer's views regarding witches.

CHAPTER **7**

The Era of Reason and Observation

The Cultural Setting

The seventeenth century must be given credit for laying the first foundations of the modern world. In the eyes of some historians the unprecedented intellectual accomplishments of this era in science, literature, the arts, and philosophy are far more significant than those of the Renaissance and the Reformation, for in the seventeenth century science became a focus of man's endeavor. A partial list of names of the men engaged in scientific work is impressive: Galileo, Brahe, and Kepler in astronomy; Boyle, Huygens, Robert Hooke, and Newton in physics; Descartes, Newton, Guyens, and Pascal in mathematics; and Thomas Sydenham and William Harvey in medicine. The social interest in science also led, in 1662, to the founding of the Royal Academy of Sciences in London, and four years later, the Academie Royale des Sciences in Paris.

As is true of all historical developments, it is impossible to ascribe to any one cause the reason why those years saw such great advances in scientific knowledge. Certain facts, however, stand out. First, the center of European cultural activity had begun to shift from Spain and Italy to England, France, and Holland. The era of overseas expansion, in which England played the most outstanding role, was well underway. In the late sixteenth century great seafarers like Francis Drake and Walter Raleigh had opened up new lands, and their adventures and new experiences had powerfully stimulated other inquisitive minds and helped to destroy adherence to economic and social traditions. Renaissance humanists had fostered man's confidence in his own intellectual faculties. The Reformation had undermined the central authority of the Pope and had successfully defied a creed that hitherto had been beyond doubt. The Reformation also emphasized that an individual had to rely on his own conscience, if not yet on his own rational insight. To a great extent, then, we may say that the seventeenth century's scientific developments were the logical consequences of the liberating effects of Renaissance humanism, the Reformation, and the exploration of the New World. The first supported the idea that men should trust their own abilities; the second reinforced this idea and also undermined central authority. One result of these changes was the rise of a rational science based on experimental observation.

Underlying the seventeenth-century advances in scientific knowledge were two intellectual approaches. The first emphasized deductive, analytical, and mathematical reasoning; the second, empirical and inductive reasoning. The first methodology is used by Descartes, Hobbes, and Spinoza; the second by Francis Bacon and John Locke. Both schools of thought share a vitally important feature—a doubt in existing knowledge and a belief that the world is governed by a rational order that is susceptible to discovery, either by deductive reasoning or by painstaking observation. The two trends found harmonious integration in the work of the greatest scientist of the era, with whom science in the modern sense begins as a novel phenomenon in human history: Galileo Galelei (1564–1642). He combined the experimental method with hypothetical intuitive assumptions, so that the experiment served to check the validity of the hypothesis. He made inroads in both approaches: he utilized the telescope for observation, and mathematical analysis of experimental and observational data for rigorous reasoning. Science in the modern sense developed from the integration of these two approaches. The process of experimental verification of hypothetical assumptions leads to new factual knowledge not included in the original theory. This necessitates the modification of the original hypothesis. The modifications of hypotheses lead to new experiments and through them to new discoveries in a never-ending, cyclic, spiraling movement that in an asymptotic curve approaches but never reaches absolute truth.

René Descartes (1596–1650), the most extreme of the deductive rationalists, was still influenced by the Middle Ages: a scholastic in spirit, he tried to resolve the world puzzle by deductive syllogistic reasoning, starting from intuitive abstractions having little connection with the world of the senses and ending with a mechanistic universe in which living organisms are complex pieces of machinery. Descartes's physiological statements lack sound foundations, nor was he a good observer of psychological phenomena. He equipped man with a "thinking substance," the soul, which, he was certain, did not interact with the body. He thus completely separated body and mind, a misleading dichotomy that still haunts the study of man.

In spite of Descartes's authority, the influence of the observationalists gradually outshone that of the rationalists. For a long while the empiricism of Bacon and Locke contributed to the development of the experimental natural sciences more than did the rationalistic trend, which nevertheless gained momentum in the eighteenth century, particularly in France. The trend toward rationalism came to full fruition only in the last years of the nineteenth century.

Descartes sought an unassailable basic starting point and found it in his famous *"cogito, ergo sum."* The fact of thinking (or self-awareness) is the safest of all statements of fact. It is an immediate experience from which one could build a system. Descartes, however, produced a system that was full of contradictions that had little resemblance to the world of reality. This indicates that hypothesis and experiment, that deductive reasoning and induction from observations, cannot be separated without paralyzing the search for knowledge.

New developments always provoke defensive repercussions. The seventeenth century, too, in which knowledge advanced more rapidly than in any previous era, was full of contradictions. Man's increasing ability to discover the secrets of nature through observation and reason resulted in a new world of self-reliance in which not everyone, however, felt comfortable. As a reaction, the longing for childish dependence and the desire to be governed by autocratic leaders and dogma were reinforced. Nothing reveals more clearly the deep contradictions of the age than the spread of witch hunts in this century of advancing naturalistic knowledge. The forces of superstition and dogma revolted against enlightened reason, which was attempting to liberate man from blind subordination to authority.

Contradictions also appear in baroque painting. The subject matter included the grandiose inflated portrayal of the nobility, the rich merchant, and the powerful politician, but also depictions of the poor, the common man in the street, the trivialities of the daily life of the village, the folk dances, the butcher shop, and the sickroom. The same painters who were commissioned to paint the leading citizens turned to subjects of more prosaic nature when following their own inclinations. Rembrandt, who glorified the rich burgher, also painted the anatomist teaching his confreres at the dissecting table.

This internal split between conflicting attitudes was clearly expressed in baroque architecture, where the struggle between rigid formalism and mannerism resulted in tortuous and tasteless exaggerations expressing a stress on freedom of form and the rejection of the shackles of classical tradition. Baroque man, in his bombastic and flaunting emphasis on force and grandeur and on the sensualism of flesh, appears as a caricature of the true individualism of the Renaissance man. The individualism of the baroque man is more of a pose, a defensive assertion of something that was waning under the corrosive influence of reason.

The prevailing values of the times were contradictory. Feudal honor, individual bravado, the dueling sword, were challenged by the burgeoning

civilian virtues of thrift, sobriety, practicality, compromise, and resourceful-
ness. The hidalgo yielded his place to the merchant. Cervantes' Don Quixote
becomes insane in fighting for the waning feudal ideals of the errant knight
against an encroaching prosaic leveling reasonableness. The two principles
are symbolized in the two protagonists: Don Quixote, the exalted dreamer,
fights for the glorious romantic past, while his earthy servant, Sancho
Panza, is the necessary exponent of empirical, practical, but, alas, pedestrian reason.

The dualism between faith and reason is seen in a great book written by
an English physician, Sir Thomas Browne (1605–1682)—*Religio Medici*.
Few books reflect the struggle of the religious against the scientific outlook
more eloquently. The *Religio Medici* was timely and a best seller. Browne
was born five years after Giordano Bruno was burned at the stake, the
same year, 1605, that Francis Bacon's epoch-making book, *Advancement
of Learning,* was published. Browne's solution to the spiritual dilemma was
not original. As his historian, Jeremiah S. Finch, aptly puts it: he accepted
"two orders of truth: that which can be discovered by the favor of man's
reason, and that which can only be known intuitively."[1] He lived in two
hermetically divided worlds: he conceded that the study of external nature
by science is permissible and at the same time testified before the tribunal
in favor of witchcraft. Yet his tortuous intellectual straddling of the fence
did not prevent his book from being put on the *Index.*

In some of the passages of the *Religio* Browne displays an intuitive
grasp of psychological motivations and particularly some of the revealing
contradictions of the mind. He states that no one can judge another because no one knows himself. He asks: Can people expect charity when they
are not charitable to themselves? He was aware of the common but contradictory coexistence of severe self-criticism and indulgence, of self-abnega-
tion and vainglory. He calls Diogenes more vainglorious than Alexander,
who rejected no honors, whereas Diogenes refused all. Such introspective
intuition into the depth of human nature was characteristic of the *grand
siècle* and can also be found in the writings of Pascal, Spinoza, Sydenham,
Burton, Shakespeare, and Cervantes. This age of contradictions—the age
of division between medieval mysticism and modern science—favored
introspection. Doubt, leading to inner conflict, forces man to turn toward
his own self in his attempt to resolve this puzzling contradiction in his
mind.

Psychological Developments

The fourteenth-century voluntarists had rediscovered man's natural desires
and feelings; Renaissance humanists and artists celebrated the individual's
earthy vitality. The contribution of seventeenth-century scientists and
philosophers to the history of psychiatry was their emphasis on the role of
reason in understanding and eventually controlling external nature.

But reason also has another function: the mastery of man's internal instinctual forces, his desires and feelings. It remained for our own time to recognize the inwardly directed functions of reason, those of self-understanding and self-mastery, which had been consistently declining since the days of Socrates, Plato, and Aristotle. The seventeenth century achieved unprecedented progress toward the understanding of nature. In the understanding of man's own nature the seventeenth century made only the first groping attempts.

Physicians interested in psychiatry in this era of the natural sciences were still inclined to explain mental illness on the basis of physiological speculation. Nevertheless, the consideration of painstaking observation as the supreme virtue could not fail to result in some advances in psychology and even in psychiatry.

Thomas Hobbes (1588–1679), a rationalist philosopher and antagonist of scholasticism, may be considered one of the originators of associational psychology. Fundamentally, his psychology is mechanistic: sense perceptions are the only source of psychic life, and perceptions are associated with each other according to the temporal sequence in which they are perceived. Hobbes was also a biologically oriented voluntarist; he believed all psychological phenomena are regulated by the instinct to preserve life and by the organism's need to seek pleasure and avoid pain. In this, as we shall see, he anticipated Spinoza, who developed the same views more comprehensively.

A philosopher who was also a physician, John Locke (1632–1704), believed, like Hobbes, that all knowledge originates in experience, that is, from sense perceptions. Locke differentiated, however, between external experience (the perception of objects) and internal experience (the perception of feelings and desires). Locke's doctrine was elaborated by his followers Bishop George Berkeley (1685–1753) and David Hume (1711–1776), who concluded that no absolute knowledge is possible since all that we know about the world is based on subjective experience transmitted through sense perceptions that do not reflect an objectively "true" picture of the world. Only through the senses can man achieve any knowledge of the world.

Impressively unbiased psychological observations appear also in the work of two great English physicians, William Harvey (1578–1657) and Thomas Sydenham (1624–1689). Their contributions to psychiatry, tangential in the sense that their main interest was in organic medicine, are nonetheless outstanding. Sydenham described the clinical manifestations of hysteria, which, because of its ubiquity, remained of central significance for the practicing physician, and Harvey described the effect of emotional tensions upon cardiac activity.

Sydenham was born at Winford Eagle, Dorsetshire, and died in London. He came from a Puritan family, and like his brothers, served in Cromwell's army in the Civil War. He studied at Oxford, where he received a Baccalaureate of Medicine in 1648; he went to Montpellier for postgraduate study and returned to London in 1661 to practice medicine. Sydenham's contributions are the result of keen clinical obervation. He stated: "In writing the history of a disease, every philosophical hypothesis whatsoever that has previously occupied the mind of the author, should lie in abeyance. This being done, the clear and natural phenomena of the disease should be noted. . . . No man can state the errors that have been occasioned by . . . physiological hypothesis. Writers, whose minds have taken a false colour . . . have saddled diseases with phenomena which existed in their own brains only; but which would have been clear and visible to the whole world had the assumed hypothesis been true. Add to this, that if by chance some symptom really coincided accurately with their hypothesis, and occur in the disease whereof they would describe the character, they magnify it beyond all measure and moderation; they make it all in all; the molehill becomes a mountain, whilst, if it fail to tally with the said hypothesis, they pass it over either in perfect silence or with only an incidental mention, unless, by means of some philosophical subtlety, they can enlist it in their service, or else, by fair means or foul, accommodate it in some way or other to their doctrines."[2]

This uncompromisingly empirical attitude combined with his gift for precise clinical observation earned him such titles as the "Prince of English Physicians" and the "English Hoppocrates." It is said that the great medical teacher of Holland, Hermann Boerhaave (1668–1738), raised his hat whenever he referred to Sydenham.

Sydenham did not trust books; he believed only what he could see and learn from his own bedside experience. In this he was a true son of his times, and the intellectual atmosphere in which he moved is best exemplified in his friendship with two of the greatest empiricists of the time, Robert Boyle, the founder of experimental chemistry, and John Locke, the philosopher whose teachings prepared the way for the French Enlightenment, and, through this powerful intellectual channel, for the French and American revolutions. What Locke preached in the abstractions of philosophy—that all knowledge came from observation—Boyle demonstrated in concrete terms by his experimentally established law concerning the behavior of gases (the equations between pressure, temperature, and volume), and Sydenham showed in his clinical descriptions. The mutual admiration of these men for each other is thus not astonishing. Locke, himself a physician, expressed his respect some years after Sydenham's death by stating that it is unfortunate that physicians instead of following Sydenham's empirical methods still prefer to argue their divergent theories of disease.

Most outstanding among Sydenham's contributions to medicine were his treatises on gout, venereal disease, St. Vitus's dance, and the use of Peruvian bark in the cure of ague. In his famous *Epistolary Dissertation on the*

Hysterical Affections, a letter to Dr. William Cole, Sydenham so precisely describes the symptoms of hysteria that even today little can be added to what he said. He maintained that it was the most common chronic disease, and he recognized that in spite of the fact that hysteria refers to the uterus (Greek, *hysteron,* uterus), males suffer from this disease also. Sydenham's sole concession to the prejudice that only women suffer from hysteria was that he called the male hysteric a "hypochondriac."

Sydenham recognized for the first time the fact that hysterical symptoms may simulate almost all forms of organic diseases. He mentions, for example, paralysis of one side of the body, which may also be caused by apoplexy, and states that hysterical hemiplegia may proceed "from some violent commotion of the mind (strong emotions)." He described hysterical convulsions resembling epileptic attacks, hysterical headaches that induced vomiting, psychogenic "palpitation of the heart," and what he called a "hysterical cough." He maintained that hysterical pain may be mistaken for kidney stones and suggested that a diagnosis that differentiates between a real stone and a hysterical disorder can be made if the psychological state of the patient is known; therefore he questions the emotional circumstances at the time of the origin of the pain.[3] Sydenham was not interested in theoretical explanations for hysteria. He still relied on the ancient concept that "animal spirits" cause disease by affecting parts of the body.

Sydenham was not the only seventeenth-century medical writer who recognized the influence of psychological factors in disease. William Harvey professed to "learn and to teach anatomy, not from books but from dissections; not from the positions of philosophers, but from the fabric of nature."[4] Harvey suggested in his writings that he might well delve more deeply into the relationship of mind and body. Had he done so with as much ingenuity as he displayed when he, for the first time in the history of physiology, described blood circulation, he might have become the father of modern psychosomatic medicine. In fact, Harvey may possibly have written much more than we know. He was a royalist, and when King Charles was beheaded many of Harvey's manuscripts were burned by frenzied antiroyalist mobs.

In his *De Motu Cordis* (1628) Harvey wrote, "Every affection of the mind that is attended with either pain or pleasure, hope or fear, is the cause of an agitation whose influence extends to the heart. . . . And hence, by the way, it may perchance be wherefore grief, and love, and envy, and anxiety, and all affections of the mind of a similar kind are accompanied with emaciation and decay, or with cacochemy and crudity, which engender all manner of disease and consume the body of man."[5] In 1649 he says of a case of heart disease: "I was acquainted with a strong man, who having received an injury and affront from one more powerful than himself, and upon whom he could not have his revenge, was so overcome with hatred and spite and passion, which he yet communicated to no one, that at last he fell into a strange distemper, suffering from extreme oppression and pain of the heart and breast, and the prescriptions of none of the very best physicians proving of any avail, he fell in the course of a few years into a scorbutic and cachectic state, became rabid and died."[6]

In 1649 Harvey further discussed the influence of the emotions on the body: "And what indeed is more deserving of attention than the fact that in almost every affection, appetite, hope, or fear, our body suffers, the countenance changes, and the blood appears to course hither and thither? In anger the eyes are fiery and the pupils contracted; in modesty the cheeks are suffused with blushes; in fear, and under the sense of infamy and of shame, the face is pale, but the ears burn as if for the evil they heard or were to hear; in lust how quickly is the member penis distended with blood and erected! . . . Such is the force of the blood pent up, and such are the effects of its impulse."[7]

The empirical orientation initiated on psychology by Bacon and Locke and by Sydenham and Harvey on medicine was not confined, of course, to England. One of the great admirers of Sydenham was a German, Georg Ernst Stahl (1660–1734). Stahl systematized both Sydenham's and Harvey's observations in *Theoria Medica Vera* (1707), which dealt with mental disturbances, extending Sydenham's ideas about hysteria into a general principle of biology. Stahl believed that the most characteristic aspect of all human living organisms, either human or subhuman, is that they are animated by a special force that is most clear in its psychological manifestations. He called this vital force "soul"; it is not distinct from the body, nor is it something separate or external that must be superimposed upon the body to make it alive. Stahl's concept of a vital force is near to present-day views of psychosomatic medicine, which do not separate the dynamic phenomena of psychology from those of physiology. Perhaps more important than Stahl's "soul" for the history of psychiatry was his idea that some mental as well as physical disturbances arise from purely psychological causes and may be differentiated from mental conditions— such as toxic deliriums—which have an organic basis. Even though Stahl made this important practical differentiation, he viewed the living organism as a psychobiological unity. Stahl's influence was negligible in his own time, so these theoretical advances had little impact until Christian Ideler (1766–1846) rediscovered them one hundred years later.

Any discussion of seventeenth-century contributions to psychological aspects of medicine would be incomplete without tribute to Baruch Spinoza (1632–1677), perhaps the greatest of pre-Freudian psychologists. This shy, ascetic inhabitant of the Jewish ghetto in Amsterdam suplied the epistemological foundation of our psychosomatic era, the identity of body and mind.

Spinoza was born in Amsterdam, into a Portuguese Jewish family

(Espinoza) that had fled the Spanish Inquisition. The son of a well-to-do merchant, from early youth he devoted all his energies to his studies, both religious and secular. In addition to the Bible and Talmud, he read the works of Arab and Jewish philosophers, particularly Maimonides, and after he learned Latin, Democritus and Epicurus, but the most direct impetus toward developing his own system came from Descartes. Spinoza's goal was to create a unified view of the world; he was both frustrated and challenged by Descartes's radical separation of mind and body, and he replaced this dualism with a concept of *psychophysiological parallelism*. His basic tenet is that mind and body are inseparable because *they are identical:* the living organism experiences its bodily processes psychologically as affects, thoughts, and desires. Psychology and physiology are two aspects of the same thing—the living organism.

Spinoza was a most consistent and uncompromising thinker for whom search for truth and the pursuit of his convictions constituted the supreme values. Judged a heretic because of his pantheism and refutations of the anthropomorphic God-image of the Jewish and Christian religions, Spinoza was publicly excommunicated by the elders of the synagogue when he was twenty-seven years old. The Jews in his community were forbidden to communicate with him in any way; they were forbidden to enter a room in which he was present or to read one line of his writings. He supported himself by teaching and by polishing lenses. He earned barely enough to live on, yet he consistently refused to accept gifts and annuities offered to him by his admirers, among them Henry Oldenbury, the secretary of the Royal Society of England, Leibnitz, the great philosopher, and Huygens, the physicist. He also refused a pension offered to him by Louis XIV, because the king expected Spinoza to dedicate his next book to him; and he turned down the chair of philosophy at the University of Heidelberg because he would not have been allowed to challenge the concepts of Christianity.

Spinoza used the prevailing vocabulary of his time, that is, he expressed himself in religious terms. His God, however, does not reside outside and above the natural world as something superimposed upon the universe; he is the universe itself. Spinoza ridiculed as primitive the idea that God can perform miracles, that is to say, acts that are contradictory to the laws of nature. His God has no other attributes than the laws of nature, laws that can be deciphered by clear mathematical reasoning. Although Spinoza speaks of the *"amor intellectualis dei"* as the supreme attitude of man, he means by this term the love of truth—the urge to understand the laws of nature. In his views he was, like Socrates, a most worldly philosopher; in his way of life he was not at all worldly. His exclusive dedication to the search for truth was as truly religious as St. Augustine's dedication to the love of God.

Nothing can exemplify more strikingly the change in Western man's outlook since the fifth century than the difference between Spinoza's and St. Augustine's "love of God," which both men considered as the supreme virtue of man. St. Augustine categorically denied man's ability to find the truth merely by reliance on his own faculties. He demanded unconditional surrender to the supernatural wisdom of God. Spinoza's "intellectual love of God" is but a parapharasing of his confidence that man, by sound and uncompromising reasoning, can decipher the laws of nature and of the mind and become free from servitude to his passions and thus achieve perfection. In the course of the twelve centuries that separate these two most dedicated thinkers, faith was dethroned and reason enthroned as the supreme virtue.

Spinoza expressed his most fundamental tenet in the succinct sentence "ordo rerum et idearum idem est": The nature of things and ideas is identical. This lucid statement postulates the identity of mind and body as two aspects, or in today's vocabulary, the subjective and objective aspects, of the same basic entity, the living organism.

Spinoza was not only a great metaphysician, he was an equally significant psychologist. In his Ethics he describes conscious mental processes with still unsurpassed detail and precision. The Ethics can be best evaluated in the light of certain semantic considerations. Spinoza was not a medical man, but a philosopher who wrote in the still prevailing jargon of the schoolmen, although in his ideas he was not in the least scholastic. The title Ethics is misleading. It is a comprehensive presentation of metaphysics, psychology, and ethics. It consists of several books. One is devoted to the relation of mind to matter and is partly epistemology, partly psychology; another, "The Nature and Origin of Affects," is pure descriptive psychology. Still another is about "The Lack of Human Freedom and the Power of the Affects." The final book deals with the power of knowledge—in modern terms, insight—which makes man free; to attain this inner freedom is the desirable goal of man. Spinoza discusses emotions, ideas, and desires in strictly objective terms without using the categories of good or bad. Values are related to the organism: "good" is what serves self-preservation, "bad" is what interferes with it. The urge for self-preservation is one of Spinoza's most fundamental concepts, and he considers it a determinant of behavior. The axis of his works is psychodynamic, or in other words, psychological causality. Just as physical events are strictly determined, so are psychological events: "There is no such thing as an absolute or free will. Every volition is determined by a cause which again is determined by another cause, and the latter again by some other cause ad infinitum. . . . The fundamental principle is the innate tendency of the body to perpetuate its being." (Thesis 48, Ethics.) This is comparable to the stability, or homeostatic, principle of Fechner, Freud, Claude Bernard, and Cannon, which will be discussed later.

Spinoza came close to the concept of the dynamic unconscious when he proposed that self-preservation motivates psychic processes: "The psyche tries as much as it is capable to become aware of those things which increase the power of the body." (Thesis 12.) And "The psyche is bent not to become aware of those things which decrease the power of the body." (Thesis 13.) This avoidance of becoming aware of certain perturbing ideas is precisely what Freud meant by repression, which he believed served to ward off anxiety and maintain homeostasis.

Spinoza believed that love also is derived from the wish to survive and that love is nothing "but pleasure connected with the idea of that thing which causes pleasure. . . ." He considered hate as displeasure connected with the idea of its cause: we hate that which threatens our existence. Freud also conceived of a life instinct but believed that hate is not in the service of the life instinct, as Spinoza taught, but on the contrary, is a manifestation of the death instinct, which is directed toward self-destruction.

Of greater interest even than these basic theoretical considerations is Spinoza's detailed analysis of different emotional qualities. In Thesis 17 he discusses in detail the phenomenon that two hundred years later Bleuler called ambivalence. "If we think of a thing which usually is connected with displeasure, but reminds us of something which used to give us an equal amount of pleasure, we hate and love it at the same time." Spinoza called this mixture of two opposite emotions "vacillation of the soul"; it bears the same relation to emotions as doubt does to ideas. Since for Spinoza emotions and ideas are intimately connected, doubt and vacillation of the soul thus differ from each other only quantitatively. The current psychoanalytic view considers the characteristic doubting of the compulsive obsessive neurotic as one manifestation of his basic ambivalence. Equally penetrating is Spinoza's analysis of hope and pity. "Hope is uncertain pleasure derived from the idea of a past or future event, about the outcome of which we are in doubt. Fear also results from the idea of something uncertain. When the doubt is lifted, hope changes into confidence and fear into despair. . . . Joy is a kind of pleasure which is derived from something about the outcome of which we were doubtful in the past. . . . Pity is displeasure which the suffering of another person arouses in us whom we feel is similar to us." This kind of pity through identification today we call empathy. Spinoza also defined (Thesis 7) the psychological mechanisms that in modern terms are called overcompensation and reaction formation: "An affect can be counterbalanced or eliminated only by another opposite and stronger affect."

Spinoza discusses the ethical aspects of his logically cohesive psychological system in the fifth and final book of *Ethics:* "The Power of the Intellect, or of Human Liberty." Freud applied his psychological theory to restore mental health through extending the activity of the conscious mind over the unconscious mental processes. For Freud the therapeutic results of psychoanalysis depend upon the replacement of unconscious mental acts by conscious ones. The ultimate therapeutic agent is increased insight into one's own motivational processes. The same is the goal of Spinoza, but he calls this goal an ethical one. What Freud calls mental health Spinoza calls the freedom of the mind. For both of them it constituted the highest value. One's mind can become free of the power of the passions only by intellectual comprehension of the total psychological situation. Spinoza calls partial insight an inadequate idea. For him, just as for psychoanalysis today, the function of the intellect is an integrative one, a comprehension of all motivations and feelings in their totality. Spinoza developed a most adequate theoretical system of personality, which had to wait until Freud for its operational implementation. Freud developed a theory of the unconscious, of repression and concepts of transference and resistance. Spinoza had only a vague knowledge of dynamic processes, what he himself would have called "inadequate ideas." His psychological descriptions of the dynamics of conscious mental processes, however, are exceptional in their completeness.

Spinoza's greatest merit is the logical cohesiveness and the strict integration of his thoughts. This makes his works difficult reading. He proposes his system in the axiomatic form of geometry; every step follows from the previous one. Moreover, his language, which is full of scholastic expressions, is medieval and stands in stark contrast with the modernity of his views. The axiomatic method of presentation, however, makes for utmost clarity in his definitions. His causal sequences are based not on geometry but on psychodynamics, and his axioms are derived from the intuitive knowledge of the logic of emotions, just as the axioms of geometry are based on the further irreducible logic of ideas.

The influence of Spinoza upon modern thought development was so pervasive that many of his basic concepts became a part of the general ideological climate that influenced Freud without his knowing its origin. This is particularly true for Freud's biological and physiological views. Johannes Müller, "the father of modern physiology," completely adopted Spinoza's theory of emotions and instincts. According to Müller, the last three books of Spinoza's *Ethics* represent the best scientific contribution to psychology. Freud in his theory of instincts adopted the then current view of the instinct of self-preservation. Though this did not originate with Spinoza—Hobbes professed the same belief—no other philosopher made it the cornerstone of his personality theory.

Spinoza's importance to the history of psychiatry lies in the fact that in his conception of the universe he considered psychological phenomena to be as significant as material processes. The influence of his concepts upon personality theory was profound, although the methodology required for the application of these ideas to individuals did not become available until the work of Freud in the nineteenth and twentieth centuries.

What was available in the seventeenth century, however, were the works of two authors who had incredible insight into the unconscious depths of the human personality—William Shakespeare (1564–1616) and Miguel Cervantes (1547–1616). As had repeatedly occurred, artistic intuition and observation anticipate scientific discoveries. These two intuitive and observant artists probed the depths of the human personality long before they were explored by psychoanalysts.

Shakespeare's masterful descriptions of the universal unconscious conflicts in man are legion. Hamlet, for instance, is, in modern terms, a compulsive neurotic personality, accurately and completely portrayed. The unconscious reason for Hamlet's compulsive hesitation in taking revenge on his uncle—namely, his Oedipus conflict—is unmistakably indicated in the text. Falstaff is another example of Shakespeare's grasp of psychological phenomena. In *Henry IV*, the unconscious background of Falstaff's psychopathic personality, his deep resistance to growing up, is highlighted by the contrasting figure of Prince Hal. Hal's regressive, playboy pretensions are at first fostered by Falstaff's uninhibited acting out, but these are modified by his identification with his king-father, who represents maturity, duty, and leadership. In *King Lear* Shakespeare touches on the deep attachment that exists between father and daughters; in *Othello* he explores in depth the psychology of jealousy.

Cervantes' grasp of the psychology of mental illness is perhaps even more striking than Shakespeare's. *Don Quixote,* one of the first psychological novels, is more than a profound parody of contemporary Spanish society, although without question this tragicomedy mirrors the dying sixteenth-century Spanish culture.

Don Quixote, however, offers far more than contemporary satire. Cervantes has deep compassion for this foolish and insane knight who becomes a martyr to his idealism and a symbol of the highest strivings of man. The profound dramatic effect of Don Quixote's story is derived from the fact that one way all mankind uses to avoid frustrating and drab reality is to return to the colorful imagery of the past, a regressive trend that is present to some degree in every healthy or sick person. When Cervantes succeeds in making the reader identify with Don Quixote he is illustrating the principle that the mentality of the psychotic includes the essential qualities of normal thinking. There is no special physiology for healthy or morbid processes of the body, and similarly there are not two kinds of psychology, one for the healthy and one for the diseased mind. The basic principles are the same in psychology and psychopathology. In psychological terms, the central theme of this novel is the escape from the unbearable present to the fantasies of the glory of the past. This form of behavior exemplifies regression, the main characteristic of psychosis.

Don Quixote and Sancho Panza, like Don Juan and Leporello, are complementary figures, personifying two aspects of one and the same person. Most psychotics, even while they are giving free rein to their wishful fantasies and falsifying reality according to their emotional needs through their hallucinations and delusions, nevertheless maintain a certain amount of practical sense that enables them to move about in the world. In a sense they live a double existence, retaining a tenuous hold on the practical world, overshadowed though it is by the self-created world of their fantasy. Sancho Panza personifies this residual rationality. He is completely dominated by his demented master, yet at the same time he helps him in practical matters and thus makes it possible for him to live by his folly. This quaint symbiosis of Don Quixote and Sancho Panza—who are really one person—gives a faithful picture of the mind of the psychotic. Fantasy, the faculty of imagining, is an essential component of thought; in psychosis this faculty of imagination is used not to master reality but to escape from it. This is one of the hidden reasons why we are emotionally so averse to a psychotic: he abuses this most distinctive faculty of man. Cervantes makes the best possible case for his psychotic in demonstrating movingly that there are extenuating circumstances in his favor. Don Quixote is indeed a man of lofty ideals and the highest principles, and we cannot help but admire his tenacity in trying to live up to them, nor can we keep from regretting that fate does not allow him to live the exemplary existence of a knight-errant. We cannot laugh at him and despise him. The worst we can say of him is that he was not cut out for this world—he was too good for it—a remark that is true for many mentally disturbed patients. It is not a coincidence that Spain, possibly the first country to unchain the psychotic patients, also produced the first novel about a psychotic hero.

Another literary description of a pathological mental state is *The Anatomy of Melancholy* (1621), written by an Oxford dean of divinity, Robert Burton (1577–1640). Burton's approach to mental illness was so advanced for his time that his book had no immediate predecessors and no immediate successors, although it influenced much of English writing in later centuries. Burton recognized the foremost psychodynamic components of melancholia and described some of the essential principles of psychoanalysis; Sir William Osler called *The Anatomy of Melancholy* "the greatest medical treatise ever written by a layman."

There is no doubt that psychological knowledge is ultimately based on subjective experience, and Bergan Evans and George Mohr (1895–1965) most convincingly conclude on the basis of *The Anatomy,* as well from Burton's life history, that Burton himself suffered from a classical case of melancholia.[8] Obviously Burton had an intimate knowledge of the emotional background of depression. This is another revelatory book, like St. Augustine's *Confessions* and Freud's *Interpretation of Dreams,* filled with astute introspection and an intuitive grasp of emotional dynamics.

Burton's book is a quaint conglomeration of ancient and current misconceptions, demonological superstitions, physiological mythologies, and a compulsive recounting of anything anyone else ever said about melancholia.

The significant parts of the *Anatomy* are those that are based almost entirely on Burton's interpretation of his own life history. He was not a clinician; most of what he knew about mental disease was derived from his own inner experiences: "Other men get their knowledge from books, I get mine from melancholizing." The outstanding biographical fact is Burton's unhappy childhood, which he attributed to lack of parental affection and which produced in him a persistent intractable dissatisfaction with the world, a never resolved embitterment that he expressed in various ways and with great literary ability. Overt and hidden sarcasm characterizes his style. His primary targets are the university scholars, who, according to him, were a cringing, intellectually dishonest lot, impractical, helpless creatures without any vision, who flattered their illiterate patrons and who possessed limited and useless knowledge. All this accusation was an attack on himself, for he was an Oxford scholar of great eminence and a recluse who perpetually dreamed of being able to participate in life. The modern view of the psychodynamic core of melancholia is that destructive hostility and resentment felt toward the world are directed against one's self. Burton illustrates this quite well, for his writing is full of direct and indirect self-depreciation; hence, at first he published his witty and erudite book anonymously, using the pseudonym Democritus, Junior; only later did he republish it under his own name.

Being himself a destructive personality, Burton's insight into the mentality of the melancholic is without peer. What differentiates Burton from the ordinary melancholic and makes him important for the history of psychopathology is that he was able to objectify his subjective insight into a comprehensive pathography of depression. He clearly recognized the emotional core of depression—relentless hostility. He also reorganized its self-destructive component. He was not, however, able to connect the two and understand that the hostility that is directed inward occurs when expressions of outwardly directed destructive tendencies are pent up and frustrated. He clearly described, however, the characteristic internal conflicts caused by an individual's constant struggle with his hostilities, and how they are manifested in jealousy, competitiveness, and ambivalence toward the opposite sex.

His therapeutic recommendations run the gamut of every remedy that had ever been suggested for melancholy from the time of the ancients up to his own day—physical exercise, sports (in bad weather, spectator sports), chess, baths, bibliotherapy, music therapy, travel, purgatives, food and drugs, diet, and moderation in sexual indulgence. "The Ordinary recreations which we have in Winter and in most solitary times to busy our minds with are cards, tables and dice, shovel-board, chess-play, the philosopher's game,* small trunks,† shuttle-cock, billiards, music, masks, singing, dancing, Yule-games, frolics, jests, riddles, catches, purposes, questions, and commands, merry tales of errant knights, queens, lovers, lords, ladies, giants, dwarfs, thieves, cheaters, witches, fairies, goblins, friars, etc., such as the owl woman told [of] Psyche in Apuleius, Boccaccio novels, and the rest, which some delight to hear, some to tell, all are well pleased with."⁹ Burton supports his advice with a flood of quotations from known and unknown sources.

Buried among the disconnected wealth of therapeutic diversions is a most remarkable chapter devoted to the value of confessing grief to a friend: "If then our judgement be so depraved, our reason over-ruled, will precipitated, that we cannot seek our own good, or moderate ourselves, as in this disease [melancholia] commonly it is, the best way for ease is to impart our misery to some friend, not to smother it up in our own breast; for grief concealed strangles the soul; but when as we shall but impart it to some discreet, trusty, loving friend, it is instantly removed. . . . A friend's counsel is a charm, like mandrake wine, it allayeth our cares."¹⁰

Burton is aware how difficult it is to find a "discreet, trusty, loving" friend, and after endless discussons he suggests a physician. Furthermore, he had an inkling that what today we call "transference" is the primary therapeutic factor in confidential and confessional self-revelation: "It is the best thing in the world, as Seneca therefore adviseth in such a case, to get a trusty friend, to whom we may freely and sincerely pour out our secrets; nothing so delighteth and easeth the mind, as when we have a prepared bosom, to which our secrets may descend, of whose conscience we are assured as our own, whose speech may ease our succourless estate, counsel relieve, mirth expel our mourning, and whose very sight may be acceptable unto us!"¹¹ In modern terminology, the patient who is so delighted by the mere sight of his therapist and is in such readiness to release his secrets and pent-up emotions is approximating the state of "positive transference." The importance of this positive relationship to therapeutic results has only in recent years become fully appreciated.

*   *   *

If the Renaissance represented Western man's first important steps toward a realistic approach to psychiatry after the long night of medieval ignorance, the Age of Reason marked a great leap forward. Through the efforts of the great scientists, philosophers, men of letters, and artists of the seventeenth century mental illness was further extricated from superstition and authoritarian error. This could occur only when inductive reasoning, based on objective and careful observations of mental illness, could ally

---

* A kind of chess.
† A kind of billiard game played with a cuestick, alos called troll-madam and pigeon-holes.

with solid intuitive judgment. In the work of Sydenham, for instance, the meticulous observations of hysteria pointed man toward an understanding of the complex relationships between mind and body. This empirical tradition, stimulated and expanded by Bacon and Locke and pursued by Stahl, Harvey, and Sydenham, is the operative foundation of modern science.

Yet the importance of the seventeenth century in the history of psychiatry would not be as great as it is without the more intuitive contributions of Spinoza. Lacking a methodology sufficient to deal with the great metaphysical and psychological problems to which he addressed himself, Spinoza still was able to crumble the Cartesian principle of mind-body dichotomy by establishing the validity of the holistic concept of the organism. This, and his brilliant analysis of emotional states, placed all subsequent students of the human mind in his debt. With such breakthroughs achieved through the use of observation and reason, the scientists of the Western world approached the next century confident that time and constant effort would yield still greater enlightenment.

CHAPTER **8**

The Enlightenment

The continuous development of scientific ideas cannot be neatly divided into centuries. It is simply a matter of convenience to label the eighteenth century the epoch of the "Enlightenment," and the reader must bear in mind that the empirical, rational, and observational heritage from the seventeenth century continued to flourish throughout the 1700's and indeed formed much of the impetus for the advances made throughout the Enlightened century. Enlightened, yes, but an era full of internal contradictions. Parallel trends, old and new, merged and comingled: although the concept of the original goodness of man was espoused, destructive instincts found outlet in bloody revolution; although the insane were unchained, the guillotine was invented.

The outstanding characteristic of the eighteenth century, however, is that belief in reason replaced tradition and faith in all aspects of society. By the early eighteenth century experimentation definitely had ousted deductive abstraction in scientific and medical investigations. Georg Stahl, a vitalist, was debating with his colleague Friedrich Hoffmann (1660–1742) at the University of Halle and losing to Hoffmann's position that experience should supplant reason in biological research. John Hunter (1728–1793), whose epitaph at Westminster Abbey proclaims him "The Founder of Scientific Surgery," wrote to his friend Edward Jenner (1749–1823), the innovator of vaccination against smallpox, "Don't think, try the experiment"; and it seemed as though all of eighteenth-century medical investigation responded to the advice of this outstanding surgeon. The objective point of view had finally dislodged the demon from human disease, and psychiatry was about to find its way into medicine through organic channels. By the early decades of the century physicians were looking for destroyed matter in the brain to explain mental disease, and concepts like the seat of the soul and "animal spirits" were gradually going into oblivion.

Progress in the exact sciences during the Enlightenment was staggering. Luigi Galvani (1737–1798), an Italian physiologist, and Count Alessandro Volta (1745–1827), an Italian physicist, pioneered in electricity. John Dalton (1766–1844), an English chemist, revolutionized physics with his atomic theory; Joseph Black (1728–1799), a Scots chemist, discovered carbon dioxide. Henry Cavendish (1731–1810), Daniel Rutherford (1749–1819), and Joseph Priestley (1733–1804) discovered and described hydrogen, nitrogen, and oxygen, respectively. Oxygen was also identified independently by Karl Wilhelm Scheele (1742–1786) of Sweden. In Germany embryology was modernized with the work of the microscopist Kaspar Friedrich Wolff (1733–1794), and in Switzerland Albrecht von Haller (1708–1777) initiated advances in physiology and compiled, in his *Elementa physiologiae corporis humani* (1757–1766), all the physiological knowledge then known. In all fields of technology, advance was added to advance. New inventions—the thresher, spinning roller, locomotive, parachute, balloon—appeared. In medicine new diagnostic tools were added to the physician's armamentarium. Stephen Hales (1677–1761), an English divine, developed a method for taking blood pressure and studied the dynamics of blood flow. Leopold Auenbrugger (1722–1809) had learned as a child that if he thumped barrels of wine he could tell the level of the fluid inside. As a doctor he thumped on the chests of his patients and left for medical posterity the valuable method of ascertaining thoracic disease by percussion. The French physician René Laennec (1781–1826) invented the stethoscope, thereby enabling physicians to hear more clearly the sounds within the chest. The beginnings of an understanding of the digestive processes were made by a French naturalist, René de Réaumur (1683–1757) and an Italian abbé, Lazaro Spallanzani (1729–1799). Diseases were more exactly diagnosed and precisely localized, and since the concept of localization is essential to the development of the history of organic psychiatry, we shall have more to say of Giovanni Battista Morgagni (1682–1771), whose anatomical findings affirmed this concept.

It is only to be expected that these developments in the natural sciences would affect philosophy and thought throughout society. Voltaire (1694–1778), for instance, wrote two books about Isaac Newton's (1642–1727) work in optics and astronomy, *Philosophie de Newton* and *Physique*. He also conducted experiments in physics and biology himself. Another philosopher, Charles Montesquieu (1689–1755), regarded history as a natural science with its own unalterable laws; he viewed social life, morals, customs, and laws as organically interconnected parts of a comprehensive total social machinery.

Psychology, too, was being approached with the same orientation. Locke had declared that all knowledge derives from external or internal experience. Étienne Condillac (1715–1780), the French philosopher, pursued this point of view and tried to demonstrate that all complicated psychological phenomena—even concepts like memory, judgment, and reasoning —derive from elementary sensations. According to this theory, man's complex abilities to abstract and differentiate depend on elementary sensations, which are the ultimate units of all psychological phenomena. Thus philosophy, history, ethics, and psychology became, at least in principle, natural sciences, and like them, subject to rational analysis and empirical observation.

From Classifying to Unchaining the Insane

The wealth of medical and scientific data established during the seventeenth and eighteenth centuries was so overwhelming that synthesis and systematization became necessary. Science has to make sense from collected facts by drawing generalizations and devising a system of order, and the eighteenth century perforce became the Age of Systems. Chemistry had been systematized by Antoine Laurent Lavoisier (1743–1794), who had also elaborated many of the essentials of combustion and respiration; and the march toward systematization continued as Carolus Linnaeus (1707–1778), a Swedish physician and botanist, applied the principles of organization to living matter in his *Systema naturae* (1735). He classified all botanical specimens into genus and species and extended his classification to the animal world, where he placed man in the order of Primates and gave him the name *Homo sapiens*.

Physicians attempting to categorize the symptoms of the mentally ill in the eighteenth century were handicapped because they had few direct observations on patients available to classify. Since codification was the order of the day, however, mental symptoms were described and categorized throughout the century, and by 1800 a large number of clinicians had meticulously reported and classified their observations. But even in the work of such sensitive men as Philippe Pinel (1745–1826) and Vincenzo Chiarugi (1759–1820) psychiatric nosology outweighed real understanding of the sources of psychological miseries; and without psychological understanding, observation of mental patients, however careful, could merely result in a more or less meaningful system of classification. Systematization does not explain the phenomena it classifies. When classifications become overextended, there is a tendency to dismiss factual data that do not fit, and the system becomes replete with errors. Methods of psychiatric treatment were affected scarcely at all by these classifiers, and in general remained methods based on a combination of primitive psychological and physiological speculations.

The most celebrated eighteenth-century teacher of these speculations was Hermann Boerhaave (1668–1738), the son of a Dutch clergyman. His fame was such that a letter—it is related—was sent to "Dr. Boerhaave, Europe," and was delivered to him in Leiden. Boerhaave himself, however, did not make any lasting contributions to medicine, but his teaching influenced dozens of prominent physicians. Although he attempted to maintain a rather eclectic point of view, Boerhaave was partial to Hippocratic doctrines and methods. Like Hippocrates, he instructed his students to observe and learn from their patients at the bedside, but his emphasis upon the Hippocratic doctrine of the four humors was a decisively retrogressive step in the history of psychiatric theory. To this most renowned teacher of the day, melancholia was nothing but a disease caused by black juices; and his students Gérard Van Swieten (1700–1772), and Anton de Haen (1704–1776), who founded the medical school at Vienna, and William Cullen (1712–1790) and John Pringle (1707–1782), who helped found the schools of medicine at Glasgow and Edinburgh, spread this doctrine throughout Europe.

To Boerhaave psychotherapy consisted of bloodletting and purgatives, dousing the patient in ice-cold water, or using some other method to put him in near-shock. Boerhaave gave the medical profession one of its first shock instruments, a spinning chair that rendered the patient unconscious. His gyrating chair was used by Charles Darwin's grandfather, Erasmus Darwin (1731–1802), a physician who believed that all diseases arose out of "disordered motions" of the nervous tissues of the body and that the rotating chair would correct the disharmony. Benjamin Rush (1745–1813), the founder of American psychiatry, was a firm advocate of the gyrating chair, since he believed that congested blood in the brain produced mental illness and that this conditon would be relieved by rotary movement.

For the most part, the physicians of the eighteenth century concerned themselves with the bizarre, the unusual, the out-of-the-ordinary features of mental disturbances. But three students of Boerhaave, George Cheyne (1671–1743), Robert Whytt (1714–1766), and Cullen, did become fascinated by the symptoms of the neurotically disturbed individual and each proposed a different classification of mental disease based on physiology. Cheyne claimed that neurotic behavior was extremely common in England and published, to prove his point, *The English Malady: or A Treatise of nervous diseases of all kinds, as spleen, vapours, lowness of spirits, hypochondriacal and hysterical distempers* (1733). Cheyne stated that there is nothing shameful about neurotic behavior and gave his own life history as a case in point. His book has none of the penetrating introspection of St. Augustine's *Confessions* or the revealing autobiographical remarks of Cardano, but it did emphasize that the most respectable of men, even a fellow of the College of Physicians at Edinburgh, could suffer from emotional disturbance and that this was not necessarily a reason to feel humiliation. However, Cheyne's classification of neurotic behavior, based on the Hippocratic theory of humors, essentially substitutes nomenclature for explanation.

Whytt divided neuroses into hysteria, hypochondriasis, and nervous exhaustion—later called "neurasthenia" by George Beard (1839–1883)— which is not far from our present clinical descriptive classification, even though his ideas were not based on detailed psychological observations. Whytt's basic theory stated the current view that disturbed motility within the nervous system produced nervous disorders. "But how much soever we may be in the dark about the immediate causes of the diseases of the nerves, yet their effects may all be reduced to some change in that sensibility or moving power which the nerves communicate to the different parts of the body."[1] Although Whytt was a painstaking neurologist—he was the first man to describe the pupillary reflex and to discuss shock following injuries to the spinal column[2]—careful clinical observation of and experimentation with reflexes simply could not reveal a real understanding of emotional disturbance.

William Cullen's classification of mental illness was the most comprehensive of all those attempted in the middle of the eighteenth century. Cullen's nosology was so impressive that Philippe Pinel later utilized it in his own system of thought. Cullen followed the methods of Linnaeus and François Boissier de Sauvages (1706–1767), a physician who had described more than two thousand diseases and arranged them into classes, orders, and genera. De Sauvages's eighth class, the *"folies,"* was a systematic and compulsive presentation of every aspect of different nervous disorders.

Cullen lectured on the theory of medicine, which we now call physiology, at Edinburgh. He became popular because he did not lecture in obscure Latin but spoke the vernacular. To make oneself understood became the motto of the day, not only for physicians, but for philosophers such as Voltaire, Diderot, Condorcet, Condillac, D'Alembert, and Rousseau. In his major work, the four-volume *First Lines of the Practice of Physick* (1777), Cullen categorized almost all of the then known diseases according to symptoms, methods of diagnosis, and therapy; four books of the second volume are devoted to mental illness.

Cullen was the first to use the term "neurosis" to mean diseases that are not accompanied by fever or localized pathology. He subdivided neurosis into Comata (conditions like apoplexy or stroke), Adynamiae (alterations of the involuntary, or what we would call today the autonomic, nervous system), and Spasmi (disturbances of voluntary muscles, such as convulsions). The fourth category of neuroses was Vesaniae, a term that he took from the ancients and by which he meant intellectual impairment. Cullen believed that neurosis was due to definite decay, either of the intellect or of the voluntary or involuntary nervous system. His clinical descriptions are remarkably accurate, and he described in detail the external signs—that is, the physiological concomitants—of what we call an "anxiety attack." The patient's actual feeling or what led to the physiological disturbance was unknown to this classifier. At the root of all neurotic afflictions, Cullen thought, there must be some sort of physiological breakdown: "Fear and dejection of mind, or a timid and desponding disposition, may arise in certain states, or upon certain occasions of mere debility. . . . The disease of melancholia, therefore, manifestly depends upon the general temperament of the body."[3] Psychiatry had reached the point of discarding the concept that an exogenous demon caused internal disharmony, but now insisted that the evil was disordered physiology. Concerning the physiological basis of melancholia Cullen remarked: "It may be observed that in it [melancholia] there is a degree of torpor in the motion of the nervous power both with respect to sensation and volition, and there is a general rigidity of the simple solids, and that the balance of the sanguiferous system is upon the side of the veins."[4] Cullen's treatments were based mostly on diet, physiotherapy, exercise, purging, blistering of the forehead, cold dousings, bloodletting, and vomiting—the customary measures used to combat physiological disturbance. Cullen, like most of his contemporaries, treated violently disturbed patients with severe restraint, threats, and strait jackets.

In 1701, the year that Boerhaave took the chair of physiology at Leiden, a medical degree was granted to a brilliant student of anatomy at Padua, Giovanni Battista Morgagni. Morgagni devoted his life to observing diseases from the vantage point of the autopsy table. He was not interested in the cadaver alone; what he wanted to know was if the symptoms of the patient could be related to the post-mortem findings, and he therefore insisted that all autopsy reports include detailed case histories. Morgagni's notes on eight hundred autopsies, compiled over a half century, were published in 1761 in one of the most important medical documents of all history: *De sedibus et causis morborum per anatomen indagatis* (*On the Seats and Causes of Disease Investigated by Anatomy*). Morgagni taught that diseases were related to particular organs, and he was especially interested in brain pathology. He demonstrated that the symptoms arising from a stroke were not due to diseases within the brain itself, but to ruptured blood vessels that affected the brain secondarily. He also observed that paralysis after a stroke involved the side of the body opposite the area of the hemorrhage in the brain. By the end of the eighteenth century, neuroanatomists, neurologists, and physicians interested in the reasons for mental illness fell under the sway of Morgagni's concept that disease could be localized and began making detailed studies of the brain. Sir Charles Bell (1774–1842) even localized the brain area responsible for the respiratory reflex. John Haslam (1764–1844), who served as superintendent of the Bethlehem Mental Asylum from 1795 to 1816, in a fervent search for the locus of mental derangement examined the brains of the deceased insane; his autopsy descriptions are so vivid that it is possible to identify one of his post-mortem findings as probably the first record of syphilis of the brain.[5] Neuropathology failed to reveal the site of mental illness, but the search continued. Approaching the closing years of the century, physicians were still turning from a revised but sterile Hippocratic physiology to the inspiring concepts of cerebral localization. Fortunately, this time the arguments of the humanitarians were affecting the men in charge of houses for the insane. It was only after the madhouse became a hospital—the greatest single step in the history of psychiatric treatment—that the psychotic could be studied and treated effectively.

One additional system of classification was advanced in the late eighteenth century by Philippe Pinel, theoretician, teacher, nosographer, and reformer. Pinel was born in St.-André in 1745, the son of a physician. He was interested first in classical philosophy, then was influenced by the writings of Locke and Condillac; he later turned to the sciences, mathematics, and physiology. He studied medicine in Toulouse, did postgraduate work at Montpellier, then lived and practiced in Paris until his death in 1826. He served as physician-in-chief at Bicêtre and at the Salpêtrière. He saw the Revolution come and go and knew many of the leading thinkers and politicians of this turbulent era. Severe and self-composed, gentle and sensitive, yet emotionally aloof, his scholarly inclination that became manifest in his early student days never left him.

Pinel's observations on his hospital patients were the basis for a practical and surprisingly simple classification of mental illness that avoided the complications and redundancies of De Sauvages's and Cullen's systems. Pinel separated psychotic illnesses into melancholias, manias without delirium, manias with delirium, and dementia—that is, intellectual deterioration and idiocy. His descriptions of mental disturbances, which of necessity had to be based on outward manifestations, are superior to those of any of his predecessors. He described hallucinations, although he did not use this term, the flight of ideas of manic patients, unpredictable mood swings, and the withdrawal of interest from the environment so characteristic of certain forms of psychosis. His descriptions of symptoms, moreover, were systematic; he distinguished between disturbances of attention, memory, and judgment, and he recognized the significance of affects. In these areas he was strongly influenced by the new science of psychology developed by Locke and his followers.

Pinel believed that the basis of mental derangement might be a lesion in the central nervous system, since he maintained traditional notions about the physical cause of mental disease. Furthermore, he believed mental illness was a natural phenomenon to be studied according to the principles which prevailed in the natural sciences—observation first, then a systematic presentation of data. Pinel was convinced that mental illness was not something superimposed upon the sufferer, but a result of heredity and life experiences.

Pinel's outspokenly psychological orientation is clearly revealed in the preface of his *Traité Médicophilosophique,* where he warns the student of psychiatry not to confuse the science of facts with metaphysical speculations and rejects meaningless physiological fictions, such as the presence of injurious materials in the heart and brain, intemperateness of the brain, cerebral hyperemia (engorgement of blood), or hardening of the nerves. He had no use for therapeutic procedures based on the indiscriminate administration of drugs or on the traditional medical procedures of purging and bloodletting. He insisted that physicians must live among the insane to be able to study their habits and personalities and follow the course of their diseases day and night, and he believed that only physicians who have some knowledge of human motivation—what he called "the history of human understanding"—are suited to work with the mentally sick. Pinel considered that, in addition to heredity, a patient's faulty education could cause mental aberration, as might also insupportable passions like fear, anger, sadness, hate, joy, and elation; he thus leaned toward ascribing mental disturbance to emotional experience.

Pinel had praise only for those psychiatrists of the past who pursued the psychological approach. In particular he commends Celsus, Aretaeus, and Caelius Aurelianus for recognizing the significance of the physician's attitude toward the mental patient and for their ability to gain the trust of their patients, toward whom they assumed the proper balance between firmness and kindness. He recognized how these hopeful beginnings of psychological medicine were retarded by Galen's dogmatic stands on anatomy and a fictitious chemistry of the "humors."

In addition to being influenced by the prevailing spirit of rational inquiry, Pinel also subscribed to another movement characteristic of the Enlightenment—a zeal for social reform and moral uplift. There was the growing belief that man could shape his destiny by social action based on the scientific knowledge of social phenomena. Pinel referred to his work in the mental asylum as "moral treatment"; his humane approach to the mentally deranged and his principles of hospital management are still valid. Many of the methods of treatment in Pinel's day were identical with those used in ancient Greece—administration of purgatives, bloodletting, and drugs such as hellebore—all methods based on crude physiological theories. His primary contribution was to change society's attitude toward the insane so that these patients could come to be considered as sick human beings deserving and requiring medical treatment. Pinel asserted that it was impossible to determine whether mental symptoms resulted from mental disease or from the effects of the chains.

Pinel's ideas were part of the times, for other men too were interesting themselves in the welfare of hitherto abused and deprived groups of people. Rousseau had warned that "man is born free, yet everywhere is in chains," and his words were taken seriously in psychiatry, as elsewhere, by men of imagination and courage. Rationalism, observation through experimentation, and classification—the three basic trends in the eighteenth century—were joined by a fourth, the *movement toward reform,* which eventually would most profoundly impress the medical world at the turn of the century. John Howard (1726–1790), the sheriff of Bedfordshire, agitated for better conditions for the prisoners in English jails; Sir John Pringle, who was an Edinburgh physician, was helping to achieve fairer treatment for prisoners of war through the work of a neutral group (the forerunner of the Red Cross); the Society for Bettering the Conditions of the Poor was established in England to provide food, shelter, and medical treatment for the desolate. By the end of the eighteenth century Johann Peter Frank (1745–1821) proposed in his "Complete System of Medical Policy" a review of the existing public-health hazards, while Christoph Wilhelm Hufeland (1762–1836), another public-health crusader, considered even mental health to be a community problem.

A spirit of optimism began to prevail. Johann Heinrich Pestalozzi (1746–1827), the Swiss educational reformer, emphasized that the miserable plight of the insane had to be drastically changed. It was three hundred years since the insane were caught up in the misogynic movement, and now they were to benefit from the opposite trend, one that would not tolerate irresponsible maltreatment of human beings. The atrocious sanitary conditions generally existing in hospitals throughout Europe were constantly being criticized; and this same optimistic fervor for reform and individual rights underlay Pinel's work in alleviating the sad plight of the inhabitants of mental hospitals.

Although the mentally sick had not been tortured at the stake for a considerable period of time, their condition during the century of the Enlightenment was still agonizing. If they were not hospitalized, they wandered through the countryside, scorned, beaten, and ridiculed. In England those who were unfortunate enough to be interned at Bethlehem Hospital, which during the medieval period had treated psychotics with some degree of kindness, had reason during the eighteenth century to regret their commitment. Bethlehem—or Bedlam, as it was called—was a favorite Sunday excursion spot for Londoners, who came to stare at the madmen through the iron gates. Should they survive the filthy conditions, the abominable food, the isolation and darkness, and the brutality of their keepers, the patients of Bedlam were entitled to treatment—emetics, purgatives, bloodletting, and various so-called harmless tortures provided by special paraphernalia. Conditions in Paris at the Bicêtre, which became a part of the General Hospital in 1660, which housed "madmen," and at the Salpêtrière, where "madwomen" were chained, were certainly no better. St. Luke's Hospital in England and the Pennsylvania Hospital in Philadelphia, founded in 1751, the Hospital for the Insane at Moscow, founded in 1764, and the Narrenthurm in Vienna, founded in 1784, offered shelter and segregation and were havens compared to Bedlam. As far as the city administrations were concerned, whether in Paris, London, or New Orleans, the police code was the same: "If a dangerous madman has no relative he shall be placed in prison."[6] This was not always a disadvantage, however; the conditions of prison life were pretty much the same as those in the established hospitals, but at least in jail the patient did not have to suffer drastic insults to his body. Under these widespread circumstances it is not surprising that when Philippe Pinel took over the administration of the Bicêtre in 1793, he himself was considered mad by his contemporaries—for he released the patients from their chains, opened their windows, fed them nourishing food, and treated them with kindness. Two years later, when he was placed in charge of the Salpêtrière, Pinel reformed it too in the same way.

It is difficult to understand the incredible inhumanity with which mentally sick citizens were treated well into the era of the Enlightenment unless three major factors are taken into consideration: the almost complete ignorance of the nature of mental illness, the deeply felt dread of the insane, and finally, the belief then current that mental disease is incurable. The contemporary physiological phantasmagorias about the causes of mental illness could not be dismissed: no one observed black humors; no one measured bodily humidity or dryness; no one observed the movements of "animal spirits"; and there was no bridge to connect anatomical knowledge with either disturbed or normal functioning of the mind. Since mental illness could never be satisfactorily explained by any of these concepts, there was no defense against the dread of the unknown, which is one of the most basic reactions of the human mind. Yet the mentally sick individual is not so different from the normal person as one would like to believe. Mental illness is made up of the same stuff as the rest of our mind—of fears and passions, desires, and hates—of the same stuff as our dreams are made. Dreams are the temporary insanity of everyday life, when the control of reason slumbers and our fantasy runs wild. The fear of mentally ill persons has another aspect: it is fear of those elementary emotional forces that everybody harbors in his unconscious mind; in other words, it is the fear of ourselves. This is why men instinctively emphasize whatever small distance divides them from the mentally ill and why they consider an insane person so alien, finding it impossible to empathize with him.

The innumerable contemporary descriptions of the miserable lot of the insane all testify to this fear. Their cruel segregation and restraint was described by Johann Christian Reil (1759–1813), one of the most advanced psychiatrists of his era: "We incarcerate these miserable creatures as if they were criminals in abandoned jails, near to the lairs of owls in bar en canyons beyond the city gates, or in damp dungeons of prisons, where never a pitying look of a humanitarian penetrates; and we let them, in chains, rot in their own excrement. Their fetters have eaten off the flesh of their bones, and their emaciated pale faces look expectantly toward the graves which will end their misery and cover up our shamefulness."[7] Excited patients were locked naked into narrow closets and fed through holes from copperware attached to chains. Beatings were common and defended by shallow rationalizations. Strait jackets and chains attached to walls or beds were used to restrain patients, since the theory was that the more painful the restraint, the better the results, particularly with obstinate psychotics. The attendants were mostly sadistic individuals of low intelligence who could not find any other employment. "The roar of excited patients and the rattle of chains is heard day and night," says Reil, "and takes away from the newcomers the little sanity left to them."[8] The unsanitary conditions, lack of nourishment, wounds inflicted by the chains, and application of drastic skin irritants to increase the torment killed a large number of these patients. The belief in the incurability of mental disease was merely one more reason for the utmost neglect of the welfare of the mentally sick. Prinz Laroche Foucault-Lianfourt stated in a report to the French Assembly: "The insane are considered incurable; they receive no treatment. Those who are considered dangerous are put in fetters as animals."[9]

In contrast to these horrifying methods of dealing with the insane, there was a more humane tradition, particularly in Spain, where the Moors had preserved the antique Roman ideas of kindly treatment. The psychiatric historian Schmitz, states: "Not Pinel, but the physicians in Valencia in 1409 were the first to remove the chains and institute moral treatment. Free exercises, games, occupation, entertainment, diet, and hygiene were used."*[10] At the Saragossa asylum, also, agricultural work was used to channel the patients' energies into constructive activity. The Valencia asylum, built at the beginning of the fifteenth century, was known throughout Europe for its advanced administration and clinical facilities. The original Valencia asylum burned down in 1545 but was replaced by a new hospital which included a special department for children. Other Spanish hospitals were built in Seville, Valladolid, Palma Mallorca, Toledo (the Hospital de Innocentes), and Granada.

Apart from their advanced mental hospitals, Spanish physicians had, over the centuries, made significant contributions to psychiatric knowledge. One of the most outstanding Spanish doctors was Arnold of Villanova (1240–1313), a professor at the University of Montpellier. He described

* Peter Bassoe (1874–1945), the Chicago neurologist, called attention to this neglected chapter of psychiatric history and confirmed the historian Ullensperger's statement that "the cradle of psychiatry was in Spain, where the first convenient and appropriate buildings were constructed for the hospitalization of the insane."

hallucinations and epilepsy and had a profound understanding of the emotional life of the mentally sick. Cristobal de Vega (c. 1510) described mania, melancholia, and erotomania, which he approached by "moral" treatment. Andres Piquer (1711–1772) discussed manic-depressive psychosis, although he may have derived this conception from a first-century Roman physician, Aretaeus of Cappadocia. The psychological perspicacity of the Spanish philosopher Vives and that of Cervantes, the novelist, has been discussed previously.

The isolation of Spain from the rest of Europe after the seventeenth century may account for the fact that the early burgeoning of psychiatry on the Iberian peninsula never developed further. Whatever the reason, the European liberation of the insane had to wait until the end of the eighteenth century, with the work of Pinel in France and the reforms of Grand Duke Pietro Leopoldo of Tuscany (1747–1792) in Italy.

Leopoldo, an enlightened absolute monarch, shared the eighteenth-century zeal for reform and was responsible for extensive social changes in his kingdom: he provided for land development, cared for delinquents, and abolished the death penalty. The first liberal "law of the insane" came into being during his reign, in 1774, and provided for medical treatment of psychotics. Leopold built the Hospital of Bonifacio in 1788 (five years before Pinel had the directorship of Bicêtre), and the following year he fortunately chose an idealistic physician, Vincenzo Chiarugi, to implement hospital reform. By the time Pinel had been appointed chief at the Bicêtre, Chiarugi had already published his most important work, *On Insanity,* in three books. Chiarugi followed the localization concepts of Morgagni and believed that psychoses are due to physical deterioration of the brain. His ideas of the psychological role of emotions in mental disease were a confused mélange derived from Descartes, Aristotle, Plato, and St. Thomas. However, Chiarugi formulated a practical classification of mental diseases almost identical with Pinel's, and his plan for treatment of the patient was similar in almost every detail. Chiarugi opposed unreasonable physical restraint and harsh measures.* "It is a supreme moral duty and medical obligation to respect the insane individual as a person. It is especially necessary for the person who treats the mental patient to gain his confidence and trust. It is best, therefore, to be tactful and understanding and try to lead the patient to the truth and to instill reason into him little by little in a kind way. . . . The attitude of doctors and nurses must be authoritative and impressive, but at the same

* George Mora, who deserves the major credit for investigating the early history of the nonrestraint movement in Italy, attempted to elucidate the reasons why Chiarugi is so little known or appreciated in contrast to Pinel. Mora points out that Chiarugi's style was difficult to understand and that many of his books were lost. In addition, Chiarugi did not have a long line of followers and successors as did Pinel.[11] Regardless of whether we consider Pinel the Chiarugi of France, or Chiarugi the Pinel of Italy, their works were similar and the time was ripe for both.

time pleasant and adapted to the impaired mind of the patient. . . . Generally it is better to follow the patient's inclinations and give him as many comforts as is advisable from a medical and practical standpoint."[12]

Another eighteenth-century humanely operated mental hospital, the Real Casa de Matti, was situated at Palermo, Sicily. A layman, Barone Pietro Pisani (1760–1837) became its administrator in 1824. He was a brilliant scholar in music, literature, and jurisprudence and had traveled widely. His motivation in becoming a humane hospital superintendent was that for many years after his son's death he had been severely depressed, and consequently, as often happens with those who have known tragedy, he empathized wholeheartedly with the plight of others suffering similar experiences.* Pisani's regulations were published in 1827 and were based on his understanding that "in spite of their mental disorders, patients respond to a frank and sincere approach and are able to experience feelings of confidence, benevolence, friendship, and pride."[13] Pisani arranged for autopsies to be performed on all the patients who died while they were hospitalized; but basically he believed that their home situations had precipitated their illnesses. Reportedly, forty percent of the patients responded to Pisani's approach by completely recovering. This was achieved without the use of narcotizing drugs, but by creating an atmosphere of understanding and affection. Without the benefit of medical training, but having learned what it was to be mentally ill, Barone Pietro Pisani stands as one of the great innovators of "milieu" treatment and of the therapeutic community, which characterizes the better mental hospitals of the modern era.

Another hospital in southern Italy, near Naples, was the Aversa, which in the thirteenth century had been a leprosarium and in 1420 was converted into a convent of St. Mary Magdalene. By 1813 the hospital had become an asylum for the mentally ill, and during the next years, under the direction of Giovanni Linguiti (1773–1825), a priest, it acquired a reputation throughout Europe as a center of enlightened moral treatment. The hospital of Magdalene reached its greatest heights under Biagio Miraglia, who completely abolished restraints of any kind and advocated such advances as ventilating systems for the hospital. Miraglia contributed to forensic psychiatry and founded the first Italian journal of psychiatry; he was also the foremost Italian phrenologist, which merely serves as a re-

* Later in the nineteenth century Dorothea Lynde Dix (1802–1887), a Boston schoolmarm, was, like Pisani, another person who was motivated by tragedies in her own life to devote herself to the welfare of others. In her thirties, after recovering from a severe bout of consumption, she dedicated herself to reforming the conditions in prisons, poorhouses, and insane asylums. With pertinacity and an unwavering devotion to her causes, she was responsible for the building or remodeling of thirty-two hospitals throughout the world, twenty of which were in the United States. The thirteen mental-hospital superintendents who formed what is now the American Psychiatric Association were directly influenced by her ideas and work.

minder that occult practices and humanitarianism are not mutually exclusive.

Some physicians east of the Rhine also were beginning to change their concepts of treatment. Anton Müller of Würzburg (1755–1827) and Johann Christian Reil were among the first of the German doctors who devoted themselves to psychiatry as a specialty and advocated a humane approach in the therapy of patients. Johann Grottfried Langermann (1768–1832), as the superintendent of an asylum near Bayreuth, Bavaria, had greater opportunity than either Reil or Müller to implement his ideas. Langermann did not believe in maintaining a cold or indifferent attitude toward his patients, nor could he agree that mental illnesses arose from damage to the nervous system. Indeed, Langermann, along with Reil, believed that even some diseases with organic findings could be attributed to psychological factors and emphasized the importance of a psychological approach to therapy. He also revived Stahl's distinction between organic and functional disturbances of the mind. Largely due to Langermann's efforts, other humanitarian hospitals were established at Seidburg and Leubus, in Prussia.

The movement toward humane treatment was based in France on the philosophy of liberation and in Germany on the concept of rationality; in England the force leading to reform was a religious one.

William Battie's *Treatise on Madness,* published in 1758, was the first extensive treatise on mental diseases in England. Battie, who was superintendent of St. Luke's Hospital, probably initiated the teaching of clinical psychiatry in England. St. Luke's had supposedly been founded because conditions at Bethlehem were so unwholesome, but the superintendents of both institutions were constantly debating in public over which hospital was managed more efficiently. The charges and countercharges continually being hurled between John Monro, who ran Bethlehem, and Battie obscured an important contribution that Battie made. He differentiated two types of insanity: diseases that are due to an "internal disorder" (today we would call them "endogenous" mental illnesses) and those that are due to extrinsic, or "exogenous," factors. Battie understood that the exogenous illnesses resulted from brain damage but did not recognize that functional mental illness results from interpersonal conflicts.

Battie, Thomas Arnold, William Perfect, and Andrew Harper published some articles in the 1780's on mental diseases, but the medical profession, as well as the public, were at a loss as to how to explain mental illness. In 1788, when King George III suffered a depressive psychosis, laymen and doctors alike argued about whether his Highness should have his skull blistered, his intestines purged, be bled, be made to vomit, or be walked around the gardens of the royal castle while he listened to soothing music. The more basic question of whether or not the mentally ill could or should be trusted without being restrained was answered by a group of religious moralists, the Quakers. In 1792 William Tuke (1732–1822), a Quaker tea merchant, founded the York Retreat. Tuke admired Pinel greatly and followed his ideas, providing an atmosphere for his patients pervaded by benevolence, comfort, and sympathy. William Tuke's son Henry Tuke (1755–1814) and his grandson Samuel Tuke (1784–1857) continued at York in the humanitarian spirit of their predecessor.

By the late 1830's, following the Tukes' lead, Robert Gardiner Hill (1811–1878) had abolished restraint at the Lincoln asylum, as had John Conolly (1794–1866) at the Hanwell asylum. Conolly was instrumental in setting up a program of instruction in clinical psychiatry at Hanwell, where he taught that restraining a patient was even worse than neglecting him. Later Conolly's ideas spread across the Continent to Russia, where they influenced Serge Korsakov (1854–1900), the great neuropsychiatrist, who spoke before his medical colleagues (1887) in Moscow "On the Non-Restraint Treatment of Patients."*14

The great psychiatric reformers Pinel, Chiarugi, Langermann, and the Tukes did not enrich our medical knowledge by singular new insights, like a Harvey or a Freud; although they were not geniuses, they were men of great devotion and courage and were true representatives of this new era that began to apply reason and observation not only to the understanding of the surrounding universe but also to man's behavior, to his social and moral conduct.

The American physicians of the eighteenth century also contributed significantly to the organization and administration of mental-hospital-reform programs. The Pennsylvania Hospital had, after 1752, admitted mentally disturbed patients; in 1775 a hospital was built at Williamsburg, Virginia, exclusively for mental patients. By the end of the eighteenth century, like their European colleagues, American psychiatrists were moving toward Morgagni's concept of brain localization and were also becoming dissatisfied with the conditions of their hospitals.

In 1812 the "first American psychiatrist," Benjamin Rush (1745–1813), in *Diseases of the Mind,* the first textbook on mental diseases written by an American, said, "In reviewing the slender and inadequate means that have been employed for ameliorating the condition of mad people, we are led further to lament the slower progress of humanity in its efforts to relieve them than any other class of the afflicted children of men. For many centuries they have been treated like criminals, or shunned like beasts of prey: or, if visited, it has been only for the purposes of inhumane curiosity and amusement. . . . Happily, these times of cruelty to this class

* Nonrestraint is still not entirely accepted. The story goes that recently an American psychiatrist was incredulous at the lack of bars on the windows and the freedom of movement of the patients in a London mental hospital. "Aren't you afraid these psychotics will go into a rage and injure themselves or other patients?" he asked. To which his decorous English colleague answered, "My dear sir, it's true these chaps may be psychotic, but remember—above all—they are Englishmen!"

of our fellow creatures and insensibility to their sufferings are now passing away. In Great Britain a humane revolution dictated by modern improvements in the science of mind, as well as of medicine, has taken place. A similar change has taken place in the Pennsylvania Hospital, under the direction of its present managers. The clanking of chains and the noise of the whip are no longer heard in their cells. [The insane] now taste the blessings of air and light, and motion, in pleasant and shaded walks in summer and in spacious entries warmed by stoves in winter, in both of which the sexes are separated, and alike protected from the eye of the visitors to the hospital. In consequence of these advantages, they have recovered the human figure, and with it their long-forgotten relationship to their friends and the public. Much, however, remains to be done for their comfort and relief."[15]

By the time he was fifteen Rush had graduated from the College of New Jersey (now Princeton), after which he spent five and a half years serving a medical apprenticeship. Then he studied at the University of Edinburgh under Cullen, to whom he was introduced by Benjamin Franklin. At twenty-three he was granted his medical diploma from Edinburgh and just a year later was made the first professor of chemistry in the first American school of medicine at Philadelphia. By 1789 he became professor of medicine at this university. At thirty-one he was one of the signers of the Declaration of Independence and a year later was one of the chief medical surgeons in the Continental Army. After he returned to Philadelphia at the close of the Revolutionary War he joined the staff of the Pennsylvania Hospital, where he served until his demise.

Rush had been born in the town of Byberry near Philadelphia, the fourth of seven children; when he was only six his father died, and his uncle, a Presbyterian minister named Samuel Finley (who later became president of the College of New Jersey), trained Benjamin in virtue, work, and responsibility. Dr. Finley inculcated his discipline not through the use of the rod but through the threat of its use. Many years later Benjamin Rush was to utilize the same principle, when necessary, to coerce his patients into changing their behavior patterns. Finley also believed that what benefited mankind was right, anything less was wrong. One could not determine right from wrong by deferring to others; one must decide this for oneself and then must take definite and positive action. Rush grew up to be a crusader against slavery, alcohol, and the death penalty. He was an advocate of public schools, free dispensaries for the indigent, higher educational facilities for women, and hospitals for alcoholics.*

Rush's medical beliefs were derived from his revered teacher, William Cullen, who believed that insanity is the result of disturbances within the

---

* In the bibliographical section of Nathan Goodman's *Biography of Benjamin Rush* it is astonishing to discover the lists of his published writings on medical, sociological, political, and theological subjects.

individual and not of mysterious outside forces that had entered the body. Cullen's concept of the physiological importance of irritability of the nervous and vascular systems was taken over by Rush. "The cause of madness is seated primarily in the blood vessels of the brain and . . . depends upon the same kind of morbid and irregular actions that constitute other circulatory diseases. There is nothing specific in these actions. They are a part of the unity of disease, particularly of fever; of which madness is a chronic form affecting that part of the brain which is the seat of the mind."[16] Rush believed that mental illnes could be caused by somatic conditions—for example, dropsy, gout, pregnancy, or tuberculosis—or by inordinate sexual activity, "gratification" as well as masturbation. Rush proposed that certain "mental states" acted on the body more "indirectly" and would eventually produce cerebral-vessel pathology; among these conditions he listed fear, anger, absence from one's "native" country, and loss of property or liberty. Rush believed that to relieve the body of vascular congestion by bloodletting, by far the most common therapeutic measure of the day, would eliminate a basic cause of mental illness.

Although Rush observed, "It will be necessary for a physician to listen with attention to [the patient's] tedious and uninteresting details of his symptoms . . ."[17] and although he realized that the patient experienced some relief from talking to the doctor, the passive role of sympathetic listener did not appeal to Rush's zealous nature. He frequently lectured to students and patients on mental illness and on "psychology," yet by and large his psychological measures were tricks reminiscent of ancient Arabian measures to compel the patient to change his thoughts or his actions. For example, if Rush had a patient who believed there was a small animal in his body and could not be convinced otherwise by reason, then Rush thought he should be given a medicine which, the patient was told, "destroys the animal"; alternatively, a small animal could be put in the patient's stool: "the deception," said Rush, "would be a justifiable one if it served to cure him of his disease."[18] A patient who believed that he could not empty his bladder should be told, Rush said, that the world was on fire and that "nothing but his water would extinguish it."[19] If these maneuvers did not work, Rush advocated terrifying the patient by dropping him into ice-cold water or by other equally drastic means. Rush used both tranquilizing and gyrating chairs on his disturbed patients. He believed it was necessary to restrain excited patients and put them in the tranquilizing chair, which he felt was more humane than a strait jacket. The tranquilizing chair consisted of leather straps around the patient's arms and legs that restricted action and thereby "calmed" the patient. The rotating, or gyrating, chair was utilized in order to relieve the patient's congested brain.

Despite these seemingly merciless devices, Rush's concern for his fellow beings was sincere. He believed in hygiene and occupational therapy for mental patients. Perhaps Rush himself had a premonition that his methods would some day fall into disrepute but wanted to leave at least the humanitarian spirit of his work when he wrote on the last page of his book: "Here the reader and author must take leave of each other. Before I retire from sight I shall only add, if I have not advanced—agreeably to my wishes—the interest of medicine by this work, I hope my labors in *the cause of humanity* will not be alike unsuccessful; and that the sufferings of our fellow creatures, from the causes that have been mentioned, may find sympathy in the bosoms, and relief from the kindness from every person who shall think it worthwhile to read this history of them."[20] Perhaps what a man writes for posterity in the last year of his life might be considered contrived, but the unqualified sincerity of what a man says to his son in the privacy of his bedchamber as he is dying cannot be questioned. Rush gave his son one last piece of advice that sums up his virtues and his philosophy: "Be indulgent to the poor."[21]

Errors, Magic, and Mesmerism

The penchant and indeed the need for classification of scientific data that was so prevalent in the eighteenth century did not always bring about scientific understanding. The era of the Enlightenment was also an era of quacks.

To begin with, let us consider Friedrich Hoffmann, who was mentioned before in connection with his controversies with Stahl. Stahl believed in an ephemeral vital substance, whereas Hoffmann considered that diseases were caused by an unspecified material substance which in excess produced spasms or tonicity and when deficient produced atony and exhaustion. This oversimplified doctrine led to two modes of therapy, energizing people and calming them down. Hoffmann prescribed "drops" for these purposes, reflecting the contemporary craze of panaceas for tenseness or nervous exhaustion. This trend has persisted to our present day, when tonics, liver pills, vitamins, and the like are used indiscriminately. A physician, John Brown (1735–1788), friend and colleague of William Cullen, further elaborated Hoffmann's doctrine of excesses and deficiencies. According to Brown's theories, the human being is bombarded with stimuli that produce an overexcited, "sthenic" state; lack of stimulation leads to nervous weakness, or "asthenia." Some patients suffering from asthenia were given such huge doses of stimulating drugs that what little life they had remaining was soon drained from them. As the medical historian Guthrie reports, Brown's system "killed more persons than the French Revolution and the Napoleonic Wars taken together."[22] In our own times stimulants (or vacations) are all too often prescribed for those patients who "feel exhausted"—a symptomatic disguise for neurotic conflict that could be treated with more permanent results by competent psychotherapy. When these patients understand their motivations they are in many cases on the road to relief from their inner tensions.

The ideas of Hoffmann and Brown were founded on the crude doctrine *"contraria contrariis,"* that a drug will be effective if its action is contrary to the symptom of the patient. This concept, also called "allopathy," later came to such disrepute that an opposite system developed under the leadership of a German physician, Samuel Hahnemann (1755–1843). Instead of giving huge doses of drugs whose actions were contrary to symptoms, Hahnemann gave very small doses of drugs whose actions were similar to the symptoms. His slogan was *"similia similibus curantur"*— similars cure similars. The best that can be said about Hahnemann's homeopathy is that if it did not cure, at least it did not kill. Homeopathy became enough of a fad so that societies were formed and journals founded to spread this doctrine.

The allopaths and homeopaths were not as popular as were followers of two other systems that appealed to the public because they looked "scientific"—phrenology, founded by Franz Joseph Gall (1758–1828), and animal magnetism by Franz Mesmer (1734–1815), both of whom were trained at the University of Vienna School of Medicine, following which they emigrated to Paris, where they were received with both wide acclaim and repudiation. Although both smacked of quackery, Gall's system led to significant developments in neurology, while Mesmer's system led to important developments in hypnotherapy, the historical godfather of psychoanalysis.

Franz Gall, a German physician from Tiefenbronn, was a dedicated medical scholar who devoted his life to the study of the brain. He described the development of the brain in the fetus, traced the development of the human brain from its early origins in the nerve ganglia of insects, and carefully dissected the white matter of the brain, tracing important fibers from the spinal cord to the cerebrum.[23] Gall, who was greatly influenced by the teachings of Morgagni, believed not only that functions of the brain could be localized in that organ but that character traits could also be attributed to certain sites within the brain. He decided that thirty-seven traits exist—for instance, cautiousness, firmness, benevolence, combativeness—and that these were localized in thirty-seven "organs" within the brain. When one day Gall noticed that the most brilliant medical students in his class were those with bulging eyes, he deduced that the organ of memory exists in the brain behind the eyes.[24] Gall then went on to make a second, more serious error: he assumed that the skull overlying the brain would have prominences over the "organs" that were overdeveloped. The obvious conclusion was that palpating the bulges and dips in the cranium could be a method of character reading. Gall's crudely materialistic theories were branded as irreligious by the Austrian government, and he was forced to leave Vienna in 1802. He lectured on his ideas for five years throughout Europe, during which time Johann Casper Spurzheim (1776–1832) became his disciple. Soon Gall became well established and developed an elite practice in Paris. Spurzheim, however, began to remodel and popularize Gall's concepts and contributed the notion that an individual's mental propensities can be changed by proper moral influences, thus diluting Gall's purely fatalistic and materialistic doctrine of cerebral localization with the tincture of hope. Spurzheim left Gall in Paris and traveled to proselytize for his new theory, which he called "phrenology." His most famous followers were a Scots barrister, George Combe, and his brother Andrew Combe, a physician. These men felt it was their duty to warn people about the dangers involved when the "moral and intellectual organs" were not strengthened by proper spiritual guidance and personal hygiene. "When the cerebellum [cerebrum] is really large," George Combe wrote, "and the temperament active, the individual becomes distinguished from his fellows by the predominance of his amorous propensities. In all his vacant moments, his mind dwells on objects related to this faculty, and the gratification of it is the most important object of his thoughts. If his moral and intellectual organs be weak, he will without scruple invade the sanctity of unsuspecting innocents and connubial bliss, and become a deceiver, destroyer and sensual fiend of the most hideous description."[25] In 1832 Spurzheim came to lecture in the United States; he died after a few months (in Boston) and was given a hero's burial. *The American Journal of the Medical Sciences* lamented, "The prophet is gone, but his mantle is upon us," to which *The London Medical Gazette,* a little less impressed with Spurzheim, retorted, "We know not on whom, if on any, his mantle will descend, but we hope nobody will be foolish enough to bring it across the Atlantic."[26] When George Combe came to America after Spurzheim died, he too won the acclaim of important citizens and medical men. Psychiatrists were enthusiastic about phrenology, and outstanding citizens like Horace Mann (who named his son after George Combe), Walt Whitman, Edgar Allan Poe, and James Garfield praised it. Such success attracted charlatans, and soon phrenologists were replacing tea-leaves readers and palmists at circus sideshows, and fortunes were being told and fortunes were being made through phrenological manipulation. The medical world and enlightened citizenry began to mock the credulity about phrenology and went along with John Quincy Adams, who had said that "he could not see how two phrenologists could look each other in the face without bursting into laughter."[27]

Phrenology itself eventually fell into disrepute, but nonetheless Gall's concepts of cerebral localization had, especially in Germany, given a tremendous impetus to the early-nineteenth-century schools of neurology. Animal magnetism and phrenology reached the shores of America in a dead heat, but the starting lines were centuries apart. The roots of animal magnetism lay in primitive beliefs. The attraction between iron and magnets was known to primitive societies, and magnets had always appealed to the magical mind. Magnetized bracelets and necklaces were worn as amulets and talismans. Paracelsus taught that not only magnets but also the heavenly bodies were able to attract and affect the human body by emitting a celestial fluid. Jan Baptista van Helmont (1577–1644), a famous Flemish chemist, believed that the power to influence distant objects resided not only in nature but also in man and that man thus was able to affect his fellows and cure them. William Maxwell (1581–1641) wrote about a "universal fluid" that was responsible for the influence of man over matter and man over man. Franz Mesmer, the originator of animal magnetism, formulated these concepts into basic propositions. Proposition I states, "There exists a mutual influence between the Heavenly Bodies, the Earth and Animate Bodies." Proposition II states, "A universally distributed and continuous fluid . . . is capable of receiving, propagating, and communicating all the impressions of movement, [and] is the means of this influence." A mysterious body fluid, mentioned in Proposition IX, "has properties similar to those of the magnet; different and opposite poles may likewise be distinguished which can be changed, communicated, destroyed, and strengthened. . . . This property of the animal body, which brings it under the influence of the heavenly bodies and the reciprocal action of those surrounding it, has by its analogy with the magnet induced me to term it Animal Magnetism." He believed that this mysterious fluid was "intensified and reflected by mirrors just like light," and that this magnetic property could be "stored up, concentrated and transported." In Proposition XXII Mesmer says, "The magnet and artificial electricity . . . have, as regards illnesses, properties which they share with several other agents provided by Nature," and by utilizing this principle one could cure "nervous disorders directly and other disorders indirectly." Mesmer's final propositions stated that "With this knowledge the physician will determine reliably the origin, nature, and progress of illness, even the most complicated." Furthermore, "This doctrine will enable the physician to determine the state of each individual's health and safeguard him from the maladies to which he might otherwise be subject. The art of healing will thus reach its final stage of perfection."[28]

The physician who made these assertions was born in the small Austrian village of Iznang. His father was chief of the forestry service under the Archbishop of Konstanz. Little is known about Mesmer's boyhood. He studied music, Latin, and divinity at a monastery, and at fifteen he went from the monastery to a Jesuit university in Bavaria. Before he entered the University of Vienna in 1759 he had already held the degree of Doctor of Philosophy. He began to study law but soon decided on a medical curriculum. In 1766 he graduated from the University of Vienna Medical School; his dissertation, "Influence of the Planets," discussed the influence of the celestial bodies upon the physiology of man.

Two years later Mesmer married a rich widow ten years his senior, which afforded him entrance into the elite Viennese society. It was not an invisible fluid that attracted Viennese ladies and gentlemen to Mesmer. It was well known that he had been a student of Van Swietan and De Haen, the famous disciples of Boerhaave, and that he could speak of philosophy, metaphysics, and science. A tall, handsome man with "a sensuous, well-molded face with high forehead, full lips and a strong chin . . . [who] talked and walked with self-confidence and radiated—perhaps the appropriate word would be—magnetism."[29]

Mesmer's burning ambition was to experiment with his theories and have them accepted by the scientific world. He enjoyed polemical free-for-alls but would never tolerate a searching analysis of his own ideas. If the vagaries within his theories were contested, Mesmer's collar would scorch and he would lose his poise and become boisterously vindictive. The first powerful ammunition for his theories came from a Jesuit priest who was court astrologer to Maria Theresa, Father Hell, who told Mesmer of the cures he had accomplished through the use of a magnet. Mesmer was convinced that the magnet was a way of "concentrating" the magic fluid, and so he used one to relieve a hysterical woman of her attacks. Father Hell used steel magnets and even gave one to Mesmer to use on his patient, but Mesmer would never acknowledge that Father Hell understood anything about the theory of animal magnetism and soon had a bitter quarrel with him. Mesmer then decided that it was not necessary actually to place magnets on the patient's body, because he believed that any inanimate object was magnetized simply by coming in contact with his own person, or as he put it, "Steel is not the only object which can absorb and emanate the magnetic force. On the contrary, paper, bread, wool, silk, leather, stone, glass, water, various metals, wood, dogs, human beings, everything that I touched became so magnetic that these objects exerted as great an influence on the sick as does a magnet itself. I filled bottles with magnetic materials just as one does with electricity."[30]

Eventually Mesmer did not have to use any object at all: a gesture with his hands was enough to make the patients feel the transmission of his magnetic force. An attractive blind pianist, Fräulein Paradies, a protégée of Maria Theresa, came to Mesmer to regain her sight, and the Viennese physicians arose in arms. They suspected that the young patient felt a strong sexual attraction toward the glamorous Mesmer. The medical world had once before been shocked by the antics of a man who touched his patients and promised cure. There would be no Irish stroker, no Valentine Greatrakes in Vienna. In 1778, by arousing the citizenry, the physicians forced Franz Mesmer to leave Vienna.* If Mesmer had been willing to give up his desire to be recognized by the medical fraternity he could have

---

* More than a hundred years later Viennese citizens were again outraged by what they considered the sexually uncouth theories of Sigmund Freud.

remained in Vienna; as it was, he accepted an offer from Louis XIV of France to come to Paris and experiment with animal magnetism.

Mesmer had an astonishing success in Paris—not in academic circles, but with hysterical ladies. For five years Mesmer treated all comers at his clinic. If they were poor there was no charge; if they were wealthy they paid an enormous fee. But even Madame Du Barry, who complained bitterly about the exorbitant fee, could not resist the great healer. Mesmer's treatment, which often was conducted on groups of patients at once, was an impressive ceremonial. The patients entered a thickly carpeted, dimly lit room that was mirrored so as to reflect every shadow; soft melodies were heard, and there was a fragrance of orange blossoms. The patients held hands in a circle around the baquet, a tub filled with "magnetized" water. Into this prepared scene would step the healer, clothed in a lilac cloak and waving a yellow wand. In the past, physicians had carried gold canes and worn red cloaks to impress their patients. Why not a purple robe and a yellow wand? Mesmer did not believe there was anything supernatural about what he was doing and explained his rituals in naturalistic terms. What he wanted to accomplish was a "crisis"—the moment when one patient would suddenly scream, break into a cold sweat, and then convulse. Mesmer knew that some of his patients, having witnessed this dramatic scene, would respond with similar symptoms. He did not realize, of course, that this was but mass suggestion. But he knew what revivalists and faith healers throughout the ages had known, namely, that soon after the violent episode tension immediately subsided. He was not aware of the fact that sexual tensions had been aroused in this atmosphere and that the "crisis" was the moment of release from these tensions.

The animal-magnetism craze—"Mesmeromania," as Stefan Zweig (1881–1942) later called it—was not professionally gratifying to Mesmer. He succeeded in convincing only one doctor, Charles d' Eslon, the physician to Louis XVI's brother, of the merits of his procedure. D'Eslon worked tirelessly and faithfully to gain acceptance for Mesmer's theory by his professional colleagues, but whenever he praised the new theory at medical meetings he was bitterly attacked. Mesmer first became discouraged and then furious. Marie Antoinette herself begged Mesmer to stay in Paris and offered him a huge grant to continue his work, but Mesmer considered her offer humiliating, since he recognized that it involved not medical recognition but becoming the pet of Parisian society. He therefore left Paris in 1781. D'Eslon stayed on to continue an unsuccessful struggle with the medical authorities; they stubbornly refused to be convinced, but he did form a secret organization of laymen, the Society of Harmony, the avowed purpose of which was to promote animal magnetism.

Mesmer later returned to Paris to meet the most devastating defeat of his life, from which he never recovered. As a result of considerable pressure by D'Eslon and other members of the Society of Harmony, Louis XVI of

France had in 1784 appointed a commission to study animal magnetism. The commission's presiding officer was Benjamin Franklin, and its membership included a famous astronomer, Jean Bailly, an outstanding botanist, A. L. de Jussieu, the chemist Lavoisier, and Dr. Guillotin, whose idea it was that a merciful execution was the right of any condemned man, no matter what his social status.* The commission eventually found that there was no such thing as animal magnetism, but only "imagination"—that is, something that did not exist—and thus symbolically guillotined Mesmer's ambitions. Soon thereafter Mesmer's holdings were confiscated by the Jacobins, who disregarded that Mesmer treated members of the laboring class and remembered only that his clientele had included the top echelon of the aristocracy. It did not help Mesmer that in a minority report Jussieu had remarked that regardless of its unsound theory, animal magnetism did seem to cure. Nor did it help that Lorenz Oken, a philosopher, and Karl Wolfhart had visited Mesmer in his last years and pleaded with him to continue his writings. It was Wolfhart who renamed animal magnetism "mesmerism." By this time Mesmer had sunk into oblivion. However, two factions developed. One was devoted to the goal of gaining acceptance of mesmerism by the medical profession; the second was formed by charlatans who saw in it a means for economic gain.

One American, Elisha Perkins (1741–1799), a graduate of Yale Medical School and a practitioner in Connecticut, adapted Mesmer's ideas and devised the Perkins Tractors, which were metal rods consisting of various alloys that supposedly could cure not only nervous affliction but also all physical maladies. Even George Washington used Perkins Tractors. Elisha's son brought the tractors to London, where he established the Perkinean Institute; but since tractors made of wood or paper or anything else were just as efficacious as metal ones, the metal-tractor fad did not last long; they were never as appealing as an invention of James Graham, O.W.L. ("Oh, Wonderful Love"), anyway. Graham's idea was a temple of health, inside which his patients reclined on celestial beds, surrounded by glass and magnetic baths; he convinced Londoners that for only a hundred pounds he could guarantee them not only everlasting health but everlasting potency. If the celestial beds, scented dancing girls, or electrical sparks could not arouse the patient's erotic imagination, then the suggestions whispered by Graham's assistants usually did.

Probably the most notorious charlatan in history was Giuseppe Balsamo (1743–1795), who called himself Count Alessandro di Cagliostro. He earned his living by practicing medicine with magnets; he also indulged in extortion and swindling and was involved in the famous "Diamond Necklace Affair," when he sold a cardinal a glistening "diamond" made al-

* During the Reign of Terror Guillotin almost lost his head on his own invention. It is ironic that Bailly and Lavoisier, members of the commission, were to die by the instrument named after their colleague of the 1784 commission.

chemically. Balsamo used animal magnetism in seances that he conducted as dramatically as Mesmer had his baquets. The participants of these seances were allowed to commune with angels and with their beloved dead through the intervention of the grand master, who was, of course, Balsamo.

In 1784, the year that the royal commission decided against Mesmer, two of his students, the Marquis de Puységur (1751–1825) and his brother, a retired army man, started "experimenting" with animal magnetism at their estate near Soissons. Their chief subject was the gardener, Victor. The marquis recorded every event of each mesmeric seance and published his observations on what he called the state of "artificial somnambulism," in which Victor could carry on intelligent and lucid conversations. Victor, ordinarily shy and retiring, was less inhibited during the "somnambulism," and the marquis concluded that the boy had great powers of clairvoyance that were brought out in the trance. In addition, the marquis described what we would call today posthypnotic suggestion, without understanding what he had observed. Like Mesmer, he believed that a universal fluid had the power to permeate the body and give the "ignorant peasant" his extraordinary powers. The brothers Puységur used nothing like Mesmer's ceremonial procedure because they were working with unsophisticated peasants, who were unaccustomed to such trappings. The peasants simply sat around a tree that had been magnetized, not with a magnet, but with a universal fluid that the Puységurs thought was electric power. The brothers did not promote convulsive crises; they simply lulled their patients to sleep and told them that when they awoke their symptoms would disappear. Some of the hocus-pocus had thus been eliminated from the new cure, even though the strange theory had not been basically revised. What they practiced was suggestion through hypnosis, a procedure still in use today.

To follow some further ramifications of mesmerism we must carry the narrative into the nineteenth century. A pupil of the Marquis de Puységur, Charles Poyen, brought animal magnetism to the United States. Poyen gave a public demonstration of magnetism in Maine (1836) that convinced a watchmaker, Phineas Parkhurst Quimby (1802–1866), of the value of mental healing. Quimby, like Poyen and the De Puységurs, believed firmly that the mesmeric phenomenon was electrical and would never perform his demonstrations of hypnosis during thunderstorms. One night he was so intent on mesmerizing a young student of his, Lucius Burkmar, that he did not notice when an electrical storm began. Burkmar, as usual, fell into his trance, and Quimby then began to doubt the validity of the electrical explanation. Quimby achieved national prominence because people flocked to see his student, who, in a trance, with clairvoyant precision, could diagnose diseases, and what was even more important, could prescribe the proper remedy. When Burkmar once advised a patient to take a costly drug and the patient protested, Burkmar countered with advice to take a less expensive drug. The patient's symptoms were alleviated when he took the cheaper drug, and this circumstance led Quimby to believe that what was occurring had nothing whatsoever to do with Burkmar's trance, his clairvoyance, animal magnetism, or invisible fluids, but that uncritical faith in his own and Burkmar's powers was what brought results. From then on Quimby was certain that cures were effected by the mind and not by electricity, and for a quarter of a century he demonstrated the value of his "mind cure."

In 1862 Quimby met a forty-year-old schoolteacher who converted his faith into dollars and his demonstrations into a cult. Mary Baker had always been a delicate, frail, tense individual, given to "seizures" and strange airs. She had been married twice before she met Quimby. This meeting was a historic one in the annals of faith healing. After her treatment by Quimby for incapacitating neurotic symptoms, she made a dramatic recovery. Mesmer had given up the magnets; Quimby had given up mesmerizing. Now Mary Baker (later known as Mary Baker Eddy after her third marriage) embarked on the crusade that led to Christian Science, a movement encompassing both faith and healing and holding that because the Lord would never make one ill, sickness was a delusion and that belief in the power of God's healing measures would destroy the illness delusion. The paradoxical spread of Christian Science in the nineteenth and twentieth centuries during the continued and spectacular advances in medical science was not due only to the fact that the followers of Mary Baker Eddy were sincere believers in their mission. This powerful irrational movement is but another testimonial to man's deep-seated wish for magic and faith.

Other followers of the Marquis de Puységur were active in Germany and England. One, Johann Kaspar Lavater (1741–1801), was a clergyman and a famous spiritual consultant. Goethe was one of his closest friends and he was in constant communication with Count Cagliostro. Lavater worked by making a "character diagnosis" on the basis of facial characteristics, and after that he began treatment based on Puységur's somnambulism. In Germany mesmerism was thus combined with physiognomy. In England John Elliotson (1791–1868), known as one of the first to use the stethoscope, led a movement to make a combination of the techniques of phrenology and animal magnetism acceptable to medical societies. Elliotson also used mesmerism for the first time to diminish pain during surgical operations, and for this radical practice he was dismissed from his official duties as president of the Royal Medical and Chirurgical Society. In India, between 1845 and 1851, James Esdaile (1808–1859) performed more than two hundred and fifty painless operations on Hindu convicts by the use of mesmerism. The use of anesthetic gases in the 1840's diminished interest in using mesmerism in surgery, but physicians had been made aware that mesmerism was more than fakery and "mere imagination." In 1843 James Braid, a Manchester surgeon, published *Neurypnology, or The*

Rationale of Nervous Sleep, in which he maintained there was nothing magical about trance states: they were simply caused by excess muscle fatigue from a prolonged period of concentration and a consequent physical exhaustion. Braid did not explain what the trance was, but he did dispel some of the air of charlatanism that surrounded mesmerism. Mesmerism now became neurypnosis; Braid then related it to the sleeping state and renamed it hypnosis (*hypnos* is Greek for sleep). Hypnosis was a reassuringly scientific term, and as the nineteenth century advanced, in the same institution where Pinel had unchained his patients, the Salpêtrière, hypnosis became a serious subject for scientific investigation under the influence of Jean Martin Charcot (1825–1893), the most important neurologist of the modern era.

In modern and recent times there are obvious examples of magical practices and charlatanism, but by and large their effect has not been widespread or as influential as that of mesmerism. In fact, what characterizes the nineteenth and twentieth centuries is the decline of the impact of magical systems on medicine and psychiatry. This is not to imply, however, that erroneous systems of thought were without consequences in scientific circles.

*   *   *

To sum up, in the Age of Enlightenment one can see three major developments that were the direct result of the intellectual events of the Renaissance and the Age of Reason. Empiricism and rationalism, along with more sophisticated methods of observation and classification, brought the problems of mental illness into sharper focus and enabled men to regard the mentally ill with more compassion. Although the passion for classification on the part of Pinel and others did not always lead to increased understanding, it did make possible a more objective approach to insanity and other mental derangements. Also, the spirit of the time added impetus to more humane treatment of the insane as exemplified in the work of Chiarugi, Rush, and the Spanish physicians. In the career of Pinel we can see this movement toward decent treatment of the insane most clearly, for Pinel was both classifier extraordinary and a liberator of the insane from their chains. In the light of these two developments—both of which indicate a triumph of reason over fear—it is almost to be expected that the third major breakthrough of the age, the elimination of magic as a major approach to psychiatry, would have taken place. Superstition has not been totally eradicated even today, but from the turn of the nineteenth century onward, the influence of magical systems on psychiatry has virtually disappeared.

CHAPTER 9

The Romantic Reaction

The philosophers of the Enlightenment had tried to create a new society based on the same rational and mechanistic principles that had successfully expanded man's understanding of the physical universe. At the beginning of the nineteenth century, however, the optimistic and victorious spirit of rationalism yielded rapidly to disillusionment, and reason was dethroned by the rediscovery of the irrational depth of the human psyche. Instinct and passion became the focal points of interest; *Weltschmerz* and withdrawal from the conquest of the external world into private life expressed the new spirit of the times. Schiller voiced the disillusionment of this new Romantic era about knowledge: *"Nur im Irrtum ist das Leben, und die Wahrheit ist der Tod"*—Life is merely error; and death is truth. The eighteenth-century idea that reason could make the world a better place to live in had come to be viewed as illusory; the consequent disenchantment with the value of rationality was a pessimistic *tedium vitae,* a *"mal de siècle"* that had seized the European mind and of which Byron became the most influential interpreter.

Thus, in the five decades between 1790 and 1840 there was a movement away from reason toward emotion and faith. This swing toward mysticism is often regarded as retrogressive, but this evaluation is too one-sided a view of progress. If progress consists merely in the intellectual mastery of the physical universe, then truly the Romantic era did interrupt the relentless advancement of the scientific credo. But if the concept of progress is not restricted solely to increasing mastery of the physical world, but is instead broadened to include increasing knowledge of man's internal life and personality, then the Romantic era's contributions are large indeed. Man's struggle with his internal self became more fascinating and challenging than his struggle with the external world, and this same internal conflict for the first time became a central intellectual issue as well. Goethe's *Werther* incarnates the disillusioned introverted neurotic, and the plays of Heinrich Kleist deal primarily with psychopathology. The life of Julien Sorel, the hero of Stendhal's *The Red and the Black,* is another example of a literary use of psychological themes. The growing disenchantment did not arise without cause.

In European politics, after the fall of Napoleon, internal affairs took precedence over great international conquests and rivalries. Led by the Austrian statesman Prince Metternich (1773–1859), the guiding spirit of the reactionary movement, Germany, Russia, and France, with the consent and tacit cooperation of England, agreed at the Congress of Vienna (1814–1815) to restore absolutism, order, and religion. The rulers of these countries saw enemies not in each other but in their own peoples, who had been aroused by the slogans of the revolution and who resisted becoming "subjects" again. The ruling class fought this internal foe by suppression. The police state, Metternich's masterwork of political suppression, appeared. Informers and secret agents lurked everywhere. Political action was replaced by words and loud but ineffective songs about freedom and the death of tyrants. Most men, however, withdrew to their homes and sought happiness in the small events of daily life: "Glück im Winkel." Interest in personal destiny replaced grandiose participation in public events and revolutionary action to reform the world. Consequently the experiences of everyday life were invested with an exaggerated emotional content so that love affairs, passionate involvements, friendships, and personal intrigues became all-important. The world citizen of the eighteenth century, actively bent on creating a new society according to the abstract universal principles of reason, was succeeded by the petty bourgeois content to creep into the secluded corner of his own small world.

Psychological Developments

In this kind of social atmosphere interest in psychology, history, and idealistic philosophy flourish, for the mind turned selfward has to become aware of the depths of the inner life.

It is no wonder, therefore, that the first half of the nineteenth century has outstanding significance for the history of psychiatry. Psychiatry deals with man as a person; its subject matter is the mind. Humanity, during its civilized history, had consistently tried to disregard the "psyche" as a matter for scientific interest and to reduce it to psychical mechanisms. These mechanisms, which Hippocrates called the humors, or dryness or moistness of the body, Morgagni identified as localized processes in the brain, and Gall believed were recognizable by the visible lumps on the skull, had stubbornly refused to be talked out of existence.

In spite of the efforts to mechanize man, the psyche reappeared again and again. It appeared in Plato's world picture populated by "ideas," in St. Augustine's introspective revelations, in the humanists' emphasis on the individual as a unique personality, in Sydenham's psychogenic explanation for hysteria, in Spinoza's metaphysical thesis about the fundamental identity of body and mind, in Stahl's vital force, and in Pinel's "moral treatment" of the insane.

The interest in explaining the psyche at the beginning of the nineteenth century, however, was more definitive than any of these earlier efforts at psychology. Its intention and result were to make psychiatry an integral part of the rest of medicine.

The first systematic treatise of psychotherapy was published in 1803 by the German physician Johann Christian Reil. Reil was one of the most vociferous promoters of hospital reform, but his most significant contribution was to advocate the psychotherapeutic approach in a consistent and imaginative way. Reil, like Pinel and other eighteenth- and early-nineteenth-century psychiatrists, was strongly influenced by the ideas of empirical psychology, but Reil was more experimental and intuitive than his contemporaries and more consistent in applying his psychological approach to the treatment of mental patients. His *Rhapsodien üher die Anwendung der psychischen Curmethode auf Geisteszerrüttungen*—Rhapsodies About the Application of Psychotherapy to Mental Disturbances—a typically Romantic title, formulates systematically for the first time the principles as well as the different techniques of psychological treatment. He is still a long way from formulating a comprehensive theory of personality; his ideas about influencing the patient's pathological manifestations by certain therapeutic techniques (exposing the silent patient to loud noises or putting the excited patient in a dark, noiseless room) are naïve and crude. He is entirely convinced, however, that mental disease is a psychological phenomenon, the cause of which requires psychological methods of treatment. "It is not too long ago that I began to apply psychic treatment methods to the cure of mental disease and recognized that it must be cured by such methods."*[1] He calls Pinel's work on insanity "overly rich" in detail but "weak in system," lacking principles and originality.

Reil clearly recognized the enormous difficulties that psychotherapy must overcome. He says that the psychotherapist needs greater talent, perspicacity, knowledge, and technical facility than physicians who deal with bodily diseases but that this should not be considered discouraging because psychology offers the physician a new instrument that can correct even bodily diseases. Reil saw clearly that an interaction exists between psychological and physiological phenomena in the organism and recognized that the healthy personality had to be explained before the diseased soul could be understood. He emphasized, however, that psychology

* Translated by authors.

should not be merely normative. He wanted it to contain all the "empirical psychological" knowledge about the mutual interaction between psychological and physiological events and to become an integral part of the science of medicine, equal in importance to pharmacology.

Reil was outspokenly convinced, and more consistently so than any of his predecessors, of the close relationship between body and mind. "Feelings and ideas, briefly, psychic influences, are the proper means by which disturbances of the brain can be corrected and its vitality can be restored."[2] This thesis is the basis of his whole psychotherapeutic system. He proposed, in a word, to cure mental diseases primarily by psychological influences—a remarkable stand in view of the fact that Reil was also an expert in brain anatomy. (A part of the brain, the "island of Reil," is named after him.) Reil considered sound clinical observation far more valuable than armchair philosophy in achieving this therapeutic goal. He also disliked indiscriminate use of pharmacological agents; for example, opiates, he says, may produce mental symptoms.

He also clearly recognized the role of sexual excitation in mental disturbances. He refers to hysterical women who become disturbed because of their inability to bear children and who develop delusions of pregnancy as a result of the frustration of their propagative instinct. For mental diseases caused by sexual problems Reil prescribes sexual intercourse. "The unworldly Platonic who has become psychotic because of his delusion about the purity of the female sex should be supplied with a prostitute who will cure his delusions by seducing him into the morass of unclean inclinations."[3] Such a statement clearly shows that Reil, the son of a minister and a man of strict moral convictions, was first of all a naturalist who visualized psychiatry as a branch of medicine based on scientific knowledge of the brain as well as of the psyche. Other methods of treatment that Reil suggests are occupational therapy, music therapy, and drama therapy; by the latter he tried to modify habitual patterns of feeling and action in his patients by having them view a play. The rationale behind this technique is that the patients became psychologically involved in the plot. Reil believed this stimulated their self-awareness. As the dangers depicted in the drama unfolded, the patient's feelings and intellect were activated, forcing him to find ways and means to rescue himself from similar imaginary dangers.

The psychology underlying Reil's diversified therapeutic procedures was little more than crude common sense; he used reward and punishment, intimidation, and appeal to reason the way parents do when they try to influence their children's behavior. However, whenever Reil used a technical device, such as frightening a patient, he presented a psychological rationale in opposition to using these techniques in a sadistic manner. He called these techniques "noninjurious torture."

Reil's contribution to psychiatry was that he outlined an empirically based therapeutic program. However, the time was simply not ripe for this program to be brought into practice. Furthermore, Reil was steeped in the philosophical bias of the Enlightenment, with its tendency to generalize. Indeed, Reil tended to overgeneralize, and he did not consider the uniqueness of the individual, who is best understood in terms of his particular life history. For example, to expose all silent patients to the noise of cannon fire—proposed by Reil—is to ignore the fact that some of these patients may have withdrawn into silence because of a frightening noise experience.

In France the men who followed Pinel continued in the tradition of this outstanding clinician and reformer. Although they recognized the central importance of the "passions"—the primary concern of the German Romantic psychiatrists—their main impact on the history of psychiatric development lay in their precise clinical implementation of hospital reform. Pinel's most outstanding pupil, Jean Étienne Dominique Esquirol (1772–1840), followed so precisely the work of Pinel that the contributions of the two men are frequently confused. Like Pinel, Esquirol did not indulge in philosophical or physiological speculations about mental illness.

In many ways his descriptions of clinical syndromes are even more precise than those of his teacher. These descriptions were often accompanied by statistics, one of the first attempts in the history of psychiatry to use this approach. Esquirol listed the precipitating psychological events that appeared significant in the mental breakdown of hundreds of his patients at the Bicêtre and the Salpêtrière. He gave the first precise description of idiocy but warned that not all intellectual defects could be subsumed under this category, for an individual's apparent lack of intelligence may result from a preoccupation with his own thoughts and feelings, thereby diminishing his ability to think intelligently about abstract matters. Esquirol, for the first time, differentiated hallucinations (a term he coined) from illusions: hallucinations are sensory impressions, for example, hearing or seeing objects that do not exist and that are entirely products of the mind; illusions are false impressions based on a misinterpretation of an actual sensory stimulus. Esquirol attempted to classify forms of mental illness according to affective monomania or a disturbance in a particular aspect of behavior, for example, homicidal and arson monomania. If one of the monomanias was connected with a depression, Esquirol used the term lypemania. Esquirol's classification is not in general use today; nonetheless, some mental patients, like paranoids or the less severely disturbed obsessive neurotics, may consistently ruminate upon one central theme to which they give their full attention, and could thereby be considered monomaniacs. Esquirol realized that man's reasoning ability is subservient to his emotional needs. This idea had been stated many times since the decline of scholastic philosophy, but it was Esquirol who specifically applied it to mental disturbances. He pointed out that criminal action may be a result of a monomania and that this type of criminal should not be punished but should be treated in a hospital for the mentally ill. Pupils of Pinel, in particular Guillaume Ferrus (1784–1861) and François Leuret (1797–1851), contributed further to forensic psychiatry by advocating treatment for the criminally insane. Leuret pointed out that strong impulses may overcome a man's conscience and force him into criminal acts. This was contrary to the popular belief at that time and is still contrary to the thinking of some present-day legal minds, who claim that all criminals are without conscience. Fortunately Leuret's ideas regarding the inability to master and contain overwhelming impulses are becoming increasingly recognized by the judiciary.

Esquirol's classic book, *Des maladies mentales considérées sous les rapports médical, hygiénique et médico-légal* (1838), was a basic text for half a century and stimulated his students to contribute new and basic definitions to clinical psychiatry. Jean Pierre Falret (1794–1870) believed that the terminology previously used to refer to mentally ill patients carried negative implications. Recognizing the sociological implications of their estrangement from society, he advocated that mental disease be called "mental alienation."[4] Physicians who attempted to reestablish the patient's contact with his social environment thus became known as alienists. Furthermore, Falret, after careful clinical observations, concluded that depressed patients frequently had alternate moods of manic excitement, which he called *de la folie circulaire* (1854). Jules Baillarger (1809–1890) called this clinical syndrome *folie à double forme*. Not since the days of the Roman Aretaeus had there been an understanding that depressive moods may be interrupted by periods of elation within the same patient. These conditions later were called by the German investigators of the late nineteenth century manic-depressive psychoses. Baillarger, like his teacher, Esquirol, became interested in hallucinatory phenomena. He described hallucinations in the hypnagogic state—when a person is midway between sleep and consciousness—and described hallucinations that occur in delirium due to alcoholism. Étienne Georget (1795–1828) was a young clinician whose descriptions of mental disturbances were so exact that he described precisely a serious form of psychosis which later was called hebephrenia. Although Georget appeared to understand that certain unacceptable ideas are not brought to consciousness and are therefore repressed, he did not further elaborate this most profound concept. It was yet beyond the scope of the followers of Esquirol to understand psychology as a state of dynamic processes of emotions and ideas that in both insane and sane persons have a meaningful continuity and interconnection. They did not yet operate consistently with the principle of psychological causality. This principle inherent in motivational psychology appeared not as a consequence of descriptive psychiatry but in spite of it, and came to fruition with the work of Freud. Nonetheless, the contribution of Esquirol's followers was to lay the foundations for a new medical discipline, that of clinical psychiatry, by introducing a scholarly and methodical approach to classifying and describing mental symptoms. Their understanding of phenomenological events led to the more comprehensive systematization of clinical entities by the German psychiatrists of the later nineteenth century. Furthermore, all these men, with true humanitarian spirit, carried on Pinel's reforms in hospital management. Their interest in psychological content was reinforced by the ideological climate of the early nineteenth century, but fundamentally their contributions reflect Pinel's classical and rationalistic point of view.

The clinical orientation of the followers of Pinel and Esquirol had both advantages and limitations. These psychiatrists did not merely talk and speculate about mental illness, but studied their patients carefully. They did write of disturbances of reasoning, affects, memory, and judgment but did not relate them to malfunctioning of the total personality. They described more or less isolated symptoms, syndromes, and behavior patterns but did not understand that these were surface manifestations of a more basic, underlying disturbance of the most vital function of the organism, namely, to coordinate its different aspects into an harmonious unity.

A step in the direction of a psychology that could view mental symptoms as manifestations of disturbances of the whole personality was made by one of the most original psychiatrists of the era, J. Moreau de Tours (1804–1884), who was also a disciple of Esquirol. Moreau and some of his contemporaries from Germany became preoccupied with the irrational, emotional, and hidden forces of the personality and thus were true representatives of the Romantic trend. They tried to understand the person as a whole, the totality of the diseased person, and the invisible psychological design behind madness. They progressed from the merely descriptive and classificatory trend of Pinel's followers and were pronouncedly more dynamic in their views. All of them anticipated certain features of psychoanalytic thought and in this regard came nearer to our present-day orientation than did their predecessors and immediate successors in the second half of the century. Moreau impressed upon his colleagues that the basis of the psychological understanding of another person is introspection. Before anyone can know what pain is, he must have experienced it, and Moreau, in order to have a firsthand experience of peculiar sensations, even went so far as to take hashish. He thus anticipated those psychiatrists in our own times who take hallucinogenic drugs in order to experience psychotic states.

Moreau pointed out for the first time that dreams offer the real clue for the understanding of disturbed mental functions. Dreams, he said, are made of the same stuff as hallucinations and thus provide a connecting link between the healthy person and the insane; dreaming is the transient psychopathology of the normal person. Moreau did not use the expression "unconscious" but came close to this concept when he wrote of two modes of existence. "It appears then that two modes of existence—two kinds of life—are given to man. The first one results from our communication with the external world, with the universe. The second one is but the reflection of the self and is fed from its own distinct internal sources. The dream is a kind of in-between land where the external life ends and the internal life begins."⁵ Moreau understood that an insane person "dreams awake"⁶ and that ". . . Delirium and dreams are not merely analogous but absolutely identical."⁷ Moreau described the completely subjective psychological phenomena that occur in the dream state, when man withdraws from the external world by shutting off external stimuli conveyed by the sense organs, and explained that the absence of the impact of external reality gives the irrational and illogical forces of the mind full sway. These free subjective psychological processes unrestricted by reality characterize the dreaming state and psychoses. The insane person is alienated from the external world and lives only his private inner life; when he hallucinates he sees and hears not what reality shows him but that which he wants to see and hear. These concepts of Moreau anticipated Freud's basic distinction between "primary" and "secondary" psychological processes. The primary processes are primitive in that the fantasy runs its own course dictated solely by wish fulfillment and uninfluenced by the impact of external reality. Freud described the secondary psychological processes as those that occur through rational thinking resulting from contact with reality, or as Moreau described earlier, resulting from "communication with the external world."

Other views of Moreau were less viable. Among these was his comparison between genius and insanity, which led up one of those blind alleys not uncommon in the history of psychiatric thought. Moreau explained that the resemblance between these two states derived from their common origin in overactivity of the mind. If this overactivity results in more intensive functioning, the quality of genius appears; if it results in greater aberration and disturbance, insanity occurs. This idea of the *dégénéré supérieur* had considerable persistency throughout the nineteenth century because it accorded with the Romantic interest in the unique individual.

The dynamic and integrative tendency exemplified by Moreau's views of psychosis, not as a circumscribed, partial aberration but as a manifestation of the total personality, was also reflected in the ideas of some German psychiatrists, among them Johann Christian Heinroth (1773–1843). Heinroth had a profound intuitive grasp of inner conflict; steeped in Lutheran tradition, he expressed his ideas about it in religious terminology. The soul was traditionally a borderline territory between theology and psychology, and even such naturalists as Aristotle could not avoid supernatural religious concepts. Aristotle ascribed to the *nous*—the intellectual principle governing nature, a divine origin. Even Spinoza retained, if nothing else, at least the expression "God" as a synonym for his completely depersonalized universe. The Protestant movement, by making man responsible to his own conscience, strengthened the psychological motif in religion, still retaining the traditional dogmatic faith in revealed truth. St. Augustine, the most penetrating of all religious psychologists, avoided giving self-understanding an independent function. Man alone without God's help cannot achieve the good life; unquestioned faith in revealed truth is the ultimate answer.

In Protestantism "individual conscience" became a new religious principle. It was not in contradiction to faith, yet man faced his God now through God's internal representative, his "individual conscience."

"Conscience," which Freud later called "superego," was to become a cornerstone of psychoanalytic psychology. Heinroth held that the ultimate cause of mental disturbance is sin, which for him was equivalent to selfishness. He expressed in religious-moralistic terminology the central concept of modern psychiatry, that of inner conflict. If Heinroth would have used the current expression, "sense of guilt," for sin, he would have been more readily recognized as a forerunner of psychoanalysis. As it is, there is a general tendency to discard him as a religious healer. When Heinroth defined mental illness as the result of sin he did not mean that all neurotics and psychotics perpetrated actual sinful acts. He referred to the sins of thought that offend our moral sense. Stated in modern terms, the source of mental disturbance is the conflict between unacceptable impulses (the id) and the conscience (the superego).

Heinroth considered that psychological processes were divided into three levels of functioning. The lowest level represents instinctual forces and feelings (in modern terms, id impulses) whose aim is pleasure. The second phase he called the ego (ich), which functions through the guidance of the intellect. The ego's aim (which is entirely self-centered) is "security in relation to the external world" and "the enjoyment of living." The main characteristic of the ego is "self-awareness." Body and psyche are but two aspects of the same thing, which appears externally in space as body and internally as psyche. That these two aspects of the self are not divisible is Heinroth's main thesis. It is no wonder, then, that he was the first to use the term "psychosomatic."

The third and highest level of mental functioning Heinroth called the conscience (Gewissen). According to him, the ego develops from the lowest level of psychological organization through the recognition of the difference between the world and the self. As will be seen, this is identical with Freud's concept of early ego development. As Freud stressed, the ego differentiates itself from the id through learning to differentiate internal stimuli from those that come from external reality. Heinroth stated that the conscience develops by a differentiation within the ego, appearing first as something alien to the ego, something that opposes the ego's self-centered strivings. This higher force, which is a part of the ego, produces a conflict within the ego.[8] For this higher force Heinroth uses the term "super-us" (Über-uns).*

The super-us is therefore a later differentiation within the ego and

* The collective nature of the commands of this higher force is probably what influenced Heinroth to use the plural super-us instead of, as Freud did later, the singular Über-ich, or superego.

represents a conflict between the basically self-centered ego and a "higher" altruistic orientation. Heinroth describes it as the divine element within man's psyche and says that not many human beings actually achieve the development of a super-us: in the majority, the voice of conscience is small, the conscience remains a foreign body within the self, and life is a continuous struggle between man's basic selfishness and his reason. The man who does achieve it lives only to serve others: "Er lebt für sich bloss um der anderen willen."

Mental health for Heinroth consisted in a full assimilation within the ego of the principles of the conscience. Only those few who accomplish this union are mentally healthy, internally "free," and happy. Mental disease is derived from the conflict with conscience.

Since Heinroth defined sin as equivalent to selfishness, he unavoidably had to pose a central question: Who can give up selfishness without giving up life itself? Accordingly, he had little hope of curing mental illness permanently. But since morality, too, is an undeniable attribute of man, Heinroth eventually accepted the Augustinian solution for reconciling these two inherent but contradictory principles: Faith in revealed truth is the remedy.

Heinroth's contributions to psychotherapy were far less original than his theoretical views concerning the nature of mental illness. Like that of his predecessors, his approach was primarily reeducational. He recommended cognitive correction for disturbances of judgment and inculcation of moral principles for disturbances of volition. However, Heinroth revealed a great deal of wisdom in the emphasis he put upon the self-curative powers of the mind. He was thoroughly Hippocratic in this point of view and gave full credit to natural healing powers. He believed in the curative powers of time and warned against trying to do too much therapy. He, perhaps more than many modern psychiatrists, was aware of the danger of overtreating and of the danger inherent in prepsychoanalytic psychotherapy, trying to help before one understands the nature of the problem.

His therapeutic armamentarium included practically all the traditional methods of physical and psychological treatment. For physical treatment he recommended electricity, warmth, bloodletting, physiotherapy, diet, and regulation of the digestive functions. His psychotherapeutic measures emphasized removal or increase of stimulation, including, for the latter, deprivation of sleep. He used restraint and punishment but also recommended relaxation—diversions and travel or, for some cases, excessive work. He did not indiscriminately apply these methods, which were based on rather general and vague psychological considerations. Heinroth was a true son of the Romantic era and strongly believed that the individuality of each patient had to be the ultimate guide for the choice of therapy. He thought that in general women needed a different psychotherapeutic approach from men and insisted that the physician's attitude had to be adjusted to the unique personality of the patient. Some patients, he said, need warmth and kindness, others firmness and strength; and patients from different countries ought to be treated differently. His opposition to routine treatment marks a most significant step toward individualized psychotherapy.

In a general appraisal of Heinroth's position in psychiatry it may be stated that in the *detailed knowledge* of personality dynamics he did not make lasting contributions, but in his *general principles,* particularly in his emphasis on understanding the patient before engaging in any special treatment, in his recognition of the individual nature of every case, in his Hippocratic trust in the natural healing powers of the mind, and above all, in recognizing the moral conflict underlying mental disturbances, he reached a remarkably advanced level of insight. In his general orientation he was one of the most modern psychiatrists of the nineteenth century and came nearer to the present spirit of dynamic psychiatry than many who followed him.

An orientation basically similar to Heinroth's characterized the writings of a number of other psychiatrists of this period. These men thought that personality functions were rooted in the instinctual and volitional forces of man. Theirs was a thoroughly biological orientation; psychological life for them was a manifestation of an organism they considered a psychobiological entity, and they viewed both normal and abnormal mental processes as manifestations of the total personailty.

Alexander Haindorf (1782–1862) wrote a textbook of psychiatry on mental illnesses (1811) in which he discussed the physiological sources of drives and their influence upon reasoning and tried to relate them to different parts of the brain. He not only considered the human organism to be a psychobiological unit, but he was one of the first to germinate the idea that emotional conflicts result in disturbing the normal functioning of that unit, leading to mental illness. Friedrich Groos (1768–1852), a philosopher who later became a psychiatrist, attempted to combine philosophical concepts with physiological reactions and proposed that man is influenced by physiological forces, of which he is unaware, that determine his reactions. If these forces are blocked and cannot find outlet, mental illness results. Freud later held a similar view and defined these forces in terms of instincts. In modern terminology, if instinctual drives are not satisfactorily relieved or sublimated, neurosis or a psychosomatic condition results. Like Groos, Karl Wilhelm Ideler (1795–1860), who was inspired by the writings of the vitalist Georg Stahl, believed that instinctual drives, which he called "passions," if intense and ungratified, can result in a breakdown in personality functioning. Ideler even anticipated a modern view when he suggested that excessive aggressiveness could be found in patients prior to a mental breakdown and that these play a decisive role in delusions of persecution when such patients become psychotic.[9]

A uniquely modern-sounding psychosomatic approach was espoused by Friedrich Eduard Beneke (1798–1854) when he proposed that ideas could become symbolized and expressed in physical reactions. This concept was reintroduced into the psychosomatic approach to medicine in recent times and improved upon when the distinction was made by Franz Alexander between reactions mediated by the sensory motor system and the autonomic nervous system.

Crucial to the psychosomatic approach were the views of Ernst von Feuchtersleben (1806–1849), who criticized the philosophers for perpetuating the mind-body dichotomy. He, like the modern psychosomaticists, regarded the body and mind as "a single phenomenon, invariably, one and indivisible."[10] Believing that mental illness was a result of personality disturbance, Feuchtersleben was one of the few Romantic writers who stressed the importance of psychotherapy for these diseases. The psychological approach to the mentally ill, he believed, would help the patient understand the development of his deviations, and therefore psychotherapy was a form of "second education." Not until the 1940's and 1950's, when the learning theory was developed, has the emphasis been so clearly placed on the view of psychotherapy as a form of relearning, or reeducation.

The psychodynamic ideas of these psychiatric Romanticists were eclipsed after the middle of the century by a resurgence of organic and clinically oriented psychiatry. The disappearance of the psychodynamic orientation was so complete that Freud's contributions appeared to his contemporaries as completely novel. But what Freud had to cope with was the descriptive classificatory approach of the writers of the latter part of the nineteenth century. Freud obviously was not acquainted with the writings of these men of the Romantic era and had to find his own psychobiological orientation. It was long after Freud's influence revolutionized psychiatry that contemporary psychiatric historians such as E. Harms, W. Riese, and G. Zilboorg recognized the significance of the psychiatrists of the Romantic period.

From the present-day perspective Romantic psychiatry appeals to us because of its dynamic orientation, its integrative grasp of the totality of the person as a psychobiological entity, and its recognition of the biological rootedness of psychological forces. This period brings into sharp relief the conceptual poverty of the next period, its purely descriptive classifications, and its therapeutic nihilism, from which we only recently have recovered. This may account for the overenthusiasm of some of the modern rediscoverers of Romantic psychiatry, who tend to overlook its inherent weaknesses. The Romantics revived the vitalist philosophy of the ancients, who viewed life as the realization of a Divine plan and the life processes as a manifestation of a mystical goal-directed force. This metaphysical bias was not the result of careful observations but of visionary speculations, and therefore a reaction against the Romantic episode was

The first psychiatrist—the witch doctor—as portrayed by a prehistoric artist in the Cave of Trois Frères at Ariège, France.

Head of Christ, adapted by the Christians from the bust of Aesculapius, the Greek god of healing (Jordan Archaeological Museum).

The medieval approach to dissection in medical training is shown at left. Mundinius lectures from a chair while an assistant dissects (New York Public Library).

right, representing the Renais-
nce revolution, Vesalius performs
e dissection himself while he lec-
res to the students gathered
ound him.

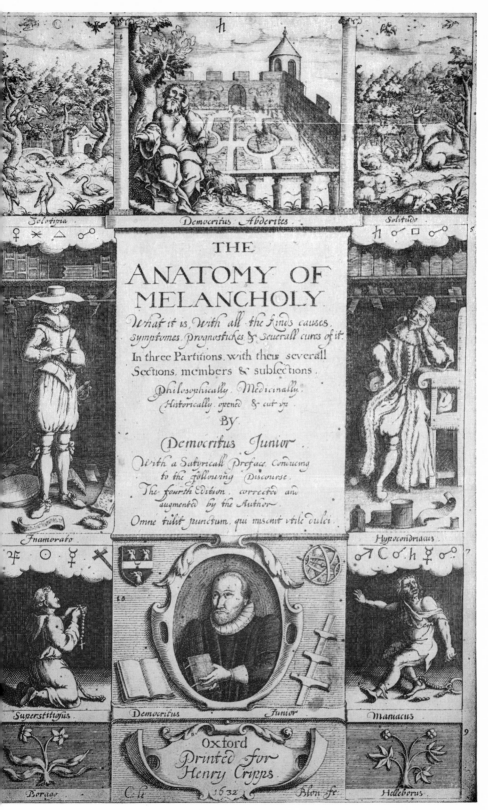

Original title page of Robert Burton's *Anatomy of Melancholy*.

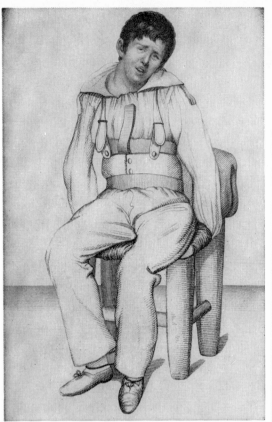

Three eighteenth-century methods
of restraining the insane.

The Madhouse, by Goya (Real Academia de Bellas Artes de San Fernando).

Pinel unchaining the insane at the Hospital of Salpêtrière.

Vincenzo Chiarugi, like Pinel, was one of the earliest champions of the humane and understanding treatment of the mentally ill.

unavoidable. For all their stimulating flashes of imagination and intuitive insight the Romantics lacked a solid foundation of clinically observed phenomena, and hence their concepts appeared as visionary flights of fancy.

Nowhere are these shortcomings of the Romantic era exposed more clearly than in the work of Karl Gustav Carus (1789–1869), originally an obstetrician, who turned his interest first toward *Naturphilosophy* and then to psychology. As far as mental disturbances were concerned, Carus had no firsthand experience; not inhibited by clinical knowledge of the way mentally diseased persons behave, he was free to indulge in unlimited speculation. His book *Psyche* (1846) consistently espouses the Romantic position, not only in regard to psychology and mental disease but also to physiology and general pathology. The central axis of Carus' philosophy, like Freud's, is the concept of the "unconscious," which Carus equated with the creative life force. This is similar to Freud's Eros and identical with Groddeck's Id, of which we shall speak later. One can easily select quotations from his book that seem deceptively modern, but also other statements that could have been written two thousand years ago. There are islands of visionary insight in his book, surrounded by an ocean of vague and confused generalizations. We read in the Introduction a most modern-sounding statement:

"The key to the understanding of the essence of conscious mental processes lies in the region of the unconscious. All the difficulties, nay, the seeming impossibility of understanding precisely the mysteries of the mind become from this point of view understandable. If it were really impossible to find in consciousness the unconscious, one should resign oneself not to understand the psyche. That is to say, ever to understand one's own self. However, should this impossibility be only apparent, then the first aim of the science of psychology should be to determine in which way the human mind can descend into these depths."*[11] Carus repeatedly asserts in the *Psyche* that what were once conscious ideas in childhood later go into the "oblivion" of the unconscious as the child matures.

Indeed, Freud wrote along similar lines a half century later. Freud, however, actually discovered an operational method of penetrating the depths of man's personality. Carus sets the problem but fails in advancing any methodological tools to achieve the goal that he stated with admirable clairvoyance. And precisely here, in this lack of operational knowledge, lies the cardinal reason why the Romantic movement had to fail in advancing psychiatry and psychotherapy.

Carus is particularly confusing when he writes of the "unconscious," which means much more than conscious mental content that sometime in the past became unconscious: the unconscious is practically equivalent

* Translated by authors.

with the whole life process, both organic and mental. Such an all-encompassing concept thereby becomes well-nigh meaningless. The unconscious animates all physiological processes; hence all organic illnesses are rooted in the unconscious mind. Organic diseases are "parasitic," alien ideas superimposed upon the healthy unconscious plan of self-realization of the organism. The source of these alien ideas—the source of disease—is not clear in Carus' writings. The conflict between the original healthy organizational design of the unconscious and these alien ideas is the essence of illness. As long as this conflict does not reach the conscious mind we deal with organic diseases; when these conflicts pervade the conscious mind mental disturbances appear. This theory resembles an erroneous current, metaphysically inclined psychiatric theory, namely, that organic disease (psychosomatic disease) is an "organ psychosis."

It is obvious that these metaphysical heights of abstract reasoning offer no glimmer of hope for dealing with clinical phenomena. In reaction to this kind of Romantic, entirely theoretical, undisciplined thought, about 1850 the pendulum of psychiatric thought swung back to the other extreme: intensive interest in arranging data into often meaningless classifications and in localizing the site of mental illness in the nervous system. Psychiatry in the second half of the nineteenth century went through a sterile period of data-gathering before the dynamic point of view could be again revived. Then it was tempered by a solidly entrenched tradition of controlled observation and rigorous reasoning. Sigmund Freud's genius lay in his mixture of speculative and scientific talents, which permitted him to synthesize these two extreme orientations.

Precursors of Neuropsychiatry

Although the first half of the nineteenth century was strongly psychological in its orientation, the beginnings of neurology fall into this epoch. Initially the disciples of Pinel and Esquirol, in the spirit of the Enlightenment, basically followed an eclectic path, stressing description and classification rather than explanation. German scholars, following the mode of the Romantic era, placed emphasis on man's psyche. Events occurring in the medical sciences brought about the gradual transition from the eclectic and Romantic to a neurological emphasis.

Toward the middle of the century medicine began to form modern concepts by incorporating the principles of physics and chemistry. Psychiatry, too, attempted to become modern and scientific by explaining disordered behavior in terms of disrupted nervous structure and function. This materialistic concept of mental disease had its roots in Morgagni's formulation in 1761 that diseases originate in localized disturbances of the bodily organs. This concept was fostered in the early years of the nineteenth century, when French physicians proposed that the focus of disease was in the tissues of the organs, and finally, in the mid-nineteenth century, when German researchers localized disease in the finite building blocks of tissues, the cells.

French scientific and artistic productivity reached new heights during the first half of the nineteenth century, and France became a center for medical knowledge. Students came from all corners of Europe and from the United States to hear lectures by the renowned clinicians, among them one of the founders of histology, Marie François Xavier Bichat (1771–1802). Pinel had remarked to Bichat that the structural unit of pathological disturbance may be more precisely localized than Morgagni had suspected. Bichat, before the development of the achromatic lens and improved compound miscroscope (c. 1825), performed more than five hundred autopsies, working with the naked eye. He identified twenty-one types of tissues. In 1800 Bichat proposed for the first time a tissue theory of disease: when tissues of an organ become weakened they become vulnerable to diseases and the diseased tissue is the primary locus of pathology.

In Germany, the country that had found Romanticism most congenial, science had to purify itself from the vague speculations of the Romantic philosophers that had begun to pervade the whole of medicine. This task was accomplished by Johannes Peter Müller (1801–1858) and his pupils, the embryologist Rudolf von Kölliker (1817–1905), Hermann von Helmholtz (1821–1894), Rudolf Virchow (1821–1902), and Friedrich Henle (1809–1885), the histopathologist. In his early years Müller was impressed by Schelling, Goethe, and other Romantic philosophers. After having earned his medical diploma at Bonn, he came to Berlin, where the leaders in the biological departments were skeptical about the value to medicine of philosophical vagaries. By the time Müller became a professor in anatomy, physiology, and pathology at Berlin, he too was firmly convinced that medical progress depended on experimentation and observation, and he encouraged his colleagues to leave their libraries and go into the laboratory and use their new microscopes, for he thought that a psychologist must also be a biologist. Müller himself was an indefatigable experimenter; he is said to have written more than fifteen thousand pages of materials describing his experiments and drawn three hundred and fifty illustrative plates.

Sir Charles Bell (1774–1842), a leading English neurologist, had proposed in 1811 that the posterior roots of the spinal cord carry sensation to the central nervous system and that the anterior roots carry away motor impulses. This very basic neurological concept had been elaborated by the French physiologist François Magendie (1783–1855). Müller's careful investigations corroborated their work, and he further proposed, in his law of specific nerve energy (1840), that each sensory organ responds to a stimulus in its own unique way.

Stimulated by Müller, physiologists began to measure neurophysiological phenomena precisely; for example, Hermann von Helmholtz actually measured the speed of a nerve impulse by experimenting with the muscles of frogs. Müller also prompted Theodor Schwann (1810–1882) to study animal tissues under the newly improved compound microscope. Schwann found in animal tissues what his close friend the botanist Matthias Jakob Schleiden (1804–1881) had found in all plant tissues, namely, a unique structure. In 1838 the Schleiden-Schwann cell theory proposed that the basic structure of all living matter is the cell and that all tissues are made up of cells. Schleiden and Schwann did not understand where cells came from, and so they theorized a primordial protein substance. The knowledge that cells come from other cells was proved by several investigators, but perhaps most conclusively by another of Müller's students, the greatest pathologist of his time, Rudolf Virchow.

Virchow's basic idea that *omnis cellula e cellula*—all cells come from cells—soon led him to the concept that all of pathology could be understood in terms of cellular disease, and he proposed that disease develops when severe stimuli disturb the life processes of the cell. For centuries medical science had tried to describe diseases in terms of a specific abnormal substance that caused the disease. Virchow's meticulous studies proved that the disease process could be described best in terms of disturbed cellular pathology. Science could now not return to the fantasies of the vitalists, who spoke of invisible ethereal substances. Under the microscope cells in a diseased body revealed undeniable concrete differences from cells found in healthy organs; and Virchow's concepts were as influential in transforming medical thought in the mid-nineteenth century as Morgagni's had been in the late eighteenth century. But the lives of these two radical men of scientific thought, Morgagni and Virchow, were strikingly different. Morgagni, with all his scientific radicalism, was a staid conservative and a noncontroversial figure in his day. Virchow, on the other hand, was as heterodox in his political beliefs as he was in his scientific views. He was a democrat in every sense of the word and an outspoken opponent of Bismarck.

Since the right wing in Germany was not inclined to tolerate opposition, Virchow's role in the Revolution of 1848 caused him to lose his position in Berlin, and he accepted an appointment in Würzburg. Frustrated in his advocacy of social and political reform, he devoted himself to expanding his concepts of cellular pathology. In 1858 he published *Die Cellularpathologie in ihrer Begründung auf physiologische und pathologische Gewebelehre* (Cellular pathology based on physiological and pathological histology), a book that marks the beginning of the modern era in medicine.

In the next year Charles Darwin (1809–1882) published his classic, *The Origin of Species by Means of Natural Selection,* which introduced into biology the rules of change and probability that had proved so useful in the physical sciences. Jean Lamarck's theory that those qualities which animals acquired during their struggle to survive were transmitted to new generations through inheritance was now replaced by a theory that could be verified by breeding experiments. Darwin proposed that chance differences between individuals belonging to the same species make some of them superior in their struggle for existence, and as a consequence of their survival, those features that have resulted in adaptation are promulgated. No longer was it necessary to explain purposefulness of living organisms from a mystical vital force that pursues preestablished goals. The gap between animate and inanimate organisms finally appeared bridgeable, and the door was opened, never again to be closed, for a vigorous attack upon the mysteries of biology by the methods of the natural sciences. The last sanctuary of the belief in a spiritual force working within the organism had been destroyed, and nothing seemed to stand in the way of scientific methods being able to explain all the mysteries of organic life and of psychology.

*   *   *

Then, the Romantic era was marked by a reaction, but a reaction in the direction of progress. In their new and enthusiastic concern over the nature of the psyche, the Romantics brought psychiatry to the threshold of modern concepts and techniques. In their furthering of humane treatment of the mentally ill—especially in seeing each sick person as an individual demanding individually patterned treatment—in their origination of ideas about the unconscious, the nature of dreams, and instincts and the complexity of the total personality, the Romantics enabled psychiatry to break away from classifications of Pinel's followers. These classifications were initially essential but tended to become sterile codifications. This breakthrough allowed psychiatry to return to a dynamic approach to mental illness and, with new discoveries in neuropsychiatry, made possible the birth of the modern age of psychiatry.

CHAPTER 10

The Modern Era

Neuropsychiatry

Although the modern era of medicine in a sense does begin in 1858 and 1859 with the works of Virchow and Darwin, medicine had already begun to utilize the principles of physics and chemistry in the two previous decades. Julius Robert Mayer (1814–1878) in 1842 had proposed the law of conservation of energy in animal organisms, which five years later was extended by Helmholtz to all matter. Modern physiological chemistry began in the early 1840's with the work of Justus von Liebig (1803–1873), when, with other chemists, he succeeded in isolating the important components of the protein molecule. In 1828 Friedrich Wöhler (1800–1882) synthetized urea. Embryology was given a great impetus by Albert von Kölliker (1817–1905) with his studies of cellular maturation and by Karl von Baer (1792–1876), who described the structure of the human ovum and the development of the spinal cord. The concept of the contagiousness of infectious diseases was inspired by the pioneering efforts of the Italian micropathologist Agostino Bassi (1773–1857), who established, also in the 1840's, that the silkworm disease was caused by a microscopic parasite.

In the next decade Louis Pasteur (1822–1895) started the bacteriological studies at the Paris École Normale that established the germ theory of disease. In the 1860's an English surgeon, Joseph Lister (1827–1912) introduced the practice of antisepsis, Ignaz Semmelweis (1818–1865) battled for aseptic technique in obstetrics, and Max von Pettenkofer (1818–1901) campaigned for hygiene in Germany.

Clinical medicine also made notable advances in the first half of the nineteenth century. Syndromes and disease entities, many of which still bear the names of the men who discovered them, were carefully described. Thomas Addison (1793–1860) described a disease of the adrenal gland, Charles Bell a paralysis of the face due to neuropathology, Richard Bright (1789–1858) a form of kidney disease, James Parkinson (1755–1824) a shaking palsy, and Thomas Hodgkin (1798–1866) a type of leukemia that attacks the lymph glands.

The early 1860's witnessed not only revolutionary events in the medical sciences but also drastic political upheavals as well. France was losing her supremacy among European nations, as the second French Empire, under Napoleon III, was weakened by internal corruption. Bismarck was unifying Germany under Prussian leadership, and the country was becoming the leading industrial, economic and military power in Europe. Germany's political and economic rise was accompanied by a vigorous growth in scientific education; the German universities were reorganized, and curricula were set up that took cognizance of the new scientific developments.

Moritz Romberg (1795–1873), a neurologist at the University of Berlin, typified the German scientific genius of this era. His *Lehrbuch der Nervenkrankheiten* (1840–1846), the first systematic book on neurology, gave the field the status of a separate medical specialty. Romberg's successor at the University of Berlin, Wilhelm Griesinger (1817–1868), had the title of professor of psychiatry and neurology. Griesinger had an all-absorbing interest in medical research, and before he was thirty he had summarized his observations in a textbook on mental disease.

During the course of his career Griesinger made outstanding contributions to the study of infectious diseases, pathological anatomy, and mental diseases. In addition to a textbook on psychiatry and one on infectious diseases, he wrote many significant articles on psychiatric diagnosis and treatment. He founded the *Archiv für Physiologische Heilkunde* as well as the Society for Medical Psychology, which was unique in that it served as a forum not only for psychiatrists but also for representatives of related fields, particularly philosophers. He advanced the cause of psychiatry as a sound medical discipline. His diversified medical interests made him one of the great synthesizers of the medical sciences, and he was always alert for meaningful relationships between anatomical and psychological phenomena. He attempted to correlate, for instance, investigations in neurophysiology, such as the work of Marshall Hall (1790–1857) on the reflex function of the medulla oblongata and the medulla spinalis, with the theories of psychological philosophers, in particular those of Johann Herbart (1776–1841). Hall had shown that motor activity is not always connected with consciousness and does not necessarily depend solely on the higher cerebral centers; Herbart, the philosopher who tried to express his philosophy in mathematics and who thus appealed to the materialistic disposition of Griesinger, maintained that behavior was not always consciously determined.

Griesinger felt that his mission was to free German psychiatry from the speculation of the Romantics. He realized that Romantic poetical speculations about insanity only produced confusion and wished to propound instead a positive approach to the etiology of mental illness. Concrete demonstrations that some mental derangements had organic causes had been made by A. L. J. Bayle (1799–1858) and J. L. Calmiel (1798–1895), who had found pathological lesions in the brain of psychotic individuals suffering from general paresis of the brain. (At that time syphilis was not yet known to be the causative agent.) Also, it had been proved that a lack of iodine could lead to hypothyroidism, cretinism, and imbecility. Griesinger's view was, therefore, that "the first step towards the knowledge of the symptoms [of insanity] is their locality: to which organ do the indications belong: what organ must necessarily and invariably be diseased where there is madness? . . . Physiological and pathological facts show us that this organ can only be the brain; we, therefore, primarily, and in every case of mental disease, recognize a morbid action of that organ."[1] Griesinger maintained this organic position even though anatomical changes in the brain had not been demonstrated in all types of insanity; he stated, ". . . although in many cases this [brain damage] cannot be ocularly demonstrated by pathological anatomy, still on physiological grounds it is universally admitted."[2] Griesinger claimed that all mental diseases should be seen as due to direct or indirect action upon cerebral cells without differentiating functional from organic psychoses, as has been done in recent times. However, his descriptions of maladaptive personality functions in cases of brain damage are valid even today.

To say that Griesinger's psychiatry was "psychiatry without psychology"[3] may somewhat oversimplify the case. Nevertheless, without question he was influential in dissipating the widespread interest in dynamic psychology evidenced in the work of the Romantic psychologists of the first half of the nineteenth century.

On the other hand, he dealt with a concept of an ego and referred to the role of repression in mental illness. "When, however, the old 'I' [ego] is vitiated, corrupted, and falsified on all sides by the morbid false ideas—when, besides, the group of perceptions of the former 'I' is so completely repressed* that, without any trace of emotion the patient has exchanged his whole personality and has scarcely any remembrance of it, then recovery is next to impossible, and only occurs in rare cases through excitation of violent emotion and thereby through a kind of mechanical training. . . ."[4] In his remarks about dreams Griesinger accurately noted the connection between mental symptoms and the dream processes.† He understood that

---

* "Repressed," the equivalent of the word *"Verdrängung,"* was used by Griesinger, probably borrowed from Herbart.
† Moreau de Tours had pointed out earlier the affinity between dreaming and mental disturbance.

wish fulfillment was basic to both mental symptoms and dreams. "To the individual who is distressed by bodily and mental troubles, the dream realizes what reality has refused—happiness and fortune. . . . So also in mental disease, from the dark background of morbid painful emotion, by sinking into a still deeper state of dreaming, the *repressed* contending ideas and sentiments, bright ideas of fortune, greatness, eminence, riches, et cetera; stand out. . . . He who has suffered loss of fortune imagines himself rich, the disappointed maiden is happy in the thought that she is tenderly loved by a faithful lover. A number of other phenomena of dreaming present an evident analogy to insanity."[5]

About some areas of psychology Griesinger had an almost premonitory understanding. He recognized that the individual's problem in mental illness was closely correlated to his loss of self-esteem and his "estrangement to himself" and that consequently physicians had to know in detail what the patient's prepsychotic personality was like in order to understand the illness. He was aware that intense internal tensions may result from seemingly surface problems. "When the individual has made certain things indispensable to his life, and when these are forcibly withdrawn, the passage of the ideas into efforts is cut off and accordingly a gap in the ego and a violent internal strife result."[6] Griesinger discussed the importance of strong affects in the case of a patient who felt guilty over his impulse to masturbate. The patient's feelings of "repentance" directly conflicted with his wish to satisfy his sexual impulses, and Griesinger remarked that the guilt was "by far more important than its direct physical effect."[7]

Griesinger's therapeutic approach was marked by his opposition to any inhumane measure, including bleeding, purgatives, emetics, and restraint, except to prevent the patient "from inflicting injury to himself or others."[8] He believed that sedative baths and narcotics alleviated excited states, that occupational activity was often instrumental to a patient's recovery, and "that cerebral activity may be modified quite effectually, directly, and immediately by the evocation of frames of mind, emotions and thoughts."[9] This statement should not be misconstrued as meaning that Griesinger had doubts about his basic tenet, namely, that cerebral pathophysiological mechanisms were solely responsible for mental illness. Nonetheless he attempted to correlate psychological with physical treatment. He explicitly stated that both the psychic and somatic methods of treatment are entitled to the same amount of attention. "Both methods of acting upon the patient have always instinctively been combined, and the most narrowminded moralistic theory cannot possibly dispute the efficacy of properly directed medicaments, baths, et cetera; while, at the same time, everyday experience has shown that almost no recovery can be perfected without psychical remedies (which may only consist of work, discipline, et cetera). . . . In spite, however, of the practical utility of this method, theoretical hypotheses have rendered it difficult for science to recognize the results of experience—the call for an undelayed combination of mental and physical remedies in mental disease on the ground of its necessity."[10] Griesinger recognized that the psychiatrist who is treating a psychotic patient must strengthen the formerly healthy integrative functions of his personality. "The old ego which in insanity for a long time is not lost, but only superficially repressed, or hidden in a storm of emotion, behind which it remains for a long time capable and ready to re-establish itself, must, as far as possible, be recalled and strengthened."[11]

Griesinger felt that therapy should fit the needs of each particular patient, but he disagreed with Rush and Reil by refusing to attempt cures for delusion by means of argument or gimmicks. He wrote, "Conversations, lectures, walks, games, tea parties, et cetera, also serve to engross and amuse the patient. These are to be regulated as much as possible to suit the different dispositions."[12]

Perhaps Griesinger's most important service to psychiatry was not in profound psychological theories but in vitalizing the hope that medical psychology would eventually become a sound medical discipline, so that psychiatry could walk hand in hand with other medical specialties as a proud equal, no longer to hide its head as a stepchild of medicine.

Henry Maudsley (1835–1918), an English psychiatrist, believed, like Griesinger, that insanity is fundamentally a bodily disease, and he had even less use for Romantic metaphysical speculations about mental illness. He maintained that character is determined primarily by the structure of the brain, yet he was not a pure materialist inasmuch as he considered physiological laws as manifestations of the "will of God." Maudsley was as highly regarded in England as Griesinger in Germany, and his *The Physiology and Pathology of the Mind* (1867) has been called a "turning point in English psychiatry."[13] Although Maudsley emphasized the importance for the psychiatrist to study the patient's life history, he rejected introspection and belongs, with Griesinger, to the same antipsychological period that was a reaction against the speculative excesses of the Romantic era.

In the latter part of the nineteenth century medical science was devoted in intensive study of pathological anatomy and biochemical investigations carried on by men of great acumen. If a physician was not actually a clinician, he had at least to be a serious student of the laboratory. No longer did he walk with a gold-headed cane and speak in weird, high-flown Latin phrases; gone were his red cape and wig. He spoke the language of his countrymen and he was respected for his knowledge and his dedication to his science. Travel and communication had improved to the point where scientists throughout the world were able to be in almost immediate contact with one another, and journals were being published that described experiments in all medical specialties. By the end of the nineteenth century it had become obvious that a nation's economic and political future depended upon its progress in science; consequently scientific investigation was not only encouraged but also subsidized by powerful nations vying for supremacy.

A representative of the new type of laboratory physician was Eduard Hitzig (1838–1907), one of Wilhelm Griesinger's most brilliant students. He collaborated, during the 1860's, with another physician, Theodor Fritsch (1838–1897), on the electrical stimulation of the brains of dogs. Their work was based on Fritsch's discovery, made while he was caring for brain wounds suffered by soldiers in the Prussian-Danish War in 1864, that stimulation on one side of the brain made parts of the body on the opposite side twitch. A paper they published in 1870 describing the "electrical excitability" of the brain launched experimental neurophysiology. The attempt to localize cerebral functions had, of course, begun with the work of Franz Gall and Spurzheim; in addition, in the early part of the century Pierre Flourens (1794–1867) and Luigi Rolando (1773–1831) had demonstrated, by excising parts of the brains of animals to see what symptoms developed, that the cerebellum is one part of the brain necessary for coordination of movement. Flourens had established the concept of excitability of the cortex; Fritsch's and Hitzig's work roughly localized the motor area of the brain cortex, and their method of stimulating the brain with electricity opened the way to more advanced studies of cerebral localization. Jean Baptiste Buillaud (1796–1881), in studying inflammations of the brain, had deduced that the temporal lobe contained the areas for speech; the precise speech area was outlined by Paul Broca (1824–1880). Other researchers working in this field in the 1870's and 1880's were David Ferrier (1843–1928) and Victor Horsley (1857–1916).* However, it must be borne in mind that knowledge of brain anatomy does not in itself lead to an understanding of psychological processes.

In addition to the research in cerebral localization, studies of the cellular architecture of the brain were being made that led to increased knowledge of the interconnections between nerve cells in the central nervous system. In 1850 Augustus Waller (1816–1870) showed that a cut nerve degenerates if it has been disconnected from its cell body, but a cut portion that remains attached to the cell body does not die. He thus showed that the cell itself nourishes its fibers. New methods of staining cell bodies and the sheaths of fibrils led, in 1891, to the concept of the neuron—the structural and functional unit of nervous tissue—by Heinrich von Waldeyer (1836–1921). The function of protoplasmic extensions from the cell body, called dendrites, was identified as bringing impulses to the cell body; another kind of protoplasmic extension, the axon, transmits the impulse away from the cell body. A formidable controversy then arose in the last years of the

* Further understanding of localization of cerebral functions in recent times had been advanced by Harvey Cushing (1869–1939), Egaz Moniz (1874–1955), C. S. Sherrington (1857–1952), Sir Henry Head (1861–1940), Wilder Penfield and others.

nineteenth century as to whether or not the neurons were continuous—joined together in a reticular network. One of the most eminent neuro-microscopists of the time, Camillo Golgi (1844–1926), supported the reticular hypothesis, but the work of Santiago Ramón y Cajal (1852–1934) established definitively that each neuron is separate from other neurons. Golgi and Ramón y Cajal shared in the Nobel Prize in 1906, at which time Golgi went down fighting to the bitter end still upholding the reticular theory. The manner in which an impulse is communicated from one neuron to the next is still the subject of research.

As these neurological and neurophysiological data accumulated, clinicians attempted to interpret them; and although emotional states could not be localized either in areas of the brain or in the brain's histological structure, physicians continued to try to link psychiatry with neurophysiology. A Russian physiologist, Ivan M. Sechenov (1825–1905), who is referred to as the father of Russian physiology, claimed, for example, in *The Reflexes of the Brain,* that psychic activity depends entirely on an external stimulus. "All psychic acts which occur along reflex lines must be studied entirely physiologically because their beginning, the sensory stimulus, and their end, the motor actions are physiological phenomena. Moreover, even the middle, or psychic, element is also strictly speaking often, if not always, not an independent phenomenon—as was formerly believed—but an integral part of this whole process."[14] Sechenov considered that the body operated like a machine, with the nervous system its central regulator.

Ivan Petrovich Pavlov (1849–1936) owed his scientific approach to Sechenov and was indebted to Darwin for his philosophical position. Pavlov was born in Riazan, the son of a priest, and first prepared himself also for the priesthood by attending a seminary; at the age of twenty-one, however, he decided to study medicine and spent some years in Germany, where he devoted himself to the study of physiology. For his experimental work on the digestive glands he received the Nobel Prize in 1904. Despite the fact that he opposed Lenin, the socialist regime recognized the value of his experimental work and supported his researches. Later in his life his political viewpoint changed and he entered into harmonious relationship with the government.

Behavioral psychologists, not only in Russia but also in the United States, base many of their theories on the Pavlovian concept of "conditioned reflexes." These are primitive patterns of reaction to a simple stimulus, which are acquired by repetitive learning. For example, when food is given to an animal, it salivates; this is an unconditioned reflex. If a bell is sounded simultaneously whenever food is given to the animal, eventually the animal will salivate at the sound of the bell alone, without any administration of food. This is a conditioned reflex: the animal has learned to connect the sound of the bell with being fed and hence reacts to the bell as it does to food. Even the most complex of the higher cerebral processes, according to Pavlov, are elaborations of simple conditioned reflexes, and he did many studies on the way in which these conditioned reflexes could be inhibited or enhanced. He was a brilliant experimentalist who worked as he lived—compulsively. For example, he always ate, drank, slept, and went on vacations at precisely the same time. Pavlov's meticulousness manifested itself also in exacting precise experimentation. Like Jackson, and later even Freud, he considered that higher processes inhibit "lower" brain functions. Thinking requires inhibition of immediate action. The complex thought processes preceding action must be carried out before action takes place, hence the inhibiting effect of the higher centers.

Pavlov's theories eventually led him to a mechanistic concept of behavior and to a classification of personality types based on how individuals handle irritating stimuli. Some, for example, react by becoming melancholics. Others are choleric, with "both strong excitatory and inhibitory tendencies, but the former are predominant."[15] "Phlegmatic" individuals have reflex activities that are relatively "rigid," and the "sanguine" type have particularly labile nervous systems. It is obvious that what we have here are Hippocratic personality types reincarnated in the framework of mechanistic reflexology. Pavlov explained conflicts in terms of neuronal arrangements that have been either overexcited or inhibited, an explanation that did nothing to bridge the gap between neuronal interconnections and psychological conflicts.

Vladimir Bekhterev (1857–1927), director of the Psychophysiological Laboratory at Kazan and founder, in 1907, of the Psychoneurologic Institute in Leningrad, was also highly influenced by Pavlov's theories and used them in his own work. Bekhterev's interests were broad, since he had studied in the psychophysiological laboratory of Wundt in Leipzig, and hypnosis with Charcot; in his own laboratory he examined physiological phenomena associated with hypnosis and even experimented with psychosurgery.

As the century wore on clinicians in Germany continued to try to do the impossible: convert medical psychology into brain psychiatry. Karl Westphal (1833–1890), a former associate of Bekhterev, more than any other German psychiatrist of the period was interested in neuroses and wrote about obsessional conditions, sexual pathology, and phobias. However, his major preoccupations were with microscopic pathology of the brain and with neurological syndromes and signs; with Wilhelm Erb (1840–1921) he discovered that the knee-jerk reflex is absent in syphilis of the spinal cord. Erb himself is known for other contributions, especially descriptions of those neurological diseases connected with muscular dystrophy. He did work on pathology of the peripheral nerves, the spinal cord, and the brain stem, and he also developed a treatment procedure, widely used in Germany, of applying low-grade galvanic and faradic currents to patients' muscles. At this time neurotic patients were being treated by neurologists in Germany, and Freud himself in his early neurological practice utilized the electric therapies of Erb, only to find them grossly ineffective and lacking any sound foundations. Freud realized that the electric-current therapy was only a form of covert suggestion and had no lasting therapeutic effect. It was because of his disappointment in these types of hit-or-miss therapies that he first began experimenting with hypnosis.

Theodore Meynert (1833–1892), a Viennese neurologist and one of the leading European histopathological investigators, identified many of the structures lying deep within the brain substance. Meynert considered that each stimulus that reached the central nervous system excited a corresponding area in the cortex of the brain. He demonstrated some pathways —association tracts—by which cortical cells communicate with one another and with deeper cells of the cerebrum, and he surmised correctly that the cells lying deeper in the brain are products of earlier phylogenetic development. Meynert was convinced that inadequate blood circulation of the brain led to states of excitement and that overflow of blood into the cerebral vessels produced depressions. (It was this sort of unsubstantiated reasoning that later was called by its critics "brain mythology.") Meynert proposed a systematic classification of mental illness based on his histopathological studies. His belief that hysteria could not exist in males indicates his thinking on neurotic disorders. Like his predecessors Cullen and Rush, his treatment measures were aimed at modifying the conditions of cerebral vessels by the use of various drugs.

Carl Wernicke (1848–1905), like his teacher, Meynert, believed that all mental diseases were caused by brain pathology. Wernicke won an international medical reputation with his book on aphasia (1874)—loss or impairment of the faculty to use language in any of its forms—and by his demonstration that one hemisphere of the brain is dominant. Wernicke also discovered that patients with organic brain damage lacked memory of recent events, whereas they retained memory of events long gone by, a point that has important diagnostic value since it helps to differentiate psychoses caused by diseases of the brain from functional psychoses. Wernicke, like other neurologists of his day, equated analysis of emotional disorders with descriptions of neurological conditions, therefore he studied psychotic conditions caused by fever and toxic agents such as morphine and alcohol. In the early nineteenth century Thomas Sutton (1767–1835) had described an alcoholic psychosis associated with delirium tremens, and Korsakov later (1887) described another common symptom of chronic alcoholism, a marked disorientation caused by patients filling in their memory gaps with confabulations. Wernicke's contribution was the discovery that some chronic alcoholics developed a disturbance of vision along with a clouding of consciousness. In addition to toxic psychosis, another group of mental disturbances—diseases resulting from senile deterioration of the brain tissue—sustained the hope that psychiatrists might be able to explain emotional phenomena from histological and gross anatomical lesions of the nervous system. States of dementia occurring in senile individuals had been well described by Esquirol, and by the end of the nineteenth century the brains of demented senile people had been carefully examined with histological methods, and definite lesions had been demonstrated. Alois Alzheimer (1864–1915) and Arnold Pick (1851–1924) found similar histological conditions in certain prematurely senile patients.

Perhaps the one disease under investigation during the nineteenth century and the early part of the twentieth century that most inspired neurologically minded psychiatrists was syphilis. The French physicians Bayle and Calmeil had clinically described general paresis—syphilis of the brain—and identified it as a disease entity, although they were unable to prove its etiology. Baillarger, Romberg, and Westphal established the clinical difference between a syphilitic infection of the spinal column and infection of the brain. In 1905 Fritz Schaudinn (1871–1906) discovered the infectious agent, a spirochete, in primary genital lesions. August von Wassermann (1866–1925) developed a blood test in 1906 to which patients who had syphilis usually reacted positively. In 1913 the *spirocheta pallida* organism was at last demonstrated in the brains of patients suffering from general paresis through the work of Hideyo Noguchi (1876–1928) and J. W. Moore. As for treatment, in 1910 Paul Ehrlich (1854–1915), after testing 606 different arsenic compounds, developed the preparation Salvarsan (arsphenamine) for the treatment of syphilis of the nervous system. Just prior to World War I Julius von Wagner-Jauregg (1857–1940), who had noted that there was a remission of symptoms when patients with syphilis were suffering from intercurrent infections, began using the malarial-fever treatment, for which innovation he received the Nobel Prize (1927) and was the only psychiatrist so honored. Not until the mid-twentieth century did Alexander Fleming (1881–1955) discover a definite chemotherapeutic agent—penicillin—that cured. At long last a psychosis—clinically demonstrable—could be thoroughly understood in terms of organ pathology and treated with a drug.

Neurologists were in the ascendancy in the United States as well as in Europe during the late nineteenth century. Silas Weir Mitchell (1829–1914), a renowned neurologist who worked as a surgeon in the Civil War, was exceedingly critical of psychological research that was not grounded in the discipline of neurology. He considered bed rest, good nutrition, comfort, and absence from occupational pressures "curative"—as had been prescribed, for that matter, by the priests in the temples of Aesculapius—and his "rest cure," like Erb's electrotherapy, became a fashionable method of treating mental disturbances.

In England the leading neurologist was John Hughlings Jackson (1835–

1911). Jackson focused his attention on epilepsy and explained many of its fundamental manifestations. Probably his interest in this malady was first aroused by the fact that his wife suffered from seizures of a localized nature (later they were to be called "Jacksonian"), although he went on to investigate generalized seizures also. Jackson derived his point of view from a physician, Thomas Laycock (1812–1876), under whom he had worked at York and from a philosopher, Herbert Spencer (1820–1903). Spencer and Laycock, a few years before Darwin's *Origin of Species,* had conceived of an evolutionary organization of the brain. (The phrase "survival of the fittest" was actually Spencer's.) Spencer thought that the nervous system could be understood in terms of evolution. "If creatures of the most elevated kinds have reached those highly integrated, very definite and extremely heterogeneous organizations they possess, through modification upon modification accumulated during an immeasurable past, if the developed nervous system of such creatures have gained a complex structure and functions little by little; then necessarily, the involved forms of consciousness which are the correlates of these complex structures and functions, must also have arisen by degrees."[16] Laycock had written a book, *Mind and Brain,* in which he also espoused the concept of evolution. Jackson's contribution was to show explicitly how evolution had occurred in the structure of the nervous system. He found that the lowest levels of the brain and spinal cord effect the simple, stereotypic movements and are the oldest in evolutionary time. The middle level—the region of the cerebrum that controls motor activities—he considered to be next oldest on the evolutionary scale. And the front part of the brain, or frontal lobe, which is the most complex and most involved in abstract and symbolic thinking and in discrimination, is the last to have evolved. The highest centers of the brain, as the last to be organized, are usually the first to be affected by disease and external agents; these higher cerebral mechanisms also inhibit the more primitive actions of the lower centers, and when they are disturbed there is a release of the more archaic behavioral patterns. This fact explains why toxic agents are able to precipitate acute regressed behavior. Alcohol is most toxic to the most recently evolved, highest areas of brain structure: when these are disturbed they fail to inhibit lower-brain activity. Jackson thought that each of the levels depended on the reflex arc and that the superior one inhibits the inferior reflex arc. In this sense Jackson's views correlate with those of Pavlov, who considered the lowest level of activity to be affected by the unconditioned reflex, the middle level by the conditioned reflex, and the highest level by thinking in symbols.

Jackson's deductions from his clinical work were tested experimentally by Charles Scott Sherrington (1857–1952). Sherrington actually did dissect out the higher levels of an animal's brain from its spinal cord and verified that then the spinal cord did become more excitable, which proved Jackson's idea about the inhibitory function of the higher centers. Sherrington also demonstrated the ways in which reflexes were integrated from the highest to the lowest level. His book *The Integrative Action of the Nervous System* (1906) synthesized concepts from neurophysiology, evolution, and clinical neurology.

Neurologists were grouping neurological symptoms into syndromes and finally into diseases; neuropathologists were localizing the lesions to explain these clinical phenomena; and duly impressed neuropsychiatrists began to apply similar principles to behavior. Some neurological diseases could be differentiated by clinical observation alone, even without the benefit of pathological investigation. Why should it not be possible, then, to systematize mental symptoms on a clinical basis in a similar manner? The brain and its appendage, the spinal column, were a rich source of new knowledge, and it appeared obvious that when their diseases were properly identified the reasons for abnormal behavior could then be categorized, and later, neuropathological confirmation of disease entities would be forthcoming. The symptoms of disordered behavior and confused thinking could be labeled and eventually linked not to philosophical vagaries disguised as psychology but to "real" medical knowledge of the pathways of the nervous system. Thus the medical and neurological advancements of the nineteenth century enticed students of behavior into the description, systematization, and classification of mental diseases.

We have noted how the trend of the Enlightenment to describe mental syndromes affected the followers of Pinel and Esquirol in the first half of the nineteenth century. Precise clinical descriptions were given for hallucinations, cyclic insanity, monomania, idiocy, and hypnagogic and alcoholic hallucinations.

The next step toward a psychiatric nosology was made in Germany with the work of Karl Kahlbaum (1828–1899), who believed that all symptoms could be organized into groups and took as his model the symptoms of general paresis. Kahlbaum introduced new terms, some of which still persist: "symptom complex," "cyclothymia" (alternating moods of depression and joyfulness), and "catatonia" (a clinical label for a psychotic individual who maintains rigid, peculiar postures and is mute).

Ewald Hecker (1843–1909), one of Kahlbaum's students, in 1871 contributed a description of a psychosis in which the individual displays inappropriate, silly mannerisms and extremely regressed behavior; he called this state "hebephrenia." Hebephrenic patients often appear to have deteriorated mentally.

This question of mental deterioration was one that intrigued nineteenth-century brain psychiatrists. On the assumption that a patient who was deteriorated must always have something amiss with his brain structure, they concluded that deterioration was related to degeneracy. The French naturalist Jean Baptiste Lamarck (1744–1829) had proposed in *Philosophie zoologique* (1809) that a change in function of an organ transforms its structure and that this changed configuration is transmitted to the next generation. His idea appealed to many neuropsychiatrists, who believed that individuals inherited their behavioral deterioration from parents. Benedict Augustin Morel (1809–1873), an Austrian pupil of Falret, was a close friend of the great French physiologist Claude Bernard, and was most impressed by the works of Darwin. Early in his career Morel proposed that there was too much emphasis on the organic aspect of mental illness and suggested that physicians study the emotional life of the parents. The spirit of the times, however, toward the organic approach and the evolutionary concepts of Darwin swayed Morel: "Degenerations are deviations from the normal human type, which are transmissible by heredity and which deteriorate progressively towards extinction."[17] Morel believed that external agents like alcohol or narcotics could predispose an individual to degeneration, and that so could a bad temperament. One generation might be simply nervous, for example; the next generation would be more nervous; the third might be entirely psychotic; the fourth generation would exhibit a full-blown degenerate state; and any future generations would be so demented that the family would become extinct.

In 1850 Morel observed deteriorated individuals similar to those that Kahlbaum and Hecker had described, but their case histories revealed that their illnesses had begun in adolescence. Morel concluded that they were suffering from a hereditary disease that invariably led to deterioration and that appeared first in the adolescent years. He called this condition "*Démence précoce*" and regarded it as a premature form of dementia; his term was later used to describe the clinical picture of dementia praecox. Another Frenchman, Valentin Magnan (1835–1916), extended this concept of degeneration by applying the description not only to individuals suffering from psychosis but also to neurotics.

The enthusiasm for the concept of degeneracy naturally led to interest in criminals. An English psychiatrist, James Prichard (1786–1848), had come to view asocial activity as a form of insanity and distinguished this particular kind of madness from that seen in mental hospitals; but Cesare Lombroso (1836–1909), an Italian anthropologist, was most responsible for the idea that criminals represent a degenerate biological phenomenon. Lombroso's theory that criminal types can be identified on the basis of physiognomy and that they are a form of inferior men has been discredited. To label the insane, the criminal, or the mentally retarded as "degenerates" blocks any approach to understanding or improvement.

The neurological emphasis on clinical observation eventually produced so much data that classification and generalization of the many ways of describing mental illness became imperative. The man whose training, personality, and dedication were right for this ambitious enterprise was on the scene—Emil Kraepelin (1856–1926).

Kraepelin was born in Neustrelitz, a rustic and serene village near the

Baltic Sea. He learned early to respect authority, order, and organization. After he assumed the directorship of a hospital and clinic there was never a question of who was the man in charge. "Imperial German psychiatry" was said to have gained its prominence under the "chancellorship" of Kraepelin, one of Bismarck's admirers.

Emil's father, an actor, supported his studious elder son, Karl, in his desire to become a teacher of the biological sciences. Karl's influence on his younger brother was evident when young Emil decided to become not only a doctor, but an academician. Emil, at twenty-eight, became chief of the mental hospital staff of Leubus.

Even before Kraepelin's graduation from the Würzburg Medical School in 1878 he was interested in the medical aspects of psychiatry. He spent the summer of 1876 in Leipzig studying under Wilhelm Max Wundt (1832–1920), a famous physiological psychologist, and shortly afterward he wrote a treatise on "The Influence of the Acute Diseases on the Origin of Mental Diseases." After graduation Kraepelin studied in Munich under the neuroanatomist Bernhard von Gudden (1824–1886) for four years and then continued his neuropathological studies in Leipzig under P. E. Flechsig (1847–1929), a famous neuroanatomist who frequently conducted autopsies on patients who had died from organic brain diseases. After a short time Kraepelin returned to experimental psychopharmacological and psychophysiological research under Wundt and was so impressed by the actions of drugs on the brain that he decided that neurophysiological research was his true calling. On the advice of Wundt and Erb, however, Kraepelin returned to clinical psychiatry and for a number of years taught at Dorpat and then Heidelberg. Finally, in 1903, Kraepelin was appointed professor of clinical psychiatry at Munich, where he spent the next nineteen years; in 1922 he retired from teaching to take a position as head of the Research Institute of Psychiatry in Munich.

Kraepelin's inclinations toward an organic approach to mental illness were encouraged by his teachers and associates, his reading of Griesinger, and his great curiosity about concrete facts. He remained continously a student of the behavioral disorders of his hospitalized patients. Kraepelin spent his years tirelessly and meticulously gathering thousands of case histories, from which he evolved a system of descriptive psychiatry that is still used to classify patients on the basis of manifest behavior. In this he continued a tradition begun by the ancient physician Aretaeus in the first century A.D. In essence Kraepelin concurred with Morel's concept of psychosis in adolescents, namely, that if an adolescent develops hallucinations and delusions and behaves in a bizarre manner and tends to get worse, he suffers from dementia praecox. Kraepelin went on to utilize the concepts of Kahlbaum and Hecker in his classification of this illness: If the patient is mute at times and violent at other times, he has catatonic dementia praecox (utilizing Kahlbaum's term "catatonia"); if he is silly and inappropriate in his verbal and behavioral responses, he is hebe-phrenic, as Hecker had suggested. If an individual has delusions of persecution, he has paranoia,* originally considered a separate illness but later included as a subvariety of dementia praecox.

Kraepelin differentiated dementia praecox from manic-depressive psychosis on the basis of prognosis. He believed that a patient rarely recovers from dementia praecox, whereas a patient may recover completely from manic-depressive psychosis, in which there are severe depressions alternating with periods of excitation as well as periods of relative normality. Kraepelin's stress on the morbid outcome of dementia praecox led to a fatalistic compliance with a predestined course. Once the label dementia praecox had been affixed to a person he became a case number awaiting the ultimate fate of deterioration. Custodial care, even though it was humane, did not change the nihilistic attitude of the staff caring for the unfortunate victim.

From the vantage point of our present dynamic era in psychiatry Kraepelin's monumental contributions require a reevaluation. There can be no doubt, however, that he succeeded in bringing into a chaotic accumulation of clinical observation a system of distinct disease entities that has stood up remarkably well into the present era. Unfortunately his systematization eventually hindered the deeper understanding of mental disturbances. What once in the past meant progress, when compared with subsequent developments, often serves as a retarding influence. The propensity of the human mind to adhere rigidly to knowledge arduously achieved in the past often interferes with further advancements.

The change in the evaluation of Kraepelin's work is one of the most striking examples of this historical sequence. He, whose authority ruled supreme at the turn of the century and the following two decades, whose Lehrbuch† became the bible of modern psychiatry, today is looked upon by the younger generation of psychiatrists as a rigid and sterile codifier of disease categories; even if these were valid, they contribute to neither understanding the causes of diseases nor their prognosis. His work is the culmination of that antipsychological era that began with Griesinger's influence and continued to dominate the scene until Freud's dynamic motivational approach revived interest in the patient as a unique person with a unique history. This interest, which the Romantic psychiatrist of the early nineteenth century initiated, went into almost complete oblivion under the influence of the steadily advancing neurophysiological knowl-

---

* "Paranoia" ("deranged" + "noūs" mind) had been used in pre-Hippocratic times and by Hippocrates himself to indicate a general or primary form of insanity. Ernest Charles Laségue (1816–1863) in 1852 had spoken of a "délire de pérsecution," but it remained for Kraepelin to give the term its modern meaning of a psychosis with states of extreme suspiciousness.

† The Lehrbuch was first published in 1883 and went through nine editions until 1927, when it came out in two volumes and 2500 pages.

edge. It became so thoroughly submerged that Freud was unaware of the fact that his basic orientation was anticipated fifty years before. The tenet that neurophysiological and psychological knowledge need not be contradictory, and that neither of them can substitute for the other in the fullest understanding of personality is still debated in our time. That the understanding and cure of mental disturbances require knowledge of the structure and functioning of the brain as well as knowledge of its psychological manifestations is still not fully recognized by many contemporary psychiatrists, who continue to insist upon either an exclusively psychological or a purely physiological approach to mental illness. Kraepelin's work is the culmination of the neurophysiological approach. He regarded psychological manifestations of mental disease as nothing but a basis for classification. At the beginning of his career he thought heredity caused mental illness; later he assumed an underlying, although undemonstrable, disturbance of body metabolism.

Because of his organic bias and his inability to think in psychological (motivational) terms, it is only natural that Kraepelin was interested in toxic conditions such as alcoholism, in which the chemical causal factor is of outstanding and demonstrable significance. His whole theoretical orientation was such as to prevent him from recognizing that repeated emotional experiences may have an even more destructive, although more subtle, effect upon mental functioning than alcohol.

It is all well and good to evaluate the effect of the contributions of one of the leading figures in the history of psychiatric thought from the advantage of a present-day perspective, but we must not lose sight of the enormous impact that Kraepelinian psychiatry had in his own time. Like Pinel and Esquirol, he demonstrated repeatedly the importance of utilizing in psychiatry the medical approach of detailed observation, careful description, and precise organization of data. Without this orientation psychiatry could never have become a clinical, disciplined specialty of medicine.

Psychological Developments

Advances in psychology during the second half of the nineteenth century were made through philosophy and literature. Stendhal, Flaubert, Balzac, De Maupassant, Dostoevsky, Shaw, and Ibsen, by virtue of their creativity and intuition, were able to penetrate depths that psychiatrists like Griesinger or Kraepelin could never touch. The progress made by the philosopher-psychologists in defining man as a personality was less impressive, and their generalizations about human nature added little to the understanding of the motivations of real persons. Nevertheless Herbart, Lotze, Fechner, Herbert Spencer, Schopenhauer, and Nietzsche, among others, helped create an intellectual climate in which important psychological work was possible. A very strong influence on late-nineteenth-century psychology came from the natural sciences, the methods of which were adapted to increase knowledge about the physiological aspects of the field.

Finally, the approach of psychiatric clinicians who concerned themselves with behavior motivated by ideas that are not conscious brought to the field of psychiatry concepts that led to the use of hypnosis as a therapeutic device. This eventuated into forms of psychotherapy hitherto unknown.

Of all the philosopher-psychologists who influenced late-nineteenth-century thinking, Johann Herbart (1776–1841) did the most toward developing psychology into a separate, empirical discipline. Herbart related psychological phenomena to the organism as a whole, spoke of energy levels of sensation, and explained the phenomenon of consciousness in terms of the intensity of internal experience. He visualized a threshold of consciousness beneath which psychological processes are not perceived, but take place "unconsciously." Herbart called conscious mental content "apperception." Below the threshold of consciousness ideas compete with each other for apperceptive attention, until one—the strongest—is victorious and becomes conscious. Herbart thus introduced a quantitative factor into mental processes.*

The impact that philosophy had upon empirical psychology is very clear in the "faculty" psychology of Friedrich Eduard Beneke. Beneke meant by "faculties" those "greater possibilities," or "powers of the soul," that differentiate human beings from animals. These faculties are similar to but not identical with what we now call ego functions.†

Gustav Theodor Fechner (1801–1887) was the first psychologist to tackle the crucial problem of the relationship between an external, physical stimulus and the resultant, subjectively experienced optical, acoustical, or tactile sensations. Fechner's work tied in with studies on sensation done earlier by Ernst Weber (1795–1878), a physiologist; the Weber-Fechner psychophysical law states that the intensity of a subjective sensation is proportional to the logarithm of the corresponding physical stimulus.‡ However, Fechner's main historical significance is not that he formulated this law but that he introduced the experimental method into the study of psychological phenomena, something that had previously been considered impossible. With his psychophysical experimentations he became a pioneer in converting psychology into a natural science.

In his metaphysical cosmological speculations Fechner is still the product of the Romantic era. Yet even in his metaphysics he is clearer and

---

* Herbart's concept of apperception is closely related to Freud's division between preconscious and unconscious processes. According to Freud preconscious content becomes conscious when the focus of attention is turned on it.

† Ego functions are discussed in the section on "Recent Developments."

‡ If added to a larger stimulus, a given stimulus is less perceptible than if added to a smaller one. Sensation increases in arithmetic progression, whereas the stimulus varies by geometric progression. The difference in light perception between ten and eleven candles is the same as between one hundred and one hundred and ten candle-power.

more consistent that his predecessors. For him the universe is a cosmic unity and the differentiation between organic and inorganic is not an essential demarcation line. Organization is the essence of life, but organization is present in the whole universe. Rather than trying to explain the emergence of organic matter from the inorganic, which is the traditional approach, he maintained that inorganic matter can be considered the result of the disorganization of previously organized systems. Psychological processes are characteristic of fully organized matter. In stressing organization as the basic attribute of life, he anticipated Claude Bernard's homeostatic principle. Freud in his *"law of stability,"* according to which the living organism attempts to maintain a stable state of organization, adopted Fechner's view and proclaimed that to maintain stable conditions within the mental apparatus is the most fundamental function of the ego.

Fechner's experimental approach inspired a number of physiologists and psychologists to the extent that a new field, physiological psychology, developed. Fechner sought to establish the relationship between the physical sensory stimulus and the resultant psychological sensation; the psychophysiologists who followed him focused on the intermediary connecting links between sensory stimulus and sensory perception—that is, the neurophysiological processes that conduct the sensory stimulus from the peripheral sense organ to the higher centers of the brain, where the optical, acoustic, tactile, or olfactory perceptions take place.

Rudolf Hermann Lotze (1817–1881), perhaps the most influential philosopher-psychologist of his time, broke the total process of perception down into three steps: first, the physical stimulation of a sensory organ; second, the conduction of this stimulus to the higher sensory brain centers; and third, the subjective sensation of light, color, smell, touch, or sound. How the physiological process in the brain centers is transformed into these subjective sensations remained an unsolved question. Lotze's main interest was in purely psychological phenomena—impulse, desire, volition, and memory—and he sharply distinguished these from physiological and physical events. However, some inklings of a biological and dynamic point of view do appear in his writings; for instance, he considered that subjective sensations like hunger and pain serve the organism because they mobilize it for necessary action. Yet Lotze's psychology was still far from being useful to understand the behavior of any individual person—normal or mentally diseased. It was equally far from connecting mental phenomena with the underlying physiological processes in the brain.

William James (1842–1910) went further toward dealing with the mind as an instrument of the organism. Although his orientation was biological, he did not attempt to explain the content of conscious mentation on the basis of physiological mechanisms. His psychological descriptions of the "stream of consciousness" with its nonfocused "fringes" are closer to reality than those of his German colleagues. His psychology, based on

careful introspection, is thoroughly empirical. At the same time, it is pronouncedly voluntaristic, inasmuch as he considered that mental processes
serve the interests of the living organism. Pragmatism well describes his
philosophical position.

James, who came from a highly intellectual family (his brother was the
novelist Henry James), earned a medical degree from Harvard but gradually moved from pure science into psychology and philosophy. However,
in his work in philosophy he always adhered to the scientific method of
careful empirical observation. He emphasized the highly personal nature of
thought processes, the ever-changing character of perceptions, which are
altered by the subjective state of the perceiving person. Mental contents do
not consist of disconnected static elements held together by associative
links. James believed them to be products of the organizing activity of the
mind, which creates a whole out of the elements. The organizing principle
is something dynamic. Behind the kaleidoscopic stream of thoughts there is
an ever-present purpose, or trend, which is adaptive; it is in the service of
the organism as a whole in its struggle to survive. Of particular interest is
James's concept that peripheral "overtones" and "fringes" are omnipresent
in the stream of thought; these consist of memories or previous experiences, unformulated intentions, and anticipations, and they direct the flow
of thought processes. James was one of the first in the modern period to
reemphasize the dynamic nature of psychological processes on the basis of
concrete introspective descriptions and not from abstractions. On the other
hand, his theory that an emotion is nothing but the subjective awareness of
physiological responses has generally been abandoned. He proposed, for
example, that anger is the awareness of increased heartbeat, changes in
respiration, and increased muscle tension (the James-Lange theory of emotion).

The voluntarist view of mental processes and personality—the notion
that instinctual needs, desires, and strivings are basic to all psychological
manifestations—is, as we have seen, deeply rooted in Western thought,
from Aristotle on. The most explicit emphasis upon volition as the basic
principle of human psychology came from two late Romantic philosophers,
Arthur Schopenhauer (1788–1860) and Friedrich Nietzsche (1844–
1900). Their ideas pervaded late-nineteenth-century society and counterbalanced the growing materialistic conception of the universe.

Schopenhauer's position was that man's most immediate knowledge
about the world is the fact that he who is a part of the world feels and
wills. He thus replaced Descartes's *cogito ergo sum* with a more dynamic
volo ergo sum—"I will, therefore I am." The fact that he feels and
strives—not that he thinks—is the most basic fact man knows. Schopenhauer also asserted that the intellect has no independent existence but is in
the service of the dynamic and irrational, or superrational, force that man
experiences as feeling and striving, which is called "will." Schopenhauer's

pessimism is derived from his recognition of will; its relentless, irrational striving, not enlightened reason and morality, is what governs the world. Under the influence of oriental philosophy, Schopenhauer came to the same doubtful solution as the Buddhists: that man should aim to rise above his dependence upon the irrational forces of volition. Through art, renunciation, and asceticism man can approach nirvana—the highest state of existence, free of striving and passions.

Nietzsche adopted the basic tenets of Schopenhauer's philosophy but came to different conclusions. He believed that instead of renouncing his irrational strivings man should cultivate will to power as the ultimate aim of life. He advocated the development of a superman who would realize all of mankind's potentialities by throwing off the restricting influence of Christian morality. Nietzsche's position, psychologically, shows more perception than Schopenhauer's because it takes into account the all-powerful influence of the irrational unconscious forces of the mind.

Both Schopenhauer and Nietzsche recognized that one limitation of natural science is that it offers no access to a most essential principle of life, the irrational nature of human existence. Neitzsche considered that modern science alienated man from his self, a view that was shared by the Danish theologian Søren Kierkegaard (1813–1855), the philosophic godfather of existentialism. Man's one-sided preoccupation with the exploration of the universe, Kierkegaard said, had made him lose contact with what is nearest to him—his own self; only a return to the original ideals of preinstitutionalized Christianity could give back to human existence the meaning that had been stripped from it by science.

The essence of the voluntarist view of the Romantic philosophers was not only this emphasis on irrational dynamic force underlying all psychological phenomena, but an extension of this universal directing force—that is, the will—to all phenomena of nature. Friedrich von Schelling (1775–1854) viewed the entire world as the creation of an all-pervading universal will. What man perceives consciously as volition is but a special case of a metaphysical universal force that forms the basis for all events in nature. Carus, a follower of Schelling, went so far as to state that all biological processes, even circulation and digestion, function according to an inherent psychological plan that basically is no different from the aims and goals that determine our conscious behavior.

This extension of the concept of will to all phenomena of nature carried with it of necessity the concept of the unconscious. Indeed the term "unconscious" was used by several authors as an alternative for the "universal will" of the natural philosophers. Carus called the directing regulative biological force the "unconscious" and differentiated three levels: the "general absolute unconscious," which is never accessible to the conscious mind; the "partial absolute unconscious," which is the directive force of all bodily processes; and the "relative unconscious," which refers to mental content that was once conscious and later became unconscious. Karl Eduard von Hartmann (1842–1906), a philosopher much influenced by Schopenhauer, contributed to this semantic shift from "will" to "unconscious mind" in his *Philosophy of the Unconscious* (1869), a book that includes a few notable examples of the existence of nonconscious mental processes. Hartmann's classification of unconscious processes is like Carus' —an absolute unconscious that is the essence of all natural phenomena in the universe, a physiological unconscious (identical with Carus' partial absolute unconscious), and finally the psychological unconscious that is the source of all behavioral patterns. Similar views were widespread among biologists. Perhaps the most articulate of these was Hans Driesch (1867– 1941), who attributed the purposeful structure and functioning of the living organism to an underlying vital force that is not conscious and is identical with the "animal spirits" of earlier thinkers.

Philosophers from Plato onward had cited the faculty of memory to demonstrate the fact that mental content is not necessarily always conscious. A memory of a past event may be recalled, but where has it been meanwhile? Obviously it has been present in a nonconscious form. This leads to the conclusion that awareness is an attribute of mental content but is not an essential. The great German physiologist Ewald Hering (1834– 1918) conceived of memory as a universal biological principle, the omnipresent characteristic of living matter; this concept of memory transcends psychological connotation . to include a postulated tendency of organic matter to recapitulate its past history. Hering's concept is based essentially on the biogenetic law of Ernst Haeckel (1834–1919), that ontogeny recapitulates phylogeny: embryological development from ovum to complex multicellular organism briefly recapitulates the developmental history of the species. Rudolph Semon adopted, expanded, and popularized Hering's philosophy and in the process gave memory, as a universal principle, a new name, "mneme."

None of these philosophical speculations about psychological and biological phenomena produced conclusions that could be validated by observation. Neither Schopenhauer's "will," Hartmann's "unconscious," Hering's "memory," nor Semon's "mneme" helped to explain observed morbid or normal psychological phenomena; however, they did strengthen the tendency to view psychological phenomena as aspects of a biological whole.

The late-nineteenth-century clinicians contributed far more specific ideas about unconscious phenomena than did the philosophers. Outstanding among them is the Frenchman Jean-Martin Charcot (1825–1893), the leading neurologist of his day. Charcot was a great observer for whom facts took priority over theories. If the facts demanded that theory be changed, Charcot did not hesitate. A native Parisian, he was educated at the Lycée Bonaparte and studied medicine at the University of Paris. One of his earliest papers, on chronic rheumatism, established him as a clinical investigator of exceptional talent. He was the first to call attention to the favorable effect of pregnancy on exophthalmic goiter (hyperthyroidism). Gradually his interest turned toward the degenerative diseases of the spinal cord and the nervous system; his studies on cerebral localization and on aphasia are classics.

Charcot was appointed physician-in-charge at the Salpêtrière in 1862, which then housed more than five thousand patients. As professor of clinical diseases of the nervous system at the Salpêtrière he became preoccupied with a large, heterogeneous group of patients who could not be put into any of the traditional clinical categories. Charcot classified this group as suffering from hysteria or neurosis; they included cases of hysterical seizures (his term for this was *"grande"* hysteria), hysterical paralyses, anesthesias (lack of sensation of touch), muscle spasms, certain choreas (diseases that produced uncontrollable movements in limbs), mutism, stuttering, intractable hiccuping, and astasia-abasia (an inability to stand straight and walk in a coordinated fashion). He also called those patients "hysteric" who suffered from mental anorexia (a malignant disturbance of the appetite), nervous disturbances of the stomach, and polyuria (frequent urination). His unbiased clinical observations on these hysterics helped to arouse interest in the role that psychological factors play in psychiatric disorders as well as in some chronic diseases. Although his work did have this effect, Charcot himself had only a limited interest in psychology and believed that hysteria was an organic disease of the nervous system.

Charcot's reputation as a neurologist was so firmly established that he could afford to turn his interest to the phenomenon of hypnosis, which was still in disrepute among most medical men. Charcot became convinced by his clinical observations that hysterical paralysis of the limbs was related to mental concepts, and he proved his point experimentally by producing paralyses in hysterical patients through hypnosis. These paralyses resembled in every detail those that he had seen occur after traumatic psychological experiences. He also succeeded in curing these experimentally induced symptoms by hypnotic suggestion. Furthermore, Charcot suspected the role of sexual impulses in the origin of hysterical symptoms.

Charcot's work on hysteria and hypnosis caused violent reactions among his contemporaries. Charcot had commented that "major hysterical" attacks occur in four distinct, consecutive phases. Hysterics had the opportunity to observe epileptic seizures, since hysterics and epileptics were housed together on the same ward. Charcot was criticized for not having taken malingering—which makes it difficult to estimate the genuineness of hysterical symptoms—into account. He was also accused of not knowing that suggestion plays a role in the development of hysterical phenomena, among them the so-called stigmata: the anesthesias of various parts of the body, particularly the throat; the reduction of the visual field, so-called tunnel vision; and other localized disturbances of the sensorium.

These criticisms were not fully justified. Pierre Marie (1853–1940), one of Charcot's collaborators and disciples, explained that the distinctness of the phases suggested that they were imitations of genuine epileptic attacks. Charcot himself said that malingering* is found in every phase of hysteria. "The patient voluntarily exaggerates real symptoms or even creates in every detail an imaginary symptomatology. Indeed, everyone is aware that the human need to tell lies, whether for no reason at all other than the practice of a sort of cult . . . or in order to create an impression, to arouse pity, etc., is a common event, and this is particularly true in hysteria."[18] And it is obviously erroneous to claim that Charcot did not recognize the role of suggestion in hysterical symptoms, particularly since he actually produced paralysis in hysterics by hypnotic suggestion and removed them later by countersuggestion.

Charcot did err, in a more fundamental aspect of hysteria, as became obvious in his controversy with Ambrose-August Liebeault (1823–1904) and Hippolyte-Marie Bernheim (1840–1919), both of the Nancy School in France. Charcot's basically organic orientation led him to conclude that the hysteric's suggestibility and hypnotizability were products of the same organic weakness of the nervous system that caused the hysteria. In fact, he actually equated hypnosis with hysteria. He insisted that only a hysteric can be hypnotized and that when he is under hypnosis his already weakened consciousness appears in pure form. Suggestion therefore was not the basis for hypnotic or hysterical phenomena; extreme suggestibility was nothing but the sign of an underlying weakness of the nervous system and indicated a lack of cohesive power. Liebeault and Bernheim, on the other hand, thought that suggestion and not an underlying organic illness was the main factor in hypnosis and maintained that many people who were not hysterics could be hypnotized. Bernheim, who was primarily a therapist, not a theoretician, explained both hysteria and hypnosis entirely on psychological grounds and unequivocally demonstrated by experiments with posthypnotic suggestion that unconscious mental content can influence behavior. Bernheim gave his hypnotized subjects commands to be carried out after awakening; when they awakened from their trances the subjects carried out these commands without remembering that the hypnotist had given these orders. Charcot's significance for the history of psychiatry lies not in his particular views about the nature of hysteria and hypnosis but in the fact that he made experimentation with hypnosis acceptable and thus paved the way for Freud's discoveries.

* In recent times, under the influence of Freudian psychology, the relationship of malingering to hysteria has been deemphasized. Rarely are hysterical symptoms the result of conscious purpose. Rather, the hysterical symptom has symbolic meaning of which the patient is unaware. The hysteric conveniently may imitate the symptom that he observes, not for the purpose of lying but as an expression or defense against expression of an unconscious wish. For example, a patient may have seen the paralysis of an arm due to a stroke; an unconscious wish to kill becomes then defended against by the development of the paralysis of his arm.

Another medical psychologist who studied under Charcot at the Salpêtri-ère and who became professor of psychiatry at the Collège de France, Pierre Janet (1859–1947), supported Charcot's theory that there was a weakness in the nervous system of the hysteric. Janet went further and proposed his own theory that this constitutional weakness contributed to inadequate psychological tension and an ensuing lack of psychic cohesive-ness. This psychic weakness, which he called psychasthenia, might follow excess fatigue or shock. Janet thus formulated the important theory that lack of integration (later considered an important ego function) results in aspects of consciousness becoming split off and resultant hysterical and dissociative phenomena. The latter referred to those processes that become separated from consciousness, causing the individual to behave as if he were completely motivated by these separate ideas—the consequence is the so-called double personality. Janet's theory, an innovation in psycho-pathology, did not include the concept of repression and thus did not concern itself with the significance of the dynamic unconscious. Freud pointed out in his autobiography that when Janet "had spoken of uncon-scious mental acts he meant nothing by the phrase—it had been no more than a *façon de parler*."[19]

Janet hypnotized many patients and discovered that under hypnosis they recalled traumatic memories that were related to the onset of their neurotic symptoms. He found that sometimes they recovered from their symptoms through the cathartic experience of relating the traumatic event. This dis-covery was also made—independently and earlier—by Josef Breuer (1842–1925), but Janet published his observations before Breuer. The consequent arguments about priority were bitter. Neither Janet nor Breuer was able to explain the recovery from symptomatology after hypnosis, since they fell back on organic explanations for the cause of neurotic symptoms.

The reawakened interest in psychology shortly before the turn of the century was by no means restricted to French psychiatry; it influenced work in England as well as Germany and reached the shores of America. Among the many men who began to write about man's emotional and instinctual life, three stand out: the German Richard von Krafft-Ebing (1840–1902), who described aberrations of the sexual drive in his *Psy-chopathia Sexualis* (1886); the Englishman Havelock Ellis (1859–1939), whose studies of sexuality in the framework of anthropology aroused great interest; and the Swiss Auguste Forel (1848–1931), whose book *The Sexual Problem* (1905) became a standard work in the field.

Naturalistic observations on sex inaugurated the belated admission that sexual phenomena had a place in medicine, although they were still con-sidered more a source of titillation that a serious scientific matter. Recogni-tion that sex is an integral part of man's daily existence and a powerful motivating force, pervading a great part of his strivings and activities, still belonged to the future. It was barely possible during these Victorian years to deal with the disturbed manifestations of the sex drive as medical or anthropological curiosities without going further into a discussion of normal adult sexuality.

The study of sexual phenomena was, however, only one offshoot of the general revival of interest in psychology. Among the great clinicians, P. J. Moebius (1853–1907) of Leipzig had a great influence because of his imaginative mind and literary ability. He, more than Charcot or Janet, believed in the psychological origin of hysterical symptoms. Moebius' interest transcended the field of medicine. His chief preoccupation was with creativity and artistic talent; he adopted the concept of the superior degenerate and considered himself to be one, and he wrote several pathographies of great men.

The Victorian denial of sexuality reinforced the age-old resistance of scientists against psychology. (Nothing demonstrates more clearly this ambivalence than the fact that Moebius, a great clinician endowed with outstanding perspicacity, was so fatalistic about psychology that he felt it offered no hope as a curative technique.) In order to avoid as much as possible facing the basic issue of sexual force, psychiatrists compromised by turning their interest toward exceptions: the psychopath, the pervert, and the degenerate genius; the comforting implication that could be derived from these studies was that what is true for these exceptions does not hold for ordinary, "normal" citizens.

This interest in exceptional psychological phenomena characterized the work of an American, Morton Prince (1854–1929), who wrote up rare cases of double personality, and a Swiss, Théodore Flournoy (1854–1920), who was fascinated not only by multiple personalities but also by telepathy and automatism, like automatic writing, as well. In addition to his interest in sexual problems, Auguste Forel worked with hypnosis and wrote a book on hypnotism in which he advanced Oskar Vogt's (1870–1959) neurological view that hypnosis was "neurodynamic inhibition" caused by "cortical exhaustion."[20]

At the end of the nineteenth century and in the first decade of the twentieth a number of psychiatrists became less concerned with psychotics and turned to the more common, and less spectacular, neurotic patients. This trend had great significance for the development of psychiatric thought, for it was easier to explain ordinary neurotic mental pathology on the basis of antecedent psychological experiences. The neurotic's mentality is more nearly normal than the psychotic's, and the step from common sense psychology to the psychology of the neurotic is much smaller.

The problems of neurotic patients seemed potentially amenable to rational psychotherapy. One of the most systematic of the attempts to treat neurotic disorders on this basis was the persuasion therapy of Paul Charles Dubois (1848–1918), who was professor of neuropathology at Bern. Dubois had been strongly influenced by Heinroth and believed that most mental disturbances have psychological causes. He emphasized that psychological functions have a physiological substratum: psychological function is "a special function of the brain" that cannot be described in physiological terms but can be influenced by psychotherapy.[21] Psychotherapy, to be effective, should be rational: the physician's task was to convince the patient that his neurotic feelings, thoughts, and behavior were irrational. Dubois's method was another form of Pinel's moral treatment and amounted to reeducation according to reason and accepted moral principles.

Dubois's rationalism was challenged by Joseph Déjerine (1849–1917), professor of psychiatry at the Salpêtrière in Paris: "*According to some authors, particularly Dubois, psychotherapy ought to be 'rational,' that is, based solely on reasoning and argument. I have always been of the opposite opinion. . . . If reason and argument were sufficient to 'change one's state of mind,' the neuropaths would find in the writings of the moralists and philosophers, and spiritual advisers, everything they would need to reconstruct their morale, and consequently their physical well-being, and therefore they would have no need of a psychotherapist. . . . Reasoning by itself is indifferent. . . . From my point of view, psychotherapy depends wholly and exclusively upon the beneficial influence of one person on another. One does not cure an hysteric or a neurasthenic nor change their mental condition by reasoning or by syllogisms. They are only cured when they come to believe in you. In short, psychotherapy can only be effective when the person on whom you are practising it has confessed his entire life, that is to say, when he has absolute confidence in you.*

"*Between reasoning, and the acceptance of this reasoning by the patient, there is, I repeat, an element, on the importance of which I cannot insist too strongly; it is sentiment or feeling. It is feeling which creates the atmosphere of confidence without which, I hold, no psychotherapy is possible, that is to say, unless reasoning produces effective action there is no 'persuasion.' I am, in fact, convinced, and have been so for a long time, that in the moral sphere the bare idea produces no effect, that it to say, the idea alone does not move one, unless it is accompanied by an emotional appeal which makes it acceptable to consciousness and thus brings about conviction. There is something analogous to faith in this, some individual element which makes the success of the psychotherapist depend upon his personality.*"[22]

Déjerine thus foreshadows present views about the predominant importance of the emotional interaction between patient and psychotherapist. In his controversy with Dubois we recognize the age-old never-settled argument about the relation of reason to emotion, the opposing views of Plato and Aristotle, of the rationalist versus the voluntarist psychologists, and finally the current controversy between the psychoanalysts who emphasize insight as the supreme therapeutic factor and those who stress that the primary therapeutic significance is the emotional experience the patient undergoes during his treatment.

Déjerine's book *The Psychoneuroses and Their Treatment by Psychotherapy* (1913), written with E. Gaukler, shows a grasp of the significance of emotional factors in functional disturbances of the gastrointestinal system, urinary and genital organs, respiratory apparatus, and skin, as well as in neurasthenia and hysteria. His references to "subconscious" determinants of neurotic symptoms are vague, but he was quite aware of the role that trauma, which he called emotional shock, played in the origin of hysterical symptoms. He cites one case of a woman who had a contracture of the right arm that suddenly appeared when she wanted to strike her husband and another of a young girl whose leg contracted after a rape attempt. From these observations Déjerine concluded: "It is evident that in these two cases it was the very nature of the emotional traumatism which determined the seat of the symptoms, and the patient became immobilized, in the latter case in a position of defense and in the former in a position of attack. When under other circumstances an hysterical paralysis is located in the limb which was hurt during the traumatism, we would again have a case where the very nature of the shock which was experienced would have determined the seat of the hysterical symptom."[23]*

Edouard Claparède (1873–1940) was perhaps one of the most inspiring medical psychologists at the turn of the century. Claparède's intellectual background was the new enlightenment of the Darwinian era. Claparède grew up in an atmosphere of free thought; his own curiosity and courage led him to explore the unknown, and his contributions to psychology were impressive because of their breadth and depth.

Claparède's cousin Théodore Flournoy introduced him to the then new experimental psychology of Fechner and Wundt. In Flournoy's laboratory Claparède met William James, who had a considerable influence on Claparède's development. In addition to Flournoy, Claparède's teachers included Déjerine, Wilhelm His (1831–1904), a renowned histologist, and Karl Ludwig (1816–1895), a famous physiologist.

Claparède's main contribution to psychology was a basic law—the law of momentary interest—which states that thinking or consciousness is a biological function in the service of the organism. Only when difficulty arises in satisfying a biological need do we become conscious of the need; only then, therefore, does the problem of gratification need solving. Dissatisfied needs are the source of both awareness and thinking. Claparède formulated this basic tenet more clearly than his predecessors: "I have attempted to show that intelligence intervenes when instinctive or acquired

* Since Déjerine's book was published after Freud's and Breuer's *Studies in Hysteria,* it is not possible to determine whether this formulation of the hysterical symptom was original or taken over from Freud. Déjerine does not refer to Freud or Breuer, and it appears from his text that he was not familiar with their writings. For example, there is no reference to dreams.

automatism is not capable of solving the problem which confronts behavior, and I have derived intelligence from the method of trials and errors of inferior animals. But, in the case of intelligence, the problem of readjustment to a new situation is solved by thought."[24] A need becomes conscious when it cannot be satisfied by automatic performance: "Consciousness intervenes when action is obstructed."[25] Claparède tried to prove this biologically founded thesis—that psychological phenomena such as thinking are means by which the organism adapts to the environment—by experimental and introspective methods. He had a profound influence on Piaget, who, as will be seen, made most significant contributions to understanding of the development of intellectual processes.

Claparède's interest in psychology was broad; he was one of the last universalists in the field. The phenomenon of sleep intrigued him greatly, particularly in terms of its biological function. In this he anticipated Freud's orientation. He saw sleep as a protective device "cutting off the individual's interest in the situation of the moment and thus stopping his activity." Sleep prevents " the organism from reaching the point of exhaustion."[26] The study of sleep led him to examine hysteria, and he decided that hysterical symptoms too are defensive reactions. He identified the equivalents of hysterical symptoms in animals and succeeded in hypnotizing goats and pigs. Indeed, he was one of the first psychologists to do experimental work with animals, work that aroused his interest in educational psychology. He founded the Rousseau Institute in Geneva, dedicated to the science of education, and his book *Child Psychology* went into four editions.

Despite the number of outstanding psychiatrists who were active at the end of the nineteenth century, the fact remains that only the men of letters, the great psychological novelists, actually penetrated below the surface manifestations of personality. These writers understood and presented not exceptional, psychotic characters but average people whose motivations and drives were clearly delineated. Stendhal's Julien Sorel was an ordinary peasant boy; Flaubert's Madame Bovary a typical provincial wife; and Balzac's Père Goriot, Eugénie Grandet, and Cousin Pons were everyday personalities, as were Ibsen's Nora, Shaw's Candida, and Goncharov's Oblomov.

Not only ordinary people but also common situations that have deep psychological meaning are presented by writers like Ibsen, who described penetrating intrapsychic conflicts before Freud made them explicit to the scientific world. This is amplified in Ibsen's *Rosmersholm* (1886), in which Rebecca West, after the death of her supposedly adoptive father, comes to live at the house of Rosmer. Subsequently she convinces Mrs. Rosmer that she has had an illicit affair with her husband. This results in Mrs. Rosmer's suicide. When Rebecca learns that Dr. West was her natural father, she immediately confesses her role in the death of Mrs. Rosmer. It becomes apparent in the drama that Rebecca had been living as Dr. West's mistress before he died. Rebecca, in attempting to atone for her guilt over her incestuous relationship with her father, confesses to the lesser crime, namely, her role in Mrs. Rosmer's suicide. Freud himself was impressed by Ibsen's perspicacity in understanding the repetition compulsion (Rebecca repeating the Oedipus entanglement with Rosmer) as well as Ibsen's understanding of the need to confess to a lesser crime out of a sense of guilt. Authors like Ibsen have the advantage over psychologists because they are able to portray in the form of fiction what could be a true story, and the reader can accept it as merely the creation of the artist's imagination and not representative of reality. The aesthetic pleasures offered by a writer's technical mastery also help to assuage righteous anger that a reader might otherwise feel about unacceptable psychological truisms.

PART **III**

THE
FREUDIAN AGE

CHAPTER **11**

Sigmund Freud

The developments of the late nineteenth century formed the background for the work of one of the most important and influential figures in the history of psychiatry, and indeed in the history of Western civilization— Sigmund Freud. Freud's contribution to the understanding of man's nature cannot be overestimated. He concluded early in his career that in order to cure mental diseases one must understand their nature and that in order to understand a phenomenon one must systematically observe it. This led to the vitally significant principle of psychoanalysis as a valid method of investigation. As a result he succeeded for the first time in explaining human behavior in psychological terms and in demonstrating that behavior can be changed under the proper circumstances. He brought about the unification of treatment and research. His principles were responsible for the emergence of the first comprehensive theory of personality based on observation and not merely on speculation.

Under Freud's championing and practice of psychoanalysis the fact that psychology—the study of personality—can have the same cumulative and operational characteristics as the natural sciences was established.

The era in which Freud began his work was dominated by the natural sciences. Nowhere was the emphasis on materialistic explanations greater than in the field of medicine. Psychology made desperate efforts to save itself from the disrepute in which philosophy as a whole began to fall. In universities, for the first time, chairs of psychology were established separate from those in philosophy. Following Theodor Fechner's lead, psychologists began to pose questions that were suited for experimental studies. Isolated functions such as sight, hearing, the tactile sensations, memory, and learning were studied by controlled experiments, the results of some of which could be expressed in simple mathematical equations. In spite of the great merits of such studies, historically this early experimental trend appears as a concession. It meant that psychology, in order to emancipate itself from philosophy, gave up the study of the big questions: What is man? From where does he come and where is he going? How does he master his own fate by making decisions? Man's isolated faculties were studied, but man as a complex system of motivational forces, as a unique personality, was not the concern of science. Man's talents and aspirations were only "epiphenomena," not worthy of attention. Even today some psychiatrists expect all answers to come from knowledge of nerve synapses and neurochemistry and visualize even history as eventually reducible to the laws of physics and chemistry. Freud himself, as a son of this era, could not fully emancipate himself from this outlook and declared that eventually psychology would be replaced by chemistry. But he refused to wait for this Utopia to come about and instead attacked the central problems of personality and its disturbances by adequate methods, those of psychology. His recognition and reconstruction of unconscious motives, on which his system of therapy for mental illness is founded, substantially extended the application of psychological causality and for the first time provided a way to affect the structure of human personality.

Yet the premature introduction into this field of pedantic and pseudo-exact-research designs could for decades have paralyzed these vigorous intellectual activities. The critics of psychoanalysis even today do not always appreciate the great merits of this period, which by conventional standards can be called unscientific. To apply statistical methods, for example, to a field in which the basic principles of the phenomena studied are lacking is certainly less scientific than the application of the more adequate so-called "naturalistic observation." To study human behavior with the methods of physics, which are suited to the study of the correlation of two or a very limited number of isolated variables, is a hopeless undertaking. Be this as it may, this early research, with all its vagueness, primarily based on intuition, produced a set of theoretical concepts, the operational possibilities of which are even today not adequately recognized.

Psychopathological behavior was not previously readily explainable through common-sense psychology because the behavior of the psychotic or neurotic does not follow psychological causality as we know it from our conscious mental processes. Why a man should react with a depression or even suicide to an advancement in his job is unexplainable by the laws of psychological causality, which we know only from subjective experience. This is the reason why, since Hippocates, man has tried to explain such unusual manifestations from physical or chemical causes, be it the black bile or—today—serotonin. The same limitations hold in the case of psychopathic criminals whose motivations appear irrational. No one would call in a psychiatrist to explain the act of a hungry man who killed to obtain food. If, however, a murder is committed without intelligible rational or emotional motives, the unenlightened judge might think of mental disturbance probably due to heredity.

The contradiction in this erroneous reasoning escapes attention unless "unconscious" mental processes are taken seriously.

What are the historical circumstances that predestined Freud to introduce successfully the psychological approach into psychiatry after previous beginnings had consistently failed? We saw how the Romantic psychiatrists only half a century earlier recognized that psychiatric illness requires psychological methods of understanding and treatment. Reil in 1803 had requested that psychotherapy and psychopathology be recognized as integral parts of medicine. Moreau de Tours had declared that dreams are made of the same stuff as psychotic symptoms and that their understanding could serve as a clue for the understanding of psychosis. Carus had postulated the all-pervasive significance of unconscious processes for both normal and abnormal behavior and went so far as to explain psychologically all biological processes. Herbart had even used explicitly the term and the concept of "repression." And yet this psychologically oriented period was short-lived. We saw how the stupendous progress of the natural sciences in general, and the advancing knowledge of the central nervous system in particular, during the second half of the nineteenth century overshadowed these psychological interests and cast suspicion and general disrepute on everything that did not fit into the materialistic-mechanistic view that had become synonymous with science. What, then, made Freud succeed where his predecessors failed?

From the perspective of the present the answer is simple: Freud made the application of psychological causality operational. What Fechner accomplished in a more circumscribed field—the study of sensory perceptions—Freud accomplished in the field of personality research, introducing into it methodical observation and a technique of inquiry that was suited to the nature of the phenomena to be investigated. Freud substituted for general philosophical speculations the concrete study of individual persons. He created the science of psychobiography by reconstructing not only the history of the patient's symptoms but also the history of the person, which threw light on the origin of his mental symptoms. He made operational what others before him—among them Pinel, more than a hundred years earlier—postulated in vague general terms: that mental illness is the outcome of a person's life experiences.

As we have said, in his scientific orientation Freud was a true representative of his time. His background was in the natural sciences, in neurology and histopathology. Histopathology and psychoanalysis may appear to be far apart, and superficially no common ground can be detected between them. The dissimilarity, however, pertains only to their subject matter. Freud's basic orientation in approaching psychological phenomena was precisely the same as the one he learned in the laboratory: careful observation and rigorous reasoning. This was why Freud so energetically protested when he was called a philosopher. His deepest devotion was to deal scientifically with the problems of personality, that is to say, to observe carefully and in detail and communicate his findings meticulously to others.

Freud knew what scientific evidence is. He insisted that his findings not be challenged on the basis of unfounded or deductive polemics, but by repeating his method of observation and testing his conclusions through factual evidence. Trained as a natural scientist, he was deeply disturbed that his psychological formulations were not given this fundamental right of every scientist. His findings were rejected by emotionally biased and psychologically ignorant critics. Instead of testing objectively the evidence he carefully presented concerning the existence of unconscious processes, infantile sexuality, and the Oedipus complex, his critics attacked him with personal vituperations, a practice long regarded as contrary to scientific ethics. Accused of being unscientific, he far outshone his opponents in the spirit of science.

In his theoretical speculative writings he was nevertheless a philosopher. He had to be, because the field of personality research had not yet developed the refined instruments of controlled studies prevalent in the physical and biological sciences. He gave clear evidence, however, that what he cherished most in his work was the solid observational basis and not the philosophical superstructure. Referring to his speculations about the structure of the "mental apparatus," he wrote: "Such ideas as these are part of a 'speculative superstructure' of psychoanalysis, any portion of which can be abandoned or changed without loss or regret the moment its inadequacy has been proved. But there is still plenty to be described that lies closer to actual experience."[1]

Freud possessed more than the merely intellectual virtues needed to travel the arduous road of a scientific pioneer. He withstood universal rejection alone without the help of confreres, which required unusual moral fortitude and deep conviction in his historical calling. No one recognized more clearly the exceptional moral fortitude of Freud than one of his earliest and most faithful pupils, Hanns Sachs, when he wrote: "In the place of insincerity, superficial amiability, and the wish to gloss over unpleasant facts, he put insistence on merciless truth, the severities of unrelenting inquiry, and the courage to 'disturb the sleep of the world. . . .' He absolutely refused to accept any statement on the strength of a higher authority. He had no patience with those who did such a thing out of intellectual laziness or cowardice or because they wanted to have it settled with the least discomfort."[2] Sachs saw in this insistence upon truthfulness the source of Freud's unflinching skepticism, which is a necessary quality of real scientists. "His strong conviction was that neither the aspiration to arrive at absolute truth nor the realization of the relative value of all attainable knowledge ought to interfere with the work and zeal of the true scientist. What mattered was to come as near to the truth as possible, to make no concession to prejudice, tradition, authority, or to one's own wishes and weaknesses. It made no difference that the approach was trifling compared with the long way ahead. The results of every science remain open to doubt in a greater or lesser degree, according to its stage of development and its peculiar methods. A [true] scientist—that is, an independent thinker—must be aware of these limitations, and after strict and repeated scrutiny must stand by his own judgment without waiting for authorization by full and absolute proof. One of Freud's favorite sayings was: 'Man muss ein Stück Unsicherheit ertragen können' (One must learn to bear some portion of uncertainty."[3] Sachs sees in "independence, courage and pride the hallmarks" of Freud's character.

There are few historical personalities about whom as much pertinent biographical data is available. Freud subjected himself to a self-analysis and had the courage to make public many of the details of this unique procedure. He also wrote a fragment of an autobiography. The most valuable part of his self-analysis came from the examination of his own dreams and is contained in his magnum opus, *The Interpretation of Dreams* (1900). Only second in importance are the numerous letters that he wrote to Wilhelm Fliess, a medical confrere and confidant. During the most significant period of his life Freud confided to Fliess in a uniquely free and uninhibited manner not only his ideas but also the internal struggles, hopes, and discouragements that accompanied his relentless efforts to create a new psychological theory of the human personality.

All this material, as well as twenty-three hundred family letters and fifteen hundred love letters exchanged between Freud and his future wife, was at the disposal of Ernest Jones, a leading follower of Freud, for the writing of Freud's biography. Jones's three volumes constitute an unprecedented document, both because it is the only complete biography written by a psychoanalytic expert in psychobiography and because of the exceptional richness of biographical data which were available to the author.

Unfortunately there is not much known of Freud's early life; most of the biographical data pertain to his adulthood. For those who knew Freud only when he was already a great leader, confident in himself and conscious of the magnitude of his accomplishments, Jones's account of his first forty-four years is a veritable revelation. In Jones's story we see a man who was continuously tormented by doubts about his abilities, who was inordinately in need of approval and emotional supports, who had a deep-seated longing to find a strong father figure on whom he could lean both intellectually and morally. He endowed his mentors with illusory qualities. In the case of the first three—Brücke, the physiologist, Charcot, the great clinical neurologist, and the eminent Viennese internist Josef Breuer—his tending to build up father images manifested itself only in exaggeration.

The great qualities of Fliess, the last in this series of father figures, are purely fictitious; they are Freud's wishful distortions. It is during the ten years of friendship with Fliess that Freud's most vulnerable side came to the fore, to which Jones refers as Freud's neurosis.

Jones attributes Freud's maturation, which took place after the turn of the century, mainly to his self-analysis. There can be little doubt that this was an important factor. There are, however, many examples of a creative genius blossoming out after having "found himself" by devoting himself to the task for which his endowments predestined him. After Freud conceived his most original and at the same time most basic ideas, which became the foundation of the new science of psychoanlaysis, he obtained a solid point of crystallization for his internal development, and his life history became closely linked to the evolution of his ideas and his work.

Freud was born in 1856 in the small industrial town of Freiberg, in the Austrian province of Moravia. His father, Jacob, was a wool merchant, and since the textile industry, which had been the economic mainstay of this town, was steadily declining, the family lived in restricted circumstances. When Sigmund was three they immigrated to Vienna. The social atmosphere of Freiberg was anything but pleasant for the Freud family. Czech nationalism against Austrian rule was on the rise, and the German-speaking Jewish minority offered an easy target for hostile feelings. The social factor indirectly influenced Freud's emotional development, for, as commonly happens in oppressed minority groups, he, the first-born son, became the focus of the family hopes for rising in the social scale.

His early boyhood ideals—Hannibal and Masséna—were replaced later by the more realistic civilian fantasy of becoming a cabinet minister. His daydreams were encouraged by his mother, to whom, during her pregnacy, it had been prophesied that her son would become a great man. Freud later generalized the impact of maternal ambitions upon his emotional development: "A man who has been the indisputable favorite of his mother keeps for life the feeling of a conqueror, that confidence of success that often induces real success."[4]

Freud's ambition to be famous remained a powerful force well into his adult years. His daydreams of heroism are frankly revealed in his letters to Fliess. In one of these he half jokingly asked Fliess whether he thinks that on the spot (in a restaurant), where he first fully understood a dream, there could be a marble tablet bearing the inscription: "Here the secret of dreams was revealed to Dr. Sigmund Freud on July 24, 1895."

Freud's excessive urge for fame was to a large degree a compensation for a blow received when, at the age of twelve, his trust in and respect for his father's strength and authority were shaken. A Gentile on the street had knocked his father's new fur cap into the mud and shouted at him, "Jew, get off the pavement." To the boy's indignant "And what did you do?" the father calmly replied, "I stepped into the gutter and picked up my cap."[5]

This spiritless resignation and lack of courage deeply disturbed Sigmund; he had to face the task of becoming what his family expected him to be without a strong father image, and it took four decades before Freud outgrew his need to replace his destroyed father ideal. He finally overcame this passive longing for a strong father only when he had actually become fully convinced of his own intellectual prowess. This point occurred at about the turn of the century. One can detect clearly in *The Interpretation of Dreams* and in *Dora: An Analysis of a Case of Hysteria* his firm confidence in his ideas and his recognition of their historical significance. From this point on Freud lived for his work.

The voluminous correspondence with Fliess is pervaded with reinforcing daydreams of these two lonely struggling individuals, both intent upon making a mark on the development of science. The difference between these two persons could not, however, have been greater. Freud was the rigorous researcher, disciplined by twenty years of solid work in neuropathology and a creative, imaginative genius; Fliess was a pedestrian clinician, absorbed by his quaint and eccentric idea of biological periodicity, which had only a meager foundation. The relation between these incongruous men, in which a potentially great man ceded the leadership to his intellectual inferior and assigned him the role of mentor and adviser, can be understood only with the help of depth psychology. The intensive friendship with Fliess apparently developed in a difficult time, when Freud needed a powerful father image on whom to lean. It was the period in which Freud already had his first glimpse into the hitherto unknown depth of man's unconscious personality and felt the challenge to explore it further, to formulate his ideas and communicate them to a world that was not yet prepared to accept them. It would be misleading to overemphasize Freud's dependency needs, which were far outweighed by his courage, persistence, and devotion to scientific truth.

CHAPTER **12**

Freud's Scientific Evolution

Freud's contributions to science were of four kinds, with a considerable chronological overlap between the first two: (1) his contributions to the anatomy of the nervous system and to neurology, achieved between 1883 and 1897; (2) his studies in hypnotism and hysteria, done from 1886 to 1895; (3) his demonstration and study of unconscious phenomena and the development of the psychoanalytic method of treatment, with which he was occupied from 1895 to 1920; (4) his systematic inquiries into human personality and the structure of society, made between 1920 and 1939. As far as subject matter and methods of research are concerned, Freud's early work in anatomy and neurology can be sharply distinguished from the rest of his scientific endeavors. Yet it is erroneous to divide Freud's scientific development into two completely independent phases, the first devoted to neurology and the second to psychological studies. A prolonged, arduous, and largely unsuccessful effort—and an effort that absorbed most of his energies for many years—to formulate his early psychological discoveries in terms and concepts of brain physiology connects them. His attempts to relate his novel contributions in the field of psychology to the prevailing anatomical and physiological orientation particularly reflects the influence of his teachers Brücke and Meynert, from whom he derived his emphasis and the necessity for validation.

Studies of the Nervous System

The reasons why Freud chose a medical career are not evident. He was never attracted by the profession and never became a conventional physician. According to Ernest Jones, Freud chose medicine as a career by a process of elimination. "For a Viennese Jew the choice lay between industry or business, law and medicine. The first of these were quickly discarded by someone of Freud's intellectual type of mind. . . ."[1] Of the remaining two, medicine was still preferred, although "without great enthusiasm." As he stated later, "Neither at that time [when he went into medicine], nor indeed in my later life, did I feel any particular predilection for the career of a physician. I was moved, rather, by a sort of curiosity, which was, however, directed more towards human concerns than towards natural objects."[2]

Curiosity about human nature was always most fundamental in him, and he considered it as a "triumph of his life" that he eventually found his way back to this interest.

Freud credited Ernst Brücke (1819–1892) with having had the greatest influence on his intellectual development. Brücke, one of the leading physiologists of the late nineteenth century, was a member of the circle of progressive scientists—Hermann von Helmholtz was another—who followed Johannes Müller. Like Müller, they believed that the principles of physics and chemistry should be applied to the study of living organisms and denied that any other force, such as some mysterious vital substance, is operative in biology. Freud thoroughly assimilated this strictly scientific attitude and never departed from it for the rest of his life.

The six years that Freud spent in Brücke's laboratory were his apprentice years in scientific investigation. He acquired a thorough knowledge of the methods of histology, published a few noteworthy articles on the gonadal cells of the eel and on the nervous system of some lower animals, and developed some ideas about nerve cells and their inner connections. He enjoyed the work but did not completely give up his philosophical inclinations. He consistently attended the lectures of Franz Brentano (1838–1917), who held the chair of philosophy at the University of Vienna, and translated a book by John Stuart Mill.

In 1881 Freud obtained his medical diploma, and for a while afterward he continued his laboratory studies in Brücke's institute, preparing himself for an academic career. He came to realize, however, that an academic career was not compatible with the necessity of earning his livelihood, and following Brücke's advice, he planned to enter private practice as a neurologist, despite his lack of interest in treating the sick. After serving as an assistant professor under Hermann Nothnagel (1841–1905), a famous professor of internal medicine, he received an appointment at the same rank in Meynert's Psychiatric Institute, where he acquired his first knowledge of clinical psychiatry. In 1885 he applied for the title of a Privatdocent in neuropathology, and on the recommendation of Brücke, Meynert, and Nothnagel, was appointed to this post. The road toward a successful career in medical practice was now open to him.

In 1884 Freud experimented with the anesthetizing action of cocaine and published a preliminary report on the effects. He hoped that this discovery would make his reputation, help him establish a practice, and enable him to marry earlier than he could otherwise expect to; however, a visit to his fiancée interrupted his work, and while he was with her, another man, Karl Koller (1857–1944), decisively demonstrated the usefulness of cocaine in ophthalmology. Freud continued to study cocaine for possible antidepressant effects, but this turned out to be a blind alley, which was fortunate, for a success in this field might have diverted him from continuing on the path that led to his psychological discoveries.

While he was at Meynert's Institute Freud acquired a knowledge of neuropathology and also learned about Herbart's dynamic psychological concepts, which had influenced Griesinger. Herbart recognized the existence of unconscious mental processes and conceived of conscious thinking as the emergence of ideas that were competing for attention. Some ideas, according to Herbart, could drive others out of awareness, and the latter could affect mood and behavior.

The first of Freud's publications on neuroanatomy concerned the roots of the neural connections of the acoustic nerve (1885). He then published a pioneering study on the sensory nerves and the cerebellum (1886) and followed with another article on the acoustic nerve (1886). Two of his contributions to clinical neurology were significant. One, a book on infantile cerebral paralysis, is considered even today an important work on the subject; the other, a book on aphasia (1891), is less well known but is more important from a theoretical standpoint.

Studies in Hypnotism and Hysteria

Freud's work in neurology overlaps his first psychopathological work in hysteria and hypnotism. His interest in the psychological aspects of medicine began in 1886, when he first went to Paris on a traveling fellowship. His reason for making this trip was that he had found the prevailing methods of treatment, particularly Erb's electrotherapy, in which patients were subjected to mild galvanic currents, of little value to his patients, most of whom were neurotics. In order to learn more about their illnesses, Freud decided to go to Paris to study with Charcot, whose fame was at its zenith. The choice to turn to Charcot was a natural one. Freud soon transferred his longing for an omniscient father from Brücke and Meynert to Charcot, whose personality fascinated him. What impressed Freud most about Charcot was his courage to contradict accepted psychiatric theory. For instance, Charcot took hysterical symptoms seriously as real, despite the usual practice of his time, which considered them merely imagined. He carefully observed and recorded hysterical symptoms and accepted the evidence that men too suffered from hysteria, which ran counter to the traditional idea that this disease was exclusively female. Most significantly, Charcot succeeded, by using hypnotic trances, in producing in some of his hysterical patients precisely the same type of symptoms they had developed in the course of their illness; and although he maintained that hysteria was caused by a basic weakness in the nervous system, he nonetheless demonstrated that the hysterical symptoms of paralysis, tremors, and anesthesias could be produced and abolished by psychological techniques. This work reaffirmed the psychogenic theory of hysteria that Sydenham had proposed two hundred years earlier.

By the time he had returned to Vienna Freud had become a militant champion of Charcot's ideas about hypnosis and its relationship to hysteria. One older colleague, Josef Breuer, listened sympathetically; otherwise, Freud's reports to the Vienna medical society about his experience in Paris were received with only mild interest and a great deal of skepticism about the validity of Charcot's description of hysterical illness. Meynert was opposed to hypnosis, and Freud's paper on male hysteria did not arouse special interest among the physicians. Freud reacted to this cool reception by withdrawing more and more from the medical community. His formerly close and friendly relationship with Meynert deteriorated rapidly and Freud soon was excluded from the laboratory of brain anatomy. The growing antagonism between Meynert and Freud had other than merely scientific aspects. Meynert resented Freud's shifting his loyalty from him to Charcot, and, according to Jones, possibly was also jealous of Freud's superiority in brain anatomy. Freud's open criticism in his book on aphasia of Meynert's theory about the relation between the cortex and the various parts of the body did not improve this antagonism, which eventually grew into open hostility. After his return from Paris the pugnacious side of Freud's character began to assert itself. He vigorously defended his own views and attacked his critics without pulling his punches. Yet he still needed a good father image to lean on. He found this eventually in the person of Josef Breuer.

Breuer assumed great importance in Freud's life. He was a successful practitioner and had repeatedly helped financially during the years when Freud was struggling to establish his career; yet Breuer's greatest contribution was neither emotional nor financial support, but a clinical observation which he had related to Freud four years before the trip to Paris. In 1880 Breuer had treated a young girl, Anna O., for classical hysterical symptoms —paralysis of the limbs, anesthesias, and disturbances of vision and speech. These symptoms had originally appeared when she was nursing her father through a serious illness. Breuer had observed that once, when the girl induced hypnosis in herself, she related in great detail the circumstances surrounding the development of one of her symptoms. Breuer thereupon began to treat her systematically with hypnosis and encouraged her in these trances to speak about the experiences that coincided with her symptoms, a technique that the patient called the "talking cure." The memories she recalled under hypnosis were accompanied by the violent expression of emotions that she had felt during the original experience but that she had been unable to express at the time; after these violent expressions of emotion (abreactions) her symptoms disappeared. Under hypnosis she could be brought back to the circumstances that had led to her symptoms. She had repressed the important events—in this case, strong feelings of resentment toward her father for being ill, feelings about which she felt great guilt—which hypnosis uncovered. However, Breuer became frightened when the phenomenon of transference occurred—his patient fell in love with him—and he quit the case. Anna O. (the pseudonym used by Breuer and Freud when they wrote up her case) may therefore justifiably be considered the inadvertent inventor of the therapeutic technique that Breuer called catharsis.

Anna O.'s case remained an isolated episode in Breuer's practice, and without his association with Freud, he may never have followed it up. Nor did Freud, when in 1882 he first heard of this case, recognize its significance, since at that time his own interest lay in explaining hysterical symptoms on an organic basis. After he had seen Charcot's experiments with hypnosis in Paris, however, he recalled Breuer's story and tried to arouse Charcot's interest in it but failed completely.

From 1886 to 1889 Freud and Breuer continued their work on cathartic hypnosis but found that some patients could not be hypnotized and others were not permanently relieved of their symptoms. Believing that their technique of hypnosis needed refinement, Freud in 1889 went to Nancy, France, where hypnosis was being used in therapeutic experimentation. Ambrose-August Liébeault, attempting to cure poor people without charge, was hypnotizing them. Also in Nancy, Hyppolyte-Marie Bernheim was experimenting with posthypnotic suggestion in which hypnotized subjects were given commands to be carried out after awakening. After witnessing these studies Freud became thoroughly impressed by the power of non-conscious psychological motivation and realized that suggestion was the psychological foundation of hypnosis.

After this second trip to France Freud translated some of the writings of Charcot and Bernheim, and his interest turned more and more to psychological phenomena. He returned to his work with Breuer on cathartic hypnosis, and the significance of the dynamic unconscious and of repression of unacceptable ideas began to take shape in his mind. In 1895 Breuer and Freud published *Studies in Hysteria,* in which they formulated the idea that hysterical patients suffer from the repressed memory of upsetting—"traumatic"—events that were so distressing that the emotions they aroused could not be faced at the time they occurred. They maintained that the secret of curing the hysterical symptoms was to give these blocked, pent-up emotions free expression.

Freud's need for a collaborator and an intellectual leader is striking in his consistent attempts to push Breuer into the foreground. He credited him with the discovery of psychoanalysis, although in fact he had to make a great effort to reawaken Breuer's interest in hypnosis and the phenomena of hysteria. He finally succeeded in doing this, but Breuer, confronted with the stark facts of the emotional involvement of the patient with his physician (*transference*), proved to be wanting in the moral courage to accept the consequences and pursue this disturbing phenomenon. Freud, unlike Breuer, continued the investigations by examining the meaning of the patient's "love" of the doctor from an objective perspective. With the understanding of transference, psychoanalysis as a therapeutic approach became established.

The Foundations of Psychoanalysis

Freud soon came to realize that, despite its usefulness, hypnosis did have therapeutic limitations. For one thing, not everyone is susceptible to being hypnotized. For another, Freud found that therapeutic results achieved by hypnosis were often transient; a symptom might disappear, only to be replaced by others. The reason this happens is that in hypnosis the subject temporarily renounces the normal functions of his ego, in particular his critical judgment, and entrusts himself completely to the hypnotist. He is therefore able to recall the painful events that his ego ordinarily would prevent his remembering; but unconscious material that is thus recalled does not become a part of his conscious personality, and on awakening the subject is usually unaware of what has happened during the hypnotic state. Recollection in hypnosis, therefore, does not eliminate the *cause of forgetting:* the resistance of the conscious personality to face unbearable repressed material. Hence the discharge of repressed emotions under hypnosis—the technical term for which is *abreaction*—does not result in a permanent cure but renders only temporary relief from the accumulated tension.

At first Freud did not understand this. Out of motives difficult to reconstruct, he began to experiment with other psychotherapeutic methods, impelled by what he called "an obscure intuition." Only later did he realize what we now know about the limitations of hypnosis. Once he did understand, he saw that the next logical step was to try to overcome, not circumvent, through hypnosis, the resistance of the conscious personality to repressed material—that is, he had to try to induce his patients to face consciously this unacceptable material. But how was he to make the patients remember in the state of consciousness these painful, forgotten experiences of the past? On the basis of Bernheim's theory that suggestion is the essence of hypnosis, Freud at first tried to use suggestion on his patients, urging them, while they were fully conscious, to recall traumatic events connected with their symptoms. After a brief period of unsuccessful experimentation with various techniques, Freud discovered in 1895 the method of free association.

Freud's new technique consisted of asking his patients to abandon conscious control over their ideas and to say whatever came into their minds. Free association takes advantage of the self-betraying tendency of unconscious material that seeks expression but is inhibited by repressing counterforces. When a patient abandons the direction of his thought processes, his spontaneous associations are guided more by the repressed material than by conscious motives; the uncontrolled train of thought thus reveals an interplay between two opposing tendencies—one to express, the other to repress, unconscious material. Free association extended over a sufficiently long period of time, Freud discovered, would lead the patient back to forgotten events that he not only remembered but also relived emotionally. The emotional abreaction in free association is essentially similar to the emotional discharge experienced during hypnosis but is not as sudden or explosive; and because these piecemeal abreactions occur while the patient is fully conscious, the conscious ego is enabled to cope with the emotions by gradually "working through" the underlying conflicts. This was the procedure that Freud called "psychoanalysis," a term he used for the first time in 1896.

Unconscious material does not appear directly during free association; instead, it influences the conscious train of thought in a way that may not always be obvious. As Freud listened to the free flow of seemingly random associations, he learned to read between the lines and gradually came to understand the meanings of the symbols through which his patients expressed this hidden material. He called the translation of the language of unconscious processes into everyday language the "art of interpretation," an art that was only fully realized after Freud discovered the significance of dreams.

He became interested in dreams when he noticed that many of his patients during their free associations began to talk spontaneously about their dreams. He therefore asked them to relate what thoughts they had in connection with elements of the content of the dreams. He noticed that these associations often revealed the dream's hidden meaning. He then attempted, by using these associations from its manifest content, to reconstruct the dream's hidden meaning—its latent content—and in so doing discovered the particular language of unconscious thought processes. He published his findings in *The Interpretation of Dreams* in 1900; this book is, without doubt, his most important contribution.

The core of Freud's theory of dreams is that dreams are attempts to relieve emotional tensions that interfere with the state of complete rest—that is, with sleep. These tensions develop from needs and wishes that have been frustrated during the preceding day, and the dreamer relieves them by visualizing their fulfillment in a hallucinatory gratification. The clearest examples of this process are the simple wish-fulfillment dreams of young children, who express as fulfilled in their dreams desires that were left unsatisfied during the preceding day. In adults the process of achieving gratification through dreams is more complex. A great many adult wishes are thwarted not by external obstacles, as the wishes of children usually are, but by inner conflicts. These inner conflicts are often the result of having rejected, during maturation, many desires that parental attitudes make unacceptable, or "ego-alien." In their dreams adults express ego-alien wishes in distorted forms. The distortions are defenses against the internal conflict that would arise if the ego-alien tendencies appeared openly. Adult dreams are, therefore, compromise formations; they satisfy ego-alien wishes, but in the disguised and symbolic, infantile language of unconscious processes—that is, in terms no longer understandable to the adult. In this way the internal conflict is avoided and the dream fulfills its sleep-protecting function.

The study of dreams offered the necessary clue for the understanding of psychopathological phenomena. Freud's technique of free association and interpretation opened a royal road to the unconscious and provided a way to understand psychopathological phenomena, for these phenomena, like dreams, are the products of ego-alien unconscious desires. Freud realized that psychopathological symptoms and dreams alike are the products of primitive ways of thinking—Freud called them "primary processes"—that take no account of the usual restrictions imposed by the physical world and the social environment. It is the nature of the unconscious to ignore limitations of time and space; the unconscious is not rational but emotional in nature; its expressions are not words but pictorial images.

Freud's study of dreams revealed a number of psychological mechanisms. One was "condensation," the combination of different ideas, all of which have some emotional common denominator, into a single symbol. For instance, the dreamer may dream of a face with the eyebrows of a father, the nose of a teacher, the mouth of a brother, and the ears of a wife, yet the composite face looks like none of these people on first inspection. If the individual with this face is killed in the dream, the death may appear innocuous, yet, unconsciously, the individuals represented are actually people toward whom the dreamer bears grudges and who are being punished.

Another of these mechanisms was "displacement." In a dream a patient can displace hate or anger or love from one person to another whom he can hate or love without internal conflict. In such a dream the dreamer might displace his wish to make love to his mother onto another woman, who would actually represent the mother by wearing shoes similar to those the mother had worn.

A great many other characteristic features of unconscious processes came to light under Freud's penetrating studies. Among these were the use of allegory, symbolism, allusion, *"pars pro toto"* (referring to one part of an object or person, but meaning the whole), and "expressing something by its opposite." To "express something by its opposite" is to negate a wish one really has because that wish is in some way undesirable. For example, a dreamer who has unconscious hostility toward his brother may wish to best the brother in competition for a job. Repugnance of the hostile wish leads him to dream that he loses the position to his brother. The object of all these dream mechanisms is to disguise the unacceptable unconscious wish.

The knowledge of unconscious processes led to enlightenment about many obscure activities of the human mind. During the first decade of the century Freud was greatly preoccupied with the demonstration of the "dynamic unconscious" as it manifested itself in slips of the tongue, use of wit, and forgetting things. In his brilliant work *The Psychopathology of Everyday Life** he showed that the seemingly fortuitous slips of the tongue, the seemingly unmotivated forgetting of words (and other parapraxias), are the results of repressed intentions.

As his ability to analyze his patients' dreams grew, Freud became increasingly aware that sexual impulses played a significant role in neurosis. He found that the ego-alien material that had been eliminated from consciousness and that consequently was being expressed in dreams and in neurotic symptoms consistently had sexual connotations. Freud was most reluctant to accept the idea that sexuality was so influential and all-pervasive, but once his observations had forced him to draw this conclusion, he courageously and defiantly refused to ignore the implications of his findings. His own self-analysis, particularly the analysis of his own dreams, gave Freud his first inkling about the Oedipus complex—the child's desire for sexual involvement with the parent of the opposite sex and his sense of rivalry with the parent of the same sex. His conclusions, corroborated by his observations of patients, were published in *Three Essays on the Theory of Sexuality* (1905). His conceptualizations about man's sexual nature became known as the "libido theory," which along with his discovery of infantile sexuality were mainly responsible for Freud's rejection by his medical confreres and the public.

The libido theory revised conventional views about the sexual instinct, which was considered an instinct of propagation. Freud concluded that there are many aspects of childhood behavior that are a source of sexually (sensually) pleasurable sensations, e.g. thumbsucking and defecation, which bear no relation to propagation. In fact, this conclusion extended the implications of sexuality beyond the concept of propagation. Freud's libido theory replaced this previous narrow definition of sexuality with a comprehensive theory of personality development in which biological (including

* First published in a German journal in 1901, in book form in 1904, and translated into English in 1914.

sexual) and psychological growth are correlated. The infant is considered to be in an "oral phase," still completely dependent on the mother for pleasures he experiences in his mouth and in a biological state character-ized by rapid growth. His psychology is dominated by the need to incorporate food and he exhibits receptive dependency; when frustrated, he becomes demanding and aggressive. The oral period is followed by the "anal phase," during which the child learns for the first time, as he under-goes toilet training, how to control his bodily functions. This phase begins at *approximately* eighteen months. Toilet training interferes with anal pleasures derived from retention and expulsion of feces, and the child's psychology is dominated by aggression, envy, obstinacy, retentiveness, and possessiveness. He acquires defenses against coprophilic tendencies (love of touching feces) such as disgust and cleanliness.

Although the phases and psychosexual development overlap and blend one into the other and cannot be considered to begin and end abruptly, the next phase is said to begin at about three years of age. It is characterized by infantile masturbation, sexual curiosity, competitive ambitious attitudes, and, above all, the Oedipus complex. These years are called the "phallic phase." Then, at about six years of age, a period of "latency" sets in, during which the child's earlier curiosity about sexual matters is replaced by curiosity about his whole environment. He attends school, and much of his energy goes into learning.

At approximately twelve years of age, with the onset of adolescence, there is a revival of sexual interest as the individual's reproductive system matures. Insecurity is a central psychological feature of this stormy period and is related to the fact that a fully matured body must be governed by an inexperienced mind. The need to test and to prove oneself becomes mani-fest in excessive competitiveness and in awkward attempts to display maturity and independence, although these attempts are undermined by underlying doubts. A revival of the Oedipal conflict occurs during these years.

Maturity, or the so-called "genital phase," is characterized mainly by self-acceptance, security, and the capacity for mature love. This behavior pattern is only possible when concern with oneself, which has hitherto been predominant, recedes. All pregenital phases are mostly self-centered, or narcissistic, because the individual is concerned with his own growth, with the mastery of his physical and mental environment. Only after the limit of growth is reached and the person is able to take himself for granted can he turn his love fully from himself to other objects.

Two of Freud's concepts, "fixation" and "regression," helped to explain the essential nature of neurotic and psychotic symptoms. Fixation is the propensity individuals have of preserving patterns of behavior, feelings, and thoughts that have served them well in the past. Regression is the tendency to return to these older successful patterns when new situations arise that require new adaptations and learning and that the ego is not yet capable of successfully accomplishing. Neurotics have more than the usual tendency to regress, and neurotic symptoms are disguised expressions of earlier ego-alien patterns that, in the present circumstances, are nonadaptive. For example, a child may learn that by screaming he can get what has been denied him. Later, when he goes to school, his teacher may refuse to allow him to play with a certain object. The child may then *regress* to his old pattern by screaming in order to get permission rather than accept the refusal or try a less violent means of accomplishing his aim.

The ego employs defense mechanisms to prevent outmoded ego-alien trends from breaking through into consciousness. Among these defenses the most important are *overcompensation,* or *reaction formation* (as when a weak person behaves as though he is very strong, even to the point of being a bully), *rationalization, turning ego-alien hostile impulses against the self* (as in the form of self-destructive attitudes and actions), and the *projection* of unacceptable tendencies by attributing them to others. Other defenses have themselves become sources of impairment.† Let us say that acceptable behavior, e.g. voyeuristic tendencies leading to the hobby of photography), and *displacement* of hostility or love felt toward inappropriate objects to acceptable ones (as when one displaces his love for his mother to love for his girl friend).* All these defense mechanisms serve to avoid conflict between the individual's social self and his inner, primitive strivings; they act, as was said above, to reduce the anxiety that arises when ego-alien repressed impulses threaten to break through into consciousness.

Neurotic symptoms, when seen in this light, could be understood as unsuccessful attempts at self-cure. They are unsuccessful because the defenses have themselves become sources of impairment.† Let us say that a person furious with his father is about to swear at him. This wish is in direct conflict with his morality, which rejects expression of anger to a parent. As a consequence he loses his voice. Now he cannot continue in his work, which requires speaking. What was a defense (loss of the voice) against the wish to berate the father has become an impairment. In this example the impairment was physical. The impairment may also be social. Let us say that a person feels that he is weak. Nobody likes a weakling, so he makes an effort to be liked by acting strong. But he may overcompensate and become a bully. Nobody likes a bully either. Thus the defense (acting very strong) against unpopularity because of weakness has become an impairment.

---

* Freud's daughter, Anna, in her book *The Ego and Mechanisms of Defense* (1936) gave a systematic and lucid description of these defense mechanisms, some of which had been described earlier by her father and his collaborators.

† This psychological concept is similar to Hans Selye's recent physiological theory, which proposes that defenses against injurious stimuli may become themselves the cause of disease.

Freud summarized these ideas, together with his theory of psychoanalytic treatment, in the first series of his *Introductory Lectures to Psychoanalysis* (1916–1917).

A crucial view in psychoanalytic treatment is what Freud called "transference." Transference is based on the fact that during treatment the patient not only remembers his past experiences, but what is more important, transfers on to the therapist the feelings he had toward significant persons in his past life—mainly his parents. He reacts to the therapist in a similar manner as he did toward his parents. Reenacting and reliving the original neurotic responses permits the patient to correct them; his past maladaptive reactions are thus brought into the treatment. In reliving his past experiences, the adult patient has an opportunity to grapple again with unresolved childhood events and emotions; his adult strength helps him solve the emotional difficulties that as a child he had found insurmountable.

Nevertheless, Freud's principal thesis was that in order to achieve a cure, recollection of past events and insight into the meaning of these events must occur.*

Revisions and Additions to Psychoanalytic Theory

For more than thirty years Freud refrained from constructing a comprehensive theory of personality, although he had made many important detailed observations in his work with his patients. He worked—and saw himself—as a scientist, not a philosopher, proceeding from observation to generalization. He refused to *begin* with speculations. Finally, in 1920, he published the first of a series of systematic, speculative writings, *Beyond the Pleasure Principle,* which was followed by a remarkable series of pamphlets that he brought together in 1933 in his *New Introductory Lectures on Psychoanalysis.* In these papers he attempted a revision of his early views about the observable manifestations of instincts: love and hate, guilt and remorse, grief and envy. He explained them in terms of the logic of emotions (psychological causality) before he began to speculate about the ultimate nature of these basic phenomena. In this, the history of psychoanalysis followed the same pattern as the development of theoretical physics: the nature of the phenomenon was comprehended at a later time than the laws of its manifestations.

At the very beginning of his studies Freud was most impressed by the conflict between the instincts of self-preservation and race-preservation—that is, between the egotistic interests of the individual and his sexual cravings. Accordingly, he differentiated between *ego* drives and *sexual*

---

* This thesis, upheld by fundamentalist psychoanalysts, has been challenged in recent times by those who emphasize not insight but the reexperiencing of emotions in relation to the therapist. (See "Recent Developments," Psychoanalytic Therapy.)

libido. Manifestations of hatred and destruction were considered to belong to the ego instincts; whereas he classified feelings of love, the drive to propagate, and other extragenital pleasure-seeking drives as sexual instincts. The phenomenon of sadism, however, did not fit into this dualistic picture, for sadism, a distinct impulse—gaining pleasure from inflicting pain—which belongs to the ego instincts, is also a source of sexual excitation and is therefore both a primitive, pregenital manifestation of libido and an ego instinct. Freud's further analysis of the so-called ego instincts—that is, the different manifestations of selfish tendencies—brought to light other contradictions to a simple, dualistic theory of the instincts. For instance, love, even sexual love, can have as its object oneself, as it does in narcissistic love. Furthermore, many of the pregenital sexual sensations are bound up with functions that are frankly self-preservative—eating and elimination, for instance. Because of these contradictions Freud revised his thinking and proposed a new scheme, based on the idea that there are two primary instincts, the life instinct, which he called "eros," and the death instinct, or "thanatos."* In his new libido theory, preservation of self and race are not the manifestations of two different instincts, but, on the contrary, they are the evidence of the same instinctive drive, love, or eros. In self-preservation the object of the eros is the individual, in the preservation of the race eros acts to unify the two sexes and form a new individual. The destructive or death instinct, thanatos, tends to separate and disrupt biological units. It acts to reduce complex living material to its components, finally achieving this aim in the process of death. It counteracts the upbuilding trend of the eros. Biological life is a continuous interaction between these two forces; the overall process of metabolism, for example, is made up of a constructive phase, anabolism, and a reductive phase, catabolism. Psychological life also involves a permanent interplay of erotic and destructive forces, which appear in mental life in mixtures. The best examples of psychological dualism are the phenomena of sadism and masochism, in both of which sexual impulses are mixed with destructive tendencies. Love and hate are polar opposites, however, and neither can be reduced to the other.†

Although there were and are objections to Freud's final dualistic theory, unquestionably this new instinct theory of Freud's accords better with observed facts. It also had great applicability in the analysis of psychosociological events. It is useful in explaining such conflicts as the individual against family, family against clan, clan against nation, and nations against

---

* Alfred Adler had called Freud's attention to the aggressive instinct, which Freud, in his papers of the early twenties, placed within the death instinct.

† The life-versus-death instinct was Freud's final dualistic theory. Prior to this formulation, in *On Narcissism* (1914), under the pressure of C. G. Jung's critique of the original-ego-instincts-versus-sexual-instincts theory, Freud arrived at an intermediate or second major dualistic theory—self-love versus object love. (See section on Jung.)

FREUD'S SCIENTIFIC EVOLUTION   [201

each other as manifestations of the destructive, or more precisely, disruptive instincts; it also helps explain why, in spite of these disruptive forces, continuous efforts are always made to form units such as family, clan, nation, and superstate.

While *Beyond the Pleasure Principle* was an attempt by Freud to revise and systematize his earlier concepts about instincts, *The Ego and the Id* (1923) was his first contribution to a general theory of personality. It was preceded by *On Narcissism* (1914). In these writings the emphasis is no longer on mental pathology but upon the structure and functioning of the normal mind. Freud had always emphasized that the human mind was not a homogeneous entity, since repression of unacceptable mental content causes a division between the conscious and unconscious parts of the personality.

According to *The Ego and the Id,* man is born with a reservoir of chaotic and conflicting instinctive demands that are not necessarily in harmony either with each other or with any given situation in external reality. This reservoir of the instinctive drives, each of which seeks gratification without respecting other instinctive drives or the possibilities afforded by reality, constitutes the id. The id follows what Freud called the "pleasure principle," that is, it seeks immediate gratification for all impulses without regard for the total organism, and it also seeks to avoid pain. As a child develops, the pleasure principle gradually yields to the "reality principle"; that is, the mental apparatus is forced to make a compromise with external reality and modify the id's instinctive demands in line with the existing possibilities of gratification in a given situation. During the process of development the child must learn to estimate the relative importance of different and conflicting instinctive demands and decide to postpone or renounce the gratification of some demands in order to assure the gratification of other more important needs. The ego is that portion of the personality which performs this coordinating function of attempting to reconcile the demands of external reality with the claims of instincts. The ego represents the brutal facts of reality; at the same time, it also serves the id, because its main purpose is to assure as many gratifications of the basic instincts as is possible under any given circumstances.

The superego, which develops after the ego, is the internal representative of the principles that regulate the child's, and the adult's, relation to the human environment, especially to the parents and the siblings. The superego is the product of education and develops through identification with the parents; their demands and attitudes are incorporated into the child's personality, and the superego becomes their inner representative. Mental life thus involves a continuous interplay among the original instinctive claims (the id), external reality, and the inner representatives of external reality, the ego and the superego. Freud explained that this inner representative of parental influence was not the same as conscience, for the reason that the function of the superego is to a high degree unconscious: it is a kind of unconscious conscience. Freud considered that the superego appears as one outcome of the resolution of the Oedipus conflict, since in achieving this resolution the child incorporates the image of the parent of the same sex. As a result, the parent with whom the child competed is made an integral part of the child's personality, and the external conflict with the parent is thus converted into an internal conflict between the superego and the ego-alien impulses of the id.

In a theoretical writing, *Inhibitions, Symptoms and Anxiety* (1925), another work on the structure of personality, Freud abandoned an earlier view of anxiety that he originally considered as a product of frustrated sexual libido. He described anxiety as a signal of approaching danger, a signal that mobilizes the ego's defenses. When the danger is external, this signal is called fear. The ego also reacts toward any threatened break-through of ego-alien impulses that have been suppressed because their expression had caused suffering in the past. The reaction to this internal danger is anxiety. Fear is, then, an alarm reaction to external danger; anxiety signalizes internal danger.

According to this formulation, anxiety is to be considered central for the theory of neurosis. When ego-alien impulses are activated, the superego reacts to them with self-punitive measures, a reaction that is perceived by the ego as guilt feelings. Guilt feelings thus consist in a fear of the superego, the internal representation of the parents, who were the original prohibitors of unacceptable impulses. Anxiety is reduced to a fear of conscience.

This new conceptualization of the personality could not fail to influence treatment procedure; however, it influenced the theory of treatment more than actual practice. Between 1912 and 1916 Freud had stressed that one of the therapist's most important functions is to analyze the patient's resistance against unconscious material, for only by reducing this resistance could the unconscious be made conscious. These later theoretical revisions implied that the reconstruction of unconscious impulses—that is, analysis of the id—was not the primary function of the therapist: instead, it was overcoming the ego's resistance—ego analysis. The aim remained the same —the extension of the realm of consciousness over hitherto unconscious parts of the personality. To achieve this goal the patient's ability to become aware of his unconscious tendencies must be increased. In other words, it requires an alteration within the ego; but how this is or can be achieved, strangely enough, was not then and is not now fully understood.

CHAPTER 13

Freud's Contributions to
Social Theory and the Humanities

Freud's ideas about group psychology have had an important influence on the fields of preventive and social psychiatry, particularly in the area of the role of cultural factors in neurosis. His first significant contributions to social theory were made in *Totem and Taboo* (1913), in which he applied his psychological theories to society as a whole. This work was followed by two others, *Group Psychology and the Analysis of the Ego* (1920) and *Civilization and Its Discontents* (1927). Ironically, these works contain most of the essentials of the sociological ideas that the neo-Freudians have embraced and that they have denied as being classically Freudian.

In *Totem and Taboo* Freud followed Charles Darwin's suggestion that the primordial human society consisted of hordes of brothers led by a powerful father. Under the influence of the universal and most focal of all human conflicts, the Oedipus conflict, the sons rebelled against and killed the chief; the horde thereupon changed into a disorganized fraternal society, a leaderless community of brothers. The need of the brothers for a powerful leader eventually led to totemism and later to religious systems—the totem and the deity being the reincarnation of the murdered father. Freud was convinced that humans have a profound emotional need for strong leadership, and this conviction is the cornerstone of all his sociological speculations. In fact, Freud had a general distrust of democratic institutions.

The essence of Freud's social theory is that a stable human society becomes possible only when the universal patricidal tendencies of the sons are overcome, so that the family—the "cell of society"—is preserved. Since the taboo against incest, which is also a component of the Oedipus conflict, makes extrafamilial marriage mandatory, different families are bound through marriage into clans, tribes, and eventually nations. The psychological nucleus of cultural development, in this view, thus lies in overcoming Oedipal strivings.

Freud supported his theory by extensive anthropological evidence, most of which he drew from *The Golden Bough* (1890), by Sir James George Frazer. Frazer's work supported his idea of the universality of both the incest taboo and the taboo against killing the totem animal, which symbolizes the father of the tribe. This sociological theory aroused a great deal of controversy among anthropologists, yet it was the first psychodynamic explanation for the ubiquitous marital laws prohibiting the different forms of incest, as well as for the great diversity of religious taboos in primitive societies.

In *Group Psychology and the Analysis of the Ego* Freud referred to a book by a French physician and social psychologist, Gustave Le Bon (1841–1931), *La Psychologie des Foules* (1895). Le Bon's main thesis is that when man becomes a part of a group he regresses to a primitive mental state. Acting as an individual, he may be cultivated and rational; acting in a group, he may behave like a barbarian, be prone to violence, abandon his critical sense, become emotional, and lose all his moral standards and inhibitions. His unique, individual features disappear, and the common ancestral heritage in man's unconscious becomes dominant. Freud explained Le Bon's description of these regressive features of mob psychology in terms of the nature of human conscience. The essence of conscience is "social anxiety," the fear of public opinion; social anxiety is naturally diminished in the members of a mob. Because the voice of the individual conscience is silent in a group, all that has been repressed, all that violates the standards of the conscience, is free to appear uninhibited.

Freud follows Le Bon in saying that the behavior of the members of the group is comparable to that of someone in a heightened state of suggestibility, as in hypnosis, but he raises a question that Le Bon does not discuss: Who is the hypnotizer? Freud contended that the leader of the group subjects its members to a hypnotic spell and that their relationship to the leader explains the relations of the members to each other. The leader becomes each individual's ego ideal, to whom he hands over all his critical faculties, just as the hypnotized individual abandons his self-determination to the control of the hypnotizer. This shared ego ideal, which ties every member of the group to the leader, also determines their interrelationship, for through their common attachment to the leader they identify with each other.

To explain the nature of the group's attachment to the leader Freud utilizes a concept of "aim-inhibited libido," or desexualized libido. The group members are bound by libidinous ties to their leader, but the leader has no emotional attachments to anybody but himself. It is precisely this narcissistic quality that makes him a leader. "He loves no one but himself, or other people insofar as they can serve his needs." He is "of masterly nature," "self-confident," and "independent." He thus represents qualities that the group members themselves cannot attain, and because he does so, he becomes their ego ideal.

By introducing the concept of libido, which ties the members of the group to the leader, Freud could dispense with Trotter's "herd instinct" as the force responsible for group cohesion. Freud's explanation clarified the mutual relationships between the members of the most elementary social group, the family. The mutual attachments between the members of the family reveal themselves as libidinous ties and do not require the invention of a special new kind of instinct. The same principle can be applied to account for bonds within the family as well as for those operative in the larger extension of the family—social groups.

Freud's theory lacks a complete definition of the emotional ties of the group members to the leader; in terms of modern psychoanalytic theory, this emotional relationship can be described as a return to the infant's dependent attitude toward his parents. The regressive nature of group behavior is then satisfactorily explained by the childlike dependence the members exhibit toward their leader, under whose spell they renounce the internalized parental images (their own consciences) and regress to the phase in which they blindly followed the guidance of their parents. Apparently most persons retain sufficient residues of childhood dependency and insecurity to be susceptible to such emotional regression. The blissful security of the Garden of Eden is a perennial motif in art and philosophy.

Freud's theory served to clarify some of the dynamics of group behavior. The concept of dependence on the leader resolves the apparent contradiction that a group, which may become ferocious and destructive, is also capable of self-sacrifice and devotion. The group attitude obviously depends upon the nature and ideals of the leader, who can influence his followers in either direction. Furthermore, by stressing the group's dependence upon the leader, we can more clearly understand the phenomenon of panic. In time of danger the group's reliance on the leader increases. Should the leader weaken, the members of the group become overwhelmed by paralyzing anxiety, for the necessary guidance is replaced by what is tantamount to desertion of helpless children by their parents. Thus, in time of danger, democratic societies are apt to sacrifice at least some of their freedoms in order to increase the authority of the government.

Freud made only the first tentative steps toward understanding the principles of social organization in his pioneering work, and his psychological descriptions are, in the main, applicable only to mob psychology. The problem of conscience, for instance, remains somewhat elusive. A social group may make man moral and yet may contribute, when there is a strong leader, to a loss of individual morality. What is there, then, about a social group that can weaken the power of the individual conscience? Freud recognized that the superego originates in social organization, for parental values as transmitted to the child are those which prevail in society. Freud tried to apply the same basic principles to the understanding of the emotional structure of firmly organized groups—the church and the army.

This choice of models was unfortunate: in the church and the army central authority is paramount; their members retain a basically childlike dependence on and obedience to leadership; the image of the central figure (the authority of higher rank) is fatherlike. Only in this does a random group under a strong leader resemble a structured group organized around a strong authority. Democratic societies differ from this formulation in that they consist of more independent, self-governing individuals who maintain a relationship of interdependence and shared sovereignty with their leaders. In such a society the members can successfully retain their own firmly internalized values. The ability of a leader to hypnotize the group members in such a society is much smaller and always tenuous. In contrast to such a situation, in which freedom of individual conscience is operative and even encouraged and in which a reversion to mob conduct means a *regression* to childlike dependence upon an hypnotic leader, the childlike dependence found in the church and the army is *fixated*.*

These fundamental contributions, with their attendant shortcomings, were of great importance, but they were only a beginning pointing the way to further study. Freud himself was fully aware that the development of human personality must be seen in terms of the influence of the prevailing social standards and values to which it is subjected. In fact, social scientists and psychologists who have felt themselves distinguished by their cultural orientation, in contrast to Freud's "nineteenth-century biological orientation," actually have added few new principles to this basic insight. Freud did not undertake comparative studies on personality development in different cultures. Such studies became possible only when psychoanalytic thought penetrated deeply into the social sciences, particularly into social anthropology. However, the basic principles of the molding influence of society upon personality development were laid down by Freud.

In *Civilization and Its Discontents* Freud focuses on man's hostile and aggressive impulses. In order to become a member of an organized social system man must renounce the unbridled expression of his individual strivings. These restrictions are the price he pays for the greater security he derives from collaboration with others. Freud explicitly states here something that he had previously always implied, namely, that the Oedipus

* Freud's theory of the group is probably a reflection of the social milieu in which he grew up—Vienna under the absolute rule of the Hapsburgs. This may also explain his perceptive recognition of the role of the leader and his tendency to overrate this role. This emphasis is not to be found in Le Bon or William McDougall (1871–1938), another psychologist who influenced Freud in his group theories.

complex is originally repressed because of destructive impulses directed toward the father and not because of its incestuous connotation. The sexual desire for the female member of the family supplies the *motive,* however, for hostility toward the father, but it is the destructive wish that is repressed by the incorporated parental image, the superego. This repression must be reinforced by external social institutions, of which social justice is an indispensable factor. Only if everyone renounces his asocial impulses can repression be maintained throughout society; if transgressions are allowed, this might mobilize into action repressed asocial impulses. Refraining from expressing asocial impulses through overt action does not relieve guilt feelings because these are aroused not only by overt acts but also by unconscious desires: not only criminal *deeds,* but criminal thoughts produce guilt feelings. This social guilt is the source of the universal discontent that, according to Freud, is an unavoidable part of social life.

This pessimistic view is essentially identical with Hobbes's social theory. Hobbes considered that human society consists of people warring against each other and that basically man is a ferocious animal who must be coerced into peaceful coexistence by a powerful tyrant. Law is essentially the law of the strong repressive leader; lacking such repressive external leadership, human beings would eventually destroy each other. Freud added to Hobbes's view the idea of an internal tyrant, the superego, which represents the originally external leader, the father. This social theory, founded on the assumption of a basic destructive instinct as an inalienable part of human nature, has been questioned by many post-Freudian theorists who do not take such a dim view of the human core.*

Freud's systematic theoretical contributions coincide with the deterioration of his physical health, which began two years before the first signs of his mouth cancer appeared. He wrote in 1921, "On March 13 of this year I quite suddenly took a step into real old age. Since then the thought of death has not left me, and sometimes I have the impression that seven of my internal organs are fighting to have the honor of bringing my life to an end.

---

* The concept of the superego had been deduced from observations made on neurotics, in whom it remains a separate entity embedded in the personality and not fully assimilated by the ego. It is a foreign body that is in constant struggle with the ego. A central feature of the neurotic is failure to integrate successfully without inner conflict into the ego the internalized social values. In the course of normal development these values become thoroughly integrated into the ego similarly as foreign protein becomes transformed into the organism's basic proteins. In the neurotic personality the ego and superego are constantly feuding. The goal of psychoanalytic therapy is to achieve an harmonious union between the two. Since nothing in nature is perfect, it can be assumed that in the deepest layers even of the mature non-neurotic person some residual asocial impulses remain still active. In the healthy person these manifest themselves primarily in dreams and have no decisive influence upon overt behavior. Even if aggressive impulses are an integral part of man's basic instincts, they can be channeled toward constructive goals. It is conceivable that in a society composed of mature individuals, people do not need external coercion by authorities or internal coercion by a harsh superego to collaborate harmoniously.

There was no proper occasion for it, except that Oliver [his son] said good-bye on that day before leaving for Roumania. Still I have not succumbed to this hypochondria, but view it quite coolly, rather as I do the speculations in *Beyond the Pleasure Principle*."[1] It is the more remarkable that both in quality and quantity his intellectual productivity during these years did not show any decline and in some respects outshone his previous accomplishments. Ernest Jones gives a most vivid picture of the moral fortitude that until his death Freud showed in these years of physical tribulation and social upheavals. Only a man who so thoroughly identified himself with his work—the immortality of which was by now insured—is capable of such a heroic posture. He felt he achieved the only form of immortality open for man, the immortality of his creations.

Soon after, he returned to his deepest concern, the origins of culture, which had preoccupied him since early youth. He writes as a postscript to his autobiography, "My interest, after making a lifelong detour through the natural sciences, medicine and psychotherapy, returned to the cultural problems which had fascinated me long before, when I was a youth scarcely old enough for thinking."[2] This interest in the origins of human society and in the humanities came to the fore intermittently in briefer writings throughout his career, but after 1921 it became more the focus of his preoccupation. Freud's interest in medicine was a detour. He was primarily a thinker, concerned with man's relation to the world and society. Natural science had a deep influence on him, but in his heart he remained above all a humanist. An indication of his aesthetic sense is to be found in the fact that his exquisite mastery of German prose earned him the Goethe Prize in 1930.

Out of his interests emerged studies in the sources of creativity and elucidations of the psychic foundations of literature. In an essay on Jensen's *Gradiva* (1907) he demonstrated with great lucidity the influence on current behavior of childhood fantasies that becomes mobilized by current adversities. In other writings he showed deep insight into the characters of Lady Macbeth, Hamlet, and Richard III, showing in psychodynamic terms what Shakespeare had grasped intuitively. His introduction to a German edition of Dostoevsky's *The Brothers Karamazov* is the most vivid among these writings. In this essay he convincingly demonstrated that all the four brothers were driven by their unconscious patricidal desires, which they expressed in four different, highly individual ways. Essays on Michelangelo's *Moses* and on Leonardo da Vinci are examples of his continued interest in the psychology of art.

The Future of an Illusion, (1928) which is devoted to religion, is perhaps the most philosophical of Freud's writings. His interest in religion was purely psychological, and in this pamphlet he traces back man's ever-present need for religion to his deeply seated and never mastered childish dependency needs, which are aroused when he faces the great unknown—the surrounding world with which he has to deal. In his *Group Psychology and the Analysis of the Ego* Freud elaborated man's need for a powerful leader—a father substitute—as the psychodynamic cement of society; in *The Future of an Illusion* he finds the same need as the deepest source of religious needs.

His last book, *Moses and Monotheism* (1939), is undoubtedly the book most motivated by Freud's own emotional needs. It was written four years before its publication, when Hitler's persecution of the Jews first cast its shadow over Europe. Freud's main thesis is that Moses was not a Jew, but an Egyptian who developed his belief in monotheism under the influence of a then prevailing Egyptian religious trend and succeeded in converting the Jews to this new concept. Finally, Moses, the angry, overpowering leader, was slain by his rebellious followers, and this murder became the source of an unconscious sense of guilt, from which the Jews never could liberate themselves. The deep emotional source of this last publication has been masterfully reconstructed by Jones in his biography of Freud. In discussing *Moses and Monotheism* Jones proposed his most original ideas about the unconscious aspects of Freud's personality. *Moses and Monotheism,* which is the least concise and lucid and the longest of Freud's books, was nevertheless the most revealing of him as a person.

Jones calls attention to a peculiar propensity of Freud's to believe that people often are not what they seem to be. Moses was not Jewish but a high-born Egyptian; Shakespeare was not the son of an uneducated English bourgeois but was (at least for a while in Freud's thought) Sir Francis Bacon or Edward de Vere, the seventeenth Earl of Oxford. Jones connects this predilection of Freud's with the conscious wish of his youth to have been the son of his English half brother, Emmanuel, which would have allowed him an easier path in life. We may add that this desire for an easier path is also expressed in what he once wrote about Einstein: "The lucky fellow has had a much easier time than I have. He had the support of a long series of predecessors from Newton onward, while I have had to hack every step of my way through a tangled jungle alone. No wonder that my path is not a very broad one, and that I have not got far on it."[3]

Freud overestimated official recognition, or, what amounts to the same, on occasion emphatically displayed an indifference to it, even at a time when he had already acquired world fame. All this together completes the picture of a never fully resolved conflict. Outwardly he heroically bore the burden of discrimination, first as a member of a minority group and later as the discoverer of the most unpopular truths about human nature, which sentenced him to live always in opposition. He never fully recognized, however, his own hidden but only too human desire for full acceptance and official recognition by the authorities. Psychoanalysts know only too well that the effect of past experiences never can be abolished completely. If in nothing else, it appears in defensive measures against these painful past experiences.

Jones does not draw explicitly the conclusion that Freud's neurosis, which was manifest in his struggling years, was at least partially responsible for the extreme fortitude and courage by which he overcame his earlier insecurity. Yet, at the same time, this "overcompensation"—Freud's extreme heroism—generated in him an occasional yearning for a less strenuous and more peaceful existence. He lived an emotionally wearing life and never yielded to the ostracism on the part of his colleagues and the authorities. And he never gave up, at least in the deep unconscious layers of his personality, playing with the fantasy that like Moses, with whom he identified himself, he really belonged on the right side of the tracks. This fantasy served as a great source of satisfaction because it enabled him to believe that it was he himself who rejected the bliss of conformity and security and chose the role of the pioneer who enforces the "truths" against the resistance of the medical world. This is indeed an even greater sign of strength than to oppose the majority as an outsider, who, because of his ancestry, is inevitably destined to fight not by his own choice but by fate.

Moses and Monotheism was written when Freud's heroism had reached its height, when he was left by his pupils alone in Vienna, facing his inevitable physical decline and foreseeing the extermination of his people. Still, he stubbornly refused to leave Vienna, even when the Nazis invaded the privacy of his home and subjected him to a degrading questioning. Finally he yielded to the pleadings of his friends, and with the help of Jones and Freud's faithful follower Princess Marie Bonaparte, left Vienna to go to London, where he died a few years later, in 1939, in the circle of his family.

CHAPTER 14

The Psychoanalytic Movement

Freud's ideas profoundly changed man's conception of his self. Inevitably they provoked a violent and initially almost universal rejection, which for ten years he had to face in what he called "splendid isolation." Gradually he attracted a handful of followers, mainly from Vienna and later from Switzerland, Hungary, and England, and these men collaborated with him in the organization of a small professional community devoted to the development of a new discipline—psychoanalysis. The present state of psychoanalytic practice and teaching is still earmarked by these events; for this reason a brief history of the early psychoanalytic movement will be given here.

During the last decade of the nineteenth century, when Freud was so isolated, he suffered from loneliness; however, as he later remarked, he was also able to concentrate on his work without being disturbed by dissensions that soon developed among his early followers and by the necessity of having to argue with uninformed opponents. In 1902 a small group of physicians interested in Freud's ideas began to meet at his house. Among them were Alfred Adler (1870–1937) and Wilhelm Stekel (1868–1940). These Wednesday-evening meetings continued for a few years; then, in 1907, in Vienna, the first formal Psychoanalytic Society was organized, with Freud as its head. This same year Freud first met Carl Jung (1875–1961), Karl Abraham (1877–1925), and Max Eitingon (1881–1943), all of whom were young psychiatrists studying with Bleuler at the Burghölzli, the public mental hospital in Zurich. (Eitingon was the first psychiatrist to undergo a training analysis with Freud, which took place during evening strolls in the streets of Vienna.) Soon Sandor Ferenczi (1873–1933) from Budapest joined the circle and became Freud's most trusted friend and his most original and imaginative collaborator.

The first international gathering of psychoanalysts was organized by Jung and took place in 1908 in Salzburg. At this conference Freud read one of his famous case histories, "The 'Rat Man': A Case of Obsessional Neurosis." The first psychoanalytic journal, the *Jahrbuch für psychoanalytische und psychopathologische Forschungen,* edited by Jung, was published in this year. In 1909 Freud accepted the invitation of G. Stanley Hall, president of Clark University in Worcester, Massachusetts, to deliver a series of lectures, and he came to America accompanied by Jung and Ferenczi.

The second international psychoanalytic congress was held in Nuremberg in 1910, at which time the International Psychoanalytic Association was founded. Latent antagonisms erupted between the Viennese and Swiss contingents. Jung was elected president of the Association. Freud consequently resigned as president of the Viennese group so that Adler could be made president. Freud also consented to have Adler and Stekel edit the monthly *Zentralblatt für Psychoanalyse.* A third publication, a bulletin to inform members of meetings, news items, and publications, also came into being.

In his biography of Freud, Jones makes the astute observation that at this meeting the hierarchical structure of the Psychoanalytic Society became apparent. Jones states that Freud felt that the Society should be organized not as in a democracy but as a hierarchy, perhaps as a reflection of the monarchistic attitude natural to a Viennese. The resulting rigidity was responsible for much of the controversy that surrounded the psychoanalytic movement, of which the first victim was Eugene Bleuler (1857–1939), professor of psychiatry at the Burghölzli Hospital.

Bleuler resigned from the International Association in 1910 for reasons that had to do with his dislike of the authoritarian manner in which the association was being run. Freud tried, but without success, to convince Bleuler to reestablish his membership; their correspondence about this matter suggests that profound differences in cultural orientation might have been a significant factor.* It is regrettable, in terms of the psychoanalytic movement and of the role that psychoanalysis played in the history of psychiatry, that these two men of supreme integrity could not collaborate, but it was, nevertheless, unavoidable.

An indication of why this break may have been inevitable is found in Bleuler's letter to Freud dated October 19, 1910: "There is a difference between us, which I decided I shall point out to you, although I am afraid that it will make it emotionally more difficult for you to come to an agreement. For you evidently it became the aim and interest of your whole life to establish firmly your theory and to secure its acceptance. I certainly do not underestimate your work. One compares it with that of Darwin,

---

* Excerpts from fifty letters from Bleuler to Freud and seven letters from Freud to Bleuler have been published by F. Alexander and S. T. Selesnick.[1]

Copernicus and Semmelweis. I believe too that for psychology your discoveries are equally fundamental as the theories of those men are for other branches of science, no matter whether or not one evaluates advancements in psychology as highly as those in other sciences. The latter is a matter of subjective opinion. For me, the theory is only one new truth among other truths. I stand up for it [psychoanalysis] because I consider it valid and because I feel that I am able to judge it since I am working in a related field. But for me it is not a major issue, whether the validity of these views will be recognized a few years sooner or later. I am therefore less tempted than you to sacrifice my whole personality for the advancement of the cause [of psychoanalysis]."[2]

Freud completely identified himself with his work. Its fate was his own. Moreover, it was natural for him to make his jealous handful of ardent followers the nucleus of an organization. Lacking the support of a university or other academic institution, he had to create his own small scientific universe, his own journals, his own press. That doing this increased the isolation of psychoanalysis and perpetuated an aura of exclusiveness and intolerance was not easy for those on the inside of the movement to see. Freud, more than his pupils, sensed the importance of the fact that through the Burghölzli psychoanalysis might be able to find entry into the academic community and therefore tried to keep Bleuler, the representative of academic psychiatry, as a connecting link. Bleuler, on the other hand, was not involved emotionally in Freud's work and visualized the development of psychoanalysis in academic terms of other scientific disciplines. He recognized the need for an association but conceived of it as a forum for discussion and research, not as a carrier of a "movement" whose "truth" had to be guarded and proselytized.

An incident involving someone else provided the impetus for Bleuler to state the issues that lay at the heart of his disagreement with Freud as well as between Freud and others who, under different circumstances, might have been Freud's allies. Dr. Maier, a psychiatrist, had been asked to resign from the Psychoanalytic Society because of differences of opinion. In a letter dated March 11, 1911, Bleuler wrote: " '. . . Who is not with us is against us,' the principle 'all or nothing' is necessary for religious sects and for political parties. I can understand such a policy, but for science I consider it harmful. There is no ultimate truth. From a complex of notions one person will accept one detail, another person another detail. The partial notions, A and B, do not necessarily determine each other. I do not see that in science if someone accepts A, he must necessarily swear also for B. I recognize in science neither open nor closed doors, but no doors, no barriers at all. For me, Maier's position is as valid or invalid as of anyone. You say he wanted only the advantages [of being a member], but wanted to make no sacrifice. I cannot understand what kind of sacrifice he should have made, except to sacrifice one part of his views. You would not demand this from anyone. Everyone should accept views only as far as they are his own views; if he accepts more he is insincere; you are, of course, of the same opinion.

"I do not believe that the Association is served by such intransigency. This is not a 'Weltanschauung. . . .'

"You think my resignation from the Society will harm psychoanalysis more than my joining helped in the past. So far as I can see, I am the only one who loses. . . .

"The introduction of the 'closed door' policy, scared away a great many friends and made of some of them emotional opponents. My joining did not change that in the least, and neither will my resignation change this fact. Your accusation that I should have considered the harm I am causing the society by my resignation seems to me, therefore, not valid."[8]

It is not possible for the historian to gauge the value of the forward thrust that the intense emotional dedication of Freud and his early followers provided as measured against the retarding influence of the early institutionalization of a young scientific doctrine. Certain it is, however, that the image of a small group of chosen heroic pioneers fighting the whole recalcitrant world is perpetuated into our present era, when the cultural climate has changed. This is an example of the cultural lag that retards progress.

Bleuler's defection from the psychoanalytic movement thus signaled the isolation of psychoanalysis from academic psychiatry and heralded its development as an increasingly centralized hierarchical organization. The retarding influence of institutionalization upon all forms of thought development is well known. In the case of psychoanalysis its progressive institutionalization outside of the universities—the traditional places of research and learning that through centuries have learned to preserve the traditional values of science—slowed down progress and perpetuated a conservative spirit from which even today psychoanalysis cannot fully emancipate itself. And so it happened that a revolutionary new way of thinking about human personality could not realize fully its inherent and almost unlimited possibilities. These historical events retarded not so much psychoanalytic thought development as its influence upon the whole of psychiatry. In Europe the influence of psychoanalysis upon psychiatry soon came to an almost complete standstill. Only in the United States, where psychiatrists were not involved in the original feud between Freud and academic psychiatry, could psychoanalysis effectively penetrate psychiatric teaching and practice.

From 1910 until the outbreak of World War I psychoanalytic thought spread throughout Europe and to the United States, India, and South America. To two already existing societies in Vienna and Zurich a third was added in 1908 by Karl Abraham, who founded the Berlin Psychoanalytic Society. In 1910 Leonhard Seif organized the Munich Society, and

James Putnam (1846–1918), of Boston, the American Society. In 1913 the Budapest Society came into being under Ferenczi, and soon after, Ernest Jones organized the first English group. In 1911, under the chairmanship of Abraham Brill (1874–1928), the New York Psychoanalytic Society was founded; in the same year a second American group, the American Psychoanalytic Association, was authorized by the International Psychoanalytic Association. Putnam was the president of the American Psychoanalytic Association, which has Canadian members, and Ernest Jones, who at that time lived in Toronto, was the secretary.

During these years the number of periodicals devoted to psychoanalysis also increased. The official journal of the International Psychoanalytic Association, the *Internationale Zeitschrift für Ärtzliche Psychoanalyse,* was founded in 1913 to replace the *Zentralblatt.* Adler had resigned as editor during the first year of the *Zentralblatt,* leaving Stekel in charge. Although Stekel was a brilliant writer and had a fine intuitive grasp of unconscious processes, he was considered unreliable and irresponsible.* Freud's dissatisfaction with Stekel's policies brought about the inception of the *Zeitschrift,* which remained in existence until Hitler dissolved it. Only a few months before, Hanns Sachs (1881–1947) and Otto Rank (1884– 1939), two nonmedical followers of Freud, established *Imago,* a journal devoted to the application of psychoanalysis to art, literature, mythology, and anthropology. After emigrating to Boston, Sachs founded a new American *Imago* in 1939, which is still in existence.

Coinciding with these vigorous developments, a number of conflicts occurred among the original followers of Freud. Adler was the first to secede; he was followed by Jung. The reasons for these two dissenters' going their own ways differed. Freud and Adler held conflicting theoretical views, and some of Adler's ideas (which will be discussed in detail later) had been proved of value. A personal motive, his stress on his own originality, was, however, an important factor prompting Adler to build a system radically different from Freud's. Freud considered Adler's system, though false, at least "consistent and coherent." The reasons for Jung's secession, however, were more complex, and, as Freud stated, scientifically less "serious." Cultural factors played an important part in Jung's dissension. There was an antagonism between the Viennese analysts on the one hand and Jung and the Zurich group on the other, even when Freud still admired Jung and entrusted him with the presidency of the newly formed International Psychoanalytic Association. After Bleuler left the Association, it was still Freud's hope that Jung would share the leadership of the psychoanalytic movement with him.

* Jones related the anecdote about Stekel's habit of illustrating psychoanalytic observations by fictitious examples. "So constantly did he comment on whatever topic came up at the weekly meetings of the Vienna Society with the words 'only today a patient of this very kind consulted me,' that 'Stekel's Wednesday Patient' became a standing joke."[4]

Unfortunately Jung's orientation toward psychology was affected by mystical and esoteric thinking; it was, as Abraham called it, a tendency to "occultism, astrology and mysticism." Furthermore, Jung's propensity toward opportunism and compromise became increasingly obvious. Jung had written to Freud from America that he was succeeding in overcoming the resistance against Freud's writings by deemphasizing the sexual factor in neurosis. Freud abhorred concessions in scientific matters and caustically replied that if he left out more the opposition would further dwindle and that by not mentioning sexual theories at all there would be absolutely no opposition. (For Jung's compromises with the Nazis, see Appendix B.)

After the defections of Adler and Jung, psychoanalytic developments were directed by a small group of staunch followers of Freud, all Viennese and Germans except for the Hungarian Sandor Ferenczi and Ernest Jones (1879–1958). It had been Jones's idea, derived from boyhood reading about Charlemagne and his paladins, to build this "specially close inner group of trustworthy analysts who should stand to Freud somewhat in the relation of a bodyguard."[5] This small group—originally Abraham, Jones, Ferenczi, Hanns Sachs, Otto Rank, and later Max Eitingon—became known as the "inner circle." Jones writes that they pledged that if any of them "felt compelled to enunciate views definitely contradictory to recognized psychoanalytic teaching, he would undertake before publishing them to submit them to a private and full discussion with the rest of us."[6] This was but the implementation of the hierarchical system that Ferenczi had proposed for the International Psychoanalytic Association in 1910; notwithstanding all the extenuating circumstances that induced this policy of internal unity and that made it a necessary measure, it did represent thought control. Unfortunately this attitude of exclusivity persisted in the psychoanalytic movement and exists to some degree even today.

The history of the psychoanalytic movement gives a revealing picture of a common historical cycle, how the early proponents of a new revolutionary scientific idea under the constant stubborn, emotionally determined opposition and vicious attacks of their opponents can be maneuvered into the position of conservative, sometimes even dogmatic, defenders rather than promoters of truth. For the pioneers who are constantly exposed to personal abuse on the part of some prejudiced and ignorant opponents, internal unity becomes more important than anything else. They consider as their greatest enemies not their frank opponents but those deviationists within their own group who cannot endure unpopularity and public criticism and are ready to compromise those basic achievements that the public rejects because of their novel and emotionally disturbing nature. Historically important is the fact that psychoanalytic societies never could fully divest themselves of this cultural heritage.

After World War I the psychoanalytic societies resumed their activities in the metropolitan centers of Europe and the United States. The older

European centers continued their steady development under the direction of the great pioneers Abraham, Ferenczi, and Jones. In Berlin Max Eitingon, Hanns Sachs (1881–1947), Sandor Rado, Franz Alexander (1891–1964), Otto Fenichel (1897–1946), Siegfried Bernfeld (1892–1953), Karen Horney (1885–1953), and Felix Böhm contributed to the organization of the first Psychoanalytic Training Institute, which attracted many American students of psychoanalysis. A year later, in 1920, a number of experienced analysts such as Paul Federn (1872–1950), Helene Deutsch, Herman Nunberg, Edward Hitschmann (1871–1957), and others organized the Vienna Institute. In London Ernest Jones soon was joined by a group of productive psychoanalysts, among them Montague David Eder (1866–1936), Edward Glover, John Rickman (1891–1951), James Strachey, Ella Freeman Sharpe, Joan Riviere and Melanie Klein. In France in the mid-twenties, after a period of relatively little activity, a vigorous group appeared, stimulated by the imaginative personality of Princess Marie Bonaparte. In Holland Van der Emden, J. H. W. Van Opphuijsen (1882–1950), and the highly gifted August Stärcke (1880–1954) were the leaders in the development of a Dutch group; and in Italy Edoardo Weiss organized a psychoanalytic society. Sporadic beginnings in the Scandinavian countries and in Belgium soon appeared. After Jung's defection Phillip Sarasin and the Rev. Oskar Pfister (1873–1956) took the lead in Switzerland, to be joined later by Heinrich Meng and Hans Zulliger.

A number of the psychoanalytic centers organized psychoanalytic training institutes, which in principle used the training system set up by the Berlin institute: theoretical and practical training were given either after or partially coincident with a compulsory personal analysis. The first official training analyst was Hanns Sachs, who was appointed by the Berlin Institute in 1921; Franz Alexander became the first analytic candidate. Committees were organized in all the training centers to screen applicants and evaluate their personalities in an attempt to select those who would be most suitable to practice psychoanalysis. Most of the present psychoanalytic institutes in the United States followed the Berlin pattern of training. After New York and Chicago, several other centers for psychoanalytic training were set up in Philadelphia, Boston, Detroit, Topeka, and San Francisco, followed later by centers in Washington, D.C., Los Angeles, Seattle, Denver, and New Orleans.

The institutionalization of psychoanalytic doctrine and practice was in full swing by the end of World War II. The psychiatric casualties during the war offered a tremendous challenge, and many physicians were attracted to psychiatry. The influence of psychoanalysis upon these developments in the United States was enormous, but it was never as rigidly separated from academic psychiatry as it was in Europe. A. A. Brill, who first translated Freud's writings into English, was highly respected by the academic psychiatrists. Smith Ely Jelliffe (1866–1945), a New York neurologist and neuropsychiatrist, and William Alanson White (1870–1937), of the St. Elizabeth Hospital in Washington, were most instrumental in bridging the gap between the psychoanalysts and university psychiatrists.

The centralization of the American Psychoanalytic Association steadily progressed. Since the inception of the psychoanalytic movement the leaders felt that it was the Association's responsibility to keep strict control and direction over psychoanalytic training. Following an old tradition originated at the Nuremberg Congress (1910), this task was entrusted to central committees. However, as soon as psychoanalysis penetrated university departments of psychiatry, a dilemma developed concerning the integration of psychoanalysis with the rest of psychiatric training. Comments on these highly significant developments, which unavoidably will have a great influence upon the further course of American psychiatry, are discussed in Appendix C.

CHAPTER **15**

The Psychoanalytic Pioneers

It has been said that no society can be better than its members. It is less often recognized that the members of a society can be much better than the society they build, which was certainly true for psychoanalysis. The same pioneers, including Freud, who founded the restrictive International Psychoanalytic Association, its branch societies, and the training institutes also worked diligently and wisely to advance this new branch of human knowledge. After Freud discovered the field of unconscious mental activity, particularly the psychology of dreams, an unlimited territory was opened up for observation and speculation. Although most of these men were clinicians, their main interest was the search for knowledge and not the treatment of the sick—in which they also followed Freud, who was not primarily a therapist but a researcher bent on enlarging basic knowledge. This tradition of research may be one reason why the method of psychoanalytic treatment has changed very little since its origination.

Karl Abraham

Undoubtedly one of the most significant of the pioneers was Karl Abraham (1877–1925). In his obituary of Abraham, Freud referred to him as *"integer vitae scelerisque purus."* No other expression better characterizes Abraham's scrupulous integrity, which extended to all aspects of his life, including his scientific work and his personal relationships with his colleagues and his family. A reserved and distinguished-looking gentleman, he had a kindly, warm expression. Abraham was born in Bremen. He acquired some psychiatric experience in Germany and then was appointed to the Burghölzli under Bleuler. Thus he was one of the first psychiatrists of the Burghölzli Asylum, along with Bleuler and Jung, who became acquainted with Freud's work.

[219

Before he took up medicine Abraham was interested in philosophy and linguistics, both of which he utilized in his later psychoanalytic work. His contributions covered a wide range of subjects: early infantile sexual development, dementia praecox, manic-depressive states, a classic paper on the female castration complex, anthropological studies, and the relation of dream psychology to mythology.

One of Abraham's most lasting contributions pertains to character formation. He contrasted the optimistic, easy-come, easy-go "oral" charac- ter with the controlling, possessive, "anal" character, descriptions that are now part of the everyday knowledge of educated persons. His pioneering work about the influence of early pregenital fixations on character forma- tion has been so thoroughly incorporated into modern psychiatric thought that its source has been almost forgotten. His most important contribution pertained to the earliest phases of psychosexual development, particularly to childish oral and anal-erotic manifestations, which helped Freud to formalize his libido theory. His penetrating remarks on mythological subjects, using dream symbolism as a clue, influenced both other psycho- analysts, such as Geza Roheim and Theodore Reik, and also Ameri- can anthropologists, among them Margaret Mead, Ruth Benedict, Ralph Linton, and Abraham Kardiner.

Abraham wrote one of the first psychobiographical essays based on a psychoanalytic approach. This essay was about the Swiss-Italian painter Segantini. These contributions, as well as his work on the psychology of mourning and melancholia, elaborated ideas that originated with Freud, and in this sense Abraham was a real disciple; but he was a disciple who exhibited an unusually strong intuitive grasp of unconscious mental proc- esses and who also possessed very high observational and reasoning powers.

The secret of Abraham's great personal influence lay in his genuinely friendly and optimistic outlook, his lack of fanatic fervor, and a trust- worthiness that impressed all who came in contact with him.

Ernest Jones

Born two years later than Abraham, in 1879, in a small Welsh village, Ernest Jones's path to psychoanalysis was quite different from that of his Central European colleagues. Torn between his admiration for the English ways and his deep loyalty to his Welsh origin, he became an advocate of the underdog and at the same time determined to become ultimately an accepted, respectable physician in Harley Street. He called himself a snob and was fully conscious of his blind determination to reach the top; on the other hand, he was keenly aware of a neurotic inability to enjoy his successes and of a self-destructive urge to fail. For Jones success meant disloyalty to his background, and therefore he could accept personal success only after he had found a more constructive form of atonement than failure. This consisted in his unswerving loyalty to Freud and the unpopular cause of psychoanalysis.

Jones acquired his medical degree in 1900 and turned his interest toward neurology. He was always attracted by social problems and, as he wrote in his autobiography, "realized that no solution could be found for any human problem, notably the social ones, unless it was based on a full knowledge of man's biological nature. . . . I was then under the illusion that this could best be studied in neurology, where it would seem that human impulses and the control of them could well be examined. . . ."[1] A man of superior intellectual prowess, unusual persistency, and great self-confidence, he was well on the way to becoming a member of the exclusive group of London's Harley Street specialists when an unfortunate incident exposed him to the false accusation of being a sexual offender. Although he was found innocent of the charge, the suspicion it caused made him welcome an opportunity he was given to emigrate to Canada in 1908.

By that time Jones had acquired some knowledge of psychiatry. The year before, he had attended a special postgraduate course in psychiatry at Kraepelin's clinic in Munich, where he studied neuropathology with Alois Alzheimer (1864–1915) and clinical diagnosis with Kraepelin himself. On his way back to England he stopped off in Zurich and visited Jung, the first psychoanalyst he had met. After he accepted the post offered him in Toronto, he went back to the Continent to study for another six months; he visited Jung in Zurich again and went to Salzburg to participate in the first psychoanalytic congress, where he met Freud. He was tremendously impressed by Freud's intellectual powers. At this congress he met other psychoanalysts and realized that his future work would be linked to the cause of psychoanalysis.

The four years he spent in Toronto were, in respect to literary output, the most prolific of his life. He believed this was due in part to the fact that his personal life in Canada was unhappy. He found the climate hard on him and the intellectual atmosphere provincial and thoroughly Victorian, like the atmosphere of his boyhood, monotonous and tedious. During these years Jones became acquainted with the leading American psychiatrists and found them more receptive toward psychoanalysis than his English colleagues had been. In England neurology was at its height and psychiatry an almost nonexistent and unimportant appendix to neurology. In America the opposite was true: neurology was uninspired, and there were a number of outstanding psychiatrists practicing, among them Adolph Meyer (1866–1950) and August Hoch (1868–1919) (both from Switzerland), William A. White, Smith Ely Jelliffe, Morton Prince, and James Putnam. A. A. Brill, one of the members of the early group that studied Freudian concepts at the Burghölzli, was highly respected by the academic psychiatrists. Jones took an active part in the organization of the American Psychoanalytic Associa-

tion in 1911. In 1914 he returned to London from Canada; the war prevented the creation of an English association, but after the war Jones
founded the British Psychoanalytic Society and remained its president and
moving spirit for more than twenty years. He also became the editor-in-chief
of the *International Journal of Psychoanalysis.*

With the exception of his biography of Freud, Jones's best contributions
were small essays, most of them applications of psychoanalytic concepts to
literature, art, anthropology, and folklore. Jones was a most erudite man,
and these essays, written in distinguished prose, are both penetrating and
sensitive and testify to the capacity of psychoanalytic concepts to deepen
our understanding of not only the primitive but also the most sophisticated
products of the human mind. One essay, a brilliant article on *The Problem
of Paul Morphy: A Contribution to the Psychology of Chess,* is a classical
study of the role that unconscious motivation can play in the fate of a
genius. Jones showed that Morphy was able to express freely his aggressive, competitive impulses in playing chess; when this sublimated outlet
was no longer available, Morphy then had to deal with these unacceptable
impulses by morbid projection, which led to his paranoid ideas and an
early death.

Jones's more technical writing was mainly devoted to the early pregenital phases of personality development; his work in this area is second
only to Abraham's.

Jones died in 1958 from coronary disease soon after the completion of
his monumental three-volume biography of Freud.

Sandor Ferenczi

Ferenczi (1873–1933), who was Freud's most intimate friend for more
than twenty-five years, was the most original thinker among the early
psychoanalysts. He had a colorful, warm personality, an irresistible
charm, and a spontaneity often lacking in those psychiatrists who preserve
their incognito toward their patients, which eventually becomes second
nature.

What most distinguished Ferenczi from his colleagues, however, was a
vital interest in therapeutic problems, an incessant urge toward therapeutic
experimentation that sprang from his dissatisfaction with the accepted
psychoanalytic technique; and it was this experimental attitude toward
therapy that eventually caused his rift with Freud. The reason why
therapeutic technique had become so sacrosanct that every attempt to
modify it was viewed with suspicion was related to the matter of who
should be entitled to call himself a psychoanalyst. The way an analyst
treated his patients—the preservation of personal incognito, the passive
attitude, and the daily uninterrupted interviews—distinguished him in the
eyes of these early practitioners from charlatans and what were called

"wild" practitioners, that is, practitioners who were in reality uninformed about psychoanalysis.

Ferenczi's technical innovations and experimentations were far from being irresponsible, "wild," or theoretically ill-founded; many of his therapeutic suggestions have proved valid over the course of years.

All of Ferenczi's technical experimentations were based on an intuitive conviction that changes in a patient's personality cannot be caused merely by interpretation, that is to say, by an understanding of the historical background of the patient's symptoms: Ferenczi tried, instead, to intensify the patient's emotional experiences during treatment. First among his attempts was what he called "active therapy," in which the therapist takes an active role in prohibiting or encouraging certain activities of the patient. This technique was frowned upon by classical analysts, who advocated a more passive role for the analyst. Ferenczi had noticed that some patients discharged repressed emotional tensions by automatic and habitual behavior patterns, such as stereotyped movements and gestures. In an effort to force inadvertantly discharged tensions to become conscious, he forbade these patients to carry out the stereotyped and automatic patterns they usually used when under emotional stress—for instance, crossing and uncrossing their legs. This technique was often successful in forcing the underlying unconscious tensions, which had been thus discharged unnoticed, into consciousness. Another active measure Ferenczi employed was to encourage the patient to carry out activities that the patient avoided because of their symbolic unconscious significance. For example, a patient who was afraid to leave his house and who had developed a phobia of the streets would be encouraged to enter the street, even in the face of his anxiety. This mobilized anxiety, which the phobia tried to prevent, would then be analyzed with the therapist. The patient, were he not to experience this anxiety, might have been content otherwise to remain as he was because he was not suffering. He also used "forced fantasies," that is, he encouraged patients to indulge in fantasies about topics that spontaneously appeared in their associations. The most active of his technical innovations, however, was in setting a termination date for treatment.

Some of these and other ideas about treatment were published in an important monograph, *Developmental Goals of Psychoanalysis,* which Ferenczi wrote in 1923 with Otto Rank. Ferenczi later retracted his recommendation about termination, but none of the other formulations contained in this publication. Among his highly significant contributions to the theory of psychoanalytic treatment was a proposal that the reawakening of forgotten memories is not an absolute requirement for the modification of neurotic patterns of thought and feeling—reliving these maladaptive patterns in relation to the therapist, transference, and recognizing that their inappropriateness may by itself be therapeutic even without remembering the past events in which these reactions originally developed. This idea created a great deal of controversy, and after its proposal Ferenczi was regarded as having abandoned some of the cardinal tenets of psychoanalysis.

In 1929 Ferenczi introduced another ingenious procedure, the principle of relaxation and neocatharsis, which also was aimed at increasing the emotional meaningfulness of treatment. This technique, which he called one of "indulgence," was in a sense the opposite of his active technique, for instead of increasing tension he tried to create a relaxed, tensionless atmosphere in which he encouraged the patient to express freely his ego-alien tendencies. Ferenczi did not mean to replace the standard "objective reserve" of psychoanalysts with these technical procedures; what he did recognize, however, was that even within the framework of the classical approach there is always present a "psychological atmosphere" and that if this atmosphere is appropriately chosen it may greatly aid the progress of treatment, particularly in cases that are at a standstill. In all these efforts Ferenczi was the forerunner of the so-called "flexible approach," which is adjusted to each patient's special problems and personality.*

Ferenczi's consistent therapeutic experimentations were thus chiefly motivated by his conviction that psychoanalysis was primarily an emotional experience, not an intellectual one; and the quality of the experience was, he felt, the essential therapeutic factor that induces the patient to change his neurotic patterns. Unfortunately his discontent with rigid approaches and his undogmatic readiness to examine all aspects of psychoanalytic treatment were responsible for the fact that he ended his psychoanalytic career as another dissenter. There is a tragic justice in this fate: he became a victim of the same control over psychoanalytic thought that he himself in his youthful enthusiasm had proposed at the founding meeting of the International Psychoanalytic Association.

Ferenczi's contributions to theory showed the same originality as his ideas about treatment. He wrote many articles dealing with the influence of unconscious motivation on everyday behavior and on personality development; his publication on "Stages in the Development of Sense of Reality" (1913) is one of the first writings in psychoanalytic ego psychology. In this article, which influenced many later psychoanalysts, Ferenczi tried to reconstruct the consecutive states—a "period of magical-hallucinatory omnipotence," a "period of omnipotence by the help of magic gestures," and a "period of magic thoughts and words as in fairy tales"—an individual goes through before he accepts the unwelcome data of his reality testing, in other words, before he adapts his feelings and thinking to the inexorable facts of reality.

The most imaginative, and at the same time most speculative, of Ferenczi's works is a book, *Thalassa,* the main thesis of which is that the

* See "Developments in Psychoanalytic Treatment" and "Psychotherapy" in Chapter 19.

origin of the sexual instinct lies in a phylogenetic craving of the living organism to reestablish its previous state of existence in the ocean, the cradle of all life. The development of the uterus, or more precisely, of the amniotic fluid, Ferenczi thought, was a re-creation of the lost ocean, the milieu from which all land animals derived. The fact that the amnion and the development of the fetus within the mother phylogenetically appear first in land animals is the basis of Ferenczi's theory. Ferenczi differentiated between *autoplastic* and *alloplastic* adaptation. As part of his cultural development, man adapts reality to his basic needs; animals, on the other hand, change their bodies to adapt to existing conditions. Man builds fires and shelters to protect him from cold; animals develop furs and subcutaneous fat deposits. The animal's method of adaptation Ferenczi called autoplastic, man's alloplastic. Although Ferenczi, like Freud, visualized phylogenesis in Lamarckian terms, these ideas may be explained equally well in Darwinian terms. In *Thalassa* Ferenczi also differentiated between two kinds of functions carried out by bodily organs—utility and pleasure. Acts of pleasure discharge energy that is not needed for the utilitarian aim of survival.*

Ferenczi died of pernicious anemia in 1933. Jones implied that Ferenczi had "a latent" psychosis that affected his later work. It is true that shortly before he died Ferenczi displayed the mental symptoms that characteristically appear when the central-nervous-system functions have become organically impaired by the ravages of pernicious anemia. However, Sandor Lorand has excellent evidence to support his claim that Ferenczi showed no signs of mental deterioration except at his very last weeks of life.[2]

---

* This concept led Franz Alexander to formulate his idea of surplus energy and thus advance an instinct theory that does not require a distinction between the sexual and destructive instincts. See "Theory of Instincts" in Chapter 19.

CHAPTER **16**

The Dissenters

Alfred Adler

In the fall of 1902 Freud was ready to emerge from his years of enforced withdrawal. He invited Kahane, Reitler, Stekel, and Alfred Adler (1870–1937) to join the Wednesday-evening discussion group that was to become the first psychoanalytic society. Adler was invited because he had publicly defended Freud's concepts.

Adler was thirty-two when he joined the small controversial Viennese group. He was thoroughly familiar with the cultural climate of Vienna and was no stranger to controversy. Born in Penzing, a suburb of Vienna, he spent his youth in the environs of Vienna and attended its university, from which he received his medical degree in 1895. His knowledge of the history of psychology and of German philosophy, especially of the works of Schopenhauer, Kant, and Nietzsche, his ability to quote the Bible, Shakespeare, and Greek tragedies, and his eloquent speaking ability accounted for his holding the center of attention at the familiar Viennese coffee-houses. Adler's gregariousness and his lively sense of humor added to his popularity.

He also had a profound social consciousness. While treating underprivileged laborers he noted the deplorable conditions under which they worked. He was particularly moved by the grievous social problems of tailors, and his pamphlet and lectures on the health of tailors so stirred public sentiment that social reforms were instituted. Struck by the frequency of eye disorders among tailors, Adler turned his medical interests to eye diseases for a brief time before entering into general practice. Then influenced by the lectures of Richard Krafft-Ebing, the president of the Viennese

Neurological Society, he turned to neurology, hoping to combine his social interests and his medical background.

Adler had been considering the roles played by organic disease as well as social conditions in the psychic life of his patients. He therefore welcomed the opportunity to participate in Freud's study group, which seemed to offer something new and stimulating to psychological thought.

In his first major publication (1907) after joining the group, Adler was still very much the medical man. He provided empirical medical observations of organic defects, while promising that "at some future time, I shall . . . make the connection"[1] between clinical medicine and psychology. Adler recorded family histories in which a tendency toward an organ or organ-system defect repeatedly occurred in its members. He noted that often when the weakness was in an unpaired organ system there existed an innate tendency for that organ to "compensate" by enlarging so as to perform more efficiently. For example, a defective heart might enlarge and thereby overcome its original handicap. When a defect occurs in a paired-organ system—for example, in one eye—the unaffected eye might compensate for the functional failure. It is as though the organism attempts to maintain optimal function in the face of organic handicap. Equally essential were psychological compensations. For example, a boy's eyeball was accidentally pierced. Though there was a constitutional weakness in his sight due to heredity (four close members of his family had weak eyes), he could overcome the handicaps of trauma and constitution by "psychical exertion."[2] Biographies of great men have revealed how they overcame handicaps through courageous effort. Demosthenes surmounted his stammering to become a great orator and Lord Byron, despite a club foot, became an expert swimmer.

Adler knew from his own personal experience the meaning of somatic defect. Because of rickets he had not walked until he was four. Soon after he could move about he developed a serious case of pneumonia. While still uncertain on his feet he was involved in several street accidents. Yet, instead of resigning himself to a life of infirmity, Adler resolved to become a doctor. While longing to join other boys in athletics, he spent his time reading the great classical writers. In his hobbies he pursued his botanical and biological interests by cultivating flowers and collecting pigeons. Because of his defect it is as understandable that Adler later became so intensely gregarious as it is that his introductory work to psychology began with the study of organ inferiority. In his 1907 work Adler stressed that failure to adapt to organic weakness led to emotional disturbances.[3]

Adler's concepts of organ inferiority were further elaborations of the homeostatic principle of the great French physiologist Claude Bernard and W. B. Cannon. Unlike inanimate matter, living organisms have a means whereby they can master internal defects. Because of this capacity, families in which there are faulty organ systems need not be eliminated by natural selection. In fact, consistent with Darwinism, a goal of the human struggle for survival is the compensation for defect.* Freud considered Adler's contribution of 1907 a "valuable work on the inferiority of organs" and expected that Adler would eventually extend his work to "The biological foundations of instincts."[4]

In 1908 Adler did turn his interests to instincts, but not as Freud had anticipated. Freud had proposed in 1905 that the basis for neurosis was a conflict between the ego instincts (the self-preservative drives) versus the sexual instincts. Adler was searching for a principle that would unify psychological and biological phenomena and still fall within the framework of an acceptable instinct theory. The aggressive drive was introduced by Adler as a unitary-instinct principle in which the primary drives, whatever they might be, lose their autonomy and find themselves subordinated to this one drive. The aggressive instinct, then, was the biological *Anlage,* or source, of psychic energy utilized when individuals overcome their organic inferiorities through compensation: ". . . unstable psychological equilibrium is always reestablished by the fact that the primary drive is satisfied through excitation and discharge of the aggression drive."[5] If there were a "confluence of drives"†—for example, if the sexual and aggressive drives occurred together—the latter was always the superordinated one. In the 1908 paper Adler proposed that drives could be turned into opposites, for example, the instinct of voyeurism could be turned into exhibitionistic behavior. Furthermore, a drive could be turned against oneself. Freud adopted these two principles in regard to instincts, calling the former "reaction formation" and the latter "turning" of the instinct "upon the subject."[6] Later, Anna Freud, in *The Ego and Mechanisms of Defense,* listed these mechanisms as two basic ego defenses.

At this point Adler was not aware that he was dealing with unconscious defensive functions of the ego. Nor was he, in his 1908 paper, attempting to create another dualistic-instinct theory. Instead, he was searching for a basic and "higher principle of motivation."[7] Even though the aggressive drive as conceived by Adler was constitutionally and biologically derived, Freud could not include it in his instinct theory. Freud considered, in the case of Little Hans, that the boy's hostile and aggressive feelings were manifestations of "aggressive propensities," which seems "a most striking confirmation of Adler's views."[8] Nevertheless, Freud believed that all instincts have the "power of becoming aggressive."[9] He could see no reason at this time to include the aggressive instinct in his duality concept

* In France in the same year as Adler's publication, Pierre Janet had proposed similar ideas in his "Sentiment de Incompletitude" (Sentiments of Incompleteness).

† Freud borrowed the phrase "confluence of drives," acknowledging that it came from Adler.[10]

or even to give it a place of preeminence, as Adler had proposed. By 1923, in *Beyond the Pleasure Principle,* Freud had placed the aggressive instinct within the death instinct, which was considered antagonistic to the life instinct. By this time Adler considered that the aggressive drive was really a mode of striving by which one adapts to arduous life tasks. Adler, when freed of the necessity to reason in terms of instincts, had sarcastically remarked that he was glad to have made a present to Freud of the aggressive drive. Adler was never to ask for the return of this gift.

It was not this paper on the aggressive instinct that initiated the break with Freud, but rather Adler's work in the years 1910 and 1911. In 1910 Adler wrote for the first time about "feelings" of inferiority and thus laid the cornerstone for his theory that the child *feels* weak and insignificant in relationship to adults.* Biological stresses and the outcome of instinctual strivings were now relegated to insignificant roles as compared to how individuals reacted to feelings of inferiority. The crucial reaction was that of the "masculine protest." The masculine position in our culture is one of strength; the feminine is one of weakness. Each of us has a feeling of weakness (femininity) and a masculine tendency to overcome it, and from this point of view we are psychologically "hermaphrodites."[11] Freud had had a similar notion some thirteen years previously, which he felt could not be validated.[12] However, another concept that Freud never disavowed was that of bisexuality. The latter, nonetheless, instinctually rooted and to be taken literally, was dissimilar to Adler's concept of hermaphroditism, which considered sex metaphorically.

Adler was now proposing that sexuality be considered in its symbolic sense. Women in our culture do not have a tendency to become neurotic because they covet the penis but because they envy the preeminence of man in contemporary culture. To women the penis symbolizes the over-exalted position of man in society. Should they wish to become men by renouncing their femininity, they will suffer from neurotic symptoms, such as painful menses, painful intercourse, or even homosexuality, all of which are expressive of their masculine protest reactions. Men who try to become excessively masculine are not reacting to anxiety over fear of castration but are overcompensating for their feelings of inadequacy as men. Adler considered that dreams constantly demonstrated the masculine protest reaction.

By 1911 Adler became bold in his criticisms of Freud's sexual theories.[13] The Oedipal situation was not to be understood as the striving of the boy to achieve sexual pleasure with his mother but instead as a symbolic battle.

* In later years when Adler surveyed family constellations and situational stresses, he added other circumstances that leave the child with feelings leading to an inferiority complex. (*Problems of Neurosis,* 1929; *What Life Should Mean to You,* 1931.)

Feeling weak and defenseless, the boy uses overcompensation to achieve superiority over the father and dominance over the mother.[18]*

In 1910 Freud had attempted to reconcile himself with the Adlerians, who resented his favoritism toward Jung.† He named Adler president of the Viennese Analytic Society and appointed Adler and Stekel as co-editors of the *Zentralblatt für Psychoanalyse.*

These measures proved temporary, since a heated polemic was brewing. Freud acknowledged that Adler had made "useful contributions to the psychology of the ego."[15] However, psychoanalysts had not yet fully resolved the problem of instinct theory and at this time were theoretically unequipped to deal with the defenses of the ego. Furthermore, Adler had not made it clear how the masculine protest differs from repression. Instead of emphasizing that the masculine protest occurs in the process of repressing feminine traits, Adler reversed the relative importance of these factors and saw repression as "only a small segment of the effects of the masculine protest."‡ It was equally unclear whether neurotic symptoms evolved because of the lack of the use of overcompensation or with the failure of that mechanism. Moreover, neurotic symptoms all appeared to have as their goal the purpose of dominating someone in the environment. To the Freudians this was not a prime cause of symptoms, but coincided with what they considered to be the pleasurable secondary gains of an illness. Adler's system, which dismissed repression and replaced causality with teleology, had relegated the libido to a no man's land. The establishment of one ego mechanism as a mainstay only led to its condemnation as an oversimplification. Freud had not toiled for more than fifteen years only to see his cherished basic concepts cast aside in favor of a system that he considered superficial. He had regarded Adler as a "remarkable intellect" and hoped he would help to develop psychoanalytic theory. Freud's disappointment was bitter as he realized the time for reconciliation had passed. In his own words: "There is room enough on God's earth, and anybody who can is fully entitled to cut any capers he likes on it without interference; but it is not a good thing for people who no longer understand one another and no longer agree to remain under the same roof together."[17]

Adler rejected Freud's insistence on adherence to basic doctrine. Freud, he believed, was behaving as the typical insecure, threatened eldest son who had to domineer tyrannically in order to protect himself against "de-

---

* Later Adler stated that "this so-called Oedipal complex is not a 'fundamental fact' but is simply a vicious unnatural result of maternal overindulgence."[14]
† Freud had invited Jones, Ferenczi, and Jung in 1909 to accompany him to the United States to speak at Clark University. At the second International Congress in Nuremberg in 1910 he had proposed that Jung be made president, with power to direct the training of analysts.
‡ These are Adler's words as recorded by the secretary of the meeting in February, 1911, in which Freud and Adler presented their differences.[16]

thronement."* Adler never would adhere to precepts that he considered provincial. As a younger man, he had abandoned the Jewish orthodoxy of his ancestors because he believed that it engendered parochial isolationism. If Judaism was believed by Adler to be constraining, Freud's group was even more restricting for him. By 1911 Adler felt he was no longer a member of an open discussion group and with nine of the thirty-five members of the Viennese Psychoanalytic Society resigned from that organization to found the Society for *Free* Psychoanalysis. With this caption they exhibited their contempt for the alleged insular policies of the Freudian circle.

In historical perspective it is unjustified to maintain that Freud was so dictatorial that he could tolerate no contrary opinion. Freud himself, in his autobiography, refers to many intelligent men who made contributions to psychoanalysis, "who have worked with me for some fifteen years in loyal collaboration and for the most part in uninterrupted friendship."[18] The disagreements that many of these workers had with Freud are recorded in the pages of this book. It is equally unreasonable to assume that Adler's sole motivation was to usurp an older brother's authority. This entirely negates Adler's intelligent system of thought and disregards the genuine dissatisfaction that he and others had with the libido theory. Furthermore, it is contradictory to the testimony of many men and women who worked with Adler and considered him least of all a power-seeking person.

In 1912 the Adlerian group changed its name to the more appropriate Society for Individual Psychology. By this title they signified their regard for man as a holistic, unique unity incapable of being subdivided into various instincts. Freed of a biological orientation, Adler's interest turned to social philosophy in order to redefine his system in terms of the individual.

He became impressed with the writings of Hans Vaihinger (1852–1933), the idealistic positivist, who had in 1911 published *The Philosophy of the 'As If'*. Vaihinger had proposed that there were social "fictions" that had no basis in reality but that nonetheless became the foundation for social action. "All men are created equal" is an example[19] of a fictitious statement that has served as an operative slogan and influenced the lives of countless people. In one of Adler's most important works, *The Neurotic Constitution,* completed in 1912 and published several years later, he individualized the concept of socially fictitious goals. He showed that man continually deludes himself by accepting fictions that become his final goals. The neurotic's character traits, his symptoms, and even his dreams could be understood as means by which individuals, compensating for their feelings of lack of self-esteem, strive for power over their fellow men in

* Adler elaborated on the manner in which the position of the child in the family (as the youngest, middle, eldest, or only child) may lead to feelings of inferiority in his work on the *Problems of Neurosis,* 1929.

order to reach the fictitious goal of completion. Because of earlier life experiences we have come to feel incomplete, imperfect. We are unaware that we have constructed a plan of life (later called "style of life"), the purpose of which is to pursue the fictional goal of superiority, by driving ourselves into positions of power over others. Adler noted that Nietzsche had expressed the view that goals of this sort are pursued with a "Will to Power." The greater the feelings of inferiority, the stronger is the need to control and overpower others.

The Adlerians, in competition with the Freudians, and as yet unaccepted in medical circles, took a defensive position and tended to utter their principles in overemphasized terms without qualifying statements. In 1913, preparing their basic concepts, they stated in Proposition One, *"Every neurosis can be understood as an attempt to free oneself from a feeling of inferiority in order to gain a feeling of superiority."*[20] In Proposition Eleven it was stated: *"All* the volition and *all* the strivings of the neurotic are dictated by his prestige-seeking policy. . . ."*[21] In several of the propositions Adler's interest in social problems was evident, and later it was to play an even more prominent role in his thinking.

His wife and his socialist friends believed that war was caused by economic tensions. For Adler this was not the full explanation, as it did not account for man's participation in war as part of his quest for egoistic gain. The ideal of peace, Adler thought, could be accessible only when man surrendered his self-centered orientation, which seeks to overcome feelings of insignificance. Even during the horrors of World War I Adler had seen remarkable examples of man's unselfish duty to his fellow beings. From those days onward Adler emphasized the importance of *Gemeinschafts-gefühl*—only through good will, not with a "will to power," could man find his full potential as a productive member of society.

In his later writings Adler stressed that the criterion of normality is reflected by the degree to which a person could direct himself to his work, love his fellow man, and fulfill his social and communal obligations. The "normal" person can place humanistic values above his selfish interests because he has overcome his compulsive egocentric goals. Adler's belief in the normal man and his capacity for social cooperativeness was summarized in his book *Social Interest*. In this he states: "The growing irresistible evolutionary advance of social feeling warrants us in assuming that the existence of humanity is inseparably bound up with 'goodness.' "[22] In the same book Adler acknowledges that individual psychology has been transforming through the years into a "psychology of values."[23] He believed that children could be helped to attain their own creativity while living in harmony with their peers if they were properly guided by their teachers and parents. Education of children was essential for the perpetuation of the social values of the community. In 1919 in Vienna he founded the first child-guidance clinic. Throughout his later years Adler remained an indefatigable lecturer to parents, teachers and the constant adviser to child-guidance clinics.

For Adler the role of psychotherapist was as meaningful as that of a teacher. It was crucial that the patient feel no inequality between himself and the therapist. The atmosphere in which a therapist sat behind a patient on the couch was not to Adler's mind, conducive to promoting parity. Facing the patient, engaging in free discussion (not free association), was the way Adler preferred to work. Sessions were fewer per week and comparatively shorter than in Freudian analysis.

He believed that the task of the therapist is to interpret, whenever it becomes apparent, how the patient deceived himself in regard to his life style. Because of the interest, warmth, and activity of the therapist, the patient's feelings of being attacked or criticized are minimized. Dreams were regarded as evidence of the patient's attitude toward something in the present—a "symbolic rehearsal of an act that the patient must soon perform in real life—and indicated his personal attitude toward the act."[24] The unconscious, although acknowledged, recedes into the background as the patient and therapist discuss the manner in which early life experiences have led to the patient's feelings of inadequacy and have resulted in his characteristic life plan. Although Adler did not consider that a person had redirected his life style until he had established social interests, his advice did not extend to specifics. A psychotherapist was not to guide a patient into a particular religion, political party, or other prescribed activity. Through insight into his patterns and through a positive experience with the therapist, the patient would become reeducated and find for himself a new and healthier mode of reaction.

Adler's approach is widely applied by contemporary counselors, group therapists, therapists of children, and by psychotherapists who practice supportive psychotherapy. Psychoanalysts and other therapists grant the usefulness of this technique with some patients but would not agree that it is universally applicable to all cases of neurosis and psychosis.

This attempt to find unity in psychological phenomena resulted in a system that oversimplifies its doctrines by recognizing only one basic mechanism of defense. There are many ways in which individuals attempt to overcome their inner conflicts, utilizing defensive patterns other than those of overcompensation. Furthermore, a teleological system does not trace the origin of a *particular* neurotic symptom or explain its unconscious meaning. Instead, all symptoms are grouped under one all-inclusive rubric, the purpose of which is, in this case, to dominate the environment. The Adlerian schema considers sexual motives as indicators of a striving for power. This does not explain the many cases of children who have actual sexual feelings and it would not account for the sexual motive seen so frequently within the context of the Oedipal situation. Adlerian psychology, although recognizing the unconscious, does not stress its influence.

234]   THE HISTORY OF PSYCHIATRY

This is understandable inasmuch as the factor that seems to be beyond the awareness of the patient is in all cases his feelings of inferiority.

Despite these shortcomings, Adler deserves a most significant position in the history of psychoanalysis and psychology because he heralded the arrival of important trends in these fields. He emphasized early two basic principles of psychosomatic medicine: that there is within the organism a basic organ vulnerability and the importance of the individual's inner image in regard to his defective functioning. In 1908 Adler stressed the importance of aggression, which is considered today to be one of the major human attributes with which clinicians must deal. Adler inadvertently proposed that the ego defends itself; he emphasized the one mechanism—overcompensation—and suggested the mechanisms of reaction formation and the turning of aggression unto oneself. These proposals were in advance of the systematic explorations of ego psychology in the 1930's and 1940's.

Although the Adlerians do not underscore transference and counter-transference as do the Freudians, Adler was one of the first to consider the relationship between doctor and patient as a meaningful experience by which an individual overcomes many of his earliest problems. In addition, there are many psychoanalysts today who concede that there are numerous instances in which the patient is more concerned with the symbolic meaning of his sexual inadequacy rather than with the literal threat to the sexual organs. A large group of psychoanalysts would concur with the Adlerians on the importance of decreasing the time of analysis and the frequency of visits.

Finally, credit must be given to Adler for the widespread influence he had had upon teachers, counselors, and educators. The inferiority complex, masculine protest, the value of social investment—all have been practical concepts that have aided professionals in dealing with human problems.

Carl Gustav Jung

Born in 1875 in Kesswil, a small Swiss village, Carl Gustav Jung was the son of a parson of the Reformed Church who was greatly interested in Oriental and classical studies; Jung's paternal grandfather and great-grandfather had been physicians.

An only child until the age of nine, Jung was lonely and withdrawn. Even in his later life he attached great importance to the dreams and events of his childhood. Jung's father tutored him in Latin from the age of six so he was far ahead of his contemporaries when he entered the Gymnasium at Basel; there he spent long hours in the library, absorbed in old books. At nineteen the young bibliophile first read Erasmus' phrase *"Vocatus atque non vocatus deus aderit"*—invoked or not invoked, the god will be present;

he inscribed these words on his bookplate and later had them carved into the stone lintel over the door of his house.[25]

Jung enrolled at the University of Basel in 1895; although his early interests were in anthropology and Egyptology, he chose to study the natural sciences, later changing to medicine. While he was in school he became engrossed in the study of spiritualism and mesmerism and attended a number of spiritualist séances. Just before his final examinations he read an introduction to a textbook of psychiatry written by Krafft-Ebing and "suddenly understood the connection between psychology or philosophy and medical science."[26] He then and there decided to specialize in psychiatry.

In 1900 Jung went to the Burghölzli, the mental hospital and university psychiatric clinic in Zurich, to study under Bleuler. He was able to compile case material that supplemented observations made previously during occult séances; he presented this material in his first book, *On the Psychology and Pathology of So-Called Occult Phenomena*. To use Jung's own words, "the split of personality in a spiritualist medium is traced to tendencies during infancy, and at the roots of the fantasy systems delusionary sexual wishes were discovered."[27] Jung refers several times to Freud's *Interpretation of Dreams* and to Breuer's and Freud's *Studies on Hysteria*. However, Jung also indicated the direction his future development would take and its divergence from Freud's position, both then and later. On the one hand, Jung saw the young somnambulist's "budding sexuality" as "the main cause of this curious clinical picture"[28]; at the same time, he was impressed with the "patient's reincarnation theory in which she appears as the ancestral mother of countless thousands."[29] There are also hints of his later teleological orientation: "It is, therefore, conceivable that the phenomena of double consciousness are simply new character formations, or attempts of the future personality to break through. . . . Somnambulisms sometimes have an eminently teleological significance, in that they give the individual, who would otherwise inevitably succumb, the means of victory."[30]

In this same early work Jung refers to the phenomenon of word associations, a subject to which he devoted much of his research during the years immediately following. He published his conclusions in *Studies in Word Association* (1906), subtitled *Contributions to Experimental Psychopathology*. The pioneer experiments in word association were made by Francis Galton (1822–1911) in 1879. Bleuler introduced the study of word associations at the Burghölzli, using the technique largely as an improved tool for description and classification. Jung recognized the larger importance of association as permitting an efficient detection of characteristic disturbances due to ideas that were emotionally charged. In the word-association test, as developed by Jung, the subject is given a word, to which he must respond with that word which springs most immediately to his mind. For example, to the given word "mother" he might respond "warm" or "big." As a control factor, the tester may offer "neutral" words, which he expects will have no emotional context for the subject. The test evaluates the subject's response to a stimulus word on the basis of the length of time between the stimulus and the response, the nature of the response word, and the behavior of the subject. A significant deviation from normal control subjects in one or all of these factors indicates that affect-laden unconscious content exists. For instance, if upon hearing the word "mother" the subject "blocks," that is, cannot think of a response word, he thereby indicates that the word contains a strong affect. Jung called this combination of the idea with its strong affect a "complex."

Since there were many psychotic patients at the Burghölzli, Jung had ample opportunity to apply his association tests to subjects with dementia praecox. Dementia praecox had undergone much study at that time and was viewed in various ways. As we have noted, Morel, who represented the French view, thought that anyone who was insane (demented) had *"démence précoce,"* meaning dementia that occurred early in life. Kraepelin said that if these people rarely recover, the proper term would be "dementia praecox," carrying the implied prognosis of dementia following soon after the onset of the illness. In 1908 Bleuler said that these people are not demented and that they may recover. He saw their illness as due to a split in psychic functioning. In 1911 he renamed the illness "schizophrenia" to indicate the split in psychic functioning, and in addition, demonstrated that the illness does not invariably lead to mental deterioration. Three years before the publication of Bleuler's classic work on schizophrenia Jung wrote: "The name [dementia praecox] is a very unhappy one, for the dementia is not always precocious nor in all cases is there dementia."[31] After three years of investigation he presented his findings in *The Psychology of Dementia Praecox* (1906), which Jones acknowledged "made history in psychiatry"[32] and of which another devotee of Freud, A. A. Brill, stated that along with Freud's studies this book "forms the cornerstone of modern interpretive psychiatry."[33] In the first quarter of the book Jung gives one of the most comprehensive surveys of the theoretical literature on dementia praecox up to that time. He based his own position on a synthesis of the concepts of many previous workers, especially Kraepelin, Janet, and Bleuler, but maintained that he was most indebted to "the ingenious conceptions of Freud."[34]

Jung cites Freud's two papers (1894, 1896) on "The Defense Neuropsychosis." In the first paper Freud reported the case of a girl forsaken by her lover; her ego rejected the idea that "he is not here" by hallucinating his voice. In this hallucinatory psychosis, as in hysteria and obsessive-compulsive disorders, Freud considered that the symptoms resulted from attempts to defend against unacceptable ideas by repression, so that in this sense they were defense neuropsychoses. In the second paper Freud used a case of paranoia (dementia praecox) to demonstrate that, as in hysteria and obsessions, the emotionally unacceptable experience or idea is partially admitted to consciousness in the compromise-symptom formation representing the return of the repressed. Jung, concurring with Freud and Bleuler, stated that a repressed idea can be linked with an affect; in the association experiments he had called this combination of a repressed idea and its affect a "complex." He defined affect as Bleuler had—a feeling, tone, mood, or emotion that is a "driving force" seeking conscious expression. It is not only the force of the complexes striving toward consciousness that results in the return of the repressed. Jung was familiar with Janet's concept that when consciousness itself is weakened, as it is, for instance, in hypnosis, unconscious processes can thereby emerge into awareness. Theoretically either strong complexes or weakened conscious perceptions may be present in both hysteria and dementia praecox; yet, mostly because of the influence of Kraepelin, dementia praecox carried a relatively poor prognosis and was considered much less reversible than hysteria. Jung consequently wrote that the results "produced by the hysterogenic complex are reparable"[35] but the effects of the dementia praecox complex are "more or less" irreparable. In his next paper (1908) on dementia praecox, *The Content of the Psychoses,* Jung was less convinced that brain degeneration always occurred. He and Bleuler together examined hundreds of psychotic patients and studied autopsy material; undoubtedly they influenced each other.

Kraepelin had postulated that brain injury due to an unknown metabolite, which he called an autotoxin, accounted for the irreversible character of dementia praecox and concluded that this toxin was the basic cause of the illness. Bleuler also believed that some organic condition—either a toxin, infection, or "glial proliferation"—was the underlying determinant in this disorder. In *The Psychology of Dementia Praecox* Jung acknowledged that Kraepelin and Bleuler might be correct but proposed that the toxin could be produced by psychological "complexes" rather than by somatic processes and suggested further that the hysterogenic complex does not release a toxin. Jung thus not only integrated the theories then current but earned the distinction of being the first to offer a tentative psychosomatic model for dementia praecox in which the brain is considered the target organ of emotional influences. Jung's theoretical concept may be summarized as follows: the complex with its powerful affect (Bleuler and Jung) produces a toxin (Kraepelin's toxin is somatic; Jung's is a psychotoxin) that injures the brain, paralyzing psychic functioning (Janet's weakening of consciousness) so that the complex is released from the unconscious and causes the characteristic symptoms of dementia praecox (Freud's return of the repressed). Although Jung gradually abandoned the toxin hypothesis and adopted the more modern concept of disturbed chemical processes, he never abandoned his belief in the primacy of psychogenic factors in schizophrenia. As late as 1958 Jung wrote ". . . psychology is indispensable in explaining the nature and causes of the *initial emotions which give rise to metabolic alterations* [Italics by authors]. These emotions seem to be accompanied by chemical processes that cause specific temporary or chronic disturbances or lesions."[36]

These proposals formulated by Jung in 1906 carried a vital impact since, on such a basis, dementia praecox could be understood within a psychoanalytic framework. By 1914 he went further, stating that "the practicing analyst knows cases where patients on the borderline of dementia praecox could still be brought back to normal life."[37] At that time Freud was not so optimistic and in the same year considered such patients "inaccessible to the influence of psychoanalysis"[38] because they had withdrawn their interests from people.

In this book on dementia praecox Jung, a respected Swiss psychiatrist, drew wide attention to Freud's theories and deplored the fact that Freud was a "hardly recognized investigator."[39] Just before he put the finishing touches on the book, in April, 1906, Jung initiated a correspondence with Freud. At the end of February, 1907, he journeyed to Vienna, accompanied by his wife and Ludwig Binswanger, who was then a volunteer physician at the Burghölzli, to meet Freud. This first meeting lasted for thirteen uninterrupted hours; as Jung recalled later, "It was a *tour d'horizon.*" He found Freud and his circle "impressive" and at the same time "peculiar" to a man of his background.[40]

Freud unquestionably must have looked forward to this meeting. He was grateful to the Zurich group for their efforts to gain recognition for psychoanalysis. He was eager to establish psychoanalysis on a broader basis than could be provided by his Viennese coterie of Jewish intellectuals. He considered Switzerland the hub of international scientific activity, whereas Vienna lay outside the great centers of Western European culture. In a letter to Abraham in the spring of 1908 Freud wrote: "It was only his [Jung's] emergence on the scene that has removed from psychoanalysis the danger of becoming a Jewish national affair."[41] Moreover, beyond considering that he was bringing respectability to psychoanalysis, Freud regarded Jung as "a truly original mind." He saw in him "the Joshua destined to explore the promised land of psychiatry which Freud, like Moses, was only permitted to view from afar."[42]

In view of all this, it is perhaps significant that Freud did not mention this first visit of Jung either in *The History of the Psychoanalytic Movement* or in his autobiography. A possible explanation of this curious omission is suggested in Binswanger's report: "The day after our arrival Freud questioned Jung and me about our dreams. I do not recall Jung's dream, but I do recall Freud's interpretation of it, namely, that Jung wished to dethrone him and take his place."[43] This fear of being displaced by Jung again became apparent in an episode that occurred when both were in Bremen in 1909. Jung wanted to make an excursion to see some relics of anthropological interest, whereupon Freud became very irritated and jumped to the conclusion that Jung's interest in the dead bodies indicated a wish for Freud's death.[44]

Freud's ambivalent feelings were paralleled by Jung's tendency to vacillate between wholehearted espousal of Freud's theories and cautious reservations. At the first International Congress of Psychiatry and Neurology in Amsterdam Jung read a paper on *The Freudian Theory of Hysteria,* intended as a defense of psychoanalysis but turning out to be almost an apology for Freud's ideas, or at least his use of such terms as "infantile sexuality" and "libido." Considering their later differences, it is interesting to note what Jung had to say at this time on Freud's sexual symbolism: "There are uncommonly far-reaching and significant analogies between the Freudian symbolisms and the symbols of poetic fantasy in individuals and in whole nations. The Freudian symbol and its interpretation is therefore nothing unheard of; it is merely something unusual for us psychiatrists."[45]

During the next few years Jung wrote a number of papers that hew precisely to the lines of classical Freudian analysis. The most clear-cut statements are found in *The Significance of the Father in the Destiny of the Individual* (1909). It may be seen that during this period Jung carried the Freudian position to an extreme, as in the following passage, omitted from later editions: "If we now survey all the far-reaching possibilities of the infantile constellation, we are obliged to say that *in essence our life's fate is identical with the fate of our sexuality*" [Italics by authors].[46] At the same time, there are glimmerings of Jung's later concept of opposing tendencies: ". . . the conscious expression of the father-constellation, like every expression of an unconscious complex when it appears in consciousness, acquires its Janus face, its positive and its negative components."[47]

There is no doubt that Jung made a considerable contribution to the budding psychoanalytic movement. A few months after his first visit to Freud he founded the Freud Society in Zurich and in 1908 organized the First International Psychoanalytical Congress at Salzburg, where the first periodical devoted exclusively to psychoanalysis, the *Jahrbuch für psychoanalytische und psychopathologische Forschungen,* was founded, with Bleuler and Freud as directors and Jung as editor. In 1909 Jung gave up his post as chief physician at the Burghölzli in order to devote himself to psychoanalytic practice and activities. At the 1910 Congress at Nuremberg, the International Psychoanalytical Association was founded, and as we have seen Jung was elected president over the angry protests of the Viennese group. According to Freud, the selection of Jung was based on his "exceptional talents, the contributions he had already made to psychoanalysis, his independent position and the impression of assured energy which his personality conveyed."[48]

Despite his prominent position in the psychoanalytic movement, Jung felt a growing uneasiness. The originality that had marked his early writing was absent in the papers he published during the years when he was primarily concerned with defending Freudian theories. Then, in 1910, he embarked on the project of extending psychoanalytic principles to subjects that had fascinated him for years, namely, material gathered from myths, legends, fables, stories from the classics, and poetic fantasies. After more than a year of research Jung published his findings in the first half of Volume III of the *Jahrbuch* (1911) under the title *Wandlungen und Symbole der Libido, Part I.** In *Wandlungen I* Jung quoted a vast number of sources in order to draw a "parallel" between the fantasies of the ancients, as expressed in myths and legends, and the "similar thinking of children."[49] He also set out to demonstrate the "connection between dream psychology and myth psychology."[50] Jung acknowledged that Rank, Franz Riklin (another early psychoanalyst), Abraham, and Jones had come to similar conclusions, albeit on the basis of fewer sources; Jung however, took a further step and arrived at the unique position that mind "possesses . . . historical strata" containing "archaic mental products" that become manifest in a psychosis when there is "strong" regression.[51] He argued that since symbols used throughout the ages are similar, they are "typical" and cannot belong to one individual alone. This sequence of ideas contains the germ of Jung's later concept of the collective unconscious.

Freud was always pleased when psychoanalytic writers delved into mythological material. He was impressed with *Wandlungen I,* and a few months after it appeared he published a statement concurring with Jung's position that dreams and neurotic fantasies are similar not only to the thinking of the child but also to the primitive mentality as revealed in ethnological research.[52]† There is no hint yet that Freud deemed it necessary to take issue with these earliest formulations of the archaic unconscious. Only in 1913, in *Totem and Taboo,* did Freud indicate his points of disagreement with this theory of Jung; in the fourth part—"The Infantile Recurrence of Totemism"—he took sharp issue with Jung and says that there is a "parallel," or "analogy," between the psychologies of primitives, children, and neurotics, whereas Jung assumes a continuity of archaic material gathered into a collective unconscious.

In the same section of the 1911 *Jahrbuch* in which *Wandlungen I* appeared, Freud discussed the mechanisms of paranoid delusion by examining the memoirs of Daniel Paul Schreber, a psychotic who had been

* The English translation by Beatrice M. Hinkle (including both Parts I and II) carries the title *Psychology of the Unconscious: A Study of the Transformations and Symbolisms of the Libido.* New York: Moffat, Yard & Company, 1916.

† In a postscript to the Schreber case, published in the second half of Volume III of the *Jahrbuch,* pp. 588–590.

president of the Court of Appeals of Saxony. Since Freud had little opportunity to study psychotic patients, it is probably true, as Jung claimed, that it was he who had called Freud's attention to Schreber's autobiography.[53] Freud, attempting to understand Schreber's "end-of-the-world" fantasy, used the explanation that his "internal" turmoil was projected outward so that he felt the world was collapsing. Schreber, Freud continued, was unable to maintain his ties to the external world because he had withdrawn his libido from the real world of things and people. But Freud himself was not fully satisfied with this explanation, since it did not clarify what happens to the ego instincts. In the absence of a "well-grounded theory of instincts," he considered two different hypotheses: it must be assumed either that the sexual libido coincides with "interest in general" or that a disturbance in the distribution of the sexual libido exerts a disruptive effect on the ego.[54] Freud's thinking evidently followed the line of the second hypothesis, since he subsequently stated in this article that the libido, after its detachment from the external world, regresses "onto the ego."

In *Wandlungen II* (1912) Jung quoted the passage that suggested the alternate hypotheses and emphasized Freud's first choice, libido coinciding with "interest in general."[55] Jung did this in order to divest the psycho-analytic libido theory of its sexual connotations. He argued that the psychotic had withdrawn not just his sexual interests but all his general interests from the external world. Although he had defended Freud's position on sexuality for a number of years, he had never totally accepted the sexual theories, and in taking this position Jung was now interpreting libido in a way that Freud had not intended. Freud had indicated that libido was not to be understood in the restricted sense of genital love as known by adults. When he first (1905) proposed his dualistic-instinct theory (ego instincts or self-preservative instincts versus sexual instincts) the term "libido" was synonymous with gaining pleasurable gratification. Freud's view of the libido, although broader than Jung's, was not so broad as the one proposed by Jung in *Wandlungen II,* which eliminated the sexual connotation. In *Wandlungen II* Jung also correctly noted that Freud had not differentiated neurosis from psychosis in the paper on Schreber and that withdrawal of libido must be presumed to occur in both. In 1913 Jung argued further that if merely the sexual libido is withdrawn on to the ego, the result would be not dementia praecox but the psychology of an ascetic whose "whole endeavor is to exterminate every trace of sexual interest." After these arguments in *Wandlungen II* Jung began to swing his ax more heavily against Freud's sexual theories. He proposed that primitive man had a primal-sexual libido that became desexualized in the course of the ages; modern man thus exhibits the paradox of a nonsexual mental life that continues to present images of primitive sexual origin that by this time, however, have been divested of their sexual connotation. "The sexuality of the unconscious is not what it seems to be; *it is merely a symbol* . . . a step forward to every goal of life, but expressed in the unreal sexual language of the unconscious and in the thought-form of an earlier stage; a resurrection . . . of earlier modes of adaptation."[56]

Jung's idea that the libido should be equated with general interest did not explain the psychology of schizophrenia any more than had Bergson's *"élan vital"* or Schopenhauer's *"Wille,"* which Jung admits are akin to his concept of the libido. He also likened libido to undifferentiated psychic energy similar to Robert Mayer's physical energy.[57]* Such a wide extension of the libido concept is tantamount to stating that an individual becomes psychotic because he hasn't normal interests! This could hardly be claimed as a psychodynamic explanation.

It took Freud over a year to respond to Jung's arguments in *Wandlungen II,* for he had to revise his libido theory to meet this challenge. He obviously could not see his libido concept entirely abandoned, for he considered it to be the only basis for an understanding of mental aberrations. Yet he must have realized the pertinence of Jung's contention that the libido theory did not sufficiently distinguish neuroses from psychoses. His answer came in *On Narcissism* (1914), in which Freud states that the psychotic affixes his withdrawn libido to his own ego and thereby returns to a state of infantile self-love (narcissism); the neurotic retains a mental image of objects from the external world and attaches his libido to this image. Thus the neurotic does not break off his "erotic relations to persons and things," whereas the psychotic loses his tie to reality by regressing to the state of narcissism. Furthermore, Freud refuted Jung's argument about the ascetic by pointing out that the anchorite may appear to have "exterminated" sexual interest, when actually he has "sublimated it to a heightened interest in the divine, in nature, or in the animal kingdom, without his libido having undergone introversion to his fantasies or retrogression to his ego."[59]

This libido controversy had an important impact on psychoanalytic theory. In *On Narcissism* Freud replaced the conflict of ego instincts against sexual instincts with a new dualism of ego-libido (narcissism, or self-love) against object-libido (love of others). On the basis of the new concept the essential issue became whether the sexual instincts turn to the self or to the outer world.

Thus the very problem that brought Jung and Freud together in the first place, namely, the psychic mechanism underlying dementia praecox, subsequently was the cause of serious differences regarding the libido theory, ultimately leading to the severance of their collaboration. Compared with this fundamental disagreement, other issues—the understanding of myths,

---

* Glover, whose statements in his "Freud or Jung?" were often exaggerated because of his bias in favor of Freud, nevertheless made a cogent argument regarding the inconsistencies of the many-faceted-libido concepts of Jung: If the "will" is noninstinctual and at the same time is equated with libido, which is presumed to be instinctual, a serious impasse results.[58]

the interpretation of symbols and dreams, and so forth—were of secondary importance. In addition, interlinked with this theoretical controversy were personal tensions that presaged the final break.

Jung felt that several events during the American lecture tour of 1909 reflected a coolness in Freud's attitude toward him. During a session of mutual analysis, for example, Freud declined to give associations to one of his dreams, saying that to do so would cause him to lose his authority.[60] This lack of frankness was seen by Jung as a loss of Freud's confidence in him and also as exposing a weakness in Freud. At any rate, Jung was convinced that from then on their personal relationship began to suffer. There is little evidence, however, that Freud's feelings for Jung had changed at that time. In the early months of 1911 he still considered Jung his "Crown Prince" and staunchly maintained: "When the empire I founded is orphaned, no one but Jung must inherit the whole thing."[61]

Later that year, however, Freud became irritated with Jung because the time he devoted to research and to a second trip to America seemed to interfere with the duties of his office as president of the International Association. Furthermore, Jung was tardy in answering Freud's letters. Other minor details, together with the fact that Jung played down the sexual theory in his Fordham lectures, were the "first signs" that prompted Freud to "withdraw his libido" from Jung, as he wrote to Binswanger on July 9, 1912.[62] Their correspondence soon became quite impersonal and restricted to business matters. In September, 1913, Jung and Freud met for the last time at the International Congress in Munich, where Jung was reelected as president of the International Psychoanalytic Association.

At this meeting Jung read a paper entitled *A Contribution to the Study of Psychological Types* in which he attempted to establish a correlation between "nosological types" on the basis of the direction of libidinal flow. In dementia praecox the patient has withdrawn his general interest from the world—designated by Jung as "introversion"—and exhibits an apathetic response to his environment. The hysteric, in contrast, has an abnormally intense level of affective investment in the external world— which Jung called "extroversion"—and presents a picture of "exaggerated emotivity." These two opposite directions of libidinal flow were assumed to be psychic mechanisms encountered in normal persons as well as in mental patients; furthermore, they also appear in the differences between various schools of psychoanalysis. Jung considered Freud's insistence on "empirical facts" and on the concept of the libido gaining pleasure from the environment as an expression of Freud's extroverted attitude. Adler, on the other hand, who emphasized the internal guiding fictions, was expressing his own exaggerated introverted tendencies. In the concluding sentence of this paper Jung spoke of his own plans for elaborating a balanced analytic psychology "which should pay equal attention to the two types of mentality."

One month after the Munich Congress Jung resigned as editor of the

Jahrbuch and in April, 1914, as president of the Association. In July, 1914, after the appearance of Freud's *The History of the Psychoanalytic Movement,* in which Freud demonstrated the incompatibility of his views with those of Adler and Jung, the entire Zurich group withdrew from the International Association.

After his parting from Freud and the psychoanalytic movement, Jung "had to establish his own values, to gain a new orientation, to be himself."[63] During the remaining years of his life he achieved an impressive literary output of more than a hundred books, articles, and reviews. He traveled far and wide to study primitive civilizations—to the Pueblo Indians in Arizona and New Mexico; to the Elgony in British East Africa; to the Sudan, Egypt, and India. He read papers at many international congresses and in 1937 delivered the Terry Lectures at Yale, taking as his subject the relationship of psychology and religion. He resumed teaching in 1933, giving weekly lectures at the Eidgenössische Technische Hochschule in Zurich. In 1944 the University of Basel created for him a chair in medical psychology, from which, however, he resigned after a short while for reasons of health. On the occasion of his sixtieth birthday he was presented with a voluminous *Festschrift* and a still more impressive one for his eightieth birthday, which was celebrated by friends and colleagues in Zurich, London, New York, and San Fransisco. The crowning honor, however, came on his eighty-fifth birthday, when the little town of Küsnacht, where he had made his home for more than half a century, elected him *Ehrenbürger* (Freeman of the township), a distinction that Jung is said to have appreciated more than even such high professional recognition as being made a Fellow of the Royal Society of Medicine of London. He became an honorary D.Sc. of Oxford University, an honorary member of the Swiss Academy of Medicine, and received honorary degrees from Harvard, the universities of Calcutta, Banaras, and Allahabad, among others. In 1958, three years before his death, a congress of analytical psychologists, the first on an international scale, took place in Zurich with one hundred and twenty participants.

On the whole Jung's psychology has found more followers among speculative philosophers, poets, and religionists than in medical psychiatry. Training centers for Jungian analytical psychology, although they require as long a teaching program as Freudian institutes, do accept nonmedical candidates. Jung admitted that he had never presented his "endeavors in psychology . . . systematically" because, in his opinion, "a dogmatic system" slips "all too easily into a certain assertive style."[64] Although he recognized the importance of Freud's causal approach, Jung considered it to be reductive and felt that mental life could be better understood by a teleological perspective. The psyche has a future as well as a past; the study of the mind should reveal not only whence a man has come but also the direction of his future. Jung maintained that the causal view is finite and therefore portends fatalism; his own teleological position holds out hope that man need not be victimized by his past.

Jung's concept of the symbol is that it represents unconscious thoughts and feelings that are able to transform psychic energy—libido—into positive and constructive values. Dreams, myths, and religions are the means of coping with conflicts through wish fulfillment as revealed in psychoanalysis; in addition, they contain hints for prospective resolutions of neurotic dilemmas. For Jung, the kind of dream interpretation restricted to revealing variations of the Oedipal theme—which is not, incidentally, the sole approach of psychoanalysis—misses the mark by its failure to recognize the creative futurity of the dream. Jung himself was repeatedly inspired by dreams or influenced by them to change the direction of his life, almost as though the dreams had oracular portent.

In his later work Jung suggested techniques of psychotherapy that are susceptible to clinical validation. His method of "active imagination," for instance, is occasionally used by non-Jungian therapists. The patient is encouraged to draw or paint whatever fantasied image has spontaneously occurred to him. As changes in the image develop, they will be noted in later drawings. The attempt of the patient to make his drawing represent more exactly the image that he visualizes may help him to associate to his preconscious or conscious imagery. Jung believed that this technique benefits the patient not only by allowing him to talk about his fantasy but also by actually doing something about it.

Jung conceded that the Freudian and Adlerian psychotherapeutic techniques may be efficacious in young persons who are concerned with sexual problems or who have a need to express their assertiveness, but he emphasized that his own method is more suitable for the older patient who is struggling with existential questions. The person past middle age who, although non-neurotic, lacks purpose may turn to religion or to the philosophy of Zen or Yoga or to the psychology of Jung for direction and solace. An individual may seek tranquillity from whatever source he chooses. However, such an approach is not effective when aimlessness is the result of serious unresolved conflicts.

Exploring the individual's potential, attempting to help a patient toward "self-realization," and evaluating neurotic patterns by taking into consideration present-day stress situations are other techniques not confined to the Jungian school alone but utilized by all conscientious psychotherapists. There are certain other phenomena recognized equally by psychoanalysts and the followers of Jung; for example, the compensatory relationship between conscious and unconscious processes has been experimentally reproduced by K. W. Bash, using Rorschach responses of subjects, both awake and in a sleeplike state.[65] A patient facing defeat in an actual life situation who dreams that he performs as a hero can be considered to be compensating for feelings of humiliation linked to earlier, similar experiences in his life; his dream does not necessarily relate to an archetypal figure.

The theoretical framework of Jung's psychology cannot be verified by any clinical means at our disposal. The many psychological tests devised to explore the introversion/extroversion concept of psychological types indicate "that both attitudes are present in varying proportions in virtually all persons"[66]—a fact of which Jung was not unaware. Labeling individuals by attitudinal type does not promote understanding of the causes responsible for such differences in personality structure; consequently this scheme is no improvement over the descriptive classifications evolved during the nineteenth century.

The concept of the collective unconscious is just as speculative. Jung divided the unconscious mind into the personal unconscious (similar to Freud's unconscious plus preconscious) and the collective unconscious, which is "the mighty deposit of ancestral experience accumulated over millions of years, the echo of prehistoric happenings to which each century adds."[67] The collective unconscious contains "primordial images" or "archetypes" that represent modes of thinking that have developed over the centuries. However, the fact that people of different centuries have used similar symbols does not prove that a specific symbol has been inherited from ancestral forebears. Man is qualitatively distinguished from other animals by being a symbolizing creature, and his basic drives and desires have not varied greatly throughout the ages. Nor are there an infinite number of symbols by which man can represent these urges. In any event, it is impossible to trace the archetypes to their origin. As Jung himself jocularly remarked, he "wasn't there when the first archetypes were laid down."[68]

Jung adopted the same terms that Freud used in psychoanalysis but gave them different meanings. This only confused things unnecessarily. For example, it would have been better if Jung had invented another term for his idea of "libido"; the same applies to his later use of "introversion." When Jung introduced the term in 1910 he gave it the meaning of the withdrawal of sexual libido from the external world. This usage was continued by Freud; but after 1911 Jung ultimately came to use this word to describe a specific psychological type rather than a pathological process. A useful term coined by Jung that has survived and is still employed by both schools is "complex."

Although at one time Jung criticized Freud for not paying sufficient attention to the actual conflict situation in which the patient finds himself, this problem became obscured as he developed his antithetical theory of the structure of the mind. The ego—the conscious, vague "I"—is opposed to the personal unconscious; the persona—the mask of oneself that is seen by the world—is opposed to the animus (the male part of the female) or the anima (the female aspect of the male) as well as to the personal unconscious and the collective unconscious; the ego opposed the shadow that is the animal side of the personality. The "self" has the goal of unifying the total personality. This task becomes most difficult if conscious sides of the personality are exaggerated without integration of the unconscious aspects. Psychotherapy—that is, Jungian "analytical psychology"—attempts to bring this "play of opposites" into harmonious integration by evaluating the polar opposites residing in the unconscious, both collective and personal, and in the consciousness. How the therapist can discriminate between the multiple antitheses and assess their relative importances becomes, however, a matter of conjecture; and furthermore, it is well-nigh impossible to detect a major and nuclear conflict in this bewildering maze of opposing interests. Unfortunately Jung does not illuminate any of these problems, since, as one authority states, "much of Jung's later work . . . is so mysterious as to be almost undiscussable."[69]*

To sum up, then, during the first decade of the century Jung made many significant contributions to psychoanalysis. His word-association experiments confirmed Freud's hypothesis of repression, and in turn Jung applied Freud's ideas to dementia praecox, and by stressing the connection between the physiological and psychological aspects of this disease, was able to construct the first psychosomatic model for it. Jung was also instrumental in bringing Freud's work to the attention of the scientific world and later played an important part in organizing the psychoanalytic movement. According to Jung it was he who suggested to Freud that all psychoanalysts should go through a training analysis. Jung's application of psychoanalytic theory to the understanding of myths and their relationship to dreams and neuroses rekindled Freud's interest in anthropology and was thus ultimately responsible for *Totem and Taboo*. Jung's most vital contribution, however, was in pointing out that Freud had failed to distinguish between neurotic and psychotic phenomena in the Schreber case. Freud, faced with the necessity of solving this problem, was spurred on to revise his libido theory. Freud's new understanding of narcissism suggested the nonlibidinal nature of parts of the ego instincts and paved the way for his final dualistic concept of the life instinct versus the death instinct. Thus Freud eventually broadened the concept of libido in his own fashion by combining it with the life instinct.

It can be said, therefore, that the ideas of both men were stimulated by the other's work; however, as far as Jung's development was concerned, Freud's theories had their major impact in the years before they met personally. In spite of his attraction to psychoanalysis and his temporary

* Jung's elusive style and his opportunism enabled racists to use his "racial unconscious" for their own purposes. In the case of national socialist ideas and policies concerning race this was facilitated by Jung's open compromises with the Nazis and his labors under their auspices. For a discussion of this side of Jung's career see Appendix B.

defense of its fundamental principles, Jung never strayed from the mysticism implicit in even his earliest work, in which the seeds of the collective unconscious are apparent. And after 1913 his elaborations of the theories that today typify Jungian thought reveal little or nothing of Freudian influence.

Otto Rank

After Jung's apostasy, the role of heir apparent fell to a brooding, sensitive Viennese intellectual Otto Rank (1884–1939), whom Freud first met when Rank was enrolled in a technical school and was supporting himself by working in a machine shop. Freud appreciated the scope of Rank's knowledge and envisioned that he could someday extend psychoanalytic theory into cultural fields. He had helped with emotional and financial support while Rank was completing his doctorate at the University of Vienna.

Rank had suffered greatly during his adolescent years. He had rheumatism; he was intensely lonely; he was estranged from his emotionally distant mother and was markedly hostile to his alcoholic father, to whom he and his brother did not speak. The diary* he kept during his late teens and early twenties contains many passages that underscore the hopeless depression that beset his tortured soul. "I grew up, left to myself, without friends, without books. I feel for most people no sympathy. I wish not to be buried, but to be burned. As a grave marker I would like a rough, unpolished block of stone. . . . I find myself constantly in a dream state and the kind of reality to which I am forced hurts me. . . . Today I bought a weapon to kill myself. Afterward the keenest lust for life and the greatest courage toward death grew up in me."[70] Rank tried to cope with these feelings of loneliness and emptiness by developing his creative potential. He had within him a burning desire to leave some worthwhile creation for posterity. These themes—separateness, creativeness, and a search for immortality—came to the forefront of his work after his defection from Freud.

Rank's treatise on artists, *Der Künstler,* was influenced by Freud's ideas and impressed Freud to such an extent that in 1906 he invited Rank into the Viennese Psychoanalytic Society. In 1907 Rank published *Der Künstler,* in which he pointed out his indebtedness to Freud, who had read the manuscript prior to publication: "According to a thought of Freud, the artist is able to restore by a peculiar roundabout way the originally pleasurable relationship to the outer world that mankind lost in attaining civilization."[71] Rank's next work was *Myth of the Birth of the Hero,*† in which he

---

* Jessie Taft, who met Rank in 1924 and collaborated closely with him, propagated many of his views in the Philadelphia School of Social Work. Part of her biographical study of Otto Rank contains his early diary.

† Translated into English in 1914.

examined the reason why in the myths of different cultures great heroes are conceived immaculately and born from the ocean. Rank applied this idea through psychoanalytic concepts of symbols and dream mechanisms. An example of symbolism is the story of Moses—a mythological hero who emerges from a box (the symbol for a womb) floating in the water (that is, birth). Dream mechanisms appear, for example, in those myths in which the true father of the hero forces the infant, who is the target of his jealousy, to leave the family. This is a reversal and projection of the son's hostility to the father, a mechanism common in dreams. Ernest Jones acknowledged Rank's special gifts for "interpreting dreams, myths and legends" and was awed by Rank's "vast erudition." Jones wrote that he was "honored when Rank praised a work of his—that the omniscient Rank should be impressed signified much."[72]

The expanding psychoanalytic society as a group was impressed with Rank's work during the next two decades, particularly his contributions to the psychoanalytic understanding of art, literature, and myths. These became especially significant when Jung, the other expert on mythology, defected. Furthermore, Rank's administrative and executive efforts within the movement were much appreciated: he functioned not only as Freud's personal secretary but also as secretary to the Viennese Psychoanalytic Society; he co-edited the journal *Imago* with Hanns Sachs from 1912 to 1924, as well as the *Internationale Zeitschrift für Psychoanalyse;* and he not only founded but also was a director of the Psychoanalytic Institute of Vienna from 1919 to 1924.

As time went on, however, Rank became less and less satisfied with his functions in the movement and came to consider them as assignments and obligations rather than expressions of his originality. Then, in 1923, he wrote, with Ferenczi, *Developmental Goals of Psychoanalysis,* which was translated into English in 1925. Although Ferenczi and Rank claimed they were "in no way differing from Freud,"[73] they first reviewed the classical psychoanalytic technique in this book and then as we have noted they made proposals for revising the analytic method. Ferenczi and Rank recommended that treatment would be shortened if in the last stage of the analysis the analyst set a termination date in order to counteract the "fixation of the patient on the therapist."[74] Their most important suggestion was that emotional experiences should be stressed in the analysis rather than intellectual reconstructions. "The final goal of psychoanalysis is to substitute, by means of the technique, affective factors of experience for intellectual processes."[75]* These proposals influenced other analysts, but Freud, in a letter to Ferenczi, said that these suggestions would lead to an

---

* The proposals to shorten the time of an analysis and the stress on emotional experience stimulated Franz Alexander to experiment with fewer analytic interviews and to emphasize the value of emotional reexperiencing in the transference (see "Developments in Psychoanalytic Treatment" in Chapter 19).

"abuse" of psychoanalytic technique.[76] Freud's coterie was not responsive to these radical suggestions and the book was attacked by many analysts, without much effect on Rank, for this brief essay was the beginning of Rank's complete revisionism.

In his next work, *The Trauma of Birth* (1924), Rank built a psychological system on Freud's statement that the infant's physiological response at the time of birth (for example, cardiac and respiratory acceleration) occurs because of overwhelming sensory stimulation and that these responses remain the prototype of later anxiety. The individual, Rank now said, is forever seeking to return to the blissfulness of intrauterine life. Healthy development occurs when through later experiences of separation from the mother (for example, weaning) the child becomes able to discharge primal anxiety, which had undergone "primal repression." Pathological states result from the fear of the womb and the wish to return to it. (It is not clear, according to Rank, why some children are not able to abreact sufficiently and work through the terrifying experiences of the brith trauma.) The young boy does not refuse to recognize the existence of the female genital because it forces him to recognize that some people have no penis (Freud's castration anxiety), but because the female womb represents the locale of his first horrifying experience. The male homosexual is so frightened of the female genital that he cannot experience pleasure from it. The sexual act itself has the primary purpose of reintroducing the male into the womb and occurs not because of libidinous drives but is a compromise solution for reentering the female body: a part of the body—the penis—returns. These formulations, based on the unproved supposition that memory traces of birth are present in the underdeveloped brain, culminated in a reinterpretation of the Oedipus complex: the child attempts to overcome the trauma of birth by attempting to rid himself of his fear of the mother's genital by wishing to penetrate it. This fails because the child is unequipped physically to reenter his mother and because the anxiety of birth—not guilt—prevents a sustained effort in this endeavor. The problem in life as well as in psychotherapy is to undo finally the horror of separation from the mother or the maternal surrogates.

Freud initially said of *The Trauma of Birth*, "It is the most important progress since the discovery of psychoanalysis."[77] The Central Committee, however, reacted unfavorably to these radical departures from theory and finally influenced Freud to admonish Rank for reducing all of psychoanalysis to one theme, and one that completely disregarded the impact of the father upon the child.* Freud finally concluded that Rank's elimination of the father from his theory was due to his personal problems. At first Rank reacted to the unfavorable criticism with great turmoil. He found it impossible at this time (1924) to leave his mentor and held analytic

---

* Many years later (1930) Rank himself recognized that he had extended the birth trauma *"ad absurdum."*[78]

conferences with Freud, after which he wrote a letter of recantation to the inner Freudian circle (December 20, 1924): ". . . my affective reactions toward the Professor and you, insofar as you represent for me the brothers near to him, stemmed from unconscious conflicts. . . . From a state which I now recognize as neurotic I have suddenly returned to myself. . . . From analytic interviews with the Professor, in which I could explain in detail the reactions based on affective attitudes, I gain the hope that I was successful in clarifying first of all the personal relationship, since the Professor found my explanations satisfactory and has forgiven me personally. . . . I shall be able to see things more objectively after the removal of my affective resistance."[79]

Finally, however, by 1929, Rank was able to separate himself from Freud's influence: he ceased making apologies and no longer wrote in the Freudian idiom. By this time he also realized the fruitlessness of analogizing from physiology to psychology and stressed not so much the birth trauma as the important periods in an individual's life, those periods in which he tries to separate himself from parental influences and thus gradually gains his own individuality. Other ideas that Rank expressed in these later works involved his concepts of will and counter-will. He stated that "Freud conceives of the individual as ruled by instinctual life [the id] and repressed by the superego, a will-less plaything of two impersonal forces. On the contrary, I understand by will a positive guiding organization and integration of self which utilizes creatively, as well as inhibits and controls, the instinctual drives."[80] The will is that part of the personality that struggles against opposing forces that attempt to inhibit the development of separateness. It develops early with the counter-will, which is directed against parental restrictions, and continues until the uniqueness of the personality becomes realized, at which time the individual has attained independence and becomes truly "creative." The average man conforms to the will of others, whereas the neurotic either rebels without a goal, thus isolating himself from the mainstream of life, or becomes overly conforming. Rank knew from his own experiences what it meant to conform out of guilt; and he considered that the role of the therapist is to help the neurotic, through the transference, to achieve the state of creative individuation. In therapy the patient is helped to accept his own will without feeling guilty for opposing the will of others and to learn through this to have a greater ability to tolerate separateness. "The last step [of psychotherapy] finally is the freeing of the acting creative self in the end phase whereby the therapist is to be given up as a leaning post."[81]

Rank's final works, *The Psychology of the Soul* (1931) and *The Art and the Artist* (1932), offer a perspective view of civilization and an interpretation of the meanings of religion and artistry; these two books go beyond the framework of individual psychoanalysis, as does also a posthumously published book, *Beyond Psychology* (1941), in which history is

THE HISTORY OF PSYCHIATRY

divided into four eras in terms of how people have tried to achieve immortality.

Rank's writings are stylistically difficult and he offers few case histories to substantiate his clinical speculations. He, like Adler, reduced all of psychology to an oversimplified and monolithic system; at the same time, some of his suggestions have proved very valuable to psychiatry, particularly the concept of a child's having to accept his own individual existence as separate from his mother.

*   *   *

All three of the men discussed in this chapter—Adler, Jung, and Rank—felt constrained by their Freudian ties and each strove for the release of his own creative potential. In the process they inevitably separated themselves from Freud's leadership. Each of them contributed to psychoanalysis and each found his own niche. Adler found his "style of life," Jung his "soul," and Rank his "creative" self-expression; but it is only fair to point out that their later philosophical speculations so abrogated rigorous adherence to systematic scientific observation that they vitiated to an extent whatever impact they may have had on psychiatric thought. In our view, Freud, in contrast, even in later philosophical writings, rarely departed from a scientific orientation.

CHAPTER **17**

Contributions from Outside
the Psychoanalytic School

By the end of the first decade of the twentieth century Freud's influence on psychiatry was by no means restricted to his followers; even his opponents could not protect themselves from the impact of his views. During these years Switzerland contributed more than any other country to psychiatric developments outside psychoanalysis. The liberal tradition of this small republic proved to be fertile soil for the study of all the vital problems of the human condition. Theodore Flournoy, Edouard Claparède, August Forel, and Eugene Bleuler were representatives of a liberal school of psychiatry whose basic orientation had much in common with psycho-analysis.

Eugene Bleuler and Schizophrenia

Of all the academic psychiatrists of the late nineteenth and early twentieth centuries, Bleuler (1857–1939) appears today to have been unquestion-ably the most advanced. His basic orientation toward mental disease and his detailed contributions to its understanding had a profound influence upon the development of the dynamic point of view that characterizes present-day psychiatry. He came independently to the conviction that the mentally sick can be studied and approached psychologically. This made him singularly susceptible to Freud's teachings.

As his son, Manfred, stated, Eugene Bleuler devoted his lifework to one central idea—recognizing the universal human component in mental dis-ease.[1] Contrary to his contemporaries who tried to understand mental disease in terms of brain pathology, Bleuler viewed the bizarre, distorted

[253

manifestations of the psychotic as essentially similar to the mental processes of normal people. Although he considered mental disease to be
basically an organic process and did not minimize the importance of brain
research, he endeavored, like Jung, to explain not the mental disease itself
but the content of its symptoms as the result of psychological—that is,
motivational and dynamic—events.

Bleuler's insistence on understanding and treating psychotics psychologically explains his intensive interest in Freud's work. Freud succeeded in
explaining neurotic symptoms in psychological terms; although these symptoms are less removed than psychotic mentation from normal psychological
processes, they are nonetheless irrational and inexplicable to common
sense. Bleuler therefore applied an approach similar to Freud's to psychotic symptoms and gave consideration to unconscious symbolic processes that are more archaic and less influenced by reality. He called these
primitive thought processes—one of the main characteristics of psychotic
phenomena—"autistic thinking." Autistic psychic processes are not influenced by reality and do not follow the laws of logic; they are primitive, are
characterized by wishful symbolic thinking, and are similar to dreaming.

Bleuler described the disturbed and inappropriate expression of emotion
(affect) and the circumstantial and tangential verbal associations of the
patient. He noted that certain psychotics experienced a simultaneous
presence of two opposing tendencies, for example, love and hate, which is
much more intense than seen in neurotics or nonneurotics. Bleuler named
this condition "ambivalence."

As we have seen, Bleuler did not agree with Kraepelin that premature
dementia was the ultimate outcome of dementia praecox. He thus renamed
the illness "schizophrenia"; Bleuler believed the central feature of the
illness to be a split in the personality brought about by morbid thought
processes. The disturbances in affect and association and the marked
autism and intense ambivalence were considered by Bleuler as the primary
symptoms of schizophrenia.

It was under Bleuler's open-minded directorship in the Burghölzli
Psychiatric Hospital that Freud's doctrine first found access into psychiatry. We have noted, however, how Bleuler could not remain identified
with the psychoanalytic movement. It was not an accident that the Burghölzli attracted so many gifted young psychiatrists whose first exposure to
psychoanalysis was under Bleuler's tutelage. Among them were Abraham,
Jones, and Eitingon, who were to play an important part in the development of Freud's teachings.

Jean Piaget and Normal Thought Development

Among the most original of the non-Freudian contributions to the understanding of mental functioning are those of another Swiss, Jean Piaget (b.
1896). He was appointed professor of philosophy at the University of

Neuchâtel in 1926, where after 1929 he held the chair of child psychology and history of scientific thought and later also of experimental psychology. From 1937 to 1954 Piaget was professor for general psychology at the University of Geneva, and for a number of years he was also professor at the Sorbonne. Since 1955 Piaget has led the International Center for Epistemology at the University of Geneva. A collaborator of Piaget has remarked that he is "by training a zoologist, by vocation an epistemologist, and by method a logician."[2] The roots of his work go back to Flournoy, Claparède, and Bleuler. He knew Freud's work, but Piaget is one of the few who have received less from psychoanalysis than they have contributed to it.

It is no exaggeration to say that what Freud accomplished for the description and understanding of the emotional development of the individual Piaget has done for the understanding of the development of man's intellectual faculties. His work has been less influential in psychiatric practice, where emotional factors have primary significance, than in normative psychology, particularly in child development.

Piaget's work can be classified primarily as basic research. The practical application of the results of basic research always comes later. Therefore, the final evaluation of the significance for psychiatry of Piaget's work is still premature and we shall concentrate on his contributions to psychology itself.

The grasping activity of the human hand serves the practical satisfaction of the subjective needs that motivate its functions, but the functions themselves can be understood only from the anatomy and physiology of the hand. Similarly, the infinitely more complex functions of grasping with the mind ultimately serve man's survival needs, yet the intellectual functions themselves can be understood only from the detailed study of the developmental stages of the thought processes that eventually culminate in the logical and rational thinking of the adult. Psychoanalysts focused on the influence that emotional needs had on the thought processes; Piaget focused on a methodical study of thinking itself and of its development. Piaget adopted Claparède's basic insight that thinking appears when new situations arise that cannot be dealt with by effortless reflexes and automatic performances learned in the past. The tension that arises when a new situation is met induces man (and also a child) to engage in groping experimentations on a trial-and-error basis. In this view, thinking is highly flexible, refined trial-and-error behavior.

Piaget considers that there are four stages of the child's thought development: (1) a sensory-motor stage, in the first two years of life; (2) a preoperational stage, from the ages of two to seven; (3) a stage of concrete operations from age seven to twelve; and (4) a stage of formal operations, beginning in the twelfth year and continuing into adulthood.

In the sensory-motor stage there appears a kind of primitive, empirical intelligence that is, however, entirely restricted to movements and perceptions without verbal explanation. The child experiments with objects and gradually connects new experiences with older ones; in other words, the child learns from experience. For example, a child learns that an unreachable object that rests on a carpet can be reached by pulling the carpet; after that he generalizes this experience to similar situations. The child of this age does not yet have a space image that contains all objects: "there is the buccal space"—the oral cavity; "the tactile kinesthetic space"—based on moving his body and touching objects with it; and finally, "the visual and auditory space." After a while, however, a kind of Copernican evolution occurs: "space becomes homogeneous, a one and only space that envelops the others."[3]

In the second, preoperational, stage symbolic functions appear in which perceived objects are represented by something else—a symbol. The most important event in this phase is that verbal signals come to be used as symbols. The perception of concrete objects may now be replaced by words, which may be experimentally manipulated in the mind in the same way that concrete objects were physically manipulated in the first stage of development.

In the third stage, that of concrete operations, the first logical operations appear and objects are classified according to their similarities and differences. In the final stage the child begins to experiment with formal logical operations, which Piaget compares to hypothesis formation. The child acquires both the logic of mathematics and the logic of propositions and tests the possible combinations between the abstractions learned in the previous stages. This form of thinking is essentially only a more flexible form of experimentation than with concrete perceptions and movements.

With these studies Piaget substantiated Freud's designation of thinking as experimentation with actions in fantasy. Piaget's detailed description of the gradual process by which the human faculty of manipulating with symbols evolves from primitive experimentation with concrete actions and objects of immediate perception was criticized because it did not pay attention to the role of emotional and instinctual factors in learning. In response to these criticisms Piaget states "that affectivity is a necessary condition for, but not a cause of intellectual development,"[4] and that affectivity may lead to "acceleration or retardation, but is not the cause of formation of cognitive structures"[5]—that is, thinking.

Piaget has attempted in his most recent work to describe in detail the interaction between emotional and cognitive factors in thought development through all the four stages he postulated. He gives a promising outline but is less successful in the formulation of general principles. Although Piaget describes adaptation as a gradual process of establishing equilibrium, it appears that he did not explicitly recognize another universal principle operative not only in thought processes but also in all organic phenomena—the principle of economy. All body processes can be understood as subject to the law of stability that was first described for physiological phenomena by Claude Bernard and for psychological processes by Freud. The organism tends to keep up constant conditions that are constantly disturbed by arising biological and emotional needs. Franz Alexander complemented this universal principle with an equally general qualifying statement: The organism attempts to restore its equilibrium with a minimum expenditure of energy. After, through trial and error, the adequate behavior patterns suitable to restore the disturbed equilibrium are found, through repetition of these successful patterns they become automatic and effortless. Thinking is also subject to this general principle of economy. The tendency to generalize, for example, is an attempt to solve many similar problems with one general formula applicable not only to one concrete problem but also to many similar ones. The tendency to build theories that contain a minimum amount of independent generalizations is another characteristic of thought development. This was demonstrated first in Ernst Mach's classical *History of Thermodynamics*. The important fact is that this tendency for economy is an integral part of those autonomous laws of thinking that Piaget tries to formulate. The economy of thought attempts to avoid disequilibrium by minimizing psychic tension, and therefore economical thought is intimately connected with affective factors and is responsible for the very processes that Piaget described in his theory. By the biological principle of economy, accordingly, not only is thinking in general motivated by emotional needs, but all the details of the thinking process are determined by the principle of effort-saving for the purpose of reducing affective factors.

Piaget's work by no means contradicts psychoanalytic findings; it complements them. Psychoanalysts are preoccupied exclusively with emotional and instinctual development. Piaget's interest has been centered on understanding the development of the highest faculty of the living organism, that of logical thinking, which is man's most powerful tool for the mastery of the environment upon which the satisfaction of his needs depends.

Alfred Binet and Intelligence Tests

Another important late-nineteenth-century development outside psychoanalysis was the evolution of techniques for psychological testing. The earliest systematized tests of variations between individuals were made by an English biologist, Sir Francis Galton, who also coined the term "eugenics." Galton had hoped to discover a relationship between heredity and intelligence by measuring certain faculties of parents and their offspring—sensory perceptions, motor coordination, and the reaction time to sensory stimuli. Galton believed that there was a significant correlation between these functions and intelligence. James McKeen Cattell (1860–1944), who was a student of Wilhelm Wundt (1832–1920), the great

German experimental psychologist, was influenced by Galton's concepts and in 1890 devised what he called "mental tests" to measure in detail an individual's ability to discriminate sensory stimuli and his capacity for memory.

In the late 1880's and early 1890's Alfred Binet (1857–1911), a distinguished French experimental psychologist, also used tests that measured sensory-motor abilities but soon realized their uselessness in estimating intelligence: children who are intellectually deficient may nevertheless have a strong grip or be able to see farther and hear better than others more intelligent. Binet maintained that intelligence involves higher mental faculties, such as the ability to abstract and generalize, and these faculties could be tested.

Binet was born in Nice and received his education in the natural sciences at the Sorbonne, from which university he received the degree of Doctor of Science. In 1892 he became director of the Psychophysiological Laboratory at the Sorbonne. Binet was one of the founders of the first French journal of psychology, *L'année psychologique*. This journal became representative of French psychological thought of that era. Binet had distinguished himself in the last two decades of the nineteenth century by his varied writings on psychology, including early studies in hypnotism (1886) and subconscious thought (1887). He went on to publish such important works as *Studies in Psychology* (1888), *Changes in Personality* (1892), *Double Consciousness* (1896), *Intellectual Weariness* (1898), *Suggestibility* (1900), and *Thoughts About Children* (1900).

In 1904 Binet was asked by the French Minister of Public Instruction to devise a test appropriate for differentiating between normal and subnormal children. The result, obtained in collaboration with Theodore Simon, a psychiatrist, was the Binet-Simon Scale (1905), a measure of judgment, ability to abstract, comprehension, and reasoning. In 1908 and again in 1911 the 1905 test was revised and standardized by ascertaining the average accomplishments of normal children of various ages; this allowed a child's intelligence to be correlated with age levels. The mental age of the child could then be determined independently of his actual age by whether or not he solved the questions that the majority of children of a certain age could solve. A five-year-old child who could answer the problems solved by most ten-year-olds had, on the Binet-Simon Scale, a mental age of ten.

The Binet-Simon tests were widely accepted throughout the world, and in 1910 Henry H. Goddard introduced them into the United States at the Training School in Vineland, New Jersey. William Stern (1871–1938) suggested that if the mental age of a child were divided by his actual age, a "mental quotient" would be obtained and that this might remain constant throughout the child's life. This mental quotient was popularized by Lewis M. Terman (1877–1956) while working at Stanford University. He called his test the Stanford Binet and utilized Stern's concept of mental quotient, which he renamed the "Intelligence Quotient," or IQ. He calculated IQ in the following way. Let us say that a ten-year-old child passes the tests of ten-year age level; his intelligence quotient is ten divided by ten, multiplied by a constant of one hundred, which equals an IQ of one hundred. This is considered normal. Should a ten-year-old pass tests that the average thirteen-year-old passes, his IQ would be thirteen divided by ten, multiplied by one hundred, equaling one hundred and thirty. IQ below seventy indicate mental deficiency.

David Wechsler devised the Wechsler-Bellevue test for adults. Adult IQ tests are based on the concept that the mental age does not increase beyond the average adult level, which is approximately the mental age of fifteen.

Intelligence tests are useful for estimating an individual's native intellectual capacity, but there are disadvantages and dangers that accompany too much reliance upon them. The more dramatic benefits of the tests apply in cases where the capacities of above-normal or subnormal persons are being examined. Yet the great bulk of individuals fall within the range of normal intelligence. Another difficulty lies in the fact that since the IQ is given in numerical terms, one can be misled by taking that factor too literally. Furthermore, the test does not indicate merely innate abilities: every individual who takes it brings to it his own experiences. An adult, in spite of a mental age of nine, is not the same individual as a nine-year-old child, since he has had years of actual living experience. In fact, lack of proper emotional or cognitive experience on the part of a child may reduce his performance on the test, since the child's background and early home environment must be essentially favorable for him to achieve his full intellectual development. It is therefore important that the imperfections of the techniques be understood and that this understanding temper one's reliance upon IQ tests.

Intelligence tests provide some estimate of native intellectual capacity, but for an overall understanding of personality, the inkblot test is a far more valuable device. Over the centuries poets and artists had observed that inkblots—like cloud formations and sand patterns—stimulated their imaginations. Leonardo da Vinci suggested to his students that a blotch of paint with no particular form could be used as a stimulus for drawing real-life scenes.[6] In 1857 Justinus Kerner (1786–1862), the German poet-physician, published *Klecksographien*, a series of inkblots accompanied by verses that the ink blots had inspired. In 1895 Alfred Binet suggested that reactions to inkblots could be used to investigate personality features, but it remained for Hermann Rorschach to develop the actual procedure.

Hermann Rorschach and Projective Tests

Hermann Rorschach (1884–1922) was born in Zurich. It is interesting that the inventor of the inkblot test was in high school nicknamed "Kleck," which means inkblot, because his father was an art instructor and Hermann himself also dabbled in ink sketches. He received his medical education in Swiss and German medical schools and completed it in Zurich, writing his doctoral dissertation under the supervision of Bleuler. While he was training in psychiatry, for the first time he tried to understand how people react to inkblots, and in a never-published study done with his friend Konrad Gehring, an art teacher, he attempted to determine whether gifted students engaged in more fantasy productions than did average students. Through Bleuler and Jung he was introduced to psychoanalysis, and although he had no formal psychoanalytic training, was elected to the vice-presidency of the Swiss Psychoanalytic Society. Rorschach remained perennially fascinated by the idea that reactions to inkblots could reveal a great deal about personality structure, and finally, after ten years of sporadic and four years of intensive work on inkblot tests, in 1921 he published his now famous *Psychodiagnostik,* based on tests administered to three hundred mental patients and one hundred normal individuals. Eight months later, in February, 1922, Rorschach died suddenly from complications following appendicitis.

In the early 1900's George Whipple, a psychologist, had published a set of standardized responses to some inkblot tests, in which he noted the time taken to react and the number and complexity of the subjects' responses, but it is doubtful whether Rorschach ever knew of his work. After experimenting with scores of inkblots, Rorschach decided to use a standard ten blots, five of which are colored; he recorded the subjects' responses to each of the blots and classified them into four categories: (1) the *location* of the response: whether the subject responds to the entire blot or a large part of it or pays attention to individual details in the blot; (2) the *quality* of the response: whether the subject reacts to a shade, a color, or what he perceives as movement within the blot; (3) the *content* of the response: whether the subject responds in terms of human, animal, animate, or inanimate objects; (4) the *degree* of conventionality of the response: whether the response is one offered by the majority of people or is ingenious or original. The testee may make as many responses as he wishes to each card, and after he has finished he is asked about why he made the responses. It is crucial, of course, that there be good rapport between the tester and testee, and the differences in the techniques or personalities of examiners may account for differences in the data.

Rorschach considered that because an individual's perceptions are influenced by his emotions and motives, the responses to the blots were valid clues to the testee's inner life. The Rorschach test is thus a "projective" test, that is, the subject projects much of his inner life into his perceptions of the blots. The free-associative method of psychoanalysis encourages the patient to reveal himself spontaneously under the influence of inner and unconscious motivations. The Rorschach test may be an invaluable adjunct to analysis, because it administers an *external* stimulus experimentally and permits comparsions between the associations of individual subjects responding to the same stimulus.

The standardization of the Rorschach test required systematic comparisons between different methods of scoring. These difficulties were partially alleviated with the organization of the Rorschach Research Exchange in 1936 under the guidance of Bruno Klopfer. A few years later the Rorschach Research Exchange became formalized into an International Rorschach Research Institute. According to Klopfer, this was founded to create "a clearing house for research and a training center in order to help satisfy a growing demand for skilled Rorschach workers in medical, psychological and educational institutions."[7] During World War I group methods of administering intelligence tests were introduced, and in World War II group methods of taking the Rorschach test were devised. In order to arrive at personality diagnoses more rapidly, a shorter test, called by Ruth Monroe "Inspection Technique," has been inaugurated. This test does not yield a complete personality assessment but indicates gross pathology.

Other projective tests besides the Rorschach have come into use. The most important clinical test is the Thematic Apperception Test (T.A.T.), introduced by H. A. Murray in 1935. The T.A.T. consists of thirty cards on which are printed various pictures, plus one entirely blank card. The subject is shown ten cards and told to make up a story around the scenes on them; he is also shown the blank card and asked to tell any story that comes to his mind. He is requested to talk about the feelings of the persons in the pictures and to relate what he thinks the outcome of the scene will be; after he is through responding, the examiner interviews him to find out the emotional backgrounds that determined his stories. As he tells what he sees in the cards, the subject reveals clues to his feelings, particularly toward important figures in his life like mother, father, sisters, and brothers. Unlike the Rorschach test, T.A.T. material, although evaluated, is not scored and is not used to compare patients with normal subjects.

In 1921, the same year that Rorschach published *Psychodiagnostik,* Florence Goodenough devised another test called the Draw-a-Man, which is used now to estimate a child's projected images of men and women and of his own self. Graphology has also been studied as a clue to personality characteristics beginning with the work of Ludwig Klages in Germany (1907). Neither the Draw-a-Man test nor graphology has attained the popularity of the Rorschach or T.A.T. methods of projective analysis. Two other often-used projective tests are the Word Association test and the Sentence Completion test. After World War II Sentence Completion tests evolved as an important clinical tool. They required that the subject complete simple sentences like "When I was a child . . ." or "I prefer to . . ."; the way he finishes these thoughts reveals his likes, dislikes, fears and resentments.

By mentioning a few of the most commonly employed psychological tests, we have not nearly exhausted the myriad of tests employed in clinical

practice.* Nor is it correct to infer that those most frequently employed—
the IQ test, the Rorschach, and the T.A.T.—could not be improved further.
Experimental research is moving rapidly to validate these techniques. What
is intended here is to demonstrate the development from assessing presumed
innate intellectual capacity, which sets the limits of educational potential
(Binet), to the understanding of the evolution of these capacities (Piaget).
Psychoanalytic ego psychology† has devoted itself to the cognitive and
emotional aspects of the individual's adjustment to his external and
internal environment. The projective tests, without being completely
standardized, nevertheless have offered objective methods to gauge ego
functions and ego defenses. The integration of these tests into the clinical
fields of diagnosis and prognosis has been the legacy of the ingenious
pioneering efforts of the brilliant work of the Swiss psychiatrist Hermann
Rorschach.

Adolph Meyer and Common-Sense Psychiatry

In addition to Bleuler, Piaget, and Rorschach, Switzerland produced yet
another influential contribution to psychological thought—Adolph Meyer
(1866–1950)—who for almost six decades dedicated himself to improving
the lot of mental patients through any approach that seemed to him sensible and practical. His was the voice of an enlightened and pragmatic European psychiatrist who had become disenchanted with neurophysiological
explanations of mental illness, and as such had special importance for the
history of psychiatry in America.

Meyer was born a few miles from Zurich; his father was a liberal and
public-spirited minister. Meyer's admiration for his uncle, a physician, and
for August Forel, with whom he studied at the University of Zurich, induced him to study medicine and particularly neurology. Meyer was especially impressed by the biological concepts of John Hughlings Jackson, the
leading English neurologist of his time, who attempted to integrate the
hierarchical levels of brain organization. Later Meyer applied Jackson's
concept of integration not only to neurological organization but also to the
personality as a whole. He also was impressed with Thomas Huxley's idea
that science is organized common sense; later he stressed the idea that
common sense should play a major role in a psychiatric clinician's approach. His earliest contact with functional mental illnesses was at home—
his mother had frequent depressive episodes—and in helping his uncle treat
some mental patients.

In 1893 Meyer decided that his professional opportunities would be
greater in America than in Europe and came to the United States to work

* There are more than four thousand tests that deal with intelligence, aptitudes, and
personality inventories.
† See "Theory of Personality" in Chapter 19.

as a pathologist at the Illinois Eastern Hospital for the Insane at Kanka-kee. Here he noted that the medical staff paid very little attention to accurate history-taking. The value of an exact biographical history of a patient began to impress the young neuropathologist. While still at Kanka-kee Meyer began giving courses in "How to Study the Human Being—for Neurologists and Alienists." Even before Freud's influence had been felt in the Midwest Meyer was already pointing out that sexual feelings develop in children and that this can lead to serious psychosocial problems. From 1895 to 1910 Meyer was chief pathologist at the Massachusetts Insane Hospital in Worcester and at the New York State Psychiatric Institute and professor of psychiatry at Cornell University Medical College. From 1910 until he retired, in 1941, Meyer was professor of psychiatry at Johns Hopkins and director of the Henry Phipps Psychiatric Clinic.

In 1902 he married Mary Potter Brooks, who soon became absorbed in her husband's work and about 1904 began to visit the families of his patients to learn more about their backgrounds. Thus Mrs. Adolph Meyer became the "first American social worker." Meyer began to emphasize more and more that in order for a psychiatrist to understand a mentally disturbed patient, he had to know about the patient's social environment and view his disorganized state as a maladjustment of the entire personality rather than the result of brain pathology. In referring to his wife's studies of the families of the mentally ill, Meyer stated, "We thus obtained help in a broader social understanding of our problem and a reaching out to the *sources* of sickness, the family and the community."[8]

Meyer was opposed to the Cartesian dualism of mind and body and regarded each person as a biological unit who experiences unique reactions to social and biological influences—an entity that Meyer called "a psycho-biological whole."* As his realistic common-sense approach developed, he felt increasingly dissatisfied with either/or methods of explaining maladaptation and refused to believe that mental illness was the result merely of the brain's being disordered or of an overwhelming environment; both had to be taken into account. For this reason Meyer introduced the term "erg-asia," by which he meant "integrated mental activity." A complete lack of integration would be "holergasia" (psychosis). He even suggested that psychiatry be called "ergasiatry." Although the concept of integration is a meaningful psychiatric concept today, these neologisms have not taken root in psychiatric literature.

In 1907 Meyer met Clifford Beers, a graduate of Yale who had suffered several severe psychotic episodes and who had received atrocious treatment in three mental hospitals. After his recovery Beers decided to devote his life to the betterment of the unfortunates incarcerated in mental hospitals.

---

* The term "psychobiology" was first used by Bernheim, of Nancy, in the late nineteenth century, but it has become connected with Meyer's basic philosophical orientation.

He described the intense suffering of being restrained in a straitjacket and the mental anguish he went through while in custodial care in *The Mind That Found Itself* (1908), a book that affected the social consciousness of the nation and helped promote better care for the mentally ill.* It led to the organization of spirited groups that Meyer called the "mental-hygiene movement." Public awareness of the needs of the mentally ill was responsible for the development of preventive psychiatry and the formation of child-guidance clinics.

In 1927 Meyer was elected president of the American Psychiatric Association and for years was considered the dean of American psychiatrists. He avoided involvement in controversies between the various schools of psychiatric thought, and even though he helped form the American Psychoanalytic Association, he never fully accepted all the tenets of psychoanalysis. Meyer was concerned with respecting the "whole range of factors" in human-personality growth. "Your point of reference," he insisted, "should always be life itself, and not the imagined cesspool of the unconscious."[10] Meyer considered mental disorders to reflect a pathology of function, and he saw no point in trying to distinguish between the psychology of the unconscious and the conscious. His feeling was that psychoanalysis was too concrete and thus contradictory to his philosophical bent of mind. One could best understand an individual by searching for all forces that react upon him and that affect his interaction with the social milieu. Regarding treatment, Meyer believed that "The patient comes with his own view of his trouble; the physician has another view. Treatment consists of the joint effort to bring about that approximation of those views which will be the most effective and the most satisfying in the situation."[11]

Meyer taught many generations of students that people fall ill because of their faulty reaction patterns. He thereby dispelled the effect of the rigid diagnostic categories of nineteenth-century psychiatry, but he nevertheless did not offer a solid theoretical basis for understanding the psychodynamics of individual patients. His approach was broad, holistic, and integrative; it did, however, lack discrimination. His principle that the individual must be understood as a complete whole, a unique entity, still prevails in psychiatric thought. He stressed sound advice, "common-sense" counseling, and

---

* A group was established by Beers in Connecticut in 1908, the National Committee for Mental Hygiene. By 1919 an International Committee for Mental Hygiene had been formed. Interest in the subject stemmed from the nineteenth century. In 1893 William Sweester wrote a book, *Mental Hygiene,* or *An Examination of the Intellect and Passions,* which attempted to interrelate mind and body. In 1880 there had been in existence a National Association for the Protection of the Insane and the Prevention of Insanity, which was one of the many social movements in the latter part of the nineteenth century in the United States. But this association lasted only four years. There were twelve charter members of the original National Committee for Mental Health, among whom were August Hoch, Adolph Meyer, Frederick Peterson, William James, and Llewellyn Barker, in 1912 Dr. Thomas Salmon was appointed director.[9]

social service. However, these in themselves do not provide insight into deeper genetic and dynamic forces that are basic to personality development. Nonetheless, his practical efforts on behalf of the mental-hygiene movement, child-guidance clinics, and the aftercare of patients; his contribution to the development of psychiatric social work; and his spirit of free inquiry forcefully advanced American psychiatry.

PART **IV**

RECENT
DEVELOPMENTS

Introduction

Dealing with contemporary developments is difficult since we no longer have on our side the verdict of history. The historian's is a hindsight wisdom; he cannot deal with the present, save on the basis of his own impressions and evaluations. In writing about present trends in psychiatry we do not offer final judgments; our references to individual contributions must of necessity be selective.

In the last three decades the activities in this field and its literature have increased astronomically. We are well aware that contributions that we consider significant may be forgotten in the future and that other presently underestimated trends will emerge as dominant in future years. We cannot try to predict whether or not the biochemical approach will eventually bury the present psychodynamic orientation or whether cybernetics will replace not only Aristotelian logic but also the knowledge of the more primitive logic of emotions that dominate the primary processes in dream fantasies. Neither can we quibble about other controversial issues, such as whether or not the broad sociological considerations will supersede the present emphasis upon understanding a person in his highly idiosyncratic uniqueness—in his own private universe—as stressed by the existentialists.

In making selections we have restricted discussion to those individual contributions that most clearly represent existing trends and to those that deviate from currently accepted concepts and practices. The latter cannot very well be dealt with summarily since they represent only the views of a single author and possibly of a small group of his followers. Thus, for example, contributions of such neo-Freudians as Horney or Fromm may be given more space than some excellent contributions of latter-day Freudians; but this should not be interpreted to mean in the least that we consider the work of the former more significant. It only means that the con-

[269

tributions of those who follow the mainstream of psychoanalytic thought are more similar to each other and can therefore be dealt with summarily. It is our hope that by giving individual consideration to some deviant authors we can provide the reader with an opportunity to apply his own judgment to these approaches.

In dealing with current developments we have found it necessary to be more technical than in previous chapters. The advancement of scientific thought in all fields is characterized by a gradual departure from what is known to common sense. We have tried nevertheless to simplify the abstract concepts of ego psychology and the theory of instincts as much as is compatible with an adequate presentation of these complex areas of modern psychiatry.

CHAPTER **18**

The Organic Approach

The Biochemist, the Psychiatrist, and the Multidisciplinary Team

Neuropsychiatry continued to make significant contributions to the understanding of mental illness during the twentieth century. Specialists also began to apply, wherever possible, newer medical theories of disease to the problems of mental illness.

Microbiology became extremely important throughout the medical world during the first three decades of the present century. Increased knowledge of microbes as major assailants of tissues was extended to mental disorders. Syphilis of the brain and its cure by induction of malaria (Wagner-Jauregg's innovation) became a model of organic mental illness and treatment. In 1917 a severe epidemic of influenza spread throughout the world. Many of the influenza victims developed viral encephalitis, which resulted in severe neurological and psychological damage. This epidemic indicated that another infectious agent could attack the brain and the brain stem and produce disease in these organs with consequent neuropsychiatric disturbance. Studies in microbiology led to the development of an arsenal of wonder drugs, among the earliest being the sulfa drugs, discovered by Gerhart Domagk in 1932, and penicillin, which was first discovered by Sir Alexander Fleming in 1928.

Work in the field of diseases that result from nutritional deficiencies produced another model for organic therapy of psychotic conditions when it was discovered that deficiencies of vitamin B lead to serious disorders, such as pellagra and beriberi, which affect brain metabolism and result in psychotic symptoms. Although treatment with vitamins has little effect on mental illness except in those cases that are definitely due to a vitamin deficiency, another aspect of vitamin research, that of the biochemical

[271

relationships between vitamins and enzymes, may yet yield valuable neuro-chemical data. Indeed, research in enzymes has already led to one of the first victories of medical science over one form of mental deficiency, that associated with ketonuria. In the middle 1930's A. Følling, a Norwegian biochemist, called attention to the fact that certain retarded children suffered from an inborn error of metabolism of two essential amino acids, plenylalanine and tryptophan. Phenylalanine normally is metabolized through enzymatic acitivity. When the enzyme (phenylalanine hydrox-ylase) is absent or inactive, phenylalanine accumulates in the blood just as sugar does in diabetes. Yet it has not been ascertained that it is the high level of phenylalanine in the blood that is responsible for the subsequent lack of brain development. Furthermore, tryptophan in this illness is not metabolized to one of its usual end products, serotonin. The role of sero-tonin for proper brain metabolism may be crucial, but as yet is not fully understood. Unmetabolized phenylalanine substances (ketones) can be detected in the urine of these children by a simple test. If a diagnosis of phenylketonuria is established, the infant can be put on a diet restricted in phenylalanine and thus may be saved from brain maldevelopment and mental retardation. Another metabolic disorder, galactosemia, that also results in mental retardation involves a congenital deficiency of galactotrans-ferase, an enzyme important in the metabolism of galactose (a form of sugar). In some cases, where liver damage does not lead to death, elimina-tion of milk products may be very helpful.

Research in heredity and genetics has led to the discovery that chromo-somal aberrations are responsible for the kind of errors of metabolism present in galactosemia and phenylketonuria. Besides the mental deficiency that is the consequence of metabolic disorders like these, hereditary factors seem to underlie another form of mental disease: mongoloid children, for example, have an extra chromosome probably the result of some sort of accident in the development of the egg. Statistical studies by Kallman have suggested that hereditary factors may be decisive in schizophrenia.

Moving with great momentum were investigations of chemical changes within tissues. Biochemists were less concerned with deficiency diseases and structural changes than with evaluating total body functioning. How the body maintains the constancy of its internal involvement, or its homeo-stasis (as W. B. Cannon called it), became a subject of scientific explora-tion. Oxygen consumption in the brain, how muscles convert chemical energy into work activity, the metabolism of nervous tissue, and the action of hormones were under investigation. It was discovered that the efficiency of certain organs can be measured electrically, since there are variations in the electric potential within their tissues. In 1929 Hans Berger showed that variations in the electrical activity of the brain could be recorded on graphs, and he invented the electroencephalogram, an invaluable tool in diagnosing brain abnormality.

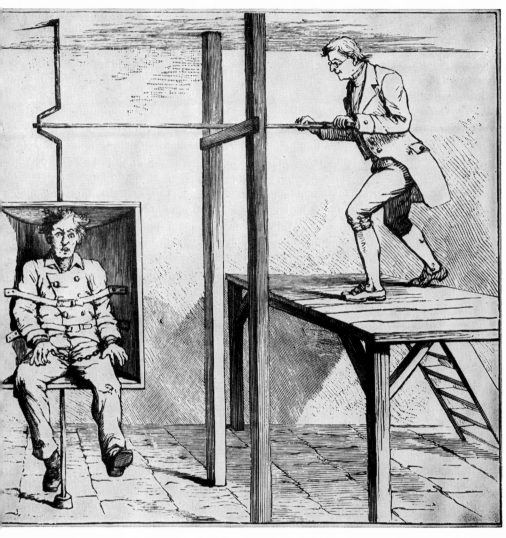

Gyrating chair, used by Benjamin Rush to increase the blood supply to the head.

Wilhelm Griesinger, who made important contributions toward the recognition of psychiatry as a medical science.

Jean Martin Charcot's clinic. The man in the apron, seated in the foreground, is presumably Freud.

SIGMUND FREUD

Das Ich und das Es

von

Sigm. Freud

1.—8. Tausend

Internationaler
Psychoanalytischer Verlag
Leipzig   Wien   Zürich

Original title page of Freud's *The Ego and the Id*.

Harlow's experiment with monkeys, showing the monkey's preference for the cloth rather than the wire mother surrogate (Courtesy of Dr. Harry Harlow).

Two kinds of treatment, as observed by students through a one-way mirror at Cedars-Sinai Medical Center, Los Angeles. Above, psychoanalysis; below, family-centered therapy.

Increasing knowledge about biochemical relationships was applied to the study of the endocrine system, which contains ductless glands that secrete hormones directly into the bloodstream. In 1884 Sir Victor Horsley (1857–1916) produced artificial myxedema (swelling of the skin) in a monkey by removing the thyroid gland. Myxedema is also present in individuals with insufficient thyroid activity. G. R. Murray in 1891 gave thyroid extracts to patients suffering from cretinism (mental retardation associated with swelling of the skin due to underactive thyroid glands). This was the first time that a patient with retarded mental faculties showed improvement by the administration of medication. It offered hope that with increasing knowledge of the complicated interplay of the endocrine glands, the physiological basis of mental illness could be understood and made accessible to effective therapy. In 1914 E. C. Kendall isolated the actual secretion of the thyroid gland (thyroxin).

The manner in which the thyroid gland is involved in metabolism has become well established in recent years. It has been demonstrated that carbohydrate metabolism is regulated by the opposing influences of secretions of insulin from the pancreas and hormones derived from the anterior pituitary and adrenal glands. Like the nervous system, the endocrine glands also regulate body functions. The governing influence of the central nervous system comes by way of nervous impulses transmitted to the body through nervous pathways; the endocrine glands regulate through transporting chemical substances via the bloodstream. The master coordinator of all the endocrine glands is the anterior pituitary.

Hans Selye explored the relationship of neurogenic and hormonal influences, proposing in his "adaptation syndrome" a typical cycle of organic responses to intense external stress stimuli. The first response is the release of metabolites in the affected tissues (the "alarm reaction"). If the alarm phase is not too severe, the metabolites will stimulate the anterior lobe of the pituitary to emit a hormone that in turn will stimulate the cortex of the adrenal gland, aiding the body in its resistance (the "countershock phase"). Should the intense stimulus continue, the adrenal cortex will persist in releasing its hormones. Prolonged exposure to this stimulus wears down the adaptive mechanisms and the individual enters a stage of exhaustion until the adrenal cortex is finally depleted and the organism dies.

The understanding of this latest model of disease, representing an interplay of biodynamic factors, is the result of continuous efforts by biochemists and physiologists to trace connected reactions occurring in living organisms. It shifts the emphasis from morphological pathology to an understanding of the functional interrelations and stresses the multifactoral etiology of diseases. As an example, the tubercle bacillus is not the only factor in the development of tuberculosis. An individual may be exposed to a virulent tubercle bacillus, yet his constitution, his inherited or acquired immunity, as well as his physiological and psychological makeup at the time of the exposure, will determine whether he will contract the disease. This latest model of disease may prove pertinent to understanding of the puzzling schizophrenic illnesses.

Another major advancement derived from modernization of technique and equipment has been the development of cranial surgery made possible by newer and safer anesthetic gases. Areas heretofore inaccessible, such as the heart and the brain, are now searchingly penetrated. The progress in the United States in neurosurgical procedures has been outstanding, especially under the leadership of Harvey Cushing (1869–1939) of Johns Hopkins University. Dr. Wilder G. Penfield of the Montreal Neurological Institute initially opened the cranial cavity to treat a localized form of epilepsy. Recently he has stimulated areas of the cortex in humans and produced vivid recall of early childhood memories. The physiological mechanism by which psychological repression occurs and by which experiences formerly repressed come into the framework of the conscious mind are problems with which future neurophysiologists, neuropsychiatrists, and their co-workers will have to grapple.

A multidisciplinary approach has become as necessary in dealing with neurophysiological problems as with other medical specialties. The psychiatrist is increasingly called upon to study psychophysiological correlations with his medical confreres. The psychiatric physician must keep abreast of neurophysiological and biochemical findings in order to be accepted by his fellow physicians as were his predecessors, the neuropsychiatrists of the nineteenth century.

Orientation to the Nervous System

In order to present adequately subsequent material that deals with recent pharmacological and surgical methods of treating mental illness, it is pertinent to review briefly our present state of knowledge about the brain and its functions.

The nervous system integrates and coordinates networks of functions that enable the organism to meet its needs efficiently and adjust to immediate as well as long-term stress situations. In other words, the main function of the nervous system is to maintain homeostatic conditions, that is, conditions of internal equilibrium, which are constantly disturbed through the very process of life. That part of the nervous system called memory stores useful patterns of behavior that, when the situation demands, can be selectively recalled and applied to new but similar situations.

The central nervous system, composed of the brain and spinal cord, is surrounded by protective layers. The brain, enclosed within the skull, is also surrounded by a fluid that acts as a shock absorber. The brain is divided into the cerebral cortex, the interbrain (the thalamus and hypothalamus), the midbrain, the pons, the medulla, and the cerebellum. (Figure A shows a brain cut in half with the plane of division along the midline bisecting the nose through its vertical axis.) These structures are divided into two symmetrical halves; by and large, one side of the brain supervises the activity of the opposite side of the body. In a right-handed person the left side of the brain is usually the dominant side; the reverse is true for a left-handed person. Exactly why one hemisphere of the brain controls the opposite side of the body is not yet understood.

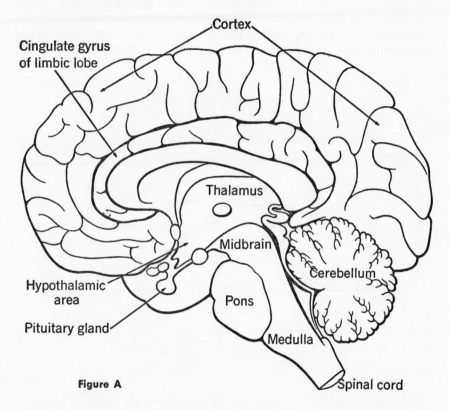

Figure A

The functional unit of the central nervous system is a kind of cell called neuron. The neuron picks up impulses through thin fibers called the dendrites; these lead into the main portion of the neuron. The impulse is transmitted to the dendrites of the next neuron through another kind of fiber called the axon. The point at which an axon of a neuron comes in contact with a dendrite of another neuron is known as the synapse. The neurons are not fused, and the impulse transmitted across a synapse reaches the next neuron through chemical mediators. One of the stimulating chemicals, acetylcholine, is produced at the nerve endings of parasympathetic nerves and in the nerves that supply skeletal muscles; sympathetic nerves release an adrenalin-like substance. Rhythmic alterations of electric potentials propagate the impulse along the neuron.

The cortex combines the functions of a filing cabinet and a computer, since it analyzes what it files. It consists roughly of four divisions, the *frontal* area, the *temporal* area, the *occipital* area, and the *parietal* area (see Figure B). The frontal lobe is concerned with higher intellectual functioning: it stores memories and is the essential organ for abstract reasoning and speech. On its intactness depends the individual's sense of morality and humor. The portion of the frontal lobe that is next to the parietal lobe is the motor area; in it originate motor impulses, which are then conducted through nervous pathways to specific areas of the body. Just behind this motor area is the portion of the parietal lobe that receives

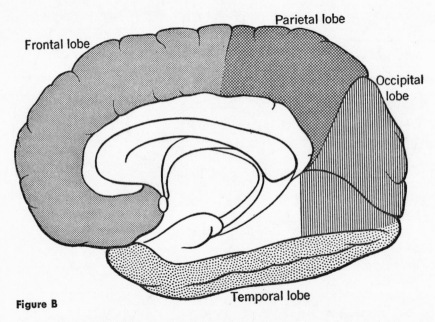

Figure B

sensory impulses. The rear portion of the cortex, the occipital lobe, receives visual stimuli. The remaining cortex, the temporal lobe, which is below the parietal lobe and in front of the occipital, correlates skin sensations and enables the individual to recognize familiar objects that he feels; it also receives auditory stimuli.

The thalamus consists of a large circular gray mass of cells that act as a relay center for sensory sensations. The latter are transmitted from the thalamus to the appropriate sensory areas in the cortex for detailed sensory discrimination. Just below the thalamus and in close relationship to the pituitary gland lies the hypothalamus (see Figure A).

The autonomic nervous system originates in the hypothalamus. The hypothalamus contains cells of origin of the autonomic nervous system; there are also cells of origin of this system in the midbrain, pons, medulla, and spinal cord. The autonomic nervous system helps regulate essential bodily functions such as heart rate, blood pressure, and gastrointestinal functions, which occur automatically and are not under voluntary control. This portion of the nervous system is delicately balanced between relaxation and stimulation. One section of the autonomic nervous system, called the sympathetic nervous system, governs actions during emergency situations when the organism is preparing for flight or fight. It regulates the blood circulation so that organs like the brain, the heart, and the limb muscles that are needed in fighting or fleeing will receive a greater supply of blood than usual; in addition, it causes dilation, or widening, of the pupil of the eye, which gives a greater field of vision. The sympathetic nervous system tends to inhibit bowel functions and emptying of the bladder, since these are unnecessary in emergency situations. Nonemergency situations are under the control of the parasympathetic system, whose actions help the organism survive over a long period of time by stimulating anabolic (upbuilding) and protective processes. The parasympathetic system stimulates digestion, regulates vegetative processes, governs the storage of sugar in the liver, and constricts the pupil to protect against light. When the body is not involved in acute emergency situations, sympathetic stimulation is minimal and the parasympathetic influence is preponderant.

The hypothalamus, together with the reticular-activating system and the limbic system, is also implicated in the expression of intense emotions, as rage. The hypothalamus is involved in the behavioral aspects of emotions; for example, tame cats become extremely savage when electrically stimulated in the hypothalamic areas on both sides of the brain. And animals that have had their cerebral cortex removed exhibit "sham rage"— that is, on the slightest provocation they become violent and may attack. When a section of the hypothalamus is removed this sham rage ceases, which indicates that the cortex inhibits this hypothalmic area.

The second essential system important to experiencing intense emotion is the reticular-activating system (r.a.s.). The r.a.s. is composed of a mass of cells extending from the brain stem to the thalamus; these cells are stimulated by sensory impulses relayed to the cerebral centers. The function of the r.a.s. is to set up these cerebral areas for the oncoming stimuli— to put the cerebral centers in a receptive state so that they are alerted or made aware of the impinging sensory impulses (see Figure C).

The limbic system, the third great neurological system involved in emotions, is as ancient as the first amphibious animal whose brain had an area able to receive olfactory impulses. This area was once called the rhinence-phalon ("rhin" means "nose," "encephalon" means "brain"), and is now called the visceral brain. It should be remembered that intense emotions, especially sexual ones, are aroused largely through smelling in the lower

r. a. s.

Reticular-Activating System

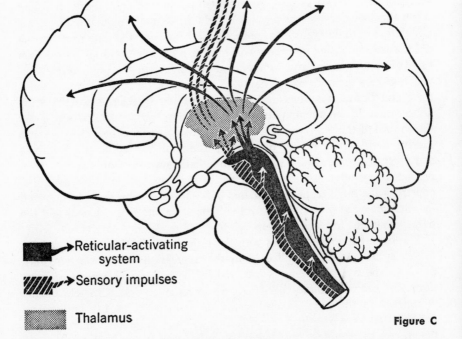

➤ Reticular-activating
system

➤ Sensory impulses

Thalamus

Figure C

mammals. The "smell brain" may be the area of the brain most involved when animals experience intense emotions. The limbic system functions as an integrated unit and is influenced by impulses reaching it from the internal organs of the body. A part of the visceral brain is an integral part of the cortex, and basic intense emotions involving visceral tensions reach cortical areas by way of the cortical portion of the limbic system, called the cingulate gyrus (see Figure A). This gyrus conducts basic emotional impulses that are received by the smell brain and merges them with the more discriminative impulses being received by the cortical areas of the brain. Although the newer cortex (neocortex) has evolved with the evolutionary increase of intellectual functioning, the visceral brain has remained the same size through the ages.

Between the pons and the hypothalamic area is the midbrain (see Figure A). Coordinated movement of the eyes depends on the proper functioning of this area. The midbrain contains a group of cells called the basal ganglia, the function of which is to regulate the automatic skeletal muscular movements involved in activities like walking. If basal ganglia are destroyed, automatic movements become erratic and rigid, and the simplest task—for example, rolling over in bed—is difficult because an individual has to roll over by making a conscious effort.

In the pons and medulla—called the brain stem—originate many of the sensory nerves that govern facial sensation and motor function. The brain stem contains cells that maintain functions vital to life, among them heart rate and respiration. The pons, medulla, and midbrain receive sensory impulses from the spinal cord and relay them to the thalamus, from which they are sent forward to the appropriate cortical areas. In response to the sensory stimuli the cortex returns impulses through the midbrain, pons, and medulla down to the spinal cord, which in turn forwards these impulses to glands and muscles.

The cerebellum is located behind the pons and medulla. The functions of the cerebellum are to ensure equilibrium and orientation in space; the cerebellum plays a key role in harmonizing muscular activity and co-ordinating muscular contracts; the finer movements of the fingers depend on an intact cerebellum.

As an example of the way the nervous pathways work, let us take the simplest kind of behavior response, the reflex arc. If you touch a hot stove, you will immediately withdraw your hand even before you consciously feel any pain, that is, before any impulse reaches the cortex. Special nerve endings for pain in the hand relay their message to neurons in the reflex arc via the dendrites; the axon of one of those neurons enters the posterior, or back, section of the spinal cord. Within the spinal cord the axon meets the dendrite of a connecting neuron, which conducts the impulse to a motor neuron in the anterior, or front, section of the spinal cord; the motor neuron relays the message back to the muscles and the hand is withdrawn. Most reflex arcs are not limited to the spinal cord but traverse the brain stem to reach the cortex. The initiating sensory impulse enters the posterior portion of the gray matter ("gray" because it consists of cell bodies that appear gray under a microscope) of the spinal cord, and there is transmitted to another neuron, which, as a rule, enters the white matter ("white" because axons are ensheathed in a white covering) of the other side of the spinal cord. This neuron traverses upward to the higher portions of the brain. When the brain reacts to the stimulus, it sends out impulses that travel downward in the white matter and eventually cross over to reach the anterior segment—the motor section—of the spinal cord, thereby relaying impulses to the appropriate muscles or glands.

Shock Treatments and Psychosurgery

The isolation, in 1922, of insulin by Frederick Banting, C. H. Best, and J. R. MacLeod brought diabetes, one of man's most dread diseases, under control. It also inaugurated the first systematized biological approach to a somatic treatment for schizophrenia. It so happened that small dosages of insulin were often used to stimulate appetite in patients with chronic illnesses, including those who were hospitalized with severe mental illnesses. Although such physicians as H. Steck in Switzerland, C. Munn in America, and H. Haack in Germany had noted beneficial effects of these insulin doses on the moods of excited psychotic patients, the idea of using insulin in the treatment of psychotics was developed by Manfred Sakel (1900–1957). Sakel had treated patients recovering from morphine addiction at the Lichterfelde Hospital, Berlin, from 1927 to 1933 and had observed that morphine abstainers became overly excited. He considered this excitement to be caused by overactivity of the adrenal-thyroid endocrine systems and reasoned that a drug antagonistic to this system would also decrease the tone of the sympathetic nervous system, which enhances overactivity of this endocrine system. He experimented with insulin and found that high dosages did indeed appear to diminish the overactive states. Sakel then decided to try using insulin in high enough dosages to produce coma in excited patients, especially those who had been diagnosed as schizophrenic. Late in 1933 Sakel reported his first experimental findings of beneficial results in schizophrenia following insulin shock.

Sakel's therapeutic endeavors were not unanimously accepted by the medical profession, in part because the theoretical rationale of his treatment method was vague. Although schizophrenic patients, especially those who had recently become ill, appeared to benefit by the treatment, it has been increasingly recognized over the years that schizophrenics in their early stage of illness respond to most treatments with benefit. Insulin, as well as other therapies, is less effective in the chronic stages of the illness. Because it was not an easy therapeutic regimen, the technique of the treatment came under attack. For maximum effect at least thirty to fifty hours of coma had to be produced; patients required continuous nursing care, and physicians had to be highly skilled in insulin administration in order to avoid such hazards as irreversible coma and circulatory and respiratory collapse. Exactly how insulin-shock treatment benefits the schizophrenic is still an open question. Recent speculations hold that the nucleoproteins in the neuron may be affected by the reduction in blood sugar caused by insulin or that the brain's enzyme systems are brought into better equilibrium, thus making the brain better able to utilize beneficial minerals circulating in the blood. These physiological hypotheses are, however, as yet unconfirmed.

Another explanation for the benefits of insulin shock depends on the idea that the reduced blood-sugar supply also reduces the amount of oxygen present in the bloodstream. If the highest brain centers require the greatest amount of oxygen, then the function of the cortex will be impaired first by any diminishment in the glucose supply, and the lower centers of the brain will thus be released from the inhibition of the cerebral cortex. In essence, then, insulin treatment encourages the individual to regress to lower and more primitive levels of adaptation. Viewed from a psychological standpoint, the patient awakens from an insulin coma in a regressed psychological state. He has to be fed intravenously or with a stomach tube and is extremely dependent on external help. This continuing physiological and psychological regression, it is presumed, gradually leads to a reshaping of higher physiological and psychological patterns as the patient responds to the great amount of attention and the hopefulness of the psychiatric team administering the insulin.

Because of its dangers, unreliable results, and high cost, insulin therapy was largely superseded during the 1940's by other forms of shocking the nervous system. The next phase in shock treatment developed as a result of investigations of epilepsy, the "sacred disease" of the ancients. In the late 1920's Ladislaus Joseph von Meduna (1896–1964), then the superintendent of the Royal State Mental Hospital in Budapest, observed that the glial tissue, which connects the cell structures of the cortex, had thickened in epileptic patients. When he compared their brains with those of deceased schizophrenic patients he noted that the latter showed a deficiency of glial structure. On the basis of these findings (which have not been subsequently confirmed) Meduna became convinced that schizophrenia and epilepsy were incompatible diseases and that a convulsive agent administered to schizophrenics would therefore cure them.*

This technique was not original with Meduna, for convulsive agents had been used by previous investigators to treat severe mental states.† Not knowing of these earlier experiments, he decided in 1933 to test camphor and soon thereafter began to use a less toxic synthetic camphor preparation, Metrazol (also called Cardiazol). Metrazol had several practical shortcomings, among them an unpredictable time lag between injection and convulsion, during which the patient was fearful and uncooperative. Also, the convulsions frequently were severe enough to cause fractures.

In 1932 Ugo Cerletti (1877–1963), at the Neuropsychiatric Clinic in Genoa, was autopsying bodies of those who had died from epilepsy; he noted a hardening in a sector of the brain known as Ammon's horn. Cerletti decided to find out whether this hardening caused or was the result of epileptic attacks. Because he assumed that drugs used to produce experi-

* In the late 1920's and early 1930's Meduna had read of statistical clinical studies purporting that schizophrenia and epilepsy rarely, if ever, occur in the same patient. These reports claimed that should a schizophrenic develop epilepsy, his psychosis could be cured.

† Dr. William Oliver in 1785 reported in a London medical journal that he had cured a case of mania by giving camphor.[1] Dr. G. Burrows made a similar claim in a book, *Commentaries on the Causes, Forms, Symptoms, Treatment, Moral and Medical, of Insanity,* published in 1828.[2] And in the eighteenth century, Auenbrugger, the discoverer of auscultation, and a Dr. Weickhardt had also recommended camphor for the treatment of mental diseases.[3]

mental convulsions might have produced the hardening in the brain, he decided to use electrical stimulation instead.[4]*

Later, in Rome, in 1935, Cerletti began collaborating with L. Bini. Cerletti learned that hogs were killed at a Roman slaugherhouse after they had been stupefied by an electrical current; Bini used these hogs to establish a safe dosage of electricity, and on April 15, 1938, Cerletti and Bini administered their first electroshock treatment to a schizophrenic patient. It soon became evident that electroshock was superior to Metrazol, since it was less dangerous, less expensive, and produced a milder convulsion. Because of its simplicity of procedure and favorable results, electroshock had, by the 1940's, also widely replaced insulin-shock treatments in schizophrenia.

Shock treatment today consists of passing seventy to one hundred and thirty volts for one tenth to five tenths of a second through electrodes attached to the patient's head. Usually three treatments a week are given; anywhere from five to thirty-five treatments may be considered optimal. For such a relatively violent procedure the side effects are mild, and the patient experiences no pain. The danger of bone fractures has been minimized by the use of curare-like drugs (by A. E. Bennet in 1941) that inhibit the production of acetylcholine at the neuromuscular junction and thus reduce muscular spasm. The patient loses consciousness immediately after the shock is administered and therefore resistance to further treatment is not connected with a recollection of physical trauma. The most striking feature of the post-treatment period is that the patient has a memory loss of a varying degree for recent events. This amnesia may last for several weeks or months following the treatment, but eventually memory is restored. Whatever brain changes do occur are reversible, and persisting brain damage is very rare.

Electroshock treatment has been proved a particularly effective measure for the severe depression—involutional melancholia—that appears in late middle age. On the other hand, shock treatments effect only a relief of symptoms. They do not reach the basic psychological disturbance underlying the illness, and patients who receive electroshock without psychotherapy—which reaches the source of the illness—frequently relapse, even

* The use of nonconvulsive electrotherapy as a method for alleviating symptoms through suggestion dates back to Scribonius Largus (c. A.D. 47), who treated the headaches of the Roman emperor with an electric eel. Nonconvulsive electrotherapy was in widespread use in the late nineteenth century, advocated by the German neurologist W. H. Erb and the French neurologist G. B. Duchenne. Probably the first electroconvulsive treatment for mental illness was administered by the French physician J. B. LeRoy in 1755 on a patient with a psychogenic blindness; almost a half century later F. L. Augustin of Germany reported a similar case. These were isolated experiments and were not followed up; the exact amount of electricity that produced convulsions without fatality was unknown. Cerletti was unfamiliar with these reports, but he did know that experimental convulsions had been produced in animals and that humans too had seizures after accidental electrical exposure.[5]

those who have psychotic depressions, for which electroshock is most effective. Despite this drawback, it must be recognized that electroshock may be imperative in cases where symptoms must be alleviated immediately in order to protect the life of a suicidal patient or the lives of others exposed to an excessively aggressive patient.

Speculations about the mode of action of electroshock treatment fall roughly into two sets of theories, one set based on possible psychological reactions to the treatment, the other on possible physiological reactions. One psychological theory maintains that the patient is so fearful of the treatment hat he "escapes into health" rather than face another treatment; another proposes that the treatment satisfies the patient's need for punishment. If this were true, however, beating or chaining the patients—as practiced in the Middle Ages—would more readily cure them. Metrazol produced a much more violent reaction and was more painful to the patient, yet its effects were inferior to electroshock. A third psychological theory holds that the patient releases his pent-up aggressive and hostile impulses through the violent muscular convulsions; but if this were true, running around the block or doing push-ups to the point of exhaustion should be equally effective. Still another psychological theory proposes that the patient experiences the electroshock as a threat to his life, against which his body mobilizes all its defenses. But if this theory were true, then psychotic patients in the analogous circumstances of facing death from cancer or other terminal illness should inevitably show signs of remission of their psychotic illness. Occasionally this does occur, but it is by no means frequent. Another theory holds that the patient's family, fearful of the treatment, gives the patient more attention and thus helps him to get better. But there are families who are consciously or unconsciously hostile to the sick person in their group and therefore would not be influenced by any such threat at all. In general it may be said that all these psychological theories may be applicable to individual patients but that they cannot hold true for all individuals.

The physiological theories about electroshock are just as speculative. Claims that electroshock stimulates the hypothalamus and therefore the sympathetic nervous system or that it stimulates adaptive responses from the adrenal cortex suffer from the observation that specific sympathetic stimulators or adrenal-cortical hormones do not cure psychotic conditions. Perhaps a plausible explanation for the efficacy of shock is that it produces a slight brain damage and thus erases the most recent neurohistological changes in the highest brain area, which stores as memories those experiences which precipitated the psychosis. In other words, as the result of shock treatment the patient completely forgets the events leading up to his symptoms and thus is put back into a predepression psychological state. The best-substantiated facts of electroshock therapy are that amnesia occurs during this period and that when the temporary memory defect based on the patient's reversible brain damage is restored, illness is apt to reoccur. The exceptions are those lucky patients whose external-life situations fortuitously improve after the shock therapy.

One speculation about the way shock treatment operates involves the concepts of feedback and reverberating circuits. After Hans Berger's discovery of the electrical potentials of the brain and his inauguration of electroencephalography, some scientists began to view the brain as a series of electrical circuits. Norbert Wiener (1894–1964) compared the brain to an electrical computer governed by mechanisms—that is, self-regulating and self-corrective devices—that allow a machine to operate according to prearranged patterns. Negative feedback keeps a machine in a state of stability; positive feedback acts to increase instability of whatever system it governs and in effect causes a machine to develop what is called a reverberating cycle in which internal control is lost. Some psychiatrists have therefore suggested that electroshock therapy breaks up a reverberating circuit in the brain that is caused by positive feedback and thereby clears the brain. The question of how far the "neurotic machines" of Norbert Wiener can be compared with a neurotic personality offers interesting areas for further research. As of the moment, the positive-feedback theory must remain in the realm of speculation.

The idea of a vicious cycle in which morbid ideas become intensified if they are not checked predated the concepts of cybernetics and was one of the theoretical concepts that led to the development of psychosurgery. Egas Moniz (1874–1955), clinical professor of neurology at the University of Lisbon, believed that "morbid" ideas stimulate and restimulate the neuron. Although no pathological changes could be detected in the synapses or in the nerve cells of patients suffering from functional psychoses, nevertheless Moniz "was particularly struck by the circumstance that certain mental patients as a type—I had in mind obsessive and melancholic cases—have a circumscribed mental existence confined to a limited cycle of ideas which, dominating all others, constantly revolved in the patient's diseased brain."[6] Moniz believed that if the frontal area of the brain were to be altered, this recurrence of unhealthy thoughts would be interrupted. He decided that the connection of the thalamus and the frontal lobes would be the most logical to work with because the thalamus is the relay center of sensory impressions, while the prefrontal lobe is concerned with interpreting sensory experiences and rendering them conscious.

Two studies influenced Moniz' interest in the prefrontal lobes. The functions of the frontal lobes had been studied at Yale by Fulton and Jacobson, who noted that monkeys whose prefrontal-lobe fibers had been severed seemed to accept frustration better and were easier to manage. Richard Brickner had removed parts of frontal lobes while removing a tumor and reported that the patient subsequently seemed less worried and less inhibited and did not appear intellectually deteriorated.[7] A Swiss psychiatrist, Burckhardt, in 1890 had also removed part of the frontal lobe in a mental patient,[8] but the work was not followed up, probably because of ethical pressure, and Moniz was thus the first to operate on a large number of patients.

Moniz' first frontal lobotomy on a psychiatric patient was performed in 1935 with the aid of Almeida Lima, a Portuguese neurosurgeon; during the 1940's psychosurgery was often advocated for patients with irretractable psychoses resistant to shock treatments. Although mortality from pre-frontal operations was only one or two percent, loud protests were raised against its use. Patients who had this kind of surgery were not merely calmer—much of the time they were reduced to being placid "zombies." Many postoperative patients lacked ambition, tact, and imagination; although the patients themselves may have felt more comfortable, their families did not. Anxiety was relieved, but at the price of a loss of self-respect and of empathy with others. Furthermore, patients with recurrent severely morbid thoughts—that is, with obsessional psychoses—were not relieved of their symptoms. A major difficulty was that psychosurgery, which mutilated irrovocably a part of the brain, was final. Not a dispensable part, such as the appendix, is removed, but an area essential to the human being—his personality—is forever destroyed. Fortunately, before the brains of too many unapproachable psychotics could be operated upon, another approach was discovered to relieve insufferable anxiety and tension—psychopharmacology.

Psychopharmacology

Primitive medicine men often used dry leaves, roots of plants, and fermented fruits to produce transient psychotic states as a way to heighten and intensify the experiences of religious ceremonials. However, only one of these naturally occurring drugs—opium, the product of poppy seeds—has been deliberately used throughout the centuries to reduce emotional stress. Theophrastus, the Greek physician-botanist, mentions opium's pain-relieving qualities; Paracelsus stored a bit of it in his walking cane; and Sydenham claimed that he could not practice medicine without it.

The drugs that have been used in medicinal therapy for disturbed emotional states can be categorized into five very general classes.

1. Drugs that do not act upon the central nervous system and do not produce changes in behavior, but that do act through suggestion—otherwise called the "placebo effect." Doctors of all periods have had their favorite remedies for ailments, and a doctor's belief that the drug will be helpful is transmitted to the patient.

2. Drugs that correct a deficiency or combat an infection that has led to disease of the central nervous system. Thyroxin, for example, helps the

mental retardation occurring in myxedema and cretinism; and states of severe confusion caused by a vitamin-B deficiency have been corrected by proper administration of vitamins. Syphilis of the central nervous system has been cited as an infectious disease that can be cured by drug therapy. Drugs that are given for these specific causes are, however, ineffective for any other mental disorder.

3. Sedatives administered to convert excited states into quiescent ones and stimulants used to produce increased activity in depressed patients. Sedatives like chloral hydrate were first synthesized about 1870 and were used in psychiatric disorders, bromides were also prescribed extensively during the nineteenth century to produce heavy sedation, and in the early twentieth century barbiturates came into use for the same purpose. As for stimulants, the effects of alcoholic beverages and of caffeine have been known for centuries. Synthetic drugs used extensively during the 1930's to treat depression were the amphetamine derivatives (Benzedrine and Dexedrine), but their disagreeable side effects—they caused loss of appetite, palpitations, and an increase in heart rate and blood pressure—interfered with widespread acceptance. Stimulants, like sedatives, act for a limited period of time; they do not produce permanent changes of mood. In the first years of this century, on the assumption that excitement interferes with clear thinking, prolonged administration of barbiturates in excited states was proposed. In 1922 Jacob Klasi recommended prolonged sedative-induced sleep, on the basis that excitement was a result of an inflammatory process in the brain that could be relieved through rest, as other inflammatory conditions were.[9] Prolonged-sleep treatment preceded insulin therapy and may be considered a forerunner of the shock treatments.

4. Drugs that facilitate verbal expression of emotions, often called narcotherapy. World War II patients suffering from traumatic war neuroses were given intravenous injections of barbiturates to help them relate the sensations they had experienced during combat. Enough of the barbiturate was given to enable a patient to speak freely without putting him to sleep. Variants of this technique continued to be used throughout the 1940's, but it is generally conceded today that this kind of treatment helps the patient to express repressed feelings and has some value in relieving acute hysterical symptoms but that it is not suited to resolving underlying conflicts. Another drug used in narcotherapy is carbon dioxide, which has also proved to have the same kind of limited value.

5. Drugs used to test pet theories about mental illness. A list of all these would fill volumes, and indeed textbooks of psychiatry used to recommend many drugs, enzymes, concoctions, extracts, hormones, and vitamins for use in mental disorders. Many of them represent desperate attempts to validate an organic explanation for psychoses, and some of them should, of course, also be considered as drugs that work by suggestion.

In general the pattern of drug therapy for mental illness has been one of initial enthusiasm followed by disappointment. Twenty years after Balard discovered bromides (1826) they were widely used in psychiatric illnesses. During the latter part of the nineteenth century and in the early years of the twentieth, physicians found that uncontrollable states of excitement could be markedly relieved by the administration of bromides. By the mid-twenties, even some psychiatrists writing in the official journal of the American Psychiatric Association were claiming that finally a drug—bromide—had been discovered that could alleviate serious symptoms of disturbed behavior. The American public, following the lead of physicians, so desired bromides that by 1928 one out of every five prescriptions was for bromides. As is usual when drugs are hailed as the solution to mental illness, disillusionment gradually set in. Patients had to be continuously maintained on bromides in order to show improvement. Nonetheless, despite the repeated shattering of the drug dream, physicians still hope eventually to alleviate man's inner strife by chemical means.

Since antiquity men have desired a state of perfect tranquillity—what the Epicureans called "ataraxia," a serene calmness. The Greeks used alcoholic beverages or narcotics to dull their senses into a state of relative peacefulness; but then, as now, they suffered eventually from confusion and hangover. In the tropical areas of the Orient, however, one drug was said to produce contentment without cloudiness. It was derived from a red-blossomed plant, about eighteen inches high, whose roots zigzagged along the ground like snakes. This plant's many names reflect its use both as an antidote for snakebite ("snakeroot plant," "serpentina," and "sarpagandha," or snake repellent) and as a treatment for moonsickness or insanity ("chabdra," or moon, and "pagla-ka-dawa," or insanity herb).[10]

The snakeroot plant was unknown to the Western world until early in the seventeenth century, when Plumier, a French botanist, first described it. He named it *Rauwolfia serpentina* after the German physician-botanist Leonard Rauwolf, who had, between 1573 and 1574, explored the medicinal plants of the Orient. It was not until the 1930's however, that any serious scientific interest was given to its medical potential. In 1931 two Indian doctors, S. Siddiqui and Rafat Siddiqui, isolated five alkaloids from the snakeroot plant, and two other Indian scientists, Ganneth Sen and Katrick Bose, described the use of *Rauwolfia serpentina* in cases of high blood pressure and also in psychoses. By the 1950's *Rauwolfia*'s ability to lower blood pressure and to calm excited patients without producing a state of confusion was known to Western physicians as well, and medication incorporating the alkaloids from its roots was being prescribed throughout the world (under many trade names, some of which are Moderil, Sandril, Serpasil, Reserpine, and Harmonyl).

Another group of potent tranquilizers, the phenothiazine derivatives, evolved as the product of meticulous laboratory investigation. One of these derivatives was used to combat parasitic worms in cattle; it also proved effective against malaria and trypanosomiasis—a form of sleeping sickness caused by a parasite in humans. Further investigation revealed that other phenothiazines were effective against some forms of allergies. In 1952 a French psychiatrist, Jean Delay, along with his co-worker, Pierre Deniker, reported the beneficial results of using chlorpromazine, a phenothiazine, for treating psychotic patients. In the 1950's the derivatives of the snakeroot plant of ancient India and chemical compounds of this new drug (sold under the trade names Thorazine, Sparine, Compazine, Stelazine, etc.) seemed to combat everything from allergy to psychosis and competed for dominance in the medical journals. Then a third drug was introduced that was to challenge the other tranquilizers in sales as a psychopharmacological panacea. Mephenesin, a glycerol derivative, was known to have a marked muscle-relaxing effect and was used extensively in the treatment of muscle spasm in acute excited conditions like delirium tremens. F. M. Berger, medical director of Wallace Laboratories, realized that Mephenesin's action was of too short a duration and in the early 1950's synthetized a related chemical compound, meprobamate, that had a more lasting effect. Meprobamate (Miltown, Equanil) had in its favor few side effects, and yet mildly tranquilized the patient.

Because these tranquilizing drugs do not significantly impair consciousness, memory, or intellectual functioning, the conclusion has been drawn that the cerebral cortex must be more or less unaffected and that the subcortical areas must be most implicated, in particular the hypothalamus, the limbic system, and the reticular-activating system.

The phenothiazines appear to inhibit significantly the alerting r.a.s., thereby diminishing awareness of disturbing stimuli. If a phenothiazine is given to a patient in a state of severe pain, for example, the patient continues to feel pain but is not as attentive to it, not as aware of it, and consequently not as troubled by it. For this reason the phenothiazines are widely used in obstetrics and surgery. These drugs are not merely effective against physical pain, however; they also reduce mental anguish and anxiety, so that individuals who usually would be driven by their inner impulses to excessive activity and excitement quiet down remarkably well after taking a phenothiazine derivative. The *Rauwolfia* compounds are less sedative than the phenothiazine derivatives and apparently have their most crucial effect upon the hypothalamus and the autonomic nervous system. They seem both to inhibit the sympathetic nervous system and stimulate the parasympathetic nervous system, which would account for some of their annoying side effects, such as pupillary constriction, increased motility of the gastrointestinal tract, and lowering of the blood pressure. Their most untoward side effect is that in many cases they produce depression.

The mildest tranquilizers, the meprobamates, seem to act in completely dissimilar fashion from both the *Rauwolfia* and the phenothiazines. They do not affect the hypothalamus or the r.a.s., but instead apparently slow down transmission of sensory impulses from the thalamus to the cortex.

The exact manner of this inhibition is uncertain, and the suppression of impulses appears to be incomplete, since if it were complete the effect would be equivalent to a chemical lobotomy, which it is not. In general the tranquilizers, with a few exceptions, have proved to be safe with relatively few side effects.

The tranquilizers have proved least effective for cases of depression, which is not surprising. Any drug that tranquilizes or inhibits alertness to stimuli could scarcely have much value for patients who are already hyper-tranquilized, inattentive, and excessively limited in their activity. However, a group of stimulating drugs, the amine-oxidase inhibitors, have proved promising for lifting the spirits of depressed patients. Amphetamines had been used during the 1930's as antidepressants, but their undesirable side effects brought them into some disfavor. Then, in the 1950's, it was observed that a drug, Iproniazid, used in the treatment of tuberculosis appeared to elate the depressed tubercular patients who took it, and research work began on using similar compounds that were less toxic than Iproniazid in the treatment of depressions. These drugs, which do not have the same undesirable side effects as the amphetamines, apparently act by inhibiting an enzyme called amine-oxidase, which seems to destroy serotonin; consequently the body is able to store up reserves of serotonin in the body. In addition to the amine-oxidase inhibitors, there are several other classes of antidepressants that are presently under full-scale investigation.

The use of the new psychotropic drugs—tranquilizers and antidepressants—has opened up new horizons for psychiatry. They have the practical advantages that they neither affect the state of consciousness to the same degree as the traditional sedatives nor have the unpleasant side effects of the amphetamines; they offer physicians the opportunity to influence specific psychic functions and shift the equilibrium between inhibitions and excitations in the desired direction. Retarded depressive patients can be stimulated; excited manic patients can be tranquilized.

Although the mode of action of these drugs is not yet fully understood, it is well established that tranquilizing drugs act primarily on the midbrain, the reticular formation, and the vegetative centers. They do not interfere with cortical functions, nor do they induce excessive drowsiness like the barbiturates. The fact that they act on the lower centers renders them therapeutically more useful than drugs that have a direct effect upon the higher centers of the nervous system: they leave integrative and cognitive functions unaffected and thus allow drug treatment to be combined with psychotherapy, which of necessity has to rely on the integrative functions of the highest centers. The very limited therapeutic usefulness of hypnotherapy and narcotherapy has shown that a genuine reconstruction of a neurotic personality cannot be achieved without involvement of these integrative functions.

Used with psychotic patients, tranquilizers reduce anxiety, restlessness, hallucinations, and delusions, which are the outward manifestations of underlying disturbances that seriously interfere with the patient's human relationships, with his functioning in life, and with psychotherapy. The manifest florid symptoms, particularly anxiety, impair the higher integrative functions. Moreover, hallucinations and delusions make contact with others more difficult and induce further withdrawal from reality. This vicious cycle is broken when drug treatment is successful. Symptomatic improvements from drugs allow for further spontaneous ego development. However, since the drug does not change the underlying personality disturbance and merely reduces its secondary manifestations, psychotherapy remains still the most incisive tool. It is still not clear, though, how far systematic and expert psychotherapy can go with psychotic patients, even when drugs have made them more accessible to intensive psychological treatment.

Whether or not psychotropic drugs should be used in cases of neurosis is a controversial issue. The secondary symptoms, such as the disturbance of the sensorium and of the thought processes that makes the psychological approach to psychotics often impossible, are much less common in neurotic patients. Reduction of extreme anxiety remains a real indication for the use of drugs in the psychoneurotic, but treatment should focus on its essential target, the underlying personality disturbance. Some psychoanalysts combine their treatment with a judicious administration of psychotropic drugs, trying to create by the reduction of disturbing excessive anxiety more favorable conditions for the psychological approach; other psychoanalysts, more fundamentalistic in their approach, believe, for technical reasons, that the use of drugs seriously interferes with their therapeutic work. These psychoanalysts maintain that to give drugs is to play the role of the magician who is trying to relieve symptoms quickly, thereby hampering his role as a psychotherapist who is trying to help the patient reveal and understand himself.

There can be no question that the psychotropic drugs have great practical value. Their use has markedly shortened the hospital stay of severely disturbed patients and has also simplified the hospital management of these patients by making them more tractable. And what is most important, the more drastic methods of treating psychotics—electroshock, insulin therapy, and psychosurgery—are less frequently used. Unfortunately most severely depressed patients respond less rapidly to the antidepressant drugs than to electroshock; nonetheless, these drugs have made it possible to humanize the hospital treatment of psychotic patients by substituting chemical for corporal restraint.

It is most tempting for a person to get relief from the unavoidable burdens and anxieties of everyday life by taking a drug rather than by facing his actual problems realistically. However, psychological habituation to a chemically induced oblivion is an unrealistic solution and a basically unreliable crutch that only compounds the problems encountered in day-to-day living. Concern about real problems induces a person to plan and strive realistically. Anxiety mobilizes both biological and psychological defenses to ensure survival. Unquestionably, under certain extremely stressful life conditions and also in pathological states of mind, tension and anxiety may hamper effectual planning and concentration. Relief by tranquilizers, even temporary relief, in such conditions may allow the person to face more realistically his internal and external problems. Only an expert psychological evaluation of the situation can lead to the correct decision whether or not administration of drugs is indicated in an individual case. Meanwhile, indiscriminate use of psychotropic drugs constitutes a definite danger for proper psychiatric care as well as for mental hygiene in general.

New drugs will come to take over for older ones, and there will be many new drug trials. It does not seem foreseeable that one drug will solve the dilemma of mental illness, but the experimentation into how drugs act on the nervous system will aid us inestimably to understand better the functioning of the brain. As we learn more about the reticular-activating system, the limbic system, and the hypothalamus, and the enzymes and the neurohormones active in the nervous system, the gap between the mind and brain becomes narrowed. Already we suspect that the cerebral cortex can block through inhibitory discharges unpleasant stimuli reaching it from other neuronal centers. We call this psychological repression. We have noted that interruption of thalamic-cortical circuits, inhibition of the r.a.s. system, or reverberations set up in the limbic lobe are not dissimilar and occur wth drug intervention. The day will arrive when the mind will come to its intended resting place, not as a structure of the brain, but as a function of it. How disturbing thoughts, feelings, and sensations, the psychological phenomenon called mind, are transmitted, stored as memories, and reacted to at a later time in life will be the legacy left by what appeared at one time to be psychopharmacological fads. Nevertheless, in the future we must be cautious lest we overevaluate valuable neurological data and claim from it more than is justified. In the final analysis, the situations that provoke emotional upsets and the subjective experience of psychic pain cannot be explained in terms of the nervous system but must be described in psychological language.

The Hallucinogens and Experimental Psychosis

The rediscovery of hallucinogens, drugs that produce transient psychotic states, has in recent years aroused the hope that chemical compounds may be found that will terminate not only experimentally induced psychoses, but other psychotic states as well. Man's attempt to produce states in himself in which he would have vivid and fantastic experiences long outdates man's attempt to cure psychosis. Over the ages men have looked for agents that would allow escape from life's pressures: opium, for instance, is such a drug, and so are alcohol and hashish. Marihuana, cohoba seed, mushrooms, and the buttons from the peyote cactus are others.

In the late nineteenth century an alkaloid isolated from the peyote cactus, mescaline, was found to produce intense perceptual disturbances, which have often been described by those who have taken it. During the 1950's mescaline was used experimentally to induce psychotic states; ut also another compound, dissimilar in structure and ten thousand tim s more potent, lysergic acid diethylamide (LSD), has also been so used.

Lysergic acid is the active ingredient of ergot, a fungus that causes the rye cereal plant to decay. Its hallucinogenic quality was discovered by accident in 1943, when, working on the derivatives of the rye ergot, a Swiss chemist, Dr. A. Hofmann, accidentally sniffed one of the synthetic products he was using. He later wrote: "I was seized in the laboratory by a peculiar sensation of vertigo and restlessness. Objects in my vicinity and also the shape of my co-workers in the laboratory appeared to undergo optical changes. . . . In a dreamlike state I left the laboratory and went home where I was seized by an irresistible urge to lie down and sleep. Daylight was felt as being unpleasantly intense. I drew the curtains and immediately fell into a peculiar state of 'drunkenness,' characterized by an exaggerated imagination. With closed eyes, fantastic pictures of extraordinary plasticity and intensive kaleidoscopic colorfulness seemed to surge towards me. After two hours this state gradually subsided."[11] Further investigations in the 1940's and 1950's brought reports of perceptual distortions, mood modulations, multicolored illusionary and hallucinatory patterns made up of glowing and beautiful geometrical designs.

Investigators have so far been unable to establish the causes of the vivid experiences that mescaline and LSD produce; both compounds appear to have similar psychological effects in man and animals. It has been theorized but not confirmed that mescaline, which is similar in structure to adrenalin, becomes converted in the body to one of the breakdown products of adrenalin, adrenochrome, which produces hallucinogenic states. The entire problem of how adrenalin is metabolized in the body has been a major concern of biological research in the past several years.

LSD on the other hand, has an indole nucleus also present in serotonin and the *Rauwolfia* compounds; LSD seems to be antagonistic to serotonin, which perhaps may underlie its psychotomimetic qualities. However, we still do not know how abnormal quantities of serotonin are related to mental illness. Some investigators postulate that by combining LSD with psychotherapy, repression might be overcome so that unconscious conflicts would reach consciousness and be communicated. The use of LSD at this time is, however, in the experimental stage, and the neurophysiological and psychological phenomena produced by these drugs remain enigmatic.

Schizophrenia—The Gordian Knot in Psychiatry

An enigma of much longer standing and perhaps much greater difficulty of solution is schizophrenia. The toll wrought by this illness is enormous. By the sixth decade of this century, it was calculated, twenty-five percent of all hospital beds in the United States had come to be occupied by schizophrenic patients. Half of the three-fourths of a million Americans hospitalized for mental illness are schizophrenic. Twenty-three percent of all patients admitted to mental hospitals are diagnosed as schizophrenic. Undoubtedly schizophrenia is one of the major health hazards in the United States.

Treatment of schizophrenia has been hampered severely by the almost unfathomable nature of the illness. Even drug treatment of the disease suffers from the fact that schizophrenia has completely eluded etiological explanation.

There are two main schools of approach to schizophrenia: the organic, which is the traditional and prevalent approach, and the psychological. Recently there has been a trend toward a more comprehensive view that utilizes information accrued from both biochemical and psychological investigations.

The biological theories of schizophrenia date back centuries, to the Hippocratic era, in which all severe mental illnesses were seen as resulting from disturbances of the humors. In modern times, as we have seen, both Kraepelin and Bleuler considered the illness to be organically based, even though Bleuler still dealt with the "fundamental" psychological manifestations—disturbed affects, loosening of associations, autistic withdrawal, and severe ambivalence.

In the 1920's attempts were made both by Ernst Kretschmer (1888–1964) in Germany and W. H. Sheldon in the United States to correlate body types with the various psychoses. Kretschmer noted that very thin people, whom he called the leptosome, or asthenic type, and whom Sheldon called ectomorphs, appeared to be more prone to schizophrenia, as compared with the rotund, pyknic people—Sheldon's endomorphs—who were more predisposed to manic-depressive episodes. The people Kretschmer called the athletic type—Sheldon's *mesomorphs*—appeared to be less prone to mental illness. There are, however, too many exceptions to these generalizations to justify acceptance of the body-type hypothesis as proof of a biological disorder. More convincing is a series of statistical studies on the occurrence of schizophrenia compiled by F. J. Kallman, which indicates that although slightly less than one percent of the overall population of the United States become schizophrenic, sixteen percent of the children of a schizophrenic parent become schizophrenic.

Furthermore, Kallman found that in those cases in which the schizophrenic was an identical twin, eighty-six percent of other twins also had the same illness.[12] There are no genetic studies that explain why fourteen percent of the other twins did not develop schizophrenia. When twins are fraternal, not identical, and one twin has schizophrenia, only fourteen percent of the other twins incur the illness, a percentage that holds for any sibling, twin or not. A study of identical twins who have been separated and therefore grew up under different environmental influences would be crucial for a full evaluation of these figures. As yet, however, there are only two reported cases of twins who have lived apart and became schizophrenic. But even in these cases separation was incomplete and there was a great deal of interaction between the twins. Identical twins who have shared the same placenta often share similar treatment from their parents. They frequently are confused not only by others but also by their parents, which may lead to problems in their feeling of unique identity. Furthermore, the close psychological association between fraternal twins is not comparable to that between identical twins. These contentions, however, have not been verified by psychological studies. The genetic factor, it would appear, is most relevant in schizophrenia. This is not to imply that malignant psychological disturbances in infancy and childhood have no effect on the later incidence of schizophrenia.

There has been an increasing interest in the importance of biochemical factors as etiological agents in mental illness, and especially in schizophrenia. For example, a Swiss biochemist, S. Akerfeldt, in 1957 found that the blood of schizophrenic patients contained a copper-carrying enzyme, ceruloplasmin; this was hailed as a way of diagnosing the illness until other investigators found that the blood of any individual who was deficient in vitamin C contained the same substance. Akerfeldt's subjects had been hospitalized for a long time and suffered from chronic deficiencies, either because their own apathy restricted their food intake or because of the poor diets they were offered. (In most hospitals the budget for the average mental patient is less than three dollars a day.) These chronic deficiencies naturally result in secondary biochemical abnormalities, and consequently biochemical findings attributed to schizophrenia are often simply the result of inadequate diet.

One of the most difficult problems of research in schizophrenia has been the fact that this diagnosis has become a waste basket. A great numbr of dissimilar illnesses are diagnosed as schizophrenia. Moreover, chronically agitated individuals suffering from intense anxiety have physiological reactions that show up in biochemical tests. The cause of the illness cannot therefore be attributed to these secondary chemical changes. Some psychiatrists argue that if the disturbed chemistry—even if it is the secondary result and not the cause of the illness—were to be restored to normal chemistry, patients would not suffer from the disturbing symptoms of schizophrenia; but before this theory can be adequately tested, a more exact understanding of the biochemistry of the human brain must be achieved.

The results of the biological studies on schizophrenia are equivocal; on the other hand, the psychological theories about the disease remain equally problematical. More than sixty percent of acute schizophrenics show improvement, and those that do not are just as infractory to psychotherapy as they are to biological treatment. Psychological theories lend themselves less readily to objective evaluation, and the bias of the psychotherapist often obscures the evaluation of results.

Freud thought that the schizophrenic patient could not effect a transference to the therapist and therefore could not be analyzed. Jung, on the other hand, who was the first to treat schizophrenic patients psychoanalytically, believed that schizophrenics are accessible to psychoanalytic treatment. And Adolph Meyer devoted himself to studying the entire life pattern of his schizophrenic patients, trying to establish stress-producing factors; he concluded that the "parergasias" (his term for schizophrenia) was caused by an accumulation of psychological stresses throughout the life of the individual.

Even more revealing than the basically descriptive work of Meyer were studies on human volunteers. These studies have shown that individuals subjected to sensory deprivation, receiving no auditory, visual, or skin sensations, suffer from delusions and hallucinations similar to those that occur in schizophrenia.

Studies on mothers and fathers have failed to reveal a consistent personality pattern by which they could be differentiated from the parents of neurotic children. A relatively new psychological view of the problem of schizophrenia is offered by the family approach. It has been found that a schizophrenic person influences all the other members of his family, so much so that frequently if the patient recovers, another member of the family suffers an emotional setback. These studies are leading to a better understanding of emotional interactions between members of a family. However, since the precise disturbances in schizophrenia have not been definitely established, it would not be appropriate at this time to discuss further the various psychotherapeutic approaches to the schizophrenic patient.

However divergent the psychological and organic orientations may seem, their integration is well on its way. The current model of etiology holds that not one but a multiplicity of causal factors produces diseases. One modern psychosomatic model proposes that psychological and organic (constitutional) vulnerabilities, together with a precipitating emotional stress, lead to a given disorder. Some cases have a strong genetic predisposition; they need only minor precipitating factors to develop mental disturbance. Where the genetic predisposition is minimal, only exceptional stress would lead to illness.

Presently research is under way to establish the relation of biological and experiential factors more concretely. A team of workers at the Mental Health Research Institute, University of Michigan, believes that biological vulnerability combined with stressful experiences during infancy and childhood lead to chemical alterations, which result in disturbed behavior when a precipitating emotional stress occurs in later life. The multidiscipline approach, studying patterns of physiological and chemical reactions, as well as psychological responses to stress situations, embodies the ideal of the modern research team. The Gordian knot of schizophrenia will not be slashed suddenly by a sword in the hands of one man but will slowly be untied by the collaboration of groups of scientists.

CHAPTER **19**

Psychological Developments

Theory of Personality

During the first two decades of the twentieth century Freud and his followers were fascinated by the newly discovered universe of the unconscious mind. Dream analysis and the method of free association proved to be most effective operational tools, and the hitherto philosophical concept of the unconscious was opened to methodical scrutiny. The demonstration of unconscious phenomena—the Oedipus complex, the castration complex, repressed sibling rivalries, and the kind of pregenital, regressive mental content revealed in neurotic and psychotic symptoms, as well as in art, folklore, and mythology—became the principle occupation of Freud and the pioneers. This was the era in which the art of interpretation flourished.

The publication of Freud's *Beyond the Pleasure Principle, The Ego and the Id,* and *Symptoms, Inhibitions and Anxiety* instituted a new era. Psychoanalysts now no longer studied merely isolated manifestations of repressed mental content; they began to place these manifestations in the context of that complex dynamic system—the total personality—that Freud liked to call the "mental apparatus." No longer was the meaning of mental content the only focus of attention; instead, analysts became interested in the dynamic interplay between the repressed and the repressing forces. The art of interpretation was taken for granted; interest turned toward the understanding of the dynamic principles of the internal organization of the whole personality. This change marks the beginnings of psychoanalytic ego psychology.

The adaptational nature of ego development had been already presaged by Freud when he distinguished between the pleasure principle and the reality principle. He considered that the reality principle resulted from the organism's gradual adaptation to the facts of external reality. An initially unorganized state of affairs in which each impulse independently seeks its own gratification regardless of the other coexisting drives is gradually transformed into an organized system in which individual impulses are harmoniously coordinated and subordinated to each other as well as adjusted to the external reality. This transformation is an adaptational process. It is the essence of maturation and is the result of the coordinating faculty of the ego.

Ferenczi, in "The Development of Reality Testing," was the first to describe the details of the early phase of this adaptational process, beginning with magical thinking and leading eventually to realistic thinking based on reality testing. This first venture in ego psychology was followed by Freud's essays, which signified his marked increase of interest in the integrative aspects of behavior.

Another early contributor to ego psychology was Herman Nunberg. In an article on schizophrenia he referred to the "synthetic functions"[1] of the ego that are disturbed in that illness, and in later writings he restated the Freudian formulation that: (1) The ego reconciles the conflicting elements in the autonomous instincts within the id and allies them one with another so that there is unanimity of feeling, action, and will (*the ego tolerates no contradiction*). (2) It brings the *instinctual* trends of the id into harmony with the requirements of reality. (3) It strikes a balance between the claims of the superego and of reality on the one hand and of the id on the other.[2] Nunberg derived the dynamic source of the synthetic functions of the ego from the life instinct—the eros.

The first systematic attempt to apply this structural-dynamic theory of personality to the understanding of neuroses and psychoses was Franz Alexander's *The Psychoanalysis of the Total Personality* (1929). In this book the author attempted to describe three psychiatric disturbances—conversion hysteria, obsessive-compulsive neurosis, and manic-depressive disease—as different forms of disturbances in the interplay between the repressive functions of the ego and the repressed tendencies. Following Freud's basic tenet that every neurotic symptom represents a compromise between the repressive forces of the ego—the superego—and the ego-alien repressed forces of the id, Alexander proposed three forms of compromise, each characteristic of one of these three mental diseases. The fully developed obsessional-compulsive neurotic shows two kinds of symptoms. One set of symptoms involves obsessive ideas of highly asocial nature, such as hitting people, having incestuous intercourse, killing near relatives, or putting disgusting objects into the mouth, which are undisguised expressions of otherwise repressed infantile impulses. The other set of symptoms are compulsive rituals, which, in contrast to the obsessional ideas, represent exaggerations of social behavior: repeated handwashings, prolonged ceremonial baths and showers (extreme cleanliness), and exaggerated meticulousness. Shoes are placed exactly parallel and symmetrically in relation to the bed. Doors and drawers are closed carefully, objects in the bathroom or pocket are scrupulously counted, all train stations between one point and another are rehearsed, the names of the Presidents are recited in order.[3] These exaggerated social rituals are paralleled by certain character trends: these neurotics are inhibited in all activities, and they are considerate, punctilious, and rigorous in observing the small courtesies and conventions of society. They suffer from a paralyzing doubt that pervades their whole personality and behavior. They look at everything from all sides and finally cannot decide to do anything. Alexander proposed that these individuals are able to express their ego-alien tendencies so directly without disguise in their obsessional ideas because their conscience is, so to speak, bribed by their overly social compulsive rituals and character trends.

A similar balance between ego-alien and social attitudes exists in manic-depressive disease. Here, however, the two kinds of symptoms follow each other in the two phases of the disease. In the depressive phase the patient is inhibited and retarded; he accuses himself of sinfulness, punishes himself with self-depreciation, and sometimes even fasts. In the manic phase he is aggressive, sexually licentious, overbearing, and unrestrained. Alexander, following the theories of Freud and Abraham, considered that in the depressive phase the individual punishes himself for his asocial excesses in thought and often in deed, but so severely that he eventually comes to the point when he feels that he has paid abundantly for his sins and therefore is again free to behave uninhibitedly, which ushers in the manic period. In the depressive phase he overpays his debts to his conscience, so that he has moral capital to spend.

Alexander applied the same dynamic principle to the explanation of the conversion symptoms of hysteria, which have a double symbolic meaning. They express both the satisfaction of an ego-alien tendency and its rejection. Hysteria is simultaneously gratification and self-punishment; the latter is expressed in the incapacitation caused by a paralyzed leg or a contracted arm. Alexander thus described three forms of psychopatho-logical mechanisms: *one-phasic,* in the simultaneous gratification of the repressing and repressed tendency of hysteria; *two-phasic,* but *simultaneous,* in obsessional-compulsive states; and *two-phasic,* but *successive,* in manic-depressive disease. In "Remarks About the Relation of Inferiority Feelings to Guilt Feelings" (1938) Alexander differentiated the psychology of guilt feelings from feelings of inferiority, that is, shame. Guilt and shame until then had been used interchangeably in psychoanalytic litera-ture; Alexander showed, however, that they have a different emotional content and entirely opposite dynamic results. Feeling guilty is a reaction for having done wrong or having wanted to do wrong to someone else and provokes the wish to be punished. The guilty person thus looks for punishment; furthermore, his guilt inhibits further aggressiveness and has a paralyzing effect. This reaction is most clearly seen in depressed patients who are inhibted and retarded and accuse themselves of sinfulness. Shame, on the other hand, is a reaction to feeling weak, ineffective, or inferior to others. The psychological reaction to shame is the opposite of that of guilt: it stimulates aggressiveness. To get rid of shame an individual has to prove that he is not weak and can beat the person who shamed him. Shame is such a primitive reaction that even animals exhibit it; but guilt feelings can arise only after an individual has acquired a conscience, that is to say, after he has incorporated the moral values of his environment. This distinction between shame and guilt has been valuable for the understanding of psychopathological phenomena, particularly the common vicious cycle that is so characteristic of many neuroses. Hostile, aggressive, ego-alien impulses provoke guilt feelings; these inhibit the person in asserting himself while competing with others. This reduction of self-assertiveness inhibits successful competition, paralyzes activity, and creates feelings of shame. Shame, in turn, mobilizes hostile aggression, which then becomes again inhibited by guilt. In this way a self-perpetuating, vicious cycle develops, which is the basis of many neurotic disturbances.

Gerhart Piers and M. B. Singer in 1953 applied Alexander's concepts in differentiating between "shame and guilt cultures," that is to say, between two kinds of societies, those in which behavior is most regulated by guilt feelings, and those in which avoidance of shame is prevalent.[4] The Japanese, whose major concern is to save face, belong to a shame culture, and the Hutterites, who exhibit a high rate of depressions due to guilt, belong to a guilt culture.[5]

Freud's theory that the personality structure consists of the ego, superego, and id was initially useful in understanding intrapsychic processes. Gradually, however, it became obvious that it was more adequate to distinguish between different functions of the mind than to divide it into airtight compartments. Alexander tried to formalize a functional theory of personality. He distinguished between four basic functions: (1) perception of subjective needs—internal perception; (2) perception of the data in the environment—external perception, or "reality testing"; (3) integration of the data of external and internal perceptions, leading to a plan of appropriate action to gratify subjective needs; (4) control of voluntary motor behavior—the executive function of the ego.[6]

This functional theory makes it possible to view psychopathology as a disturbance of one or more of these basic ego functions. Massive repression, for example, is a disturbance in the capacity of internal perception. Excluded from consciousness, repressed tendencies cannot be integrated and therefore cannot result in a planned voluntary execution, a situation common in hysteria. The integrative function is the one primarily disturbed in compulsive-obsessional states: the ego-alien tendencies penetrate into consciousness but remain isolated like foreign bodies without being integrated with the rest of the mental content. In behavior disorders the executive function is conspicuously disturbed, particularly in one important aspect, that of control over impulses. In psychoses, reality testing is conspicuously impaired. In all mental disturbances, however, every one of these functions is to greater or lesser degree disturbed.

Most of the work discussed thus far focused on the mental apparatus as a complex dynamic system; they were attempts to reconstruct the interaction of various ego functions and construct a comprehensive personality theory along basic Freudian lines. We now turn to two significant contributions of a more descriptive nature, dealing with the empirical foundation of that elusive abstraction to which the different authors refer as the ego: the work of Paul Schilder (1886–1940) and Paul Federn (1872–1950). Paul Schilder's significant descriptive elaboration of the concept of the body image made the notion of the ego more concrete. Schilder conceived of the ego as an irreducible entity in which the awareness of the body and its functions is a significant component: that is, a person realizes that the movements of his body are subordinated to his will. Schilder maintained that for a creature that could not move, body and world would be completely identical. "The term ego is meaningful only insofar as it refers to something constant and unchanging. . . . If I say, 'Yesterday I was a different man,' I cannot possibly mean that my ego has changed: only the experience of the ego and its modes of experiencing have changed. The ego is constant and unchanging in time; furthermore, we ascribe to every ego a particular uniqueness. *My* thinking, feeling, acting, are *a priori* completely different from those of a you. . . . The ego thinks, feels, perceives, has a past and a present. One cannot say that experiences are attributes or parts of the ego, because every experience presupposes an ego; the ego lives in its acts, independent of their objects. The fact that the unity of the ego is preserved in spite of the multitude of its acts can only be described, not be further explained."[7] In these statements Schilder anticipated the concept of the sense of ego identity, which was further eleborated by Erik Erikson in *Childhood and Society*.

The awareness of one's body is, however, not dependent on actual sensory perceptions. This Schilder demonstrated by citing the well-known fact that patients who have lost a limb by amputation continue to experience the presence of the no longer existing limb and have sensations and pains that they localize in this nonexisting part of their body. In his far-reaching formulations about the body image Schilder drew from the classical studies of Goldstein and Gelb on cases of psychic blindness and on patients with brain injuries. He in turn influenced Thomas Szasz, who, in his book *Pain and Pleasure*, further elaborated these observations and drew theoretical conclusions from them.

Other contributions of significance in the psychological analysis of the ego were made by Paul Federn. Schilder emphasized that the ego is such an omnipresent component of consciousness that it is not perceived as are other objects of awareness; in other words, one is not *specifically* aware of something of which one is *continuously* aware. Federn postulated further that the concrete study of the ego can be meaningful only by observations of severe disturbances of ego feelings. According to Edoardo Weiss, an authority on the works of Federn, "The sense of ego, which is omnipresent, is not ordinarily recognized, and slight disturbances and variations subside unobserved. Yet a moment of introspection will demonstrate that variations in intensity of ego feeling are a matter of common experience. When tired or drowsy, we feel numb; upon waking from a refreshing sleep, or upon receiving exciting news, we feel an invigorated sense of ego. Such dynamic variations point, as Federn recognized, to the existence of an 'ego cathexis,' which he examined from many aspects."[8] In his commentaries on Federn, Weiss concluded that Federn made an important contribution to ego psychology by his "precise and minute description of inner experience, rather than theoretical hypotheses."[9]

Federn helped to explain the psychological importance of ego boundaries. According to him, the awareness of an ego is not static, but is subject to constant dynamic fluctuation depending on what Federn calls "libido cathexis," that is, an emotional investment or charge. If the ego withdraws this investment from an object, that is to say, if the ego withdraws its interest, the object appears strange. A similar estrangement from one's own self is the feeling of *depersonalization,* a well-known phenomenon in certain neurotic and psychotic states. Depersonalization (the loss of the sense of the reality of one's self) often affects one's body image. Insufficient investment in either body or mental ego may be caused by different psychological (emotional) reasons. To quote Edoardo Weiss on this subject, "The ego may react to an external situation presenting a conflict by withdrawing itself from the sense organs, thus causing the outer world to seem unreal; and it may withdraw itself similarly from a body organ which has become the source of unpleasant sensations, or from some objectionable wish or affect."[10]

The interest in ego psychology received strong impetus from Anna Freud's lucid descriptions in *The Ego and Mechanisms of Defense* (1936), which explains the ego's various defense mechanisms by which it keeps ego-alien tendencies out of consciousness. The key defense mechanism is repression, which Sigmund Freud had conceived as the principal means by which the child's weak ego defended itself from impulses that in the past had brought him into conflict with the environment. The child has not yet learned to control impulses of which he is aware: whatever impulse enters his consciousness is acted on immediately. Hence the child finds that the only way to keep himself out of trouble is to repress, which is in itself an unconscious process, and thus protect himself from temptation that he could not resist if his dangerous impulses became conscious. In addition to repression, auxiliary defense mechanisms exist: a partial list might include overcompensation, rationalization, projection, turning impulses against the self, and isolation (of ideas from feelings).* Anna Freud's systematic description of these defensive processes marked a turn of interest from the content of repressed material—id analysis—toward the study of the dynamic processes by which the ego tries to preserve its integrity.

It had become clear that not only the specific content of unconscious ego-alien impulses but also the methods of defense the ego employs against them determine the nature of psychopathology. Projection, for instance, is the typical defense mechanism in paranoid conditions; an unacceptable hostile impulse that breaks through the barrier of repression and enters into consciousness is attributed to another person: "It is not I who wants to attack him. He is afer me." Turning aggressive impulses against the self is the central defense in depressive conditions, suicide being the most extreme example. Anna Freud described for the first time another common defense mechanism, identification with the aggressor. Fearful of expressing rage toward the overpowering aggressor, the individual identifies with his tormentors and discharges his rage toward the helpless victims. This mechanism was later observed in concentration camps, where some inmates behaved as brutally toward the rest of their co-sufferers as the guards did against all of the prisoners.

More recently, Anna Freud has emphasized the adaptational aspects of personality functions. Normality depends upon the intactness of the ego's capacity to reconcile id impulses with the superego's demands and with the impact of the environment and also upon the ego's controlling function.[11] Her ideas about the ego's tasks may be summarized as the mediation, supervision, and control of impulses, which corresponds to a great degree with Alexander's concepts of the four basic ego functions.

In 1939 Heinz Hartmann attempted to clarify some fundamental aspects of ego psychology. Hartmann's main point was that ego functions had been studied by psychoanalysts almost exclusively from the point of view of the ego's role as a mediator between instinctual demands and value judgments incorporated into the superego. Hartmann proposed to focus on those ego functions that do not deal with the resolution of such internal conflicts, but with the adaptation of the individual to his environment, such as "perception, intention, object-comprehension, thinking, language, recall phenomena and productivity . . . the well-known phases of motor development, grasping, crawling and walking; and to the maturation of learning processes implicit in all these and many others." He does not claim that these adaptive processes "remain untouched by psychic conflicts or are not inwoven into other conflicts."[12] Yet he feels it advisable to consider these

---

* See "Freud's Scientific Evolution," page 188, for other mental mechanisms.

activities as belonging to a "conflict-free" ego sphere and calls them "autonomous" functions.

Hartmann's delineation of conflict-free autonomous ego functions was a corrective reaction to the neglect of those adaptive, rational processes by which the ego eventually learns to master its environment. Adaptive functions obviously have fundamental significance: the ego's biological task consists in more than the resolution of internal conflicts alone. Freud's *Ego and the Id* was responsible for viewing the ego as an internal regulatory apparatus that tries to retain constant, optimal conditions within the organism. This internal stability is disturbed by subjective needs that often conflict with each other, with socially imposed and internalized normative principles, and with the external environment. It is true that exernal adaptive functions are less influenced by specific internal conflicts; yet they constitute a constant struggle with the exigencies of reality. In other words, adaptations both to the *internal* and *external* environment are basic functions of the ego. To designate the disharmony between subjective needs and the superego as conflict and then call the problems of external adaptation "conflict free" is misleading. This distinction interferes with developing an ego theory applicable to the function of the ego—to adapt to the internal as well as to the external environment. The ubiquitous struggle with reality must be also considered as conflict if one wants to preserve the fundamental meaning of the term "conflict."

Hartmann's emphasis on autonomous ego functions, on the other hand, accords well with general biological principles. All body functions have their own specific, autonomous functions. Grasping with the hand has its own technology, which has to be learned, just as does locomotion. Internal conflicts may disturb such learning; nonetheless, complex physical performances have their own inherent principles based on mechanics—the transformation of chemical energy into mechanical work—and the specific anatomy and physiology of the particular organs involved. The ego's adaptive functions are also based on their own principles, the most complex of which are the psychological laws of thinking, which have only recently become objects of psychological inquiry. (One of the most important of these studies, that of Piaget, has already been mentioned.) Hartmann brings out the point that a most important aspect of these autonomous body functions is that they are not always for the satisfaction of biological needs, but may also be practiced for their own sake as a source of pleasure. For example, a colt frolicking in a field, running in circles, derives pleasure from that stimulating, purposeless activity. It is valid to speak of autonomous functions of the ego in this sense. A concept of "functional pleasure"[13] introduced by the Viennese psychologist Karl Buhler (1879–1963) was utilized by Robert Waelder and Franz Alexander for the understanding of play, and later led to proposed revisions in the theory of instincts.[14] (See "Theory of Instincts," this chapter.)

Ernst Kris and Rudolf Loewenstein collaborated with Hartmann in attempts to apply the conclusions of ego psychology to the conduct of psychoanalytic treatment. Kris introduced a useful concept—regression in the service of the ego—that throws light upon the creative processes of art and literature, an area that has been conspicuously neglected by psychoanalysts. He considered that the unconscious not only contains ego-alien tendencies repressed from consciousness because of their unacceptable nature, but also is the generator of creativeness that the integrative activity of the ego can activate.

This increasing emphasis upon dynamic concepts produced further elaborations of Freud's structural theory of personality. Melanie Klein's speculations about the early phases of ego development will be discussed below. She was primarily interested in the process by which early parental images are introjected in the ego, particularly the so-called "bad" images by which the child feels persecuted. A most elaborate revision of Freud's structural concepts was advanced by a British psychoanalyst, W. Ronald Fairbairn (1889–1964), who proposed in *An Object-Relations Theory of Personality* (1954) a systematic reformulation of ego psychology, based on the idea that the theory of impulses should be revised in terms of structural theory. He drew special attention to the fact that (as in the case of Freud's theory of the ego) the whole conception of internalized objects had been developed without any significant modification of the psychology of impulses originally adopted by Freud. Fairbairn explains repression as being caused by a split within the ego that occurs before the Oedipus complex and the formation of the superego. This split is due to the introduction of bad and good objects; the battle between these introjected good and bad objects is the essence of his personality theory. This early split does not involve moralistic considerations and predates the formation of the superego. "Repression originates as a defense against internalized bad objects, and . . . the establishment of the superego represents an additional and later defence ('the moral defense') corresponding to the attainment of a new level of structural organization, beneath which the old level persists."[15] Fairbairn maintains that the schizophrenic split can be derived from the defenses against these originally internalized bad objects incorporated into the personality. They are either "exciting" or "rejecting" objects. In spite of their speculative nature, Fairbairn's views represent an important challenge for further clarification of prevailing concepts about early ego development.

In our opinion, the structural points of view have been somewhat over-elaborated by speculative assumptions about static structural units within the ego. As mentioned before, even the concept of the superego is yielding more and more to that of superego functions, replacing the idea of a circumscribed, more or less static compartment within the personality. Structural hypotheses about early ego developments, on the other hand, if not taken too literally, may be useful in conceptualizing the complex intra-psychic conflicts observed in depressions, in schizophrenic processes, and particularly in the rare cases of multiple personality

In spite of a continued interest in structural speculations, the adaptational orientation in particular, Freud's stability principle has come more and more to the forefront of attention. In *Beyond the Pleasure Principle* Freud described a form of regression that differed from the first type of regression he had recognized. Originally he had spoken of a person evading an unresolved present conflict by regressing to an earlier, satisfactory stage of development in which he had still been happy. The individual, in a sense, retreats in his feelings and behavior to "the good old days" when he still felt secure. Certain repetitive dreams of patients suffering from traumatic neuroses of the war suggested to Freud that another form of regression exists—the return to an unresolved conflict of the past. Freud observed that some patients who had suffered severe shocks during their wartime experiences frequently conjured up in their dreams the same traumatic situation, which was anything but a satisfactory or pleasurable experience. These dreams obviously contradicted the pleasure principle. Freud explained this seemingly paradoxical phenomenon as a belated attempt of the ego to master a situation that originally had overwhelmed it by massive stimulation. Freud thus identified the principle of "subsequent mastery," which is a basic attribute of the ego and the means by which the ego tries to preserve its homeostatic equilibrium.

Abraham Kardiner, in a comprehensive monograph on the *Traumatic Neuroses of War* (1941), further elaborated the principle of belated mastery. He recognized the central significance of the ego's attempt at mastery as a manifestation of its homeostatic function, its attempts to restore the equilibrium disturbed by the massive impact of external stimuli breaking through its stimulus barrier. Kardiner differentiated two kinds of mastery: *active mastery*—the utility of an object for the organism is exploited or obstacles are successfully overcome; and *passive mastery*—when the organism uses flight from, escape from, or avoidance of a noxious object.[16]

In another writing Kardiner explained the symptoms of traumatic neurosis as being unsuccessful results of the ego's adaptive efforts. These symptoms are mainly reactions of avoidance. In this work Kardiner used Sandor Rado's formulation of *traumatophobia*—the idea that the traumatized ego tries to escape from and avoid further traumatic experiences. Most of the symptoms of traumatic neurosis, such as loss of consciousness, speech, locomotion, and coordination of movements are, in fact, avoidance reactions. In casting off these faculties the individual regresses to the state of a helpless infant; he behaves as if he refuses to continue his independent adult existence if it means becoming involved in dangerous combat experiences.[17]

Thomas French has made promising contributions to the understanding of the ego's integrative functions, beginning with a description of goal-directed behavior from the point of view of biological adaptation. French introduced a most useful concept, that of *goal structures,* which are either end goals or subsidiary goals. To achieve a final goal necessitates breaking up the task into a number of simpler ones. At first subsidiary goals must be reached in order to achieve the final goal. For instance, in order to eat, we must first go to a store, buy food, and prepare and cook it. Such a complex pattern of action can be executed only after one has a "practical grasp of the total situation." This is a complex integrative act, and yet it is a faculty—common sense—that every normal person possesses and which therefore has been taken for granted. French tried now to analyze what appeared to be something obvious. History has shown that accepting the obvious retards scientific advancement. As long as one took for granted that the apple falls to the earth "because it is heavy," the theory of gravitation could not develop.

French sees *common sense* as the basic factor not only in goal-directed behavior but also in understanding of motivation and in psychoanalytic interpretation. This emphasis on common-sense understanding was first proposed by Alexander in 1931 in a lecture given before the Harvey Society. His thesis then was that scientific psychology should develop and refine the common-sense faculty that every healthy individual possesses. Common-sense understanding of the motivations and behavior of other people is based on the faculty of self-awareness: one person understands another person's motives because he knows what his own reactions in a similar situation would be. People are able to communicate their internal psychological states to each other by verbal symbols simply because the observer and observed are similar systems. This is the one advantage that psychology has over other sciences, and any psychological method that does not recognize and exploit this advantage will necessarily have limited value for the study of the human personality.[18] The best example is Behaviorism, which neglected to use and to develop the common faculty of understanding the *mental* process of other persons.

French has developed an ingenious technique of comparative dream analysis, the application of which can extend and improve the way in which this intuitive kind of common-sense understanding is used in psychoanalytic interpretation. His work on the integrative aspects of human behavior opens up new avenues for developing the science of motivational psychology and making it less dependent upon individual intuition.

The essence of French's work is that he considers goal-directedness to be common for all forms of behavior. Goal-directed behavior is motivated either by the wish to escape from a disturbing stimulus or by the hope for positive satisfaction: remembrance of previous success leads to hope for immediate satisfaction and stimulates the mechanisms of integration to form a method for reaching the desired goal. In fact, the integrative capacity is based on hope, just as the integrative task arises out of needs. Expectation of success makes it possible to withstand painful frustration and pressure of other disturbing needs while concentrating the motor discharge on efforts to achieve the desired goal.[19]

In order to accomplish an integrative task, the integrative capacity of a person must exceed or at least be sufficient to solve the problem at hand. Moreover, an optimum of motivational pressure is needed to activate and sustain the effort for goal-directed thinking and planning. If the motivational pressure is too great the result may be an unintegrated discharge of tension in the form of an uncontrolled-rage attack; if the pressure is not sufficient, effort needed for the integrative act will not be activated.

French's main emphasis is on the problem-solving function of the ego, which he thinks is active not only in conscious but also in unconscious phenomena, particularly in dreaming. This is probably his most controversial proposition, since it contradicts a rigid distinction between primary and secondary processes. According to the Freudian view, the primary processes of the unconscious have no problem-solving functions. They are motivated by wishful fantasies; they are not influenced by the facts of external reality, and they follow their own primitive laws. They appear to be almost random phenomena that cannot be described by the laws governing conscious thought processes. French has eschewed this Aristotelian dichotomy between the primary and secondary processes and instead conceives of the two as a continuum. He describes primary processes as merely being less organized than the secondary processes and thinks that fundamentally they both follow the same psychological laws. He cites the fact that complex problems like chess puzzles are sometimes solved in dreaming; it is equally true that solutions for scientific problems have often appeared in dreams. French convincingly demonstrates the problem-solving function of dreaming by showing, in a meticulous analysis of a series of his patients' dreams, how the dreamers tried to resolve conflicts between opposing attitudes. Each dreamer first tried one solution to a problem by dreaming it; after the solution had been analyzed and proved unworkable, each patient then dreamed of another approach. French concludes that the problem-solving function of the mental apparatus is used in both rational goal-directed behavior and the resolution of internal conflicts; this conclusion implies Hartmann's idea that the ego functions may be used in an autonomous fashion independent of their utility for the total organism.

The adaptational approach to ego functions, which considers them as the means by which the organism maintains that dynamic equilibrium we call life, inevitably meant that psychoanalytic theory had to incorporate material from three contemporary psychological developments: Gestalt psychology, learning theory, and cybernetics. French, who was influenced by Gestalt psychology, is considered one of the foremost exponents of "integrating" psychological theories into psychoanalysis.[20] French's concept of the total grasp of a situation is closely related to the Gestalt psychologist's emphasis that perception is more than a registration of details, but an active psychological act of organization by which a total gestalt is grasped.

Theories Related to Learning

Most of the ego's adaptive functions are learned during the individual's maturation, and for this reason ego psychology unavoidably has had to make use of learning theory. We must therefore discuss some highlights of those contributions in this field that have an immediate pertinence to contemporary personality theories and particularly to psychiatry.

Learning can be defined as the acquisition of changes in behavior resulting from past experiences. The object of learning theory is to establish how such acquired changes come about, and the psychological or neurophysiological processes responsible for them. Most theorists, explicitly or implicitly, assume that the living organism's responses to the environment are adaptive. Some of these adaptive responses are inherited unconditioned reflexes such as those involved in respiration, sucking, and swallowing; others are acquired by learning during the organism's postnatal development. This assumption is independent of the question of whether or not adaptive patterns are always successful and useful. Some inherited reflexes may no longer be adaptive and may even be harmful—like the one exhibited by a moth flying into a flame. There are also learned responses, previously useful for survival, which have lost their usefulness with changing conditions: a mouse, for instance, that has learned to master one maze to find food and then is put into a different maze possesses learning that is no longer adaptive, that is to say, its learning is no longer useful for satisfying its hunger. Adaptive behavior, whether successful or not, is a universal biological phenomenon, and in living organisms is referred to as the instinct of *self-preservation,* or the *constancy principle.*

The assumption of a self-preservation tendency, however, does not explain the process by which adaptive behavior is learned. The trend to maintain life does indeed propel the drive to learn, but it does not in the least explain the process of learning itself. It explains why but not how we learn.

According to Ernest Hilgard, learning theories may be divided into two groups: mechanical, "stimulus-response" theories and "cognitive theories."[21] These two kinds of learning theories are more complementary than contradictory, since each deals with different aspects and different forms of learning.

The simplest form of learning is the acquisition of conditioned reflexes, a phenomenon explored by Pavlov and Bechterev. Because of its fundamental nature their work is a convenient place to start into the labyrinth of learning theory. Setting aside the finer distinctions between the various stimulus-response theories, we may begin by saying that the observation on which they all are based is the simple process of conditioning.

The sight and smell of food activates the unconditioned reflex of salivation. If the sight of food is synchronized with the sounding of a bell and these two events are repeated, the sound of the bell alone will eventually elicit salivation. This is the classical experiment on conditioned reflex. A variant is the American method of "instrumental conditioning." A hungry cat must select one lever to push in order to reach its food. After trial and error the cat finally finds the correct lever. By repetition he learns the proper movement, and a voluntary action has become a conditioned action.

The Pavlovians tried to explain conditioning on mechanistric-neurophysiological grounds, avoiding psychological concepts as much as possible. Their aim was to objectify psychology and reduce it to neurophysiology, so that dealing with data of subjective awareness is made superfluous. In animal experiments this was not only possible but also imperative, because one cannot talk with dogs. If a frustrated dog exhibited manifestations of anger, only the objective, and preferably measurable, aspects of that rage were considered. In Pavlov's laboratory I. Shenger-Krestovnikova went on to confuse dogs by slightly changing the stimulus to which they were conditioned, thereby producing what Pavlov called experimental neurosis. For example, a dog conditioned to respond to the representation of a circle was shown an ellipse, which the dog could not differentiate from the circle and which did not earn him food when he responded to it. Pavlov observed that in this perplexing situation the dog became agitated, whined, and then, exhibiting signs of neurosis, attacked the apparatus.*

Pavlov's mechanistic neurophysiological speculations were never completely confirmed, but his observational findings did become the foundation of a learning theory based on the concept of *contiguity,* the simultaneous stimulation of different nerve centers. According to this theory, all learning consists in creating new connections—new complex conditioned reflexes—between different brain centers.

It was, however, not Pavlov, but E. L. Thorndike (1874–1949) who first formulated the mechanical principle of "connectionism." He applied the old concept of association psychology not only to connecting ideas with other ideas that have been experienced in contiguity with each other, but also to connecting actions with their results. When the result of an action is

* H. S. Liddell of Cornell University, following the observations of Pavlovians, produced experimental neuroses in animals. He found that the emotional rapport between the animal and the experimenter was an essential factor in relieving neurotic symptoms in the experimental animal.[22] W. Horsley Gantt and Jules Masserman also noted that neurotic behavior experimentally produced in animals was less marked in the presence of the experimenter with whom the animal had developed a trusting relationship.

rewarding, it gratifies the need that initiated the action (for example, hunger); this reinforces the learned behavior pattern. Animals and humans learn through trial and error. When a successful need-satisfying behavior pattern is finally found by chance it is repeated and thus reinforced. This was Thorndike's "law of effect,"[23] which later Pavlov independently discovered and called "reinforcement." The connection thus established between action and motivation was conceived as being merely a mechanical connection, although Thorndike did not speculate as much as Pavlov did about the possible neurophysiological basis of such connections. Thorndike consistently emphasized motivational factors—for example, the interest inherent in the tasks and the degree of attention paid to them. Thorndike substantiated his formulations with animal experiments, mainly with cats, and demonstrated that learning curves showed the influence of repetitions on the speed of learning.[24] His observations about learning by trial and error and the repetition of successful actions have remained the basis of all later learning theories. Even those theorists who repudiate the concept of a mechanical connection between isolated actions and their results must take Thorndike's observations into account, however they may evaluate them.

In animal experiments, motivations cannot be observed directly. When the hungry cat tries persistently to open the door leading to food, the experimenter can only assume that its behavior is motivated by hunger, since hunger can be experienced only introspectively. The early learning theorists followed the basic principles of the natural sciences, describing only what they could see by direct observation; they considered that psychological phenomena—such as needs, wishes, desires, hopes, disappointments, and emotion—were outside the scope of their interests, although, of course, they could not avoid making tacit use of them. John B. Watson (1878–1958) advocated most forcefully the principle that learning theory should describe only "objective," observable behavior, and hence is regarded as the founder of what is called Behaviorism. B. F. Skinner is today Behaviorism's most consistent exponent. Skinner is not so much interested in formulating a general theory of learning as he is in making precise, predictable, and repeatable experiments on Thorndike's law of reward and in working out the laws of "stimulus discrimination" and "response differentiation."

Behaviorists have, then, contributed a number of experimentally confirmed facts to learning theory, as well as an analysis of some of the basic factors in learning: contiguity or association between motivations and actions and between external stimuli and responses; the principle of trial and error; and the reinforcement of correct solutions. It is, however, difficult to explain their avoidance of the role that psychological phenomena like motivation, anxiety, and rage play in the learning process. It is obvious that much important information should come from man's own subjective experiences while he is learning. A game of chess cannot be behaviorally described without accounting for the thought processes that motivate the player to make his moves. Man has access to his own intellectual processes while solving problems through introspection. Only he can give an accounting of the mental processes that result in his actions. Studying learning in itself is a complex learning process, and it is a fundamental fallacy to use intellectual faculties in studying learning and at the same time try to exclude them from learning theories. Behaviorists underestimate the value of the most direct way man has to study behavior, that is, through man's own faculty of self-awareness.

The main contribution of Gestalt psychology to learning theory was to show that perception is an active function: that is, perceiving is an organizing function and not simply a passive registration of external stimuli. The Gestalt approach began with a study of the principle underlying motion pictures, done by three German psychologists, Max Wertheimer (1880–1943), Wolfgang Kohler, and Kurt Koffka (1886–1941). They found that the viewer fills in the short time gaps between the separate pictures that make up a film, and in effect perceives an illusory continuity, although in reality he is looking at a series of distinct, disconnected pictures.

Perception is seen by the Gestaltists as the result of a complex organizational act of the perceiving mind. The mind actively does something to the elements of the sensory stimuli it receives: it makes of them an organized whole.

The Gestalt psychologists went on to apply this observation to the more complex psychological phenomena of cognition and learning. They focused their interest on the cognitive organization of all the pertinent factors involved: external stimuli, behavioral responses, and motivation, which, of course, amounts to understanding the whole situation. The main thesis of Gestalt psychology has by now been generally accepted, namely, that learning consists of an active integrative act and is more than a simple molding of the learner's mind through repeated experiences of blind trial-and-error activities.

It should, however, be stressed that both types of learning exist— learning by trial and error and cognitive learning through insight—and that they are not quite so contradictory as it may appear. Similar laws that have been described for trial-and-error activity prevail also in mental activity, in experiments with thoughts. Essentially the law of reward and punishment holds both for trial and error and for the cognitive search for solutions, although in the latter case it is more difficult to define the nature of the reward. That learning without insight exists is proved by the fact that infants learn before they acquire those integrative functions that are needed for cognitive learning. Their learning can be better accounted for by the stimulus-response theories. The fundamental principles described by Thorndike, on the other hand, give a very incomplete and unrealistic picture of the learning process of normal human adults.

Recent experimental operational methods have been proposed that may in the future help to unify learning theory with other areas of psychological knowledge. Clark L. Hull (1884–1952) was strongly influenced by the methods of theoretical physics. He applied mathematical methods to set up psychological postulates, from which he deduced that there were certain conclusions that could be tested. Even though his methodology is rather complicated, it is a model that psychological theoreticians respect. Influenced by the Behaviorists, Hull believed that learning is a result of rewarded behavior.

Edward C. Tolman (1886–1959) stressed that immediate rewards were not necessary to learning. He believed that if an animal learned that a portion of an environment has reward-giving possibilities, then when placed in this setting it would behave in terms of its "expectancy" of getting a reward. A rat in a maze may learn the significant elements in the maze in spite of the fact that there is no ostensible reward, like food. Its latest behavior in the maze would be a function of its expectancy. Why the animal has this "expectancy behavior" is a matter of speculation.

Kurt Lewin (1890–1947), like Hull, used mathematical terminology to describe his field-theory system, using a topological system (maplike representations). He outlined the reward-giving (positive valence) and the punishment-giving (negative valence) regions in the individual's psychological "life space" (world as perceived). The direction of a person's behavior—his avoidances and efforts at approach—could be deduced from a view of the topological survey of his life space. Lewin's emphasis on motivation made learning theory more relevant to psychological ego theory and served as a guide for a number of psychoanalysts, among them Thomas French.

In recent years the interchange between experimental psychologists and psychoanalysts has sometimes been reciprocal. It is obvious that psychoanalysis can offer learning theory much information about motivation and the effect of emotions upon the learning process and that learning theory reciprocally offers psychoanalysis an experimental approach for dealing with the mind. In fact, the psychotherapeutic process can be described in terms of a learning process. The specific problem in therapy consists in finding an adequate interpersonal relation between therapist and patient. Initially this is distorted because the patient applies to this specific human interaction feeling patterns and behavior patterns that were formed in the patient's past and that do not apply either to the therapeutic situation or to his present life situation. During treatment the patient is helped to overcome the propensity to old learned patterns of behavior that have become maladaptive, and insights gained aid him in generalizing to new situations. This complex process of relearning follows the same principles as the more simple relearning process hitherto studied by experimental psychologists. It contains elements of cognition as well as learning from interpersonal experiences that occur during the therapeutic interaction. These two components are intricately interwoven. They were described in psychoanalytic literature with the undefined, rather vague term "emotional insight." The word "emotional" refers to the interpersonal experiences, the word "insight" to the cognitive element. Present research studies, in which psychoanalytic treatment is being observed through one-way mirrors, are attempting to focus on this problem of emotional insight, which is a central factor in every learning process, including psychoanalytic treatment.

Judd Marmor, a psychoanalyst who attempted to relate psychoanalytic therapy to theories of learning, points out that several of these research studies have shown that nonverbal as well as the verbal reactions of the therapist act as positive and negative reinforcing stimuli, thereby encouraging or discouraging certain responses. These reactions on the part of the therapist act as "reward-punishment cues or conditioning stimuli." The analyst tacitly approves of mature patterns of reactions, and his disapproval tends to inhibit less mature patterns. Marmor continues, "This process requires frequent repetition before the previous over-learned conditioned-responses become extinguished, and the new conditioned responses (habit patterns) become firmly established."[25]

Every intellectual grasp, even when it concerns entirely nonutilitarian preoccupations, such as playful puzzle-solving efforts, is motivated by some kind of urge for mastery and has tension resolution as its reward. In psychotherapy the reward consists in less conflictful, more harmonious interpersonal relations, which the patient achieves first by adequately relating to his therapist, then to his environment, and eventually to his own ego ideal. However, an impasse may occur in therapy when the patient's symptoms in themselves become pleasurable, or as the analysts say, there are "secondary gains" from the neurosis. Learning theory suggests that originally the neurotic pattern had some adaptive value. But the pattern tends to become "overlearned" and the neurotic symptom gains "positive reinforcement" so that it becomes more "resistant to extinction."[26]

When collaboration between learning theorists and psychoanalysts, which holds great promise for developing an improved personality theory, has been retarded, it has been mainly for two reasons. First, there is professional distrust on the part of the experimenter for the less operational and less precise concepts of psychoanalysis. Nevertheless, experimenters neglected to deal with the most central problems of human behavior because these could not be approached by experiment. Equally, or perhaps more important, the psychoanalytic institutes, with a few exceptions, confined their activities to the training of psychiatrists for the practice of psychoanalysis and were not active in the advancement of psychoanalysis through research. They accepted only in exceptional cases research psychologists or social scientists for training in research—a policy that only most recently has been relaxed.

In spite of this unfortunate barrier that has divided psychologists from psychoanalysts, a most promising beginning has been made by a few psychologists familiar with both fields, particularly John Dollard and Neal E. Miller. In animal studies they demonstrated that hostility results from frustration. This hostility spreads from the original object to others in what they called "generalization of response," or in psychoanalytic terminology, use of displacement mechanisms. When frustrating objects cannot be attacked for either external or internal reasons, displacement is a common mechanism of discharge. It is precisely what is entailed in transference feelings when a child generalizes from a frustrating experience with his mother to the point where he feels that all women are basically frustrating. Habit patterns then develop in which the individual reacts in a hostile way to all women as though they were his frustrating mother.

Dollard and Miller have applied learning theory to a central phenomenon of human psychology, repression. Repression is a learned phenomenon. The expected reward that reinforces repression lies in the fact that repression attempts to free the conscious mind from anxiety caused by ego-alien wishes. One of the general theses proposed by earlier learning theorists was that successful behavior patterns attained by learning reduce the need that originated the learning process. The reduction—in this case, the reduction of anxiety through repression—is the reward for the arduous process of learning.

The idea that motivational pressure is reduced by need satisfaction is related to the concepts of cybernetics, the science of self-regulating feedback mechanisms. The best-known example of a self-regulating feedback mechanism is the thermostat. When the temperature reaches a certain point, the thermostat feeds back a message to the heat-supplying furnace; the heat supply is shut off, and eventually the temperature drops. When it goes below the desired level, the thermostat feeds this information to the furnace and turns it on again. Living organisms operate with many similar feedback mechanisms, by which they ensure constant internal conditions. When blood sugar, for example, rises above the normal level, a message is sent to the carbohydrate-regulating center, and the supply of sugar is cut off until the surplus in the bloodstream is used up. A baby who is learning movements—walking or grabbing, for instance—at first overshoots or does not use its muscles properly. These mistakes are corrected by feedback mechanisms based on man's kinesthetic sense, which registers the position and tension of the muscles, until eventually the movements become entirely correct and then automatic. Internal regulatory mechanisms are based on the transmission of messages from one organ to another within the organism. Similar transmission of messages and feedbacks are also common between human beings. This is the point at which it becomes possible to apply the laws of communication, derived mostly from electrical engineering, to psychology and specifically to learning.

Three of the ego's functions—external perception, internal perception, and the integration of the messages received by perception—consist of conducting messages from one system to another. These functions, as Anatol Rapoport has pointed out, do not consist of energy transformations, but message transportation, which requires only small amounts of energy, and involve problems of coordination and combination of messages by coding.[27] The possibility of describing the intrapsychic and inter-personal communicative aspects of ego functions in terms of cybernetics seems extremely alluring, although, as Rapoport has emphasized, it is fraught with the danger of making an unwarranted application of concepts derived from communication theory to psychology. The conceptual system of cybernetics still has to be adapted to psychological phenomena; nonetheless, some limited applications are already being made, particularly by Jurgen Ruesch and James Miller.

Lately John von Neuman's and O. Morgenstern's mathematical theory of games has come to the attention of psychologists. In everyday life man is constantly called upon to make decisions. The same is true, of course, for animals. According to the game theory, man chooses the most utilitarian mode of behavior from among the many possibilities open for him. Making such advantageous choices is the essence of playing games. This decision-making process can be expressed in mathematical formulas, in which the available possibilities, probabilities, and the "utility value" of each choice are contained in their relationship to each other. To account by mathematical formulas for the extreme range of values that motivate human behavior and influence human decision outside of the field of economics presents obstacles, but those may not be insuperable.

Game theory recognizes that there are probabilities of choice alternatives that are also important in psychotherapy.[28] Neurotic individuals too often behave as though they have only one choice—a self-defeating one—and all too often accept this choice. The psychotherapeutic process for these people is to allow them to gain understanding of alternative choices measured in terms of risks and gains.

The field of ego psychology, together with these newly built bridges to learning theory and communication theory, has become a focal point of study in recent years. This interdisciplinary work may lead to the formulation of general principles that go far beyond the present boundaries of psychoanalysis, which until very recently has been preoccupied with deciphering the meaning of unconscious mental content.

Theory of Instincts

The psychoanalytic theory of instincts has in recent years undergone a gradual reevaluation, which has striking similarities with developments in theoretical physics. Heat and electricity at first were conceived as materials, fluids. A colder object in contact with a warmer one heats up as the result of the fluid that flows from the warmer into the colder one. What the warmer body loses, the colder one gains. Electricity too, as the term "juice" shows, was conceived as a fluid that flows from objects with higher electric potential to lower ones. These older "substance" theories have been gradually replaced by dynamic views. Heat turned out to consist in the kinetic energy of moving molecules, and the electric fluid gave place to the concept of the electric field. What is important in these developments is that many of the earlier-discovered quantitative laws of heat and electricity retained much of their validity even when the more adequate, newer theories were generally accepted. This is because the laws governing natural phenomena are often correctly described before their ultimate nature is agreed upon. The best example is the phenomenon of light. The ultimate nature of light until very recently was a riddle to physicists. The corpuscular theory gave way to the newer wave theory. Recently, however, both theories have been used, since certain aspects of light, such as radiation, cannot be explained from the wave theory, while interference can be explained only by it (Niels Bohr's principle of complementarity). Many quantitative laws of optics, however, remained valid, independent of the changing views concerning the ultimate nature of light.

Originally libido, the sexual instinct, was vaguely thought of in terms of a circulating "substance"; this idea has been replaced by an inclination to think of the motivating forces behind behavior in functional terms. The view that when a person falls in love some fluidlike substance flows away from his reservoir of self-love is no longer held; however, the distinction between narcissistic libido and object love is as valid today as when it was originally described by Freud in 1914. Many modern critics who try to replace the original libido theory by a functional theory make a grave mistake; they confuse Freud's hypothetical superstructure with the solid foundations of his clinical observation. The "ultimate nature" of instincts is far from being known, but the observable psychodynamic laws of behavior will remain unaffected by theory. Newer insights into culturally conditioned modifications of man's behavior do not contradict but only complement our previous knowledge about the biological functions of behavior. And similarly, further exploration of the physiological substratum of behavior will neither invalidate nor detract from the value of psychodynamic knowledge.

Looking upon the newer developments in instinct theory from this point of view, one finds little that has to be revoked from the earlier observations. More recent theoretical views, however, open up new approaches and allow new questions to be asked and tested by observation.

In the beginning, motivational forces were viewed in the frame of reference of adaptation, which brought ego psychology and instinct theory close to each other. Freud's adaptational point of view was first applied to ego psychology. As a result, the concept of ego instincts was replaced by one of partially inherited, partially learned ego functions that could be best understood as adaptive performances necessary to maintain the organism's equilibrium. Instead of speaking of an ego instinct, one spoke of the functions that maintained a constant dynamic equilibrium in the organism. The ego's primary function, in this view, consists precisely in the preservation of this equilibrium through perception, reality testing, integration, and execution of action. Thus the ego instinct is reduced to coordinating functions that consist partially of inherited automatisms and partially of learned behavior patterns. These ego performances are obviously based on complex neurophysiological processes. Internal perception has its neuro-anatomical substratum in the sensory portions of the nervous system, just as reality testing depends upon special sense perceptions. The integrative faculties depend upon the complex network between the highest centers of the nervous system, and the executive function depends on the motor centers of the brain and the peripheral-motor-nerve connections.

Representative of the trend to reduce instincts to general dynamic principles, such as homeostasis, is Lawrence Kubie's article *Instincts and Homeostasis*. Kubie analyzed different aspects of internal equilibrium and then concluded that "the classification of instincts must rest on a physiological rather than on a psychological basis, and that instincts represent the demands which the body makes on the mental apparatus."[29] Although instincts are direct or indirect expressions of inherited biochemical processes, he stressed that they are still modifiable through experience.

The theory of libido has been less susceptible to reevaluation than the theory of ego instincts. Intellectual functions, as we mentioned in our discussion above, consist of the transportation of messages and not of energy transformations, and as such require minimal amounts of energy. Instincts, on the other hand, are the motivating forces of motor behavior and consequently involve expenditure of effort, although the precise quantities cannot be measured. This quantity, which somewhat resembles physical energy, is what psychoanalytic instinct theory means by "libido."

Libido was conceived by Freud as something somatic, originating within the organism and at the same time possessing psychological content. Libido takes human beings as its objects, toward whom it is directed in the form of love or desire. Its psychological aim is sexual gratification. It seeks discharge. After Freud gave up his original distinction between ego instincts and the erotic instinct—that is, libido—he still believed there were two kinds of energies: the eros and the thanatos, the life instincts and the death instincts. Erotic instincts encompass all acts that sustain life and build up higher units from smaller elements. Eros was conceived as a combining force. Much of what Freud originally considered ego instinct has come now to be placed into the category of the eros. Hunger, for example, serves to build up the organism; hence, it should be regarded as an erotic instinct.

The death instinct opposes this combining force. Psychologically it manifests itself in hate and destructiveness. This destructive force operates within the organism as a death instinct; when it is directed outward, it is hostility. The internal action of the death instinct is to disrupt living substance into its components—the catabolic phase of metabolism. The outward manifestation of the death instinct is the destruction of obstacles in the external environment; it destructively disrupts social units, be it the family, the clan, the nation. War, for example, according to Freud, is a manifestation of this disintegrative force. The fact that the aggressive impulse is observed mostly in the service of the life instinct, as, for example, when an animal kills its prey to satisfy hunger, creates a conceptual problem that Freud tried to resolve by a rather vague and nonoperational concept of a mixture of erotic and death instincts. What can be stated is that energy gained from catabolic processes in which more complex molecules are decomposed into their constituent parts is used for those mostly destructive motor activities that are needed to wrench food from the environment. Food becomes incorporated, split into its elements, and through anabolic processes is built up again into living matter. These complex processes of metabolism can hardly be described as a mixture of two kinds of instincts, but as a coordination of integrative and disintegrative processes: not so much as a battle between two instincts but as a highly organized dynamic equilibrium between upbuilding and disintegrating processes. The energy gained from the disintegrative process is utilized for replacing the disintegrated units by building up new ones from material incorporated from the environment.

This was the line of reasoning that motivated French and Alexander to view the life process as a combination of integrative and disintegrative processes instead of a struggle between two instincts. They came to this consideration independently, French from the study of integrated goal-directed behavior, Alexander from somewhat more general considerations and particularly from the study of sexual phenomena and of play.

French was struck by the disintegration of goal-directed behavior that occurs when an organism faces tasks beyond its integrative capacity, that is to say, which it cannot master by appropriate, adjusted, goal-directed behavior. This disintegration of adapted goal-directed behavior manifests itself in rage, a chaotic discharge of motivational pressures. It seemed obvious that a destructive rage attack, which is but the disintegration of constructive goal-seeking motivations, cannot involve the transformation of one instinct into another one. Goal-directed intelligent behavior aimed at satisfying the organism's need serves survival, and according to the Freudian dual-instinct theory, belongs to the life-maintaining function of the eros. In a rage attack it is not the *quality* of the instinct that changes; what happens is merely that a different form of discharge is used. French's analysis of behavior leads, then, not to a qualitative differentiation between two instincts, but to a distinction between a more organized and a less organized discharge of motivational pressure.

The question is: Does the task of adaptation, which is necessary for homeostasis, fully describe all aspects of human and animal behavior? Obviously, adaptive functions are for the purpose of maintaining the status quo, that is to say, maintaining the constant conditions within the organism that make life possible. But what can be said about growth and propagation? Growth represents a continuous change within the organism; propagation obviously leads to the creation of a new organism, which has not existed before. A principle that maintains status quo cannot explain phenomena that constitute change. In order to account for these two conditions Alexander introduced the concept of *surplus energy*. Growth consists in taking in more than the organism expends; otherwise, growth would not be possible. But every organism reaches its limits of growth; it becomes mature, incapable of further aggrandizement. At this point propagation takes place. Propagation, then, is the manifestation of a surplus that can no longer be handled by the organism. It is growth beyond the limits of the organism. When the organism has reached the limits of individual growth, it must divide. This division is simple and symmetric in monocellular organisms; it is asymmetric in the complex multicellular organisms. The psychological counterpart of these biological events manifests itself in a change of emotional attitudes. Psychologically, an immature, growing human being is "narcissistic"; he is concerned with his own development and with the perfection of his own faculties, and his attitude toward others expresses the wish to be loved and helped. In contrast, a mature human being, finished with his growth, does not need the same support from outside. His cup is full and overflows. This overflow leads to what Freud called object love, which at least partially replaces narcissistic, or self-directed, love. Narcissism, then, is the expression of the biological state of immaturity; object love is the psychological counterpart of maturity, a state during which a surplus that cannot be applied anymore to individual growth is expended biologically in propagation, psychologically in heterosexual love and creative activity.

However, the state of surplus is not restricted to the mature individual. The child whose biological needs are to a great degree satisfied by parental care also has a constant need to discharge surplus energy, which he does through the playful exercise of his physiological faculties, an activity that is connected with pleasurable sensations (functional pleasure). He climbs and negotiates obstacles, for example, simply to exercise and enjoy his physical powers. Freud called this playful discharge of surplus energy the pregenital manifestation of sexuality—oral eroticism, anal eroticism, and so on. Playful practices are not yet integrated into the service of survival. Instead, each of these functions is practiced for its own sake, for the functional pleasure derived from it. They are not yet integrated in the service of utilitarian survival functions. The child becomes more independent as these faculties become gradually coordinated into useful adaptive functions. (This concept is close to what Hartmann called "autonomous ego functions," although he did not identify them with pregenital and extra-genital libido.) Ferenczi, on the other hand, differentiated between useful and pleasure functions and maintained that the organism expresses sexual tensions that it need not coordinate for useful purposes. Alexander later restated this concept by saying that sexuality discharges any surplus excitation regardless of the quality of the drive, a view best exemplified in adult perversions in which emotional tendencies—curiosity, hostility, pride, suffering—become the focus of sexual gratification.

Practically every emotional trend—love, curiosity, the need to call attention to oneself, aggressiveness, and the need for suffering—can be expressed either nonsexually or sexually. When an impulse is discharged in an isolated fashion without being subordinated to a more complex goal structure, it assumes a sexual connotation. Such isolated emotional dis-charges of surplus energy occur in states of excess excitation, when there is a surplus of motivational pressure beyond that which is necessary for coordinated utilitarian, self-preservative functions. An excess of oral crav-ing, beyond what is psychologically conditioned by hunger, is precisely what we call oral eroticism. Excessive accumulated aggressive impulses that are not necessary for survival may be discharged in the form of sadism.

The sexual nature of an emotional discharge depends upon a special condition, whether the discharge takes place as an isolated gratification that serves as a goal in itself or whether it becomes a component part of a goal structure that serves the interest of the total organism. Killing, if it seems to satisfy hunger, is not sadism. When destruction or inflicting pain become aims in themselves, they assume a sexual connotation in the form of sadism.

The question must then be asked: Under what circumstances does an emotional content assume the quality of sexual excitement? Observational data indicate that every gratification of an impulse has an erotic character if it is performed for its own sake and is not subservient to the needs of the organism as a whole.

Sexuality in all its multiple manifestations may thus be considered a special form of discharge of impulses, and there is no need to postulate two instincts of different quality. Any impulse loses the quality of sexuality as soon as it becomes organized as a constituent part of a utilitarian complex structure, which French appropriately calls "goal structure."

Developments in Psychoanalytic Treatment

It is a striking fact that psychoanalytic treatment has undergone few changes since its guiding principles were formulated by Freud between 1912 and 1915. No medical practitioner would attempt to treat his patients today with the methods of fifty years ago; yet the standard psychoanalytic treatment being taught today in psychoanalytic institutes has remained essentially unchanged. Is the standard procedure, then, so excellent that it does not require reevaluation and improvement? Or are there reasons for this conservatism? A contemporary student of psychoanalytic history finds it difficult to account for this inertia, particularly if he has devoted his efforts to the advancement of psychoanalytic treatment and thus cannot be completely objective. It is safe to say that the role of reformer of psychoanalytic treatment has never been popular. Rejection by outsiders forced the pioneer psychoanalysts to stress conformity within their own group. Perhaps more important than the cultural need to conform is the bewildering complexity of the psychodynamic processes of treatment. The insecurity that these intricate processes necessarily provoke creates a defensive dogmatism. Almost any statement about technique can at best be merely tentative. Tolerance of uncertainty is generally low in human beings, and a dogmatic reassertion of a traditionally accepted view is a common defense against the ensuing anxiety.

There are, nonetheless, areas of the essential psychodynamic principles on which most psychoanalytic treatment rests. Briefly, they consist of the following observations and evaluations:

1. During treatment unconscious, repressed material becomes conscious. This increases the action radius of the conscious ego: the ego becomes cognizant of unconscious impulses and then able to coordinate and integrate them with conscious content. As a result, the ego can modify hitherto unconscious impulses and include them in conscious voluntary behavior without internal conflict. However, the patient resists recognizing unconscious content, and overcoming this resistance is a primary technical problem of treatment.

2. The mobilization of unconscious material leading to its becoming conscious is achieved mainly by two basic therapeutic circumstances: material that emerges during interpretations of free association, slips of the tongue, and dreams; and the patient's emotional interpersonal experiences in the therapeutic situation. Sooner or later the neurotic patient directs his typical neurotic attitude towards his therapist. He develops a transference—the repetition of interpersonal attitudes that characterized his childish feelings about his parents or other significant people in his life. This process of transferring these feelings to the therapist is favored by the therapist's encouraging the patient to express himself as freely as he can during the sessions. The therapist's objective, nonevaluative attitude helps mobilize unconscious material during the process of free association and at the same time facilitates the manifestation of transference. The original neurosis of the patient, which is based on his childhood experiences, is thus transformed into an artificial "transference neurosis," which is a less intensive repetition of the patient's "infantile neurosis," that is to say, his

early unresolved conflicts. The resolution of these repeated, reexperienced feelings and behavior—the resolution of the transference neurosis—becomes the aim of treatment.[30]

There is little disagreement about these fundamentals of psychoanalytic treatment. Controversies have pertained primarily to the technical means by which the transference neurosis can be resolved; suggestions for therapeutic modifications have merely emphasized certain aspects of the treatment. It is most difficult to evaluate all the suggested modifications because it is generally suspected that authors' accounts about their theoretical views do not precisely reflect what they are actually doing while treating patients. The reason for this discrepancy lies in the fact that the therapist is a "participant observer," who is called upon constantly to make decisions on the spot. The actual interactional process between therapist and patient is much more complex than the theoretical accounts about it.

In regard to psychoanalytic techniques, in general, there have been two main emphases: on cognitive insight as a means of breaking up the neurotic patterns, and emphasis upon the emotional experiences the patient undergoes during treatment. These are not mutually exclusive, yet most controversial discussion centers on the relative importance of cognitive or experiential factors.

One exponent of the value of cognitive insight was Edward Bibring: "In psychoanalysis proper, all therapeutic principles are employed to a varying degree, in a technical, as well as in a curative sense, but they form a hierarchical structure in that insight through interpretation is the principal agent and all others are—theoretically and practically—subordinate to it."[31] Otto Fenichel, on the other hand, believed that insight imparted to the patient by interpretation has no great therapeutic value if it is not accompanied by emotional experience. Purely cognitive interpretations, he believed, supply "dynamically ineffective knowledge."

Alexander considered the central therapeutic factor to be *the corrective emotional experience,* that is, the difference between the original conflicts and the actual doctor-patient relationship, which he explained in this way: "The new settlement of the old unresolved conflict in the transference situation becomes possible not only because the intensity of the transference conflict is less than that of the original conflict—but also because the therapist's actual response to the patient's emotional expressions is quite different from the original treatment of the child by the parents. The therapist's attitude is understanding but at the same time *emotionally detached.* His attitude is that of a physician who wants to help the patient. He does not react to the patient's expression of hostility either by retaliation, reproach, or signs of being hurt. . . . The fact that the patient continues to act and feel according to outdated earlier patterns whereas the therapist's reactions conform to the actual therapeutic situation makes the tranference behavior a kind of *one-sided shadowboxing.* The patient has the opportunity not only to understand his neurotic patterns, but at the same time to experience intensively the irrationality of his own emotional reactions. The fact that the therapist's reaction is different from that of the parent, to whose behavior the child adjusted himself as well as he could with his own neurotic reactions, makes it necessary for the patient to abandon and correct these old emotional patterns. After all, this is precisely one of the ego's basic functions—adjustment to the existing external conditions. As soon as the old neurotic patterns are revived and brought into the realm of consciousness, the ego has the opportunity to readjust them to the changed external and internal conditions."[32] However, recent observation of psychoanalytic treatment has revealed that the "emotional detachment" of the therapist is less complete than this idealized model postulates.

The contrast between the transference situation and the actual relationship between patient and physician has long been considered as an essential therapeutic factor. Richard Sterba pointed out that the intellectual counterpart of this emotional discrepancy occurs when the transference situation is interpreted and the patient recognizes that his attitude toward the therapist is rooted in childhood and is not an appropriate reaction to the therapist. Sterba called this double attitude—the transference feelings and the simultaneous rational attitude to the therapist—"a dissociation within the ego."[33] James Strachey emphasized the therapeutic significance of the patient's recognition of the difference between the "archaic fantasy object," that is, the transference attitude, and the "real external object."[34] All these considerations mentioned so far were theoretical evaluations of the therapeutic factors that are operative in psychoanalysis.

Derived from these considerations, Alexander proposed technical innovations aimed at intensifying the emotional experiences of the patient. One of them was reducing the number of interviews in appropriate phases of the treatment in order to make the patient more vividly conscious of his dependency needs by frustrating them. Another of Alexander's suggestions pertains to the ever-puzzling question of termination of treatment. The traditional belief is that the longer an analysis lasts the greater is the probability of recovery. Experienced analysts came more and more to doubt this, for treatments lasting over many years do not seem to be the most successful ones. On the other hand, many so-called "transference cures,"* after very brief contact, have been observed to be lasting. There are no reliable criteria for the proper time of termination. Improvements observed during treatment often prove to be conditioned by the fact that the patient is still being treated. Neither the patient's own inclination to terminate the treatment nor his wish to continue is always a reliable indication. The complexity of the whole procedure and our inability to

---

* Cures occurring after brief contact with the therapist resulting from the patient's intense emotional reactions toward the therapist.

estimate precisely the proper time of termination induced Alexander to employ the method of experimental temporary interruptions, a method that in his experience is the most satisfactory procedure. This is a modification of Ferenczi's and Rank's previously discussed enforced final termination by setting a date. The technique of tentative temporary interruptions is based on trust in the natural recuperative powers of the human personality, which are largely underestimated by many psychoanalysts.* There is an almost general trend toward "overtreatment." A universal regressive trend in human beings has been generally recognized by psychoanalysts. Under sufficient stress everyone tends to regress to the helpless state of infancy and seek help from others. The psychoanalytic-treatment situation caters to this regressive attitude. As Freud stated, treatments often reach a point where the patient's will to be cured is outweighed by his wish to be treated.

In order to counteract this trend, continuous pressure on the patient is needed to make him ready to take over his own management as soon as possible. During temporary interruptions patients often discover that they can live without their analyst, and when they return the still-not-worked-out emotional problems come clearly to the forefront. This type of "fractioned analysis," which was practiced in the early days of the Outpatient Clinic of the Berlin Institute, is an empirical way to find the correct time for termination.†

Furthermore, Alexander called attention to Freud's concepts of regression, which were discussed before. Often we find that the patient regresses in his free associations to preconflictual early infantile material as a maneuver to evade essential pathogenic conflicts. This material appears as "deep material," and both patient and therapist in mutual self-deception spend a great deal of time and effort analyzing this evasive material. Alexander even believes that the recent trend to look for very early emotional conflicts between mother and infant as the most common source of neurotic disturbances is the result of overlooking this frequent regressive evasion of later essential pathogenic conflicts.

Another technical issue that has received attention is the therapist's neglect of the patient's life situation in favor of a preoccupation with his past history. This is based on the tenet that his present life circumstances merely precipitate and mobilize the patient's infantile neurosis. In general,

* Judd Marmor has recently pointed to learning-theory studies that would bear out the efficacy of periodic vacations from analysis: "Intermittent and irregular reinforcements are more effective than frequent or regular ones in changing patterns of behavior."[35]

† L. Szondi has also described a modification of standard psychoanalysis, the aim of which is to overcome long periods of stagnation during treatment. He calls this method "Active Hammerblow Association Technique." He repeats words or sentences of a dream content or association material vigorously and quickly and does this so often that the patient somehow abandons his resistance. Szondi uses this *Psychoshock-Therapie* only within the framework of "orthodox passive Freudian analysis."[36]

of course, the present is always determined by the past; still, many contemporary analysts believe that there is an unwarranted neglect of actual life circumstances. The patient comes to the therapist when he is at the end of his rope, so entangled in emotional problems that he feels he must have help; the analyst should never allow the patient to forget that he came to him to resolve these problems. The interest in past history at the expense of the present is the residue of the historical period when research in personality dynamics was of necessity a prerequisite for developing a rational treatment method. However, some of the so-called neo-Freudians went to the opposite extreme and did not believe in the necessity for the therapist to delve into the past history of the patient.

These recent controversial issues will have to wait for the verdict of history. Their significance cannot yet be evaluated with finality. There has thus been a growing inclination to question the validity of some traditional and habitual practices and a coincident trend toward greater flexibility in technical procedures, so that technical details are adjusted to the individual patient and his problems.

Even though there has been considerable controversy over matters like frequency of interviews, interruptions, termination, and the mutual relation between the intellectual and emotional factors in treatment, there seems to be a universal consensus about the significance of the therapist's individual personality for the results of the treatment. Interest in this question was first manifested in several contributions dealing with the therapist's own emotional involvement in the patient—the so-called countertransference phenomenon, a term Freud first used in 1910. Not until about 1940, however, were the therapist's unconscious, spontaneous, or studied reactions toward the patient explored. The reasons for this neglect were both theoretical and practical.

Freud had originally likened the analyst's role in the treatment to a blank screen; he was to keep his neutral personality so that the patient could project onto him, as onto a blank screen, any role—the image of his father, say, or of his mother, or of any other significant person in his past. In this way the patient would thus be able to reexperience the important interpersonal events of his past undisturbed by the personality of the therapist. It is now generally recognized, however, that in reality the analyst cannot and does not remain a blank screen or an uninvolved intellect, but is perceived by the patient as a concrete person who reacts to the patient in many different ways.

The question is how to evaluate these countertransference phenomena. Some analysts view countertransference as an undesirable complication. They cling to Freud's ideal model of treatment: that the patient should reveal himself through free association without controlling the train of his ideas and should consider the analyst only an expert who is trying to help him. The therapist at the same time should have only one reaction to the patient—the wish to understand him and give him an opportunity to readjust through the insight offered by interpretations.

This view—that the analyst's own emotional reactions should be considered a disturbing factor in treatment—at present prevails. Some authors, among them Edith Weigert, Frieda Fromm-Reichmann (1899–1957), P. Heimann, and Therese Benedek, however, have asserted that countertransference has certain therapeutic assets and have pointed out that the analyst's knowledge of his countertransference attitudes gives him a particularly valuable tool for understanding the patient's transference reactions. As to the therapeutic significance of the countertransference, Michael and Alice Balint consider whatever impurity it introduces into the treatment as negligible for the therapeutic process; Benedek believes that the therapist's personality is the most important agent of the therapeutic process. There is general agreement that a too intensive emotional involvement on the therapist's part is a seriously disturbing factor. The analyst's self-learning in his own personal analysis should help free him from unwise emotional participation in the treatment. This is, indeed, the most important objective of the training analysis; it helps the analyst learn how to control and possibly even change his spontaneous countertransference reactions. Alexander believed that the countertransference may be helpful or harmful, depending on whether they are different from or the same as the parental attitude that contributed to the patient's emotional difficulties. For this reason he believed that the therapist must be keenly aware of his own spontaneous feelings to the patient and try to replace them by an interpersonal climate that is suited to correct the original neurotic patterns.*

One of the most systematic revisions of the standard psychoanalytic procedure has been offered by Sandor Rado. His critical evaluation of psychoanalytic treatment and his suggested modifications deserve particular attention because he is one of the most thorough students of Freud's writings.

More and more dissatisfied with the practice and methods of teaching psychoanalysis, Rado proposed a technique based on "adaptational psy-

* Alexander believed that the therapist, in order to increase the effectiveness of the corrective emotional experience, should attempt to create an interpersonal climate suited to highlight the discrepancy between the patient's transference attitude and the actual situation as it exists between patient and therapist. For example, if the original childhood situation that the patient repeats in the transference was between a strict, punitive father and a frightened son, the therapist should behave in a calculatedly permissive manner. If the pathogenic factor was the father's doting, all-forgiving attitude toward his son, the therapist should take more of an impersonal and reserved attitude. This suggestion was criticized by some authors, who maintain that these consciously and purposely adopted attitudes are artificial and will be recognized as such by the patient. Alexander maintained, however, that the therapist's objective and emotionally detached attitude is in itself artificial inasmuch as it does not exist between human beings in actual life. This controversy will have to be decided by further experiences of practitioners.

chodynamics." As is true of many other innovators, much of Rado's formulations consist of new terminology. Some of his newly emphasized ideas are nonetheless highly significant. He is most concerned with those features of the standard technique of psychoanalysis that foster regression without supplying a counterforce toward progression, that is to say, toward the patient's successful adaptation to his actual life situation. Rado raises the crucial question: Is the patient's understanding of his past development sufficient to induce a change in him? "To overcome repressions and thus be able to recall the past is one thing; to learn from it and be able to act on the new knowledge, another."[37]

As a means of promoting the goal of therapy, Rado recommends bringing the patient from his earlier, childlike, faulty adaptations to an appropriate adult level, so that the patient, as much as is feasible, cooperates with the physician at an adult level. The patient, for example, following his regressive trend, "parentifies" the therapist; but the therapist should counteract this trend and not allow himself to be pushed into the parent role. Because he believes that loss of self-confidence is the main reason why the patient builds up the therapist into a powerful parent figure, Rado's main principle is to "bolster up the patient's self-confidence on realistic grounds."[38]

He also stresses the importance of dealing with the patient's actual present-life conditions in all possible detail. "The patient must learn to view life, himself, and others in terms of opportunities and responsibilities, successes and failures. He must learn to understand his doings in terms of motivation and control, to evaluate his doings in terms of the cultural context, and to understand his development in terms of his background and life history." Interpretations must always embrace the conscious as well as unconscious motivations. "Even when the biographical material on hand reaches far into the past, interpretation must always begin and end with the patient's present life performance, his present adaptive task. The significance of this rule cannot be overstated."[39]

Rado considers his adaptational technique but a further development of the current psychoanalytic technique, not something basically contradictory to it. It should be pointed out that although he criticizes the standard psychoanalytic procedure, he is criticizing only current practice, not theory. According to accepted theory, the patient's dependent—in Rado's term, "parentifying"—transference should be resolved. The patient during treatment learns to understand his own motivations. This enables him to take over his own management. He assimilates the therapist's interpretations so that gradually he becomes able to dispense with the therapist, from whom he has received all he needs. The therapeutic process thus recapitulates the process of emotional maturation; the child learns from the parents, incorporates their attitude, and eventually no longer needs them for guidance. Rado's point is supported by the fact that current procedure does not always achieve this goal, and, we may add, unnecessarily prolongs the procedure, because the exploration of the past becomes an aim in itself, and indeed the goal of the treatment. Rado's view is that this exploration of the past should be subordinated to a total grasp of the present-life situation and serve as the basis for future adaptive accomplishments. The goal of both Rado and Alexander is the same: to minimize the danger of encouraging undue regression and evasion of the current adaptive tasks.

The reformers discussed above have remained within the fold of psychoanalysis and retained its basic theoretical orientation; other critics, however, have moved farther away from the Freudian school and proposed more radical changes, principally about theory rather than practice.

Psychotherapy

Coinciding with the reform movements within psychoanalysis itself, psychoanalytic principles were applied more and more to other forms of psychotherapy. From the point of view of practice, this is the most significant trend in present-day psychiatry. This development became known through such synonymous terms as psychoanalytically oriented psychotherapy, dynamic psychotherapy, and—a much less fortunate expression—brief psychoanalysis. This gradually evolved from the daily practice of experienced psychoanalysts, many of whom came to recognize the limited applicability of the standard psychoanalytic procedure. Rigid technical rules (e.g. the patient should be seen four or five times per week for many years and should be on a couch and freely associate) became shackles instead of helpful guides. Rado limits his adaptive variety of psychoanalysis to those patients "who are capable and desirous of self-advancement by extensive learning and maturation." One is reminded of the *aperçu* attributed to Freud, that psychoanalysis is an excellent therapy, particularly for healthy persons. In the course of time it became evident that different types of patients required modified technical approaches that could be based on psychodynamic principles formulated by psychoanalysis. The first such modification of technique was the *play therapy* used with children, which will be discussed later. After that came application of psychoanalysis first to severe behavior disorders, then finally to psychotics.

Since schizophrenia represents an unsolved enigma of psychiatry, therapeutic approaches to it necessarily have had to remain highly empirical and experimental. Harry Stack Sullivan's "interpersonal" approach to the disease influenced Frieda Fromm-Reichmann. In her book *Principles of Intensive Psychotherapy* she emphasized the importance of establishing a meaningful relationship with the patient. After such a relationship is established, she believed that "psychoanalytically oriented psychotherapy" can be successful in many cases. A workable emotional relationship with the patient is instrumental in reversing the psychotic's tendency to withdraw from the environment. Since this withdrawal is the essence of the schizophrenic process, a meaningful personal relationship may initiate a new acceptance of reality on the part of the patient and become the crystallization point of the patient's recovery.

——Another exponent of a psychoanalytic approach to schizophrenia is John Rosen. According to him the therapist is a loving omnipotent protector and provider for the patient. Rosen believes that the psychotic patient sees the therapist as an idealized mother and will accept his deep interpretations of instinctual reactions. Accordingly, he gives a great number of deep interpretations in the hope that some of them will click. He also tries to involve the patient in a strong emotional relationship by spending almost unlimited time with him. At present it is difficult to evaluate the effectiveness and meaningfulness of these and a great number of other therapeutic experiments using the psychological avenue of approach to psychotic patients.

Now let us return to the modifications of the psychoanalytic approach to neurotics, an area where the classical psychoanalytic approach is more prevalent.

Many arguments center about the question of whether or not it is possible to draw a sharp line between psychoanalysis proper and psychotherapy based on psychoanalytic principles. Some authors would like to make a clear-cut differentiation. For example, Bibring and many others see the main characteristic of psychoanalysis in its principal reliance on interpretations. According to them, all other therapeutic measures are subordinated to insight that the patient obtains through the therapist's interpretations, which the patient "works through." Others, like Alexander, emphasize that in all psychotherapies different factors are unconsciously or inadvertently utilized, such as support and abreaction. In psychoanalysis emotional support rendered by daily contact with the "parentified" (Rado) analyst is perhaps even greater than in so-called supportive therapies. Furthermore, in supportive therapies the patient obtains insight because as soon as his anxiety is reduced spontaneous insight becomes possible. Alexander suggested that the difference between psychotherapies is gradual, that they differ according to the extent to which insight, emotional experiences, support, and free expression of pent-up affects (abreaction) play a part in the therapeutic process. Alexander did not see the need for a rigid distinction between psychoanalysis and therapies based on the same scientific principles. From the practical point of view, nevertheless, it became customary to differentiate between uncovering and supportive types of treatment. The former try to mobilize repressed material; the latter try to satisfy the disturbed patient's need for dependency and attempt to increase the ego's integrative capacity by reducing anxiety. There is agreement that more supportive therapy is indicated where an otherwise adequate ego's functions are only temporarily disturbed by traumatic experiences of later life (situational neuroses). Supportive therapy is also indicated in cases of severe psychotic disturbances, such as schizophrenia. Chronic personality disturbances (character neurosis) that develop early in life require uncovering treatments, the most exacting form of which is psychoanalysis.

It must be said again that developments in the field of psychotherapy have been and are still hampered by the fact that psychoanalytic institutes are slow to recognize the great significance of broadening the therapeutic applications of psychoanalytic knowledge and continue to restrict their teaching almost exclusively to the practice of the standard psychoanalytic procedures. This orientation is to a large degree the effect of Freud's metaphorical statement in which he compares the "pure gold" of psychoanalysis with the "cheaper alloys" of psychotherapy. The psychoanalytic institutes maintain this conservative viewpoint, even though over the years it has not been the standard analytical procedure that is richer, but the solid psychodynamic knowledge, the therapeutic applications of which are broader than originally envisioned by Freud. Moreover, it appears today that the gold of the standard procedure itself needs to be further purified from its nontherapeutic components preserved by custom and tradition.

Based on one or another of the learning theories, interesting experimental and distinctive therapeutic approaches have evolved. Among them are those proposed by Andrew Slater in *Conditioned Reflex Therapy* (1949), by Joseph Wolpe in *Psychotherapy by Reciprocal Inhibition* (1958), and by A. Bandura in *Behavioristic Psychotherapy* (1963). These therapeutic designs practiced by some psychologists are not based on theories of unconscious motivation, nor do they consider internal subjective experiences, and have not been adopted by psychiatric or psychoanalytically oriented practitioners. They are thus not in the scope of this presentation. On the other hand, men like John Dollard and Neal Miller in *Personality and Psychotherapy* (1950) tried to correlate learning theories and psychoanalysis, a trend that may become a fruitful area of future work.

There have evolved in recent times some other nonanalytic psychotherapies that have totally deemphasized insight and have stressed the recognition by the patient of his feelings or have stressed the real (not transference) relationship between the patient and the therapist. Also, in recent years some new nondynamic psychotherapeutic approaches have been used that may be of value to a particular patient or to some patients under special circumstances. However, all too often the advocates of these approaches have recommended them to all patients under all circumstances, while denying the relevance of psychoanalytic principles.

Among the most significant of the current psychotherapeutic developments not based on principles of psychoanalysis is the client-centered, or nondirective, therapy originated by the psychologist Carl Rogers. It was conceived as a therapy in which the therapist makes little demand upon the patient, offers an atmosphere free of threats, and does not direct the patient into any particular channels. The therapist's role is to clarify what the patient is thinking and feeling. Rogers assumes that there are innate forces striving toward growth within the individual and that it is the therapist's primary function to create conditions that enable the client—that is, the patient—to express and explore himself freely and without fear. The therapist must feel and communicate an "unconditional positive regard" toward the client and show that he understands the client's feelings. By verbalizing the client's emotional experiences the therapist helps him to deal more objectively with them; however, the client-centered therapist limits his remarks to the experience actually communicated by the client and does not offer any interpretation or direction. The goal of client-centered therapy, in line with Rogers' self-concept theory of personality, is to achieve a greater congruence between the client's image of himself as he is, that is, his real self, and as he would like to be, his ideal self.

It would appear that for the therapist always to relay unconditional regard may contradict a principle of learning theory, namely, that it is better to give approval for desired behavior but to withhold it if the behavior is undesirable. In these terms a distinction could be drawn between basically accepting the patient and unnecessarily approving all his behavior.[40] Furthermore, Rogers stresses that the therapist's primary requisite is to be capable of expressing empathy and that psychiatric or psychological information may even be unnecessary. This is an over-exaggeration of the importance to therapy of the therapist's attitudes and personality.

Rogers was an original contributor to research in the psychotherapeutic process. He and his students were among the first therapists to make tape recordings and movies of therapeutic sessions so that the therapeutic process could become accessible to observation.

Beginning in the mid-fifties several psychiatric centers in the United States undertook the taping and filming of therapeutic sessions and have been gathering information about the crucial problem of the influence of the therapist's personality in treatment.

Most of our knowledge about the psychological processes in treatment has been derived from the—usually—incomplete records of the therapist, who, as a participant observer, cannot hope to be objective about his own reactions. The opportunity to observe a therapist's behavior through recordings and films has proved to be more informative than anecdotal statements. In addition, the recordings of hundreds of interviews have considerable value as a tool for teaching the art of psychotherapy, comparable, in effect, to clinical demonstrations of medical and surgical performances.

In England, Anna Freud and her associates have introduced a different systematic approach to the study of clinical case material collected at the Hampstead Clinic, a therapeutic and research center for child therapy. This approach is called the "Index" project because the psychoanalytic material obtained in the clinic's work is categorized and classified on index cards. This project is also an attempt to preserve and systematize clinical observations and make them available for study by research workers. The Hampstead project obviously is struggling with the same difficulty inherent in methodical clinical research as the American studies, namely, to bring by meaningful generalizations some order into the chaotic and vast variety of individual observations.

CHAPTER **20**

Social Psychiatry

Group Therapy, Family Therapy, and the Therapeutic Community

An increasing recognition of the fact that the patient as a member of society is subject to influences by his social environment has gradually led to the development of psychotherapeutic techniques aimed at treating the patient within a group. One practical consideration for group therapy is that the traditional one-to-one relationship of patient to therapist greatly limits the number of patients any one therapist can treat; this is a matter of great concern especially in institutions for the mentally ill where a few therapists must handle enormous populations. Hospital psychiatry has for this reason long included treatment of small groups in therapeutic sessions as well as the treatment of great numbers of patients in a "therapeutic community." Freud did not treat patients in groups; however, *Group Psychology and the Analysis of the Ego* offers a theoretical framework for understanding the cohesion within a group: it is the members' identification with the same authority figure.

Treatment of groups by inspirational psychology is as old as the primitive witch doctor, who influenced his tribe collectively through ritualistic performances. Mesmer conducted his hypnotic seances for groups as Émile Coué did in his sessions on autosuggestion and positive thinking. A more recent but still typical kind of inspirational group is Alcoholics Anonymous, whose group members share common experiences during sessions and thus help each other in the expression of feelings about their common problem of alcoholism.

The development of psychotherapeutic group work began in the United States in 1905, when J. H. Pratt held educational meetings aimed at raising the morale of his tuberculous patients at the Boston Dispensary. In Vienna in 1919, Alfred Adler, who was then working in one of the first child-guidance clinics, sometimes interviewed children in the presence of other children, teachers, or their parents. A follower of Adler, Rudolph Dreikurs, began working with groups of adults during the 1920's. Dreikurs has pointed out that his group approach was a natural outgrowth of Adlerian philosophy, which "always considered man as a social being and socially motivated (in contrast to the psychoanalytic and other psychologic approaches)."[1] Another early pioneer in group therapy was Edward W. Lazell, who in 1919 attempted to educate groups who appeared inaccessible to psychoanalysis by giving lectures on psychoanalysis at St. Elizabeth's Hospital in Washington. In New York in 1930, L. C. Marsh also lectured his hospitalized psychiatric patients on diverse subjects, but not on psychoanalysis. He felt that the encouragement derived from group discussions led to a feeling of group solidarity and that individuals felt supported and encouraged by their fellows. J. W. Klapman later used similar methods in working with groups of psychotic patients, encouraging discussions on subjects interesting to the group but not necessarily personal.[2] Group work was used in the late 1920's in Vienna by J. L. Moreno, who began to use dramatic classes with disturbed children. Samuel R. Slavson also utilized play therapy in his group work with children at the Jewish Board of Guardians in New York in the 1930's.

Psychodynamically oriented group therapists use techniques similar to those of individual therapy. The technique the therapist chooses to use depends on the nature of the group, that is, the ego strength of the individual members. If a group consists of psychotic patients, for instance, the therapist assumes a supportive role until the patients develop strong enough egos so that he can interpret unconscious resistance and help them achieve insight. As is also true of psychotherapists who do individual psychotherapy, the degree of participation of the therapist who works with groups will depend a great deal on his theoretical orientation and on his own personality.

The advantage of group over individual psychotherapy, according to group therapists, is that the patient in individual treatment may consciously suppress or unconsciously repress certain attitudes and experiences that a group may elicit as live and spontaneous reactions to group pressures. Group therapists maintain that patients form transference reactions to the group therapist, who usually represents a parent figure, and that they also reenact transference reactions to other members of the group in accordance with their previous attitudes toward their siblings. The mobilization of feelings by group interaction may bring relief through catharsis and may even help the patient to achieve insight. For withdrawn patients who need to interact, this experience may be particularly beneficial.

On the other hand, some problems occur that are unique to group psychotherapy. Perhaps the most important of these is that the multiplicity of reactions that arise within a group gives the therapist, especially one who is inexperienced, a feeling of being overwhelmed by the complexity of group psychodynamics; he then may react in the group as he might in any other social situation and either identify himself with the aggressors or come prematurely to the defense of the underdog. Experience and training in group therapy, however, as well as personal analysis, mitigate these countertransference problems.

The concept that each patient is also a member of a group has far-reaching implications for hospitalized patients. Ever since 1939, when Abraham Myerson described what he called a "total push" for treating chronic hospitalized patients, there has been a continual and increasing concern for organizing hospital activities in such a way that the individual patients do not vegetate in back wards. One recent development in this trend is the idea of the "therapeutic community"—a concept popularized by Maxwell Jones at the Dingleton Hospital, Melrose, Scotland.* Jones writes: "In a therapeutic community all of the patient's time spent in a hospital is thought of as treatment. Treatment to be effective, will involve not only the handling of the individual's neurotic problems, but also an awareness of the fresh problems, which the fact of being in a neurosis hospital would create for the patient. . . . The patient, the social *milieu* in which he lives and works, and the hospital community of which he becomes temporarily a member, are all important and interact on each other."[4] Jones thus advocates that in the mental hospital every activity of the patient should be integrated into a program that will be therapeutic for that particular individual.

This approach must depend on an understanding of the patient's basic problems in psychosocial living. Information about the patient is collected and correlated by an integrated-team approach involving social workers, psychologists, the hospital staff, and other patients, as well as the psychotherapist. The social worker gathers all the information he can about the patient's background from the family. The psychologist tests the patient to help define his underlying psychodynamics. Careful observations are made by nurses and attendants on the patient's behavior in the hospital and his reactions to other individuals in the ward. The psychiatrist then discusses with these staff members the patient's problems and decides on what he feels will be a therapeutic program for the patient. Occupational therapy, for example, is not prescribed merely to pass time, but in a way that will

---

* As early as 1946 T. F. Maine organized a mental hospital in the city of Birmingham, England. His idea was that the hospital and the city should have no barriers between them and that the hospitalized patient would receive full participation from the staff in his resocialization; Maine called this program "a therapeutic community."[3]

influence the patient: a shy, withdrawn individual will be encouraged by the therapist and other patients to participate in dancing or in athletic games; a patient who fears his own aggressions can be helped to sublimate by activities like punching a bag or using hammers and other tools to build things. Some hospitals set up as therapeutic communities have facilities where patients can do remunerative work that gives them a feeling of productivity and consequently raises their self-esteem. Some hospitals help patients find jobs during the day in a nearby community as a step toward rehabilitating them. Other hospitals have day-care sections, that is, the patients are treated in the hospital during the day and spend the night at home with their families. Alternatively, a patient may be assigned to night-care facilities, that is, either working in the hospital and participating in the program or working on the outside during the day and sleeping in the hospital because he is not yet ready to live full time at home. Most therapeutic-community hospitals recognize the importance of patient organizations run by patients elected by their peers; for instance, the patients may have their own committees to make recommendations to the hospital administration in regard to hospital policy. The therapeutic community thus encourages social interaction between patients and facilitates the reassurance and encouragement that patients can offer to each other. These principles of the therapeutic community are being utilized not only in the mental hospitals but also in other hospitals.

One of the most important features of recent developments has been the gradual acceptance of the psychiatrist and his team in general hospitals. Psychiatrists are often consulted by other medical staff members regarding their medical patients.

In the United States the federal government is coming to recognize mental illness as a responsibility of the entire community. The National Institute of Health now has a division, the National Institute of Mental Health, which allocates large sums of money yearly for research and treatment of mental illness. Many states are subsidizing clinics for the treatment of mental illness in the communities, with the underlying philosophy that it is better to treat the mentally ill within the community than to isolate them from their loved ones. In fact, the trend indicates that in the future not bigger and better mental hospitals will be constructed but better facilities will be available for the emotionally distressed in their own communities.

The attempt to understand the patient not just in terms of his intrapsychic dynamics but as a living member of a community has been one of the most enlightened developments in the treatment of the mentally ill. It heralds a period of psychiatric advance that we may well call "social psychiatry," which, incidentally, is the British title of Maxwell Jones's book on the therapeutic community.

Another recent development in psychiatry that has broad implications for research and therapy is "family-centered therapy." In this technique an entire family is treated at the same time by one or more therapists. It has never been uncommon for a psychotherapist to confer once or twice with the spouse of a patient or with other therapists who might be treating other members of the patient's family. What is new in family-centered therapy is the idea of treating the family in one place at the same time. One of the first to undertake treatment of an entire family was John Bell. In 1934 Clarence Oberndorf described his experiences with the concurrent analysis of married couples, but this work attracted little notice until the 1950's, when Bela Mittelmann reported his experience in analyzing husbands and wives concurrently.[5] Nathan Ackerman, a leading proponent of the family method of treatment, has pointed out that the classical one-to-one relationship of psychotherapy tends to isolate the individual without a consideration of the roles the patient plays in his family, so that the therapist has no chance of learning the important methods of communication within the family. One problem in using the family approach is that it takes an inordinate amount of skill on the part of the therapist to refrain from becoming a judge and arbiter of family squabbles during therapeutic sessions; if he falls into this countertransference pitfall, he will be unable to make therapeutically beneficial comments.

One facet of family therapy is the concurrent treatment of the schizophrenic patient and his entire family. An important goal of this type of treatment is to correct distorted interpersonal communication between the members of the family. Don Jackson, Gregory Bateson, and their colleagues have postulated that the schizophrenic is caught in an "unescapable double bind": the schizophrenic receives conflictual messages from important members of his family who express two orders of message, one of which denies the other. For instance, the schizophrenic may hear assertions of love from his parents; while his parents are making these assertions, they may be also clenching their fists or showing tension that betrays to the patient a contradictory message of hatred. These investigators do not claim that this is the only psychological cause underlying the development of schizophrenia but do emphasize that distorted communication between the sick patient and his family is an important factor. Furthermore, they have remarked on the fact that the sick member of the family plays an important role in family equilibrium, so much so that improvement of the schizophrenic patient changes the whole intrafamilial situation. In the late 1950's and early 1960's Murray Bowen, Lyman C. Wynne, and Theodore Lidz have also pioneered in utilizing family therapy both as a diagnostic tool and as a method of treatment for schizophrenic patients.

In family-centered therapy various recent trends in psychiatry converge: the trend toward treating patients as members of a group, the trend toward recognition of the importance of the family as a therapeutic community, and the trend toward utilizing the latest concepts of communication and field theories.

Psychiatric Problems of Aging (Geriatrics)

There are few more timely problems in psychiatry than those related to man's inevitable fate of having to grow old. Until recently psychiatry had focused upon the mental diseases—for instance, the senile psychoses—that are caused by the progressive deterioration of the brain; more recent developments, however, have put an increasing emphasis on the psychological and sociological factors inherent in the mental problems of the aged.

It is estimated that by 1975 more than ten percent of the population of the United States will be sixty-five or older. We are obviously succeeding in prolonging the life of our citizens, but the advances in medicine responsible for this lengthened life span have not been matched by equal progress in our institutions, most of which make it clear that we have little use for the aged in our society. For instance, take the prevailing policy of forced retirement based solely on chronological age; its widespread application totally disregards the fact that there are varying rates of aging, depending on each individual. Many persons at eighty are physically and mentally more efficient than others at fifty; nonetheless, most are forced into idleness at the same chronological moment. Nor has our society yet adjusted to the increasing number of senior citizens or learned to make constructive use of their talents. It is becoming clear that this discrepancy between our ability to proglong life and our inability to deal with the fact that this ability will create an ever-higher proportion of old people in our society is the core of the geriatric issue.

It has been known for a long time that the progressive decline of body functions affects mental functioning, although physiological decline is not paralleled in any simple way by psychological decline. An individual's emotional attitude, on the other hand, can influence his physiological processes and with it the aging process; this psychological attitude depends to a very high degree on cultural factors. In societies in which the old are held in great respect and in which being old has a positive connotation, the word "old" itself need not be avoided and replaced by euphemisms like "senior citizen." In cultures where old age has prestige—for example, in the Far East and to some degree also in Europe—the old person may be more animated than his American counterpart. He faces a challenge from his social environment: his society venerates and respects him and also expects him to be wise and set an example. This challenge, the feeling of being needed and respected, counteracts biological decline. This is borne out by a fact that is well known to physicians, that often after retirement all the psychological and physical symptoms typical of aging that before retirement were present only in traces suddenly appear full-blown. The prematurely retired person may become irritable, cranky, and depressed and lose his interest in life; he also shows signs of gradual physical decline. This set of syndromes has been described as a "retirement neurosis," and in many cases the reactions appear with remarkable suddenness and may lead to premature death. Unfortunately the many pertinent anecdotal observations of physicians and psychiatrists about this phenomenon have not yet been subjected to statistical analysis; in addition, the psychosomatic aspects of aging still remain almost entirely unexplored.

One important aspect of aging closely related to mental health is endocrinological decline. The endocrine glands—the adrenal system, the thyroid, the pituitary, the gonads—are all ultimately influenced by emotional processes. The clearest demonstration of this influence occurs in those animals that ovulate under the stimulus of sexual excitement. On a far more complex level, but still reflecting the same relationship of endocrines to emotions, we may say that an individual's emotional processes influence practically all of his body processes. His attitude to his job, to the members of his family, to his associates, and to the society in which he lives, his expectations of himself and people's expectations of him—all these circumstances have either a depressing or an energizing, vitalizing effect that is mediated through the same endocrine system that also regulates the physiological processes involved in aging. Obviously no one can stop the relentless march of aging entirely, but there is good clinical evidence that full, active, zestful participation in the life of the community keeps people younger much longer.

Of particular interest to geriatric psychiatry are the effects of sensory deprivation. The normal functioning of the central nervous system requires a steady input of sensory stimuli. Horace Magoun and his co-workers have thrown light upon this phenomenon by their exploration of the reticular-activating system. The r.a.s. has an activating function upon sensory input, and the state of consciousness probably depends upon its activity. If the functioning of this activating system is interrupted, the organism becomes apathetic and goes to sleep, which seems to indicate that sensory stimulation is essential to alert and adequate psychological activity. D. O. Hebb's work on sensory isolation has also indicated that prolonged sensory deprivations or prolonged exposure to a monotonous environment may produce severe mental disturbances. Thought processes are affected, hallucinations appear, visual functions are disturbed, and emotional responses become abnormal.[6] Obviously people create artificial, fantasy stimulation as compensation for stimulation they no longer receive from the real environment.

The impairment of sensory perceptions—of sight and hearing, for instance—that occur in old age also leads to a kind of physiological isolation from the environment and may be at least partly responsible for mental disturbances in old age. This sensory deprivation is reinforced by the social isolation resulting from the exclusion of older people from active participation in social functions. Our society thus promotes the physiological process of aging by not supplying the old with the environmental stimulation necessary to their mental and physical health.

Increasing knowledge about the influence of psychological factors upon body functions raises significant questions about the best way to manage aging persons. At present psychiatrists are only beginning to become aware of the problems involved. Although bodily functions decline in old age, at the same time, wisdom, knowledge, and sound judgment based on experience increase. It is interesting that insurance companies set a higher rate today for those under twenty-five years old—although the reflexes of the young are extremely fast—than for people who are over sixty-five. Obviously the slowing of the reflexes is counteracted by greater wisdom, greater experience, and better judgment. Some functions even improve with age. One cannot extrapolate from the visible and tangible manifestations of physical decline and assume that the elderly person is declining in all his functions. This factor offers hope in the solution of the problems concerning the aged.

Alcoholism and Drug Addiction

With the growing social consciousness of our time, alcoholism—excessive consumption of alcohol—has in recent years become a focus of medical interest. Alcohol, far more than any other psychologically active drug, has traditionally been used to reduce emotional tensions. And the study of alcoholism is a paramount example of why a comprehensive multidisciplinary approach has become necessary for psychiatry. The problems of describing alcoholism, of understanding it, and of approaching it therapeutically demand that its biological, psychological, and sociological aspects be considered as a totality.

We have recently learned a great deal from neurophysiology and biochemistry about the impact of alcohol upon bodily functions, particularly on liver functions, metabolism, endocrine balance, the autonomic nervous system, and the higher nervous centers that affect perception and muscular coordination. Although these studies have contributed to a more effective treatment of acute alcoholic episodes, more attention has in recent years been paid to the psychological motivations underlying alcoholism both in individuals and in social groups than to physiological effects of overdrinking. As for the sociological factors of alcoholism, in general these vary from one subcultural group to another within our society. Certain subcultures enthusiastically approve of drinking; others look upon it with reservation; others frown upon it; and among certain minorities it is strictly outlawed. This variance in cultural acceptance makes a medical definition of alcoholism difficult. The answer to the question of when alcoholism should be considered a medical or a psychiatric problem depends to a high degree upon culturally determined value judgments. An alcoholic's status financially and socially usually determines society's reaction to his drinking problem. An affluent alcoholic is not, for instance, a public charge, whereas a poor one is. Allowed to run their course, the effects of alcoholism would be the same for each person, but whereas the poor man will in all likelihood find little help for his problem, the affluent one may be helped through a private sanatorium or by a psychiatrist. Thus the recognized nature of the individual's problem and its cure may well depend on nonmedical and nonpsychiatric criteria.

A descriptive behavioral and statistical approach toward alcoholism had until recently been dominant in clinical psychiatry; it is best exemplified by Kraepelin's treatment of this subject. From him we learn that alcoholism is found in more than forty percent of epileptics and traumatic neuroses, is very common among arteriosclerotics, and is much less common among dementia-praecox patients, hysterics, and manic-depressives. No attempt is made to differentiate between etiological or secondary correlations. The studies of Kraepelin and his followers also tell us that alcoholism is more common among men than women and among the Germanic nations than Moslems, Buddhists, or Mormons. Other nineteenth-century statistical studies reported that chronic alcoholism seems to have an effect upon descendants; stillbirths and miscarriages were found to be more prevalent in alcoholic families and idiocy more common in children who were conceived during alcoholic excesses. Alcoholic families produced thirty-five percent of beggars and vagrants and 44.7 percent of prostitutes.[7] It may safely be said that these chaotic and uncritical correlations of highly undifferentiated and heterogeneous variables threw little real light on the complexities of alcoholism; they even cause a great deal of confusion and faulty conclusions.

In the past the greatest research emphasis has been on the effects of alcohol on the brain and on bodily functions, as well as on the clinical, particularly psychiatric sequelae of chronic alcohol consumption, of which delirium tremens and Korsakov's psychosis (characterized by memory gaps) are outstanding examples. Some serious neuropsychiatric complications associated with chronic alcoholism and consequent poor dietary habits, such as Wernicke's syndrome (loss of motor coordination, clouding of consciousness, and difficulties in vision), and alcoholic neuritis, are due to vitamin-B deficiencies. Treatment procedures, like the use of antibuse to "condition" against the intake of alcohol by causing severe gastrointestinal disturbance and vomiting when alcohol is ingested while the drug is in the body, are available. However, if they are undertaken without attention paid to psychosocial factors, they become dismal failures.

The consumption of alcohol is a voluntary act that is both consciously and unconsciously motivated; therefore, the psychological approach is a natural point of departure for a systematic analysis of the etiological variables involved. The paramount questions about alcoholism are: How does an individual become a chronic drinker? What function does alcohol play in his emotional household? What circumstances perpetuate his drinking habit? These cannot be answered by superficial statistical correlations of overt behavioral manifestations, but only by intensive studies of individual drinkers. The statistician may discover, for instance, that orthodox Jews drink less than Irish Catholics, but only an intensive biographical study of representatives of these two groups can reveal why this statistical finding is valid.

Early psychoanalysts who discussed alcoholism stressed the disinhibiting effect of the drug: it reduces repressions and permits the freer expression of ego-alien, mostly infantile, cravings. Alcohol thus acts to lift the controls on behavior acquired during biological and social maturation; in addition, under its influence speech becomes less coherent, muscle coordination diminishes, and thinking regresses in the direction of the primary process. All the shackles imposed by the progressive organization of behavior, the adaptation to biological independence, and the acceptance of cultural standards are loosened, and a less responsible, less self-reliant, childish kind of happiness is temporarily recaptured. Observations of these phenomena are so numerous that it is needless to belabor the point by citing authorities; to sum them up it is enough to say that alcohol obviously favors the ever-present regressive trend to escape from the hardships of relentlessly recurring adaptive tasks that are integral to the serious business of living.

Among the repressed tendencies that early psychoanalytic investigators observed to be mobilized under alcohol were oral-dependent and latent, passive homosexual cravings. Since passive-homosexual trends are, as a rule, superimposed upon oral trends, the latter seem to be the more specific psychological factor. Repressed or inhibited heterosexual and hostile impulses were also mentioned by several observers. Sandor Rado postulated a regression to a very early quasi-orgastic sensation in which the whole alimentary tract is involved and called this phenomenon "alimentary orgasm." The "narcotic superpleasure," according to Rado, is a "derivative of alimentary orgasm."[8]

Alexander, Robert Knight, and Rado were impressed by the cyclic effects of drinking. The first phase consists of elation, lack of inhibitions, and a freer expression of inhibited or repressed trends; these phenomena reflect the fact that alcohol first affects the higher brain centers, which in general are inhibitory and controlling. As drinking continues, the alcohol gradually paralyzes the lower brain centers too, and the second phase, which is depressive in tone, develops. When the drinker has sobered up, he enters a third phase, the hangover. The original stressful situation for which he had tried to get relief by drinking then returns, compounded by additional stress, namely, a sense of guilt and shame over his alcoholic excess. He reacts to the hangover by starting to drink again, both because he wants to feel elated again and also because he hopes to dull his self-accusations and guilt.

An important motivational factor in alcoholism seems to be the oral-incorporative urge: the trend toward returning to the earliest gratification of the nursing situation. Knight believes that this oral fixation is frequently due to the specific family configuration of an indulgent mother married to an inconsistent father.[9] An orally indulged child does not learn self-control and reacts with rage to every frustration. An inconsistent father aggravates the child's emotional instability by an unpredictable, first indulgent, then tyrannically forbidding attitude. Both parents' characteristic behaviors mutually reinforce the child's intolerance for frustration and predispose him toward oral fixation.

Two other distinct motivational factors may be perceived in the alcoholic: (1) a desire to escape from stress and (2) a desire for the regressive gratification of repressed or inhibited impulses. Alcohol is able to relieve temporarily almost any kind of emotional stress, be it anxiety, shame, guilt, or generalized feelings of insecurity. When an individual suffering from shyness and inferiority feelings resulting from excessive inhibitions, pent-up and never-expressed resentments, or inhibition of sexual cravings discovers that alcohol makes him feel self-confident, daring, and enterprising, the stage is set for recurrent drinking. The freedom from emotional restrictions is itself highly gratifying, but the essential attraction consists in the relief from his self-defeating inhibitions and their emotional consequences; and if adverse events in life—such as failures of professional ambitions or of love relations—increase his emotional frustrations, the lure of alcholic indulgence may become irresistible. The gratification component of drinking involves the reestablishment of the bliss of an oral-dependent satiation, as well as of infantile omnipotence.

According to Knight, a strong urge to gratify oral cravings is the distinguishing mark of the most malignant cases, which he calls "essential alcoholics"; in what he calls "reactive alcoholics" this oral fixation is less significant, and they drink to escape stress situations occasioned by traumatic events in their lives.*

It appears logical to distinguish between these groups of alcoholics. One group escapes from a vague but pressing emotional-stress situation; this escape is achieved because the alcohol acts pharmacologically to cloud

---

* Jules Masserman and K. S. Yum have demonstrated the escape factor in alcoholism. They administered alcohol to cats and succeeded both in abolishing conditioned responses and in protecting them from developing experimental neurosis. Ingestion of alcohol in these animals led to temporary disintegration of complex "neurotic" and psychotic behavioral patterns induced experimentally, leaving rela-

discriminatory and self-critical functions and thus relieves the emotional distress caused by external vicissitudes. This group can clearly be contrasted with a second group, who drink primarily to achieve regressive gratification, the gratification of oral impulses.*

There is an increasing attempt to relate psychological and sociological factors in the occurrence of alcoholism. For example, Abraham Myerson in 1944 called attention to the relative infrequency of alcoholism among ascetic Protestant sects and orthodox Jews, in contrast to its relative frequency among nonascetic Protestants and Irish Catholics.[13] Members of these ascetic social groups are inculcated through lifelong education with a supreme social ideal of self-control, together with contempt for uninhibited indulgence; it appears, although it has not yet been demonstrated, that the psychodynamic mechanism responsible for their high abstinence is successful repression. Such group influences in themselves are of a psychological nature, just as the individual influences prevailing in each family depend upon the idiosyncratic qualities of the parents. The origin of group ideals itself is, however, not a purely psychological problem. They can be understood only in the light of the total structure of the prevailing social institutions, as viewed from a historical perspective. Group ethos is the result of the history of a culture, just as individual personality is the outcome of the person's life history. Their influence upon the individual in preparing the soil for alcoholism is, however, a strictly psychological problem.

The influence of the group can be well observed in the therapeutic successes of Alcoholics Anonymous. Identification with a group that does not condone alcohol and yet is neither punitive nor contemptuous toward the alcoholic allows him to gratify his dependency needs without inner conflict—something he could never do in the past—and without shame or rebellion toward the persons upon whom he depends. In time he becomes a helper himself, which restores his internal equilibrium by elevating his self-esteem. Shame for his childish dependency, guilt reactions, reactive hostility, and rebellion—the main source of guilt feelings—are eliminated. He finds emotional support that, importantly, is distributed among the whole

---

tively simpler adaptive patterns intact. After this, the neurotic animals spontaneously sought and ingested alcohol until their neuroses were relieved by various procedures analogous to those employed in clinical psychotherapy. Also albino rats under the effect of alcohol overcame quickly their fear of approaching the feeding box that gave them electric shocks whenever they came in contact with it. These rats obviously became more daring under the influence of alcohol, similarly as do humans who take alcohol to overcome lifelong inhibitions acquired through interpersonal experiences.[10]

* Rado well characterized the gratification the alcoholic experiences as the bliss derived from the reestablishment of the innocent omnipotent feeling of the infant.[11] G. Lolli saw the essence of the alcoholic's fulfillment in the experience of an undifferentiated pleasure of body and mind in union.[12]

group and that emanates, as they view it, eventually from a Supreme Being.

In focusing on psychosocial factors, we cannot neglect those biological factors that may be decisive in the most malignant cases of alcoholism. Reliable clinical observations indicate there is a striking difference in susceptibility toward alcohol in different persons that does not seem to be fully explicable on the basis of differences in personality structure caused by postnatal experiences. Furthermore, advanced alcoholics present another physiological complication that plays an even more important role in other drug addictions—their physiological dependence on the drug that may be partially responsible for their uncontrollable craving.

One further set of experiments tends to show that oral fixation itself may be related to a nutritional deficiency, due to a type of metabolic block attributable to an individual's enzyme structure. This is assumed to be the case by Roger Williams in his "genetotrophic" theory of alcoholism. His experiments on rats have led him to conclude that the tendency of the animals to consume alcohol can be increased by feeding them a diet deficient in specific elements; it can be reduced by supplying the rats with the omitted nutritional components.[14] Even if Williams' experiments are interpreted as showing merely an increase of an incorporative urge caused by metabolic factors, it is quite consistent with our present knowledge of conditioning to conclude that if this undifferentiated craving becomes coupled through repetition with a pleasurable sensation following the ingestion of alcohol, a specific yearning for alcohol might develop.

It is most probable, of course, that a biological factor would not in most instances lead to chronic, malignant drinking unless interpersonal experiences occur that contribute to and reinforce the development of oral fixation and lack of internal discipline. Moreover, it is entirely possible that both a genetotrophic factor and bad early interpersonal experiences could be counteracted by cultural influences that emphasized self-control and an aversion to self-indulgence. The complexity of the problem should warn us against trying to isolate one single category of factors in the etiology of alcoholism.

The integration of biological, sociological, and psychodynamic viewpoints, so necessary for an understanding of alcoholism, is also required to understand and treat addiction to other drugs, which most often are opiates. The treatment of the drug addict is further complicated by his body's adaptation to the drug: this adaptation consists of overcompensating innervations directed against the inhibitory effects of the drug. These overcompensatory mechanisms are responsible for the great physical anguish that is felt when the drug is withdrawn. The sociopsychological sources of the craving for drugs is only slowly earning serious recognition, and as yet little advance has been made in combating this grave behavior problem.

Although many drugs, such as barbiturates, tranquilizers, and marihuana, have been considered habit-forming, the term "drug addiction" usually refers to habitual use of opium derivatives like heroin. The characteristics of addiction are psychological dependence on the drug, the development of a tolerance for it so that increasingly greater amounts are needed to achieve the same effect, and a growing physical dependence on the drug so that withdrawal symptoms occur upon cessation of use.

The typical American pattern of addiction begins with usage of barbiturates or marihuana in adolescence and progresses to the use of heroin in the early twenties. This differs from the typical British pattern of addiction, which usually begins in the thirties or forties as the result of medical usage of drugs for relief of pain. Furthermore, although British narcotics clinics have met with some success in helping addicts, American clinics have not, mainly because the American addict psychologically differs from his English counterpart. He tends to be extremely dependent, passive, isolated, afraid of responsibility, and suspicious. His habit more often than not stems from his inability to cope with the myriad problems of life. A further complication is the American addict's tendency to increase his maintenance dose. This factor, which poses serious problems for a clinic dispensing narcotics, has prevented such clinics from gaining public or governmental sanction in the United States.

Federal narcotics hospitals, at Fort Worth, Texas, and Lexington, Kentucky, have been hampered in effectiveness because patients who go there voluntarily are free to leave after a short period of hospitilization. Furthermore, there are not adequate follow-ups on patients who leave these hospitals for different parts of the country. A study in new York, based on 912 patients discharged from the Public Health Service Hospital in Lexington, disclosed that because addicts face the psychological obstacles mentioned above, they need constant contact with a resource that can provide step-by-step support and constant supervision to help them sustain their efforts to discontinue the drug.[15] A conclusion of the study was that addiction must be viewed as a chronic illness in which only limited progress is now being achieved.

Some techniques have shown promise. Work with families has been found to be important, since modifications of family attitudes are urgently needed if the patient is to have a chance for recovery. Unannounced calls on the addict also improve the quality of follow-up supervision. An aid in determining whether an addict has resorted to the use of heroin again is the drug Nalline, which causes pupillary changes following the intake of the narcotic. An innovation involving a unique private effort at rehabilitating addicts has been of great help. The Synanon organization maintains several residences for addicts in which they can receive intensive support from fellow ex-addicts in order to keep them "clean."

However, in order to find better solutions to the problem of narcotics addiction, there must be better follow-up studies, continued research into a therapeutic approach, and more factual information disseminated to the public. In addition, it has been advocated by most authorities on the subject that the federal hospitals be given greater control over the addict by making civil—not criminal—commitment compulsory.

Psychiatry and the Law

A major complication in treating narcotics addiction is due to the position of the law. As we have come to know more about the causes and nature of drug addiction, we have recognized that current legal attitudes, which regard addicts primarily as criminals to be punished, may be misplaced and may even aggravate the narcotics problem. As psychiatry and sociology have become more sophisticated and as we have improved our understanding of man's conscious and unconscious motivations, the relationship between psychiatry and the law has broadened. This relationship involves not only drug addiction but also adult crime, juvenile delinquency, and sexual psychopathy. In fact, nowhere is the relationship between psychiatry and social problems more apparent and more in urgent need of clarification than in forensic psychiatry.

The law and psychiatry both concern themselves with the behavior of individuals, but whereas the law seeks primarily to protect society from antisocial behavior, psychiatry seeks to help the individual transgressor. Still, psychiatric information often opens the way to understanding the motivations for crime and thus aids the law in assessing innocence or extent of guilt and in determining just punishment. Since the law seeks to safeguard society from crime, psychiatry can be of immense help in such protection through the rehabilitation of criminals. Psychiatric understanding may enhance human rights by helping to eliminate punishment of the mentally ill for crimes for which they are not truly responsible or for acts that should not properly be viewed as crimes at all.

The psychiatrist is frequently asked to render testimony to help the courts decide in cases where an individual may be disabled because of a psychic trauma. In cases of wills and contracts, the psychiatrist may bring light to the matter of the competence of the signer; he also may testify as to the sanity of one of the marital partners in divorce suits or about the competency of a parent in a case involving guardianship of a child. Although the relevance of psychiatric testimony in such cases is by no means uncontested, there has been an increased reliance on it in recent years.

Much greater controversy over relevance exists in cases of criminal responsibility. The central issue is whether mental illness on the part of the alleged criminal precludes punishment for his act. Closely associated is the broader question of what mental illness is, for not even at this stage of psychiatric evolution has a suitable definition of mental illness been made part of the law.

This problem has long beset the jurist. As early as the third century A.D., Domitius Ulpianus (170–228), a Roman jurist, claimed that an insane person is not responsible for a criminal act. Henry de Bracton (d. c. 1268), an English churchman and jurist, followed Ulpianus in not holding a madman accountable for his acts. This doctrine, that a madman lacks reason and does not know what he is doing, has been carried down to modern times, but not as much in Anglo-Saxon courts as in Continental law. In France and Belgium especially the principle reigns that no matter what the extent of the mental illness involved, the mentally ill person is not punishable.[16] It should be remembered about English legal tradition, however, that as recently as the seventeenth century mental illness was considered inimical to criminal intent and therefore not punishable.

Unfortunately these early flexible and liberal conceptions did not survive in England and American law to the present day. Dominant instead is the M'Naghten rule. Daniel M'Naghten had a delusion that the home secretary had perpetrated an injustice upon him. By mistake he killed the secretary's clerk. In 1843 M'Naghten was acquitted by reason of insanity. In essence, the M'Naghten rule states that for the perpetrator of a crime to be considered innocent by reason of insanity he must have had a defect in his reasoning powers so as not to know that what he did was wrong. The "right-and-wrong test" did not refer to any issue other than his alleged crime. The M'Naghten rule exists as the criterion for acquittal on the basis of insanity in almost all of the states in America today. It has led to innumerable conflicts between psychiatric authorities and legal minds. Psychiatrists point out that the court requires that they state whether the person knew right from wrong. This question is a moral question and not a scientific one. Furthermore, the "right-and-wrong" doctrine applies only to a cognitive feature of the mind. It does not take emotional factors into consideration.

Nineteen states have attempted to consider emotional factors by adding the "irresistible-impulse doctrine" of 1834 to the M'Naghten rule. This doctrine raises the question of whether the accused was a "free agent in forming the purpose to kill." In other words, was he overwhelmed with an impulse to kill that destroyed his reason. Wilfred Overholzer, a psychiatric authority on problems of legal matters, points out that the irresistible-impulse doctrine does consider an emotional component; however, it considers only one aspect of an emotion, its propensity to overwhelm the individual's faculty of reason. But it is as difficult to claim that the defendant labored under "an uncontrollable impulse, as it is to say, that he lacked capacity to recognize the difference between right and wrong."[17]

These tests of insanity were criticized as early as 1838, when Isaac Ray, one of the founders of the American Psychiatric Association and the first great American forensic psychiatrist, criticized the M'Naghten rule. As a result of the influence of Isaac Ray, in 1869 the Supreme Court of New Hampshire contradicted the M'Naghten rule, which had implied that an insane person must have a total loss of reason. The New Hampshire ruling introduced the question of whether the criminal act was a product of a mental illness, for if such was the case, then "criminal intent" was not present. The most important subsequent development occurred in 1954, when in the District of Columbia the Durham decision was rendered. This decision was not explicit on the question of criminal intent, but repeated the New Hampshire ruling that if an act is a result or product of a mental disease, criminal responsibility does not exist. Overholzer decries the fact that only New Hampshire, the District of Columbia, and Alabama have followed the reasoning outlined in the Durham decision. He points out that there is a vagueness to the Durham decision not found in the M'Naghten rule. However, the Durham rule does allow the psychiatrist freer rein in his evaluation and testimony, because he can give the facts to the jury without having to limit himself to moral questions of right and wrong. The jury may then decide the question in the light of the evidence provided by the psychiatrist, also without being tied to the either/or limitations of "right" and "wrong."

Another recent trend in legal procedure, embodied in the English Homicide Act of 1957, recognizes gradations of mental illness and is taken from the Scottish doctrine of "diminished responsibility," which holds that the degree of a crime and therefore the degree of punishment may be diminished when there is mental illness that is not classified as insanity. This rule was rejected by the United States Supreme Court; however, from a practical standpoint, in many American states an individual who is believed to have a mental illness is prosecuted under the principle of diminished responsibility.

One of the most enlightened approaches to the problem of mental disease in criminals was made in 1921 in the Massachusetts "Briggs law," which applied to individuals indicted for a capital offense or who were convicted previously of a felony. In such cases the accused receives a routine psychiatric examination by an expert—serving as a "friend of the court"—who testifies regarding the presence or absence of a mental disease. This has eliminated the problem of the contests between psychiatric expert witnesses for the defense and the prosecution. Although it had been feared that appointed psychiatrists under the Briggs law would find mental illness too often and thus excuse too many criminals, only nineteen percent of more than sixty-six hundred examined subjects were judged to be mentally abnormal.[18]

There are those, even within the psychiatric profession, who believe that the psychiatrist cannot aid the court to understand the mental status of accused criminals. There are others, however, who believe that the only true expert on mental illness is the psychiatrist and that he has a responsibility to present the facts as he finds them in the individual subject. In order to guide the psychiatrist in his testimony, Manfred Guttmacher, an outstanding forensic psychiatrist, has defined the role of the psychiatric expert in the court in the following way: "1.) A statement should be made as to whether the defendant is suffering from definite and generally recognized mental disease and why and how this conclusion was reached. 2.) If it had been asserted that the defendant suffered from a mental disease, its name and its chief characteristics and symptoms, with particular emphasis on its effect on an individual's judgment, social behavior and self-control, should be given. 3.) There should then follow a statement of the way and degree in which the malady has affected the particular defendant's behavior, especially in regard to his judgment, social behavior, and self-control. 4.) The psychiatrist should then be asked whether the alleged criminal act was, in his opinion, the result of, or was committed under the influence of, his disease."[19]

Furthermore, as Overholzer points out, the expert should not accept fees contingent on his findings; the experts on both sides of the question should be in contact with one another and allowed to examine each other's reports, and the court should be particularly careful to screen the qualifications of the experts.[20]

Since the cardinal question to be answered in all criminal cases pertains to motivation, the psychiatric expert who is trained to think in terms of psychodynamics and motivations obviously can aid the court even more than by merely stating a diagnosis. The same criminal act can be the result of self-defense, negligence, or intent; therefore, the motivation of the perpetrator is what decides society's reaction to the act. If Freud's thesis that human acts are determined by both conscious and unconscious motivation is true, the offender will be able to offer only a partial explanation of why he did what he did; he cannot account for his often decisive unconscious motivations. Freud's brief article "Criminality from a Sense of Guilt"[21] deeply influenced the thinking of psychoanalysts about criminal behavior. In it Freud suggested that guilt feelings originate from repressed antisocial cravings, primarily Oedipal tendencies, and that these cravings and feelings are often the chief determinants of criminal acts. Extending this thesis, Franz Alexander defined the neurotic character and the neurotic criminal who constitutes a subgroup of the neurotic character. Alexander went on to become one of the first to challenge from a psychoanalytic frame of reference existing legal methods of dealing with offenders. The neurotic character who may express his neurosis in criminal acts is beset with unconscious guilt resulting from forbidden unconscious wishes. The transgressions he commits are minor in terms of the superego, compared to the forbidden unconscious wish. When he is punished for his transgressions he is relieved temporarily from the unconscious sense of guilt. In other words, such an individual possesses austere conscience and therefore is more afraid of his own inner moral judgment than of the secular court.*

Alexander first studied psychoanalytically unconscious motivations for criminal acts when he was called in by a German court for expert testimony in the case of a young female kleptomaniac who had been under his psychoanalytic treatment shortly before she had committed several thefts. The presiding judge had been puzzled when he learned that the girl had stolen worthless objects; those objects that had some value she had thrown into a river. Her preference was for cheap reproductions of paintings of the Madonna with the Child. Alexander told the court that the girl was a deprived orphan who had decided to become an actress. While studying for the stage she became the girl friend of a wealthy bachelor who had made it clear to her that he would never marry her. She wanted desperately to have a child, but prudence prevented her from giving up birth control. This conflict drove her to gratify symbolically her desire and to identify with the Virgin Mary, who could have a child by virgin birth. During the treatment the girl became aware of the connection between her longing for motherhood and her stealing and succeeded in controlling her kleptomania. The judge, convinced by this argument, gave the girl a suspended sentence, with the stipulation that she continue her psychoanalysis.

Impressed by the willingness of usually conservative judges to take psychiatric factors into consideration, Alexander and a Berlin lawyer, Hugo Staub (1886–1942), studied a series of cases in which they suspected unconscious motivations as predominant factors. Their thesis, published in 1929 in *The Criminal, the Judge and the Public,* was that man, born asocial, acquires his social attitudes only during the process of emotional maturation. As the child accepts and internalizes parental attitudes he renounces some of his asocial wishes, particularly aggressive hostile impulses; the equilibrium he achieves between gratification and renunciation is what is perceived as a "sense of justice." If gratifications for his renunciations are not forthcoming, the individual feels unjustly treated; he feels that society owes him something. If he sees another person going unpunished for asocial or antisocial behavior, *his sense of justice is also disturbed.* Since he complies with the accepted restrictions of asocial tendencies, why should another person be able to exhibit antisocial behavior and get away with it? Hence he demands that the offender be punished. This psychodynamic formula explains a well-known phenomenon: the arousal of public sentiment if an offender does not receive what the public regards as his deserved

---

* About the same time, and independently, Theodor Reik in his book *Geständniszwang und Strafbedürfnis* (*The Compulsion to Confess and the Need for Punishment*) also explained the urge of some criminals to confess their offense as an attempt to relieve an unconscious sense of guilt.

punishment; it also gives the clue for the emotional involvement of the judge, the jury, and the general public in court procedure. This revenge motive, or wish for retribution, is a source of demands for punishment for the offender.

There are two other and more rational and constructive reasons for incarcerating offenders: to deter potential or actual criminals from breaking the law by setting an example and to rehabilitate offenders. Alexander and Staub strongly advocated psychotherapeutic treatment for all offenders who can be rehabilitated. At the time, this orientation may have seemed a soft, Utopian attitude of "coddling the criminal." However, Alexander and Staub also recommended that incurables be incarcerated, with an undetermined sentence, for as long as they constitute a menace to society.

Alexander and Staub discussed only offenders who were "neurotic criminals." Theoretically, neurotic symptoms are in a sense a person's private affairs, but in real life, behavior often has serious consequences for the environment. If unconscious trends are aggressive in nature, they are frequently expressed in antisocial behavior. Freud pointed out that the neurotic (particularly the compulsive neurotic) is at the same time antisocial and overly social. His symptoms satisfy, in fantasy, his antisocial tendencies; but he atones for them in the self-inflicted suffering that his neurosis causes him. The neurotic character acts out, not in fantasy but in real life, both his unacceptable unconscious tendencies, his criminal acts, and also his need for suffering, being caught and punished. After punishment, which relieves his guilt feelings, he feels free once again to offend the social order; hence the tendency toward recidivism.

As sociologists and psychiatrists have studied criminality, they have also categorized certain criminals as belonging to the nonneurotic category and have compared them with individuals having personalities that were nonconflictual and nonguilt-ridden. The most perplexing problem facing penology today is how to protect society from individuals who are proven criminals, as well as to provide for persons who can be rehabilitated. Sociologists are in agreement that punishment is not a deterrent to criminal acts and that it is not a suitable means of bringing about rehabilitation.* Unfortunately society is still more concerned with punishing an offender— making him "pay his debt to society"—than with helping him to overcome his criminal propensities. It is commonly believed that minimal punishment should be given for minimal crimes and severe punishment for greater crimes. Not enough attention is given to whether or not the offender still remains a danger to society. Ideally, criminals should be treated psychiatrically in order to help them overcome their motivations in committing crimes. This would be especially true in the case of the neurotic criminal. The practical problem here is a lack of sufficiently trained personnel and

---

* Learning theory explains that punishment may temporarily cause behavior to cease but does not eliminate the "propensity" toward it as effectively as does the judicious use of reward.

techniques for influencing antisocial behavior. It is also difficult to decide whether or not an individual still represents a menace to society. It would appear that such a question could better be answered by students of the behavioral sciences than by lay groups.

In spite of powerful resistance, there are modern trends in penology where the age-old, conservative, disciplinary, nonpsychological procedures seem to be changing. And there is slow progress. Pioneering studies are gradually penetrating into outdated conceptions. In some states, such as California, the orientation is changing so that the stress is on attempting to rehabilitate rather than to punish. In California, there is a program under proposal to develop "community correctional centers." These centers would function as halfway houses to which prisoners would be sent for guidance in such practical matters as occupational and loan opportunities in their local communities before they fully reenter society. Should a parolee commit a minor violation of his parole, the existence of these centers would preclude his being returned to prison in that he could return instead to these centers.

Parallel with the growth of interest in penal procedures has been the continuation of the search for better understanding of the motivational background of criminal behavior. This is extremely fortunate, for crime prevention will ultimately have to rest on a solid grasp of the dynamics of motivational forces. In no field is this more important than in that of juvenile delinquency.

A major contribution to a theoretical understanding of delinquency was the work done by Stanislaus Szurek and Adelaide Johnson (1905–1960), who studied the causes underlying the delinquency of juveniles who came from "good families." In some of their cases they noted a defect in the superego structure of one or both of the parents, defects termed "superego lacunae." Parents who exhibited these lacunae consciously, or more often unconsciously, condoned their children's delinquent behavior because they themselves received some sort of vicarious gratification from the antisocial acts and deeds. In other words, they secretly and unconsciously encouraged their children's delinquent behavior as a way of expressing their own antisocial tendencies.[22]

Today even more effort is going into sociologically oriented attempts to prevent crime than into psychotherapeutic and rehabilitative treatment for individual criminals. Clifford Shaw's statistical studies highlight the influence of environmental factors on crime. He found that in Chicago certain areas of the city act as criminal centers; some of these areas may spawn twenty times as many criminals as other Chicago districts. These centers, which are the slum districts where immigrants settle, are characterized by low social standards. Shaw's findings illustrate that those members of the population who have the least interest in the existing social order also are most inclined to break it.[23]

Sheldon and Eleanor Glueck have also studied the sociological and psychological factors of crime. Their subjects were five hundred delinquent and five hundred nondelinquent juveniles, on whom they collected sociological data and to whom they gave psychiatric interviews and Rorschach tests.[24] Their results confirmed a clinical observation that the mental health of a delinquent boy's family is likely to be poorer than that of a nondelinquent's family. They also found that although both delinquent and nondelinquent boys have emotional conflicts, delinquents are more likely to solve their conflicts by some kind of direct action, whereas neurotic juveniles express their conflicts in the form of socially harmless symptoms. Furthermore, the delinquent boys had had less opportunity during childhood to identify themselves with suitable parental images.

The Gluecks were able to confirm statistically another conclusion previously reached by clinicians: that severe neglect and severe punitive treatment favor the development of delinquent tendencies. Either undeserved or overly severe punishment and suffering weaken the restrictive influence of conscience and favor asocial behavior; but being neglected and forgotten is just as painful—or even more painful—for the child, so that a neglected boy may become delinquent in order to be punished, regarding punishment as a sign of concern and interest. That is why the adolescent delinquent eagerly looks for the newspaper reports of his criminal activities, reports that put him—the neglected, forgotten member of society—into the limelight. The Gluecks' study clearly shows that the psychological and sociological approaches are not in conflict with each other but are complementary.

Penetrating studies have come from Melitta Schmideberg, the daughter of the famed child analyst Melanie Klein. With admirable persistency she organized in New York the Association for Psychiatric Treatment of Offenders. She emphasizes psychodynamic understanding of criminals and maintains that control of antisocial behavior is essential to rehabilitation. She advocates close liaison between the parole officer and the psychotherapist of the parolee and insists that those parolees who omnipotently deny that they can be caught must not be allowed to reinforce this denial by using their psychotherapy as a sanctuary to escape the consequence of their behavior.

Recent developments in the approach to delinquency in England are similar to those in the United States. The struggle of psychiatrists to replace the antiquated legal orientation of punishment with a psychological approach encountered there the same resistance as in the United States. However, English reformatory and correctional practices have found support in the evolution of the so-called Borstal system. Borstal is an English village that gives its name to a system of correctional procedure that claims to be less impersonal than the larger American correctional institutions. In a Borstal institute fewer than three hundred and fifty delinquent youths are housed, which compares favorably with the usual American correctional school, which houses more than two thousand persons. George Mohr points out that the American diagnostic studies are more penetrating but that although "the American criminologists may know objectively more about their delinquent and criminal population . . . they do less about it than the English whose investigations seem more superficial."[25]

Even more archaic and punitive than laws affecting criminals are those that concern sexual psychopathy and especially homosexuality. For example, during World War II homosexuals were drafted into the military service, and then, after they were discovered to be homosexual, received "undesirable" discharges from the service and were denied G.I. benefits. Judd Marmor, in an article on homosexuality, *The Problem of Homosexuality: An Overview,* points out that the homosexual in the United States is even barred from obtaining civil-service employment. He is considered a security risk, Marmor points out, because he is subject to blackmail, and this is because society's condemnation of him makes him vulnerable to exposure. According to Alfred Kinsey, approximately one third of American males at one time or another have had overt homosexual experiences; there are somewhere between two and four million males who now practice overt homosexuality. In every state in the United States homosexual acts between males (but not always between females) are considered criminal. The same is true in England. In 1954 in England, a special committee appointed by the House of Lords filed the Wolfenden report, which stated that if homosexual behavior involved adults who freely participated and thereby consented in private to the homosexual act, a crime was not committed. Behavioral scientists throughout the world concurred with the Wolfenden report and supported its findings; nevertheless, in 1960 the House of Commons defeated the proposals recommended by the report.

When homosexual acts are carried out in private, where there is no minor involved and where there is no violence or coercion, the privacy and freedom of choice of the individual are interfered with by the existing penal codes in Anglo-Saxon countries. Austria and Germany are the only European countries in which legal means are implemented to punish homosexual acts between consenting adults. Thomas Szasz points out that so long as people seek through their legislatures and by means of the criminal law to influence the private sexual conduct of the adult members of society, it will be impossible to differentiate adequately between sexual acts that offend the public safety and welfare and those that do not.[26]

Furthermore, to impute irresponsibility and lack of trustworthiness to homosexuals is to generalize with a kind of prejudice similar to that noted in racial prejudice. As Judd Marmor states, "The 'dependability' of a homosexual . . . depends on whether or not he is a responsible human being with an adequate superego, and that factor is the only one to be evaluated; otherwise his homosexuality is neither more nor less relevant than is the heterosexuality of a male counselor in a girls' camp."[27]

All the available psychiatric knowledge indicates that a person may exhibit deviant behavior in one aspect of his life but may be quite adequate in his overall functioning. A person who has recurrent headaches from psychogenic reasons may still be a productive artist or an efficient administrator. Furthermore, the social prejudices against the homosexual, like social prejudices against other discriminated groups, in themselves lead to a vicious cycle of secondary problems. One of the important tasks of maturation is that of overcoming the feelings of inadequacy the child feels in the world of bigger people. When social forces ostracize, belittle, and berate individuals, regarding them as strange, peculiar, and inferior, their feelings of inferiority and inadequacy are only reinforced. It is all the more remarkable that despite the fact that they have been subjugated to tyrannical laws and other abuses, gifted and creative homosexuals have wrought brilliant achievements.

The source of legislation that is aimed at the homosexual who has not seduced children or been coercive has the same psychological source as the physical brutality displayed by individuals toward homosexuals: the deep fear of homosexuality within ourselves that we must punish in others so as to deny its source within our own psyche. It has been argued that homosexuality is a crime because it is contrary to the concept of biological survival. By the same token, then, contraception should be a crime. Furthermore, we might consider, as Szasz points out, that "biological survival is threatened by too much procreation, not by too little," and that "normal heterosexual procreative sexuality (for example, in juvenile marriages) does more demonstrable harm to society than homosexual practices between consenting adults." Szasz raises another important concept regarding the "threat" that the homosexual poses for a heterosexual society: "Because he rejects heterosexuality, the homosexual undermines its value. So, of course, does the priest. The homosexual, however, rejects one type of sexual conduct in favor of another, whereas the priest eschews the pleasures of the flesh to emphasize the value of the spirit. The homosexual thus threatens the heterosexual on his own grounds. He makes the heterosexual fear not only that he too may be homosexual, but also that heterosexuality itself is not as much 'fun' as it has been made out to be. Many people behave as if sexual satisfaction were one of their main interests in life. If the value of their favorite game is undermined, they may lose interest in it, and then what will they do? . . . Of course, the homosexual himself is a victim of this sexual obsession. Preoccupied with an intent on homosexual cravings and gratifications, he is the mirror-image of the ever-lustful, ever-frustrated heterosexual."[28]

One of the perplexing problems from a psychological standpoint in attempting to understand the phenomenon of homosexuality is its definition. Perhaps the clearest and most empirical definition is that proposed by Marmor: ". . . the clinical homosexual, therefore, [is] one who is motivated in adult life by a definite preferential erotic attraction to members of the same sex, and who usually (but not necessarily) engages in overt sexual relations with them."[29] This definition does not exclude those who have intense sexual longings for members of the same sex, yet because of moral considerations do not indulge in overt activity. This definition does exclude those individuals who engage in occasional homosexuality because of situational circumstances, such as prisoners or soldiers, but who do have a basic preference for sexual experience with women. It is impossible to describe any one particular pattern that leads to the preference for sexuality with the same sex. Most vulnerable are those children who cannot identify with the adult of their own sex or who fear contact with members of the opposite sex. Although there may be, in some cases, a biological factor, this finding has not been completely validated.

The fact that one fourth to one half of all homosexuals who seek psychotherapeutic treatment can effect a reversal of their sexual interests attests that at least in these cases early psychogenic influences were most important in the development of the condition. It should be stressed, however, that forcing a homosexual, just as forcing a neurotic or any individual, to undergo psychotherapy cannot be expected to achieve successful results. Yet, imprisonment is not an alternative to the "rehabilitation" of the homosexual. We should be reminded of the point made in 1948 by B. Karpman that prison life reinforces homosexual patterns rather than weakens them.[30]

Homosexuality is, of course, only one aspect of the general problem of sexual psychopathy. The problem is compounded on a nationwide basis by the lack of uniform legal definition of sexual psychopathy. California has arrived at a legal definition that may well be the most explicit and practical of those offered. It stresses "predisposition" and "menace" in setting forth five characteristics, all of which must apply to the individual under consideration. First, the individual must have been convicted or have pleaded guilty to a crime, though not necessarily to a criminal sexual offense. Second, the criminal offense must be one not punishable by death. Third, the individual must be afflicted with a mental disorder or a pronounced departure from normal mentality, or he must possess a "psychopathic personality." Fourth, he must be predisposed to the commission of sexual offenses. And fifth, the degree and nature of his predisposition must be such as to constitute the individual a menace to the health and safety of others.[31]

Once the offender has met these criteria, he is committed to a hospital for sexual offenders indefinitely, until the hospital staff believes that he is cured. In a five-year study of almost two thousand sexual offenders, seventy-five percent of those studied have remained free of police contact after having been treated at the Atascadero State Hospital in California.[32]

These results indicate that proper identification and treatment of offenders can offer society and the afflicted individual greater protection than simple punishment under archaic laws.

We have seen how difficult it is for the alcoholic to combat the pressures of his condition under the hostile influence of prevailing social attitudes. How much more onerous, then, must be the efforts at rehabilitation of the sexual psychopath, the addict, the delinquent, and even the criminal when these cruel attitudes are embodied in punishment and merciless imprisonment. If we are to protect society—and this means each individual in society—from these diseases of our society, we need to marshal all our *effective* weapons to the purpose. And we must be prepared to scrap all our outmoded, ineffective, and harmful weapons, if only for the sake of improving this protection. Bad laws do not make a good society. We desperately need to bring into wide view what we now know about human behavior, and just as desperately we need to bring out laws into harmony with our knowledge. As long as our institutionalized attitudes—our laws— lag behind our expanding enlightenment, our society can only work against itself. To eliminate this lag would not be the revolutionary act that some fear it would be. The outmoded laws on which we now rely were established on the basis of what we *then* knew of behavior and motives. Although they may even then have been warped by ignorance and prejudice, they represented man's effort to conform in law to his knowledge of himself. In sweeping away prejudice and ignorance and bringing our laws into harmony with what we now know, we will only be carrying on an ancient and worthy tradtion. If one of the noblest aspects of man's history has been his struggle to know himself, then no less exalted should be his determination to be just to himself.

CHAPTER **21**

The Culturalist School
and the Neo-Freudians

Freud recognized that man cannot be understood unless viewed in the social framework in which he has matured. He defined the superego as the imprint upon the personality of the prevailing social values that are transmitted to the child by parental influences. However, Freud did not make comparative studies of human development in different types of society. Studies like these have been the main contribution to psychiatry of the men and women who are discussed in this section.

Freud was interested in the two features common to all societies: the regulation of sexual relations through marital laws and the tabooing of hostile, aggressive impulses directed against the father. Social regulations in different cultures that prohibit incest take many different forms; so do the totemistic taboos against patricidal impulses. Nonetheless, these extremely variable social regulations all coincided with what Freud generally found in his individual patients, that is, the Oedipus complex. Freud recognized, although he did not explicitly so state, that the Oedipus complex has both a social origin and a social function. It protects the basic cell of society, the family, from disruption, for only when incest and patricide are outlawed can the family and hence society survive. Patricidal and incestuous wishes are manifestations of man's biological nature, not products of society. Freud's theory of personality accordingly took cognizance of man's innate impulses as well as of the social structure that regulates the expression of those impulses. Man, however, is more than his Oedipus complex. The impact of society is directed toward more than merely controlling sexuality and hostility arising from jealousy; it must influence all aspects of personality development.

Essentially, however, most of the later meaningful sociological contributions to personality theory are based on these solid biological and sociological foundations laid down by Freud. As will be seen, those authors who tried to ignore either the biological or the sociological factors failed in formulating a viable theory. This is only because man is a biological organism and at the same time a member of a social organization.

Some of the authors who became interested in the social aspects of personality development remained in the psychoanalytic fold and tried to develop their ideas along psychoanalytic lines of thought. In contrast, many "neo-Freudians" opposed the Freudian views and maintained that their work on social influences invalidated Freud's original theory.

We shall begin by considering the work of the first group. Freud, Abraham, Jung, and Rank in their early works, and later Theodor Reik, pointed out similarities among the symbolisms of psychopathological phenomena, dreams, mythology, and the rites of primitive cultures. Their work thus began to connect the fields of psychoanalysis and anthropology. One of the first anthropologists to take up their ideas was Geza Roheim (1891–1953). Equipped with a thorough knowledge of psychoanalytic psychology, he undertook pioneering field studies in Melanesia. Roheim's main thesis was that culture and neurosis are the products of the same psychological mechanisms and owe their existence to the "prolonged infancy" of the human species. The fundamental principles of unconscious fantasy-activity are the same in normal and abnormal processes, the same in neurosis, psychosis, art, dreams, and rituals. The "dominant" ideas that every culture has are determined by the infantile situation. Roheim's theory fails to take into account the fact that the culture-producing members of society are not infants, but adults. Consequently, his views appear dubious to most anthropologists, who believe that the entire structure of a culture, rather than different kinds of infantile situations, determines the individual's social attitudes. The social organization as a whole determines the typical parental values and child-rearing practices, and these in turn influence the responses and behavior patterns of the infant.

Although there existed a weakness in some of Roheim's social theories, he made an interesting contribution to the psychological origins of economic life. He stated that practical inventions are not at first brought into use for utilitarian aims, but are developed from "playful" activities, from idle hobbies, and later secondarily exploited for economic purposes. The application of this hypothesis to "technological discoveries" is feasible. For example, flying was originally a "playful" activity of adventurous persons who had merely vague dreams of its future practical significance. This experimentation was motivated primarily by a yearning to rise toward the skies, often appearing in dreams of expressing the wish for power, freedom, and mastery. Originally the wish to fly was neither for the purpose of commercial travel nor for a means of dropping bombs upon enemies. Pursuing Roheim's theory, we arrive at the seemingly paradoxical conclusion that culture is the product of man's leisure and not the sweat of his brow: when he is relieved from the necessities of the struggle for survival, his productive abilities become liberated.[1]

Theodor Reik had basically the same psychoanalytic orientation as Roheim. He wrote stimulating essays on the psychology of religious rituals in which he carefully demonstrated their origins in the unconscious. Like Roheim, he did not view the phenomena in the context of the culture in which they originated; instead, he applied the same psychodynamic mechanisms that had been observed in individual patients to group phenomena. He believed that each total cultural configuration, which evolves as the result of historical evolution, develops, from the immense register of all psychodynamic possibilities, its characteristic symbolisms and values. The specific aspects of any one culture cannot be deduced from universal human nature. Why courage becomes the highest virtue for nomadic tribes and thrift for settled agricultural nations is a complex question that requires an approach different from Roheim's and Reik's.

American social anthropologists, some of whom had been trained by Franz Sumner and Franz Boas (1858–1942), were able to apply psychoanalytic tools to anthropological material in a most rewarding way. Ruth Benedict (1887–1948), for example, was able to show that every culture has a consistent cohesive ideological pattern—the "ethos of culture"—and that this pattern has a determining influence both upon child-rearing and upon the adult's social functions. The ethos comprehends the prevailing social values that determine social influences upon a person's mental development. National traits, according to her view, are therefore not determined by heredity but by the social milieu as it manifests itself in the all-pervading ethos of a society.

Psychoanalysis most affected social anthropology through the work of Margaret Mead. In their book, *The Balinese Character,* Mead and Gregory Bateson gave a vivid account of the child-rearing practices of the Balinese and demonstrated how their custom of methodically intensifying sibling rivalry contributes to the stoic quality of the Balinese character. The Balinese mother deliberately shows an older child that she is breastfeeding a younger one; this action is designed to provoke extreme jealousy in the older child and forces him to learn at an early age to control his violent jealousy. In *Male and Female* Margaret Mead demonstrated how certain characteristic American traits are culturally conditioned by the traditionless, ever-changing, and forward-looking nature of our social climate. She ascribes to American marriages the specific difficulty of a lack of traditional patterns of life, which places a "strain on the couple" asked to build "a whole copy of life" in a future-oriented culture for which there are no guideposts.[2]

Abram Kardiner, in collaboration with an anthropologist, Ralph Linton,

worked out his concept of the "basic personality" as an elaboration of
Ruth Benedict's thesis of the cultural ethos. Kardiner described national
character, using more psychodynamic emphasis than did Benedict. His
methodology is in a sense the direct opposite of Roheim's: instead of
trying to explain specific social institutions, rituals, and myths on the basis
of an individual's unconscious mechanisms, Kardiner conceives of personality as having been molded by social institutions developed under
the influence of geographically and economically determined national
problems. His approach is based on the functional theory of social
institutions, according to which cultural institutions and attitudes are
determined by the particular methods a specific society adopts to solve its
problems of survival and perpetuation. Institutions and value systems of
nomadic societies are different from those of agricultural societies because
these two economic-survival techniques require different attitudes from the
individuals who use them. Every culture, however, has some nonadaptive
components. The latter, at least partially, represent outmoded cultural
patterns transmitted from earlier periods.

While Kardiner centered his attention on the adaptive, culturally determined basic aspects of personality structures in primitive, static societies,
Alexander attempted to reconstruct the psychodynamic structure of the
rapidly changing Western democracy. Alexander viewed man's behavior as
dominated by two opposing trends: one toward stability and security, the
other toward creation, adventure, and exploration of the unknown. The
conservative trend toward security stems from the principle of self-preservation and is manifested in securing and retaining the necessities for
survival. The progressive or expansive trend toward exploration of the
unknown stems from the principle of growth and propagation. Although
both tendencies have always marked man's social aspirations, each major
period of history has been dominated by one or the other of them,
depending on whether man's energies must be bent toward obtaining
security or whether he is secure enough to allow his energies to range
beyond his current limitations. The feudal era, for example, was governed
by a preoccupation with establishing stability and mutual protection. A
shifting economic and social structure made possible, and even necessary,
the development of that bold, venturesome spirit that marked the general
creative surge that was the Renaissance.

Alexander, using the vantage point of psychodynamics to view historical
developments, also concerned himself with the problem of what he called
the "cultural lag." In his book *Our Age of Unreason* he described the
tensions between social structure and opposing attitudes, and in *The
Western Mind in Transition* he dealt with the dangers involved in the
emergence of the "mass man."

The *cultural-lag* concept was first developed by William Ogburn, a
social scientist. As introduced by Ogburn and further developed by Alex-

ander, the concept is that attitudes tend to become so solidly rooted in society that they outlive the sociological structure that created them. Modern technology, for instance, has been creating social changes at a faster rate than our prevalent conservative attitudes and social institutions have been able to keep up with. Furthermore, since emotional attitudes tend to lag behind changes in social structure, the discrepancy between them—the cultural lag—results in social disorganization. In the individual this discrepancy leads to emotional conflicts and contributes to a tendency toward neurotic disturbances.

Among more recent attempts to relate individual psychological developments with cultural influences, Erik Erikson's work is outstanding. He combines concepts of libido theory with ego psychology and also with sociological considerations in discussing the difficulty encountered by present-day youth in finding an "ego identity."[3] Man's most human faculty is his awareness of his identity of himself as a distinct person who exists in a continuum of past, present, and future and who plans and shapes his own fate with a sense of self-determination. A feeling of identity emerges as the result of a continuously progressing integrative process. Erikson has attempted to reconstruct this complex psychological process through infancy, childhood, latency, adolescence, and adulthood, each of which involves characteristic biologically determined changes in libido organization. Erikson points out that sociopsychological influences in the human environment affect personality development and that each new phase of development, which he calls a "crisis," requires new adaptive tasks to harmonize the changing libidinal forces with changing expectations of the environment toward the growing individual. Adolescence, the most profound of these crises, is the best example. Erikson demonstrates that adaptational problems are common to particularly vulnerable groups, such as immigrants and minorities, and, like Alexander and Fromm, he thinks rapid social change, by fostering "ego-diffusion," makes it difficult to establish ego identity. Because his sociologically oriented work is based on clinical observations, it is more applicable to clinical practice than the philosophically conceived writings of the neo-Freudians.

As psychoanalysts dealt with individual life histories and emphasized the impact of a particular family constellation upon personality formation, anthropologists and culturally oriented psychoanalysts were emphasizing the common influences operating on every family living within a given culture. Alexander regarded these two points of view as complementary; hence, he tried to synthesize their concepts. He took the position that since the constituent parts of what is called society are individual human beings, then logically the nature of social organization will be dependent on the nature of these constituent units, that is, human nature. The interrelationships between members of society are determined by the social system in which the individuals live. This system consists in a specific mode of survival—through agriculture, for instance, or hunting, nomadism, or militarism—and this system determines the values and the educational principles within the group. Culture, so to say, makes use of the infinite range or possible behavior patterns according to its needs, which vary from social system to social system within the same culture. But this does not preclude enormous individual differences. The sociologist is interested in the cultural system as a whole, the clinical psychoanalyst in specific individuals. What psychoanalysis offers to sociology is the knowledge of a great variety of psychological mechanisms, but it cannot explain which psychological mechanism and which emotional attitudes of all possible ones will develop at a certain historical moment in a certain group. Such an explanation must be based on the sociologist's investigation of the actual structure, the prevailing and historical traditions, of the society as a whole.

For the psychotherapist, however, it is not sufficient to know the common features prevailing among members of the same cultural group. If the psychoanalyst begins to think in sociological terms like "competitive civilization" in treating his patients, he will most likely be satisfied with such generalizations and neglect the study of specific competitive situations. In clinical work the understanding of each individual must be based on the assessment of his specific experiences and not on knowledge of averages as represented by cultural patterns.

Harry Stack Sullivan (1892–1949) was an early proponent of the point of view regarding analysis characterized by an emphasis on what he called *interpersonal relationships*. He considered mental illness to consist of, as well as to stem from, disturbed interpersonal relationships. Freud had defined psychosis as a conflict between the person and the external world that leads to his withdrawal, and neurosis as intrapsychic disturbances between the id, ego, and superego. On the basis that the external world consists of other human beings, Sullivan pointed out that the basic conflict is between the individual and this human environment. This statement holds true for both psychosis and neurosis, since intrapsychic conflicts originally were interpersonal conflicts that become intrapsychic when the original adversaries—usually the parents—participating in these conflicts are internalized. Sullivan's emphasis on interpersonal relations is the main reason why neo-Freudians consider him one of their group: nonetheless, he actually had no particular sociological sophistication, and his major contributions were all to clinical psychiatry. Moreover, he shared Freud's biological orientation and believed in the significance of instincts.

Sullivan had extensive clinical experience applying dynamic psychotherapeutic techniques to schizophrenics. He possessed a special ability to communicate with this alienated group of mental sufferers, and his psychological descriptions of their behavior are unparalleled in their clarity. Sullivan's position on schizophrenia is that in this illness the rational, reality-adjusted mental functions are repressed but not irreparably disrupted. Repression of the reality-adjusted functions is the means by which the psychotic withdraws from reality; with proper treatment, Sullivan felt, the repression could be lifted.

Most of the neo-Freudians are identified as such by their criticism of standard psychoanalytic ideas, particularly the libido theory. Some of their attacks have been both necessary and constructive, and they have stimulated progress in psychiatry. They have not, however, always been able to come up with better concepts to take the place of those they have criticized.

Karen Horney (1885–1952), for instance, tried to rewrite psychoanalytic theory and failed, yet many of her critical considerations of weak points in psychoanalytic theory were well taken. Strongly influenced by Adler, she subjected the role of sexuality in neurosis and the libido theory to a much-needed scrutiny; nonetheless she was unable to offer any satisfactory new ideas. She merely replaced the idea of a vague biological substance, the libido, with an equally vague sociological concept, culture. For dialectic reasons Horney tried to create the effigy of a one-sided biologically oriented Freud. Then, in order to destroy this effigy, she became extremely one-sided in the opposite (antibiological) direction. Thus she overlooked some fundamental facts of human psychology: that not only is the human being born with a psychophysiological dynamic structure, but that even his later development is influenced to a high degree by rigidly predetermined biological growth. Therefore, to try to understand the psychology of puberty or senescence without paying attention to the biological changes in the organism would be a procedure just as one-sided as to try to understand an individual as a complex structure of innate libidinal drives that operate in him without regard to external influences.[4]

Horney also attacked an overemphasis of childhood situations and of childhood memories to the neglect of understanding the patient's real-life current emotional problems. She correctly pointed out that a regressive repetition of a childhood pattern of behavior is never a precise repetition but is necessarily modified by later experiences, by the maturation of the patient, and by his altered life situation. Then, however, she misused this proper conclusion to minimize the clinical significance of regression. She went even so far as to underestimate the therapeutic importance of a biographical reconstruction of the patient's past in order to understand him in his present difficulties.

Horney's books are full of excellent and realistic descriptions of typical conflict situations. Her "masochistic," "perfectionistic," and "narcissistic" characters are clinical pictures masterfully abstracted from a wealth of observations. Her theoretical ideas, however, are far weaker than her clinical contributions. In one respect she deserves unqualified credit for her insistence that patients ought to be considered in terms of detailed psychological realities instead of theoretical abstractions. This viewpoint cannot be overemphasized in a field in which there is such a temptation to replace a real understanding of the living person with less troublesome theory.

So far as cultural factors are concerned, Horney singles out one conflict that is characteristic for our present Western culture—the contradiction between the high evaluation of success in our competitive society and the Christian principle of neighborly love and need for affection. In the *Neurotic Personality of Our Time* she describes the neurotic person as the victim of this pervading conflict of values.

Erich Fromm is another neo-Freudian who has had much attention from social scientists and the general public. His book *Escape from Freedom* is particularly well known. In it he expounds the emotional difficulties prevalent in free societies—the burden of self-responsibility these societies impose, which mobilizes the regressive urge to be led and dominated. In general Fromm's ideas about "social character" are similar to Kardiner's concept of basic personality. In his later work Fromm has become more and more interested in basing social reform on psychodynamic considerations. He has adopted the old concept of immutable natural laws that logically prescribe what a "sane society" should be. In his belief in an absolute set of ethical standards, he differs markedly from the other neo-Freudians, who take the relativistic view that prevailing values vary from society to society.

The neo-Freudians broadened the perspectives of personality research by including a consideration of social factors to which all members of a cultural group are exposed. Consequently their contributions may affect social science more than clinical psychoanalysis; they may eventually facilitate the development of a yet nonexisting preventative psychiatry, as, for example, the prevention of delinquency. However, individual psychotherapy, particularly in Western society, the unique fate of each individual and the highly diversified specific constellation in each family must remain the main considerations. This is particularly true for our Western society. In totalitarian societies that discourage individual differences and aspire to produce uniform men whose destiny is determined by centrally planned principles and measures, the aims of psychotherapy will have to change accordingly. In such societies personality research will focus on types and not on unique individuals.

CHAPTER 22

Philosophical Vistas

Existentialism, a thoroughly European post-World War II phenomenon, is a general orientation toward the self and the world that is the diametrical opposite of the behavioristic orientation. It exalts self-awareness as man's most basic experience: experiencing one's own existence. Why has this philosophical orientation, which Søren Kierkegaard (1813–1855) and Friedrich Nietzsche (1844–1900) promulgated in the last century, been revived in the last few decades? And what relationship does it bear to psychiatry? It appears that this philosophical trend is one of the many manifestations of the European man's disillusionment with his extroverted interest in the physical universe and the values that have inspired him since the Renaissance. Two world wars, followed by social, economic, and spiritual collapse, initiated not only opposition against those in power but also a general ideological revolt against the values and beliefs that man felt brought about the catastrophe. Science became the natural target of this revolt, since man intuitively grasped that the world in which he lived and which was collapsing was primarily the product of science and technology. The popularity of existentialism indicates that man has turned his back on the world, which he has explored and dominated so successfully, especially through science, during the last three hundred years, and has begun to look into his own self. Psychoanalysis is the scientific manifestation of an introverted interest in the self; existentialism is its philosophical counterpart. This is why in the last two decades many European psychiatrists have adopted its tenets as their basic orientation. The best-known American representative of the existentialist school is Rollo May, who edited a volume entitled *Existence: A New Dimension in Psychiatry and Psychology.*

It is difficult to establish what the existential psychiatrist stands for other than an insistence that each patient must be understood in his own right, or in their vocabulary, "in his own universe." This position, of course, is no different from that of psychoanalysts. Existentialists seem to think, however, that because psychoanalysis puts an emphasis on technical rules and regulations and has strong commitments to theoretical formulations, it has so become the victim of modern "scientism" that the uniqueness of each individual patient is neglected. Existentialists refer to this as "methodolatry," or the deification of technique.

Existential psychiatrists derived much of their vocabulary from the German philosopher Martin Heidegger, who was a pupil of Edmund Husserl (1859–1938), the founder of the phenomenological school of philosophy. Heidegger felt that to describe the elusive contents of man's self-awareness, literary expressions are more suitable than the usual technical terms of psychology. Central among these are the expressions "being in the world" and being "thrown into the world," referring to man's primary experience of finding himself in the world as a self-reflecting being. This "experiencing of being" is always coupled with the threat of not being, not existing. This is the source of a universal anxiety, or the existential "despair."

A contention of the existentialist psychiatrists that has greater significance for psychotherapy is that in the therapeutic situation two concrete human individualities interact, and not, as the theory maintains, a patient and a blank screen upon which the patient projects his own feelings. The existentialists call the interaction of the therapeutic situation an *encounter* and try to understand and describe it phenomenologically. As has been mentioned, recently some psychoanalysts independently came to the same conclusion, and Alexander's theory of the corrective emotional experience is based precisely on this view. The development of transference is not denied by the existentialists, but they stress that the transference and countertransference do not account for the richness of the therapeutic encounter, which includes much more than repetitive modes of emotional reactions between patient and therapist. The therapist represents for the patient parental images or members of the patient's family who once played an important role in his emotional development; but at the same time, he is also a concrete person to whom the patient reacts as an individual.

Existential psychiatry has not yet proposed a systematic therapeutic procedure, but has tried to modify the psychoanalytic approach. This is certainly true of the best-known Swiss existential analysts, Meddard Boss and Gustav Bally. Another Swiss existentialist, Ludwig Binswanger, knew Freud well and was deeply influenced by him. His existentialist inspiration, however, stems from Husserl. Binswanger, as well as V. E. von Gebsattel, is distinguished mostly for the phenomenological description of subjective experiences during treatment. J. Zutt, a German, believes that man can overcome the gap that exists between the essential core of his personality and that of another person through the "aesthetic area of life." Those who are not versed in the characteristically obscure German philosophical style of writing and thinking will not find it easy to follow Zutt's work. Essentially, however, he strives to describe accurately the encounter between the two personalities of therapist and patient. Erwin Straus, a German, is psychologically a most sensitive existential psychiatrist. His work describes the subjective determination of man's awareness of the surrounding world in an outstanding fashion. Of the French psychiatrists, Henry Ey has been somewhat influenced by psychoanalysis, but more by existentialist philosophy. His writings are both lucid and erudite; he has an encyclopedic knowledge of older and current psychiatric literature, which he is able to synthesize in a rational manner.

The central emphasis in existential psychiatry is on a vivid description of the patient's emotional moods. Their insistence on phenomenological description may be responsible for the existentialists' neglect of the unconscious determinants of behavior, since unconscious motivations cannot be directly observed and described but have to be reconstructed from analyzing such material as dreams, slips of the tongue, and free associations. Recent interest among some psychiatrists in Zen Buddhism goes even one step beyond existentialism in the direction of self-awareness. Zen is a Chinese derivative of Indian Buddhism and probably began with the teachings of the Chinese patriarch Bodhi-Dharma, who lived in the sixth century A.D. and adapted Gautama Buddha's teachings to the Chinese cultural scene.[1]

Zen refers essentially to an inner mystical experience, "satori," which cannot be well described in rational terms. It can only be subjectively experienced. In satori the conventional distinction between inner and outer world disappears and man becomes one with the universe. Authorities on Zen insist that Zen is not an intellectual system and that its essence, the satori experience, escapes conceptualization and must be described in aphorisms and parabolic poetic references. Suzuki, who is mainly responsible for introducing Zen to the American public, states: *"Satori may be defined as an intuitive looking into the nature of things in contradistinction to the analytical or logical understanding of it. Practically, it means the unfolding of a new world hitherto unperceived in the confusion of a dualistically-trained mind. Or we may say that with satori our entire surroundings are viewed from quite an unexpected angle of perception. Whatever this is, the world for those who have gained a satori is no more than the old world as it used to be; even with all its flowing streams and burning fires, it is never the same one again. Logically stated, all its opposites and contradictions are united and harmonized into a consistent organic whole. This is a mystery and a miracle, but according to the Zen masters such is being performed every day. Satori can thus be had only through our once personally experiencing it."*[2]

The goal of Zen is psychotherapeutic in the sense that it aims to provide a sense of finality and contentment for those who are dissatisfied with life. The revelatory and introspective experience of satori has a Christian parallel in the conversion experiences of mystics. Jakob Böhme's (1575–1624) conversion experience is an outstanding example. One day Böhme saw a reflection of the sun in an old pewter dish. The entire sun was contained in this worthless object, and Böhme suddenly understood that the key to the mysteries of the world lies in one's own internal experiences. His experience, as he described it, was the same as those that the followers of Zen describe as satori; similar exalted moments have also been repeatedly described by mental patients as turning points in their disease. Zen's anti-intellectual quality makes it difficult for Western man to grasp, since he is raised in the Greek rational tradition and its modern revival. The anti-intellectual emphasis explains the strange nonsensical answers—calculated non sequiturs—that the Zen masters give their pupils who try to penetrate into the mysteries of satori. With this provocative nonsense given in a highly authoritative manner, they try to discourage reasonable thought.

Typical are such dialogues: "Ummon, quoting an ancient Buddhist philosopher who said 'Knock at the emptiness of space and you hear a voice; strike a piece of wood and there is no sound'; took out his staff and, striking space, cried, 'Oh how it hurts!' Then tapping at the board, he asked, 'Any noise?' A monk responded, 'Yes, there is a noise.' Thereupon the master exclaimed, 'Oh you ignoramus!' "[3] or "Hyakujo one day went out attending his master Baso. A flock of wild geese was seen flying and Baso asked: 'What are they?' 'They are wild geese, sir.' 'Wither are they flying?' 'They have flown away, sir.' Baso abruptly taking hold of Hyakujo's nose gave it a twist. Overcome with pain, Hyakujo cried aloud: 'Oh! Oh!' 'You say they have flown away,' Baso said, 'but all the same they have been here from the beginning.' This made Hyakujo's back wet with cold perspiration. He had *satori*."[4] This nonsensical dialogue is a kind of brainwashing aimed at discouraging rational logical thought, which interferes with direct intuitive experiencing of one's innermost self. Reason and logic may be useful in understanding the world around us, but they interfere with experiencing one's own being.

In trying to characterize satori, Suzuki enumerates eight features: irrationality, intuitive insight, authoritativeness, affirmation, sense of the beyond, impersonal tone, feeling of exaltation, and momentariness.[5]

For someone raised in the Western tradition of thinking, it is not easy to evaluate the possible significance of Zen for psychiatry. Erich Fromm, who has written on Zen Buddhism and psychoanalysis and who is a student of Suzuki, maintains that satori undercuts intellectualization, which is also a goal of psychoanalysis. However, the intuitive grasping of one's true nature in psychoanalysis leads to a rational understanding, which is inimical to the Zen Buddhist thinking.

Fromm, following Suzuki's ideas, has claimed that there is a striking

similarity between Zen Buddhist practices and psychoanalysis. He dis-
agrees with our contention that satori is a regression to a narcissistic state.
He claims that both Zen Buddhism and psychoanalysis have an ethical
orientation and that they attempt to overcome unhealthy character developments, for example, immaturity or greediness. Both systems rely on
severance from the authority figure (the analyst and the master) for
ultimate success. Both the master and the psychoanalyst have themselves
experienced the procedure (satori for the master, psychoanalysis for the
psychoanalyst); both systems attempt to rid the individual of excessive
rationalizations and intellectualizations.[6]

However, it is difficult for the Western mind to understand how the
satori experience leads to the achievement of humility, love, and compassion, the end goals of Zen Buddhist doctrines. The obvious similarities
between schizophrenic regressions and the practices of Yoga and Zen
merely indicate that the general trend in Oriental cultures is to withdraw
into the self from an overbearingly difficult physical and social reality. Only
the future can tell how much Western psychiatry will learn from this
Oriental bent of thought, which for centuries coexisted with the more
outward-directed Western mentality, without the two influencing each other
to any appreciable degree. Contemporary existential philosophy offers a
Western counterpart to Zen emphasis upon self-awareness as a deep source
of knowledge. Western interest in Yoga and Zen may perhaps most
hopefully be interpreted as a sign of the gradual dwindling of isolation
between these two cultures. Cultural cross-fertilization is the next inevitable step in thought development.

CHAPTER **23**

Developments in Child Psychiatry

Child psychiatry received its impetus from several social movements: in particular, educational reforms that emphasized the educability of mentally retarded children, mental-hygiene and child-guidance movements, and the attention given to the delinquent child. Until Freud's influence became widespread, psychologists' observations of normal children had more impact on the development of this field than the writings of psychiatrists.

Early Writings

Psychiatrists in the early nineteenth century were primarily interested in classifying the psychoses of children. Esquirol differentiated the mentally defective from the psychotic child in his *Maladies Mentales* (1838) and reported several interesting case histories of children with homicidal impulses. Wilhelm Griesinger devoted part of his influential book *Pathologie und Therapie der Psychischen Krankheiten* (1845) to the psychiatric problems of children. Griesinger noted that many of the conditions that he had described in adults—for example, mania and melancholia—were also found in children. He classified the mental illnesses of children under the same headings as adult illnesses and believed that there were both psychological and organic predisposing causes. Henry Maudsley, a contemporary of Griesinger, devoted thirty pages of his book *Physiology and Pathology of the Mind* (c. 1867) to "Insanity of Early Life." Like Griesinger, Maudsley classified childhood mental diseases under headings used for adult diseases; unlike Griesinger, who advised using educational methods to cure childhood mental illness, Maudsley did not recommend any form of treatment. In the last two decades of the nineteenth century, discussions by leaders in the field were "restricted by fatalism which saw in the reported [childhood] disorders the irreversible results of heredity, degeneracy, excessive masturbation, overwork, or religious preoccupation."[1]

It is unfortunate that one of the most illuminating late-nineteenth-century presentations of child psychiatry had little influence. In 1887 Hermann Emminghaus published *Psychic Disturbances of Childhood.* Emminghaus' work, according to Ernest Harms, a psychiatric historian, was "one of the very few attempts made up to that time to give a systematic over-all presentation of child psychiatry. . . . Mental diseases in children [were] described as 'incommensurable' with those of adults, and a clearcut separation of scientific study in the two fields [was] called for."[2] Emminghaus began his book with a statistical epidemiological study of abnormal mental conditions of childhood as he found them in Germany. He divided the psychoses into those resulting from physical causes, such as diseases of the brain, and those caused by psychological factors, such as excessive fear or anxiety. Emminghaus noted that poor home conditions, poor education, and unhealthy social situations produced mental illnesses in children; he discussed pathological disturbances in thinking and imagination and presented a systematic survey of various pathological entities. Emminghaus' enlightened point of view extended to the delinquent child, whom he considered to be suffering from an illness rather than from poor morals, and needing to be understood and helped rather than punished. Unfortunately Emminghaus' ideas were ignored; and later, influential textbooks of psychiatry by Kraepelin and Bleuler omit any reference to childhood mental disturbances per se. The tendency in psychiatric literature had been established: children were to be regarded as miniature adults and were therefore not entitled to a distinctive approach.

Toward the end of the nineteenth century there were some studies, though not by psychiatrists, that attempted to explain children's behavior and psychology. Charles Darwin wrote a descriptive treatise, *A Biographical Sketch of an Infant* (1876) that stimulated similar work elsewhere. William Preyer in Germany published an important observational work called *The Mind of the Child,* which elaborated the child's developmental patterns of growth and behavior. A psychologist, James Scully, wrote a comprehensive book, *The Studies in Childhood* (1895), in which he noted that play reveals a great deal of the child's mental processes. Milicent Shinn, in *Notes on the Development of a Child* (1893), gave a careful description of the day-by-day development of a newborn infant. In 1891 Stanley Hall founded the *Pedagogical Seminary,* a journal for the publication of studies on children; the articles in it continued to advocate the idea that the understanding of children must be based on an appreciation of normal behavior.

The study of normal development was most advanced in the United States by Arnold Gesell (1880–1961), who began his career as a psychology student under Hall at Clark University and then later earned a medical degree from Yale. In 1925 Gesell published a comprehensive systematic outline of the normal developmental pattern in children, *The Mental Growth of the Pre-School Child: A Psychological Outline of Normal Development from Birth to the Sixth Year, Including a System of Developmental Diagnosis.* The impact of Gesell's work on clinical practice lay in its insistence that one must understand normality before one can comprehend deviation. Gesell and his associates at Yale emphasized that each successive period of development derives from the preceding one; they also attempted to show on a behavioral level how development proceeds.

Education and the Mental Defective

We must return to the latter part of the eighteenth century to trace the concepts of education that have played a part in child psychiatry. Eighteenth-century children were educated according to a rigidly imposed curriculum. Then, in 1762, Jean Jacques Rousseau published *Emile,* a book that inspired educational reform. Rousseau emphasized the importance of permitting children to learn by actively doing things for themselves unhampered by rigid external restrictions. Rousseau's ideas influenced Johann Heinrich Pestalozzi (1746–1827), a Swiss educator who devoted his life to teaching the children of the poor. Pestalozzi always emphasized, like Locke and Condillac, that knowledge stems from observations, which in turn stimulate the development of man's innate potential.* The revolutionary educational views of Rousseau and Pestalozzi had already begun to stimulate the imaginations of teachers and scientists when the first attempts to deal humanely with the education of a retarded person were made.

In 1798, near Aveyron, France, a wild teen-age boy was found by a group of hunters. He could not speak and behaved like a savage; he was turned over to Jean Itard, the chief medical officer at the Institution for the Deaf and Dumb in Paris. Philippe Pinel believed that the boy was a mental defective and that he could not be educated; Itard, however, believed that the boy simply appeared defective because he had never known any civilizing influence. The boy probably was mentally defective; nevertheless, Itard, who spent five years trying to educate the boy by humane methods, was able to demonstrate that the boy, who never became normal, could improve in his social behavior. Itard's experiment was thus the first effort ever made to train a mentally retarded individual.

Edward Seguin, a Christian socialist, wished to educate mental defec-

---

* Later in the nineteenth century the ideas of Rousseau and Pestalozzi greatly influenced Friedrich Froebel (1782–1852), a German educationist who taught that a child, like a flower, blossoms best when nurtured by an interested gardener. He advocated free play wherein children engaged in field trips, nature study, and handiwork under the permissive guidance of a teacher. This Froebel called a "kindergarten."

tives for sociopolitical reasons, since "the task of educating the idiot was part of a wider movement for the abolition of social classes and the establishment of a just society."[3] In 1846 Seguin published a treatise, *Idiocy and Its Treatment*. With unrealistic optimism he believed that retarded people could be completely cured because they were merely children with "prolonged" infancies. Seguin's method of teaching was to foster perceptual faculties before conceptual functions, a principle still applied today in educating both defective and normal children. In 1842 Seguin had systematized the teaching of mental defectives at the Bicêtre, and by 1848, when he brought his ideas to America, because he believed that a democratic society would be most receptive to his liberal educational views, the movement to educate subnormals was well under way. In the 1840's schools for retarded children were founded in Abendberg, Switzerland, by J. Guggenbuhl; in Berlin by C. M. Seagert; in Bath, England, by John Conolly. The first state school in the United States for retarded children was opened in Massachusetts under the guidance of Samuel Ridley Howe. In 1896, at the University of Pennsylvania, Lightner Witmer, who coined the term *clinical psychology,* opened the first psychological clinic to use remedial educational methods to treat defective children. Witmer also investigated those factors that interfere with normal children's ability to use their intellectual potential. Also at the end of the nineteenth century, Walter Fernald, a pioneer in developing methods for aiding the retarded in the United States, founded the first scientific association for the study of treatment methods for the feeble-minded.

These educational efforts for the feeble-minded lacked a method of assessing the intellectual capacity of a retarded child; obviously less ought to be expected from a severely impaired child than from one only mildly retarded. To fill this need, the French Minister of Public Instruction, as we have already mentioned, asked Alfred Binet to devise a method of testing intelligence. The role of Binet, Simon, Goddard, and Terman in devising standardized intelligence tests, and Piaget's work on the development of rational thought in the child, all of which are essentially related to the beginnings of education for retarded children, have also been discussed.

Delinquency and the Child-Guidance Movement

By the end of the nineteenth century progressive educators, in line with the contemporary concern with public hygiene, were beginning to be concerned with the problems of delinquency. In 1909 the National Committee for Mental Hygiene was organized under the guiding influence of Clifford Beers, Adolph Meyer, and William James, and in the same year the child-guidance movement—a specifically American contribution to child psychiatry—was launched.

Also about this time a Chicago philanthropist, Mrs. W. F. Dummer, commissioned Dr. William Healy to study the work then being done on the causes and prevention of delinquency. Dr. Healy found only two American clinics—Witmer's clinic, at the University of Pennsylvania, and another under Goddard's direction at Vineland—that were concerned enough with this problem to give children psychological tests. Mrs. Dummer then underwrote a research clinic, the Juvenile Psychopathic Institute, founded in 1909, under Healy's direction. After a six-year study, Healy published *The Individual Delinquent: A Textbook of Diagnosis and Prognosis,* a classic exposé of the socioeconomic roots of delinquency and a book that laid to rest the idea that the causes of delinquency were defective genes or defective mentality or "degeneracy." In the meantime, several other important centers for child study had also been established. In 1912 the Boston Psychopathic Hospital was organized under Elmer E. Southard (1876–1920), who, together with Mary Jarett, was responsible for introducing the psychiatric social worker into the psychiatric child-guidance team. Southard's concept of the function of the social worker, which was to study the child both in school and at home, was influenced by Adolph Meyer, who had encouraged his wife to visit the homes of his patients.

The sociological roots of delinquency and its relationship to later criminal behavior were on the way to being firmly established. The psychoanalyst Bernard Glueck published a report of the results of his psychiatric examinations of inmates at Sing Sing, including relevant data concerning their earlier life histories. In 1922 Clarence Darrow published *Crime, Its Causes and Treatment,* which supported a basic premise of the mental-hygiene movement, namely, that punishment was not a cure for delinquency and that the prevention of crime rested on the understanding of the sources of delinquency. In 1922, also, the National Committee for Mental Hygiene, financed by the Commonwealth Fund, inaugurated a five-year program for fellowships at child-guidance centers; it also arranged for schools to have staff psychiatrists and for liaisons between courts and psychiatric teams.* This work helped further an interdisciplinary method of studying the factors that lead to conduct disorders by combining psychological testing, social information, and psychiatric diagnosis.

In 1924 the American Orthopsychiatric Association was established. Its members included sociologists, criminologists, psychologists, social workers, psychiatrists, and other professionals who were interested in understanding and treating delinquency. Over the years, orthopsychiatry—the word means "straight-mindedness"—has extended its sphere of interest beyond delinquency to all forms of maladaptive behavior, including neurotic disorders of children.

The recognition that an aggressive predelinquent child or even a delin-

---

* An important aspect of child guidance is the investigation and treatment of disorders of infancy. The first clinic that was devoted to this problem was in Boston in the early twenties under the directorship of Douglas Thom.

quent adolescent is not an individual who is innately "bad," that he cannot be handled through punitive measures, and that antisocial behavior may represent a behavioral manifestation of an underlying neurosis led to attempts to treat aggressive individuals directly. One of the first men to try this in a residential setting was a Viennese educationist turned psychoanalyst, August Aichhorn (1878–1949).* As a youth Aichhorn developed an understanding of and an empathy with delinquent behavior through carousing with ruffians who used to hang around his father's bakery. He became a schoolteacher noted for being able to deal successfully with aggressive youngsters. He established and directed two reformatories, the first at Ober-Hollabrunn in 1918, the second at St. Andra in 1920. Anna Freud become impressed with Aichhorn's work and suggested he would have greater insight about these children if he had psychoanalytic training. Aichhorn went to the Viennese Psychoanalytic Institute; after completing his psychoanalytic training, he published *Wayward Youth* (1925; English version, 1935). In this book Aichhorn pointed out that the personality development of a child who has an unsatisfactory relationship with a parent will be adversely affected and such a child will then have difficulty establishing relationships with other people. This is the matrix around which "latent delinquency" forms. If external influences continue to be unfavorable, the latent delinquent becomes an overt delinquent.

The way, then, to deal with the delinquent, Aichhorn decided, would be to help him establish a relationship with a trusting adult upon whom he can rely and with whom he can at last find a meaningful identification, that is, an ego ideal. Aichhorn's warmth, his empathy with delinquent children, his steadfast adherence to the principle that punishment is useless, and his patience aided him enormously in the task he had set himself. When they first met him, his charges would consider Aichhorn weak because he did not take punitive, retaliatory measures against their aggressive outbreaks, but then they grew to trust, respect, and eventually love the man whose life was devoted to understanding and helping them. And when they had finally identified themselves with Aichhorn, they were able to integrate with their group and also progress in their schoolwork.

Aichhorn also demonstrated with a second group that adolescents could be influenced by increasing their respect for an authority figure. These boys were not openly violent like the aggressive youngsters; they were more like adult "con" men. Aichhorn believed that the fathers, whom these boys had taken as ego ideals, had led lives of deceit themselves; consequently Aichhorn decided he ought to "unmask" the parental models by making himself superior to them so that eventually he could help the boys depreciate their original ego ideals. Aichhorn managed this by exhibiting his own character strength, but in such a way that he never provoked fear

* We are indebted to Dr. George J. Mohr, who studied under Aichhorn, for information about him.

in the boys. First the boys were awed by Aichhorn's methods, then they became dependent on him, and finally they showed typical neurotic reactions in their transference relationship to him. Once the neurosis came out, the abnormal behavioral patterns diminished and Aichhorn could treat the boys with a technique similar to the interpretive method of psychoanalysis. His therapeutic secret thus involved engaging the boys in an emotionally powerful relationship, making it possible for their neuroses to become manifest in the transference situation rather than in behavior disorders, and then using modified psychoanalytic treatment.

Aichhorn's work inspired the founding of residential treatment centers not only for behaviorally disordered children but also for children with other forms of emotional disturbances. One of these centers is the Sonia Shankman Orthogenic School at the University of Chicago. Bruno Bettelheim, its director, published accounts of his treatment of very disturbed children in *Love Is Not Enough*. Bettelheim bases his approach on psychoanalytic theory; he points out that feigning love or giving lip service to loving a child "falls short of its purpose . . . without the appropriate or genuine emotions."[4] Fritz Redl and David Wineman also contributed to aiding residential children by their descriptions of how and why children's defenses break down and how a therapeutic milieu may help their reorganization.

Psychotherapy of Children

Psychoanalytic treatment of children with neurotic disorders was inaugurated by Sigmund Freud. In *Three Essays on the Theory of Sexuality* (1905) Freud delineated his theoretical concepts about childhood neuroses. Three years later Freud was consulted by the father of a five-year-old boy called little Hans, who had a severe phobia in regard to horses and who was constantly ruminating about penises. Freud encouraged the boy's father, a physician, to undertake the psychoanalytic treatment of the child under Freud's supervision. Freud saw the father in consultations and explained to him what the child feared. Much of the analysis of the phobia dealt with the fear that the horse, which the child unconsciously equated with the father, would castrate little Hans in retribution for the boy's hostility to the father. As a result of the treatment, the boy was relieved of his symptoms.

In 1919 Hermione von Hug-Hellmuth, a Viennese psychoanalyst who had realized that a child expresses himself more directly in play than verbally, published *A Study of the Mental Life of the Child,* in which she showed that a child's free play represented fantasy production and offered a way to understanding his unconscious processes. Her work marks the beginning of play therapy.

Hug-Hellmuth did not treat children under six, nor did she evolve any system for treating children; Melanie Klein (1882–1960) did both these things. Her technique replaced the free associations used in analysis of adults with play. She had studied under Ferenczi in Budapest and Abraham in Berlin; her book *The Psychoanalysis of Children,* which she dedicated to the memory of Karl Abraham, was first published in 1932. She extrapolated Freud's concepts about the unconscious life back to the earliest life of the infant. At first Klein visited the homes of her child analysands (one was as young as two years and nine months) in the belief that the child's play was really a symbolic way of mastering anxiety by re-creating family situations. Later she discontinued psychoanalytic investigations at the children's homes and instead offered her patients toys in her office.

On the basis of her work with children, Melanie Klein concluded that Oedipal hostility and guilt existed even prior to the third to sixth year of life, when Freud presumed that the Oedipal complex emerged. She was the first to draw attention to the fact that even an infant could feel hostile and aggressive to the parent of the opposite sex. Furthermore, she believed that because the mother's breast frequently frustrated the infant, as well as fed it, the breast was not only an object of love but of hostility. Klein believed that a child's paranoid feelings—caused by the fear that he will be destroyed by the father, who is his Oedipal rival, or the mother, whom he feels has frustrated him—originate in infancy. She considered that the child had knowledge of his parents' sexual relationship. To her, for instance, the child who bumped two play cars together was expressing symbolically his unconscious knowledge of parental sexual intercourse, even though he had never witnessed the primal scene. She considered, however, that psychoanalysis could protect all children from hostile and aggressive impulses that cause them unbearable guilt.

She advocated immediate and direct interpretation of the unconscious motivations of the child, arguing that a transference neurosis develops between the therapist and the child in which the child reenacts toward the therapist all the feelings displaced from the original parents and that this reenactment, just as in the psychoanalysis of adults, should be interpreted by the psychoanalyst. Klein took very little interest in the daily life of a child as reported by the parent or in the relationship between the child's mother and father. In essence, she felt that the young child's neurosis was dependent upon his own inner difficulties in handling his aggression; if the instinctual drives of the young child were interpreted as early as possible, she thought, his ego would be strengthened.

Klein developed an elaborate theoretical system about early psychodynamic processes that was modeled on clinical observations made on adults, even including such phenomena as paranoid and depressive reactions that subsume the preexistence of guilt feelings. The Oedipus complex, the superego, and the child's fear of retaliation for destructive impulses, according to Klein, develop at the beginning of extrauterine life.

Anna Freud, who came to England in 1938 with her father to escape the Nazis, works with children but holds some views that contrast with those of Melanie Klein. She believes that analysis is only "appropriate in the case of an infantile neurosis,"[5] and she has taken issue with Klein in respect to transference. She pointed out that although generally the child will transfer feelings that he has about his parent to the analyst, he does not develop a full-blown transference neurosis, as Klein believed, because the original parental love object is still influential while the child is being analyzed. The child is constantly interacting with the parents and therefore will not always transfer his inner fantasy life onto the analyst.

Another important distinction between the approaches of these two analysts centered around the utilization of interpretation. The Freudians are unwilling to interpret immediately deep material from the unconscious; they will utilize information from the play for later interpretation only after a meaningful therapeutic relationship has been established with the child. Anna Freud noted that, unlike adults, most children come to analysis with little or no motivation. As a rule, they have been forced to come by their parents. Before the child can be analyzed, a strong positive relationship with the analyst must develop, and the child must respect the analyst— otherwise interpretations will have no value. As an example, Anna Freud reports the case of a recalcitrant child with whom in order to establish a relationship she would do various things. If the child was interested in tying knots, Anna Freud tied more complicated knots so that the child would come to admire her. Winning the child's confidence as an important initial step in child therapy is generally accepted today by child analysts.

Anna Freud recognized that by playing the child adapts himself to reality. Play does not always reveal deep unconscious conflicts: if a child bumps two cars together, it does not necessarily mean that he is reenacting the primal scene. He may be reenacting an actual accident that he had seen that had caused him some consternation. Other analysts, such as Erik Erikson, believe that play is not merely a method of working out unconscious problems, but that in play the ego masters anxiety situations by recreating traumatic incidences. Anna Freud works closely with the parents, who report to her the daily events that might affect the content of the child's play. Perhaps the greatest difference between these two schools of child psychiatry is that the Kleinians proceed much in the way classical Freudians do with adults in interpreting the deepest layers of the unconscious, believing that this is the most important therapeutic factor, whereas Anna Freud and her school believe that the child's ego structure is still developing and that therefore the analyst not only should make appropriate interpretations but also should exert an educational influence on the child.

In her elaborations of the differences between child and adult analysis Anna Freud maintains the position that the child represents an "open system" in which spontaneous cures may occur because of the natural maturational process. She recognizes the significance of the corrective emotional experience as a therapeutic factor but restricts it to child analysis. She assesses maturity on the basis of the child's speech, control of the excremental functions, ability to orient to a strange environment without excessive fear, degree of emancipation from the mother, relation to other children, and ability to use toys constructively. She assesses pathology by establishing whether repression is temporary or persistent. Correction of early maternal deprivation is of great therapeutic significance, and she feels that only when faith in the mother is established can separation from her be tolerated. Most sound is her emphasis on flexibility of treatment, changing the technique from day to day to fit the situation.[6]

American workers have advocated certain other techniques of play therapy. David Levy introduced what he calls "relationship therapy." Like Anna Freud, Levy allies himself with the child and assumes a permissive attitude, so that, hopefully, the child will feel freer with the therapist than with his parents in discussing his innermost feelings. Levy believes that treatment aimed at insight should be the approach with children only when other methods have not worked. Levy has also introduced a "controlled play"; the therapist encourages the child to reenact situations that are believed to have been traumatic. This method allows the child to express the affect connected with the traumatic incident and serves as a release. Levy does not use the free-play technique of Anna Freud; instead he uses dolls that represent persons in defined situations and takes a more active role in the therapeutic procedure. This method is essentially based on the theory that by playing the child learns how to master certain interpersonal situations.

Frederick Allen (1890–1964) followed Aichhorn's therapeutic approach in presenting himself to the child as a warm human being and an ego ideal; once the child had identified with Allen, he was prepared to transfer these positive feelings to other adults in his environment and thereby improve his social relations. Allen did not interpret the meaning of play in terms of past experiences. He focused on the here and now and gave the child an opportunity to work out his feelings toward the therapist. Even though Allen's technique was similar to Aichhorn's, their theoretical orientations were different. Aichhorn believed that the child's basic drives are asocial and that he becomes a social creature only through education. Allen, on the other hand, assumed that the child has a creative potential within himself, and, if he is undisturbed, he will achieve a healthy development.

One of the leading American child psychiatrists in the United States, Lauretta Bender, also minimizes intellectual interpretations and stresses the importance of a permissive atmosphere wherein the child feels free to express his feelings. She uses puppets to reenact traumatic situations. Bender's technique allows the child more choice than does Levy's, which more actively controls the content of the play; in this respect Bender's approach is similar to Anna Freud's.

We have noted an interesting approach, popularized by Samuel Slavson, which involves observing and treating children in groups. Bender has shown puppet shows to groups of children with beneficial therapeutic results. J. L. Moreno has also used his psychodrama technique, with children portraying dramatic roles in group psychotherapeutic sessions. Moreno believes that the child who acts a role that derives from either his past experience or his fantasy is able to discharge pent-up affects through his participation in the drama. Since the audience at psychodramas may participate as freely as they choose, the child who is acting is brought into close emotional relationship with the group, which improves intragroup relatedness.

The foregoing account makes it apparent that the main trend in child psychotherapy is away from analyzing children with classical psychoanalytic techniques. One final warning about child therapy and child raising may be cited: the work of Margaret Gerard (1894–1954), who was one of the pioneers in the field of child psychiatry and who made important observations on psychosomatic symptoms, particularly enuresis, in children. Gerard emphasized that free play was to be distinguished from an unrealistic, overly permissive attitude that encourages the child to give vent to all of his chaotic impulses. She pointed out that complete license to express any and all feelings without some sort of structuring would lead to "character disintegration."

The field of child psychiatry developed from nineteenth-century attempts to improve the educational possibilities for mental defectives. It was advanced by work on psychological tests that were designed to determine the innate intellectual potentiality of all children. This led to the child-guidance movement in the United States, which was finally followed by play therapy inspired by psychoanalytic theory.

Mother-Child Relationships and Recent Research

The early mother-child relationship is so important for ensuing pathology that it has probably received more attention than any other aspect of child psychiatry. In the past two decades the mother-child unity has been studied by direct observation on lower animals as well as humans. These experiments contrast markedly with early psychoanalytic studies, which were based solely on adult patients' retrospective reports of their childhood experiences.

Leo Kanner, whose *Child Psychiatry* (1935) was the first textbook in English on the subject, described one kind of infant pathology that he claimed was closely related to the early mother-child relationship—the autistic child, who from birth appears withdrawn from social contact. Such a child either never or only late develops the ability to speak comprehensively. According to Kanner, this type of child is extremely skillful when dealing with objects—in fact, his dexterity may be excellently developed —but he is unable to relate meaningfully to people. Kanner found the mothers of these children to be intelligent but cold and very much emotionally removed from their children. Kanner thus considered autism a kind of childhood schizophrenia traceable to maternal influence.

Kanner's view is opposed by Lauretta Bender, who believes that schizophrenia has a biological foundation. Bender proposed that a "maturational lag" in the embryo is the real cause of the illness and that a later crisis situation merely precipitates an overt schizophrenic reaction in a child already genetically predisposed. Bender divides the childhood schizophrenias into three groups. Children who belong to the first group cannot talk and appear defective; it is these children she would call "autistic." The second group, the "pseudoneurotics," seem to be neurotic, but under closer scrutiny are found to be psychotic. The third group, who are also really psychotic, appear psychopathic because they are prone to delinquency.

Rene Spitz compared the development of babies from two different types of foundling homes. In one the infants received little attention or stimulation, although they were provided with proper nourishment. In the other (an institution for children whose mothers were in penal institutions), the mothers were permitted to fondle and play with the infants frequently. Spitz found that the infants in the first institution developed far more poorly than those in the latter and concluded that their lack of development was caused by "hospitalism"—living in an environment without proper maternal stimulation.[7] Spitz also described a condition he called "anaclitic depression," seen in children who as infants were denied proper maternal care. They tend to weep, withdraw, lose weight, become susceptible to infection, and may even die.[8]

Two other New York psychoanalysts, Margaret Fries and Margaret Ribble, who have worked extensively with infants believe that although there is a difference in the activity levels of infants from birth, the way in which the mother handles the child in the nursing period determines whether or not the child will become hyperactive or inactive. Ribble points out that "Painful tension states develop readily in babies who do not have appropriate and consistent psychological mothering."[9] She states that a disturbance in the mother-child relationship frequently leads to "exaggerated forms of autoerotism, such as prolonged thumb-sucking, retaining of stools, breath holding, and a variety of automatic movements which interfere with the development of the individual. . . ."[10] Ribble emphasizes that a warm mother-child relationship in the first year of life protects the child from many forms of physiological disturbance and that an unmothered infant will attempt to stimulate himself with rhythmical types of body movements, such as head-banging and excessive rocking. Ribble stresses that one of the mistakes in our present system of caring for newborns is that after being with the mother briefly the infant is taken away to the hospital nursery until the next day.

It has been established by now that rejecting or indifferent mothers often have tense and negativistic infants who may even fail to suck and in some cases become extremely withdrawn and semistuporous. Also, even a child's future intellectual capacity is apparently adversely affected by maternal deprivation. A notable study by Mary Leitch and Sybylle Escalona details what is stressful to an infant and how he reacts to the stress. They show that tenseness of the mothering person directly affects the level of tension of the infant.[11]

Another leading authority on the results of maternal separation or deprivation is John Bowlby, an English psychoanalyst. Two of his books, *Child Care and the Growth of Love* and *Maternal Care and Mental Health,* have had an influence on professional and lay people alike. Bowlby points out that the child separated from his mother goes through three phases— protest, despair, and finally detachment. During the protest stage he is angry that his mother has gone away; then he begins to lose hope that she will return; finally this despair turns to withdrawal and he becomes unresponsive. Bowlby relates these stages to mourning and maintains that the psychopathology of the infant is similar to Freud's classic description, *Mourning and Melancholia* (1917).[12] Bowlby points out that premature separation from mother evokes pathological forms of mourning similar to those seen in older children or in adults. Not every child is permanently crippled by being separated from his mother; Bowlby explains that damage from early deprivation depends on the age at which it begins, how long the deprivation persists, and what kind of substitute care is provided.[13] He agrees with Melanie Klein that the way in which a child reacts at the time of deprivation will determine how he reacts later in life to the loss of a loved one; but he does not accept her idea that the aggression the infant shows is in the service of the death instinct or that the infant is fearful of retaliation.

Another unfavorable form of mother-child relationship is "maternal overprotection," the kind of smothering love that can be so detrimental to personality development. David Levy analyzes the consequences in his book *Maternal Overprotection*. He categorizes overprotective mothers as either "indulgent" or domineering. Indulgent mothers allow their children to rule the roost and rarely impose disciplinary action; their children remain infantile in their demands and expectations. The children of the domineering mothers show a less conspicuous lack of character growth but exhibit more signs of neurosis, such as shyness, fear, anxiety, and exces-sively submissive behavior.[14]

The dissemination of information concerning the importance of the early mother-child bond has in many instances resulted in a tacit intimidation of mothers. Psychiatrists have been aware of this adverse result, and books such as Kanner's *In Defense of Mothers: How to Bring Up Children in Spite of the More Zealous Psychologists* have been written in order to counteract this trend. Fortunately, psychologically sophisticated pediatricians like Charles Aldrich and Benjamin Spock have informed the public about the psychological care of the infant.

The early mother-infant relationship has been examined in monkeys by Harry F. Harlow, who arranged for one group of baby monkeys to be fed from bottles attached to a wire "surrogate" mother and another group fed from bottles attached to terry-cloth surrogates. The wire mother was biologically adequate, but the monkeys fed in this manner showed more signs of emotional disturbance than those fed by the cloth figure and were less advanced than those fed by real monkeys. Harlow also observed that monkeys deprived of real mothering, if brought in contact with other monkeys early in life, can make a good adjustment. Thus, contact with other monkeys, be they mothers or peers, is essential to monkey adaptation.[15] Another animal study by H. S. Liddell showed the importance of early cutaneous contact with the mother. One of Liddell's animals was deprived of maternal contact, whereas its twin grew up normally under the mother's care. The animal that was isolated from the mother was far less able in later life to withstand experimentally induced trauma.[16] Ethological studies of imprinting in animals centered on the innate pattern of behavior in the offspring are pointing to critical periods when a lack of proper stimulation might result in striking perceptive, conceptual, or affective difficulties later in development.

Another important trend in recent psychiatric research has been the attempt to understand the influence of the father in the family, for example, how he indirectly affects the child in the nursing period by his attitude toward his wife. Furthermore, current research (by means of family therapy) into intrafamilial dynamics—the manner in which members of the family interact with each other—will undoubtedly reveal important psychological principles relevant to child psychiatry. Recent studies on psychosomatic conditions of childhood—ulcerative colitis, asthma, and rheumatoid arthritis—offer promising leads into understanding the influence of psychological stress upon specific organ dysfunction.

Although future research must certainly continue to explore the causes and treatment of retardation, great attention will also be directed to the question of creativity and the investigation of means to enhance the development of the creative child. It must also be borne in mind that the normal child, as well as the exceptional one, will benefit in the future from the application of psychological methods to education. Efforts are now under way to use group consultations to disseminate information from psychiatric experts to educators, religious teachers, and others. Sociologists are focusing on areas such as increasing urbanization and desegregation that force us to be keenly aware of the impact of these trends on our children.[17] Studies by men such as B. Pasamanick have undertaken to trace the course of mental disease in individuals from before birth to the onset of mental disturbance. These studies will concern all phases of the subject's life, including environment, culture, physical health, and other factors.

The greatest hope for the future is that this multidisciplined approach will not only lead to more effective treatment of psychological disorders in children but also will open the way to successful preventive child psychiatry for all economic groups.

CHAPTER **24**

The Psychosomatic Approach
in Medicine

Systematic clinical and experimental study of the interaction between mind
and body, one of the most recent developments in medicine, became
possible only after philosophical confusions about the two had been cleared
away.

As we have seen, the Western view that body and mind are separate
parts of man is as old as written history; although this fateful confusion
was codified by Descartes, it had existed long before he wrote and has
affected psychiatry more than any other field. Mythologies, religions, and
philosophies have been concerned with the relationship of body to mind,
but different ages and different thinkers evaluated it differently. The
Platonic notion was that the mind rules over the body, which is but the
executor of desires and ideas. Hippocrates, on the other hand, considered
psychological processes nothing but epiphenomena, insignificant reflections
of bodily processes that themselves were subject to the universal laws of
the physical universe.

Primitive man explained natural events in psychological terms. Modern
man first discarded this supernatural and spiritual view of the inanimate
world and then tried also to deanimate his view of himself to the point
where human personality was considered unimportant to the scientific
study of man. Only at the end of the nineteenth century did this particular
pendulum begin to swing back and personality—man's emotions and
motivations—become a legitimate object of methodical and controlled,
that is to say, scientific, inquiry. The psychosomatic approach in medicine
is the first attempt to extend past personality into the mind-body problem
itself.

Bodily reactions to emotions are among the most common experiences of everyday life. One feels afraid: his pulse becomes faster and his breathing deeper. One feels anger: his face flushes and his muscles tense. One feels disgust: his stomach begins to churn. Relieved from suspense, one reacts with a deep sigh. A clown makes our diaphragms go into spasmodic contractions, our facial muscles contort: we burst into laughter. We witness a tragic event or experience bereavement: our lachrymal glands begin to secrete tears and we weep.

Subjective sensations such as fear, anger, disgust, merriment, and sorrow thus mobilize highly complex bodily processes such as changes in the heart rate and blood circulation, in respiration, in stomach and bowel activity, in the muscle system, and in the glands. Because these phenomena belong to our everyday experience, we take them for granted and do not recognize that when we laugh or weep we are involved in one of the greatest mysteries of biological science. All such processes, in which the first links in a chain of events are perceived *subjectively* as emotions and the subsequent links are *objectively* observed as changes in body functions, are called psychosomatic phenomena. Their partially subjective, partially objective nature has led to the prevalent confusion about the dichotomy of mind versus body. The rise in blood pressure and increased heartbeat that accompany rage or fear can be studied objectively through measurement. Yet the rage and fear themselves can be experienced only subjectively and by the person involved. This fact of physiological *and* psychological events occurring in the same organism was interpreted in terms of a division of man into a psyche (soul) and a soma (body), and the study of man likewise was separated into these two general approaches, which remained separate and unbridged for centuries.

As we have just described, our feelings continuously influence our bodily functions. But experiences that work the opposite way are equally common, that is, bodily changes have an effect upon our psychology. This traffic goes both ways. We imbibe alcohol, which changes our bodily chemistry: we promptly react with changes in mood. Some of us lose our inhibitions and become aggressive, others become sentimental and weepy. Sedatives affect us physiologically: as a result, we feel sleepy. Tranquilizers relieve our emotional tensions. High fever makes us feel delirious.

It is obvious, therefore, that we are indivisible organisms. It is only the vantage point from which we choose to view ourselves that makes us seem otherwise. From the psychological point of view we take advantage of the fact that living beings are subjectively aware of much of what goes on within themselves: they feel hunger when the stomach is empty, pain when the normal body processes are disturbed, pleasure when needs are satisfied. In addition, human beings can communicate these internal psychological events by using words to describe subjectively perceived states of mind. The faculty of verbal communication is what makes the precise psychological study of human beings possible. The physiological point of view in general ignores subjective communication in favor of rigidly mechanical measurement of observable, very often external, reactions.

Because man is a complex physiological apparatus and at the same time a self-aware individual capable of verbal communication, he should be studied psychologically and physiologically at the same time. To reconcile the results of these two kinds of observation is the essence of the psychosomatic approach.*

Methodological Advancements

The development of psychosomatic medicine depended on certain advances in methodology and concepts, for even if some physicians since antiquity may have suspected that a patient's emotions influenced the course of his disease, they had no vocabulary adequate to describe the idea. Some physicians did attribute organic symptoms to emotional tensions—for example, a change in heartbeat due to emotional factors—but their training had prepared them to observe and describe only the physiological changes; they had no equally precise way of identifying or describing the causative emotional factors. They had to content themselves with meaningless generalities like "nervousness," "worry," or "overwork." And their psychological prescriptions had to be equally primitive and meaningless, such as "Don't worry," or "Relax," or "Cut out all this nonsense." Their clinical preparation simply did not prepare them to deal with emotional-stress situations that they suspected were underlying the physical symptoms.

Freud's method of free association for the first time allowed a precise study of causal sequences of psychological phenomena, because it focused on the hitherto neglected unconscious links that connect ideas. Free association not only permits the reconstruction of unconscious motivational links; it often brings these links into consciousness so that they could be very precisely observed. Thus the way was prepared for adequate study of both conscious and unconscious emotional stresses that might be contributing to an organic disease.

Another aspect of Freud's psychoanalytical theory also bore directly upon the field of psychosomatic medicine—the conclusions he drew from his experiments in hypnosis about the disappearance of hysterical physical symptoms† after hypnotized patients had expressed repressed emotions. These hysterical symptoms, Frued decided, were unusual bodily expressions of emotional tensions that for some reason were unacceptable or

---

* Formal recognition of this was evidenced when the *American Journal of Psychosomatic Medicine* was founded in 1939.

† Although hypnosis did not survive as a generally applicable treatment in chronic neuroses, because it does not alter the underlying causes, it found a medical application in pain reduction (obstetrics, dentistry, etc.) and in acute neuroses immediately following traumatic episodes (war neurosis, shell shock).

unbearable and hence had been excluded from consciousness and normal expression. They took symbolic expression in disturbed bodily functions. The price the hysterical patient pays for not facing his repudiated emotions is that the emotion disappears from consciousness and a dynamic substitute, the organic symptom, consisting in the disturbed function of an organ, arises in its place. Hence the expression "conversion hysteria."

This explanation for hysteria has since been validated by extensive clinical experience, but it explains only psychogenic symptoms occurring in muscles under voluntary control—for example, in the extremities or in sense organs like the eye, that receive perceptual or sensory stimuli.

Pioneers in psychosomatic medicine—Georg Groddeck (1866–1934) and Ernst Simmel (1882–1947) in Germany, Felix Deutsch (1884–1964) in Vienna, Smith Ely Jelliffe (1866–1945) in the United States, and Angel Garma in Argentina—uncritically attempted to explain all symptoms, even those affecting the visceral functions, as the direct expression of highly specific repressed ideas of fantasies. The internal vegetative organs entrusted with basic biological functions are not, however, constructed to express details of psychological content, unlike those organs—such as the vocal apparatus and facial muscles—that are voluntarily controlled and that express and communicate ideas. Furthermore, internal organs do not react to specific repressed ideas such as those that underlie hysterical symptoms, but to general emotional qualities. Neither do they, like conversion symptoms, *discharge* emotional tensions. The elevation of blood pressure in rage does not relieve the rage, but is sustained by it. Alexander in 1948 made this distinction between hysterical-conversion reactions and adaptive changes in vegetative functions called forth by emotional tensions.[1] He pointed out that the extension of the theory of conversion hysteria to all psychosomatic reactions is a typical example of an error that is common in the history of sciences—uncritically taking over concepts from one field in which they are valid and applying them to another field in which they are not applicable.

Emotional Factors in Disease

The development of our knowledge about the influence of emotions upon organic processes that are not under voluntary control had to wait until an American physiologist, Walter Cannon (1871–1945), introduced a new concept derived from his ingenious investigations into the bodily effects of rage and fear. Cannon showed that the organism responds to emergency situations with certain adaptive changes in its total physiological economy and demonstrated that emotional states activate physiological functions that prepare the organism for the situation that these emotions signalize. Fear and rage stimulate the adrenal glands; the adrenals activate the carbohydrate metabolism, so that sugar becomes readily available for energy. Both blood pressure and the distribution of blood change in such a way that blood flows increasingly to those organs needed for flight or "fight."[2] Simultaneously, anabolic and storing functions such as digestion and assimilation are inhibited: an organism that must mobilize all its resources to meet an emergency involving fear or rage cannot indulge in the luxury of digesting and storing food.

When Cannon's work on the mechanisms by which emotions influence the functions of the internal vital organs was applied to the study of emotional stress in chronic organic diseases, the psychosomatic era in medicine truly got under way. There was particular interest taken in emotional factors in organic diseases in Germany after World War I. One of the clearest of the thinkers and observers was Leopold Alkan, who consistently emphasized that chronic emotional tensions may produce physical alterations that become manifest as chronic organic diseases. Emotions may, for instance, produce lasting contractions and spasms in hollow organs, thus altering blood supply and eventually leading to atrophies. Spasms may lead also to such enlargements as dilatation of the esophagus or hypertrophy of the left ventricle of the heart in essential hypertension. Emotional stimulation of the endocrine glands may lead to tissue change, as it does in psychologically conditioned thyrotoxicosis. Alkan even considered that emotions played a causative role in diabetes, although he was not able to substantiate this experimentally as a primary etiological mechanism.

Felix Deutsch and Georg Groddeck were the most consistent proponents of the significance of emotional factors, not only in hysterical conversion symptoms but also in chronic organic diseases. Groddeck's theory is essentially similar to that of Carus, who preceded him by more than half a century. Groddeck was perhaps the most extreme representative of a panpsychological orientation. He took the position that the unconscious (*Das Es,* or the id) is the formative principle of all normal and abnormal bodily processes.* Organic diseases accordingly ultimately have a psychological nature, since they are the expressions of unconscious conflicts. Felix Deutsch's early point of view was not much different, since he applied Freud's concept of conversion to all dysfunctions of the body. Other men interested in psychosomatic phenomena were Karl Fahrenkamp, who demonstrated the influence of emotions on fluctuations of blood pressure and made a strong case for the psychogenic origin of essential hypertension; G. R. Heyer and Fritz Mohr, who published comprehensive books on the psychological treatment of organic diseases; and Viktor von Weizsäcker (1886–1957), professor of medicine in Heidelberg, whose thinking was strongly influenced by Freudian views. Weizsäcker believed that emotions influence bodily disturbances; he also pointed out that bodily disease affects the psyche. His most instructive contributions were his

* Freud borrowed the expression "id" from Groddeck.

brilliant case presentations, in which he impressively demonstrated the emotional components and antecedents of bodily diseases. The respectability of the psychosomatic approach was enhanced when Kurt Westphal and Gustav von Bergmann (1878–1955), suggested that most duodenal ulcers had a neurotic origin.

This German interest in psychosomatic medicine was brought to America by Alexander, who in 1932 initiated, at the Chicago Psychoanalytic Institute, the first systematic collaborative research in psychoanalysis focused on psychosomatic problems. Patients suffering from different forms of gastrointestinal disturbances, such as ulcer, colitis, and constipation, were given psychoanalytic treatment by analysts from the Chicago Institute team, who then looked for any psychological features that might be typical for the different diseases. Concurrently Flanders Dunbar (1902–1959) was also studying large numbers of patients with organic diseases, and both studies uncovered striking psychological similarities in patients suffering from the same organic disease. Dunbar formulated these similarities into her personality profiles; she described the ulcer personality, the coronary personality, and the arthritic personality, as well as a great many others.

The Chicago studies identified circumscribed conflict patterns characteristic for certain diseases that may appear in different kinds of personalities. The results were formulated as a vector theory, based on the general direction of the conflicting impulses involved in the disturbances. Alexander distinguished between three vectors: (1) the wish to incorporate, receive, or take in; (2) the wish to eliminate, to give, to expend energy for attacking, for accomplishing something, or for soiling; and (3) the wish to retain or accumulate. These concepts were taken over from the psychoanalytic theory of libido development. The emotional attitudes that are linked with the basic biological processes of intake, retention, and expenditure are easily recognizable as the emotional components of the functions of the gastrointestinal tract. Intake of food is related to oral impulses, passive receptiveness, aggressive incorporation, and biting. Elimination of the waste products is related to anal evacuation and the tendency to accumulate and retain, or anal retention. The psychological factors in the different gastrointestinal disturbances were described as conflicts among these three vectors. Stomach functions, for example, seemed to be disturbed in some patients who reacted with shame to their wish to receive help or love or to lean on another person. In others the conflict expressed itself as guilt about wanting to take something away from another person by force, as occurs in sibling rivalry among children who want to possess parental love alone and who also envy the possessions of their siblings. The reason why the stomach functions are vulnerable to this type of conflict was found in the well-established finding that eating constitutes the first gratification of the receptive incorporating urge. In the child's mind the wish to be loved and the wish to be fed become deeply linked. When in later life the wish to be helped by another person provokes shame, which is not an unusual reaction in a society that places a premium on the self-made man, the wish to be helped finds regressive gratification by an increased urge toward oral incorporation. This urge stimulates stomach secretion, and chronic hyper-secretion in disposed individuals may eventually lead to ulcer formation.[3]

In addition to the characteristic conflictual patterns found in duodenal-ulcer patients, psychodynamic constellations typical for six other chronic diseases were also described—ulcerative colitis, asthma, hypertension, rheumatoid arthritis, neurodermatitis, hyperthyroidism.

In disturbances of the bowels—psychogenic diarrhea and the different forms of colitis—the conflicts typically found centered around emotional difficulties (hopeless efforts) about accomplishment. Like patients with stomach troubles, these patients also show unconscious dependent tenden-cies, and they too try to compensate for them by the urge to give something in exchange for their receptive desires; however, they lack the self-confidence to realize these ambitions. When they lose hope of ever accomplishing what they have undertaken to do, their bowel disturbance appears. Other studies on ulcerative colitis have led to the suggestion that repressed destructive impulses and disturbances in or loss of a key relation-ship, accompanied by a feeling of hopelessness or despair, may also be factors underlying the illness. George L. Engel published a comprehensive review of the literature on ulcerative colitis and subjected the different theories to a careful critical evaluation.

In cases of rheumatoid arthritis the Chicago group found a conspicuous emotional emphasis upon muscular expression of emotions, an expression, however, that is extremely tightly controlled. In asthma the most specific psychological conflict centers around communication with key persons. The early mother-child relationship is disturbed; this disturbance expresses itself in the small child in a suppression of the impulse to cry; later the child is unable to establish frank, trusting verbal communication with the mother or mother substitutes.

In the cases of essential hypertension—chronic elevation of blood pressure characterized by the absence of a discernible organic cause, such as heart or kidney disease—the most conspicuous psychological pattern is an inhibition against the free expression of resentments felt toward other people because of a desire to be loved. These patients are like boiling volcanoes of pent-up, never fully expressed hostilities and resentments. As youths they may have been bullies, but then they discovered that they alienated others by their vindictiveness and consequently suppressed their hostile feelings. Patients with neurodermatitis had a conspicuous longing for physical contact that had been frustrated by undemonstrative parents; they showed, simultaneously, conspicuous exhibitionistic tendencies. And, finally, in the thyrotoxic patients, a basic fear for survival was established as having been the fundamental psychological stimulus—a finding that confirmed the old clinical observation of the sudden onset of this disease after an overwhelming traumatic experience. Thyrotoxic patients often experience psychological trauma early in life when they lose a loved one upon whom they depended. They then attempt to handle their dependency yearning by early attempts at achieving maturity, for example, by taking care of others instead of remaining in a dependent position.

Although most patients in the Chicago study showed psychological features that were characteristic for their disease, not everyone with the same characterological features develops the corresponding organic symptoms. It is obvious therefore that the presence of the psychological features alone do not explain the disease. Some other factors—most probably vulnerabilities of the affected organs that are either constitutional or acquired very early—must be present at the same time. This was called the "x factor": these organ vulnerabilities plus the specific psychological constellations are together responsible for the development of the organic symptoms. Moreover, these two factors are not necessarily two independent variables. This view of double causation—the coincidence of somatic and psychological factors—has been supported by the studies of Arthur Mirsky, who has identified the somatic factor in duodenal ulcer as a constitutional tendency to gastric hypersecretion.[4] Mirsky has been able to predict successfully which of a large sample of soldiers would later develop duodenal ulcers: they were all hypersecretors who at the same time displayed emotional conflict over their dependent leanings.

A psychophysiologic theory of *specificity* (relating specific emotional conflicts to specific organ systems) appears plausible inasmuch as there are striking psychophysiological correlations. In the thyrotoxic patient who strives toward early maturity, an organ that secretes a metabolic accelerator has become diseased. Chronically preparing to fight, the hypertensive individual has a dysfunction of the circulatory apparatus. The arthritic is one who gets ready to strike but inhibits the urge: his symptoms occur in joints that are closely related to the musculo-skeletal system. The patient with neurodermatitis, longing for physical closeness, has disturbances in the organ of contact. The asthmatic is inhibited in verbal communication, and an organ necessary for this function (the lung) is disturbed. The peptic-ulcer patient longs to be fed, and a lesion in the upper gastrointestinal tract develops. Only in ulcerative colitis are there as yet no direct psychophysiological correlations.[5]

The presence of these two factors—that is, constitutional or acquired organ vulnerability and a characteristic emotional-conflict pattern—still does not fully explain the actual onset of the symptoms. Both organic and psychological predispositions exist long before the disease actually develops. What, then, is responsible for the precipitation of the disease? Alexander and his collaborators proposed, in addition to the psychological configuration and the x factor, a third condition, the onset situation, which is defined as the precipitating life situation as it affects the patient. The onset situation is strictly a psychological concept. The same life situation—for example, being left by one's spouse—may be felt as a relief by one person and a catastrophe by another. A person with a specific organ vulnerability and a characteristic conflict pattern develops the corresponding disease only when a fortuitous turn of events in his life mobilizes his central conflict, leading to a breakdown of his psychological defenses. The candidate for thyrotoxicosis must be exposed to a perilous situation that threatens his survival before he develops any symptoms. The duodenal-ulcer candidate will develop his symptoms when his need for leaning on another person is frustrated beyond his tolerance; his ulcer symptoms are equally likely to appear if his wife leaves him or if he is promoted to a position that involves added responsibilities. With some luck, and if the proper situation never occurs, despite a predisposing physiological vulnerability and psychological pattern, an individual may never develop the disease to which he is both psychologically and organically susceptible.

During the last few decades there have been many other psychiatric and psychoanalytic investigations of patients suffering from the diseases discussed and from other chronic diseases as well. Some of these studies also indicate that chronic organic diseases have not only a specific organic pathology, but that the individual suffering from them also has a specific psychopathology. In other words, diseases of the body are closely correlated with characteristic disturbances of the emotional life. These studies also reveal that emotional factors participate in the causation of organic diseases, although by no means are they solely responsible for them. Some studies emphasize psychological factors specific to the organic illness, other than those identified by the Chicago group. Other investigators do not agree that there are characteristic emotional factors involved in the different diseases and maintain instead that a person with a vulnerable organ system might develop a disease of that system under the influence of any kind of emotional stress.

Alexander and French were not satisfied with impressions gained through clinical studies because it is often tempting to read a dynamic pattern into a case history. Some twelve years ago they inaugurated a blind diagnostic study of a large number of patients. Subjects with one of the seven so-called psychosomatic diseases were interviewed. The transcripts of the interviews were rigorously censored to exclude medical clues as well as to safeguard against the possibility that the interviewer might inadvertently reveal the diagnosis. A team of internists deduced the illness at a slightly higher rate (25 percent) than chance (14.4 percent). A team of psychoanalysts recognized the illness correctly almost twice as frequently as the internists (45 percent).[6] Even though this is a significant statistical finding, certain questions arise. Why was not the percentage of correct deductions by the analysts even greater? A reasonable answer would be that the specific dynamic formulations are not yet well enough refined or in some instances perhaps not explicit enough. On the other hand, certain specificity hypotheses perhaps need to be revamped.

In another study of emotional and physiological interactions, Therese Benedek and B. B. Rubinstein, with the help of daily temperature charts and vaginal smears, established the consecutive phases of the ovarian cycle in a group of women who at the same time were undergoing psychoanalysis. Independently, the psychoanalytic records were scrutinized and the changes in the emotional attitudes of the women—particularly the content of their dreams—were described during the consecutive phases of the menstrual cycle. A striking correspondence between the physiological phases of the menstrual cycle and psychoanalytic dream material was found.

Benedek and Rubinstein formulated these conclusions: "(1) The emotional manifestations of the sexual drive, like the reproductive function itself, are stimulated by gonad hormones; (2) parallel with the production of estrogen,* an active, extraverted heterosexual tendency motivates the behavior; (3) parallel with the progestin phase,† the psychosexual energy is directed inwardly as a passive-receptive and retentive tendency; thus (4) parallel with the hormonal cycle an emotional cycle evolves. The hormonal and emotional cycles together represent the *sexual cycle*."[7]

The Need for Experimental Corroboration of Psychosomatic Theories

One way of obtaining a more complete understanding of the psychological influence on body processes is to create in a laboratory setting different kinds of emotional-stress situations and directly observe their physiological sequelae. Some investigators have used the technique of so-called stress interviews, during which they discuss with the subjects upsetting episodes of their past lives and at the same time observe changes in blood circulation, respiration and nasal functions, stomach activity, and endocrinological responses. Other investigators have taken advantage of stressful real-life situations and studied the physiological responses of such subjects as students before examinations and paratroopers during training.

One of the most impressive psychosomatic studies was that of Thomas Holmes, Helen Goodell, Stewart Wolf, and Harold Wolff on nasal responses to threat and conflict. The authors, on the basis of both clinical and experimental studies, concluded that humiliation, frustration, and

* One of the female hormones important to the development of female sexual characteristics.
† Another female hormone, which is produced in larger quantity at the time of menstruation and during pregnancy.

resentment may produce nasal responses consisting of redness of the mucous membrane of the nose, marked swelling of the nasal turbinals, profuse secretion, and obstruction. These reactions are similar to those found when the person is exposed to local stimuli noxious to the nose and also when the integrity of the whole organism is threatened. They concluded that these local nasal reactions are attempts of the organism to shut out an unfavorable environment. In another publication Harold Wolff and his collaborators reported that in cases of anxiety and emotional conflict, a nasal hyperfunction ensues that intensifies common-cold symptoms and the magnitude of the mucous membrane's response to pollens.

Among the experimental studies of the physiological consequences of emotional stress, those of D. H. Funkenstein and his collaborators are significant. In the laboratory they created emotional-stress situations in their experimental subjects and succeeded in establishing differences in physiological responses to anger and fear. Whereas Cannon considered the overall physiological reactions to anger and fear as being the same, Funkenstein was able to differentiate between the physiological responses to fear and anger. These studies confirmed the views of Von Euler and some other investigators that rage increases the nor-adrenalin production of the adrenal medulla, whereas anxiety mobilizes adrenalin production. The generally accepted view that endocrinological secretions are influenced by emotional stress now became enriched by a more precise knowledge of the specific nature of these psychoendocrinological processes.

Another recent and most promising experimental approach to psychophysiological processes pertains to the study of sleep, in particular to the psychological and bodily effects of sleep deprivation and dream deprivation. Louis Jolyon West and his collaborators succeeded in experimentally producing psychotic states by continuously depriving normal persons of sleep. After the fifth sleepless day the basic ego function of reality testing began to fail. The subjects began to hallucinate and developed delusional ideas. At the same time, they became extremely suggestible. West and his collaborators suspected that sleep deprivation has been used in totalitarian states for brainwashing of prisoners. The results of sleep deprivation appear to be more closely related to actual psychotic states than the ones obtained by hallucinogenic drugs such as lysergic acid.

Of equal significance are the investigations by Charles Fisher and William C. Dement on dream deprivation. Kleitman and Dement in earlier experiments succeeded in demonstrating changes in electroencephalographic tracings and eye movements that occur synchronously with dream activity. In ingenious experimental studies Dement and Fisher consistently awakened their subjects whenever they began to dream. They then demonstrated that on subsequent nights in these subjects a compensatory dream activity developed, "dream deficit," which created tension and anxiety, "difficulty in concentration," "irritability," "motor incoordination," "disturbances in a time sense and in memory." They suggested that dream deprivation carried out intensively might even lead to dreamlike states while awake, to hallucinations, delusions, and other psychotic symptoms. By these studies they supplied evidence for Freud's views that dreams have a psychobiological function as vents through which psychological tensions are at least temporarily relieved.

Since the early 1930's Jules Masserman and his associates at Northwestern University, as a part of a comprehensive study integrating biological and psychological correlates ("biodynamics"), have been developing experimental methods for studying principles of psychotherapeutic interventions in animals. The animals were subjected to experimental procedures that created conflicts, and therefore neuroses, in them. For example, the animals were placed in a stress situation whereby they were forced to choose between mutually incompatible patterns for survival. A monkey was conditioned to go to a feedbox after a signal, then a toy snake was placed in the feedbox. Monkeys have an instinctual fear of snakes; they were thus faced with the prospect of starvation in order to avoid a mortal enemy. Masserman and his colleagues found certain procedures curative to these animals with experimentally induced neuroses. These methods are similar to those employed by psychiatrists in treating human beings under stress. They are as follows:

1. Satisfaction or a diminution of one of the conflictful biologic needs, such as frustrated hunger or frustrated sex.

2. Removal to a less stressful environment.

3. Forcing the solution by direct stress kept within the organism's tolerance. The example in humans would be to help an individual who is afraid of heights by gradual stages until he attains an imposing height.

4. Using social relationships to help the organism to adopt better patterns of behavior. An analogy would be sending a "problem child" to a "good school" where children behave in a culturally approved manner.

5. Employing "positive-transference" influence in helping to retrain the neurotic organism to healthier methods of adaptation. A gentle experimenter can gradually help an animal to overcome his resistance to approaching a conflictual stimulus. Interestingly, if the animal is consistently afraid of the experimenter, he cannot be retrained. In the same sense, a patient who associates the therapist with some figure who had a negative influence on him in the past ("negative transference") will be unable to improve until this situation is changed. The importance in animal therapy of the leverage supplied by a positive relationship between the neurotic animal and the experimenter (therapist) has been repeatedly demonstrated by the Masserman experiments.

6. Furnishing opportunities for the utilization of acquired skills for remastering a previous conflict situation. An analogy in humans is the

encouragement of a pilot who has been in a plane crash, but who was not injured, to fly again.

Masserman's experiments are examples of how animal studies, which are often suspect to the clinician, can yield meaningful practical information. In fact, the experimental production and cure of illnesses in animals has traditionally been a basic source of scientific medical knowledge. It is therefore understandable that psychoanalysts like Masserman, have interested themselves in basic research with neurotic animals.

It is still too soon to predict all the implications for medical theory and practice of these studies on the relation of physiological and psychological processes. As our knowledge advances, we are learning that emotional factors have an influence on practically every disease; they contribute even to the precipitation of such well-defined organic diseases as tuberculosis. Moreover, the importance of emotional stress varies from case to case, and it is not possible at present to estimate the relative significance of organic versus psychological factors.

The term "psychosomatic" should therefore be reserved to a general method of approach pertaining to the entire field of medicine. Every patient has a personality; his emotional tensions have an influence upon all processes of the body. The personality can be considered as a central government that is connected through *nervous* and *endocrine* pathways with all other parts of the body. It receives information from all parts of the body and can send out executive messages to all organs. Just as every citizen is affected if Washington changes the tax rate, so are all organs influenced by those central processes we call personality functions.

Knowledge of the interaction between emotional factors and the basic organic functions of the body is still in its beginnings, but its potential value is immense, since emotional factors are involved in all diseases. Precise knowledge of psychosomatic interaction will mean that a more direct and active psychotherapy can be intelligently coordinated with the general medical management of the patient.

The psychosomatic approach entails teamwork. During the acute phase of the illness and during hospitalization, treatment of necessity must center around the medical management of the patient. This portion of the comprehensive medical management is carried out by medical specialists. When the acute symptoms are under control, ideally the focus of attention shifts to systematic psychotherapy carried out by psychiatrists, who try to relieve those chronic emotional stresses that contribute to the illness.

In treating chronic diseases discussed in this section, medical management alone seldom can bring about permanent relief. If the emotional stress resulting from unresolved conflicts persists, the patient will unavoidably relapse. The chronic emotional stimuli resulting from conflicts must also be eliminated, or at least reduced, to ensure permanent cure. Close collaboration between medical specialists and psychiatrists must be based on mutual understanding of and respect for each other's specialized knowledge; so far it exists only in a limited number of medical centers. That it exists at all is probably one of the significant advancements in modern medicine.

It still occurs that a patient suffering from an organic disease in which emotional factors are suspected to have an etiological role must go secretly to a psychiatrist, hiding this fact from his treating physician so as not to arouse his ire; and some psychiatrists treating patients suffering from chronic organic conditions frown upon the patient's continued contact with an organicist as something that would interfere with the psychiatric treatment. This antagonism between the organicist and the medical psychologist is an indication of one of the most common weaknesses of the human mind—to seek either-or solutions. Fortunately, monocausal explanations are gradually losing ground in all fields of medicine.

The prevailing trend in the United States toward the establishment of psychiatric departments in general hospitals is indeed encouraging. Pioneering physicians in such hospitals—psychiatrists as well as organicists—are frequently successful in bringing about a meaningful integration of the somatic and psychological management of both psychiatric and organic cases. The mental asylum that is isolated both geographically and ideologically from the medical centers is being looked upon by many as only a vestige of the past.

CHAPTER **25**

Outlook

Human motivations—love, hate, hope, despair, revenge, the actual content of a person's life, all his most significant and real experiences—can be meaningfully explained only psychologically. The basic position of the present-day psychosomatic approach is that man's personality and body constitute an indivisible whole and that medicine must approach personality problems and their bodily effects with a combination of psychological and somatic methods of treatment. The psychological approach is but another avenue to influence the organism. Psychology and biology deal with the same complex organism and they represent but two different aspects of it.

There is little doubt that in building the bridge between the knowledge of brain structure, on the one hand, and of behavior, on the other, the new science of cybernetics and communication theory will play a preeminent part. This contribution comes primarily from technology. Brain processes as well as thought processes can be well visualized as transmission of coded messages in a complex communications system governed by basic universal principles. The next step in these developments obviously will be the understanding of the transmission not only of signals but also of meanings, something that even the most ingenious minds working in these fields cannot now accomplish. In view of these developments, it can be expected that the coming years will be characterized by a growing collaboration among psychiatrists, psychoanalysts, experimental psychologists, physiologists, and engineers, leading to a comprehensive view of human and animal behavior. The multidisciplinary approach, furthermore, will study man not only as a biological organism and an individual personality but also as a member of a higher system—society. How the whole social configuration, the institutions and values prevailing in a society, contributes to the shaping of personality is a question that will attract the attention of the best minds in the fields of psychiatry, anthropology, and the social sciences.

In spite of recent strides toward such integration, the field of psychiatry is still in a state of flux. These different approaches coexist but have not been unified into a cohesive system. We may visualize, however, future development in at least four directions.

First, a continued and growing interest in the psychological approach, which will consist of a more precise description and psychodynamic understanding of the psychotherapeutic process. The crucial step will come from breaking through the incognito barrier of the therapist, who to date has been—as a participant observer—the sole source of knowledge of the intricate interpersonal relationship between therapist and patient. Exposing the treatment procedure, including the therapist, to nonparticipant observers and recording all the happenings of the therapy, all verbal and nonverbal communication, will make this material approachable to study and restudy by others.

Second, there is every indication that psychosomatic interest will continue as one of the main avenues of integration of psychological and physiological phenomena. The old philosophical mind-body dichotomy is already being rapidly liquidated. New developments will come from an increasing emphasis on experimental procedures in which the emotional-stress situations as they occur in everyday life will be realistically reproduced and studied as they affect the whole organism. One may expect further ingenious experimental use for research of art—particularly motion-picture films—by which all the existing human conflicts can be aroused in the viewer.

Third, recent advances in pharmacology, because of their great practical value for the management of hospitalized patients, will enrich our ability to regulate the intensity of excitations in the different parts of the nervous system. The theoretical yield of these developments cannot yet be fully visualized, but it does not seem probable, as some authors believe, that pharmocological and biochemical methods will throw more light upon the complex phenomena of interpersonal relationships and replace psychological methods of treatment. It appears rather that the psychological approach cannot be replaced but will remain the principal method.

Fourth, the sociological point of view necessarily will grow in significance.

We live in an era of collaboration and integration. The solitary man of the nineteenth century with his impregnable self-sufficient system of values is rapidly yielding his place to the communal, the so-called other-directed person with a soul, searching vainly for his own identity. The imprint of this cultural shift upon psychiatry manifests itself in the growing interest in group dynamics and its sociological aspects. Consequently future developments will consist in a growing integration of the biological, psychodynamic, and sociological approaches and the emergence of a comprehensive psychiatry no longer trying to solve the great mystery of human behavior from one single restricted point of view, but by each approach trying to enrich itself by considering contributions coming from the other avenues of approach.

This need for integration is the latest in the great chain of needs that has marked the evolution of psychiatry through the ages. As other needs have been met, so will this, and as a result other challenges will come into being. In this study we have seen how man has met the pervasive need to know himself. In the living stream of influence from Plato to St. Augustine to Spinoza to Vives to Heinroth to Freud, we have seen man's recognition and increased understanding of the vital principle of psychic reality, and we have watched man delve into the strange realm of his deepest motivations. Similarly, beginning with Hippocrates and continuing with Plater, Sydenham, Esquirol, and Kraepelin, we have seen mental illness brought under the framework of clinical medicine. Finally, in the persons of Soranus and Cicero, the medieval monks, the courageous Weyer, and men of mercy such as Pinel, Chiarugi, and the Tukes, we have seen psychiatry free the mentally ill from the lashes of misunderstanding and the chains of brutalization and make available to them methods of psychotherapy aimed at actual cure. We have seen this line of development move from Reil, with his techniques of persuasion, to the moral therapists and then to the work of Charcot and Bernheim and to the revolutionary breakthrough wrought by Freud. All these developments, those that succeeded and those that failed, were in answer to man's unending challenge to come to terms with himself as he wishes to be and as he really is.

The challenge is unending because psychiatry, having just come of age, has much more to learn. New and dynamic concepts are being offered, and opposition to established principles is being raised. There is even a movement to cast aside some sixty years of knowledge and ideas amassed through the Freudian approach. It must be for psychiatry to retain its sense of proportion, to recognize that although the Freudian approach has its limitations, it would be absurd not to make use of the great work that has grown out of Freud's legacy.

And the challenge will continue because today only a relatively small number of men, women, and children who need psychiatric help can obtain it. Lack of money, lack of facilities, and lack of enlightened public policy still conspire with man's ancient prejudices to keep the emotionally disturbed in chains of neglect and misery. Not until all people, whatever their wealth, race, creed, locale, or status, can find the help psychiatry can offer will the great psychiatric tradition truly come into its own.

The Founders of the American Psychiatric Association

On October 16, 1844, thirteen physicians who were also superintendents of mental institutions met in Philadelphia and formed the American Association of Medical Superintendents. This organization later became the American Psychiatric Association. The thirteen founders were:

Samuel Woodward (1787–1850), who served as the first president. One of the founders of the Hartford Retreat in Connecticut and former legislator from that state, Woodward had an active interest in the treatmentment of alcoholics and was the author of *Essays on Asylums for Inebriates* (1838).

Samuel White (1777–1845), who was the first vice-president, inaugurated the Hudson Lunatic Asylum in New York.

Thomas Kirkbride (1809–1883), superintendent of the Pennsylvania Hospital and guiding spirit of "model-hospital" building, was the first secretary-treasurer.

Amariah Brigham (1798–1849) was the founder and first editor of the *American Journal of Insanity,* which later became the *American Journal of Psychiatry.* He was superintendent of the first public institution for the mentally ill in New York State—the Lunatic Asylum at Utica.

Isaac Ray (1807–1881), superintendent of the State Hospital at Augusta, Maine, published in 1838 his *Treatise on the Medical Jurisprudence of Insanity,* which was the first text written in English on forensic psychiatry.

---

* Most of the information in this appendix has been taken from Nolan Lewis, "American Pyschology from Its Beginnings to World War II, *Handbook of Psychiatry,* Vol. I, pp. 5–7. Ed. by S. Arieti. New York: Basic Books, Inc., 1959.

Pliny Earle (1809–1892), the superintendent of the Bloomingdale Hospital in New York, occupied one of the first professorships of psychological medicine, at the Berkshire Medical Institution in Pittsfield, Massachusetts. He wrote the influential and optimistic *Curability of Insanity* (1877).

Luther Bell (1806–1862), superintendent of the McLean Asylum in Somerville, Massachusets, wrote on acute psychotic conditions and on other medical subjects.

William Awl (1799–1876) was an organizer of the Ohio State Asylum.

Nehemiah Cutter (1787–1859) organized a private hospital, the Pepperell Asylum, in Massachusetts.

Francis Stribling (1810–1874) was superintendent of the Western Lunatic Asylum of Virginia.

John Butler (1803–1890) was superintendent of the Boston Lunatic Asylum and later superintendent of the Hartford Retreat (after Brigham).

John Galt (1819–1862), the first superintendent of Williamsburg Asylum, published *The Treatment of Insanity* (1846), a compilation of all the known facts about mental illness.

Dr. Charles Stedman (1805–1866) followed Butler as superintendent of the Boston Lunatic Hospital and edited a translation of the phrenologist Spurzheim on the anatomy of the brain.

APPENDIX B

Jung and the National Socialists

After Hitler came to power, Jung made concessions to the Nazi racial philosophy, which supports the impression that he lacked Freud's uncompromising moral fortitude and also Freud's scientific objectivity. Moreover, this episode in Jung's career illustrates the perversion of Freud's ideas by the National Socialists.

In 1933 the New German Society of Psychotherapy was organized by Hitler's appointee, Dr. M. H. Göring, a relative of the Nazi leader, Hermann Göring. In the same year, Professor Kretschmer, the president of the Society, resigned and Jung took over the presidency, along with the editorship of the official journal of the Society, *Zentralblatt für Psychotherapie.*

The Society and its journal officially accepted the Nazi outlook. Göring pronounced this change in unmistakable words in the first issue of the reorganized journal: "This Society has the task of unifying all German physicians in the spirit of the National Socialistic government . . . particularly those physicians who are willing to practice psychiatry according to the 'Weltanschauung' of the National Socialists."[1]* Jung wrote a brief introductory statement to the same issue in which, among other politically ambiguous sentences, he states: "The factual and well-known differences between Germanic and Jewish psychology should no longer be blurred, which can only benefit science."[2] In the next issue of the same journal, in a confused article, "The Present Situation of Psychotherapy," Jung severely attacked Freud's views concerning the significance of the infantile roots of neurosis. In this article Jung attacked also the "Jewish theory" of Adler about the will for power as the basic motivating force. Comparing his own emphasis upon the creative aspects of the unconscious mind with Freud's hedonistic views (the pleasure principle), he accused Freud and Adler of

* Translations from the *Zentralblatt* by the authors.

seeing only the shadowy sides of human nature. He attributed the popularity of Freud's treatment method to the fact that the psychoanalyst underevaluates the patient's personality, "hits the patient in his vulnerable spot and this way he cheaply gains superiority. . . . There are really decent people who are not cheaters and who do not use ideals and values for the beautification of their inferior personality. To treat such persons reductively* and to attribute to them ulterior motives and to suspect behind their natural purity an unnatural dirt is not only sinfully stupid, but criminal."[3]

That Jung, who knew better, could put on paper such a demagogic falsification of Freud's views can be explained only as an attempt to justify in pseudoscientific language the Nazi's views about the lowness of Jewish mentality.

Jung writes, "The Jews have this similarity common with women: as the physically weaker ones they must aim at the gaps in the opponent's defenses, and because of this technique which was forced upon them through centuries, the Jews have the best defenses where others are most vulnerable. . . . Because of their ancient culture they are capable quite consciously even in the most friendly and tolerant environment to indulge in their own vices, while we are too young not to have 'illusions' about ourselves. . . . The Jew, a cultural nomad, has never and probably will never create his own cultural forms because all his instincts and gifts depend on a more or less civilized host nation. The Arian unconscious has a higher potential than the Jewish; this is an advantage and a disadvantage of a youthfulness which still is nearer to barbarism."[4] Jung considers the Aryan's psyche both more barbarian and more creative: "The unconscious mind of the Arian contains tensions and creative elements to be realized in the future. It is dangerous and not permissible to de-evaluate these creative forces as childhood's romanticism. . . . In my opinion it was an error of the hitherto existing medical psychology that it applied unwittingly the Jewish categories—which are not even valid for all Jews—to Germans and Christian Slavs. The most valuable secret of the German personality, its creative intuitive soul, was declared to be a childlike-banal morass. At the same time my warning voice was suspected as anti-Semitism. This suspicion originated with Freud. He knew the German soul as little as his German idolators knew it. Did they learn something from the powerful appearance of National Socialism upon which the whole world looks with amazed eyes: Where was the unprecedented tension and momentum when National Socialism did not yet exist? It was hidden in the German soul, in its depth, which is anything else but a wastebasket for unfulfilled childhood desires and unsettled family resentments. A movement which takes hold of a whole nation must have become rife in each person."[5]

Ernest Harms in an article, "Carl Gustav Jung—Defender of Freud and

* The word "reductively" refers to Freud's genetic explanations that the later, "higher" aspirations of man develop from more primitive, originally nonsocial trends.

the Jews," makes an elaborate but most unconvincing effort to vindicate Jung's activities during this period. His emphasis is that Jung was not anti-Semitic and that he tried to defend Freud and the Jewish psychiatrists in general as much as it was possible in those days. Harms does not dispel the impression, however, that Jung saw in the National Socialist movement an opportunity to get back at Freud and to liquidate Freudian psychoanalysis in Germany by declaring it unacceptable to the German personality. Jung refers to psychoanalysis as a "soulless materialistic movement," the product of a noncreative race, which cannot grasp the depths of the creative intuitive German genius. Jung was not a German citizen and had no excuse for becoming the leader of a new kind of Germanic psychiatry and the editor-in-chief of a journal that openly and officially subscribed to the philosophy of National Socialism. Accepting leadership in this new psychiatric movement, which had a decided political orientation, Jung actually became the leader of psychiatry in Middle Europe. His motives were neither anti-Semitism nor a real conviction about the principles of National Socialism. In a letter to a colleague, quoted by Harms, Jung tries to refute the rumor about his anti-Semitism. He ends his letter with the following highly self-revelatory sentence: "The next thing people will invent is that I suffer from a complete lack of principles and am neither an anti-Semite nor a Nazi."[6] This is exactly what Jung himself demonstrated in the rest of his letter. The question inevitably arises: What, then, motivated Jung to declare that Freud's psychology was unsuited for non-Jews, a psychology to which he himself contributed and that he extolled and defended in previous years? And what moved him to play a prominent role in a new racially oriented psychological movement? Since it was obviously neither racial prejudice nor Nazi conviction, what was it, then? It is difficult to evade the answer that it was sheer *opportunism*. Freud's suspicion was that Jung, to achieve acclaim, was not immune to allowing his views to be influenced by public opinion. This is strongly supported by Jung's activities and writings during the Hitler era.*

---

* E. A. Bennet, in *C. G. Jung* (London: Barrie & Rockliff, 1961), takes issue with the remarks in Appendix B (on pp. 56–62).

The Organization of Psychoanalytic and Psychiatric Teaching, Practice, and Research

The Psychoanalytic Movement

In the last thirty years, particularly in the United States, the institutionalization of psychoanalysis has made rapid advances. Psychoanalytic institutes have thoroughly organized the training of psychiatrists for the practice of psychoanalysis.

The first American psychoanalytic institute was founded in New York in 1931. A year later the Chicago institute was set up and after that seventeen institutes in various cities, plus three training centers, were created. All the institutes now operate under the supervision of a central national educational body, which has established compulsory minimal standards and which has the last word, through its membership committee, about the eligibility of students for membership in the American Psychoanalytic Association. This membership is equivalent to certification as a psychoanalytic specialist and corresponds to certification in a medical specialty by a medical specialty board. One important difference does exist, however, between the certification of a physician in a medical specialty and admission of a student of psychoanalysis to the American Psychoanalytic Association: specialty boards subject applicants to a thorough professional-competence examination, whereas the membership committee of the American Psychoanalytic Association decides on the applicant's qualifications on the basis of written reports from teachers with whom he had studied at his institute.

This centralization and standardization of training, which went into effect in the 1940's only after considerable controversy, is unique to American psychoanalytic organization. When the controversy raged, a minority group held the position that psychoanalysis had not yet advanced to the point where it could afford a rigidly enforced, centralized training setup. Those who advocated the creation of a centrally controlled national teaching system argued that the profession had no protection against unqualified and self-styled psychoanalysts and no way to protect the public from unscrupulous therapists. Although conformity has been imposed successfully by the Association, many analysts still have reservations about its desirability.[1]

A number of psychoanalysts expressed misgivings about the spirit of "indoctrination" that prevails in psychoanalytic institutes. Edward Glover, one of the leaders of psychoanalysis in England, thus expressed his reservations: "It is scarcely to be expected that a student who has spent years under the artificial . . . conditions of a training analysis and whose professional career depends on overcoming 'resistance' to the satisfaction of his training analyst, can be in a favorable position to defend his scientific integrity against the analyst's theory and practice . . . for according to his analyst, the candidate's objections to interpretations rate as resistance. In short, there is a tendency in the training situation to perpetuate error."[2]

In several writings Alexander expressed reservations about the premature standardization and rigidity in teaching carried out in most psychoanalytic institutes.* He maintained that the essential questions are: How do the numerical rules and uniform standards influence the moral aspects of training? How do they influence the morale of the teachers and of the students? More specifically, the question is whether or not these numerical regulations introduced a greater evil than the individual laxities of the past. What is it, then, in our educational system that requires a change? It is not the details of our system that require revision, but its spirit. The institutes teach well the principles of psychodynamics, psychoanalytic psychopathology, dream theory, and practice of dream interpretation, the known facts of personality development. Our educational system requires fundamental improvement in basic orientation suitable for preparing sound practitioners who can use theoretical knowledge for therapeutic purposes, unimpeded by traditional, untested rules and regulations. The central core of all these weaknesses of our educational system is that in teaching we are more past-than future-oriented. Not as individuals, but as an organized group of teachers we do not stress sufficiently to our students that psychoanalysis— particularly its therapeutic application—does not represent a static system

* Institutes require a minimum number of hours to be spent in a training analysis, which is basically a therapeutic analysis conducted by senior members of the institute who have been designated as training analysts. The latter also supervise students (other than those whom they analyze) in their analyses of patients. There is a minimum number of sessions that the candidate must have with his supervisors.

of well-substantiated rules of procedure, but that it is a steadily developing field, pregnant with uncertainties, and that it requires steady revision. *What we can teach to the students without reservation is the science of psychodynamic reasoning demonsrated on live clinical material.*[3]

In 1955 some psychoanalysts, as a reaction against the conformist trend prevailing in the American Psychoanalytic Association, founded a scientific forum called the Academy of Psychoanalysis. Its aim was to serve as a platform for exchanging ideas of common interest for psychoanalysts and representatives of related disciplines. It is not a union type of professional organization of practitioners, but furnishes a meeting place for the exchange of ideas for those who have been trained and recognized by different psychoanalytic training institutes.

In sum, then, the American Psychoanalytic Association has, through its efficient organizational measures, preserved and taught effectively the basic tenets and practices of the Freudian school. However, with few exceptions, people sufficiently trained in scientific research, such as experimental psychologists, have not participated in psychoanalytic training programs. Therefore, this system, although successful in preserving the important contributions that psychoanalysis in the past introduced into psychiatry, has slowed the further advancement of psychoanalytic research.

One of the most pressing problems at present consists in the need for the coordination of psychiatric training of residents in universities with their training in psychoanalytic institutes.

Training of Psychiatrists

During the last thirty years the United States has taken over leadership in psychiatric training and research. The training of psychiatrists has, during the last decades, become consolidated and formalized in university departments of psychiatry and a few teaching hospitals, where a three-year curriculum for psychiatric residents has been established. This curriculum involves some theoretical instruction; most of it is supervised clinical work with patients. Psychiatric residency programs are not as rigidly formalized as the programs of the psychoanalytic institutes; they are somewhat more experimental and differ from training center to training center.

One problem that has still not been solved satisfactorily arises when a psychiatric resident wants to acquire psychoanalytic knowledge. If he enlists as a candidate in a psychoanalytic institute he must thereafter divide his time between two institutions. The coordination of these two kinds of training for the practice of psychiatry is imperative, but so far full integration has not been achieved.

However, in spite of the powerful influence of the traditional isolation of psychoanalytic training in independent institutes, the separation of this training from residency training is less marked. Once proper training staffs, including training analysts who can participate in theoretical instruction and who can undertake both the preparatory analysis and the supervision of the candidates' work, can be established, there is no reason why such specialized training cannot be offered within the same department of each existing medical school.

Notes

CHAPTER 3. *Contributions of the Ancients*

1. Mackenzie, D. *Infancy of Medicine*. London: Macmillan & Co., 1927.
2. Sigerist, H. *History of Medicine*, Vol. I, p. 175. New York and London: Oxford University Press, 1951.
3. Robinson, V. *The Story of Medicine*. New York: The New Home Library, 1944.
4. Gordon, B. L. *Medicine Throughout Antiquity*. Philadelphia: F. A. Davis Co., 1949.
5. Sigerist, *op. cit.*, p. 490.
6. *Medicine and Pharmacy: An Informal History of Ancient Egypt*. Bloomfield, N.J.: Schering Corp., 1955.
7. Castiglioni, A. *A History of Medicine*. New York: Alfred A. Knopf, 1947.
8. *Ibid.*, p. 57.
9. Gold, H. R. *Psychiatry and the Talmud*, Vol. I, No. 1. Jewish Heritage, 1957.
10. Sotah 42, as quoted by Gold, *op. cit.*, p. 11.
11. Atkinson, D. *Magic, Myth and Medicine*. Cleveland: World Publishing Co., 1956.
12. Whitwell, J. R. *Historical Notes on Psychiatry*, p. 28. London: H. K. Lewis & Co., Ltd., 1936.
13. Gordon, *op. cit.*, p. 299.
14. Zilboorg, G., with G. W. Henry. *A History of Medical Psychology*, p. 32. New York: W. W. Norton & Co., Inc., 1941.

CHAPTER 4. *The Classical Era*

1. Edelstein, L. and E. *Aesculapius*, Vol. II. Baltimore: Johns Hopkins Press, 1945.
2. Leonardo, R. A. *The History of Medical Thought*, p. 16. New York: Froben, 1946.
3. Heidel, W. A. *Hippocratic Medicine*. New York: Columbia University Press, 1941.

[415

4. Chadwick, J., and W. Mann. *Hippocrates,* p. 148. London: Blackwell, 1950.

5. Peterson, W. P. *The Hippocratic Wisdom,* pp. 44, 45. Springfield, Ill.: Charles C Thomas, 1946.

6. Gordon, B. L. *Medicine Throughout Antiquity.* Philadelphia: F. A. Davis Co., 1949.

7. Robinson, V. *The Story of Medicine,* pp. 83–84. New York: The New Home Library, 1944.

8. Robinson, *op. cit.,* p. 119.

9. Gordon, *op. cit.,* p. 711.

10. Cicero, M. T. *Tusculan Disputations,* p. 225. Trans. by J. E. King. London: William Heinemann; New York: G. P. Putnam's Sons, 1927.

11. *Ibid.,* p. 237.

12. Cicero, M. T. *The Academic Questions, Treatise de Finibus, and Tusculan Disputations,* p. 410. Trans. by C. D. Yonge. London: George Bell and Sons, 1878.

13. *Ibid.,* p. 431.

14. Aurelanius, C. *On Acute Disease and On Chronic Disease,* p. 39. Trans. by I. E. Drabkin. Chicago: University of Chicago Press, 1950.

15. *Ibid.,* p. 43.

CHAPTER 5. *The Medieval Period*

1. MacKinnzy, L. C. *Early Medieval Medicine,* p. 50. Baltimore: Johns Hopkins Press, 1937.

2. Wright, E. *Medieval Attitudes Toward Mental Illness,* p. 356. Bulletin, History of Medicine, Vol. VII, 1939.

3. Walsh, J. J., *Medieval Medicine,* p. 201. London: Black, 1920.

4. *Brett's History of Psychology,* p. 215. Ed. by R. S. Peters. London: George Allen and Unwin, Ltd.; New York: The Macmillan Co., 1953.

5. St. Augustine, *Confessions,* pp. 166–167. Trans. by E. B. Pusey. New York: The Modern Library, 1949.

6. *Ibid.,* pp. 190–192.

7. *Ibid.,* p. 7.

8. *Ibid.,* pp. 9, 10.

9. *Ibid.,* pp. 10, 11.

10. *Ibid.,* p. 15.

11. *Ibid.,* p. 17.

12. *Ibid.,* p. 19.

13. *Ibid.,* pp. 29, 31.

14. *Ibid.,* p. 34.

15. *Ibid.,* p. 67.

16. *Ibid.,* p. 55.

17. Browne, E. G. *Arabian Medicine,* p. 83. Cambridge: The University Press, 1921.

18. Martí-Ibáñez, F. *Centaur-Essays on the History of Medical Ideas,* p. 90. M.D. Publications, 1958.

19. Robinson, V. *The Story of Medicine,* p. 192. New York: The New Home Library, 1944.

20. Browne, *op. cit.,* p. 84.

21. Robinson, *op. cit.,* p. 162.

22. Martí-Ibáñez, *op. cit.,* p. 92.

23. Browne, *op. cit.*, p. 85.

24. *Ibid.*, p. 89.

25. Zilboorg, G., with G. W. Henry. *A History of Medical Psychology*, p. 126. New York: W. W. Norton & Co., Inc., 1941.

26. Ackerknecht, E. H. *A Short History of Psychiatry*. Trans. by S. Wolff. New York and London: Hafner Publishing Co., 1959.

27. Whitwell, J. R. *Historical Notes on Psychiatry*, p. 195. London: H. K. Lewis and Co., Ltd., 1936.

28. Havelock Ellis as quoted by Bromberg, W. *The Mind of Man*, p. 51. New York: Harper & Brothers (Torchbooks), 1959.

29. Zilboorg, G. *The Medical Man and the Witch During the Renaissance.* Baltimore: Johns Hopkins Press, 1935.

30. Institoris, H. *Malleus Maleficarum*, p. 87. Trans. by the Rev. Montague Summers. London: Pushkin, 1928.

31. *Ibid.*, p. 47.

32. Zilboorg, G., with G. W. Henry. *A History of Medical Psychology*, p. 161.

CHAPTER 6. *The Renaissance*

1. Russell, B. *A History of Western Philosophy*, p. 495. New York: Simon and Schuster, 1945.

2. Robinson, V. *The Story of Medicine*, p. 249. New York: The New Home Library, 1944.

3. Malraux, A. *The Voices of Silence*. Trans. by S. Gilbert. New York: Doubleday and Co., Inc., 1953.

4. Ortega y Gasset, J. *Man and Crisis*, p. 186. New York: W. W. Norton & Co., Inc., 1958.

5. Osler, W. *Evolution of Modern Medicine*, p. 120. New Haven, Conn.: Yale University Press, 1921.

6. "Hand and Medicine," *M.D. Magazine*, March, 1960, p. 90. Ed. by F. Martí-Ibáñez.

7. Ore, O. *Cardano: The Gambling Scholar*, p. 25. Princeton, N.J.: Princeton University Press, 1953.

8. *Ibid.*, p. 47.

9. Gorton, D. A. *History of Medicine*, p. 205. New York and London: G. P. Putnam's Sons, 1910.

10. Laurence, R. M. *Primitive Psychotherapy and Quackery*, p. 255. Boston: Houghton Mifflin, 1910.

11. Robinson, *op. cit.*, p. 269.

12. Sigerist, H. *The Great Doctors*, p. 98. New York: Doubleday and Co., Inc., 1958.

13. Bromberg, W. *The Mind of Man: The History of Psychotherapy and Psychoanalysis*, p. 64. New York: Harper & Brothers, 1959.

14. Ehrenwald, J. *From Medicine Man to Friend*, p. 240. New York: Dell Publishing Co., 1956.

15. *Ibid.*, p. 241.

16. Zilboorg, G. *The Medical Man and the Witch During the Renaissance*, p. 192. Baltimore: Johns Hopkins Press, 1935.

17. Zilboorg, G., with G. W. Henry. *A History of Medical Psychology*, p. 228. New York: W. W. Norton & Co., Inc., 1941.

CHAPTER 7. *The Era of Reason and Observation*

1. Finch, J. S. *Sir Thomas Browne.* New York: Henry Schuman, 1950.
2. Latham, R. G. *The Works of Thomas Sydenham, M.D.,* Vol. I, p. 14. Trans. from Latin edition of Dr. Greenhill. London: The Sydenham Society, 1848.
3. *Selected Works of Thomas Sydenham, M.D.,* with a short biography and explanatory notes by J. D. Comrie, p. 135. London: John Bale and Sons, Danielson Ltd., 1922.
4. *The Works of William Harvey,* p. 7. Trans. by Robert Willis. London: C. J. Adlard for the Sydenham Society, 1847.
5. *Ibid.,* p. 70.
6. *Ibid.,* pp. 7, 127–128.
7. *Ibid.,* pp. 128–129.
8. Evans, B., and G. J. Mohr. *The Psychiatry of Robert Burton,* p. 122. New York: Columbia University Press, 1944.
9. Burton, R. *The Anatomy of Melancholy,* Vol. II, p. 81. Ed. by F. Dell and P. Jourdan-Smith. London: J. M. Dent and Sons, 1961.
10. *Ibid.,* p. 107.
11. *Ibid.,* pp. 108–109.

CHAPTER 8. *The Enlightenment*

1. Whytt, R. "Observations on the Nature, Causes and Cure of Those Disorders which have been commonly called nervous, hypochondriac or hysteric" (as quoted by W. Riese, "History and Principles of Classifications of Nervous Diseases," *Bulletin of the History of Medicine,* p. 472).
2. Wechsler, I. S. *The Neurologist's Point of View.* New York: A. A. Syn, 1950.
3. Cullen, W. *First Lines of the Practice of Physic,* pp. 327, 330. Edinburgh: Bell and Bradfute, 1812.
4. *Ibid.,* p. 330.
5. Haslam, J. *Observations on Insanity with particular remarks on the disease and an account of the morbid appearance on dissections.* London: 1798. (As noted by Zilboorg, *A History of Medical Psychology,* p. 302.)
6. Police Code of 1808, p. 369, as quoted in *Louisiana State Mental Journal,* "The Care and Treatment of the Mentally Ill in Louisiana," Vol. 110, No. 11 (November, 1958).
7. Kraepelin, E. "Hundert Jahre der Psychiatrie," *Zeitschrift für die gesamte Neurologie,* Vol. 38 (1918), p. 162.
8. *Ibid.,* p. 172.
9. *Ibid.,* p. 173.
10. Bassoe, P. "Spain as the Cradle of Psychiatry," *American Journal of Psychiatry,* May, 1945, pp. 731–738.
11. Mora, G. "Bi-Centenary of the Birth of Vincenzo Chiarugi (1749–1820): A Pioneer of the Modern Mental Hospital Treatment," *American Journal of Psychiatry,* Vol. 116 (September, 1959), pp. 267–271.
12. Mora, G. "Vincenzo Chiarugi (1759–1820) and His Psychiatric Reform in Florence in the Late 18th Century," *Journal of the History of Medicine,* Vol. 14 (October, 1959), p. 431.
13. Mora, G. "Pietro Pisani (1760–1837): A Precursor of Modern Mental

Hospital Treatment," *American Journal of Psychiatry*, Vol. 117, No. 1 (July, 1960), p. 79.

14. Raskin, N. "Non-Restraint," *American Journal of Psychiatry*, Vol. 115, No. 5 (November, 1958), p. 471.

15. Rush, B. *Medical Inquiries and Observations upon the Diseases of the Mind*, 4th ed., pp. 241–242. Philadelphia: J. Grieg, 1830.

16. Rush, B. *Medical Inquiries and Observations upon the Diseases of the Mind*, 5th ed., pp. 15–16. Philadelphia: Gregg and Elliott, 1835.

17. *Ibid.*, p. 104.

18. *Ibid.*, pp. 106–107.

19. *Ibid.*, p. 108.

20. *Ibid.*, p. 365.

21. Goodman, N. *Benjamin Rush*, p. 346. Philadelphia: University of Pennsylvania Press, 1934.

22. Guthrie, D. *A History of Medicine*, p. 219. London: Nelson, 1958.

23. Lewis, N. *Short History of Psychiatric Achievement.* New York: W. W. Norton & Co., Inc., 1941.

24. Davies, J. *Phrenology: Fad and Science*, p. 7. New Haven, Conn.: Yale University Press, 1955.

25. Combe, G. *Functions of the Cerebellum*, p. 19, Introduction. Edinburgh: Madachlan and Stewart, 1838.

26. Davies, *op. cit.*, p. 20.

27. *Ibid.*, p. 71.

28. Mesmer, F. A. *Mesmerism.* Trans. by V. R. Myers, Introduction by Gilbert Frankau. London: MacDonald, 1948. (Originally published 1779.)

29. Freeman, L., and M. Small. *The Story of Psychoanalysis*, p. 16. New York: Pocket Books, Inc., 1960.

30. Goldsmith, M. *Franz Anton Mesmer*, p. 64. New York: Doubleday and Co., Inc., 1934.

CHAPTER 9. *The Romantic Reaction*

1. Reil, J. Rhapsodien über die Anwendung der psychischen Curmethode auf Geisteszerrüttungen, p. 30. Halle: Curt, 1803.

2. *Ibid.*, p. 50.

3. *Ibid.*, p. 187.

4. Zilboorg, G., with G. W. Henry. *A History of Medical Psychology*, p. 395. New York: W. W. Norton & Co., Inc., 1941.

5. Moreau (de T.) J. *Du Hachisch et de l'alienation mentale*, p. 41. Paris: Librairie de Fortin, Masson et Cie, 1945.

6. *Ibid.*, p. 42.

7. *Ibid.*, p. 31.

8. Heinroth, J. A. *Lehrbuch der Stoerungen des Seelenlebens.* Leipzig, 1818.

9. Zilboorg, G., *op. cit.*, p. 476.

10. Zilboorg, G., quoting Feuchtersleben's *Lehrbuch der Ärztlichen Seelenkunde* (Vienna, 1845), *op. cit.*, p. 477.

11. Carus, K. G. *Psyche, Zur Entwicklungsgeschichte der Seele*, p. 1. Pforzheim: Flammer und Hoffman, 1846.

CHAPTER 10. *The Modern Era*

1. Griesinger, W. *Mental Pathology and Therapeutics*, p. 1. Trans. by C. L. Robertson and J. Rutherford. London: New Sydenham Society, 1867.

2. *Ibid.*, p. 4.

3. Zilboorg, G., with G. W. Henry. *A History of Medical Psychology*, p. 437. New York: W. W. Norton & Co., Inc., 1941.

4. Griesinger, *op. cit.*, p. 59.

5. *Ibid.*, pp. 108–109.

6. *Ibid.*, pp. 165–166.

7. *Ibid.*, p. 173.

8. *Ibid.*, p. 491.

9. *Ibid.*, p. 461.

10. *Ibid.*, p. 460.

11. *Ibid.*, p. 483.

12. *Ibid.*, p. 489.

13. Lewis, A. "The 25th Maudsley Lecture—Henry Maudsley: His Work and Influence," *Journal of Mental Science*, Vol. XCVII, April, 1951.

14. Wortis, J., quoting Sechenov, *Soviet Psychiatry*, p. 18. Williams and Wilkins Co., 1950.

15. *Ibid.*, p. 31.

16. Magoun, H. W. "Concept of Brain Function," Northwestern Medical School's *Quarterly Bulletin*, Vol. XXXIII, p. 324.

17. Ackerknecht, E. H. *A Short History of Psychiatry*, p. 48. New York and London: Hafner Publishing Co., 1959.

18. Guillain, G. *J. M. Charcot, His Life, His Work*, p. 139. Trans. by P. Bailey. New York: Hoeber Medical Division, Harper & Row, Publishers, Incorporated, 1959.

19. Freud, S. *An Autobiographical Study, The Complete Psychological Works of Sigmund Freud*, Vol. XX, pp. 30–31. Trans. by J. Strachey. London: The Hogarth Press, 1950.

20. Bromberg, W. *The Mind of Man: The History of Psychotherapy and Psychoanalysis*, p. 193. New York: Harper & Brothers, 1959.

21. Dubois, P. *The Psychological Origin of Mental Disorders*, p. 64. New York: Funk and Wagnalls, 1913.

22. Déjerine, J., and E. Gauckler. *The Psychoneuroses and Their Treatment by Psychotherapy*, pp. vii–viii. Trans. by S. E. Jelliffe. Philadelphia and London: J. B. Lippincott Co., 1913.

23. *Ibid.*, pp. 267, 268.

24. "Edouard Claparède," trans. by D. Beineman, in *A History of Psychology in Autobiography*, Vol. I, ed. by C. Murchison, p. 80. New York: Russell and Russell, 1961.

25. *Ibid.*

26. *Ibid.*, p. 78.

CHAPTER 11. *Sigmund Freud*

1. Freud, S. *An Autobiographical Study, The Standard Edition of the Complete Psychological Works of Sigmund Freud*, Vol. XX, pp. 32–33. Trans. by James Strachey. London: The Hogarth Press, 1959.

2. Sachs, H. *Freud, Master and Friend*, pp. 36, 146. Cambridge, Mass.: Harvard University Press, 1944.

3. *Ibid.*, pp. 146, 147.

4. Jones, E. *The Life and Work of Sigmund Freud*, Vol. I, p. 5. New York: Basic Books, Inc., 1953.

5. *Ibid.*, p. 22.

CHAPTER 12. *Freud's Scientific Evolution*

1. Jones, E. *The Life and Work of Sigmund Freud,* Vol. I, p. 27. New York: Basic Books, Inc., 1953.
2. Freud, S. *Gesammelte Werke,* Bd. I/III, p. 281. London: Imago, 1940–1952. As noted by Ernest Jones in *The Life and Work of Sigmund Freud.* Ed. and abr. in one volume by Lionel Trilling and Steven Marcus, pp. 21–22. New York: Basic Books, Inc., 1961.

CHAPTER 13. *Freud's Contributions to Social Theory and the Humanities*

1. Jones, E. *The Life and Work of Sigmund Freud,* Vol. III, p. 79. New York: Basic Books, Inc., 1957.
2. Freud, S. *An Autobiographical Study: The Standard Edition of the Complete Psychological Works of Sigmund Freud,* Vol. XX, postscript, p. 72. Trans. by James Strachey. London: The Hogarth Press, 1959.
3. Jones, *op. cit.,* p. 131.

CHAPTER 14. *The Psychoanalytic Movement*

1. Alexander, F., and S. T. Selesnick. "Freud-Bleuler Correspondence," *Archives of General Psychiatry,* January, 1965, pp. 1–9.
2. *Ibid.,* p. 5.
3. *Ibid.,* p. 5.
4. Jones, E. *Free Associations: Memoirs of a Psychoanalyst,* p. 219. New York: Basic Books, Inc., 1959.
5. *Ibid.,* p. 227.
6. *Ibid.,* p. 227.

CHAPTER 15. *The Psychoanalytic Pioneers*

1. Jones, E. *Free Associations: Memoirs of a Psychoanalyst,* p. 98. New York: Basic Books, Inc., 1959.
2. Lorand, S. "Sandor Ferenczi (1873–1933)," *Psychoanalytic Pioneers.* Ed. by F. Alexander, M. Grotjahn, and S. Eisenstein. New York: Basic Books, Inc., in press.

CHAPTER 16. *The Dissenters*

1. Adler, A. *Studie über die Mindertwertigkeit von Organen.* Vienna: Urban und Schwartzenberg, 1907. (English translation: Study of Organ Inferiority and Its Psychical Compensation: A Contribution to Clinical Medicine. New York: Nervous and Mental Diseases Publishing Company, 1917.)
2. *Ibid.,* p. 4.
3. *Ibid.,* p. 23.
4. Freud, S. *Collected Papers,* Vol. I, p. 339. Ed. by Ernest Jones. London: The Hogarth Press and the Institute of Psychoanalysis, 1953.
5. Adler, A. "Der Aggressionstrieb im Leben und in der Neurose," *Fortschritte der Medizin,* Vol. XXVI, pp. 577–584 (1908). As quoted by H. and R.

Ansbacher, *The Individual Psychology of Alfred Adler,* 1st ed., p. 35. New York: Basic Books, Inc., 1956.

6. Freud, S. "Instincts and Their Vicissitudes," *Collected Papers,* Vol. IV, pp. 69, 72.

7. Ansbacher, H. and R. *The Individual Psychology of Alfred Adler,* 1st ed., p. 44. New York: Basic Books, Inc., 1956.

8. Freud, S. *Collected Papers,* Vol. III, p. 281.

9. *Ibid.,* p. 282.

10. *Ibid.,* p. 281.

11. Adler, A. "Der Psychische Hermaphroditismus im Leben und in der Neurose," *Fortschritte der Medizin,* Vol. XXVIII (1910), pp. 486–493.

12. Jones, E. *The Life and Work of Sigmund Freud,* Vol. I, p. 402. New York: Basic Books, Inc., 1953.

13. Adler, A. (a) "Die Rolle der Sexualität in der Neurose" (1911). Reprinted in *Heilen und Bilden; ärztlich-pädogogische Arbeiten des Vereins für Individualpsychologie* (with Carl Furtmüller, ed.), pp. 94–103. Munich: Reinhardt, 1914. (b) " 'Verdrängung' und 'Männlicher Protest'; ihre Rolle und Bedeutung für die neurotische Dynamik" (1911). Reprinted in *Heilen und Bilden,* pp. 103–114.

14. Adler, A. *Social Interest: A Challenge to Mankind,* p. 21. London: Faber and Faber, Ltd., 1938.

15. Freud, *Collected Papers,* Vol. I, p. 341.

16. Colby, K. "On the Disagreement Between Freud and Adler," *American Imago,* Vol. VIII, 1951, p. 235.

17. Freud, *Collected Papers,* Vol. I, p. 340.

18. Freud, S. *An Autobiographical Study,* pp. 97–98. Trans. by James Strachey. International Psychoanalytic Library, 1950.

19. H. and R. Ansbacher, *op. cit.,* p. 77.

20. Adler, A. *New Leading Principles for the Practice of Individual Psychology,* p. 23. Trans. by P. Radin. Ed. by C. R. Ogden. Paterson, N.J.: Littlefield, Adams & Co., 1959.

21. *Ibid.,* p 24

22. Adler, A. *Social Interest: A Challenge to Mankind,* p. 48.

23. *Ibid.,* p. 38.

24. Woodworth, R. *Contemporary Schools of Psychology,* p. 197. New York: Ronald Press Co., 1948.

25. Bennet, E. A. *C. G. Jung,* p. 146. London: Barrie and Rockliff, 1961.

26. *Ibid.,* p. 147.

27. Jung, C. G. "Referate über psychologische Arbeiten schweizerischer Autoren (bis Ende 1909)." *Jahrbuch für psychoanalytische und psychopathologische Forschungen,* Vol. II, 356–388 (1910).

28. Jung, C. G. "On the Psychology and Pathology of So-Called Occult Phenomena," *Collected Works,* Vol. I, p. 70. New York: Pantheon Books, 1960.

29. *Ibid.,* p. 69.

30. *Ibid.,* p. 79.

31. Jung, C. G. "The Psychogenesis of Mental Disease," *Collected Works,* Vol. III, p. 161. New York: Pantheon Books, 1960.

32. Jones, E. *The Life and Work of Sigmund Freud,* Vol. II, p. 30. New Work: Basic Books, Inc., 1957.

33. Brill, A. A. Introduction to English translation of Jung, *The Psychology of Dementia Praecox.* Monograph No. 3, p. ix. New York: Nervous and Mental Diseases Publishing Co., 1936.

34. Jung, C. G. *The Psychology of Dementia Praecox*. Monograph No. 3, p. iii. New York: Nervous and Mental Diseases Publishing Co., 1936.

35. *Ibid.*, p. 31.

36. Jung, C. G. "Letter to the Chairman of a Symposium on Chemical Concepts of Psychosis," *Collected Works*, Vol. III, p. 272.

37. Jung, C. G. "The Content of the Psychoses," Introduction to Second Edition, *Collected Works*, Vol. III, p. 156.

38. Freud, S. "On Narcissism," *Collected Papers*, Vol. IV, p. 31. Trans. by James Strachey. London: The Hogarth Press and Institute of Psychoanalysis, 1949.

39. Jung, C. G. "The Psychology of Dementia Praecox," *Collected Works*, Vol. III, p. 26.

40. Bennet, *op. cit.*, p. 148.

41. Jones, *The Life and Work of Sigmund Freud*, Vol. II, p. 48.

42. *Ibid.*, p. 33.

43. Binswanger, L. *Sigmund Freud: Reminiscences of a Friendship*, p. 2. New York: Grune & Stratton, 1957.

44. Bennet, *op. cit.*, p. 44.

45. Jung, C. G. "Freud and Psychoanalysis," *Collected Works*, Vol. IV, pp. 10–24. New York: Pantheon Books, 1961.

46. *Ibid.*, p. 320 *n.*

47. *Ibid.*, p. 321 *n.*

48. Freud, S. *The Complete Psychological Works of Sigmund Freud*. Trans. by James Strachey, Vol. XIV, "On the History of the Psychoanalytic Movement," p. 43. London: The Hogarth Press, 1957.

49. Jung, C. G. *Psychology of the Unconscious*, p. 27. Trans. by Beatrice Henkle. New York: Moffat, Yard & Company, 1916.

50. *Ibid.*, p. 29.

51. *Ibid.*, p. 37.

52. Freud, *Collected Papers*, Vol. III, p. 470.

53. Clark, R. A. "Jung and Freud: A Chapter in Psychoanalytic History," *American Journal Psychotherapy*, October, 1955, p. 608, *n.* 2.

54. Freud, S. *Collected Papers*, Vol. III, p. 461.

55. Jung, C. G. "Wandlungen und Symbole der Libido, II." *Jahrbuch für psychoanalytische und psychopathologische Forschungen*, Vol. IV (1912), p. 173.

56. Jung, C. G. *Psychology of the Unconscious*, p. 433.

57. *Ibid.*, p. 138.

58. Glover, E. *Freud or Jung?* p. 59. New York: Meridian Books, Inc., 1956.

59. Freud, S. "On Narcissism," p. 38.

60. Bennet, *op. cit.*, p. 40.

61. Binswanger, *op. cit.*, p. 31.

62. *Ibid.*, p. 45.

63. Bennet, *op. cit.*, p. 63.

64. Jung, C. G. Foreword to Jolan Jacobi, *The Psychology of Jung*, p. v. New Haven, Conn.: Yale University Press, 1943.

65. Bash, K. W. "Zur experimentellen Grundlegung der Jungschen Traumanalyse," *Schweiz. Z. Psychol. Anwend.*, Vol. XI (1952), pp. 282–295. Cited in C. S. Hall and G. Lindzey, *Theories of Personality*, p. 110. New York: John Wiley & Sons, Inc., 1957.

66. Hall, C. S., and G. Lindzey. *Theories of Personality*, p. 108. New York: John Wiley & Sons, Inc., 1957.

67. Jung, C. G. *Collected Works,* Vol. VIII, "Analytical Psychology and 'Weltanschauung,' " p. 376.

68. Jung, interviewed by Richard Evans, of the University of Houston, filmed in Zurich in 1957; presented by the Analytic Psychology Club of Los Angeles, Oct. 27, 1960.

69. Peters, R. S. (ed.). *Brett's History of Psychology* (abridged), p. 695. New York: The Macmillan Company, 1953.

70. Taft, J. *Otto Rank,* pp. 20–29. New York: Julian Press, 1958.

71. *Ibid.,* p. 57.

72. Jones, *The Life and Work of Sigmund Freud,* Vol. II, p. 160.

73. Rank, O., and S. Ferenczi. *The Development of Psychoanalysis.* Trans. by Caroline Newton. New York and Washington: Nervous and Mental Diseases Publishing Company, 1925.

74. *Ibid.,* p. 13.

75. *Ibid.,* p. 62.

76. Jones, E. *The Life and Work of Sigmund Freud,* Vol. III, p. 57. New York: Basic Books, Inc., 1957.

77. *Ibid.,* p. 59.

78. Taft, J., *op. cit.,* p. 150.

79. *Ibid.,* pp. 110–111.

80. Rank, O. *Will Therapy and Truth and Reality,* pp. 111–112. New York: Alfred A. Knopf, 1950.

81. *Ibid.,* p. 183.

CHAPTER 17. *Contributions from Outside the Psychoanalytic School*

1. Bleuler, M. "Schizophrenia: Review of the Work of Professor Eugene Bleuler," *Archives of Neurology and Psychiatry,* Vol. XXVI (1931), pp. 611–627.

2. Bolgar, H. "Jean Piaget and Heinz Hartmann: Contributions Toward a General Theory of Mental Development," *Science and Psychoanalysis,* Vol. VII, Ed. by J. Masserman, p. 40. New York: Grune & Stratton, 1964.

3. Piaget, J. "Intellectual Development of the Child," *Bulletin of the Menninger Clinic,* Vol. XXVI, No. 3, p. 123 (May, 1962).

4. Piaget, J. "Effect and Intelligence in Mental Development," *Bulletin of the Menninger Clinic,* Vol. XXVI, No. 3, p. 134 (May, 1962).

5. *Ibid.,* p. 130.

6. "Ink Blot Investigations," *M.D. Magazine,* Vol. V, No. 2, p. 176 (February, 1961).

7. Klopfer, B., and D. Kelley. *The Rorschach Technique,* p. 6. Yonkers-on-Hudson, New York: World Book Company; 1942, 1946.

8. Meyer, A. "A Historical Sketch in Outlook of Psychiatric and Social Work," *Hospital Social Service Quarterly,* Vol. V (1922), p. 22.

9. Lewis, N. "American Psychiatry from Its Beginnings to World War II," in *American Handbook of Psychiatry,* Vol. I, p. 11. Ed. by S. Arieti. New York: Basic Books, Inc., 1959.

10. Lief, A. *The Common Sense Psychiatry of Adolph Meyer,* 1st ed., Foreword, p. x. New York: McGraw-Hill Book Company, 1943.

11. Muncie, W. "The Psychobiological Approach," in *American Handbook of Psychiatry,* Vol. II, p. 1319. Ed. by S. Arieti. New York: Basic Books, Inc., 1959.

CHAPTER 18. *The Organic Approach*

1. Kalinowsky, L. B., and P. H. Hoch. *Shock Treatments, Psychosurgery, and Other Somatic Treatments in Psychiatry*, p. 4. New York: Grune & Stratton, 1952.

2. Cobb, S. "One Hundred Years of Progress in Neurology, Psychiatry and Neurosurgery," *Archives of Neurology and Psychiatry*, Vol. 59 (1948), p. 79.

3. Von Meduna, L. "The Convulsive Treatment: A Reappraisal," in *Great Physiodynamic Therapies in Psychiatry*, p. 86. Ed. by A. Sackler and F. Martí-Ibáñez. New York: Harper & Brothers, 1956.

4. Cerletti, U. "Electro-Shock Therapy," in Sackler and Martí-Ibáñez, *op. cit.* New York: Hoeber Division, Harper & Row, Publishers, Incorporated, 1956.

5. Cerletti, U. "Old and New Information About Electro-Shock," *American Journal of Psychiatry*, pp. 87–94.

6. Moniz, E. "How I Succeeded in Performing the Prefrontal Leukotomy," in Sackler and Marti-Ibañez, *op. cit.*, p. 131. New York: Hoeber Division, Harper & Row, Publishers, Incorporated, 1956.

7. Alexander, L. *Treatment of Mental Disorders*, p. 75. Philadelphia: Saunders, 1953.

8. Sargant, W., and E. Slater. *An Introduction to the Physical Methods of Treatment in Psychiatry*, 3rd ed., p. 239. Baltimore, Md.: Williams and Wilkins Co., 1954.

9. Diethelm, O. "An Historical View of Somatic Treatment in Psychiatry," *American Journal of Psychiatry*, Vol. 95 (July-March, 1938–1939), pp. 1165–1179.

10. Moore, R. B., W. J. Pierce, and A. D. Dennison, Jr., "The Story of Reserpine," *Journal of the Indiana State Medical Association*, Vol. 47, No. 8 (August, 1954), p. 854.

11. Jarvik, M. "Mechanisms of Action of Lysergic Acid Diethylamide, Serotonin and Related Drugs," in *Psychopharmacology*, p. 145. Ed. by N. Kline. Washington, D.C.: American Association for the Advancement of Science, 1956.

12. Kallman, F. J. "Genetic Aspects of Psychoses," in *Biology of Mental Health and Disease*. New York: Hoeber Division, Harper & Row, Publishers, Incorporated, 1952.

CHAPTER 19. *Psychological Developments*

1. Nunberg, H. "The Course of the Libidinal Conflict in a Case of Schizophrenia," *Practice and Theory of Psychoanalysis*, Nervous and Mental Disease Monographs, No. 74, 1948. "Verlauf des Libidokonfliktes in einem Falle von Schizophrenia," *Internationale Zeitschrift für Psychoanalyse*, Vol. 7, p. 30, 1921.

2. Nunberg, H. "Ego Strength and Ego Weakness," *American Imago*, Vol. 3, pp. 25–40, 1942.

3. Alexander, F. *Fundamentals of Psychoanalysis*, p. 219. New York: W. W. Norton and Co., Inc.

4. Piers, G., and M. B. Singer. *Shame and Guilt*. Springfield, Illinois: Charles C Thomas, 1953.

5. Eaton, J., and R. Weil. "The Mental Health of the Hutterites," in *Mental Health and Mental Disorder: A Sociological Approach*, pp. 223–237. Ed. by A. Rose. New York: W. W. Norton & Co., 1955.

6. Alexander, F., and H. Ross (eds.). *Dynamic Psychiatry*, p. 10. Chicago: The University of Chicago Press, 1952.

7. Schilder, P. *Medical Psychology*, pp. 299–300. Trans. by D. Rapaport. New York: International Universities Press, Inc., 1953.

8. Weiss, E. *The Principles of Psychodynamics*, p. 37. New York: Grune & Stratton, 1950.

9. *Ibid.*, p. 39.

10. *Ibid.*, p. 43.

11. Freud, A. "The Concept of Normality," medical faculty lecture, the University of California at Los Angeles, April 2, 1959.

12. Hartmann, H. "Ego Psychology and the Problem of Adaptation," in *Organization and Pathology of Thought*, p. 365. Ed. by D. Rapaport. New York: Columbia University Press, 1951.

13. Waelder, R. "The Psychoanalytic Theory of Play," *Psychoanalytic Quarterly*, Vol. II (1933), pp. 208–224.

14. Alexander, F. "A Contribution to the Theory of Play," *Psychoanalytic Quarterly*, Vol. XXVII (1958), pp. 175–193.

15. Fairbairn, W. R. *An Object-Relations Theory of Personality*, pp. 167, 169. New York: Basic Books, Inc., 1954.

16. Kardiner, A. "The Traumatic Neuroses of War," *Psychosomatic Medicine*, Monograph II and III, No. 4, 1941.

17. Kardiner, A. "Traumatic Neuroses of War," in *American Handbook of Psychiatry*, Vol. I. Ed. by S. Arieti. New York: Basic Books, Inc., 1959.

18. Alexander, F. *Psychoanalysis and Medicine: The Harvey Lectures, 1930–1931*. Baltimore: Williams & Wilkins Co., 1941.

19. French, T. M. "The Reintegrative Process in a Psychoanalytic Treatment," in *The Integration of Behavior*, Vol. III, p. 25. Chicago: The University of Chicago Press, 1958.

20. Selesnick, S. T. "Franz Alexander and Thomas French: Psychoanalysis Integrated and Expanded," in *Science and Psychoanalysis*, Vol. VII. Ed. by J. Masserman. New York: Grune & Stratton, 1964.

21. Hilgard, E. R. *Theories of Learning*. New York: Appleton-Century-Crofts, 1948, 1956.

22. Liddell, H. S. "The Alteration of Instinctual Processes Through the Influence of Conditioned Reflexes," *Experimental Medicine*, Vol. 4 (1942), pp. 390–395.

23. Thorndike, E. L. "A Proof of the Law of Effect," *Science*, Vol. 77 (1933), pp. 173–175.

24. Thorndike, E. L. "Animal Intelligence: An Experimental Study of the Associative Processes in Animals," *Psychological Review Monograph*, Supplement 2, No. 8 (1898), pp. 1–16.

25. Marmor, J. "Psychoanalytic Therapy and Theories of Learning," in Masserman, *op. cit.*, p. 271.

26. *Ibid.*, p. 267.

27. Rapaport, A. "Mathematics and Cybernetics," in *American Handbook of Psychiatry*, Vol. II, Ed. by S. Arieti, pp. 1743–1760. New York: Basic Books, Inc., 1959.

28. Neuman, J. von, and O. Morgenstern (1944). *Theory of Games and Economic Behavior*, rev. ed., Princeton, N.J.: Princeton University Press, 1947.

29. Kubie, L. S. "Instincts and Homeostasis," in *Psychosomatic Medicine: Experimental and Clinical Studies*, Vol. X. New York: Hoeber Division, Harper & Row, Publishers, Incorporated, 1948.

30. Alexander, F. *The Scope of Psychoanalysis*, "Unexplored Areas in

Psychoanalytic Theory and Treatment," Part II, pp. 319–335. New York: Basic Books, Inc., 1962.

31. Bibring, E. "Psychoanalysts and the Dynamic Psychotherapist," *Journal of the American Psychoanalytic Association,* Vol. 2 (1954), pp. 762.

32. Alexander, F. *Psychoanalysis and Psychotherapy,* pp. 74–75. New York: W. W. Norton & Co., 1956.

33. Sterba, R. "The Fate of the Ego in Analytic Therapy," *International Journal of Psychoanalysis,* Vol. XXVIII (1947).

34. Strachey, J. "The Nature of the Therapeutic Action of Psychoanalysis," *International Journal of Psychoanalysis,* Vol. XV (1934).

35. Marmor, *op. cit.,* p. 272.

36. Szondi, L. "Die Anwendung der Psychoshock-Therapie in der Psychoanalyse," *Acta Psychotherapeutica,* Basel and New York: S. Karger, Vol. V., Fasc. 1 (1957).

37. Rado, S. "Recent Advances in Psychoanalytic Therapy," *Psychiatric Treatment,* Vol. XXXI, pp. 42–58. Proceedings of the Association for Research in Nervous and Mental Diseases. Baltimore: Williams & Wilkins Co., 1953.

38. *Ibid.,* p. 53.

39. *Ibid.,* p. 54.

40. Marmor, *op. cit.,* p. 273.

CHAPTER 20. *Social Psychiatry*

1. Dreikurs, R. "Early Experiments with Group Psychotherapy," *American Journal of Psychotherapy,* Vol. 13 (1959), p. 884.

2. Walker, N. *A Short History of Psychotherapy in Theory and Practice.* New York: The Noonday Press, 1957.

3. Maine, T. F. "The Hospital as a Therapeutic Institution," *Bulletin of the Menninger Clinic,* Vol. 10, No. 3 (1946), pp. 65–70.

4. Jones, M. *Therapeutic Community,* p. 53. New York: Basic Books, Inc., 1953.

5. Grotjahn, M. "Individual and Family Dynamics," in *Science and Psychoanalysis,* Vol. II, pp. 90–101. Ed. by J. Masserman. New York: Grune & Stratton, 1959.

6. Hebb, D. O. *The Organization of Behavior: A Neuropsychological Theory.* New York: John Wiley & Sons, Inc., 1949.

7. Kraepelin, E. *Psychiatrie,* 8th ed. Leipzig: I. Band Barth, 1909.

8. Rado, S. "Narcotic Bondage," *American Journal of Psychiatry,* Vol. 114, Part I (August, 1957).

9. Knight, R. P. "The Psychodynamics of Chronic Alcoholism," *Journal of Nervous and Mental Disorders,* Vol. 86 (1937), p. 538.

10. Masserman, J. H., and K. S. Yum. "An Analysis of the Influence of Alcohol in Experimental Neuroses in Cats," *Psychosomatic Medicine,* Vol. 8 (1946), p. 36.

11. Rado, S. "The Psychic Effects of Intoxicants: An Attempt to Evolve a Psychoanalytic Theory of Morbid Cravings," *International Journal of Psycho-Analysis,* Vol. 7 (1929), p. 396.

12. Lolli, G. "Alcoholism as a Disorder of the Love Disposition," *Quarterly Journal of Studies on Alcohol,* Vol. 17 (1956), p. 96.

13. Myerson, A. "The Treatment of Alcohol Addiction in Relation to the Prevention of Inebriety," *Quarterly Journal of Studies on Alcohol,* Vol. 5 (1944), pp. 189–199.

14. Williams, R. *Nutrition and Alcoholism.* Norman: University of Oklahoma Press, 1951.

15. "Rehabilitation of Drug Addiction." U.S. Department of Health, Education and Welfare. Mental Health Monograph No. 3, May, 1963. Project Director, Leon Brill.

16. Overholser, W. "Psychiatry and Some Problems of Criminal Responsibility," *Archives Suisses de Neurologie, Neurochirurgie et de Psychiatre,* Vol. 91, Fasc. 1. (1963), pp. 316–322.

17. *Ibid.,* p. 319.

18. Overholser, W. "Major Principles of Forensic Psychiatry." *American Handbook of Psychiatry,* Vol. II, p. 1898. Ed. by S. Arieti. New York: Basic Books, Inc., 1959.

19. Guttmacher, M. "Why Psychiatrists Do Not Like to Testify in Court," *The Practical Lawyer,* Vol. I, No. 5 (May, 1955).

20. Overholser, W. "Major Principles of Forensic Psychiatry," p. 1898.

21. Freud, S. "Criminality from a Sense of Guilt: Some Character Types I Have Met With in Psychoanalytic Work," *Collected Papers,* Vol. IV, pp. 342–344. London: The Hogarth Press, 1925.

22. Johnson, A., and S. Szurek. "The Genesis of Antisocial Acting Out in Children and Adults," *Psychoanalytic Quarterly.* Vol. 21 (1952), p. 323.

23. Shaw, C., and H. McKay. *Delinquency Areas.* Chicago: The University of Chicago Press, 1929.

24. Glueck, S. and E. *Unraveling Juvenile Delinquency.* New York: Commonwealth Fund, 1950.

25. Mohr, G. J. "Review of *Criminal Youth and the Borstal System,* by William Healy and Benedict Alper." (The Commonwealth Fund, 1941.) *Psychoanalytic Quarterly,* Vol. 12 (1943), pp. 419–422.

26. Szasz, T. "Legal and Moral Aspects of Homosexuality," in *The Sexual Inversion,* pp. 124–132. Ed. by J. Marmor. New York: Basic Books, Inc., 1965.

27. Marmor, *op. cit.,* p. 19.

28. Szasz, T. *op. cit.,* p. 135.

29. Marmor, *op. cit.,* p. 4.

30. Karpman, B. "Sex Life in Prison," *Journal of Criminal Law and Criminology,* Vol. 38 (1948), pp. 475–486.

31. Rapaport, W., and D. Lieberman. "The Sexual Psychopath in California," *California Medicine,* Vol. 85 (1956), p. 232.

32. "Risks of Parole of Sex Offenders," *Medical Tribune,* April 13, 1964.

CHAPTER 21. *The Culturalist School and the Neo-Freudians*

1. Alexander, F. "A Contribution to the Theory of Play," *Psychoanalytic Quarterly,* Vol. 27 (1958), pp. 175–193.

2. Mead, M. *Male and Female.* New York: Morrow, 1949.

3. Erikson, E. *Childhood and Society.* New York: W. W. Norton & Co., Inc., 1950.

4. Alexander, F. *The Scope of Psychoanalysis,* pp. 145–155, "Psychoanalysis Revised." New York: Basic Books, Inc., 1961.

CHAPTER 22. *Philosophical Vistas*

1. Suzuki, D. T. *Zen Buddhism,* p. 52. Ed. by W. Barrett. New York: Doubleday & Co., Inc. (Anchor), 1956.

2. *Ibid.,* p. 84.

3. *Ibid.*, p. 23.
4. *Ibid.*, p. 92.
5. *Ibid.*, pp. 103–108.
6. Suzuki, D. T., E. Fromm, and R. De Martino. *Zen Buddhism and Psycho-Analysis.* New York: Grove Press, 1960.

CHAPTER 23. *Developments in Child Psychiatry*

1. Kanner, L. *Child Psychiatry,* p. 17. Springfield, Ill.: Charles C Thomas, 1945.
2. Harms, E. "At the Cradle of Child Psychiatry," *American Journal of Orthopsychiatry,* Vol. 30 (1960), p. 187.
3. MacMillan, M. B. "Extra Scientific Influences in the History of Child Psychopathology," *American Journal of Psychiatry,* Vol. 116, No. 12 (June, 1960), p. 1093.
4. Bettelheim, B. *Love Is Not Enough,* p. 5. New York: The Free Press of Glencoe, 1950.
5. Freud, A. *Psychoanalytic Treatment of Children,* p. 3. London: Imago Publishing Co., 1946.
6. Freud, A. "Assessment of Childhood Disturbances," in *Psychoanalytic Study of the Child,* Vol. XVII, pp. 149–158. New York: International Universities Press, 1962.
7. Spitz, R. "Hospitalism: A Follow-up Report," in *Psychoanalytic Study of the Child,* Vol. II, pp. 113–117, 1947.
8. Spitz, R. "Anaclytic Depression," in *Psychoanalytic Study of the Child,* Vol. II, pp. 313–342.
9. Ribble, M. "Anxiety in Infants and Its Disorganizing Effects," in *Modern Trends in Child Psychiatry,* p. 23. Ed. by N. Lewis. New York: International Universities Press, 1945.
10. *Ibid.*, p. 24.
11. Escalona, S., and M. Leitch. "The Reactions of Infants to Stress: A Report on Clinical Findings," in *Psychoanalytic Study of the Child,* Vol. 3–4, pp. 121–140, 1947.
12. Bowlby, J. "Childhood Mourning and Its Implications for Psychiatry," *American Journal of Psychiatry,* Vol. 118, No. 6 (1961), pp. 481–499.
13. Bowlby, J. *Maternal Care and Mental Health,* p. 11. Geneva World Health Organization, 1951.
14. Levy, D. "Maternal Over-Protection," in N. Lewis, *op. cit.,* p. 30.
15. Harlow, H. and N. "The Effect of Rearing Conditions on Behavior," *Bulletin of the Menninger Clinic,* Vol. 26, No. 5 (1962), pp. 213–224.
16. Liddell, H. "Conditioning and Emotions," *Scientific American,* Vol. 190 (1954), pp. 48–57.
17. Selesnick, S. T. *Historical Perspectives in the Development of Child Psychiatry in Current Theories.* Ed. by J. Masserman. New York: Grune & Stratton, 1965.

CHAPTER 24. *The Psychosomatic Approach in Medicine*

1. Alexander, F., and T. M. French. *Studies in Psychosomatic Medicine.* New York: The Ronald Press, 1948.
2. Cannon, W. B. *Bodily Changes in Pain, Hunger, Fear and Rage.* New York: Appleton, 1920.

3. Alexander, F. *Psychosomatic Medicine,* pp. 85–132. New York: W. W. Norton & Co., Inc., 1950.

4. Mirsky, I. A. "Physiologic, Psychologic and Social Determinants in the Etiology of Duodenal Ulcer." Reprinted, *Journal of Digestive Diseases,* New Series, Vol. 3, No. 4 (April, 1958). New York: Hoeber Division, Harper & Row, Publishers, Incorporated.

5. Selesnick, S. T. "Franz Alexander and Thomas French: Psychoanalysis Integrated and Expanded," in *Science and Psychoanalysis,* Vol. VII, p. 63. Ed. by J. Masserman. New York: Grune & Stratton, 1964.

6. Pollock, G. Panel on experimental study of psychophysiological correlations. Preliminary report. Presented at American Psychosomatic Society, Atlantic City, N.J., May, 1959.

7. Benedek, T. "The Functions of the Sexual Apparatus and Their Disturbances," in Alexander and French, *op. cit.*

APPENDIX B. *Jung and the National Socialists*

1. Göring, M. H. "Mitteilung des Reichsführers der Deutschen Allgemeinen Ärtzlichen Gesellschaft für Psychotherapie," *Zentralblatt für Psychotherapie,* Vol. 6 (1933), pp. 140–141.

2. Jung, C. G. Introduction to Goring, *op. cit.,* p. 139.

3. Jung, C. G. "Zur Gegenwärtigen Lage der Psychotherapie," *Zentralblatt für Psychotherapie,* Vol. 7 (1934), p. 11.

4. *Ibid.,* pp. 8–9.

5. *Ibid.,* p. 9.

6. Harms, E. "Carl Gustav Jung, Defender of Freud and the Jews," *Psychiatric Quarterly,* Vol. 20 (1946), pp. 199–230.

APPENDIX C. *Organization of Psychoanalytic and Psychiatric Teaching, Practice, and Research*

1. Alexander, F. *The Western Mind in Transition.* New York: Random House, 1960.

2. Glover, E. *An Investigation of the Technique of Psychoanalysis.* Baltimore: Williams & Wilkins Co., 1940.

3. Alexander, F. "Psychoanalytic Education for Practice," in *Psychoanalysis and Human Values.* Ed. by J. Masserman. New York: Grune & Stratton, 1961.

Bibliography

GENERAL BIBLIOGRAPHY

The selected bibliography, which is not exhaustive, is intended to supplement the articles and books used as direct references (Notes) and to aid the reader who may wish to pursue further the subject matter of each chapter.

There are several books that were used by the authors so frequently that they deserve special notation. They are included here and deal with the following subject headings:

History of Psychiatry

ACKERKNECHT, E. H. *A Short History of Psychiatry*. Trans. by S. Wolff. New York and London: Hafner Publishing Co., 1959.

ALTSCHULE, M. *Roots of Modern Psychiatry*. ("Psychiatry: Essays in the History of Psychiatry.") New York: Grune & Stratton, 1957.

BROMBERG, W. *The Mind of Man: The History of Psychotherapy and Psychoanalysis*. New York: Harper & Brothers, 1959.

LEWIS, N. *A Short History of Psychiatric Achievement*. London: Chapman and Hall, 1942.

SCHNECK, J. *History of Psychiatry*. Springfield, Ill.: Charles C Thomas, 1960.

WHITWELL, J. R. *Historical Notes on Psychiatry*. London: H. K. Lewis & Co., Ltd., 1936. Early times to end of the sixteenth century.

ZILBOORG, G., with G. W. Henry. *A History of Medical Psychology*. New York: W. W. Norton & Co., Inc., 1941. (The most outstanding and thorough book, written in English, which covers the period from primitive times to the mid-nineteen-thirties.)

History of Medicine

CASTIGLIONI, A. *A History of Medicine*. New York: Alfred A. Knopf, 1947. A very comprehensive study of the subject.

GARRISON, F. H. *History of Medicine*, 4th ed., Philadelphia and London: W. B. Saunders, 1960.

LEONARDO, R. A. *The History of Medical Thought.* New York: Froben, 1946.
MAJOR, R. H. *A History of Medicine.* Springfield, Ill.: Charles C Thomas, 1954.
ROBINSON, V. *The Story of Medicine.* New York: The New Home Library, 1944. A short history, written whimsically without distorting the facts.
SIGERIST, H. *The Great Doctors.* Trans. by Eden and Cedar Paul. New York: Doubleday & Co., Inc., 1958.

History of Psychology

BORING, E. G. *A History of Experimental Psychology.* New York: Appleton-Century-Crofts, 1950.
FLIEGEL, J. L. *A Hundred Years of Psychology* (1833–1933). Andover: Duckworth, 1948.
MURPHY, G. *Historical Introdoction to Modern Psychology.* New York: Harcourt, Brace & Co., 1949.
PETERS, R. S. (ed.). *Brett's History of Psychology.* London: George Allen and Unwin, Ltd.; New York: The Macmillan Co., 1953. (A scholarly and complete study of the subject.)

History of Science

BISHOP, P. W., and G. SCHWARTZ. *Moments of Discovery* (2 vols.). New York: Basic Books, Inc., 1958.
NORDENSKIÖLD, ERIK. *The History of Biology: A Survey.* New York: Tudor, 1949.
SARTON, G. *Introduction to the History of Science* (3 vols.). Washington: Carnegie, 1931.
SINGER, C. *Studies in the History and Methods of Science* (2 vols.). Oxford: Clarendon Press, 1917, 1921.
THORNDIKE, L. *History of Magic and Experimental Science* (2 vols.). New York: The Macmillan Co., 1929, 1941.

History of Thought Development

BRINTON, C. *Ideas and Men: The Story of Western Thought.* Englewood Cliffs, N.J.: Prentice-Hall, Inc., 1950.
ORTEGA Y GASSET, JOSÉ. *Toward a Philosophy of History.* New York: W. W. Norton & Co., Inc., 1941.
RUSSELL, B. *A History of Western Philosophy.* New York: Simon and Schuster, 1945.
SELIGMAN, K. *History of Magic.* New York: Pantheon, 1948.
TAINE, H. A. *The Ancient Regime.* Trans. by J. Durand and Peter Smith. New York: Henry Holt and Co., Inc., 1931.
WINDELBAND, W. *Lehrbuch der Geschichte der Philosophie.* Tubingen: J. C. B. Mohr, 1928.

Collections of Classical Essays by Contributors to Psychiatric Knowledge

HUNTER, R., and IDA MACALPINE. *Three Hundred Years of Psychiatry* (*1535–1860*). London: Oxford University Press, 1963.

SHIPLEY, THORNE (ed.). *Classics in Psychology.* New York: Philosophical Library, 1961.

There are many books that refer to psychiatric developments outside the United States or are written in languages other than English, such as:

ADAM, H. *Über Geisteskrankheit in Neuer Zeit.* Regensburg: Rath, 1928.

DE BOOR, W. *Psychiatrische Systematik. Ihre Entwicklung in Deutschland seit Kahlbaum.* Berlin: Springer Verlag, 1954.

DORER, M. *Historische Grundlage der Psychoanalyse.* Leipzig: Meiner, 1932.

ELLENBERGER, H. *La Psychiatrie Suisse.* Aurillac, 1953.

FOUCAULT, M. *Folie et Déraison. Histoire de la Folie a l'Âge Classique.* Paris: Editions Plon, 1961.

KIRCHOFF, T. *Grundriss einer Geschichte der deutschen Irrenpflage.* Berlin, 1890.

KOLLE, K. (ed.). *Grosse Nervenaerzte* (3 vols.). Stuttgart: Thieme, 1956, 1959, 1963.

LEIBBRABD, W., and A. WETTLEY. *Der Wahnsinn. Geschichte der abendländlischen Psychopathologie.* Freiberg-Munich: Alber, 1961.

MARTHE, R. *La revolution psychoanalytique. La vie et l'oeuvre de Freud* (2 vols.). Paris: Editions Payot, 1964.

SCHULTZ, J. *Psychotherapie. Leben und Werke grosser Aerzte.* Stuttgart: Hippokrates Verlag, 1952.

SEMELAIGNE, R. *Les pionniers de la psychiatrie française avant et après Pinel* (2 vols.). Paris: Bailliere, 1930, 1932.

TUKE, D. H. *Chapters on the History of the Insane in the British Isles.* London, Paul, Trench & Co., 1882.

ULLERSPERGER, J. *La historia de la psicologia y de la psiquiatria en España.* Madrid: Alhambra, 1954.

SELECTED BIBLIOGRAPHY

CHAPTER 2. *The Three basic Trends in Psychiatry*

ACKERKNECHT, E. H. *A Short History of Medicine.* New York: Ronald Press, 1955.

CLEMENTS, H. *Magic, Myth and Medicine.* London: Health for All, 1952.

EHRENWALD, J. *From Medicine Man to Freud.* New York: Dell Publishing Co., 1956.

ELLENBERGER, H. "The Ancestry of Dynamic Psychotherapy," *Bulletin of the Menninger Clinic,* Vol. 20 (1956), p. 288.

FRAZER, J. G. *The Golden Bough.* London: Macmillan & Co., 1910–1915.

FREUD, S. *Totem and Taboo.* London: George Routledge and Sons, Ltd., 1919.

HAGGARD, H. W. *Mystery, Magic and Medicine.* New York: Doubleday, Doran, 1933.

LIPS, J. E. *The Origin of Things.* New York: Win Inc., 1947.

MALINOWSKI, B. *Magic, Science and Religion.* New York: Doubleday & Co., Inc. (Anchor), 1955.

OSLER, W. *The Evolution of Modern Medicine.* New Haven, Conn.: Yale University Press, 1921.

ROHEIM, G. *Magic and Schizophrenia.* New York: International Universities Press, 1955.

SIGERIST, H. *History of Medicine,* Vol. I. London: Oxford University Press, 1951.

WRIGHT, J. "The Medicine of Primitive Man," *Medical Life*, Vol. 31 (1924), p. 483.

CHAPTER 3. *Contributions of the Ancients*

ALEXANDER, F. "Buddhistic Training as an Artificial Catatonia," *Psychoanalytic Review*, Vol. 18 (1931), pp. 129–145.

CHI-MIN WANG and LIENTÊ WU. *History of Chinese Medicine*. Shanghai: National Quarantine Service, 1936.

DAHL, R. A. "A Brief History of Faith Healing," *Quarterly Bulletin*, Northwestern University Medical School, Vol. 34 (1960), pp. 64–71.

FRIEDENWALD, H. *The Jews and Medicine* (2 vols.). Baltimore: Johns Hopkins Press, 1944.

GARRISON, F. H. "Persian Medicine and Medicine in Persia," *Bulletin of Institute of History of Medicine*, Vol. 1 (1933), p. 4.

GORDON, M. D. "Medicine Among the Ancient Hebrews," *Isis*, Vol. 33 (1941), p. 4.

JAYNE, W. A. *On Healing Gods of Ancient Civilization*. New Haven, Conn.: Yale University Press, 1925.

KAGAN, S. R. *Jewish Medicine*. Boston: Medico-Historical Press, 1952.

LEDERER, W. "Primitive Psychotherapy." *Psychiatry*, Vol. 22 (1959), pp. 255–265.

MURRAY, M. *The Splendour That Was Egypt*. New York: Philosophical Library, Inc., 1949.

MUTHU, D. C. *The Antiquity of Hindu Medicine and Civilization*. New York: Hoeber Division, Harper & Row, Publishers, Incorporated, 1931.

PETRIE, W. M. F. *A History of Ancient Egypt*. London: Methuen & Company, Ltd., 1924.

REINACH, S. *Orpheus: The History of Religions*. New York: Liveright, 1930.

SNOWMAN, J. *A Short History of Talmudic Medicine*. London: Bale, 1935.

SUN, J. G. "Psychology in Primitive Buddhism," *Psychoanalytic Review*, Vol. 11 (1924), pp. 39–47.

THOMPSON, R. C. *Devils and the Evil Spirits of Babylonia*. London: Luzac, 1903.

VEITH, ILZA. "Ancient Japanese Medicine," *Ciba Symposia*, Vol. 2 (1950), p. 1191.

———. "Psychiatric Thought in Chinese Medicine," *History of Medicine and Allied Sciences*, Vol. 10 (1955), p. 261.

CHAPTER 4. *The Classical Era*

ADAMS, F. *The Genuine Works of Hippocrates*, Vols. I and II. New York: Wood, 1886.

ALBUTT, T. C. *Greek Medicine in Rome*. London: Macmillan & Co., 1921.

DICKENSON, G. L. *The Greek View of Life*. New York: Doubleday, Doran, 1925.

DRABKIN, J. E. "Remarks on Ancient Psychotherapy," *Isis*, Vol. 46 (1955), p. 223.

EDELSTEIN, L. "Greek Medicine in Its Relation to Religion and Magic," *Bulletin of the Institute of History of Medicine*, Vol. 5 (1937), p. 201.

JELLIFFE, S. E. "Notes on the History of Psychiatry: 15 Papers Dealing with

Greco-Roman Psychiatry," *Alienist and Neurologist,* February, 1910, to February, 1917.

LEWIS, N. "Historical Roots of Psychotherapy." *American Journal of Psychiatry,* Vol. 114, No. 9 (March, 1958).

RAYMOND, A. *Sciences in Greek and Roman Antiquity.* London: Methuen & Company, Ltd., 1927.

ROSTOVTZEFF, M. *A Social and Economic History of the Roman Empire.* New York and London: Oxford University Press, 1926.

SINGER, C. "The Failure of Inspiration. Science, the Handmaid of Practice: Imperial Rome (50 B.C.–A.D. 400)," in *A Short History of Scientific Ideas to 1900.* New York: Oxford University Press, 1959.

VEITH, ILZA. "Medical Ethics Throughout the Ages," *A.M.A. Archives of Internal Medicine,* Vol. 100 (1957), p. 504.

WITHINGTON, E .T. "The Aesclepiadiae and the Priests of Asclepius," in *Studies in the History and Method of Science,* Vol. 2. Ed. by C. Singer. Oxford: Clarendon Press, 1921.

CHAPTER 5. *The Medieval Period*

CAMBELL, D. *Arabian Medicine and Its Influence on the Middle Ages* (2 vols. London: Kegan Paul, 1926.

DURANT, WILL. *A History of Medieval Civilization,* Vol. IV: *The Age of Faith,* A.D. 325–1300. New York: Simon and Schuster, 1950.

FORT, G. F. *History of Medical Economy During the Middle Ages.* New York: Bonton, 1883.

HUIZINGA, H. *The Waning of the Middle Ages.* New York: Doubleday & Co., Inc. (Anchor), 1954.

LAWRENCE, B. M. *Primitive Psychotherapy and Quackery.* Boston: Houghton, 1910.

MARTÍ-IBÁÑEZ, F. *Centaur: Essays on the History of Medical Ideas,* pp. 81–109. New York: M.D. Publications, 1958.

MURRAY, M. A. *The Witch-Cult in Western Europe, A Study in Anthropology.* Oxford: Clarendon Press, 1921.

RIESMAN, D. *Medicine in the Middle Ages.* New York: Paul B. Hoeber, 1936.

WALSH, J. J. *Medieval Medicine.* London: A. & C. Black, 1920.

CHAPTER 6. *The Renaissance*

BURCKHARDT, J. *The Civilization of the Renaissance in Italy.* London: Phaidon Press, 1951.

CASTIGLIONI, A. *The Renaissance of Medicine in Italy.* Baltimore: Johns Hopkins Press, 1934.

ECKMAN, I. *Jerome Cardan.* Baltimore: Johns Hopkins Press, 1946.

HAGGARD, H. *The Doctor in History.* New Haven, Conn.: Yale University Press, 1934.

HEARNSHAW, F. J. C. *The Social and Political Ideas of Some Great Thinkers of the Renaissance and Reformation.* London: C. C. Harrap & Co., 1925.

MACHIAVELLI, N. *The Prince in the Historical, Political, and Diplomatic Writings,* Vol. 2. Trans. by Christian E. Detmold and J. R. Osgood. Boston, 1882.

WITHINGTON, E. T. "Dr. Johann Weyer and the Witch Mania," in *Studies in the History and Method of Science.* Ed. by C. Singer. Oxford: Clarendon Press, 1917.

CHAPTER 7. *The Era of Reason and Observation*

ALEXANDER, B. "Spinoza und die Psychoanalyse," *Chronicon Spinozanum,* Vol. 5 (1927), pp. 96–103.

CLARK, G. M. *The Seventeenth Century.* New York and London: Oxford University Press, 1929.

DENONAIN, J. J. *Sir Thomas Browne, Religio Medici.* London: Cambridge University Press, 1955.

FULTON, J. F. "The Rise of Experimental Methods," *Yale Journal of Biology and Medicine,* March, 1931.

HUNTER, R. A., and IDA MACALPINE. "William Harvey: His Neurological and Psychiatric Observations," *History of Medicine and Allied Science,* Vol. 12 (1957), p. 26.

LECKY, W. E. H. *History of the Rise and Influence of the Spirit of Rationalism in Europe* (2 vols.). London, 1910; New York, 1914.

SCHNECK, J. "Thomas Sydenham and Psychological Medicine," *American Journal of Psychiatry,* Vol. 113 (1957), p. 1034.

CHAPTER 8. *The Enlightenment*

ACKERKNECHT, E., I. GALDSTON, and G. ROSEN. "Mesmerism," *Ciba Symposia,* Vol. 9, No. 11 (1948).

BECKER, C. L. *The Heavenly City of the 18th Century Philosophers.* New Haven, Conn.: Yale University Press, 1932.

BUTTERFIELD, L. H. (ed.). *Letters of Benjamin Rush,* Vol. I. Philadelphia: American Philosophical Society, 1951.

CASSIRER, E. *The Philosophy of the Enlightenment.* Trans. by F. C. A. Koelin and J. P. Pettegrove. Princeton, N.J.: Princeton University Press, 1951.

CUTTEN, G. B. *Three Thousand Years of Mental Healing.* London: Hodder and Stoughton, 1910.

DE SAUSSURE, R. "French Psychiatry of the 18th Century," *Ciba Symposia,* 2nd series, 1950.

MAJOR, R. *Faiths That Healed.* New York: D. Appleton-Century, 1940.

MEYER, A. "Reevaluation of Benjamin Rush," *American Journal of Psychiatry,* Vol. 101 (1945), p. 433.

MORA, G. "Biagio Miraglia and the Development of Psychiatry in Naples in the 18th or 19th Century," *Journal of the History of Medicine,* Vol. XIII (1958).

RIESE, W. "History and Principles of Classifications of Nervous Diseases," *Bulletin of the History of Medicine,* December, 1945.

———. "Philippe Pinel, His Views on Human Nature and Disease, His Medical Thought," *Journal of Nervous and Mental Diseases,* Vol. 114 (1951), p. 313.

RUSH, B. *The Autobiography of Benjamin Rush.* Ed. by G. W. Corner. Princeton, N.J.: Princeton University Press, 1948.

SHYROCK, R. H. "The Psychiatry of Benjamin Rush," *American Journal of Psychiatry,* Vol. 101 (1945), p. 429.

TEMPKIN, O. "Gall and the Phrenological Movement," *Bulletin of the History of Medicine,* Vol. 21 (1947), p. 275.

VEITH, ILZA. "Medical Ethics Throughout the Ages." *A.M.A. Archives of Internal Medicine,* Vol. 100 (1957).

WILLEY, B. *Eighteenth Century Background: Studies on the Idea of Nature in the Thought of the Period.* London: Chatto and Windus, 1940.

WITTELS, F. "The Contribution of Benjamin Rush to Psychiatry," *Bulletin of the History of Medicine,* Vol. 20 (1956), p. 157.

WOLF, A. *A History of Science and Technology and Philosophy of the 18th Century* (2nd ed.). Rev. by D. McKie. London: George Allen and Unwin, Ltd., 1952.

ZWEIG, S. *Mental Healers.* Trans. by Eden and Cedar Paul. London: Cassell & Co., Ltd., 1933.

CHAPTER 9. *The Romantic Reaction*

BARUK, H. "Moreau de Tours: precurseur in psychopathologie et en psychopharmacologie," *Bulletin de l'Academie National de Medicine,* Paris, Vol. 144 (1960), p. 852.

CARLSON, E. T., and N. DAIN. "The Psychotherapy That Was Moral Treatment," *American Journal of Psychiatry,* Vol. 117 (1960), p. 519.

COBB, S. *Foundations of Neuropsychiatry.* Baltimore: Williams & Wilkins Co., 1941.

ELLENBERGER, H. "The Unconscious Before Freud," *Bulletin of the Menninger Clinic,* Vol. 21 (1957), p. 3.

EULNER, H. H. "Johann Christian Reil," *Neue Zeitschrift Ärztl. Fortbild,* Vol. 49 (1960), p. 472.

HARMS, E. "An Attempt to Formulate a System of Psychotherapy in 1818," *American Journal of Psychotherapy,* Vol. 13 (1957), p. 269.

———. "The Early Historians of Psychiatry," *American Journal of Psychiatry,* Vol. 113 (1957), p. 749.

LEWIS, N. D. C. "Historical Roots of Psychotherapy," *American Journal of Psychiatry,* Vol. 114 (1958), p. 795.

NEUBERGER, M. "British and German Psychiatry in the Second Half of the 18th and Early 19th Century," *Bulletin of the History of Medicine,* Vol. 18, p. 121.

RIESE, W. "The Pre-Freudian Origins of Psychoanalysis," in *Science and Psychoanalysis.* Ed. by J. Masserman. New York: Grune & Stratton, 1958.

SIGERIST, H. "Psychiatry in Europe in the Middle of the 19th Century," in *One Hundred Years of American Psychiatry.* Ed. by J. K. Hall. New York: Columbia University Press, 1944.

WHYTE, L. *The Unconscious Before Freud.* New York: Doubleday & Co., Inc. (Anchor), 1962.

CHAPTER 10. *The Modern Era*

ALPER, L. "The History of Neurology During the 19th Century," *Bulletin, University of Miami School of Medicine,* Vol. 14 (1960), p. 75.

BRACELAND, F. J. "Kraepelin, His System and His Influence." *American Journal of Psychiatry,* Vol. 113 (1956), p. 871.

BRAZIER, M. "The Historical Development of Neurophysiology," in *Handbook of Neurophysiology.* Ed. by J. Fields. Washington: American Physiological Society, 1959.

COBB, S. "One Hundred Years of Progress in Neurology, Psychiatry and Neurosurgery," *Archives of Neurology and Psychiatry,* Vol. 59 (1948), p. 89.

FREUD, S. "Some Character Types Met With in Psycho-Analytic Work (Those

Wrecked by Success)," in *Collected Papers*, Vol. IV, pp. 323–341. London: The Hogarth Press, 1949.

GANTT, W. H. *Russian Medicine*. New York: Paul B. Hoeber, 1937.

HAYMAKER, W. *The Founders of Neurology*. Springfield, Ill.: Charles C Thomas, 1953.

KAHN, E. "Emil Kraepelin," *American Journal of Psychiatry*, Vol. 113 (1956), p. 289.

MEYER, A. "Obituary of August Forel," *Archives of Neurology and Psychiatry*, Vol. 26 (1931), p. 1303.

RIESE, W. "History of Neurology." *MD Publication*, 1959.

———. "The Impact of Nineteenth Century Thought on Psychiatry." *International Review of Medicine*, Vol. 173 (1960), p. 7.

WALSHE, F. "The Evolution of Ideas in Neurology During the Past Century and the Future of Neurological Medicine," *Journal of the Royal Institute of Public Health*, Vol. 23 (1960), p. 33.

WECHSLER, I. S. *The Neurologist's Point of View*. New York: A. A. Wynn, 1950.

WINKLER, J. R., and W. BROMBERG. *Mind Explorers*. New York: Reynal and Hitchcock, 1939.

CHAPTER 11. Sigmund Freud

ALEXANDER, F., and HELEN ROSS. *The Impact of Freudian Psychiatry*. Chicago: The University of Chicago Press, 1961.

ELLENBERGER, H. "Fechner and Freud," *Bulletin of the Menninger Clinic*, Vol. 20 (1956), p. 201.

FREUD, E. L. *Letters of Sigmund Freud*. Ed. by Ernst L. Freud. Trans. by Tania and James Stern. New York: Basic Books, Inc., 1960.

FREUD, M. *Sigmund Freud: Man and Father*. New York: Vanguard Press, 1958.

FREUD, S. *The Origins of Psycho-Analysis* (Letters to Wilhelm Fliess, Drafts and Notes, 1887–1902). Ed. by Marie Bonaparte, Anna Freud, and Ernst Kris. Trans. by Eric Mosbacher and James Strachey. New York: Basic Books, Inc., 1954.

FROMM, E. *Sigmund Freud's Mission*. New York: Harper & Brothers, 1959.

GRINKER, R. "Reminiscences of a Personal Contact with Freud," *American Journal of Orthopsychiatry*, Vol. 10 (1940), p. 850.

JONES, E. *Sigmund Freud: Four Centenary Addresses*. New York: Basic Books, Inc., 1956.

WITTELS, F. *Freud and His Time*. New York: Liveright, 1931.

CHAPTER 12. *Freud's Scientific Evolution*

ALEXANDER, F. *Fundamentals of Psychoanalysis*. New York: W. W. Norton & Co., Inc., 1948.

BREUER, J., and S. FREUD. *Studies in Hysteria*. New York: Nervous and Mental Diseases Publishing Company, 1956.

FENICHEL, O. *The Psychoanalytic Theory of Neurosis*. New York: W. W. Norton & Co., Inc., 1945.

FREUD, A. *The Ego and the Mechanisms of Defense*. London: The Hogarth Press, 1937.

FREUD, S. *The Basic Writings of Sigmund Freud*. Trans. by A. A. Brill. New York: Modern Library, 1938.

FREUD, S. *Collected Papers*, Vols. I–V. Trans. by Joan Riviere. London: The Hogarth Press, 1924–1953.

FREUD, S. *The Standard Edition of the Complete Psychological Works of Sigmund Freud*, Vols. II–XXIII. Trans. by James Strachey. London: The Hogarth Press, 1953–1964.

GLOVER, E. *Psychoanalysis*, 2nd ed. London: Staples Press, 1949.

OBERNDORF, C. P. (ed. and trans.). "Autobiography of Josef Breuer (1842–1925)," *International Journal of Psycho-Analysis*, Vol. 34 (1953), p. 64.

WAELDER, R. "The Historical Development of Psychoanalytic Thought," in *Basic Theory of Psychoanalysis*, Part I, pp. 33–93. New York: International Universities Press, 1960.

CHAPTER 13. *Freud's Contributions to Social Theory and the Humanities*

ALEXANDER, F. "Adventure and Security in a Changing World," pp. 462–473; Introduction to "Group Psychology and the Analysis of the Ego," by S. Freud, pp. 473–483; "On the Psychodynamics of Regressive Phenomena in Panic States"; in *Scope of Psychoanalysis*. New York: Basic Books, Inc., 1961.

FREUD, S. *The Standard Edition of the Complete Psychological Works of Sigmund Freud*, with special reference to Vols. XIII, XVII, XXI, and XXIII. Trans. by James Strachey. London: The Hogarth Press, 1953–1964.

CHAPTER 14. *The Psychoanalytic Movement*

EHRENWALD, J. "History of Psychoanalysis," in *Science and Psychoanalysis*, pp. 145–152. Ed. by J. Masserman. New York: Grune & Stratton, 1958.

NUNBERG, H., and E. FEDERN (eds.). *Minutes of the Vienna Psychoanalytic Society*, Vol. I, 1906–1908. Trans. by M. Nunberg. New York: International Universities Press, 1962.

OBERNDORF, C. P. *History of Psychoanalysis in America*. New York: Grune & Stratton, 1953.

THOMPSON, CLARA. *Psychoanalysis: Evolution and Development*. New York: Hermitage House, 1950.

CHAPTER 15. *The Psychoanalytic Pioneers*

ABRAHAM, K. *Selected Papers on Psychoanalysis* (2 vols.). Trans. by D. Bryan and A. Strachey. New York: Basic Books, Inc., 1957.

DE FOREST, ISETTE. *The Leaven of Love: A Development of the Psychoanalytic Technique of Sandor Ferenczi*. New York: Harper & Brothers, 1954.

FERENCZI, S. *Final Contributions to the Problems and Methods of Psychoanalysis*. Ed. by M. Balint. Trans. by E. Mosbacher, et al. New York: Basic Books, Inc., 1955.

———. *Further Contributions to Theory and Technique of Psychoanalysis*. Compiled by J. Riekmann. Trans. by J. I. Suttie, et al. New York: Basic Books, Inc., 1952.

———. *Sex in Psychoanalysis: Contributions to Psychoanalysis*. Trans. by E. Jones. New York: Brunner, 1950.

———. *Thalassa: A Theory of Genitality*. New York: Psychoanalytic Quarterly, Inc., 1938.

————, and O. RANK. *The Development of Psychoanalysis*. New York: Nervous and Mental Diseases Publishing Co., 1925.

FREUD, S. "Sandor Ferenczi," obituary, *International Journal of Psycho-Analysis*, Vol. 14 (1933), pp. 298–299.

JONES, E. *Essays in Applied Psychoanalysis*, Vols. I and II. London: The Hogarth Press, 1951.

————. *Papers on Psychoanalysis*. Baltimore: Williams & Wilkins Co., 1950.

CHAPTER 16. *The Dissenters*

ADLER, A. *Neurotic Constitution*. Trans. by B. Glueck and J. Lind. New York: Moffat, Yard and Co., 1917.

————. *The Practice and Theory of Individual Psychology*. Trans. by P. Radin. New York: Humanities Press, 1951.

ALEXANDER, F. "Review of *The Development of Psychoanalysis*, by Otto Rank and Sandor Ferenczi," *International Journal of Psycho-Analysis*, Vol. 6 (1925), p. 484.

BOTTOME, P. *Alfred Adler: A Portrait from Life*. New York: Vanguard Press, 1957.

FERENCZI, S. "Kritiken und Referate, C. G. Jung: Wandlungen und Symbole der Libido," *Internationale Zeitschrift für Ärztl. Psychoanalysis*, Vol. 1 (1913), p. 391.

FREUD, S. "The Defence Neuro-Psychoses." *Collected Papers*, Vol. I. London: The Hogarth Press, 1924.

————. "Further Remarks on the Defence Neuro-Psychoses." *Collected Papers*, Vol. I. London: Hogarth Press, 1924.

FROMM, E. "An Evaluation of Jung's Memories, Dreams and Reflections," *Scientific American*, September, 1963.

HALL, C. S., and G. LINDZEY. *Theories of Personality*. London: John Wiley & Sons, Inc., 1957.

JUNG, C. G. *Collected Works* (13 vols.). Ed. by H. Read, et al. Trans. by R. F. C. Hull. New York: Pantheon Books, 1953–1964.

————. *Memories, Dreams, Reflections*. Trans. by Richard and Clara Winston. New York: Pantheon Books, 1963.

————. *Modern Man in Search of a Soul*. New York: Harcourt, Brace & Co., 1933.

KARPF, F. B. *Psychology and Psychotherapy of Otto Rank*. New York: Philosophical Library, 1953.

LEWIS, A. "Jung's Early Work," *Journal of Analytic Psychology*, Vol. 2 (1957), p. 119.

MULLAHY, P. *Oedipus Myth and Complex, A Review of Psychoanalytic Theory*. New York: Hermitage Press, 1948.

MUNROE, RUTH L. *Schools of Psychoanalytic Thought*. New York: The Dryden Press, 1955.

ORGLER, H. *Alfred Adler: The Man and His Work*. London: C. W. Daniel, Co., Ltd., 1947.

PROGOFF, I. *The Death and Rebirth of Psychology*. New York: Julian Press, Inc., 1956.

RANK, O. *Art and Artist*. Trans. by Charles Francis Atkinson. New York: Alfred A. Knopf, 1932.

————. *Beyond Psychology*. Scranton, Pa.: Haddon Craftsmen, 1941.

————. *The Myth of the Birth of the Hero*. Trans. by F. Robbins and Smith E. Jelliffe. New York: Basic Books, Inc., 1952.

————. *Psychology and the Soul.* Trans. by William D. Turner. Philadelphia: University of Pennsylvania Press, 1950.

————. *The Trauma of Birth.* New York: Basic Books, Inc., 1952.

————. *Will Therapy and Truth and Reality.* New York: Alfred A. Knopf, 1950.

RAYNER, D. "Adler and His Psychology—Seen Through His Early Memories," *Mental Health,* Vol. 16 (1957), p. 58.

SCHICK, A. "The Cultural Background of Adler's and Freud's Work," *American Journal of Psychotherapy,* Vol. 18 (1964), p. 7.

SELESNICK, S. "Alfred Adler" and "C. G. Jung." *Psychoanalytic Pioneers.* Ed. by F. Alexander, M. Grotjahn and S. Eisenstein. New York: Basic Books, Inc., in press.

————. "C. G. Jung's Contributions to Psychoanalysis," *American Journal of Psychiatry,* Vol. 120 (1963), p. 350.

THOMPSON, CLARA. *Psychoanalysis: Evolution and Development.* New York: Hermitage House, 1950.

WALKER, N. *A Short History of Psychotherapy in Theory and Practice.* New York: Noonday Press, 1957.

WAY, L. *Adler's Place in Psychology.* New York: The Macmillan Co., 1950.

WHITE, R. "Is Alfred Adler Alive Today?" *Contemporary Psychology,* Vol. 2 (1957), p. 3.

CHAPTER 17. *Contributions from Outside the Psychoanalytic School*

ABT, E. L., and L. BELLAK. *Projective Psychology.* New York: Alfred A. Knopf, 1950.

ANTHONY, E. J. "The Significance of Jean Piaget for Child Psychiatry," *British Journal of Medical Psychology,* Vol. 29 (1956), p. 20.

BEERS, C. *A Mind That Found Itself.* New York: Doubleday & Co., 1908.

BINET, A. "Attention et Adaptation," *L'Année Psychologique.* Vol. 6 (1899), p. 268.

————, and V. HENRY. "La psychologie individuelle," *L'Année Psychologique,* Vol. 2 (1896), p. 411.

BLEULER, E. "Dementia Praecox or the Group of Schizophrenias." Trans. by J. Ziskin. New York: International Universities Press, 1950.

————. *Textbook of Psychiatry.* Trans. by A. A. Brill. New York: The Macmillan Co., 1924.

DIETHELM, O. "Obituary of Adolph Meyer," *American Journal of Psychiatry,* Vol. 107 (1950), p. 78.

ELLENBERGER, H. "The Life and Work of Hermann Rorschach (1884–1922)," *Bulletin of the Menninger Clinic,* Vol. 18 (1954), p. 173.

FLAVELL, J. H. *The Developmental Psychology of Jean Piaget.* Princeton, N.J.: D. Van Nostrand Co., Inc., 1963.

FREEMAN, F. N. *Mental Tests: Their History, Principles, and Applications.* Boston: Houghton Mifflin, 1939.

HUNT, J. McV. *Intelligence and Experience.* New York: Ronald Press Co., 1961.

LOWREY, L. "Obituary of Adolph Meyer," *American Journal of Orthopsychiatry,* Vol. 20 (1950), p. 424.

McKOWAN, ROBIN. *Pioneers in Mental Health.* New York: Dodd, Mead & Co., 1961.

MEYER, A. *Collected Works of Adolph Meyer* (4 vols.). Ed. by E. E. Winters. Baltimore: Johns Hopkins Press, 1950–1952.

————. *Psychobiology: A Science of Man*. Compiled and trans. by E. E. Winters and A. M. Bowers. Springfield, Ill.: Charles C Thomas, 1958.

MUNCIE, W. "The Psychobiological Approach," in *American Handbook of Psychiatry*, Vol. II. Ed. by Silvano Arieti. New York: Basic Books, Inc., 1959.

PIAGET, J. *The Child's Conception of Physical Causality*. Littlefield, 1960.

————. *The Child's Conception of the World*. London: Humanities Press, 1951.

————. *The Growth and Logical Thinking from Childhood to Adolescence*. New York: Basic Books, Inc., 1958.

————. *The Language and Thought of the Child*. London: Humanities Press, 1959.

————. *Logic and Psychology*. New York: Basic Books, Inc., 1957.

————. *The Moral Judgment of the Child*. New York: The Free Press of Glencoe, 1948.

————. *Play, Dreams and Imitation in Childhood*. New York: W. W. Norton & Co., Inc., 1951.

RAPAPORT, D. *Diagnostic Psychological Testing*, Vol. II. Chicago: Year Book Medical Publishers, Inc., 1946.

RORSCHACH, H. *Psychodiagnostics*. Ed. by W. Morgenthaler. Trans. by Paul Lemkau and Bernard Kronenberg. New York: Grune & Stratton, 1949.

ROSENZWEIG, S., with collaboration of Kate Kogan. *Psychodiagnosis*. New York: Grune & Stratton, 1949.

SCHAFER, R. *Psychoanalytic Interpretation in Rorschach Testing, Theory and Application*. New York: Grune & Stratton, 1964.

TERMAN, L. M., and M. A. MERRILL. *Measuring Intelligence*. Boston: Houghton Mifflin, 1937.

VARON, EDITH J., *The Development of Alfred Binet's Psychology*. Princeton, N.J.: Psychological Review Company, 1935.

WECHSLER, P. *The Measurements of Adult Intelligence*. Baltimore: Williams & Wilkins Co., 1944.

WOLFF, P. H. "Developmental and Motivational Concepts in Piaget's Sensorimotor Theory of Intelligence," *Journal of the American Academy of Child Psychiatry*, Vol. 2, No. 3 (April, 1963).

————. "The Developmental Psychologies of Jean Piaget and Psychoanalysis," in *Psychological Issues*, Vol. II, No. 1, Monograph 5. New York: International Universities Press, Inc., 1960.

ZILBOORG, G. "Eugen Bleuler and Present Day Psychiatry," *American Journal of Psychiatry*, Vol. 114 (1957), p. 299.

CHAPTER 18. *The Organic Approach*

ARIETI, S. *Interpretation of Schizophrenia*. New York: Robert Brunner, 1955.

BERGER, F. M. "Meprobamate: Its Pharmacological Properties and Clinical Uses," *International Record of Medicine and G. P. Clinics*, Vol. 169, No. 4 (April, 1956).

COHEN, S. *The Beyond Within: The LSD Story*. New York: Atheneum, 1964.

————. "Notes on the Hallucenogenic State," *International Record of Medicine*, Vol. 173 (1960), p. 380.

FREEMAN, W. "Psychosurgery," in *Handbook of Psychiatry*, Vol. II. Ed. by S. Arieti. New York: Basic Books, Inc., 1959.

HARMS, E. "Origin and Early History of Electrotherapy and Electroshock," *American Journal of Psychiatry*, Vol. 12 (1955), p. 933.

HIMWICH, H. E. "Effect of Shock Treatment on the Brain," in *The Biology of Mental Health and Disease*, Milbank Memorial Fund Conference. New York: Paul B. Hoeber, 1952.

HOCH, P. "Drugs and Psychotherapy," *American Journal of Psychiatry*, Vol. 116 (1959), p. 305.

HOLLISTER, L. "Drugs in Emotional Disorders, Past and Present," *Annals of Internal Medicine*, Vol. 51 (1955), p. 1032.

JACKSON, D. (ed.). *The Etiology of Schizophrenia*. New York: Basic Books, Inc., 1960.

KETY, S. "Biochemical Theories of Schizophrenia," *Science*, Vol. 129 (1959), pp. 1528–32 (June 5), pp. 1590–96 (June 12).

KRETSCHMER, E. *Physique and Character*. London: Kegan Paul, 1925.

MORGAN, C. T., and E. STELLER. *Physiological Psychology*. New York: McGraw-Hill Book Company, 1950.

RINKEL, M., and H. HIMWICH. *Insulin Treatment of Psychiatry*. New York: Philosophical Library, 1959.

SHELDON, W. H. *Varieties of Human Physique*. New York: Harper & Brothers, 1940.

UHR, L. M., and J. G. MILLER (eds.). *Drugs and Behavior*. New York: John Wiley & Sons, 1960.

WIKLER, A. *The Relation of Psychiatry to Pharmacology*. Baltimore: Williams and Wilkins Co., 1957.

WORTIS, J. (ed.). *Recent Advances in Biological Psychiatry*. New York: Grune & Stratton, 1960.

WRIGHT, W. W. "Results Obtained by the Intensive Use of Bromides in Functional Psychoses," *American Journal of Psychiatry*, Vol. 5 (1926), p. 365.

CHAPTER 19. *Psychological Developments*

ALEXANDER, F. *Fundamentals of Psychoanalysis*. New York: W. W. Norton & Co., Inc., 1948.

———. *The Psychoanalysis of the Total Personality*, Monograph Series No. 52. New York: Nervous and Mental Disease Publishing Co., 1959.

———. "The Relation of Structure and Instinctual Conflicts," *Psychoanalytic Quarterly*, Vol. 2 (1933), p. 181.

———. "Three Fundamental Dynamic Principles of the Mental Apparatus and of the Behavior of Living Organisms," in *Scope of Psychoanalysis*. New York: Basic Books, Inc., 1961.

ARLOW, J., and C. BRENNER. *Psychoanalytic Concepts and the Structural Theory*. New York: International Universities Press, 1964.

BANDARA, A. *Behavioristic Psychotherapy*. New York: Holt, Rinehart & Winston, Inc., 1963.

BENEDEK, THERESE. "On the Organization of Psychic Energy: Instincts, Drives and Effects," in *Mid-Century Psychiatry—An Overview*. Ed. by R. Grinker. Springfield, Ill.: Charles C Thomas, 1953.

BIBRING, E. "The Development and Problems of the Theory of the Instincts," *International Journal of Psycho-Analysis*, Vol. 22 (1941), p. 102.

BURTON, A. (ed.). *Psychotherapy of the Psychoses*. New York: Basic Books, Inc., 1961.

BYCHOWSKI, G. *Psychotherapy of Psychosis*. New York: Grune & Stratton, 1952.

————, and J. DESPERT. *Specialized Techniques in Psychotherapy.* New York: Basic Books, Inc., 1952.

CARSON, I., and S. SELESNICK. "Ego Strengthening Aspects of Supportive Psychotherapy," *American Journal of Psychotherapy,* Vol. 13 (1959), p. 298.

DEUTSCH, F. *Applied Psychoanalysis.* New York: Grune & Stratton, 1949.

DIETHELM, O. *Treatment in Psychiatry.* Springfield, Ill.: Charles C Thomas, 1950.

DOLLARD, J., L. W. DOOB, N. E. MILLER, and R. R. SEARS. *Frustration and Aggression.* New Haven, Conn.: Yale University Press, 1939.

MILLER, N. *Personality and Psychotherapy.* New York: McGraw-Hill Book Company, 1950.

ERICKSON, E. *Childhood and Society.* New York: W. W. Norton & Co., Inc., 1950.

FENICHEL, O. *The Collected Papers of Otto Fenichel.* New York: W. W. Norton & Co., Inc., 1953.

FROMM-REICHMANN, FRIEDA. *Principles of Intensive Psychotherapy.* Chicago: The University of Chicago Press, 1950.

GANTT, W. H. *The Origin and Development of Behavior Disorders in Dogs.* New York: Psychosomatic Monograph, 1942.

GLOVER, E. *The Techniques of Psychoanalysis.* New York: International Universities Press, Inc., 1958.

HARTMANN, H., E. KRIS, and R. M. LOWENSTEIN. "Comments on the Formation of Psychic Structure," in *Psychoanalytic Study of the Child,* Vol. II. New York: International Universities Press, 1946.

HULL, C. L. "Conditioning: Outline of a Systematic Theory of Learning," in *The Psychology of Learning.* National Social Studies Education, 41st yearbook, 1942.

KNIGHT, R. P., and C. R. FRIEDMAN. *Psychoanalytic Psychiatry and Psychology.* New York: International Universities Press, Inc., 1954.

KOFFKA, K. *Principles of Gestalt Psychology.* New York: Harcourt, Brace & Co., 1935.

KOHLER, W. *The Mentality of Apes.* Trans. by E. Winter. New York: Harcourt, Brace & Co., 1925.

LEWIN, K. "Field Theory and Learning," in *Psychology of Learning.* National Social Studies Education, 41st yearbook, 1942.

LORAND, S. *Techniques of Psychoanalytic Therapy,* New York: International Universities Press, 1946.

MASSERMAN, J. H. *Behavior and Neuroses.* New York and London: Hafner Publishing Co., 1964.

————. *Dynamic Psychiatry.* Philadelphia and London: W. B. Saunders Co., 1955.

MENNINGER, K. "Regulatory Devices of the Ego Under Major Stress," *International Journal of Psycho-Analysis,* Vol. 35 (1954), p. 1.

————. *Theory of Psychoanalytic Technique.* New York: Basic Books, Inc., 1958.

NUNBERG, H. *Principles of Psychoanalysis.* New York: International Universities Press, 1955.

PAUL, L. (ed.). *Psychoanalytic Clinical Interpretation.* New York: The Free Press of Glencoe, 1963.

PAVLOV, I. P. *Conditioned Reflexes.* Trans. by G. V. Anrep. London: Oxford University Press, 1927.

REICH, W. *Character Analysis.* New York: Orgone Institute Press, 1949.

REIK, T. *Listening with the Third Ear.* New York: Farrar, Straus & Co., 1949.

ROGERS, C. R. *Client-Centered Therapy.* Boston: Houghton Mifflin, 1951.

ROSEN, J. M. *Direct Analysis.* New York: Grune & Stratton, 1953.

RUESCH, J. *Disturbed Communication.* New York: W. W. Norton & Co., Inc., 1957.

SKINNER, B. F. *The Behavior of Organisms.* New York: Appleton-Century-Crofts & Co., 1938.

SULLIVAN, C. *Freud and Fairbairn: Two Theories of Ego Psychology.* Doylestown, Pa., Doylestown Foundation, 1963.

SZASZ, T. "On the Psychoanalytic Theory of Instincts," *Psychoanalytic Quarterly,* Vol. 21 (1952), p. 25.

———. *Pain and Pleasure: A Study of Bodily Feelings.* New York: Basic Books, Inc., 1957.

TOLMAN, E. C., B. F. RITCHIE, and D. KALISH. "Studies in Spatial Learning: Response Learning vs. Place Learning by the Non-Correction Method," *Journal of Experimental Psychology,* Vol. 37 (1947), p. 285.

WERTHEIMER, M. *Productive Thinking.* New York: Harper & Brothers, 1945.

WIENER, N. *The Human Use of Human Beings.* Boston: Houghton Mifflin, 1954.

WOLBERG, L. *The Technique of Psychotherapy.* New York: Grune & Stratton, 1954.

CHAPTER 20. *Social Psychiatry*

ACKERMAN, N. W. *The Psychodynamics of Family Life.* New York: Basic Books, Inc., 1959.

AICHHORN, A. *Wayward Youth.* New York: Viking Press, 1935.

ALEXANDER, F. "The Neurotic Character," *International Journal of Psychoanalysis,* Vol. 9 (1930), p. 11.

———, and W. HEALY. "Roots of Crime," in *Psychoanalytic Studies.* New York: Alfred A. Knopf, 1935.

ALEXANDER, F., and H. STAUB. *The Criminal, the Judge and the Public.* New York: The Free Press of Glencoe, 1956.

ALLEN, C., and C. BERG. *The Problem of Homosexuality.* New York: Citadel Press, 1958.

ARING, S. D. "Senility," *A.M.A. Archives of Internal Medicine,* Vol. 100 (October, 1957), p. 519.

BACH, C. *Intensive Group Psychotherapy.* New York: Ronald Press, 1960.

BELL, N. W., and E. F. VOGEL. *The Family.* New York: The Free Press of Glencoe, 1960.

BIEBER, I., et al. *Homosexuality.* New York: Basic Books, Inc., 1952.

BOWEN, M. "A Family Concept of Schizophrenia," in *The Etiology of Schizophrenia.* Ed. by Donald Jackson. New York: Basic Books, Inc., 1960.

CLAUSEN, J. A., and R. N. WILSON (eds.). *Explorations in Social Psychiatry.* New York: Basic Books, Inc., 1957.

COHEN, A. *Delinquent Boys: The Culture of the Gang.* New York: The Free Press of Glencoe, 1955.

CORY, D. W. *The Homosexual American: A Subjective Approach.* New York: Castle Books, 1960.

COWDRY, E. V. *Problems of Aging.* Baltimore: Williams & Wilkins Co., 1952.

DAVIDSON, H. *Forensic Psychiatry.* New York: Ronald Press, 1952.

DE RIVER, J. P. *The Sexual Criminal: A Psychoanalytical Study.* Springfield, Ill.: Charles C Thomas, 1949.

DONNELLY, J. "Psychiatric Therapy in the Geriatric Patient," *Journal of the American Geriatrics Society,* Vol. 2 (1954), p. 655.

DOUGLAS, W. O. *Law and Psychiatry.* New York: William Alanson White Institute of Psychiatry, 1956.

EDELSON, M. *Ego Psychology, Group Dynamics and the Therapeutic Community.* New York: Grune & Stratton, 1964.

EISSLER, K. (ed.). *Searchlights on Delinquency.* New York: International Universities Press, 1949.

FOULKES, S. H. *Introduction to Group Analytic Psychotherapy.* London: Heinemann, 1948.

FRANK, J. D. *Group Therapy in the Mental Hospital,* Monograph Series No. 1. Washington: American Psychiatric Association, Mental Health Service, 1955.

GREENLEIGH, L. "Some Psychological Aspects of Aging," in *Social Casework.* New York: Family Service Association of America, 1955.

————. "Timelessness and Restitution in Relation to Creativity and the Aging Process," *Journal of the American Geriatrics Society,* Vol. VIII, No. 5 (1960).

GROTJAHN, M. *Psychoanalysis and the Family Neurosis.* New York: W. W. Norton & Co., Inc., 1960.

GUTTMACHER, M. *Sex Offenses: The Problem, Causes and Prevention.* New York: W. W. Norton & Co., Inc., 1951.

————, and H. WEIHOFEN. *Psychiatry and the Law.* New York: W. W. Norton & Co., Inc., 1952.

KAPLAN, J. *Mental Disorders in Later Life.* Stanford, Calif.: Stanford University Press, 1956.

KLAPMAN, J. W. *Group Psychotherapy, Theory and Practice.* New York: Grune & Stratton, 1946.

KRUSE, H. D. (ed.). *Alcoholism as a Medical Problem.* New York: Hoeber Division, Harper & Row, Publishers, Incorporated, 1956.

LIDZ, T., and S. FLECK. "Schizophrenia, Human Integration, and the Role of the Family," in *The Etiology of Schizophrenia.* Ed. by Donald Jackson. New York: Basic Books, Inc., 1960.

LORAND, S., and M. BALINT. (eds.) *Perversions: Psychodynamics and Therapy.* New York: Random House, 1956.

MORENO, J. L. "Psychodrama," in *American Handbook of Psychiatry,* Vol. II. Ed. by Silvano Arieti. New York: Basic Books, Inc., Vol. II. 1959.

NYSWANDER, M. *The Drug Addict as a Patient.* New York: Grune & Stratton, 1956.

OVERHOLSER, W. *The Psychiatrist and the Law.* New York: Harcourt, Brace & Co., 1953.

REIK, T. *Geständniszwang und Strafbedürfnis: Probleme der Psychoanalyse und der Kriminologie.* Leipzig: Internationaler Psychoanalytischer, Verlag, 1925.

SCHMIDEBERG, M. "The Offender's Attitude Towards Punishment," *Journal of Criminal Law, Cirminology and Police Science,* Vol. 51 (1960), p. 328.

SLAVSON, S. R. (ed.). *The Fields of Group Therapy.* New York: International Universities Press, 1947.

STERNS, A. W. "Isaac Ray, Psychiatrist and Pioneer in Forensic Psychiatry," *American Journal of Psychiatry,* Vol. 101 (1945), p. 573.

THEWLIS, M. W. *The Care of the Aged (Geriatrics)*. St. Louis: Mosby, 1954.
THOMPSON, G. N. (ed.). *Alcoholism*. Springfield, Ill.: Charles C Thomas, 1956.
WALLERSTEIN, R. S. *Hospital Treatment of Alcoholism*. New York: Basic Books, Inc., 1957.
WEAKLAND, J. H. "Double Bind Hypothesis of Schizophrenia and 3-Party Interaction," in *The Etiology of Schizophrenia*. Ed. by Donald Jackson. New York: Basic Books, Inc., 1960.
WIKLER, A. *Opiate Addiction*. Springfield, Ill.: Charles C Thomas, 1953.
WYNNE, L. C., L. M. RYCKOFF, J. DAY, and S. I. HIRSCH. "Pseudomutuality in the Family Relations of Schizophrenics," *Psychiatry*, Vol. 21 (1958), p. 205.

CHAPTER 21. *The Culturalist School and the Neo-Freudians*

ALEXANDER, F. "Adventure and Security in a Changing World," in *Medicine in a Changing Society*. Ed. by I. Galdston. New York: International Universities Press, 1957.
————. *The Age of Unreason: A Study of the Irrational Forces in Social Life*. Philadelphia: J. B. Lippincott Co., 1942.
————. "Psychoanalysis Revised," *Psychoanalytic Quarterly*, Vol. IX (1940). Also in *The Scope of Psychoanalysis*, pp. 384–411. New York: Basic Books, Inc., 1961.
————. "Psychoanalysis and Social Disorganization," American Journal of Sociology, Vol. XLII, No. 6 (1937). Also in *The Scope of Psychoanalysis*, pp. 137–164. New York: Basic Books, Inc., 1961.
————. Review, Geza Roheim's *The Origin and Function of Culture*, *Psychoanalytic Review Quarterly*, Vol. 24 (1945), p. 3.
————. *The Western Mind in Transition*. New York: Random House, 1960.
BENEDICT, RUTH. *The Chrysanthemum and the Sword*. Boston: Houghton Mifflin, 1946.
————. *Patterns of Culture*. Boston: Houghton Mifflin, 1934.
BIRNBACH, M. *Neo-Freudian Social Philosophy*. Stanford, Calif.: Stanford University Press, 1961.
FROMM, E. *The Art of Loving*. New York: Harper & Brothers, 1956.
————. *Escape from Freedom*. New York: Rinehart & Co., 1941.
————. *The Sane Society*. New York: Rinehart & Co., 1955.
HORNEY, KAREN. *Self-Analysis*. New York: W. W. Norton & Co., Inc., 1942.
————. *Neurotic Personality of Our Time*. New York: W. W. Norton & Co., Inc., 1937.
————. *New Ways in Psychoanalysis*. New York: W. W. Norton & Co., 1939.
KARDINER, A. "Adaptational Theory: The Cross Cultural Point of View," in *Changing Concepts of Psychoanalytic Medicine*. Ed. by S. Rado and G. E. Daniels. New York: Grune & Stratton, Inc., 1956.
LINTON, R. *The Concept of National Character, Personality and Political Crisis*. Ed. by Alfred H. Stanton and Stewart E. Perry. New York: The Free Press of Glencoe, 1951.
MEAD, MARGARET, and G. BATESON. *Balinese Character*. New York: New York Academy of Sciences, 1942.
ROHEIM, G. *The Origin and Function of Culture*. Nervous and Mental Disease Monograph No. 69, 1943.
————. *Psychoanalysis and Anthropology*. New York: International Universities Press, 1950.

SALZMAN, L. *Developments in Psychoanalysis.* New York: Grune & Stratton, 1962.

SULLIVAN, H. S. *The Interpersonal Theory of Psychiatry.* Ed. by Helen S. Perry and Mary L. Gawel. New York: W. W. Norton & Co., Inc., 1953.

CHAPTER 22. *Philosophical Vistas*

BINSWANGER, L. "Existential Analysis and Psychotherapy," in *Progress in Psychotherapy*, Vol. I. Ed. by Frieda Fromm-Reichmann and J. L. Moreno. New York: Grune & Stratton, 1956.

BOSS, MEDARD. "Daseinanalysis and Psychotherapy," *Progress in Psychotherapy*, Vol. II. Ed. by J. Masserman and J. L. Moreno. New York: Grune & Stratton, 1957.

HEIDEGGER, M. *Sein und Zeit.* Halle: Niemeyer, 1927.

KIERKEGAARD, S. *The Concept of the Dread.* Trans. by Walter Lowrie. Princeton, N.J.: Princeton University Press, 1944.

MAY, R., E. ANGEL, and H. ELLENBERGER. *Existence: A New Dimension in Psychiatry and Psychology.* New York: Basic Books, Inc., 1958.

RUIDENBECK, H. (ed.). *Psychoanalysis and Existential Philosophy.* New York: Dutton, 1962.

WATTS, A. *The Way of Zen.* New York: Pantheon Books, 1957.

CHAPTER 23. *Developments in Child Psychiatry*

AICHHORN, A. *Wayward Youth.* New York: Viking Press, 1935.

ALLEN, F. *Positive Aspects of Child Psychiatry.* New York: W. W. Norton & Co., Inc., 1963.

———. *Psychotherapy with Children.* New York: W. W. Norton & Co., Inc., 1942.

BENDER, LORETTA. *Child Psychiatric Techniques.* Springfield, Ill.: Charles C Thomas, 1952.

CAPLAN, G. *Principles of Preventive Psychiatry.* New York: Basic Books, Inc., 1964.

CRUTCHER, ROBERTA. "Child Psychiatry, A History of Its Development," *Journal of Psychiatry*, Vol 6. (1943), p. 191.

DEUTSCH, A. *The Mentally Ill in America.* New York: Doubleday, Doran, 1937.

GERARD, M. "Direct Treatment of the Child," in *Orthopsychiatry 1923–1948: Retrospect and Prospect*, pp. 498–499. Ed. by L. Lowrey and V. Sloane. New York: American Orthopsychiatry Association, Inc., 1948.

GLOVER, E. "Examination of the Klein System of Child Psychology," in *The Psychoanalytic Study of the Child*, Vol. I. New York: International Universities Press, 1945.

HARLOW, H. "The Nature of Love." *American Psychologist*, Vol. 113 (1958), p. 677.

HESS, E. "Imprinting in Animals," *Scientific American*, Vol. 198 (1958), p. 81.

KANNER, L. *In Defense of Mothers*, 4th ed. Springfield, Ill.: Charles C Thomas, 1958.

KLEIN, MELANIE. *Psychoanalysis of Children.* Ed. by Ernest Jones. Trans. by A. Strachey. International Psychoanalytic Library. London: The Hogarth Press, 1954.

———. "The Psychoanalytic Play Technique," *American Journal of Orthopsychiatry*, Vol. 25 (1955), p. 223.

LEVY, D. "Use of Play Techniques as Experimental Procedure," *American Journal of Orthopsychiatry,* Vol. 3 (1933), p. 266.

LEWIN, B. "Child Psychiatry in the 1830s," in *Psychoanalytic Study of the Child,* Vol. III–IV, p. 489, 1949.

LEWIS, N. (ed.). *Modern Trends in Child Psychiatry.* New York: International Universities Press, 1945.

MOHR, G. "August Aichhorn," in *Psychoanalytic Pioneers.* Ed. by F. Alexander, M. Grotjahn, and S. Eisenstein. New York: Basic Books, Inc., in press.

PASAMANICK, B., and H. KNOBLOCH. "Epidemiologic Studies on the Complications of Pregnancy and the Birth Process," in *Prevention of Mental Disorders in Children: Initial Exploration.* Ed. by G. Caplan. New York: Basic Books, Inc., 1961.

REDL, F., and D. WINEMAN. *Children Who Hate.* New York: The Free Press of Glencoe, 1951.

———. *Controls from Within.* New York: The Free Press of Glencoe, 1952.

SCHRUT, A. "Suicidal Adolescents and Children," *Journal of the American Medical Association,* Vol. 188 (1964), p. 1103.

WITMER, H. L. *Psychiatric Interviews with Children.* Cambridge, Mass.: Harvard University Press, 1946.

CHAPTER 24. *The Psychosomatic Approach in Medicine*

ALEXANDER, F. "The Logic of Emotions and Its Dynamic Background," *International Journal of Psychoanalysis,* Vol. 16 (1955), p. 399.

———. "Preliminary Report on a Psychosomatic Study of Rheumatoid Arthritis" (with Adelaide Johnson and Louis B. Shapiro), *Psychosomatic Medicine,* Vol. 9 (1947), p. 295.

ALKAN, L. "Anatomische Organkrankheiten aus seelischer Ursache." *Med., Klin.,* Vol. 27 (1931), p. 457.

BELLAK, L. (ed.). *Psychology of Physical Illness: Psychiatry Applied to Medicine, Surgery and the Specialties.* New York: Grune & Stratton, 1952.

BERGMANN, G. VON. "Ulcus duodeni und vegetatives Nervensystem," *Berliner Klinische Wchnschr.,* Vol. 50 (1913), p. 2374.

DEMENT, W. "The Effect of Dream Deprivation," *Science,* Vol. 131 (1960), p. 1705.

———, and N. KLEITMAN. "Cyclic Variations in EEG During Sleep and Their Relation to Eye Movements, Bodily Motility, and Dreaming," *EEG Clin. Neurophysiology,* Vol. 6 (1957), p. 673.

———. "The Relation of Eye Movements During Sleep to Dream Activity: An Objective Method of the Study of Dreaming," *Journal of Experimental Psychology,* Vol. 53 (1957), p. 339.

DONIGER, M., E. D. WITTKOWER, et al. "Psychophysiological Studies in Thyroid Function," *Psychosomatic Medicine,* Vol. 18, No. 4 (1956).

DUNBAR, FLANDERS. *Emotions and Bodily Changes.* New York: Columbia University Press, 1954.

ENGEL, G. L. "Studies of Ulcerative Colitis." I: "Clinical Data Bearing on the Nature of the Somatic Process," *Psychosomatic Medicine,* Vol. 16 (1954), p. 496.

———. "Studies of Ulcerative Colitis." II: "The Nature of the Somatic Processes and the Adequacy of Psychosomatic Hypotheses," *American Journal of Medicine,* Vol. 16 (1954), p. 416.

———. "Studies of Ulcerative Colitis." III: "The Nature of the Psychologic Processes," *American Journal of Medicine,* Vol. 19 (1955), p. 231.

———. "Studies of Ulcerative Colitis," IV: "The Significance of Headaches," *Psychosomatic Medicine,* Vol. 18 (1956), p. 234.

———, F. REICHSMAN, and H. L. SEGAL. "A Study of the Infant with a Gastric Fistula," *Psychosomatic Medicine,* Vol. 18 (1956), p. 374.

FAHRENKAMP, K. *Die Psychophysischen Wechselwirkungen bei den Hypertonie-Erkrankungen.* Stuttgart: Hippokrates Verlag, 1926.

FISHER, C., and W. C. DEMENT. "The Utilization of Psychoanalytic Method of Theory in Psychiatric Research: Studies on the Psychopathology of Sleep and Dreams," presented at the joint meeting of the American Psychiatric and American Psychoanalytic associations, Toronto, Canada, May, 1962.

GRINKER, R. *Anxiety and Stress.* New York: McGraw-Hill Book Company, 1955.

HALLIDAY, J. L. "Concept of a Psychosomatic Affection," *Lancet,* Vol. 2 (1943), p. 692.

HAM, G., F. ALEXANDER, and H. G. CARMICHAEL. "A Psychosomatic Theory of Thyrotoxicosis," *Psychosomatic Medicine,* Vol. 13 (1951), p. 18.

HEYER, G. R. *Das Körperlich-Seelische Zusammenwirken in den Lebensvor-gängen.* Munich: J. F. Bergman, 1925.

HOLMES, T. H., T. TREUTING, and H. G. WOLFF. "Life Situations, Emotions and Nasal Disease: Evidence on Summative Effects Exhibited in Patients with Hay Fever," *Psychosomatic Medicine,* Vol. 13 (1951), p. 71.

MOHR, F. *Psychophysische Behandlungsmethoden.* Leipzig: Hirzel, 1925.

SELESNICK, S. T. "Separation Anxiety and Asthmatic Attacks Related to Shifts in Object Cathexes," in *The Asthmatic Child.* Ed. by H. Schneer. New York: Hoeber Division, Harper & Row, Publishers, Incorporated, 1963.

———, and Z. SPERBER. "The Problem of the Eczema-Asthma Complex: A Developmental Approach," in *Psychoanalysis and Current Biological Thought.* Ed. by N. Greenfield and W. Lewis. Madison, Wis.: University of Wisconsin Press, 1965.

SELESNICK, S. T., D. B. FRIEDMAN, and BERNICE AUGENBRAUN. "Psychological Management of Childhood Asthma," *California Medicine,* Vol. 100 (1964), p. 406.

SPERLING, M. "Psychoanalytic Study of Ulcerative Colitis in Children," *Psychoanalytic Quarterly,* Vol. 15 (1946), p. 302.

WEISS, EDOARDO. "Psychoanalyse eines Falles von Nervoesem Asthma," *Interna. Zeitschrift für Psychoanal.,* Vol. 8 (1922), p. 440.

———, and D. S. ENGLISH. *Psychosomatic Medicine.* London: W. B. Saunders, 1957.

WEIZSACKER, V. VON. *Fälle und Probleme.* Stuttgart: Ferdinand Enke Verlag, 1886.

———. *Der Kranke Mensch.* Stuttgart: K. F. Koehler Verlag, 1951.

WEST, L. J., H. H. JANSZEN, B. K. LESTER, and F. S. CORNELISOON, JR. "The Psychosis of Sleep Deprivation," *Annals of the New York Academy of Sciences,* Vol. 96 (1962), p. 66.

WESTPHAL, K. "Untersuchungen zur Frage der Nervoesen Entstehung Peptischer Ulcera," *Deutsches Archiv Klin. Med.,* Vol. 114 (1914), p. 327.

APPENDIX C. *The Organization of Psychoanalytic and Psychiatric Teaching, Practice, and Research*

ALEXANDER, F. *Psychoanalysis and Psychotherapy.* London: George Allen & Unwin, Ltd., 1957.

BLAIN, D. "The Organization of Psychiatry in the United States," in *Handbook of Psychiatry*, Vol. II. Ed. by S. Arieti. New York: Basic Books, Inc., 1959.

LEVIN, M. "The Impact of Psychoanalysis on Training in Psychiatry," in *Twenty Years of Psychoanalysis*. Ed. by F. Alexander and H. Ross. New York: W. W. Norton & Co., Inc., 1953.

————, and H. LEDERER. "Teaching of Psychiatry in Medical Schools," in *Handbook of Psychiatry*, Vol. II. Ed. by S. Arieti. New York: Basic Books, Inc., 1959.

MENNINGER, K. "The Contributions of Psychoanalysis to American Psychiatry," in *A Psychiatrist's World*. Ed. by B. H. Hall. New York: Viking Press, 1959.

WHITEHORN, J. (ed.). *The Psychiatrist, His Training and Development*. Washington: American Psychiatric Association, 1953.

INDEX

Index

About the Authors

Dr. Franz G. Alexander was born in Budapest in 1891. He earned degrees from the University of Budapest (1912) and the Berlin Psychoanalytic Institute (1919). In 1930 he became Visiting Professor of Psychoanalysis at the University of Chicago, the first of several positions of increasing importance in this country. In 1932 Alexander founded the Chicago Institute for Psychoanalysis and was its director for twenty-five years. During 1938–39, he was president of the American Psychoanalytic Association and ten years later he became president of the American Society for Research in Psychosomatic Medicine. He joined Cedars-Sinai Medical Center, in Los Angeles, where he became head of the Psychiatric Department and Director of the Psychiatric and Psychosomatic Research Institute in 1956. At the time of his death, in 1964, he was president of the Academy of Psychoanalysis. He wrote more than 250 articles and sixteen books, including the classic *Roots of Crime, Psychoanalysis and Psychotherapy,* and *The Scope of Psychoanalysis.*

Dr. Sheldon T. Selesnick was born in Detroit, Michigan, in 1925. Receiving his medical degree at Indiana University School of Medicine (1950), he then served his internship at the Los Angeles General County Hospital and took his psychiatric training in Chicago and Los Angeles. He has had further training in psychoanalysis and child psychology, and has become well regarded for his numerous publications on psychiatric history, child psychiatry, and especially on psychosomatic disorders. He is a diplomate and fellow of the American Psychiatric Association, a fellow in the Academy of Psychoanalysis, and a member of the American Psychoanalytic Association and the American Psychosomatic Society. A student and colleague of Dr. Alexander at Cedars-Sinai Medical Center, he is now in charge of Psychosomatic Research at that hospital. He is on the teaching faculties of the Southern California Psychoanalytic Institute and the Department of Psychiatry at the University of Southern California School of Medicine.